INDO-EUROPEA

Indo-European Poetry and Myth

M. L. WEST

OXFORD
UNIVERSITY PRESS

OXFORD
UNIVERSITY PRESS

Great Clarendon Street, Oxford OX2 6DP

Oxford University Press is a department of the University of Oxford.
It furthers the University's objective of excellence in research, scholarship,
and education by publishing worldwide in

Oxford New York

Auckland Cape Town Dar es Salaam Hong Kong Karachi
Kuala Lumpur Madrid Melbourne Mexico City Nairobi
New Delhi Shanghai Taipei Toronto

With offices in

Argentina Austria Brazil Chile Czech Republic France Greece
Guatemala Hungary Italy Japan Poland Portugal Singapore
South Korea Switzerland Thailand Turkey Ukraine Vietnam

Oxford is a registered trade mark of Oxford University Press
in the UK and in certain other countries

Published in the United States
by Oxford University Press Inc., New York

First published 2007
First published in paperback 2008

British Library Cataloguing in Publication Data
Data available

Library of Congress Cataloging in Publication Data
Data available

Typeset by SPI Publisher Services, Pondicherry, India
Printed in Great Britain
on acid-free paper by
CPI Antony Rowe, Chippenham, Wiltshire

ISBN 978–0–19–928075–9 (Hbk.) 978–0–19–955891–9 (Pbk.)

5 7 9 10 8 6 4

Preface

SINCE my programmatic article 'The Rise of the Greek Epic' (*JHS* 108 (1988), 151–72) much of my work has been related to the Homeric poems and the tradition behind them. My 1997 opus *The East Face of Helicon* began as an investigation of the extent to which that tradition was modified under the influence of Near Eastern poetry, though in the event the volume grew to take in more than Homer. The present work may also be seen as part of a series of 'Prolegomena to Homer', or, if you like, to Greek literature.

However, Greece is not here the central point of reference. My subject is the Indo-European poetic and narrative tradition as a whole, and while Greek poetry supplies part of the evidence, it is not itself the object of inquiry. That is one reason why it would not have been appropriate to call the book *The North Face of Helicon.* Another reason is that a different kind of relationship is involved. Helicon, once it was colonized by the Muses, did face east and did not face north; the Indo-European element was a heritage from the past, not a continuing irradiation.

It remains the case that I write as a professional Hellenist, as much an amateur in Indo-European studies as in oriental. I have furnished myself with a working knowledge of some of the relevant languages. I have explored the literatures, roaming far and wide through unfamiliar landscapes, some rugged, some lush, a stranger in Paradise with a clipboard. But when it comes to the reconstruction of proto-Indo-European roots constipated with hypothetical laryngeals, I defer to the authority of the pundits—those black-belt analysts whom I personally hold in the highest admiration, but whom some may view as the unreadable in pursuit of the unpronounceable.

Specialists may look askance at my practice of quoting the Vedic texts with punctuation and capitalized initials for names, and adjusting them as necessary to restore the metre where it has suffered in transmission. I see no merit in the convention of transcribing the verses exactly as transmitted in the *saṃhitā* text, that is, often unmetrically (where it is obvious that an older form has given way to a newer one) and with no punctuation to guide the reader. We do not do this with Greek or Latin texts; why do it with Indian ones? It may be argued that punctuation and capitalization prejudice the interpretation. But if one is going to make use of a text, one must at some point come to an opinion on its articulation and interpretation; usually this will be uncontroversial, and in any case it is only reasonable to share it with the reader, using the means customary with texts in other languages.

The East Face of Helicon was written during my tenure of a Senior Research Fellowship at All Souls College. Most of the present work was too (until my retirement date arrived), and I will once again voice my gratitude to that excellent institution for its benign (but watchful) support. Of individuals, my thanks are due especially to Calvert Watkins and John Penney, who willingly read the chapters as I produced them and gave me the benefit of their expert comments and criticisms. No sensible person would infer that they endorse everything in the final version. I am further indebted for help on occasional questions to Margaret Clunies Ross, Stephanie Jamison, Ann Matonis, Michael Meier-Brügger, Alexis Sanderson, and Gerald Stone.

Calvert Watkins is of course himself the author of a big book with kindred subject matter. It will be apparent how much I owe to it. Mine is different enough in scope and timbre to avoid (I hope) the charge of flogging a dead dragon. Neither he nor I will claim to have exhausted the subject. The field is so large, and its boundaries so far from being set, that it is impossible to read everything that might be relevant. I may well have overlooked ancient texts and modern scholarly works that I would have thought important if I had seen them. I have indeed found it impossible to accommodate everything that I have read while imposing something like an orderly structure on the book. What is presented here, accordingly, is to be regarded not as a compendium of all the material that I and previous researchers have accumulated, but as a selection representing a personal vision, or rather vista.

Vista is the better word, because the object of perception is not something at a fixed distance like a line of hills on the horizon. Vistas have depth. As I will explain in the Introduction, the elements of shared inheritance that can be abstracted from the extant Indo-European literatures cannot all be followed back to proto-Indo-European. Much the greater number lie in the foreground or the middle distance, corresponding to pools of common tradition that must have extended over wide areas of Europe or Eurasia in the later Bronze or early Iron Age. Perhaps they reach further back, but we cannot see; the mists come and go.

M.L.W.

Oxford
New Year, 2006

Contents

Abbreviations

AJP	*American Journal of Philology*
Anat. St.	*Anatolian Studies*
ANET	J. B. Pritchard (ed.), *Ancient Near Eastern Texts relating to the Old Testament*, 3rd edn. (Princeton 1969)
ARW	*Archiv für Religionswissenschaft*
ASPR	G. P. Krapp and E. V. K. Dobbie, *The Anglo-Saxon Poetic Records*, 6 vols. (New York 1931–53)
AV	Atharvaveda (Śaunaka recension)
AV Paipp.	Atharvaveda (Paippalāda recension)
BoTU	E. O. Forrer, *Die Boghazköi-Texte in Umschrift*, 2 vols. (Leipzig 1922–6)
BSL	*Bulletin de la Société de Linguistique de Paris*
CEG	P. A. Hansen, *Carmina Epigraphica Graeca*, 2 vols. (Berlin–New York 1983–9)
CHLI	J. D. Hawkins and others, *Corpus of Hieroglyphic Luwian Inscriptions*, 2 vols. (Berlin–New York 1999–2000)
CIL	*Corpus Inscriptionum Latinarum*
CPB	Gudbrand Vigfusson and F. York Powell, *Corpus Poeticum Boreale*, 2 vols. (Oxford 1883)
CQ	*Classical Quarterly*
CTH	Emmanuel Laroche, *Catalogue des textes hittites* (Paris 1971) (cited by text number)
Edd. min.	*Eddica minora.* Dichtungen eddischer Art aus den Fornaldursögur und anderen Prosawerken zusammengestellt und eingeleitet von Andreas Heusler und Wilhelm Ranisch (Dortmund 1903)
EIEC	J. P. Mallory and D. Q. Adams (edd.), *Encyclopedia of Indo-European Culture* (London–Chicago 1997)
FGrHist	Felix Jacoby, *Die Fragmente der griechischen Historiker* (Berlin–Leiden 1923–58)
GGA	*Göttingische Gelehrte Anzeigen*
GRM	*Germanisch-romanische Monatsschrift*
GVI	Werner Peek, *Griechische Vers-Inschriften*, i (Berlin, 1955)
Gylf.	Snorri Sturluson, *Gylfaginning* (the first part of the Prose Edda)
HS	*Historische Sprachforschung*

HSCP	*Harvard Studies in Classical Philology*
IEW	Julius Pokorny, *Indogermanisches etymologisches Wörterbuch* (Bern–Munich 1959–69)
IF	*Indogermanische Forschungen*
IG	*Inscriptiones Graecae*
Igor	*Slovo o pŭlku Igorě*, ed. by Henri Grégoire, Roman Jakobson, Marc Szeftel, *La geste du Prince Igor'* (New York 1948)
IIJ	*Indo-Iranian Journal*
Il.	*Iliad*
JAOS	*Journal of the American Oriental Society*
JAs.	*Journal Asiatique*
JCS	*Journal of Cuneiform Studies*
JHS	*Journal of Hellenic Studies*
JIES	*Journal of Indo-European Studies*
JIESM	*Journal of Indo-European Studies Monograph Series*
JRAS	*Journal of the Royal Asiatic Society*
KBo	*Keilschrifttexte aus Boghazköi*
KUB	*Keilschrifturkunden aus Boghazköi*
LD	Krisjanis Barons, *Latvju daiņas*, 8 vols. (Riga 1894–1915, 2nd edn. 1922) (cited by text number)
MAMA	*Monumenta Asiae Minoris Antiqua*
MBh.	*Mahābhārata* (cited from the Poona edition)
MGH	*Monumenta Germaniae Historica*
MIE	'Mature' Indo-European (see Introduction, p. 5)
Mír Curad	Jay Jasanoff and others (edd.), *Mír Curad: Studies in Honor of Calvert Watkins* (Innsbruck 1998)
MSS	*Münchener Studien zur Sprachwissenschaft*
NGG	*Nachrichten der Gesellschaft der Wissenschaften zu Göttingen*
Od.	*Odyssey*
OGIS	Wilhelm Dittenberger, *Orientis Graeci Inscriptiones Selectae* (Leipzig 1903–5)
PBA	*Proceedings of the British Academy*
PIE	Proto-Indo-European
PMG	D. L. Page, *Poetae Melici Graeci* (Oxford 1962)
PMGF	Malcolm Davies, *Poetarum Melicorum Graecorum Fragmenta*, i (Oxford 1991)
RC	*Revue Celtique*

RE	Pauly–Wissowa, *Real-Encyclopädie der classischen Altertumswissenschaft* (Stuttgart 1894–1980)
Rh. Mus.	*Rheinisches Museum*
Rm.	*Rāmāyaṇa*
Roscher	W. H. Roscher (ed.), *Ausführliches Lexikon der griechischen und römischen Mythologie* (Leipzig–Berlin 1884–1937)
RV	Rigveda
ŚB	*Śatapatha Brāhmaṇa*
SCHS	A. B. Lord and others (edd.), *Serbo-Croatian Heroic Songs* (6 vols. published: nos. 1–4, 6, 14, Belgrade–Cambridge, Mass. 1953–80)
SEG	*Supplementum Epigraphicum Graecum*
SH	H. Lloyd-Jones and P. J. Parsons, *Supplementum Hellenisticum* (Berlin–New York 1983)
SIG	Wilhelm Dittenberger, *Sylloge Inscriptionum Graecarum*, 3rd edn. (Leipzig 1915–24)
SIGL	*Studia Indogermanica Lodziensia*
Skáldsk.	Snorri Sturluson, *Skáldskaparmál* (the second part of the Prose Edda)
SLG	D. L. Page, *Supplementum Lyricis Graecis* (Oxford 1974)
SSL	*Studi e Saggi Linguistici*
Táin (I)	*Táin bó Cúailnge*, recension I, ed. by Cecile O'Rahilly (Dublin 1976)
Táin (L)	*Táin bó Cúailnge*, Book of Leinster recension, ed. by Cecile O'Rahilly (Dublin 1967)
TAPA	*Transactions of the American Philological Association*
TPhS	*Transactions of the Philological Society*
TrGF	Bruno Snell, Richard Kannicht, Stefan Radt (edd.), *Tragicorum Graecorum Fragmenta* (Göttingen 1971–2004)
TS	*Taittirīya Saṃhitā*, ed. by A. B. Keith, *The Veda of the Black Yajus School entitled Taittirīya Saṅhitā*, i (Cambridge, Mass. 1914)
Vd.	*Vidēvdāt* (Avesta)
Wb. d. Myth.	H. W. Haussig (ed.), *Wörterbuch der Mythologie* (Stuttgart)
Y.	*Yasna* (Avesta)
Yt.	*Yašt* (Avesta)
ZA	*Zeitschrift für Assyriologie*
ZCP	*Zeitschrift für Celtische Philologie*
ZDMG	*Zeitschrift der Deutschen Morgenländischen Gesellschaft*
ZPE	*Zeitschrift für Papyrologie und Epigraphik*
ZVS	*Zeitschrift für Vergleichende Sprachforschung*

Standard abbreviations are used for Greek and Latin authors and works. Any puzzlement should be easily resolved by reference to a Classical dictionary.

Note on Translations Quoted

Most translations offered for quoted passages (Vedic, Avestan, Greek, Old Norse, etc.) are my own. For the Indian epics I normally use the available volumes of the Chicago translation of the *Mahābhārata* and the Princeton translation of the *Rāmāyaṇa*;[1] for *MBh.* 10, W. J. Johnson, *The Sauptikaparvan of the* Mahābhārata (Oxford 1998); for other books of *MBh.*, the old version by K. M. Ganguli published under the name of P. C. Roy, *The Mahabharata of Krishna-Dwaipayana Vyasa* (Calcutta 1884–94). For the *Shāh-nāma* I have generally used the abridged version by Reuben Levy (see Bibliography). The Armenian oral epic *Sassountsy David* is quoted from the translation by A. K. Shalian, *David of Sassoun* (Athens, Ohio 1964), the *Táin bó Cúailnge* from Cecile O'Rahilly's bilingual editions (see Abbreviations list), and *Y Gododdin* from J. T. Koch's version in Koch–Carey (2000) (Bibliography). Sources of other translations used are indicated as they occur.

[1] *MBh.* 1–5 by J. A. B. van Buitenen, 11–12. 167 by J. L. Fitzgerald (Chicago 1973–2004); *Rm.* 1 by R. P. Goldman, 2–3 by S. I. Pollock, 4 by R. Lefeber, 5 by R. P. and S. J. S. Goldman (Princeton 1984–96).

Introduction

'Indo-European' is primarily a term of historical linguistics. It refers to the great family of languages that now extends across every continent and already two thousand years ago extended across the whole breadth of Europe and large tracts of central and southern Asia; or it refers to the hypothetical ancestral language from which all the recorded Indo-European languages descend.

That affinities existed among various of these languages, including Persian and Sanskrit, was often observed from the sixteenth century on. In the seventeenth, the idea emerged of an extinct parent language, generally identified as 'Scythian' or 'Japhetic', as the source of the historical tongues.[1] The scientific study of linguistic relationships began early in the nineteenth century, pioneered by scholars with monosyllabic names such as Rask, Bopp, Grimm, and Pott. It was at this time that the terms 'Indo-Germanic' and 'Indo-European' were coined; they are first recorded in 1810 and 1813 respectively.[2] The two centuries since then have seen steady advances in knowledge and understanding, and the progress achieved is now cumulatively enormous. All serious students operate on the assumption of a single parent language as the historical source of all the known Indo-European languages.

This is still a hypothesis, not an observable fact, but it is an inescapable hypothesis. Of course, when this proto-Indo-European was spoken, it was itself only one of many languages that existed at that time, and it was no doubt related to some of the others. Some scholars argue for affinities with

[1] For the early comparatists see the survey of Sergent (1995), 21–7, who cites an ample bibliography.

[2] See K. Koerner, *IF* 86 (1981), 1–29. 'Indo-Germanic' was meant to define the family by reference to its eastern and western extremities; that Celtic belongs in it was not discovered till the 1830s. 'Indogermanisch' continues to be the prevalent term among German-speakers, for whom it has the merit of greater euphony as well as appealing to national feeling, but in the rest of the learned world the more inclusive 'Indo-European' is now standard.

Semitic, Caucasian, and Uralian, and gather all of these, together with Indo-European, into a super-family dubbed 'Nostratic'. This shimmering construct is of no consequence for the present study. But it is good to bear in mind that Indo-European was not a unique, original entity like the primal cosmic atom before the Big Bang. As a historical reality, it necessarily existed in a historical context.[3]

If there was an Indo-European language, it follows that there was a people who spoke it: not a people in the sense of a nation, for they may never have formed a political unity, and not a people in any racial sense, for they may have been as genetically mixed as any modern population defined by language. If our language is a descendant of theirs, that does not make them 'our ancestors', any more than the ancient Romans are the ancestors of the French, the Romanians, and the Brazilians. The Indo-Europeans were a people in the sense of a linguistic community. We should probably think of them as a loose network of clans and tribes, inhabiting a coherent territory of limited size. It has been estimated that in prehistoric conditions the largest area within which a single language could exist without dividing into mutually unintelligible tongues (as Indo-European, of course, eventually did) might be of up to a million square kilometres—roughly the size of Ontario—but was probably a good deal less.[4]

A language embodies certain concepts and values, and a common language implies some degree of common intellectual heritage. Within the original common territory,[5] which we may call Eurostan, there no doubt existed local diversities: differences of material culture, of dialect, of cult and custom. But so long as the dialects remained mutually intelligible and there was easy communication across the whole area, we might suppose there also to have been a measure of shared tradition in such spheres as religion, storytelling, and general ideology. If the evidence assembled in the present work is not illusory, this theoretical expectation is fulfilled.

Indo-European studies have long spilled beyond the confines of purely linguistic analysis and reconstruction. By the middle of the nineteenth century some scholars—the pioneer was Adalbert Kuhn—had started to make inferences from the linguistic evidence about the people who spoke the proto-language: about their habitat, their conceptual world, their social

[3] Typological similarities with other language families are reviewed by B. Comrie in Ramat (1998), 74–97.

[4] Mallory (1989), 145 f., cf. 64.

[5] It should be understood that 'original' here does not mean 'occupied from the beginning of time', but refers to the initial area from which the later diversification of Indo-European languages proceeded; in other words, the territory occupied by the Indo-Europeans in the last phase of development before they and their one language began to divide.

institutions, their mythology.[6] From 1853 onwards Kuhn, Theodor Benfey, and others began to identify parallel poetic phrases in different branches of the Indo-European tradition, especially in Greek and Indic: phrases composed of words that corresponded etymologically in the different languages, and expressing concepts such as would not have had a place in ordinary everyday speech but only in an elevated formal type of discourse, in poetry or high rhetoric. The inference was that the Indo-Europeans had had poetry and a poetic language, some relics of which survived long enough in traditional usage to be still recognizable in texts available to us.[7] In 1860 there appeared the first attempt to reconstruct Indo-European forms of versification by comparing Greek and Vedic metres.[8]

The comparative mythology that took flight at this period, associated especially with Kuhn and Müller, stalled within fifty years and made a forced landing. This was partly because some of its most striking conclusions were based on equations of names that turned out to be untenable as more exact linguistic rules were established by the so-called Neo-grammarians, and partly because of its practitioners' propensity for explaining almost every myth or mythical personage as an allegory of the sun, moon, storm, or some other natural phenomenon. There continued to be sober surveys of the evidence for Indo-European culture, and numerous attempts, based on ecological appraisals and data from prehistoric archaeology, to determine the whereabouts of the *Urheimat*, the original homeland. But it was in the linguistic field that the clearest progress was being made. The Neo-grammarians, whose leading figure was Karl Brugmann, achieved what seemed to be a fairly complete and definitive account of the Indo-European languages and their evolution from the parent tongue. Then in the first two decades of the twentieth century further horizons opened up through the discovery of two hitherto unknown branches of the Indo-European family, represented by Tocharian and Hittite.

[6] Adalbert Kuhn, *Zur ältesten Geschichte der indogermanischen Völker* (Progr. Berlin 1845), expanded in *Indische Studien* 1 (1850), 321–63; id. (1859); Jacob Grimm, *Geschichte der deutschen Sprache* (Leipzig 1848; 4th edn. 1880); various works of Friedrich Max Müller, from his *Essay on Comparative Mythology* (1856) to his *Science of Mythology* (1897); Pictet (1859–63); Michel Bréal, *Hercule et Cacus* (Paris 1860); Victor Hehn, *Kulturpflanzen und Haustiere* (Berlin 1870); August Fick, *Die ehemalige Spracheinheit der Indogermanen Europas* (Göttingen 1873); Otto Schrader, *Sprachvergleichung und Urgeschichte* (Jena 1883), translated as *Prehistoric Antiquities of the Aryan Peoples* (London 1890). Already in 1788 Sir William Jones (*Asiatic Researches*, i. 422 f.) had found common elements in Greek, Roman, and Hindu religion and postulated a historical connection.

[7] For an account of the progress of this line of inquiry from Kuhn onwards see Schmitt (1967), 6–60. The first to speak explicitly of 'traces of Indo-Germanic poetry' was Adolf Kaegi, *Der Rigveda. Die älteste Literatur der Inder* (2nd edn., Leipzig 1881), 128 n. 12, cf. 158 n. 82.

[8] See the section on metre in Chapter 1.

The year 1924 saw the first of a long series of publications by Georges Dumézil that were to give comparative mythology a fresh direction and a fresh esteem. While pursuing philological equations of names as far as they went, he held that they were not necessary for establishing connections between myths in different traditions, as new names had often been substituted for old ones. More significant, in his view, were parallel structures. In the 1930s he developed his famous theory of the three *fonctions*, the sacral, the martial, and the economic. This gave him a structural formula that he was able to find in myths, pantheons, and rituals all over the place. At first he thought that it derived from a real threefold division of Indo-European society into holy men, warriors, and peasants. Later he retreated from this position and presented the system rather as a feature of Indo-European thought, a habit of organizing things in terms of those three categories.

Dumézil's work has been enormously influential. Some researchers continue to operate within the framework of his tripartite ideology, and to refer to the First, Second, or Third Function as if they had the same truth-status as the first, second, or third declension in Latin. Others have been strongly critical. As the system is essentially a theoretical taxonomy, it is hardly capable of proof or disproof. You may find it illuminating and useful, or you may not. Personally I do not. But one must acknowledge Dumézil's breadth of learning and combinatorial brilliance, and give due credit for his real discoveries.[9]

Meanwhile the more strictly philological approach to the quest for Indo-European poetry and culture made unspectacular but steady progress under the pens of such scholars as Paul Thieme, Bernfried Schlerath, Jaan Puhvel, Calvert Watkins, Marcello Durante, Enrico Campanile, and Wolfgang Meid. Something of a milestone was set in 1967 by Rüdiger Schmitt's *Dichtung und Dichtersprache in indogermanischer Zeit*, a major synthesis of what had been achieved up to that date in the field of Indo-European poetics and poetic language. Schmitt did not concern himself with theology and myth, and his focus is somewhat restricted also in that Celtic and Anatolian evidence remains outside his purview.

In the last thirty or forty years Indo-European studies of every kind have gained energy and mass. A journal devoted to their less austerely linguistic aspects was founded in 1973 and has thrived, calving numerous monographs by the way. There have been ever more frequent conferences resulting in bulky

[9] On Dumézil and his development see C. Scott Littleton, *The New Comparative Mythology* (Berkeley–Los Angeles 1966; 3rd edn. 1982); W. W. Belier, *Decayed Gods. Origin and Development of Georges Dumézil's Idéologie Tripartite* (Leiden 1991) (strongly critical); Sergent (1995), 328–33; B. Schlerath, *Kratylos* 40 (1995), 1–48; 41 (1996), 1–67 (critical); Polomé in E. C. Polomé (ed.), *Indo-European Religion after Dumézil* (*JIESM* 16, Washington, DC 1996), 5–12; W. W. Belier, ibid. 37–72.

volumes of proceedings, Festschriften and Gedenkschriften for distinguished Indo-Europeanists, and other substantial books. Since 1997 we have had an imposing and decidedly useful (if uneven) *Encyclopedia of Indo-European Culture.*

THE INDO-EUROPEANS IN SPACE AND TIME

In assessing the evidence from the diverse literatures and traditions of the Indo-European peoples, we shall need to have a notion of their historical relationships. Just as in reconstructing a manuscript archetype one cannot simply take agreements between any two or three manuscripts as reflecting the archetype reading, but must consider their stemmatic relationships, and the degree to which these relationships are confused by cross-contamination, so with Indo-European.

The first question concerns dialect groupings within Indo-European.[10] There is a growing consensus that the Anatolian branch, represented by Hittite and related languages of Asia Minor, was the first to diverge from common Indo-European, which continued to evolve for some time after the split before breaking up further. This raises a problem of nomenclature. It means that with the decipherment of Hittite the 'Indo-European' previously reconstructed acquired a brother in the shape of proto-Anatolian, and the archetype of the family had to be put back a stage. E. H. Sturtevant coined a new term 'Indo-Hittite' (better would have been 'Euro-Hittite'), and at a recent conference Robert Drews advocated using this for the larger construct and reserving 'Indo-European' for what remains after the separation of Anatolian.[11] The great majority of linguists, however, use 'Indo-European' to include Anatolian, and have done, naturally enough, ever since Hittite was recognized to be 'an Indo-European language'. They will no doubt continue to do so. For the time being we lack a convenient term to denote the non-Anatolian side of the family. I shall call it 'Mature Indo-European' (MIE), and use 'Proto-Indo-European' (PIE) for the archetype of the whole family (Drews's PIH).

[10] Among recent works on this topic see Gamkrelidze–Ivanov (1995), 325–74; *EIEC* 550–6 s.v. Subgrouping; Berkeley Linguistic Society: *Proceedings of the Twenty-fourth Annual Meeting: Special Session in Indo-European Subgroupings* (Berkeley 1998).

[11] In Drews (2001), 250. It may be mentioned here that some scholars regard Etruscan as representing another branch of the family, related to Anatolian. See F. R. Adrados, *JIES* 17 (1989), 363–83; F. C. Woudhuizen, *JIES* 19 (1991), 133–50 and 29 (2001), 505–7; doubted by E. Neu, *HS* 104 (1991), 9–28; response by Adrados, *HS* 107 (1994), 54–76.

Within MIE, the clearest major sub-group is an eastern one characterized by a series of linguistic innovations and represented by Indo-Iranian, Armenian, Phrygian, and Greek. It is sometimes called Graeco-Aryan.[12] To the north, Slavonic and Baltic seem to be closely related to each other, and in the west Celtic and Italic. But overall one finds a network of multiple overlapping links connecting different languages and groups, especially where they are neighbours, or have been at some time in the past: for example connecting Slavonic with Iranian, or Germanic with Italic or Celtic on the one side and with Baltic on the other. Linguistic changes (especially phonetic changes) frequently cross dialect and language boundaries and so blur them, and it may come about that a dialect of one language shares features with neighbour languages that other dialects do not.[13] When one bears in mind that most peoples have had different neighbours at different times, and so been exposed successively to different linguistic influences, it is not surprising if the outcome is a complex layered pattern that resists instant stemmatic analysis.

An example of an isogloss that once appeared fundamental for language grouping, but is now seen to be of secondary importance, is the celebrated *satem* shift. This is the generalized change of palatal velar consonants to sibilants, as illustrated by the [s] in Avestan *satəm* 'a hundred' corresponding to the [k] in Latin *centum* or Greek *ἑ-κατόν*. In the nineteenth century Indo-European languages were routinely divided into *centum* and *satem* languages, and this was taken to be a basic dichotomy. As we now understand, the absence of the *satem* shift is not a significant indicator of a relationship between languages. Its presence does make a link, but only a superficial one, as the shift was an areal phenomenon which affected a number of languages that were in contact at the time, cutting across older established and more basic divisions. The *satem* languages include Indo-Iranian, Armenian, and Slavonic, but not Greek or Phrygian. The shift thus affected only a part of the Graeco-Aryan territories, together with some other lands adjoining them.

The central part of the Indo-European area is represented by little-known ancient languages such as Illyrian, Thracian, and Dacian, and by modern Albanian. Some regard Albanian as descended from ancient Illyrian, while others connect it rather with Dacian. Thracian and Albanian, and probably the other two, are *satem* languages. Dacian and Thracian are considered to be

[12] On the term Aryan, which in modern usage refers to Indo-Iranian, see p. 142. For the Graeco-Aryan grouping cf. Kretschmer (1896), 168–70; Durante (1976), 18–30; Euler (1979), 18–23 (history of views since 1858); James Clackson, *The Linguistic Relationship between Armenian and Greek* (Oxford 1994), who contests the belief often encountered that Greek and Armenian have a specially close relationship within the group.

[13] Kretschmer (1896), 24 f., 411.

closely related, and to show some affinities with Baltic.[14] Links have also been seen between Thracian and the Anatolian languages Lydian and Luwian.[15]

For the most part the pattern of affinities and distances between the various Indo-European languages and language groups corresponds fairly well to the geographical relationships of their earliest recorded speakers. The striking exception is Tocharian, a language, or rather two kindred languages, spoken in the second half of the first millennium CE around the Tarim basin in Chinese Turkestan. It shows no close connections with the languages of the east.

Chronological parameters

In Anatolia, from about 1650 BCE, we find the earliest attested Indo-European language, Hittite, together with two related languages, Luwian and Palaic. The personal names attested in Assyrian traders' records from Kültepe (the ancient Kanesh, 20 km. north-east of Kayseri) show that the dominant population of that area was already Hittite at the beginning of the second millennium, and that Hittite already had a distinct profile separating it from Luwian. Clearly these Indo-European peoples were well established in Anatolia before 2000 BCE. But they were hardly autochthonous, for there were also many non-Indo-European speakers in the land. The native language of the central region was Hattic, which is thought to have Caucasian affinities. Further east there was a solid front of non-Indo-European languages, Hurrian and Semitic. It was in the west and south of Anatolia that the languages of the Indo-European group prevailed. This geographical distribution points strongly to the Indo-European speakers' having entered the country not from the east via the Caucasus, but from the west, from the Balkans, as the Phrygians and Galatians did in later times.[16]

We shall see shortly that Graeco-Aryan must already have been differentiated from MIE by 2500 BCE. We have to allow several centuries for the development of MIE after its split from proto-Anatolian and before its further division. The secession of proto-Anatolian, then, must be put back at least to the early third millennium, whether or not it was synchronous

[14] Kretschmer (1896), 213 f.; I. Duridanov, *Thrakisch-dakische Studien* (Sofia 1969), 99 f.; M.-M. Rădulescu, *JIES* 12 (1984), 82–5 and 22 (1994), 334–40. Cf. also E. C. Polomé in *The Cambridge Ancient History*, iii(1). 866–88; Gamkrelidze–Ivanov (1995), 805 f. (who claim Albanian affinities with Graeco-Aryan); Sergent (1995), 94–9.

[15] H. Birnbaum, *JIES* 2 (1974), 373.

[16] G. Steiner, *JIES* 18 (1990), 185–214; Sergent (1995), 409. For the Kültepe tablets see Annelies Kammenhuber, *Die Arier im Vorderen Orient* (Heidelberg 1968), 27–9; Gamkrelidze–Ivanov (1995), 757–9.

with the migration into Anatolia. There is in fact archaeological evidence that would be consistent with its introduction to Anatolia at that period.[17] It is possible that its carriers could have crossed from Europe by a land bridge, the Black Sea being still an enclosed lake; at any rate the Black Sea's water level appears to have been much lower then than it is now.[18]

It has come to be widely accepted that Greek-speakers were preceded in Greece by speakers of an Indo-European language of the Anatolian type, similar to Luwian.[19] These were the people responsible for the numerous place-names ending in *-nthos* and *-ssos*. Parnassos, for example, is happily explicable in terms of the Luwian *parna-* 'house' and possessive suffix *-ssa-*, and Hittite and Luwian texts attest an Anatolian town (or towns) of the same name, Parnassa. We may call this pre-Hellenic language Parnassian. From the distribution of the names, it seems to have been current in the Early Helladic II period, which began around 2800. I take it to betoken not an invasion from Anatolia, but a parallel movement down from Thrace by a branch of the same people as entered Anatolia, the people who were to appear 1,500 years later as the Luwians.

The first speakers of Greek—or rather of the language that was to develop into Greek; I will call them mello-Greeks[20]—arrived in Greece, on the most widely accepted view, at the beginning of Early Helladic III, that is, around 2300.[21] They came by way of Epirus, probably from somewhere north of the Danube. Recent writers have derived them from Romania or eastern Hungary.[22]

The Phrygians, whose language shows a number of noteworthy similarities to Greek,[23] crossed into Anatolia after 1200. Previously they had been

[17] See W. H. Goodenough in Cardona (1970), 261 (appearance of battle-axes in western Anatolia); M. M. Winn, *JIES* 2 (1974), 120 f. (east Balkan Chalcolithic cultures antecedent to Troy I); J. Mellaart, *JIES* 9 (1981), 135–49 (spread of north-west Anatolian cultures to the later Luwian lands around 2700–2600); Sergent (1995), 409 f.

[18] The Early Bronze Age site of Kiten on the Bulgarian coast, now ten metres under water, was still inhabited in 2715 ± 10 BCE (dendrochronological date), when its last pilings were driven: P. I. Kuniholm in Drews (2001), 28.

[19] L. R. Palmer, *TPhS* 1958, 36–74; id., *Mycenaeans and Minoans* (2nd edn., London 1965), 321–57; Alfred Heubeck, *Praegraeca* (Erlangen 1961); Sergent (1995), 140–4; O. Carruba, *Athenaeum* 83 (1995), 5–44; R. Drews, *JIES* 25 (1997), 153–77; M. Finkelberg, *Classical World* 91 (1997), 3–20. Note the reservations of Anna Morpurgo Davies in Gerald Cadogan (ed.), *The End of the Early Bronze Age in the Aegean* (Leiden 1986), 109–21.

[20] From Greek *μέλλω*, 'I am going to be'.

[21] Cf. West (1997), 1 with n. 2.

[22] Sergent (1995), 413–15; J. Makkay, *Atti e memorie del Secondo Congresso Internazionale di Micenologia* (Rome 1996), 777–84; id., *Origins of the Proto-Greeks and Proto-Anatolians from a Common Perspective* (Budapest 2003), 47–54.

[23] G. Neumann, *Phrygisch und Griechisch* (*Sitz.-Ber. Österr. Ak.* 499, 1988); Sergent (1995), 122 f.

residing in the south Balkans. They may have retreated from there under pressure from Thracian tribes coming down from further north, from beyond the Dnieper.[24] It was formerly assumed that Phrygians and Thracians were closely related, and compound adjectives such as 'Thraco-Phrygian' used to be freely used in various connections. In fact there is no special affinity between the two. It is to be observed that Phrygian, like Greek, was a *centum* language, whereas Thracian was *satem*, like Slavonic and Iranian.

Armenian too is a *satem* language, and not closely related to Phrygian, even though both belong to the Graeco-Aryan group. In historical times the Armenians were located far away to the east of the Phrygians, and Herodotus (7. 73) was told that they were a Phrygian colony. Perhaps someone had observed a similarity to the Phrygian in their language or culture. But if we set aside this dubious western connection, their geographical situation is much easier to understand on the hypothesis that they came there by way of the Caucasus. They first appear in history in the seventh century BCE; there is no sign of them earlier, despite our having Urartian inscriptions from the area from the immediately preceding centuries. Their arrival may be connected with the burning of the main Urartian fortresses in around 640.[25] This was just at the time when the Cimmerians had come down from north of the Caucasus and were causing havoc throughout Asia Minor. There seems much to be said for the view that the Armenian influx was part of the same movement.[26] If so, the Armenians had previously lived in the north-east Pontic area, in the immediate neighbourhood of other *satem*-speakers such as the Scythians (who drove out the Cimmerians according to Herodotus 1. 15).

The Iranian and Indic languages are closely related to each other, and must be traced back to a common Indo-Iranian or Aryan. The period of Indo-Iranian unity may be put in the late third to early second millennium, and its territory located north and east of the Caspian Sea. From an archaeological point of view it seems a good fit with the Andronovo culture which developed in northern Kazakhstan between 2300 and 2100 and later spread southwards and eastwards.

Indic was already differentiated from Iranian by the sixteenth century, when a horde of Aryan warriors established themselves as rulers of the land of Mitanni in north Syria. Their personal names, their gods, and other evidence of their speech show that they were Indic-speakers. We may suppose that Indic had been the dialect of the southern Aryans, and that they had made a major southward movement down the east side of the Caspian. Then, faced

[24] Cf. Sergent (1995), 423–5.

[25] Paul Zimansky in Drews (2001), 23 f.

[26] Cf. Feist (1913), 65; Schramm (1973), 164–217.

with the vast uninhabitable desert region of eastern Iran, they divided right and left: one group headed west between Mt Elbruz and the sea and eventually made its fortune in Mitanni, while the main body proceeded east through Afghanistan and reached the Punjab before the middle of the millennium.

An Iranian migration followed some centuries later, again moving south and dividing at the desert. The ones who turned right camped in the Zagros mountains and eventually expanded further south to become the Medes and Persians, peoples first mentioned in Assyrian records in the ninth and eighth centuries. The ones who turned left became the East Iranians of Bactria and Sogdiana. Other Iranians stayed in the north and roamed widely across the steppes, to appear in the mid-first millennium as Scythians and Sarmatians.[27]

If Indo-Iranian already had a distinct identity in central Asia in the last quarter of the third millennium, and mello-Greeks were entering Greece at the same period, we must clearly go back at least to the middle of the millennium for the postulated Graeco-Aryan linguistic unity or community. This was presumably situated in the east Balkan and Pontic regions.

We are beginning to get a sense of overall chronology, or at least a set of *termini ante quos*: divergence of Anatolian from the rest of Indo-European by 2900 at latest, perhaps some centuries earlier; emergence of a distinct eastern dialect (Graeco-Aryan) by 2500; individuation of Greek, Indo-Iranian, and no doubt other languages in the group by 2300; differentiation of Indic and Iranian by 1600.

It is more difficult to reconstruct developments in other parts of the Indo-European world. Historical evidence for the northern and western peoples—Balts and Slavs, Germans, Celts, Italics, and the rest—becomes available much later than it does for the Anatolians, Indics, and Greeks. By the seventh century BCE we can see that a clear differentiation of Italic languages has occurred; a common Italic must surely be put back into the second millennium.[28] We may assume that at least a proto-Celtic and a proto-Germanic also existed by the same date. But this is more than a millennium after the epoch when MIE began to break up. To bridge the gap we are reduced to poring over the archaeological record, trying to identify prehistoric cultures that might have evolved by continuous development into what we know to have been a Celtic culture, an Italic one, and so on.

[27] On Indo-Iranian migrations cf. R. Heine-Geldern, *Man* 56 (1956), 136–40; P. Bosch-Gimpera, *JIES* 1 (1973), 513–17; T. Burrow, *JRAS* 1973, 123–40; D. W. Anthony, *JIES* 19 (1991), 203; *EIEC* 308–11; A. Hintze in Meid (1998), 139–53. On the Iranianness of the Scythians cf. Kretschmer (1896), 214 f.; Sergent (1995), 429.

[28] Cf. H. Rix in Alfred Bammesberger and Theo Vennemann (edd.), *Languages in Prehistoric Europe* (Heidelberg 2003), 147–72.

Those practised in this form of endeavour tend to agree that three large culture complexes in the third millennium are likely to be relevant to the early history of the Indo-European dispersal: the Yamna(ya) or Pit-grave culture which extended from the Danube to the Urals, a Balkan-Danubian complex in south-east Europe, and the Corded Ware culture extending from the Rhine across Germany and southern Scandinavia eastwards to the upper Volga. One adept has written recently:

> No one has yet figured out a coherent linguistic history of Europe without assuming that both the Corded Ware and the Yamnaya cultures were predominantly Indo-European speaking, and yet there is no general agreement about the relationship between these cultures.[29]

His own model seems entirely plausible. His original Indo-Europeans are represented by the Sredny Stog and Khvalynsk cultures in the Ukraine and middle Volga regions. About 4400 BCE, following depopulation in the Balkans, they spread westward. The division between the Anatolians and the rest perhaps took place in the lower Dnieper region in the first half of the fourth millennium, before the invention or general currency of the wheel, as the Anatolian word for a wheel is not from the same root as that current in other branches of Indo-European.[30] The Anatolian party might be represented by the Usatovo and other hybrid cultures found west of the Black Sea down to 3500; this area had close ties across the Bosporos. In the third millennium what later appears as the Luwian area shows a sequence of destruction and depopulation, followed by a switch to a more pastoral economy: this would be the work of the incoming Indo-European groups. The MIE peoples would be represented by the Yamna and Corded Ware cultures together. Evidence is cited for population movements from the steppe into north and central Europe between about 3500 and 3200.[31]

This scenario implies a higher (but not much higher) chronology than the *termini ante quos* proposed above. In placing the last phase of Indo-European unity no earlier than the late fifth to early fourth millennium, it is in accord with arguments drawn from the Indo-Europeans' apparent familiarity with the domesticated horse, ox traction, and the woolly sheep.[32] It also suggests an incipient division between east and west Indo-European in the late fourth millennium. The eastern variety would be ancestral to Graeco-Aryan.

[29] B. J. Darden in Drews (2001), 212.

[30] The earliest evidence for wheeled vehicles is from Poland and dated to 3530–3310. See D. W. Anthony, *JIES* 19 (1991), 199 f.; K. Jones-Bley, *JIES* 28 (2000), 445; Darden in Drews (2001), 204–9. On the vocabulary see *EIEC* 640 f.

[31] Darden, ibid. 184–228.

[32] Cf. *EIEC* 157, 276, 648 f.; E. W. Barber in Drews (2001), 6, 13; Darden, ibid. 193–200, 204.

SOURCES

In the search for Indo-European poetry and myth we have to draw on sources of very various character and very various date, from hymns and ritual texts of the second millennium BCE to songs and folk-tales recorded in the nineteenth century CE. It might be thought that nothing sound could possibly be built from such diverse materials. But Indo-European linguists are in a similar boat. They work on the one hand with Hittite and Vedic texts that are over three thousand years old, on the other hand with Albanian or Lithuanian, which were first recorded no more than five or six hundred years ago. Yet from data of such unequal antiquity they are able to forge unshakeable structures. The reason is simple. Although languages undergo enormous changes over two or three millennia, and to the casual eye are transformed out of recognition, they may also preserve many highly archaic elements. Even modern English, which cannot compare with Lithuanian as a conservator of ancient morphology, is full of Indo-European vocabulary; it preserves unchanged, almost alone, the original sound [w]; it preserves such old features as ablauting verbs (sing, sang, sung) and free-range preverbs (not easy to get away from). Such things are identifiable as old by surveying the whole system. Similar principles will apply in the present investigation.

As in linguistic reconstruction, we seek to work back to prototypes by comparing data from different branches of the Indo-European tradition. The more widely separated and historically independent the branches, the further back in time their concord should carry us. Within each branch we shall pay greatest attention to the oldest available material, as that is where inherited elements are most likely to appear, and where what seem like significant elements are most likely to be inherited. In some cases, naturally, a genuinely inherited motif may turn up only in a later source, but our emphasis must be on the earlier ones.

The oldest extant texts in Indo-European languages are those in the **Anatolian** languages Hittite, Luwian, and Palaic, starting in the seventeenth century BCE, and written either in cuneiform or in Luwian hieroglyphs.[33] The greatest number are in Hittite and date from the New Kingdom, *c.*1350–1200. The majority are prescriptions for rituals; there are also state documents of various kinds, royal annals, prayers, laws, treaties, correspondence,

[33] The cuneiform texts are identified by reference to Emmanuel Laroche, *Catalogue des textes hittites* (Paris 1971) (*CTH*); the hieroglyphic ones by reference to J. D. Hawkins and others, *Corpus of Hieroglyphic Luwian Inscriptions*, i–ii (Berlin–New York 1999–2000) (*CHLI*).

instructions to officials, omen texts, oracles, and a limited number of mythological narratives. The myths, however, mostly seem to be taken over from other, non-Indo-European peoples of the region (Hattics, Hurrians, Babylonians, Canaanites), and have little to offer for the present enterprise. The ritual texts sometimes contain embedded hymns, prayers, or incantations, which may be more relevant. The vocabulary of the languages themselves can throw valuable lights.

Hieroglyphic Luwian inscriptions continue into the first millennium, being most frequent in the first quarter. From later centuries we have inscriptions in other languages of Asia Minor that belong to the Anatolian family, such as Lydian, Lycian, Carian, and Sidetic. They have little to offer in terms of content, but I shall have occasion to mention some of them in the section on metre in Chapter 1.

Of comparable antiquity to the Hittite and Luwian material, and of much richer interest for our purpose, is the **Indic**. Of prime importance are the 1028 hymns of the Rigveda (RV), thought to have been composed in the Punjab in the period between 1500 and 1000 BCE. The collection is arranged in ten books, of which 2–7 are the oldest: these are the so-called Family Books, attributed to poets from half a dozen specific families. Books 1 and 10 are the latest. A second large collection, the Atharvaveda (AV), probably overlaps in time with the later parts of the Rigveda, from which much material is repeated. It is more magical in character, consisting largely of curses, blessings, and charms for various purposes. It exists in two recensions. The better known is that of the Śaunaka school, which contains 581 hymns. The other is that of the Paippalādas (AV Paipp.), only parts of which have so far been edited. A later Vedic text that I have occasionally cited is the Black Yajurveda in the recension of the Taittirīyas (*Taittirīya Saṃhitā* = TS). Later still is the *Bṛhaddevatā*, an index of the deities of the Rigveda, of interest for the myths that it relates about them.

Apart from this Vedic and para-Vedic literature, India's two great epics, the *Mahābhārata* and the *Rāmāyaṇa*, are of some significance. Although later in language and versification than the Vedas and certainly composed at a later time—they grew over a long period, conventionally put between about 400 BCE and 400 CE—they clearly continue traditions of narrative poetry going back many centuries.[34]

[34] The subject of the first, the war of the Bhāratas, should have taken place (if it was a historical event) around the ninth century BCE. For an account of the epics see Puhvel (1987), 68–81 and 89–92, and in general Brockington (1998). He reviews Indo-Europeanists' efforts with the *Mahābhārata* on pp. 67–81.

The oldest documents of **Iranian** literature are the seventeen hymns of Zarathushtra (Zoroaster) known as the *Gāthās*. They are transmitted as part of the Avesta, the corpus of Parsi sacred books. The three largest components in what has survived of the collection are the *Yasna* liturgy (Y.), the *Yašts* or hymns of praise (Yt.), and the *Vidēvdāt* or *Vendidād* (Vd.), a book that sets out (in the words of R. C. Zaehner) 'dreary prescriptions concerning ritual purity' and 'impossible punishments for ludicrous crimes'. The *Gāthās* form chapters 28–34, 43–51, and 53 of the *Yasna*. Their language is about as archaic in Indo-Iranian terms as that of the Rigveda, and this persuades some scholars to date them to before 1000 BCE; others put them as late as the sixth century. The truth very likely lies between these extremes. Next in age is another section of the *Yasna*, the '*Gāthā* of the Seven Chapters' (Y. 35–41). The remainder of the Avesta, known collectively as the Younger Avesta, dates probably from between the eighth and fourth centuries BCE, the *Vidēvdāt* being the latest part.

Zarathushtra lived in eastern Iran, perhaps Drangiana in the south-western part of what is now Afghanistan, and the Avestan language is east Iranian. West Iranian is represented by Old Persian, the language of the royal inscriptions promulgated by Darius I (reigned 521–486) and his successors down to Artaxerxes III (359–338).[35]

For anything in the nature of Iranian epic we have to wait for the *Shāh-nāma* of Firdawsi, a lengthy verse history of the Iranian empire composed about 975–1010. It does not continue a native tradition of epic, but it does embody much ancient myth and folktale.[36]

From another corner of the Iranian world we have an interesting body of legend recorded at a still later date. This is the heritage of the Ossetes, who form an Indo-European enclave in the ethnic mosaic of the northern Caucasus, speaking a language of the Iranian family. They are believed to be a remnant of the Alans, who were powerful in the region until the eleventh century. Their mythology, which is concerned with a legendary race of heroes called the Narts, was first brought to wider attention by Dumézil, and collections of the material have been published by others more recently.[37]

35 These are cited from the edition of R. G. Kent, *Old Persian. Grammar, Texts, Lexicon* (New Haven 1953).

36 See Puhvel (1987), 117–25.

37 Georges Dumézil, *Légendes sur les Nartes* (Paris 1930); id., *Le livre des héros. Légendes sur les Nartes* (Paris 1965); id. (1968–73), i. 441–575; id. in *Wb. d. Myth.*, i. 4: Mythologie der kaukasischen und iranischen Völker (1986); Sikojev (1985); Colarusso (2002). See also the highly erudite and informative chapter by H. W. Bailey in A. T. Hatto (ed.), *Traditions of Heroic and Epic Poetry* (London 1980–9), i. 236–67.

The remaining Indo-European language in which we have texts from the second millennium is **Greek**. However, these early, non-literary documents in the Linear B script yield little that we can use. A far more rewarding source for Indo-European inheritance is the corpus of Homeric and Hesiodic poetry. Most of it was fixed in writing in the seventh century BCE, but some of the material it contains, and the traditional language in which it is expressed, have more ancient roots, reaching back at least into the Mycenaean age. Next in importance are the lyric poets of the period 650–450. It is one of the latest of these (also the most extensively preserved), the Boeotian Pindar, who has the greatest amount of interest to offer. Calvert Watkins has called him 'in many ways the most Indo-European of Greek poets'.

The other languages of the Graeco-Aryan group are Phrygian and Armenian. The **Phrygian** material is epigraphic, and comes from two separate periods: from the eighth to the fourth century BCE (Old Phrygian), and the second to fourth century CE (New Phrygian). Some of the inscriptions are metrical or contain metrical phrases, and certain formulae of elevated diction are recognizable.[38] The literary attestation of **Armenian** begins after the Christianization of the country in the fourth century. There are eight fragments of pre-Christian oral verse on mythological and heroic themes, preserved in quotation, and some other evidence of ancient beliefs.[39] Popular oral heroic poetry survived into the twentieth century, and 1939 saw the publication of a national 'folk epic' *Sassountsy David*, put together from poems transcribed from bardic recitations. It deals with the lives and adventures of four generations of legendary kings who founded and ruled in the city of Sassoun (now Sasun in Turkey). From the formal point of view this *Grossepos* is an artificial construct, but the materials represent authentic oral tradition.[40]

For the ancient **Thracian** and **Illyrian** peoples the source material is extremely scanty. It consists largely of personal and place names, a few glosses from Classical sources, and one or two inscriptions. To these can be added a larger body of inscriptions from south-east Italy in the Messapic language,

[38] Texts are collected by Haas (1966); Claude Brixhe and Michel Lejeune, *Corpus des inscriptions paléo-phrygiennes*, i–ii (Paris 1984); Vladimir Orel, *The Language of Phrygians. Description and Analysis* (New York 1997).

[39] Collected and translated by L. H. Gray, *Revue des Études Arméniennes* 6 (1926), 159–67. See also J. R. Russell, ibid. [new series] 20 (1986/7), 253–70; id., *Acta Antiqua* 32 (1989), 317–30; Ishkol-Kerovpian (1986).

[40] Cf. C. M. Bowra, *Heroic* Poetry (London 1952), 357. I cite the work by page from the translation by A. K. Shalian, *David of Sassoun* (Athens, Ohio, 1964).

which is generally considered to be Illyrian, and a number of statements by Classical authors about Thracian religion.[41]

Among the **Italic** languages Latin naturally takes pride of place. But Latin literature is so pervasively influenced by Greek that it can only be used with the greatest caution as a separate witness to Indo-European tradition. The most promising sources are the earliest poets, who, while by no means innocent of Greek influence, at any rate were the least far removed from older native traditions; religious ritual and language, insofar as they are not based on Greek models; and popular and subliterary material such as charms and incantations. Outside Latin the most notable text is the series of bronze tablets from Iguvium (Gubbio) containing the proceedings of a college of priests, the Atiedian Brethren, with ritual prescriptions and regulations. They date from between 200 and 50 BCE, and constitute the principal document of the Umbrian language. Occasional mention will be made of other Italic dialects such as Marrucinian and Venetic.

Celtic evidence, coming as it does from the most westerly of the Indo-European territories, is of especial interest and value as a complement to what can be gathered from Graeco-Aryan sources. There is a gap in time between the continental Celtic material and the insular. The first, consisting of Lepontic, Gaulish, and Celtiberian inscriptions, comes from the Roman period and fades out in the third century CE. The Gaulish inscriptions are the most significant, giving us many names of local deities and sometimes other things of religious interest. Further information on the Celts and their ways is provided by Greek and Latin writers such as Diodorus, Strabo, and Caesar, who were all indebted to the Stoic Posidonius, and some others who were not.[42]

The insular Celtic material consists mainly (apart from some primitive Irish inscriptions in the Ogam script) of Irish and British literature, and it begins around 600 CE. On the Irish side, besides a not very large quantity of early poems and poetic fragments collected by Kuno Meyer and Enrico Campanile, the main body of pertinent material is narrative prose (with some embedded verse) dealing with heroic and legendary subject matter and dating from the eighth to twelfth centuries. There are four major groups, known as the Ulster and Fenian Cycles, the Cycle of the Kings, and the Mythological

[41] See Clemen (1936), 83–92; Detschew (1957); Krahe (1955–64); Mayer (1957–9); Haas (1962); C. Brixhe and A. Panayotou, 'Le thrace', in Françoise Bader (ed.), *Langues indo-européennes* (Paris 1997), 181–205; C. de Simone and S. Marchesini, *Monumenta Linguae Messapicae* (2 vols., Wiesbaden 2002).

[42] Zwicker (1934–6); Michel Lejeune, *Lepontica* (Paris 1971); id. and others, *Recueil des inscriptions gauloises*, i–iv (Paris 1985–2002); Meid (1994); id., *Celtiberian Inscriptions* (Budapest 1994); Jürgen Untermann, *Monumenta Linguarum Hispanicarum*, iv: *Die tartessischen, keltiberischen und lusitanischen Inschriften* (Wiesbaden 1997); Lambert (2003).

Cycle. The most celebrated single work, from the Ulster Cycle, is the *Táin bó Cúailnge* or *Cattle-raid of Cooley* (sometimes referred to simply as 'the *Táin*', though there are also other *Cattle-raids*). According to Thurneysen it was already known in the first half of the eighth century, but it is preserved in later recensions of the ninth and eleventh.[43] Other works to be mentioned by name, all from the twelfth century, are the *Dindshenchas*, which are prose and verse texts concerned with the lore and legend attached to place names, the *Acallam na Senórach* (*Conversation of the Ancients*), a collection of numerous stories and poems with a narrative frame, and the *Lebor Gabála Érenn* (*Book of the Invasions of Ireland*), an antiquarian mythical history.

From Britain we have a poetic and prose literature in Early and Middle Welsh—we call it Welsh, but until the Saxons confined it to Wales it was the language of large areas of England and southern Scotland too. The earliest poems are associated with the late sixth-century bards Taliesin and Aneirin. Taliesin was the court poet of Urien, king of Rheged (Cumbria with Dumfries and Kirkcudbright), a champion of the British against the English. Aneirin was a younger contemporary of Taliesin and court poet in Strathclyde. He is credited with *Y Gododdin*, sometimes misdescribed as a heroic poem, in fact a collection of short praise poems mostly relating to the historic Battle of Catraeth (Catterick).[44] The most important prose source is the *Mabinogion*, a collection of eleven mythical narratives from the tenth and eleventh centuries. Mention will also be made of the *Triads of the Isle of Britain*, a twelfth-century collection of miscellaneous lore expressed in the form of lists of three.

Finally there is a Gaelic oral tradition represented by songs collected from the Western Isles in the nineteenth century by Alexander Carmichael (*Carmina Gadelica*, 6 vols., Edinburgh 1928–59). They contain some remarkable survivals of pagan piety.

The earliest evidence relating to the **Germanic** world comes from Classical authors, most notably from Tacitus' *Germania*, which drew on a lost work of Pliny the Elder on the German wars. Tacitus mentions the existence of traditional poetry as the Germans' only form of record of the past, and in another work he refers to songs in which the national hero Arminius was commemorated.[45] Later, after Christianity brought literacy, we find four separate branches of Germanic poetic tradition: Old High German

[43] For surveys of this literature see Thurneysen (1921; on its chronology, 666–70); Dillon (1946), (1948); Koch–Carey (2000).

[44] I cite *Y Gododdin* by the line-numbering of Sir Ifor Williams, *Canu Aneirin* (1938), which is followed by Koch–Carey (2000), 307–41. The transmitted text is thought to be a mixture of recensions of the seventh and ninth centuries, see Koch–Carey (2000), 304–6.

[45] Tac. *Germ.* 2. 2, *Ann.* 2. 88; passages from other authors in Clemen (1928).

(Alemannic and Bavarian), Old Saxon, Old English (Anglo-Saxon), and Old Norse. These show mutual similarities of metre and diction that point to a common origin. Insofar as their subject matter is heroic, they look back to the Gothic world of the fourth and fifth centuries; the Gothic lays of that time probably stood in a common line of tradition with those of which Tacitus had written.

Germanic heroic poetry is represented by two stray pages from the Old High German *Hildebrandslied*, by the likewise eighth-century *Beowulf* and a few other Old English pieces such as the *Finnsburh* and *Waldere* fragments, the *Battle of Brunanburh*, and the late *Battle of Maldon*, and by a number of Norse poems of the ninth to twelfth centuries. Most of these last are included in the so-called Elder or Poetic Edda, others are preserved in the prose sagas or other sources, and one, the *Biarkamál*, in a Latin hexameter version in Saxo Grammaticus' *History of the Danes*. The ninth- or tenth-century Latin epic *Waltharius* may also be noticed for its Germanic subject matter, related to that of *Waldere*.

The Edda further contains mythical poems about the gods and gnomic poetry. Besides the Edda there is a large body of verse by the skalds, professional court poets, composed in a less archaic, highly elaborate style. Two ninth-century skaldic poems of importance for mythology are Thiodolf's *Haustlǫng* and Bragi's *Ragnarsdrápa*. The Old English corpus includes narrative poems on Christian subjects, reflective and gnomic poems, riddles, and spells. Two spells and a prayer in Old High German, the Merseburg Charms and the Wessobrunn Prayer, will also engage our attention.

Complementing this poetic literature, two substantial prose works of the early thirteenth century are of especial importance. Snorri Sturluson's Prose Edda consists of three parts: *Gylfaginning*, a delightfully written compendium of Nordic myths about the gods, based on older poetic sources; *Skáldskaparmál*, a survey of poetic language, with much reference to mythical material; and *Háttatal*, a treatise on verse-forms. Saxo's *History*, mentioned above, is a Latin work in sixteen books, of which the first nine in particular are a precious repository of Danish legend.

The **Baltic** countries were not converted to Christianity till a comparatively recent date—Latvia in the thirteenth century, and Lithuania in the fifteenth—and then only superficially. The consequence is on the one hand that there is no native literature until even later, but on the other hand that pagan gods and mythology remained alive in the popular consciousness long enough to be reported by Christian writers and to leave many traces in songs and ballads. The tradition of these songs is very abundant, especially in Latvia, where over 60,000 were recorded in the nineteenth century. There have also been collections of folk-tales, riddles, and the like. Pagan cult practices were also slow to disappear. Some of them could still be documented in nineteenth-century Latvia.[46]

The **Slavs** were converted much earlier, in the ninth and tenth centuries. Again most of the earliest evidence for their native religion and beliefs comes from outsiders' reports. By way of poetic tradition there is an obscure and peculiar Russian epic from 1185–6, the *Lay of Igor*, besides the oral heroic verse represented by the Russian *byliny* and the much ampler products of the Serbo-Croat bards. The folklore of the Slavonic peoples is a further source of material.[47]

Albania has its own poetry and folklore, though it is doubtful how far they can be regarded as representative of a distinct branch of Indo-European tradition, since they are not clearly separated from those of neighbouring lands. The oral epics parallel those of the South Slavs and are in some cases composed by bilingual poets, while the folk-tales often resemble those found in Greece. There remains nevertheless a residue of national mythology.[48]

CONSIDERATIONS OF METHOD

Many who have written on Indo-European poetics, mythology, and religion have tended to proceed in a rather naive way, ignoring historical and geographical coordinates. As soon as they find a parallel between two individual traditions, say between Greek and Indian myth, they at once claim it as a reflex of 'Indo-European', without regard either to the groupings of the Indo-European dialects or to the possibilities of horizontal transmission. Greater sophistication is needed.[49]

In the light of the earlier discussion it will be seen that application of the comparative method can take us back to different levels of antiquity, depending on the location of the material compared. Schematically:

[46] The fullest collection of the external sources was made by Wilhelm Mannhardt and published posthumously under the title of *Letto-Preussische Götterlehre* (Riga 1936); cf. also Clemen (1936), 92–114. For the songs cf. Rhesa (1825); K. Barons, *Latvju daiņas* (1894–1915, 2nd edn. 1922; 8 volumes) (*LD*), from which 1,219 stanzas with variants are edited and translated in Jonval (1929); folk-tales etc. in Schleicher (1857). The evidence for the Lithuanian pantheon is laid out by Usener (1896), 79–119, with the help of Felix Solmsen. See also Mannhardt (1936); Gimbutas (1963), 179–204; Biezais–Balys (1973); H. Biezais, *Baltische Religion* (Stuttgart 1975); Greimas (1992); P. U. Dini and N. Mikhailov, *Mitologia baltica* (Pisa 1995).

[47] C. H. Meyer (1931) collects sources in non-Slavonic languages. See further Unbegaun (1948); Gimbutas (1971), 151–70; N. Reiter, 'Mythologie der alten Slaven', in *Wb. d. Myth.* i(2). 165–208; Váňa (1992) (survey of literary sources: pp. 29–34).

[48] Lambertz (1973).

[49] Cf. Meid (1978), 6 f.

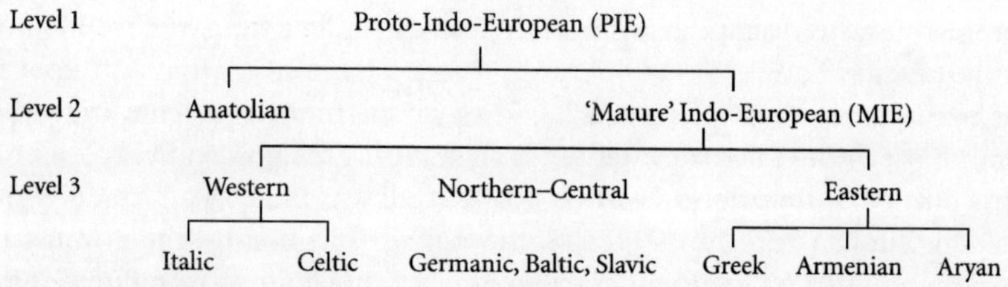

It is to be noted that these levels are stemmatic, not synchronic. A significant parallel observed between Homer and the Rigveda should take us back to Level 3 and (according to the argument presented earlier) to about 2300 BCE, the time of the Sixth Dynasty in Egypt; one between Italic and Celtic will likewise take us to Level 3, but perhaps only to 1300 BCE, contemporary with Mycenaean Greece or early Vedic India. An agreement between Celtic and Iranian will take us back to Level 2, sometime in the first half of the third millennium. To get back to the deepest level, to PIE, we shall require a comparison involving Anatolian.

An archaeologist is interested not only in the deepest layer of his site but in all the others too. 'Indo-European' in the title of my book is a shorthand term. I am not concerned only to reach the PIE stratum, throwing aside whatever does not fulfil the criteria for reaching it. Levels 2 and 3 are just as interesting, indeed more so, as the finds are more abundant, varied, and coherent. In practice it will not be very often that we can reach Level 1: it requires the PIE material to have survived on both sides of the stemma for two thousand years or more from the time of the Anatolian secession to the time of our earliest direct evidence, and much of the Indo-European heritage was lost on the Anatolian side under the influence of alien cultures. Most of the time, therefore, the evidence will take us no further than Level 2 or 3. It would be very tiresome if I were to point this out explicitly on every occasion, so I ask the reader to note it and not to impute my economy to negligence.

Sometimes I am aware, or the reader may discover ahead of me, that certain things which I attribute to Indo-European (PIE or MIE) are also to be found in Semitic or other non-Indo-European cultures. That does not lessen the value of the results, as my object is to identify whatever is Indo-European, not just what is distinctively or exclusively Indo-European. As another researcher in the field has written, 'since the aim of the present work lies solely in the reconstruction of a culture and not in its evaluation in comparison with other cultures, the question whether individual features of Indo-European culture can or cannot also be found among non-Indo-European peoples is entirely outside our concern'.[50] Nor is the reconstructive method invalidated by objections on the lines 'the parallel motifs that you note in this and that source need not imply a common Indo-European prototype, because they occur all over the world'. If a motif is indeed universal, all the more likely that it was also Indo-European.

There are of course standards to be applied. The parallels used must be specific and detailed enough to indicate a historical connection; and we have to discount those where the historical connection looks likely to be horizontal rather than the result of common descent from primeval times. The Indo-Europeans did not simply divide and divide into more and more separate peoples who proceeded to develop in isolation from one another. Most of them were in communication with neighbouring peoples over long periods, and with different ones at different times. In some cases parts of their populations undertook long migrations that brought them among quite new neighbours. Wherever peoples were together, it was possible for elements of language and culture to cross the frontiers by diffusion. In such cases philologists speak of a linguistic area or *Sprachbund*, and they describe a change (such as the *satem* shift) that affects contiguous rather than cognate languages as an 'areal' phenomenon.[51] They are usually able, on phonological or morphological grounds, to identify elements that a language has acquired by horizontal transmission and not by inheritance, for example Iranian loan-words in Armenian or Celtic ones in German. It is not so easy in the case of myths and motifs, unless they are tied to specific names.

According to our stemma, significant parallels between Homer and the Rigveda ought to take us back to the time of the Graeco-Aryan language or *Sprachbund*. The premise is that all contact between mello-Greeks and mello-Aryans was severed by about 2300 BCE. However, the archaeologist János Makkay has marshalled a series of plausible arguments for the thesis that a band of Iranian-speaking invaders from the steppes occupied Mycenae itself at the beginning of the Late Helladic period, around 1600.[52] This would have

[50] Campanile (1990b), 11. See also Müller (1897), 185–9.

[51] Cf. Watkins (1995), 218 f.

[52] J. Makkay, *The Early Mycenaean Rulers and the Contemporary Early Iranians of the Northeast* (Budapest 2000). This might account for the presence in the Homeric language of Iranian loan-words such as *τόξον* 'bow' (this already in Linear B) and *γωρυτός* 'bowcase'. So Durante (1976), 30: 'certo è che un ethnos iranico ha intrattenuto rapporti con la grecità nella fase micenea, se non ancor prima. Testimonia in tal senso la voce *τόξον* . . . La perfetta corrispondenza con pers. *taxš* "arco", di cui si ha un antecedente nell'antroponimo scitico *Τόξαρις*, rivela che si tratta di un iranismo.' Cf. ibid. 31, 36, on the name of the Dana(w)oi and its possible relationship to Avestan *dānav-* 'river', Vedic *dā́nav-* 'dripping water', and the river-names Danube, Don, Dnestr, etc. According to myth ('Hes.' fr. *128), it was the Danaai who made Argos well-watered. Danae and her son Perseus recall the names of Iranian tribes, the Turanian Dānavas (Yt. 5. 72–4, 13. 37 f.) and the Persians.

been a southward swoop parallel to that of the Indic group who took over Mitanni at the same period. If it really happened, it would provide a channel by which Aryan poetry might have directly influenced early Mycenaean poetry, short-circuiting the stemma. It is hardly likely that all Greek–Indic and Greek–Iranian parallels could be so accounted for, but it remains a theoretical consideration to be borne in mind.

Both in the Mycenaean age and in subsequent centuries Greece was much exposed to contacts with the Near East, including Anatolia. So if we find parallels between Greek and Hittite myth, religion, or idiom, we must ask whether it is a case of independent inheritance from Indo-European or of horizontal transmission. At a later period the problem is similar with regard to Greece and Italy.

Under the Roman empire there were extensive trade connections linking southern with northern Europe. The literacy that gave us our Celtic and Germanic texts was the gift of a clergy schooled in Latin letters. Some scholars have sought to derive as much as possible in these literatures from Classical models and to play down the element of native tradition. They have certainly gone too far in this, but the possibility of Classical influence must always be considered. The Germans were also subject to Celtic influences from an early date, certainly from well before the beginning of the Christian era to long after.[53]

Let me give an example of horizontal transmission. The doctrine of metempsychosis is both Greek and Indian. The Greek and Indian doctrines must be historically connected, because they correspond point for point. Souls pass into the body of a higher or lower creature according to their conduct in their previous incarnation; this cyclical process continues over thousands of years; pure conduct will eventually lead to the divine state; the eating of meat is to be avoided. Such a system is not reliably attested for any other people. But we cannot regard it as Graeco-Aryan heritage, because it is absent from the earliest stratum of Indian literature, the Vedas, and equally from the earliest Greek literature, and it stands out in sharp contrast to earlier Indian and Greek ideas about death. It appears as it were from nowhere in both countries at about the same time, around the sixth century BCE, and we must suppose that it reached them from a common source, probably across the Persian empire, even though no such doctrine is attested in Iran.[54]

It is not only contacts between Indo-European peoples that come into question. In some cases others may have functioned as middlemen. Certain shamanistic elements common to Nordic and Indian myth may have come to

[53] Cf. Feist (1913), 483; de Vries (1956), i. 64, 137, 171.

[54] Cf. West (1971), 61–7.

both areas from the neighbouring Finno-Ugric peoples of north and central Asia.[55] Some myths that occur both in India and in Greece can be traced to the far-reaching influence of Mesopotamia. For instance, in one of the poems of the Greek Epic Cycle, the *Cypria*, it was related that once upon a time Earth was oppressed by the excessive numbers of people milling about on top of her. Zeus took pity on her and conceived the plan of lightening the burden by means of the Trojan War. A similar myth is found in the *Mahābhārata*. The earth once complained to Brahmā of the ever-increasing weight of mankind, and Brahmā created death to alleviate the problem. Some have inferred from the coincidence that an Indo-European tradition lies behind the story, although it appears only in a late phase of the Greek epic tradition and at an even later date in India. What is more to the point is that a similar myth is attested over a thousand years earlier in Mesopotamia. The natural conclusion is that the Greek and the Indian poets were both using a motif somehow derived from Mesopotamia, not one inherited from Graeco-Aryan antiquity.[56] Similar considerations apply to the Hesiodic and Indian Myths of Ages, or to the currency of the animal fable in both Greece and India.[57]

When we have parallels that extend all the way from India or Iran to the Celtic world, their probative value may be rated particularly high, because horizontal transmission seems virtually ruled out. But even then we must be cautious. The heroic traditions of both India and Ireland portray warriors using horse-drawn chariots. We might be tempted to infer that this was an Indo-European style of warfare. Similarly, as we shall see in Chapter 5, the myth of the Sun's horse-drawn chariot is widely diffused among Indo-European peoples, and we might well conclude that this was an Indo-European myth. But it cannot be so, for archaeology tells us that the war-chariot with spoked wheels—the only type of vehicle light enough for horses to pull at speed—first appeared east of the southern Urals around 2100–2000 BCE, long after the Indo-European cultural continuum had been broken up. Chariot warfare as a military reality and as a heroic motif, and the myth of the solar chariot, must have spread across the Indo-European territories long after the Indo-European peoples themselves had done so. These novelties were no doubt widely disseminated in the space of a few centuries; it is likely enough that chariot-borne warrior bands were instrumental in their rapid

[55] Cf. Lorenz (1984), 259 f.

[56] *Cypria* fr. 1; *MBh.* 1. 58, 3. 142, 11. 8. 20–6, 12. 248–50, etc.; V. Pisani, *ZDMG* 103 (1953), 127 f. = Schmitt (1968), 156 f.; id. (1969), 64 f.; Durante (1976), 61; W. Ruben, *Sitzb. Ak. Wiss. DDR* 1973 (24), 50–5; C. Vielle in L. Isebaert and R. Lebrun (edd.), *Quaestiones Homericae* (Louvain–Namur 1998), 275–90; West (1997), 480–2.

[57] Myth of Ages: West (1997), 312–19. Animal fable: ibid. 319 f., 502–5.

diffusion. But they cannot, as they stand, go back to the archetypal mythology of the proto-Indo-Europeans.[58]

This is a devastating result for us seekers of Indo-European mythology. If ideas and myths could spread so far and so fast over lands that had been Indo-Europeanized long before, how can we ever know if we are getting back to an original common heritage? Perhaps we cannot. Perhaps we must content ourselves with identifying 'isomyths', elements shared by a particular pair or a particular constellation of peoples, acknowledging that they may date only from a comparatively late phase in the long history of the diaspora.

CONCLUSION

Comparative Indo-European mythology remains and is bound to remain a poor relation of comparative Indo-European philology. It is easy to see why. People change their gods and their mythologies more readily and quickly than they change their declensions and conjugations, and more capriciously. Rules can be formulated to predict how a given Indo-European phoneme will turn out in Old High German or Pale Dry Tocharian, but the mutations of divinities or of mythical motifs are subject to no rules. The validity of a comparison, therefore, cannot be tested in the same way, by reference to a standard, but has to be judged on its intrinsic appeal. The total harvest will certainly be modest in comparison with the quantity of linguistic material available for the reconstruction of Indo-European speech.

As the various Indo-European tribal groups spread into new lands and contacts between them weakened, they became exposed to other cultural influences of many kinds. The Hittites came into the cultural orbit of the Hattic, Hurrian, and Mesopotamian civilizations, and their society, religion, and mythology were transformed as a result. The Greeks absorbed much from previous Aegean culture and from contacts with the peoples of the Near East. If we take the principal gods of the Homeric Olympus—Zeus and Hera, Leto, Apollo and Artemis, Poseidon, Athena, Ares, Hephaestus, Hermes, Aphrodite—we find that only one of them, Zeus, has a clear Indo-European ancestry. The rest either developed on Greek soil or were taken over from other peoples with whom the Greeks came in contact. Zeus himself has

[58] Cf. Durante (1976), 15. On the origin of the spoke-wheeled chariot see Robert Drews, *The Coming of the Greeks* (Princeton 1988), 107–57; D. Anthony and N. Vinogradov, *Archaeology* 48(2) (1995), 36–41; *EIEC* 627 f.; E. W. Barber, *The Mummies of Ürümchi* (London 1999), 203 f.; E. E. Kuzmine, *JIES* 29 (2001), 12–17.

evolved some way from his Indo-European beginnings. Similar considerations apply to the traditions of the other peoples that fall within our purview.

However, the case of Zeus and his many cognates in the other traditions (Chapter 4) proves that some elements of Indo-European theological heritage were preserved in widely separated regions. One factor that favoured their survival was the persistence of poetic traditions of a conservative nature. We shall see in the next two chapters how shared features of poetic theory, diction, and imagery and of stylistic and metrical technique attest the continuity of these traditions from a common origin. It is reasonable to hope for the preservation in them of at least some mythological themes of equal antiquity.

1

Poet and Poesy

Axiom: all peoples at all times have had poetry and song. It follows that the Indo-Europeans must have had them, and that a continuous tradition linked their poetry and song with those of the historical successor peoples.

This *a priori* conclusion is in itself empty. We shall endeavour to give it substance by comparison of the documented poetic traditions. We are interested, not just in establishing that the Indo-Europeans had poetry, but in finding out, so far as may be possible, what kinds of poetry they had, what were its characteristics, and how they conceptualized it.

What do we mean by poetry? The term will cover all verse, that is, all composition constrained within some kind of metrical form. But for the present purpose a wider definition is called for. Much of the evidence for Indo-European poetry comes from the identification of what appears to be 'poetic' diction. When we characterize it as poetic, the implied antithesis is not with prose but with 'normal' or everyday speech. Prose (*prosa oratio*) is not a meaningful category where there is no written literature. The opposition is between 'unmarked' and 'marked' language: on the one hand, ordinary, idiomatic speech; on the other, a style which diverges from the ordinary by using elevated or archaic vocabulary, ornamental epithets, figures of speech, a contrived word order, or other artificial features. It is this 'marked' language that it will be convenient to call poetic. But its use may not have been confined to compositions in verse. There is some likelihood that it was also deployed for high-flown narrative or rhetorical utterances that lacked metrical form.[1]

[1] Cf. Meid (1978), 11: '"Dichtung" ist im Grunde genommen jede über das bloß Umgangssprachliche hinausgehende stilisierte Rede, jeder in irgendeiner Absicht sprachkünstlerisch gestaltete Stoff; die Formung mußte nicht unbedingt eine metrische sein.'

THE POET

In traditional Indo-European societies poetry was not a diversion to be taken up by anyone who happened to be visited by the lyrical impulse. Knowledge of the poetic language and technical command of the verbal arts were the province of specialists. These specialists were of more than one kind, for they performed a variety of functions, as priests, seers, eulogists, and so forth. Accordingly there was, so far as we can see, no single Indo-European word for 'poet', but different words corresponding to the different roles that poets played. It is difficult to reconstruct specific terms, because requirements and designations changed over time in different societies. It is nevertheless possible to discern elements of vocabulary that link separated peoples and point back to the terminology of remote eras.

It is convenient to start from the Celtic world, where a remarkable conservatism of tradition is observable in regard to poetic institutions for well over a thousand years from the time of the earliest records.

Classical sources, going back to Posidonius in the early first century BCE, report that the continental Celts had poet-singers called Bards (*bardoi*), philosopher-priests called Druids (*dryidai* or *drouidai*), and diviners called *vates*. The Bards sang songs of praise or blame, accompanying themselves on instruments resembling lyres; in particular they celebrated the brave deeds of warriors in 'heroic verses'. The Druids were venerated for their wisdom and holiness, presiding over sacrifices, performing judicial functions, and checking immoderate behaviour. According to Caesar they educated many of the young men and made them learn a large quantity of oral verse. The Vates foretold the future from augury and sacrifical omens.[2]

All three terms reappear in insular Celtic, as Old Irish *bard* (Welsh *bardd*), *druí* (Welsh *derwydd*), and *fáith*. The *bard* was a reciter and a composer of lower sorts of poetry. The *druí*, having lost his sacerdotal functions with the advent of Christianity, was no more than a sorcerer; his role as a learned poet had been taken over by the *fili*, of whom more below. The *fáith* was concerned with spells and divination (*fáth*).

The word *bard*, proto-Celtic **bardos*, is analysed as an old compound going back to *g^w*r̥*h_2-$d^h$$h_1$-*o*- and meaning 'praise-maker'. The first element is related to Vedic *gír* 'praise-song', *jaritár-* 'singer', and the verb *gr̥* 'sing, praise',

[2] Strabo 4. 4. 4; Diodorus 5. 31. 2–5; Athenaeus 246cd (Posidonius F 34. 4, 169. 31, 172 Theiler); Timagenes (*FGrHist* 88 F 2) ap. Amm. Marc. 15. 9. 8 (where the *vates* are replaced by *euhages* following a corruption in the Greek source: *ΟΥΑΤΕΙC* > *ΕΥΑΓΕΙC*); Caesar, *Bell. Gall.* 6. 13–14; Lucan 1. 447–58; Festus p. 31. 13 L.

Lithuanian *gìrti* 'praise'. The second element is the very common verbal root meaning 'set in place, create', as in Greek *τίθημι*. What is particularly significant is that the same two roots are combined phrasally in Indo-Iranian, in Vedic *gíras . . . dhā* and Avestan *garō . . . dā* 'offer praises'.[3] This phrase at least, if not the compound noun designating the eulogist, can be assumed to go back to (Mature) Indo-European, and so can the idea that it expresses of conferring praise through poetry, whether on god or man.

The other Gaulish and Irish terms do not take us so far back, but they do point to connections extending beyond the Celtic sphere. *Dru-(w)id-* should mean 'oak-seer': it is reported that a tall oak served the Celts as an image of 'Jupiter', and we cannot help but recall the ancient mantic oak of Zeus at Dodona in Thesprotia (an Illyrian rather than a Greek institution).[4] If *druidai* had been recorded as the name of the priest-prophets of Dodona, nothing would have seemed more apt.

The *fili* (plural *filid*) who inherited the druid's role in Ireland also has a title to do with the seer's function. It is related to Welsh *gweled* 'see' (cf. *telewele* 'television'), and perhaps to Latin *voltus* 'visage'. It reappears in the name of the German prophetess Veleda, who enjoyed immense esteem in the time of Vespasian.[5] For the semantic nexus we may compare the Vedic *kaví-* 'sage, seer, priest-poet', Avestan *kəvi-*, Lydian *kaveś* (a priest), Samothracian *koiēs*, all related to a root **keu-* 'see, behold'.[6]

The term *vatis*, Irish *fáith*, appears in Latin as *uātēs* 'seer, prophet, inspired poet', which, however, is under strong suspicion of being a Celtic loan-word.[7] Related forms occur in Welsh *gwawd* 'cause, theme, poem, prophecy', and outside Celtic in Old Church Slavonic *vĕtiji* 'orator' and in a set of Germanic words that link the ideas of poetry and possession: Gothic *woþs* 'possessed', Old High German *wuot* 'frenzied', Old English *wōd* 'frenzied', *wōð* 'song', Old Norse *óðr* 'possessed, inspired; mind, poetry'.[8]

[3] RV 8. 96. 10; Y. 41. 1, cf. 45. 8; E. Campanile, *SSL* 20 (1980), 183–8; Watkins (1995), 117; J. Uhlich, *TPhS* 100 (2002), 414.

[4] The Celtic oak: Val. Flacc. 6. 90; Max. Tyr. 2. 8. Dodona: *Od.* 14. 327; [Aesch.] *Prom.* 830–2. For Celtic and other sacred groves cf. Chapter 7.

[5] Tac. *Hist.* 4. 61, 65; *Germ.* 8. 2; Stat. *Silv.* 1. 4. 90.

[6] Greek *κοέω*, Latin *caueo*; *IEW* 587; cf. R. Gusmani in *Studi Triestini di Antichità in onore di Luigia Achillea Stella* (Trieste 1975), 255 f.; Watkins (1995), 88; Gamkrelidze–Ivanov (1995), 734 f.

[7] If the underlying form is **wō-ti-*, this must be the case, as the change [ō] > [ā] is Celtic, not Italic. E. Hamp in *Papers from the Thirteenth Regional Meeting of the Chicago Linguistic Society* (1977), 149, offers a different account.

[8] Hence the god Woden or Odin has his name (p. 137). See further K. von See, *GRM* 14 (1964), 2; H. Wagner, *ZCP* 31 (1970), 46–57 = *Studies in the Origins of the Celts and Early Celtic Civilisation* (Belfast–Tübingen 1971), 46–58; Meid (1991), 25 f.; Watkins (1995), 118; Gamkrelidze–Ivanov (1995), 734; *EIEC* 493b.

A similar linkage of ideas, with different vocabulary, can be found in Graeco-Aryan tradition.[9] The hymns of the Rigveda were the work of priest-poets called Rishis (*ŕṣi-*); Zarathushtra uses the corresponding Avestan word *ərəši-* of himself (Y. 31. 5). It is related to Armenian *heṙ* 'anger', Lithuanian *aršùs* 'violent', and German *rasen* 'to rage', so its basic meaning will have been 'one who goes into a frenzy'. Another Vedic word for a poet or singer is *vípra-*, which means 'inwardly stirred, inspired, wise'. The Greek word for a seer, *mántis*, is derived from the verbal root *man-* 'make/be mad, frenzied'.

In his role as eulogist the Vedic poet is a *stotŕ̥*; the Avestan equivalent is *staotar*, and the verb to which these are the agent nouns appears in Homeric Greek as στεῦται, 'he claims, boasts'. Another Vedic term for a praise-poet is *kārú-*, and this too has a Greek cognate in the shape of κήρυξ 'herald'. '(Travelling) poet' is presumably the older meaning, and the concepts remained close enough for Pindar to declare that 'the Muse raised me up as her chosen κάρυξ of skilful verses for Hellas'.[10]

We see that while terminology diverged in different parts of the Indo-European world, two specific roles in which poets appeared can be identified in both east and west. They functioned on the one hand as bestowers of praise, whether on men or gods, and on the other as prophets or seers, gifted with special knowledge, perhaps through an altered state of consciousness. Both of these solemn offices naturally called for a heightened form of utterance, that is, for 'poetic' diction. Both roles could be combined in the service of the gods: Zarathushtra designates himself both as an *ərəši* and as Ahura Mazdā's *staotar*, his praise-singer, and the Vedic Rishis likewise use *stotŕ̥* of themselves in appropriate contexts.

Status, training, rewards

These functions were important to the community and to its ruler (or whoever was the poet's patron), especially as he and/or his ancestors were principal beneficiaries of the finely formed public praises that the poet could bestow or withhold. And such services could not be performed by any Tom, Dick, or Harry. They called for special knowledge, skill, and training. Consequently a master poet enjoyed a high status, and in some cases felt able to address his prince or patron almost as an equal. Pindar is notable for the lack of deference with which he dispenses advice to his aristocratic paymasters. In

9 Durante (1960), 231 f. ~ (1976), 167; Schmitt (1967), 303.

10 F. Specht, *ZVS* 64 (1937), 3; P. Thieme, *ZDMG* 107 (1957), 85; Schmitt (1967), 301 f.; Pind. fr. 70b. 23, cf. *Nem.* 4. 74; Bacchyl. 13. 231; Solon 1. 1.

corresponds exactly in form to the Indic *vácas-*, which in the Rigveda can mean 'word, speech' but mostly refers to the pronouncements that make up the song, or to the song as a whole. The feminine *vāc-* (corresponding to Latin *uōx*) is used similarly, and there is another word from the same root meaning 'hymn', *ukthám*.[19] In Avestan a strophe of the *Gāthās* was called a *vacatašti-*, literally a 'fashioning of the utterance'. Tocharian A *wäktasurñe* 'eulogy' and Old High German *giwahan, giwahanen* 'mention, tell of', *giwaht* 'fame, remembrance', give further hints of the use of this root in connection with formal or poetic utterance. Most remarkable is the Irish term *anocht* for a type of metrical fault; it means literally 'not (to be) uttered', the counterpart of Vedic *anukta-*, and it must be a very ancient survival, as the **wek*ʷ root was defunct in Celtic.[20]

English 'say' goes back to the Indo-European root **sek*ʷ. This appears to have been appropriate to declarations or recitals made before an audience, as derivatives in various languages are used in connection with public discourses or narratives in prose or verse: Greek ἐν(ν)-έπω, used in the imperative in Homer in asking the Muse to relate a particular matter; Latin *in-sequo*; Old Irish *sc-ēl* 'story', *in-sce* 'discourse', *ro-sc(ad)*, a form of alliterative composition; Middle Welsh *chw-edl* 'recitation'; Lithuanian *pā-saka* 'story, legend'.[21]

Of several words for singing, one that is common to east and west is **geh₁*: Vedic *gā* 'sing', *gā́thā* 'song' (Avestan *gāθā*); Lithuanian *giedóti* 'sing', *giesmẽ* 'song of praise'; Slavonic *gudú* 'sing with a stringed instrument'; Old English *gieddian* 'sing', *giedd, gidd* 'song, poem, saying, riddle, tale'. The root **seng*ʷʰ which provides the common Germanic word (Gothic *siggwan*, German *singen*, English *sing, song*, etc.) must once have had a wider distribution, as, besides Church Slavonic *sętь*, it lies behind the Greek poetic word ὀμφή < **song*ʷʰ*ā*. In the Homeric language this is used only of prophetic utterances issuing from a god, but the Doric lyric tradition preserved its older sense of musical sound from voices or instruments. The root **kan* prevailed only in Italic and Celtic, where it is associated with charms and spells as well as poetry: Latin *cano, carmen* < **can-men*; Old Irish *canaid* 'sings', *cétal* 'song', Welsh *cathl*, < **kan-tlon*. But it has left traces in Greek καν-αχή 'clangour' and in the Germanic word for 'cock', Gothic *hana*, modern German *Hahn*.[22]

[19] I normally cite Vedic and Avestan nouns in the stem form, but in the case of neuter *o*-stems I give the ending *-am/-əm* as an economical way of indicating the gender.

[20] Watkins (1995), 87 n. 0, 119. On the derivatives of **wek*ʷ cf. Gamkrelidze–Ivanov (1995), 733 f.

[21] Ernout–Meillet (1959), s.v. *insequo*; Meid (1978), 22 n. 36.

[22] Cf. the obscure gloss in Hesychius, ἠϊκανός· ὁ ἀλεκτρυών. On these words cf. *IEW* 525 f.; Watkins (1963), 214 = (1994), 369; *EIEC* 519b.

Another word-set shared by Italic, Celtic, and Germanic is that represented by Latin *laudo* 'praise, mention (honourably)'; Old Irish *luaidim* 'I celebrate, mention', *lóid* 'song'; Gothic *liuþōn* 'sing, praise', Old Norse *lióð*, Old High German *leod, liod,* Middle High German *liet* 'stanza' (in the plural 'song'), modern *Lied,* Old English *lēoþ*. The semantic development from 'praise, commemoration' to 'song of praise or commemoration' and 'song' generally is easily understood. It is already apparent in Cato's notice that Roman banqueters used to sing *clarorum uirorum laudes atque uirtutes.*[23]

One of several Old Norse words for the art of poetry is *bragr*. Some favour relating this to the root of Vedic *brah-mán-* 'priest', *bráh-man-* 'prayer', and to Gaulish *brictom, brixtia,* 'magic', Irish *bricht* 'incantation, spell, charm; octosyllabic metre'.[24] If they are right, a very ancient lexical item would be implied. But the Brahman's connection with poetry is contingent, and other scholars uphold the alternative etymology that equates him with the Roman *flamen*. We shall return to this elsewhere.

Within Graeco-Aryan we can trace the etymological connection of Greek ἀείδω 'sing' with Vedic *vad-* 'speak, tell of, sing of' (specifically with the reduplicated present *vā́vadīti*), and that of Armenian *erg* 'song' with Vedic *arká-* 'song of praise; singer', Sogdian **ni-γrāy-* 'sing (of)', and Ossetic *arğaw* 'tale'.[25]

Poetry as recall

More universal among Indo-European peoples than any of the above designations is the use, in relation to poetic activity, of words based on the root **men* 'think (of), call to mind'.[26] In composing a new poem or reciting an old one, the poet must call to mind things that he knows. When someone who is speaking or singing calls something to mind, it is at once expressed in words, so that **men* may also refer to utterance, as in Vedic *mányate* 'think; mention', Lithuanian *menù, miñti,* or Latin *mentionem facere.*

The Vedic verb is used of composing a hymn, as in RV 5. 13. 2 *Agné stómam manāmahe,* 'we think out a laudation for Agni'; 5. 35. 8, 48. 1; 8. 29. 10, 90. 3. The *mánas-* or *manīṣā́-* (mind, intellect) is engaged in the process (RV 1. 171.

[23] Cato, *Origines* (fr. 118 Peter) ap. Cic. *Tusc.* 1. 3; 4. 3; *Brutus* 75; Varro, *De vita populi Romani* (fr. 394 Salvadore) ap. Non. Marc. p. 77. 2 M. *carmina antiqua in quibus laudes erant maiorum.*

[24] Mayrhofer (1953–80), ii. 452–6; id. (1986–2001), ii. 236–8; *contra,* P. Thieme, *ZDMG* 102 (1952), 126; cf. Schmitt (1967), 305; Bader (1989), 52–5.

[25] A. L. Sihler, *New Comparative Grammar of Greek and Latin* (New York–Oxford 1995), 86; Gamkrelidze–Ivanov (1995), 822; *EIEC* 449a.

[26] Watkins (1995), 68 f., 72, 73; Gamkrelidze–Ivanov (1995), 393 f., 713, 734 n. 3; B. W. Fortson IV in *Mír Curad,* 138; *EIEC* 575.

2; 5. 81. 1; 9. 100. 3, al.). The song or formula is a *mánman-* or a *mántra-* (Avestan *mąθra-*). It can also be referred to as a *sumatí-* or *sumnám*, both meaning literally 'good thought, good disposition'. It has been proposed to derive the Greek ὕμνος from the same elements, **su-mn-o-*;[27] this has its attractions, though it is hard to account for ὑ- instead of the normal Greek εὐ- unless on the assumption (historically conceivable—see pp. 21 f.) that the word came into Mycenaean from an Iranian source.

The poets of the Homeric Hymns often conclude with the formula 'I will bethink me (μνήσομαι) both of you (the god addressed) and of other singing'. Similarly the Maidens of Delos are described as first hymning Apollo, Leto, and Artemis and then, 'bethinking themselves (μνησάμεναι) of the men and women of old, they sing a song (ὕμνος) that charms the peoples' (*Hymn. Ap.* 160 f.). The Muses can assist by putting the poet in mind of the relevant material (*Il.* 2. 492 μνησαίατο; Pind. *Pae.* 14. 35). This is why they are called the daughters of Memory, Mnemosyne. The word Muse itself is derived from the **men* root: Μοῦσα < **món-t-ih*$_2$ or **mon-tu-h*$_2$.[28]

When Livius Andronicus translated Homer's Μοῦσ' ἐδίδαξε as *Diua Monetas filia docuit* (fr. 21 Blänsdorf), he was adopting the Greek filiation of the Muse to Mnemosyne. But *Moneta* does not mean 'memory'; it signifies the goddess who *monet*, who puts in mind, *moneo* being a causative formation from **men-*. Virgil employs it in asking for the Muse's help at *Aeneid* 7. 41: *tu uatem, tu diua mone* (cf. Ovid, *Fasti* 5. 447). This usage cannot be accounted for from the Greek models, but must come from native Italic tradition.

Old English and Norse poetry provides further evidence. After Beowulf has killed Grendel, a poem about the exploit is composed by one of Hrothgar's thanes, a man with a memory for tales (*gidda gemyndig*), who recalled (*gemunde*) a multitude of old legends (*Beowulf* 868–70). In *Widsith* (54 f.) the poet says 'I can sing, therefore, and tell a tale, and recall (*mǣnan*) before the crowd in the mead-hall . . .', while *The Whale* begins 'Now will I once more in a song . . . make known in words, with poetic craft, by mental recall (*þurh mōdgemynd*) . . .'. The Eddic Sibyl of *Vǫluspá* begins her prophecy with a general call to attention: Odin has asked her to recount the ancient histories, 'those earliest that I recall' (*um man*). 'I recall (*ec man*) the giants . . . I recall nine worlds . . .'. Odin himself, as a god of poetic inspiration, is attended by two ravens called Huginn and Muninn, Thought and Recall (*Gylf.* 38).

[27] A. Kuhn, *ZVS* 2 (1853), 131; 4 (1855), 25; Durante (1976), 155–60; cautious approval in Euler (1979), 66 f. See above for an alternative etymology.

[28] Watkins (1995), 73, 110. Cf. also Tyrt. 12. 1; Sappho fr. 55; Pind. *Ol.* 8. 74, *Nem.* 1. 12, 7. 15, 9. 10, *Isth.* 8. 62; fr. 341 μνα<μο>νόοι Μοῖσαι; Theoc. 16. 42–5. According to Plutarch, *Quaest. conv.* 743d, the Muses were in some places called the Mneiai.

In Slavonic tradition too poetry is concerned with the renewal of memory. In the *Lay of Igor* (4) we read how the great poet Boyan 'used to recall (*pomnyašetĭ*) the words and the dissensions of the early times'. Salih Ugljanin in two of his oral epics, *The Song of Baghdad* and *The Captivity of Dulić Ibrahim*, used the formulaic line *davno bilo, sada pominjemo*, 'long ago it was, and now we remember it'. In a Bosnian version of an Albanian song about Marko and Musa, he sang:

> This will ever be remembered (*s' pominje*) to the end of time,
> as long as mankind and time endure,
> and as long as these endure, Marko will be remembered,
> Marko Kraljević will be remembered.[29]

By an inversion of the standard notion of being mindful, the poet may instead speak of not being unmindful. One of the Homeric Hymns begins 'I will bethink me, and not be unmindful, of Apollo the far-shooter'. Another concludes, 'there is no way to adorn sweet singing while heedless of you'. Similarly there are early Irish poems beginning 'It is not fitting to forget . . .', and the British praise-poem for Gwenabwy mab Gwen begins 'It would be wrong to leave unremembered him of the far-reaching feats'.[30] If this is not itself an Indo-European formula, it could readily have developed independently in Greece and the Celtic area from the primary one.

Poesy as construction

It is not enough to recall. The poem must be crafted. In many Indo-European traditions poetic composition is expressed by words meaning 'make', 'fashion', and the like, or by terms drawn from specific manufacturing crafts such as carpentry or weaving.

In Greece from the archaic period we find the most basic words for 'make', τεύχειν and ποιεῖν, used of poetic creation; ποιητής became the ordinary word for 'poet'. τεύχειν is a poetic vocable, in other words an archaism. Its application to 'making' poetry has been linked with the cognate Old Irish *duan* 'poem', from **dʰ(e)ugʰnā-*.[31] In other languages too we find the plainest words for 'make' employed for poetic composition: in Latin *facere* (*uersus*, *carmen*, etc.), in India *kṛ*, as in RV 9. 114. 2 *mantrakṛ́tām* 'of song-makers'.

[29] *SCHS* ii, nos. 1. 9, 4. 8; i. 360–4, lines 159–62.

[30] Hymn. Hom. 3. 1; 7. 58 f.; cf. Pind. fr. 94b. 36; K. Meyer (1913), 16/18, 20; *Y Gododdin* 292, cf. 75.

[31] Durante (1960), 234 ~ (1976), 170; Bader (1989), 24. τεύχειν: *Od.* 24. 197, Pind. *Isth.* 1. 14, al.; Nünlist (1998), 86 f. ποιεῖν: Solon 20. 3, Theognidea 771, etc. On the whole range of manufacturing imagery applied to poetic composition in Greek see Nünlist, 83–125.

This latter root also appears in Middle Irish *creth* 'poetry' (< $^*k^wrto$-) and Welsh *prydydd* 'poet'. It can have associations with sacral and magical activity, as in Vedic *kártram* 'spell, charm', Lithuanian *keraĩ* 'magic', *keréti* 'bewitch', and Church Slavonic *čaro-dějĭ* 'magician'.[32]

Not all making requires special skills, but composing poetry does. It is a craft, a job for professionals. As with other crafts, its practitioner is in a position to earn profits from his work. Early Welsh has a word *cerdd* meaning both generally 'craft, profession' and more specifically 'poetry, poem, music'. Its Old Irish equivalent *cerd* has similar meanings, and may also stand for 'craftsman' or 'poet'. These words have a Greek cognate in *κέρδος* 'gain, profit'.[33]

Poesy as weaving

In Indo-Iranian, Greek, Celtic, and Germanic we find poetic composition described in terms of weaving.[34] From the Rigveda we may quote:

asmā́ íd u gnā́ś cid devápatnīr
Índrāya arkám ahihátya ūvuḥ.

For him, for Indra, the women, the wives of the gods,
have woven a song at his killing of the dragon. (1. 61. 8)

tatám me ápas tád u tāyate púnaḥ.

My work (previously) stretched out (sc. as on a loom) is being stretched out again. (1. 110. 1)

mā́ tántuś chedi váyato dhíyam me.

Let the thread not break as I weave my poem. (2. 28. 5)

víśvā matī́r ā́ tatane tuvāyā́.

All my mindings/songs (*matī́s*, root **men*) I have stretched out for thee. (7. 29. 3)

anulbaṇáṃ vayata jóguvām ápaḥ.

Weave ye the singers' work without a knot! (10. 53. 6)

[32] Durante (1960), 234 f. ~ (1976), 170 f.; Watkins (1963), 214 = (1994), 369; (1995), 117; E. Hamp in *Papers from the Thirteenth Regional Meeting of the Chicago Linguistic Society* (1977), 148.

[33] Campanile (1977), 37; Watkins (1994), 677 f.; (1995), 75 f.

[34] Cf. T. Aufrecht, *ZVS* 4 (1855), 280; Pictet (1863), 481 f.; Schmitt (1967), 298–301; Durante (1960), 238–44 ~ (1976), 173–9 (the most thorough study); H. Wagner, *ZCP* 31 (1970), 50–4; Campanile (1977), 36 f.; John Scheid–Jesper Svenbro, *The Craft of Zeus: Myths of Weaving and Fabric* (Cambridge, Mass. 1996), 111–55; Nünlist (1998), 110–18.

In Avestan the verb *vaf*, by origin 'weave', has come to mean 'sing of, hymn'. Thus Zarathushtra sings *yə̄ vå Aṣ̌ā ufyānī manascā vohū apaourvīm*, 'I who will hymn You, Truth, and Good Thought as never before' (Y. 28. 3); *yavat̰ ā θβā, Mazdā, staomī ufyācā*, 'insofar as I praise and hymn Thee, Wise One' (43. 8).

In Greek the metaphor is familiar. ὑφαίνω 'weave' (from the same root as the Avestan verb) and the semantically close πλέκω 'plait' are repeatedly used by Pindar and Bacchylides with objects such as 'songs' or 'words', for example:

> ἦ σὺν Χαρίτεσσι βαθυζώνοις ὑφάνας ὕμνον ἀπὸ ζαθέας
> νάσου ξένος ὑμετέραν ἐς κλυτὰν πέμπει πόλιν.
>
> Having woven a song with the deep-girdled Graces, from his god-blest
> island your friend sends it to your celebrated city. (Bacchyl. 5. 9)

In the following pages it will become increasingly apparent that these two fifth-century exponents of the Dorian tradition of choral song were heirs to a repertory of Indo-European or at least Graeco-Aryan imagery that is hardly visible in the Ionian epic and Lesbian lyric traditions. However, in the present case we can cite Sappho's reference (fr. 188) to Eros as a plaiter of tales, μυθόπλοκος.[35]

In two or three places, as in the above example from Bacchylides, ὑφαίνω appears in association with the noun ὕμνος, perhaps with a sense of word-play, as if ὕμνος were derived from the ὑφ- root. Scholars used to take this etymology seriously, but it is nowadays rejected on phonological grounds. We have already adverted to two other etymologies of this interesting word.

From Irish Enrico Campanile adduced an example from the early text *Amrae Choluimb Chille* (§52 Stokes): *fáig ferb fithir* 'the master wove words'. At a much later date a member of a hereditary poetic family attached to the O'Neills could write:

> Not spinning the threads of wisdom
> nor tracing our branching peoples
> nor weaving a graceful verse . . .
> Men of base trade look down
> on our woven rhetorical songs.[36]

[35] For ὑφαίνω cf. further Pind. *Nem.* 4. 44, fr. 179; Bacchyl. 1. 4?, 19. 8; *PMG* 955?; *CEG* 660. 4 (fourth century); Call. fr. 26. 5; for πλέκω, Pind. *Ol.* 6. 86, *Pyth.* 12. 8, *Nem.* 4. 94, *Pae.* 3. 12; *PMG* 917b. 3; Critias fr. 1. 1 Diels–Kranz.

[36] Fear Flatha Ó Gnímh (early seventeenth century) in Thomas Kinsella, *The New Oxford Book of Irish Verse* (Oxford 1986), 164 f.

In Welsh *gweu* 'weave' was often used of poetic composition.[37] The Old English poet Cynewulf writes in the epilogue to his *Elene* (1237) *þus ic fród and fús . . . wordcræft wæf and wundrum læs*, 'Thus I, old and ready to go, wove word-craft and gleaned wonders'. Snorri Sturluson quotes a Norse skald's verse in praise of Earl Skúli Bárðarson: 'Skúli was most outstanding . . . The eulogy shall not be delayed; I am putting together a many-stranded encomium (*mærð fiǫlsnærða*) for the generous prince.'[38]

Poesy as carpentry

The Latin evidence is deliciously ambiguous. The Latin for 'weave' or 'plait' is *texere*, and this is applied to poetic and other literary composition at least as early as Plautus, *Trinummus* 797, *quamueis sermones possunt longei texier.* Hence comes the word 'text', which has won its place in many modern languages. But *texere* is also employed of building ships or other wooden structures, and this is certainly an old use, as its cognates in other Indo-European languages are associated above all with carpentry. The underlying root is **teḱs*. In Vedic we have *tákṣan-* 'carpenter' and the corresponding verb *takṣ*; in Avestan the equivalents *tašan-* and *taš*; in Greek τέκτων 'carpenter, builder', τεκταίνω 'construct, fashion', and τέχνη (< **teḱs-nā*) 'craft'.[39]

In all these languages words from the **teḱs* root are used of poetic composition,[40] so that the Latin use of *texere* may belong in the same tradition and may have had, at least originally, the corresponding sense of 'build'. In the Rigveda we have, for example,

> evā́ te Gṛtsamadā́ḥ śūra mánma . . . takṣuḥ.
>
> So the Gṛtsamadas have fashioned a song for thee, mighty one. (2. 19. 8)
>
> abhí tā́ṣṭeva dīdhayā manīṣā́m.
>
> I have thought out the song like a carpenter. (3. 38. 1)
>
> ápūrviyā purutámāni asmai . . . vácāṃsi . . . takṣam.
>
> Unprecedented, original words will I fashion for him. (6. 32. 1)

[37] L. C. Stern, *ZCP* 7 (1910), 19 n.; J. Vendryès, *RC* 37 (1917), 281; H. Wagner, *ZCP* 31 (1970), 50–4.

[38] *Háttatal* st. 68, trs. A. Faulkes.

[39] See further Ernout–Meillet (1959), s.v. *texo*; Chantraine (1968–80) s.v. τέκτων; Gamkrelidze–Ivanov (1995), 611, 734.

[40] Cf. T. Aufrecht, *ZVS* 4 (1855), 280; Pictet (1863), 481 f.; J. Darmesteter, *Mémoires de la Société de Linguistique de Paris* 3 (1878), 319–21 = *Études iraniennes* ii (Paris 1883), 116–18 (German version in Schmitt (1968), 26–9); Durante, (1960), 237 f. ~ (1976), 172 f.; Schmitt (1967), 14, 296–8; Campanile (1977), 35 f.; Nünlist (1998), 101 f.

The expression at 7. 7. 6 *mántraṃ yé . . . átakṣan*, 'who fashioned the song' (cf. 1. 67. 4; 2. 35. 2), has its Avestan counterpart at Y. 29. 7 *təm āzūtōiš Ahurō mąθrəm tašat̰*, 'the Lord fashioned that chant of the ghee-libation'. As mentioned earlier, a strophe of the *Gāthās* was called a *vacatašti-*, a 'fashioning of the utterance'; a half-strophe was a *naēmō-vacatašti*.[41]

Pindar is again in the van of the Greek poets who illustrate this metaphor: *Pyth.* 3. 113 ἐπέων κελαδεννῶν, τέκτονες οἷα σοφοί | ἅρμοσαν, 'resounding verses such as skilled carpenters have joined together'; *Nem.* 3. 4 μελιγαρύων τέκτονες κώμων, 'carpenters of honey-voiced encomia'. Cratinus began a lyric of his comedy *Eumenides* (fr. 70) with an invocation of τέκτονες εὐπαλάμων ὕμνων, 'O carpenters of skilful hymns'. The derived verb τεκταίνομαι appears in a similar connection in a fragment of Democritus (21 Diels–Kranz), 'Homer, having a nature in contact with the divine, fashioned an array of verses of every kind', and in one of the Hellenistic poetess Boio (2 Powell), who wrote of the legendary prophet Olen as the first who 'fashioned the song of ancient verses'. The epigrammatist Nicarchus praises Homer's supremacy in τεκτοσύνη ἐπέων (*Anth. Pal.* 7. 159. 3). This phrase, like Pindar's ἐπέων . . . τέκτονες and Democritus' ἐπέων κόσμον ἐτεκτήνατο, conjoins the same roots as the Vedic *vácāṃsi takṣam* and Avestan *vacatašti-*.

The **teḱs* root has been lost from Celtic, but the concept survives in another lexical form.

The Welsh bards called themselves the carpenters of song, *seiri gwawd* or *seiri cerdd*, and claimed as their own all the tools and technical terms of the craftsman in wood, e.g. the axe, knife, square. When a rival imitated their themes or methods they told him bluntly to take his axe to the forest and cut his own timber.[42]

This reminds us of the Greek and Latin use of 'timber' words (ὕλη, *materies*, *silua*) for the subject matter of literary compositions. In Irish, linking alliteration was called *fidrad freccomail* 'staves of joining', and types of internal rhyme were called *uaitne* 'pillar' and *salchubaid* 'willow-rhyme, post-rhyme'.[43]

In Old Norse the craftsman who works in wood, metal, or stone is a *smiðr*, and the term is also applied to poets in such compounds as *lióðasmiðr* 'songsmith', *galdasmiðr* 'spellsmith'; Bragi is *frumsmiðr bragar*, 'proto-smith

[41] Christian Bartholomae, *Altiranisches Wörterbuch* (Berlin 1904), 1037, 1340.

[42] Sir Ifor Williams, *Lectures on Early Welsh Poetry* (Dublin 1944), 7. Cf. RV 10. 53. 10, 'Sharpen now, O poets (*kavayaḥ*), the axes with which you do joinery (*tákṣatha*) for the immortal one'.

[43] S. N. Tranter in Tristram (1991), 261 f. In Norse too the alliterating words were called 'staves'. Another Irish term for alliteration was *uaim* 'stitching'.

of poetry'.[44] That carpentry is the particular craft in view appears in two passages from the tenth-century poet Egill Skallagrímsson and another from the twelfth-century poet Hallar-Stein:

Easily smoothed by my voice-plane are the praise-materials [timbers] for Thori's son, my friend, as they lie selected in twos and threes on my tongue.

I carry forth from the word-shrine praise's timber leafed with utterance.

I have smoothed with poetry's plane, painstaking in my work, my refrain-ship's beak.[45]

The vigour of the imagery in Nordic literary theory is further demonstrated in a passage from the thirteenth-century work by Óláfr Þórðarson Hvítaskáld known as the *Third Grammatical Treatise* (16 f.):

Paranomeon [*parhomoeon*] is when several words have the same initial letter, as in *sterkum stilli styriar væni*. This figure is much used in the art of eloquent speech that is called rhetoric, and it is the first principle of that poetic form that holds Norse versification together, in the way that nails hold a ship together that a craftsman makes and that otherwise goes in loose order, timber from timber: so too this figure holds the form together in versification by means of those staves that are called props and head-staves.[46]

The ship of song

The most elaborate objects made by joiners in early times were firstly boats and ships, from at least the Mesolithic period, and secondly wheeled vehicles: block-wheel wagons from sometime before 3300 BCE and spoke-wheeled chariots from around 2000. Both ships and chariots appear figuratively in Indo-European traditions in connection with poetic activity. But just as in the real world these artefacts, once made, tend to be valued as means of transport rather than just as fine specimens of carpentry, so in poetry they are represented not so much as things the poet makes as conveyances to travel on.

Let us first consider ships.[47] In a hymn to the Aśvins the twin gods beyond the sea are invited to 'come in the ship of our mindings/songs to reach the opposite shore' (RV 1. 46. 7); the perfected hymn is imagined as the conveyance that will enable them to come into the worshippers' presence. Another

[44] *Skáldsk.* 10; Durante (1960), 237 = (1976), 172 f.

[45] Egill, *Arinbiarnarkviða* 15; *Sonatorrek* 5. 3 f.; Hallar-Stein in *Skáldsk.* 47 (st. 203).

[46] Cf. Gerd Kreutzer, *Die Dichtungslehre der Skalden* (2nd edn., Meisenheim 1977); S. N. Tranter in Tristram (1991), 255–9; W. Sayers, 'Scarfing the Yard with Words: Shipbuilding Imagery in Old Norse Poetics', *Scandinavian Studies* 74 (2002), 1–18.

[47] Cf. Durante (1958), 8 f. ~ (1976), 128 f.; for Greek, Nünlist (1998), 265–76; for Latin poets, E. J. Kenney in N. I. Herescu (ed.), *Ovidiana* (Paris 1958), 206.

Rishi says to Indra, 'I come to you with prayer, as to the ship of eloquence in the (poetic) contest' (2. 16. 7). And another: 'For Indra and Agni I set my eloquence going: I drive it forwards like a ship on the river with my songs' (10. 116. 9; cf. 9. 95. 2). In 10. 101. 2 the images of weaving and the ship are juxtaposed: 'Make your thoughts gladsome, stretch them out (as on the loom); make a ship, to ferry them across!'

Pindar and Bacchylides play with nautical images in various ways. Bacchylides in the opening of one poem (16) announces that the Muse has sent him a cargo ship from Pieria, laden with songs, and in another (12) he prays her to steer his mind like a skilled helmsman, if she has ever done so before. Pindar resorts to this imagery especially in those passages where he changes tack in mid ode with an injunction to himself: 'Ease oar, plant anchor quick to ground from prow to avoid rocks!' (*Pyth.* 10. 51 f.). 'Has some wind thrown me off course like a boat at sea?' (*Pyth.* 11. 39 f.). 'My heart, to what alien headland are you diverting my voyage?' (*Nem.* 3. 26 f.). 'West of Cadiz there is no crossing: turn the ship's rig back to Europe's land' (*Nem.* 4. 69 f.). In a couple of other places (*Pyth.* 4. 3, *Nem.* 6. 28 f.) he desires the Muse to direct or strengthen the songs' *οὖρος*, the following wind that helps a ship on its way.

Ship imagery reappears in the Latin poets, but there is no guarantee that it is independent of Greek models. It is perhaps more noteworthy that we find traces of it in the North. One skaldic expression for poetry was *skip dverga*, the Dwarfs' ship. Egill Skallagrímsson, whom I quoted above, has the remarkable line

> hlóðk mærðar hlut munknarrar skut,
>
> I loaded the stern of my mind-ship with a portion of praise,

where the mental ship, the *mun-knǫrr*, has its prow from the **men* root previously discussed.[48]

The chariot of song

Evidence for the chariot image is limited to Graeco-Aryan, except for its currency in the Latin poets, where the same consideration applies as in the case of the ship.[49] In the Rigveda it occurs frequently. In several passages it is a straightforward symbol of the poet's craftsmanship:

[48] *CPB* ii. 62. 23; Egill, *Hǫfuðlausn* 1. 4.

[49] Cf. F. Edgerton, 'The metaphor of the car in the Rigvedic ritual', *AJP* 40 (1919), 175–93; Durante (1958), 9–11, 13 f. ~ (1976), 129–33; Campanile (1977), 35 f.; for Greek, Nünlist (1998), 255–64; for Latin poets, E. J. Kenney as above (n. 47).

asmā́ id u stómaṃ sáṃ hinomi
rátham ná táṣṭeva tátsināya.

For him I deliver the praise-song
as a joiner does a chariot to him who commissioned it. (1. 61. 4)

imā́ bráhmāṇi . . . yā́ tákṣāma ráthām̐ iva.

These prayers which we have built like chariots. (5. 73. 10)

Similarly 1. 94. 1, 130. 6; 5. 2. 11, 29. 15; 10. 39. 14.

In other places the poets imagine the car being harnessed and set in motion. Sometimes they are in competition for a prize, and the poetic contest is likened to a chariot race:

ī́ḻe Agníṃ suávasaṃ námobhir . . .
ráthair iva prá bhare vājayádbhiḥ;
pradakṣiṇín Marútāṃ stómam ṛdhyām.

I call on Agni the gracious with homage . . .
As if with racing chariots I am borne onward;
with him on my right hand may I make a success of the Maruts' praise-song.
(5. 60. 1)

Cf. 2. 31. 1–4; 5. 66. 3; 7. 24. 5; 8. 3. 15, 80. 4–8; 10. 26. 1/9. It is not necessarily the poet who rides in the car. In 2. 18. 1–7 the poet harnesses the horses to the chariot and urges Indra to mount it and come in it, and similarly in 3. 35. 4. In 5. 61. 17 the goddess Night is besought to convey the poet's praise-song to his patron, 'like a charioteer'.

Chariot imagery appears twice in the *Gāthās*. At Y. 50. 6 f. Zarathushtra prays:

may He who gives wisdom to be the charioteer of my tongue
teach me his rules with good thought.
And I will yoke you the swiftest steeds,
ones widely victorious in your laudation,
Wise One, in truth sturdy with good thought:
ride ye with them, and may ye be there for my succour.

Here are combined three of the concepts seen in the Vedic passages: the hymn as a chariot to be guided, the chariot-team as a contender for victory, and its yoking by the poet for the god to ride in. At 30. 10 the prophet declares that when his religion triumphs, 'the swiftest (steeds) will be yoked from the fair dwelling of Good Thought, of the Wise One, and of Truth, and they will win good fame'.

In the Greek poets the chariot is usually identified as that of the Muse or Muses. Empedocles (fr. 3. 5 Diels–Kranz) asks her to drive it 'from (the dwelling-place of) Piety', which makes a curious parallel to the last Gathic passage. Bacchylides (5. 176 f.) calls on her to halt 'the well-made car' when he wants to make a transition. Pindar sees himself as travelling in it (*Ol.* 9. 81, cf. *Isth.* 2. 1 f.); it is yoked by his patron (*Pyth.* 10. 65); it speeds on to celebrate the athlete's victory (*Isth.* 8. 61).[50]

A more elaborate picture is developed in the proem of Parmenides' philosophical apocalypse (fr. 1. 1–25 D.–K.). The poet is borne along on a car drawn by mares that take him as far as his desire reaches. Sun-maidens show him the way on the path that leads the enlightened man anywhere. This perhaps draws on a distinctive strand of mystic tradition that grew out of the more general theory of poetic charioteering. It finds its closest parallel not in the Veda but in the *Rāmāyaṇa* (3. 33. 19 f., cf. 6, 10; 46. 6; 49. 14), where it is explained that those who have conquered higher worlds by asceticism possess chariots that fly where one desires.

The Greeks had a musical form associated with dactylic rhythm and called the Chariot Nome, *ἁρμάτειος νόμος*; it is said to have been used by Stesichorus and invented by the piper Olympus. The term goes back in any case to the fifth century BCE.[51] It may have been coined to describe the bucketing rhythm of dactylo-epitrite lyric. But it can hardly be dissociated from the idea of the poet's chariot of song. Neither can the term *πεζός* 'pedestrian', which in the fifth century was used as the antithesis of 'sung, melodic' and subsequently came to designate prose discourse as opposed to verse.[52] 'On foot' must have been meant to contrast with 'on horseback' or 'in a conveyance'.

The song takes off

Even apart from the imagery of horses and chariot we find in Graeco-Aryan poetry the idea that the song is something that moves forward and travels a course.[53] Hesiod recalls that the Muses of Helicon 'set me on the path of song', *ἐπέβησαν ἀοιδῆς* (*Op.* 659). The Phaeacian bard Demodocus, invited to perform, 'set forth and began from the god', *ὁρμηθεὶς θεοῦ ἤρχετο*.[54] Both poets and prose writers refer to themselves as 'going on' to a new point,

[50] See also Pind. *Ol.* 6. 22–5, *Nem.* 1. 7, *Isth.* 5. 38, *Pae.* 7b. 12–14, fr. 124ab. 1, 140b. 8; Bacchyl. 10. 51; Ar. *Vesp.* 1022; Choerilus of Samos fr. 1. 4–5; Call. fr. 1. 25–8; Lucr. 6. 47, 92 f.; Virg. *G.* 2. 541 f., etc. For the 'yoking' image applied more generally to songs and words in Vedic and Greek cf. Wüst (1969), 57–9.

[51] See M. L. West, *CQ* 21 (1971), 309–11.

[52] A. C. Pearson, *The Fragments of Sophocles* (Cambridge 1917), i. 14 (on fr. 16); Eduard Norden, *Die antike Kunstprosa* (3rd edn., Leipzig–Berlin 1915), i. 32–4.

[53] See Durante (1958), 3 f. ~ (1976), 123 f.; Nünlist (1998), 228–54.

[54] *Od.* 8. 499. In the next line, usually read *ἔνθεν ἑλών* 'taking it from there', Bergk proposed *ἐλῶν* 'driving', which would imply the chariot metaphor; cf. Pind. *Isth.* 5. 38 *ἔλα νῦν μοι πεδόθεν*; Bacchyl. 10. 51 *τί μακρὰν γλῶσσαν ἰθύσας ἐλαύνω | ἐκτὸς ὁδοῦ;*

or as 'returning' to an earlier one. But in the poets, both Indian and Greek, we find more graphic images.

According to RV 9. 10. 6 'the poets of the past open the doors of mindings/songs', presumably enabling the songs to come forth. Similarly Bacchylides (fr. 5): 'One becomes skilled (as a poet) from another; it was ever so. For it is not the easiest thing to discover the gates of unspoken verse.' And Pindar (*Ol.* 6. 27): 'the gates of song must be opened for them'. In Parmenides the gates of Night and Day are opened for his car to pass through, so that he can learn the truth that will form the subject matter of his poem.

The poem needs an open, smooth road for its advance. 'As in the past, make the paths conducive for the new hymn' (RV 9. 91. 5). 'Broad are the approaches from every side for story-men to glorify this famed island' (Pind. *Nem.* 6. 45 f., cf. *Isth.* 3. 19, Bacchyl. 5. 31). 'It is no rocky or uphill path, if one brings the Muses' honours to the house of men of high repute' (*Isth.* 2. 33 f.).

When all is ready, one can say 'let the song go forth!'

prá Víṣṇave śūṣám etu mánma.

Let the song go forth sonorously for Vishnu. (RV 1. 154. 3)

prá śukrá etu devī́ manīṣā́ asmát sútaṣto rátho ná vājī́.

Let the shining, divine song go forth from us like a well-built prize-winning chariot. (7. 34. 1)

prá Mitráyor Váruṇayo stómo na etu śūṣíyaḥ.

Let our praise of Mitra and Varuna go forth sonorously. (7. 66. 1)

The third-person imperative *etu* corresponds to Greek ἴτω, and the formula resembles Greek examples such as Aesch. *Sept.* 964 ἴτω γόος· ἴτω δάκρυ, Soph. fr. 490 ἴτω δὲ Πυθιὰς βοά, Eur. *Phaethon* 101 ἴτω τελεία γάμων ἀοιδά, Ion of Chios fr. 27. 7 ἴτω διὰ νυκτὸς ἀοιδή.

Besides travelling by road or by ship, the song may fly (**pet*) through the air.[55]

párā hi me vímanyavaḥ
pátanti vásyaïṣṭaye
váyo ná vasatī́r úpa.

For forth my sentiments
fly to find success
like birds to their nests. (RV 1. 25. 4)

The Danaids in Aeschylus' *Supplices* (656) sing 'So from our suppliant mouths let the honorific prayer fly forth' (ποτάσθω). In Homer we have the

[55] Durante (1958), 5–8 ~ (1976), 124–8; Nünlist (1998), 279–83.

formula ἔπεα πτερόεντα, 'winged words', and the ἄπτερος μῦθος, the utterance that fails to fly. Lyric poets describe their songs as 'winged' or 'flying',[56] or as causing the person celebrated to fly.[57]

In a more pointed image the song is conceived as a bolt shot from a bow.[58] 'Like an arrow on the bow the minding/hymn is set' (RV 9. 69. 1). 'Like an archer shooting his shaft clear beyond (his rivals), proffer him the praise-song' (10. 42. 1). 'O singer, bring forth the hymn . . . just as an archer aims his arrow, address this prayer to the gods' (AV 20. 127. 6). 'From the mouth fly forth the arrows of speech' (*MBh.* 5. 34. 77). Once again Pindar provides close parallels:

> Many are the swift shafts under my elbow, within the quiver,
> that speak to those who understand, but for the generality
> require interpreters . . .
> Come, my spirit, aim the bow at the target! Whom do we hit this time
> with our arrows of glory discharged from gentle heart?[59]

The arrow is his favourite metaphorical missile, and presumably traditional, but sometimes he varies it by speaking of throwing a javelin (*Ol.* 13. 93, *Pyth.* 1. 44, *Nem.* 7. 71, 9. 55) or a discus (*Isth.* 2. 35).

VERSIFICATION

Scholars have long looked for genetic relationships between the metrical systems used by different ancient Indo-European peoples. Rudolf Westphal made the first such attempt in 1860, and a meritorious effort it was.[60] He compared Vedic and Avestan metres with some of the standard Greek ones, and fastened on to a number of important points. Others in the nineteenth century tried to reconstruct an *Urvers* from which the Latin Saturnian and Germanic alliterative verse could also be derived by postulating developments *ad hoc*, but they failed to add much of significance to what Westphal had achieved.[61]

[56] Pratinas, *PMG* 708. 5; Pind. *Pyth.* 8. 34, *Nem.* 7. 22, *Isth.* 5. 63; Anon. *PMG* 954b.

[57] Theognis 237 f.; Pind. *Pyth.* 5. 114, *Isth.* 1. 64; cf. Ennius' claim in his epitaph, *uolito uiuus per ora uirum*, 'I fly living across the mouths of men'.

[58] See Durante (1958), 7 f. ~ (1976), 128; Nünlist (1998), 145–8.

[59] *Ol.* 2. 83–90; see also *Ol.* 1. 112, 9. 5–12, *Nem.* 6. 28, *Isth.* 2. 3, 5. 46 f., fr. 6a (g).

[60] 'Zur vergleichenden Metrik der indogermanischen Völker', *ZVS* 9 (1860), 437–58.

[61] K. Bartsch, *Der saturnische Vers und die altdeutsche Langzeile* (Leipzig 1867); F. Allen, 'Ueber den Ursprung des homerischen Versmasses', *ZVS* 24 (1879), 556–92; H. Seiling, *Ursprung und Messung des homerischen Verses* (Progr. Münster, Nördlingen 1887); Hermann Usener, *Altgriechischer Versbau* (Bonn 1887). Cf. Schmitt (1967), 7 f.

A real advance was made by Antoine Meillet, who based his conclusions mainly on a careful comparison of Vedic with Greek metres.[62] Without mentioning Westphal, he made many of the same points; but whereas Westphal's eye had focused, for the Greek side, on the hexameter and the iambic dimeter and trimeter, Meillet found better comparanda in the metres of the Lesbian lyricists. And whereas Westphal (and the other Germans) could not comprehend any metre except in terms of a regular beat, the Francophone Meillet, writing at a time when music was coming to be written more often without bar lines, understood that quantitatively patterned verses may be taken at face value and need not be divisible into feet of equal duration.

While there have been a few sceptics, most investigators since Meillet have accepted that his conclusions form a sound basis for further work. The two major extensions to his edifice have been the analyses of Slavonic metre by Roman Jakobson and of Old Irish metre by Calvert Watkins.[63] Continuing efforts have been made to bring Italic and Germanic verse under the same umbrella, and there have been various claims for the recognition of Indo-European elements in specimens of Hittite, Luwian, Lycian, Lydian, Sidetic, Phrygian, Gaulish, Celtiberian, Welsh, and Tocharian verse. The following survey must necessarily be succinct, concentrating on the main facts and leaving aside much subsidiary detail.[64]

Graeco-Aryan metre

It is still Greek and Vedic that show the clearest relationship. This may be because they are two of the oldest attested and bear the best witness to an original system that had become deformed by the time the evidence from other branches comes into view. Or it may be because Graeco-Aryan had developed a particular system that never existed in the same form in other parts of the Indo-European area. In any case the best procedure will be first to see what can be established about Graeco-Aryan metre, and then to inquire how far the results can be extended to MIE or PIE.

The governing principles of prosody and versification are essentially identical in Vedic and early Greek. The unit of composition is a verse containing a

[62] Meillet (1923), foreshadowed in previous publications. On the development and influence of Meillet's views see Françoise Bader, 'Meillet et la poésie indo-européenne', *Cahiers Ferdinand de Saussure* 42 (1988), 97–125.

[63] R. Jakobson, 'Studies in Comparative Slavic Metrics', *Oxford Slavonic Papers* 3 (1952), 21–66 = id. (1962–88), iv. 414–63; Watkins (1963), 194–249 = (1994), 349–404.

[64] Cf. Schmitt (1967), 307–13; West (1973), 161–87; Durante (1976), 62–5, 70; Gamkrelidze–Ivanov (1995), 738–40; Watkins (1995), 19–21, 54.

determinate number of syllables.[65] The boundaries of the verse do not cut into a word or accentual unit; very often the end of the verse coincides with a syntactic pause. For prosodic purposes the verse is a continuum, the words within it being treated as an unbroken stream of sound, divided into syllables without regard to word division or sense pauses. Between verses this continuity is broken.

There is a clear opposition of long and short syllables, a syllable being long if it contains a long vowel or diphthong or if it ends in a consonant. A single consonant between vowels is assigned to the second of the two syllables, but where two or three consonants occur together (other than at the beginning of the verse) they are divided between syllables, making the prior syllable automatically long.[66] Where a short final vowel occurs before an initial vowel, the two syllables are generally reduced to one, whether by amalgamation (Vedic) or by elision of the first (Greek).[67] Other short vowels may in certain circumstances be lengthened *metri gratia.* A long final vowel before an initial vowel generally remains but is shortened by correption. The semivowels i/i̯ and u/u̯, as the second element of a diphthong, are treated as consonants when the diphthong is word-final before an initial vowel.

A verse is given a recognizable identity firstly by the grouping of words within it, so that in a longer verse there is usually a word-break or 'caesura' after a set number of syllables, and secondly by some degree of regulation of the sequence of long and short syllables, particularly in the latter part of the verse. Word accent plays no part.

Much the commonest species of verse in the Rigveda are:[68]

(i) An eight-syllable line of the form × × × × ∪ – ∪ – ‖, used in three- or four-line stanzas (called respectively *gāyatrī* and *anuṣṭubh*). A variant type, preferred in some early hymns, has the 'trochaic' cadence $\underline{\cup}$ ∪ – – ‖.

[65] In many types of Greek verse (such as the Homeric hexameter) and in later Sanskrit verse the number is subject to variation due to the optional substitution of two short syllables for one long or vice versa. But this is not true of the Vedic hymns, nor of Lesbian lyric, which in this as in some other respects evidently represents the older state of affairs.

[66] In Greek there was an increasing tendency not to divide plosive + liquid groups ([pr], [kl], etc.), so that a preceding short open syllable remained unlengthened, especially if word-final. But this was clearly a secondary development.

[67] Cf. J. Kuryłowicz in Cardona et al. (1970), 425 f.

[68] For full details see Hermann Oldenberg, *Die Hymnen des Ṛigveda*, i (Berlin 1888), 1–162; E. V. Arnold, *Vedic Metre* (Cambridge 1905); B. A. van Nooten and G. B. Holland, *Rig Veda. A Metrically Restored Text* (Cambridge, Mass. 1994), vii–xviii and 577–667; on prosody see also Kuryłowicz (1973), 42–96. In the metrical schemes that follow, the symbol × denotes 'indifferent quantity', $\underline{\cup}$ 'mostly long', and $\bar{\cup}$ 'mostly short'. The final position in a verse is shown as long, but it may always be occupied by a short syllable, the full length being made up by the pause at line-end. The dividers | ‖ ||| represent respectively regular word-end (caesura), verse-end, and strophe-end.

(ii) An eleven-syllable line with a caesura after four or five syllables and the cadence ⏑ – – ‖, used in four-line stanzas (*triṣṭubh*) or to conclude a song in twelve-syllable lines. The second, fourth, and eighth syllables tend to be long, and the two syllables following the caesura short. The typical schemes are (*a*) × ⏓ × ⏓ | ⏒ ⏒ ⏓ ⏓ ⏑ – – ‖, (*b*) × – ⏒ – ⏓ | ⏑ ⏑ ⏓ ⏑ – – ‖.

(iii) A twelve-syllable line, also used in four-line stanzas (*jagatī*), resembling the eleven-syllable except that it has an extra short syllable in the cadence, ⏓ ⏑ – ⏑ – ‖ instead of ⏓ ⏑ – – ‖.

The relationship between (iii) and (ii) is matched exactly in Greek verse, where very frequently, besides lines ending in . . . ⏒ – ⏑ – ‖, there occur (often to conclude a sequence) others that differ only in ending . . . ⏑ – – ‖. The latter are called catalectic in relation to the former, and the former acatalectic. This systemic parallel is one important point of correspondence between Greek and Vedic.

A second feature is that in both traditions the regulation of quantities is strictest in the cadence of the verse and least strict at the beginning. Greek verses in historical times are fairly closely regulated throughout, but—as already noted by Westphal—what seems to be a relic of original freedom at the start of the verse appears in the so-called 'Aeolic base' of certain Lesbian metres, where the first two syllables may be indifferently long or short.

The most typical of these metres, one that can be followed through Greek poetry for many centuries, is the eight-syllable glyconic, × × – ⏑ ⏑ – ⏑ –. Apart from its slightly more fixed scheme, this is very much like the Vedic octosyllable, which indeed may appear in a form identical to the glyconic. Out of the thirty octosyllables that make up RV 6. 54, for example, ten are good glyconics, as in stanza 5ab:

Pūṣā́ gā́ ánu etu naḥ,	– – – ⏑ ⏑ – ⏑ – ‖
Pūṣā́ rakṣatu árvataḥ.	– – – ⏑ ⏑ – ⏑ – ‖

There also occur, particularly in early hymns, seven-syllable verses which in some cases appear as a catalectic version of the eight-syllable (× × × × ⏑ – – ‖), in others as a foreshortened or headless ('acephalic') version (× × × ⏑ – ⏑ – ‖).[69] Both have counterparts in common Greek verses, the pherecratean (× × – ⏑ ⏑ – –) and the telesillean (× – ⏑ ⏑ – ⏑ –) respectively. There is a catalectic form of the latter known as the reizianum (× – ⏑ ⏑ – –).

In the Lesbian poets the glyconic and other such units are used as

[69] See B. Vine, *ZVS* 91 (1977), 246–55.

components of stanzas of two, three, or four lines. We do not find, as in the Veda, stanzas composed of three or four lines of the same form; at least one will be different. In Sappho fr. 94, for instance, the stanza consists of two glyconics and a third line which is an expanded glyconic, × × – ⏑ ⏑ – ⏑ ⏑ – ⏑ – ‖. In fr. 98 it is two glyconics and a third line in which a glyconic is prefixed with – ⏑ –. The same principle of an extended third line is seen in the so-called *uṣṇiḥ* metre of certain early Vedic hymns (e.g. RV 3. 10; 8. 12–13, 15, 18, 23–6; 9. 102–7) in which the third of the three octosyllables is extended by a repetition of the four-syllable cadence: × × × × ⏑ – ⏑ – | ⏑ – ⏑ – ‖.

This iambic tetrasyllabic element has some similarity to the first part of those eleven- and twelve-syllable verses in which the caesura falls after four syllables, since they tend to have the second and fourth syllables long. What follows the caesura then resembles the independent octosyllable or its catalectic heptasyllabic counterpart. Where the caesura comes after five syllables, what precedes it may be identified as the pentasyllabic colon × – ⏓ – × | which can also appear, in duplicate, to form a recognized type of verse called *dvipadā virāj*; the rest of the line is equivalent to a headless octosyllable or heptasyllable.

In other words, if we designate the standard octosyllable as G, its catalectic and acephalic versions as $G_{\wedge}$ and $_{\wedge}G$, and the tetra- and pentasyllabic complements as 4 and 5, we can analyse the eleven-syllable verse as 4 | $G_{\wedge}$ ‖ or 5 | $_{\wedge}G_{\wedge}$ ‖, the twelve-syllable as 4 | G ‖ or 5 | $_{\wedge}G$ ‖, and the *uṣṇiḥ* stanza as G ‖ G ‖ G | 4 ‖|.

Similar formulae can be applied to Greek lyric verse, with G here realized as the glyconic (gl), 4 as the iambic metron × – ⏑ – (ia), and 5 as the penthemimer × – ⏑ – × (pe). For instance, Alcaeus' fragments 140 and 358–60 Voigt are composed in stanzas made up of gl + gl + ia (G G 4), while in fragments 70 and 117b the first and third lines of the strophe consist of ia + gl (4 G). The combination of ia + telesillean (4 $_{\wedge}G$) forms the first two lines of the frequently used Alcaic stanza.

The iambic dimeter, × – ⏑ – × – ⏑ – (2ia), can be regarded as an alternative realization of the G pattern. Again, the Vedic octosyllable may take this form. Examples from the same hymn as cited above (RV 6. 54) are 1b *yó áñjasānuśā́sati*, 3a *Pūṣṇáś cakrám̐ ná riṣyati*, 6a *Pū́ṣann ánu prá gā́ ihi*. The iambic trimeter (3ia) then appears as the counterpart of the Vedic twelve-syllable line, particularly in its 5 | $_{\wedge}G$ ‖ form, as it too normally has its caesura after the fifth syllable. When Archilochus (frs. 172–81) and Hipponax (fr. 118) use stanzas composed of trimeters and dimeters in alternation, this is entirely parallel to Vedic strophes of the forms 12 ‖ 8 ‖ 12 ‖ 8 ‖| (called *satobṛhatī*), 12 ‖ 12 ‖ 8 ‖| (*kṛti*), 12 ‖ 8 ‖ 8 ‖| (*pura-uṣṇiḥ*), etc.

I have limited myself here to the most salient points of comparison.[70] The sum of correspondences, not only in the structure of individual lines but also in their relationship to one another and in the patterns in which they are combined, is sufficient to show the persistence both in the Rigveda and in Greek poetry of forms already established at any rate by the Graeco-Aryan period.

We have, of course, early evidence for another branch of Graeco-Aryan, namely Iranian. Zarathushtra's *Gāthās* are in verse, and we should expect their metres to show some relationship to the system reflected in Vedic and Greek. And so they do, inasmuch as they are based on lines with a fixed number of syllables and a caesura, arranged in strophes of three, four, or five lines. On the other hand there is no regulation of quantities. In view of the agreements between Vedic and Greek, we must suppose that such regulation had existed at an earlier stage but lost its significance. Kuryłowicz has argued that its role had been taken over by a stress accent on the penultimate syllable of every word and of the verse.[71] A prosodic difference from Vedic and Greek is that the meeting of a final with an initial vowel never results in syllabic loss. This may be connected with the fact that, according to the oral tradition as recorded in the Sasanian orthography, all final vowels had come to be pronounced long, as was also the case in Old Persian.

The lines are of the following varieties: 7 | 9 (Y. 28–34, three-line strophes); 4 | 7 (Y. 43–50, five- and four-line strophes); 7 | 7 (Y. 51, three-line strophes), and in a more complex strophe (Y. 53) 5 | 7 twice, followed by 7 | 7 | 5 twice. They all involve a seven-syllable colon. The 4 | 7 and 5 | 7 combinations can be directly compared with the Vedic eleven- and twelve-syllable lines, the four-line strophe of 4 | 7 corresponding to the Indian *triṣṭubh*. If Kuryłowicz's stress theory is right, the original cadence . . . ∪ – – ‖ has been replaced by . . . × ×́ × ‖. In the Younger Avesta, as for example in the Hymn to Mithra (Yt. 10), the commonest metre is an octosyllable, varied occasionally by lines of ten or twelve syllables.

There have been several attempts to find metre in some of the Phrygian inscriptions, especially the Neo-Phrygian epitaphs from the Roman period, where a number of recurrent and probably traditional formulae appear. Most recently I have pointed out that several of these appear to show metrical patterns resembling the Greek glyconic and pherecratean, in some cases

[70] For fuller surveys of Greek lyric cola and their interpretation in terms of the same system see Watkins (1963), 195–210 = (1994), 350–65; West (1973), 165–70; Gasparov (1996), 54–64.

[71] J. Kuryłowicz, *L'accentuation des langues indo-européennes* (2nd edn., Paris 1958), 369–80; id., *BSL* 67 (1972), 47–67; id. (1973), 102–38. On Gathic metre see also Christian Bartholomae, *Die Gāθās und heiligen Gebete des altiranischen Volkes* (Halle 1879), 1–19; J. Hertel, *Beiträge zur Metrik des Awestas und des Ṛgvedas* (Leipzig 1927); J. Gippert, *Die Sprache* 32 (1986), 257–75.

prefixed by a four-syllable element (– ⏑ ⏑ – | or × – ⏑ – |) or followed by a pentasyllabic one (| × – ⏑ – –). I have given reasons for thinking that these patterns were not borrowed from Greek models but inherited from the time when the Phrygians' Bronze Age ancestors lived near those of the Greeks.[72]

The remaining branch of Graeco-Aryan is Armenian. The metres of classical Armenian poetry are derived from Greek. But the fragments of older, pagan poetry are versified on a different, syllable-counting principle. As in Iranian, syllabic quantities are no longer regarded. The poem on the birth of Vahagn begins with four seven-syllable lines; then, after two of nine syllables, there are two more of seven and two more of nine. Other fragments show hepta- and octosyllables, and sequences of 7 | 6 and 6 | 9 verses.[73] We must reckon with the possibility that these metres developed under the Iranian influence to which Armenian culture had long been subject. But they may equally represent a native tradition.

Other Indo-European metre

We have now reconstructed the outlines of a Graeco-Aryan metrical system, characterized by quantitative prosody and lines of determinate length. There were shorter lines of seven or eight syllables, ending in the cadences . . . ⏑ – – ‖ or . . . ⏑ – ⏑ – ‖, and longer lines made by prefixing these with a four- or five-syllable element, × ⏓ × ⏓ | or × ⏓ ⏑ ⏓ × |. Simple strophes were built, usually from three or four similar lines, but sometimes by alternating lines of different length. This summary account, it should be stressed, does not necessarily encapsulate the whole of Graeco-Aryan metrics, only those details that we are able to reconstruct from the extant evidence.

The next step is to inquire how much of this picture, if any, can be taken back to Level 2 (MIE) or Level 1 (PIE). To what extent can the same features be recognized, firstly in the other ancient European poetic traditions and secondly in the Anatolian?

Taking the European traditions in chronological order of attestation, we begin with the Italic evidence, which consists primarily of the Latin Saturnian metre and other odds and ends of early Latin verse; we ignore, of course, the classical Latin metres borrowed from Greek.[74]

The basic scheme of the Saturnian may be represented as

[72] 'Phrygian Metre', *Kadmos* 42 (2003), 77–86.

[73] See L. H. Gray, *Revue des Études Arméniennes* 6 (1926), 160 f., 164–7.

[74] Cf. T. Cole, 'The Saturnian Verse', *Yale Classical Studies* 21 (1969), 3–73; West (1973), 175–9; Watkins (1995), 126–34; P. M. Freeman, 'Saturnian Verse and Early Latin Poetics', *JIES* 26 (1998), 61–90.

× × × × | × ⏓ × | × × × × ×́ × ‖

—a seven-syllable colon, usually with caesura after the fourth syllable, in syzygy with a six-syllable colon of which the penultimate syllable is stressed (and most often long). There are many irregularities in the number of syllables, most of which can be explained by special rules or put down to faulty transmission, but this description may be taken as the basis for discussion.

In the extant material, the oldest of which dates from the third century BCE, the accentual rules of classical Latin apply.[75] At an earlier period the stress had fallen on the initial syllable of every word. At that time the caesura after four syllables would have entailed a stress on the fifth, and the verse would have had the form

× × × × ×́ × × | × × × × ×́ × ‖

The pattern is strikingly analogous to the type of acatalectic + catalectic pairing typical of Graeco-Aryan quantitative verse:

× × × ⏑ – ⏑ – | × × × ⏑ – – ‖

We have already suggested that in Avestan, with stress having come to be a significant factor in versification, the original cadence . . . ⏑ – – ‖ was replaced by . . . × ×́ × ‖. If a parallel development occurred in proto-Italic, the Saturnian can be satisfactorily explained as the continuation of a prototype of the form $_{\wedge}$G | $_{\wedge}$G$_{\wedge}$ ‖.

Another verse found in the early Latin material, in the Arval and Saliar hymns and in certain traditional charms, is an octosyllable with medial caesura and penultimate stress: *diuom deo supplicate*; *nouom uetus uinum bibo*. This cannot be equated with the ordinary Graeco-Aryan G verse, but it could correspond to the Vedic trochaic *gāyatrī* type.

Attempts have been made since the nineteenth century to identify and analyse verse in other Italic dialects such as Oscan, Paelignian, Faliscan, and South Picene. Some of these analyses appear wholly arbitrary; others seem possible but too uncertain to assist the argument, and I pass over them here.[76]

We move north to the Celtic lands. Here the oldest extant verses are perhaps to be found in a Gaulish curse-tablet from Chamalières, dating from the first century of our era. The text begins: *andedíon uediíumi diíuion risunartiu Mapon Arueriíatin*, 'by virtue of the Lower Gods I invoke Mapon

[75] Except that words scanning ⏑ ⏑ ⏑ × were presumably still stressed on the first syllable, as in Plautus and Terence.

[76] See F. Bücheler, 'Altitalisches Weihgedicht', *Rh. Mus.* 33 (1878), 271–90; 'Altitalische Grabschrift', ibid. 35 (1880), 494 f.; P. Poccetti, 'Eine Spur des saturnischen Verses im Oskischen', *Glotta* 61 (1983), 207–17; H. Eichner, *Die Sprache* 34 (1988/90), 198–206; Watkins (1995), 126–34; P. M. Freeman, *JIES* 26 (1998), 77–9.

Arveriatis'. This certainly seems to show poetic diction and word order, and it can be arranged into three verses of seven or eight syllables with quantitative cadences in . . . ⏑ – – ‖ or . . . ⏑ – ⏑ – ‖.[77] The similarity with the prototypes reconstructed for Graeco-Aryan is remarkable.

Irish verse does not come into view until half a millennium later, but the high proportion of words that are exclusively poetic is a sign of the antiquity of the tradition behind it.[78] In this poetry an initial stress accent has replaced quantity as a formative factor. In the earliest epic and gnomic poetry the commonest type of verse is a heptasyllable of the form

× × × × | ×́ × × ‖

This closely resembles the heptasyllable that forms the first half of the Latin Saturnian, and we can derive it in just the same way from the $_{\wedge}$G prototype.

Freely alternating with the heptasyllable, or sometimes as the fourth line of a quatrain, we find a verse that differs from it only in having one more syllable before the caesura. This would correspond to the full G. There is also a longer verse, apparently very archaic and soon abandoned, in which the heptasyllable is preceded by a protasis of four or (less often) five syllables, marked off by caesura:

(×) × × × × | × × × × | ×́ × × ‖

This is exactly parallel to the construction of longer verses in Graeco-Aryan by prefixing 4 | or 5 | to G, $_{\wedge}$G, etc.

If these Irish verses ending in . . . | ×́ × × ‖ go back to acatalectic prototypes, we should expect that catalectic ones would appear with an ending . . . | ×́ × ‖, as they do in Latin and (without the consequential caesura) in Avestan. Such verses in fact occur. Indeed a complete series of 'acatalectic' and 'catalectic' measures can be found: 5 | 3 and 5 | 2 (= G: G$_{\wedge}$), 4 | 3 and 4 | 2 ($_{\wedge}$G: $_{\wedge}$G$_{\wedge}$), 3 | 3 and 3 | 2, 2 | 3 and 2 | 2. When members of these pairs are combined in a stanza, the 'acatalectic' ones precede. Thus Watkins cites stanzas of the forms 4 | 3 ‖ 3 | 2 ‖ 4 | 3 ‖ 3 | 2 ⦀, 3 | 3 ‖ 3 | 2 ‖ 3 | 2 ‖ 3 | 2 ⦀, 2 | 3 ‖ 4 | 2 ⦀, and 2 | 3 ‖ 2 | 3 ‖ 4 | 2 ⦀. This is in accord with the predominantly clausular character of the catalectic type in Vedic and Greek.

77 W. Meid, *Zur Lesung und Deutung gallischer Inschriften* (Innsbruck 1989), ad fin.; id. (1990), 47 f. For the Chamalières *defixio* see Lambert (2003), 152–61. In another major Gaulish text, the lead tablet from Larzac (Lambert, 162–74), G. Olmsted finds metre (*JIES* 17 (1989), 155 ff.; 19 (1991), 280–2), while Meid (1990), 48 finds 'eine teilweise rhythmisierte Prosa mit einem hohen Anteil an lautfigurativen Elementen'.

78 Thurneysen (1921), 56. In the account that follows I rely on Watkins's seminal paper (as above, n. 63), while noting that it has been subjected to some strong criticism: see E. Campanile, *ZCP* 37 (1979), 193–7; K. Klar, B. O Hehir, and E. Sweetser, *Studia Celtica* 18/19 (1983/4), 47–51; McCone (1990), 38–41, 45. Cf. also Kuryłowicz (1973), 159–71.

In early British poetry the picture is not quite so sharp, but it fits sweetly enough into the same frame. It has long been a matter of controversy how its metrical practice should be understood, but according to an authoritative modern study syllable-counting gives better results than accentual analysis. The characteristic three-line stanza, the *englyn*, typically consists of seven-syllable lines; sometimes the first has eight syllables.[79]

Germanic verse does not contribute very much to the argument. We can certainly speak, on the basis of strong similarities between Norse, Old English, Old Saxon, and Old High German verse-forms, of a common Germanic tradition. There is a standard four-stress line that divides into two halves, linked by obligatory alliteration. The first half tends to be longer than the second, but the number of syllables is very variable. In Old Norse the verse is mainly used in four-line stanzas in what is called 'ancient style' (*fornyrðislag*). There is also a longer type of line with three stresses in each half, and in Norse and English there is a form of strophic composition in which a four-stress line alternates with a single three-stress colon.

It is not hard to suggest ways in which these measures might have evolved from quantitative prototypes such as we have postulated. The dimensions of the four-stress line would suit an origin from the combination of an eight- or seven-syllable verse (G or $_{\wedge}$G) with its catalectic counterpart. But here we are only observing that the data are compatible with our theory. We cannot claim that they corroborate it.

When it comes to Slavonic metre, we are dealing with material recorded in much more recent times. But the static nature of the forms as far back as they can be traced, together with their diffusion throughout the Slavonic lands, encourages the assumption that they represent a common heritage of considerable antiquity.[80]

Here again accentual developments in the languages have affected versification to a marked degree. However, the Serbo-Croat ten-syllable epic line preserves a recognizable quantitative cadence in performance, and more noticeably so in poems recorded in the eighteenth century. The underlying scheme is

$$\times\times\times\times \mid \times\times\cup\cup - \times \parallel,$$

with the principal stresses on the first, fifth, and ninth syllables. The ninth tends to be prolonged in recitation, and this feature is also recorded from Moravia and Bulgaria. The ten-syllable line occurs further in Slovakia, Poland, Belarus, and Ukraine.

[79] Rowland (1990), 308–19.

[80] Here and in what follows my information is drawn from Jakobson (as above, n. 63). See also Watkins (1963), 210–12 = (1994), 365–7; Gasparov (1996), 15–35.

The caesura after the fourth syllable suggests analogy with the Vedic, Avestan, Greek, and Irish long lines formed with a four-syllable protasis. What follows the caesura is an exact fit with our $_{\wedge}G_{\wedge}$ prototype. That it is to be assigned to our catalectic category is confirmed by the existence in Russia of an acatalectic equivalent, an eleven-syllable verse, no longer with the caesura, but still with the ninth syllable stressed and prolonged. We may infer that proto-Slavonic had the two types, acatalectic × × × × | × × ⏔ ∪ – ∪ – ‖ and catalectic × × × × | × × ⏔ ∪ – – ‖.

Another common Slavonic verse, used for epical-historical narratives, is of eight syllables, with stress on the sixth. By the principles applied above, this should correspond to the G prototype, × × × × ∪ – ∪ – ‖. If we take the Russian form of this verse, where the third syllable is also stressed, and apply the same method, we arrive at × × – ∪ ∪ – ∪ – ‖, which is exactly the Greek glyconic and a frequent manifestation of the Vedic octosyllable. Outside Russia, however, the stresses in the first half of the verse fall rather on the first and fourth (Bulgaria) or the second and fourth syllables. There is also a caesura after the fifth.

Another kind of octosyllable, associated with laments, is characterized by trochaic rhythm and thus penultimate stress. This suggests the catalectic category, and again there is a Russian acatalectic equivalent with an extra syllable at the end to provide confirmation. There is also, in Russian and Serbo-Croat, a longer form of the line, with an extra four-syllable colon at the beginning—the now familiar protasis element.

The Lithuanian songs make use of cola of four, five, six, and seven syllables in various combinations.[81] The penultimate syllable tends to be long and stressed, the distribution of other stresses being irregular. We find strophes consisting of two, three, or four heptasyllables; strophes of two or four lines of 5 | 5, or four of 5 | 4; of 5 | 5 | 7; of four of 4 | 6, or two of 4 | 4; of 4 | 4 | 6. In a folk-tale published by Schleicher a horse utters a series of octosyllables (4 | 4), concluding, as it were catalectically, with a heptasyllable.[82] The 4 | 6 combination resembles the Slavonic decasyllable.

The Latvian folk singers use three types of metre. The most frequent is the 4 | 4 octosyllable. Its rhythm is strongly trochaic, as Latvian has an initial stress and monosyllables may not be placed in the fourth and eighth positions (which are normally short). Sometimes the hemistich takes a catalectic form, ×́ × – | instead of ×́ × × ∪ |. Secondly, there is also a 3 | 3 verse with dactylic rhythm: ×́ × ∪ | ×́ × ∪ ‖, again with catalectic variants. Gasparov suggests that

[81] Rhesa (1825), 334–47; P. Trost in *Poetics. Poetyka. Poètika*, i (Warsaw–The Hague 1961), 119–26; Kuryłowicz (1973), 200–10; Gasparov (1996), 13 f.

[82] Noted and quoted by Meillet (1923), 77 f.

this may derive from a longer, twelve-syllable verse broken down into hemistichs. Thirdly, there are strophes in which the octosyllable alternates with a six-syllable line without caesura, the most popular arrangement being 6 ‖ 6 ‖ 8 ‖ 6 ‖‖.[83]

Albanian oral poetry, according to a nineteenth-century scholar, was non-strophic and unrhymed, consisting of a series of loose octosyllables, among which seven- or six-syllable lines sometimes appeared. There is also epic verse in 4 | 6 decasyllables similar to those of the neighbouring Serbo-Croat tradition.[84]

Finally, I should not wish to be reproached for overlooking the Tocharians, who are believed to have migrated to their historical seat in Chinese Turkestan from the west and ultimately from Europe. Their verse appears to be purely syllabic.[85] Cola of between three and eight syllables are combined in long lines. The commonest are of twelve syllables (4 | 4 | 4 or 5 | 7), fourteen (7 | 7), and eighteen (7 | 7 | 4). Less common are fifteen (5 | 7 | 3 or 7 | 8 or 8 | 7), seventeen (6 | 6 | 5), and twenty-five (5 | 5 | 8 | 7). Lines of equal or unequal length are grouped in four-line strophes.

These structures might be derived from the same set of prototypes as those discussed above; the prevalence of four-, five-, seven-, and eight-syllable cola, and the occurrence of such conjunctions as 5 | 7 and 8 | 7 among the rest, are suggestive. Watkins notes that the heptasyllable commonly has a caesura after four syllables. But one cannot build anything firm on these foundations.

If the Tocharian, Baltic, and Germanic evidence is inconclusive, the Italic, Celtic, and Slavonic traditions provide positive encouragement to think that the metrical principles extrapolated from Vedic and Greek were not valid only for Graeco-Aryan but, by and large, also for the rest of Europe; in other words, for MIE. It remains to ask whether indications of a similar system can be detected in Anatolia (apart from Phrygian, which does not belong to the Anatolian but to the Graeco-Aryan group). If they can, the inference will be that it can be attributed to PIE.

The usable material is disappointingly slight. We have a small number of extended mythological narratives in Hittite that are clearly poetic in nature, but they are translated or adapted from Hurrian originals, and it is not clear

[83] V. J. Zeps in *A Festschrift for Morris Halle* (New York 1973), 207–11; Gasparov (1996), 11–13.

[84] Alberto Straticò, *Manuale di letteratura albanese* (Milan 1896), 60; J. Kolsti in C. E. Gribble (ed.), *Studies presented to Professor Roman Jakobson by his Students* (Cambridge, Mass. 1968), 165–7. Examples of octosyllabic songs can be found in Auguste Dozon, *Manuel de la langue chkipe ou albanaise* (Paris 1878), 85 ff.

[85] Emil Sieg and Wilhelm Siegling, *Tocharische Sprachreste*, i. A (Berlin 1921), x–xi. Cf. C. Watkins in H. Eichner and H. C. Luschützky (edd.), *Compositiones Indogermanicae in memoriam Jochem Schindler* (Prague 1999), 601–14, especially 604 f.

whether the Hittite versions are themselves metrical. If they are, the versification seems to be based on a general balance between syntactic cola, as in Akkadian, Ugaritic, and Hebrew verse, and not on any measurement by syllables.[86]

For syllabic verse we must look elsewhere. Watkins has adduced a plausible example in an Old Hittite funeral song, perhaps as old as the seventeenth century BCE, where three lines of 4 | 4 or 5 | 4 are each followed by a five-syllable refrain.[87] He has also drawn attention to certain Luwian fragments, quoted in Hittite ritual texts, which certainly look like verse: they show signs of alliteration, rhyme, and poetic word-order. One is what he has sensationally interpreted as the first line of an epic lay about Troy:

ahh-ata-ta ālāti awenta Wīlusāti,

rendered as 'When they came from steep Wilusa'. This can be seen as a two-colon line, 7 | 7 (or, assuming an elision, 6 | 7), with distraction of epithet and noun so as to give rhyming endings to the hemistichs. A parallel line in another fragment shows the words differently arranged so as to keep a similar length of cola: *ālāti-ta ahha zītis awīta* [?*Wīlusāti*], 'When the man came from steep [?Wilusa]'. Another piece divides easily into 7 | 7 | 7 | 11 (= 7 | 4), where the first two heptasyllables are the same and the third rhymes with them.[88]

From the fourth century BCE we have a small body of verse inscriptions in Lydian, notable for their consistent use of a kind of rhyme: throughout each poem the last syllable of every line contains the same vowel. In one case the lines are arranged in three-line stanzas. The line is normally of twelve syllables, but sometimes eleven, with a regular caesura before the fifth or sixth syllable from the end. It can be analysed in terms of four trisyllabic 'feet', in each of which the last syllable is accented. An accented syllable may also stand in the first position in the line, less often in the fourth, and occasionally in the seventh.[89] It is difficult to relate this pattern in any persuasive way to what we have found elsewhere. But the fact that the metre shows constraints based on the syllable-count and on syllabic weight does bring this Lydian verse into some connection with other Indo-European systems, even if the relationship cannot be more closely defined.

[86] Such was the conclusion of H. G. Güterbock, who attempted a metrical transcription of the *Song of Ullikummi*: *JCS* 5 (1951), 141–4. Cf. I. McNeill, *Anat. St.* 13 (1963), 237–42; S. P. B. Durnford, ibid. 21 (1971), 69–75; West (1997), 103; H. C. Melchert in *Mír Curad*, 483–94.

[87] *KBo* 3. 40 = *BoTU* 14*α* 13′–15′; H. Eichner, *Denkschriften der Österreichischen Akademie* 236 (1993), 100–6; Watkins (1994), 418 f.; (1995), 248. The nine-syllable lines can be reduced to eight syllables if *kata arnut* is read with crasis or elision, *kat'arnut* (Eichner, 104).

[88] Watkins (1994), 714; (1995), 146 f., 150; for others see Eichner (as n. 87), 112 f.

[89] M. L. West, *Kadmos* 11 (1972), 165–75; 13 (1975), 133–6; H. Eichner, *ZVS* 99 (1986), 203–19; id., *Die Sprache* 32 (1986), 7–21; id. (as n. 87), 114–27; cf. Gusmani (1975).

Together with the extremely scanty Hittite and Luwian evidence, this suggests that proto-Anatolian poets may have practised composition in verses or cola of commensurate length, including some of seven or eight syllables, and sometimes arranged them in three- or four-line strophes. We cannot establish whether there were definite quantitative patterns that they favoured, or if they were familar with the catalectic–acatalectic opposition. Proto-Anatolian, of course, is not the same as proto-Indo-European, and if its metre was indeed less finely chiselled than that of MIE, it remains an open question which of the two more faithfully reflects the PIE situation.

Alliteration

Watkins has noted some instances of alliteration in the Luwian fragments. It is also noticeable in the Lydian documents, not as an invariable feature but as an intermittent ornament. As such it is observable in most of the Indo-European poetic traditions.[90] It is often conspicuous in Vedic;[91] sometimes in the *Gāthās* and the pre-Christian Armenian fragments; rarely in Greek, though examples can be found.[92] In western and northern Europe it was cultivated especially where an initial stress-accent developed, in Italic, Irish (but not Celtic overall), Germanic, and to a lesser extent Latvian. In historical Latin verse, although the generalized initial accent no longer prevailed, many words still did have it, and alliteration is a prominent feature in the early period. So it is in Irish, and we have seen that the terminology applied to it both in Irish and in Norse acknowledges it as having a structural significance in composition. In Germanic versification it had long been obligatory and governed by definite rules. These were already in operation by the time of the earliest runic inscription (*c.*200 CE), and probably before Tacitus' time.[93]

In view of this diffusion there is every likelihood that alliteration was an occasional, though not a constitutive, feature of Indo-European verse. We shall see in the next chapter that the choice and arrangement of words formed

[90] Cf. Wackernagel (1943), 5; Schmitt (1967), 40 n. 259; Watkins (1994), 714–16; (1995), 109–14, 188; Gamkrelidze–Ivanov (1995), 735–7.

[91] E.g. RV 1. 67. 6 *priyā́ padā́ni paśvó ní pāhi; viśvā́yur Agne guhā́ gúhaṃ gāḥ*, 10. 14. 7 *préhi préhi pathíbhiḥ pūrviyébhir, yátrā naḥ pū́rve pitáraḥ pareyúḥ*. Cf. W. Krause, *ZVS* 50 (1922), 121–3; J. Gonda, *Acta Orientalia* 18 (1939), 50–79; id. (1959), 177–200; S. Sani, *SSL* 12 (1972), 193–226.

[92] Cf. M. S. Silk, *Interaction in Poetic Imagery* (London 1974), ch. 8. A noteworthy instance is Hes. *Op.* 25 f. καὶ κεραμεὺς κεραμεῖ κοτέει καὶ τέκτονι τέκτων, | καὶ πτωχὸς πτωχῶι φθονέει καὶ ἀοιδὸς ἀοιδῶι, where the verbs in each line are chosen to alliterate with the nouns.

[93] Cf. West (2004), 48.

an important part of Indo-European verbal art and often expressed itself in figures characterized by assonance of one sort or another.

Metrical terminology

Indo-European poetry was a craft practised by professionals and handed down from one to another. The techniques of versification had to be mastered; in the case of the Irish *filid* we know that they progressed through a series of metres in the course of their years of training. It would not be surprising if a technical vocabulary relating to metre and versification developed among such specialists at an early date. There are in fact certain elementary parallels between Indo-Iranian and Greek terminology that suggest the existence of such a technical language at least in the Graeco-Aryan world.

In the Rigveda the verb *mā* 'measure' is used in connection with the composition of the poem. In the epilogue of 1. 38 there is a series of imperatives (13–15): 'Hymn Brahmanaspati with extended song . . . Measure out (*mimīhí*) the laudation with your mouth, sheet it like Parjanya, sing the song of eulogy! Praise the Maruts' horde!' In 8. 76. 12 the poet declares, *vā́cam aṣṭā́padīm ahám návasraktim . . . mame*, 'I have measured out an eight-step, nine-cornered hymn.' This refers to the hymn's *gāyatrī* metre, eight-syllable lines in three-line strophes that are themselves grouped in triads. 'Eight-step' does not mean 'consisting of eight steps', but 'in steps of the eight(-syllable) type', since the term *padám* 'footstep' denotes a whole verse, whether of eight or eleven or some other number of syllables. Compare 1. 164. 23 f.,

yád gāyatré ádhi gāyatrám ā́hitaṃ,
traíṣṭubhād vā traíṣṭubhaṃ nir-átakṣata,
yád vā jágaj jágati ā́hitam padáṃ:
yá ít tád vidús, té amṛtatvám ānaśuḥ.
gāyatréṇa práti mimīte arkám,
arkéṇa sā́ma, traíṣṭubhena vākám,
vākéna vākáṃ dvipádā cátuṣpadā;
akṣáreṇa mimate saptá vā́ṇīḥ.

That *gāyatra* is laid down upon *gāyatra*,
or that *triṣṭubh* was built from *triṣṭubh*,
that the *jagat* step is laid down on *jagat*—
they who know this have escaped death.
With the *gāyatra* one measures out the stanza,
with the stanza the song; with the *triṣṭubh* the verse;
with the two-step or four-step verse the poem.
By syllable they measure out the seven tones.

In later Sanskrit both *padam* and *pādaḥ* 'foot' are used to mean 'verse'. The usage seems to go back to Indo-Iranian times, as we find a corresponding use of *pada* or *paδa* in the Avesta. But is it mere coincidence that in Greek too 'foot', πούς, is the traditional name for the smallest unit of analysis apart from the syllable? Scholars have hesitated to make the connection, because there seemed to be a divergence of meaning: the Indian term refers to a whole verse, the Greek one to a subdivision of a verse, usually of only two or three syllables. But while this use of πούς is standard from Aristoxenus on, in the earliest extant example of the word in a metrical sense, at Aristophanes, *Frogs* 1323, it appears to refer to a whole glyconic verse, the Greek cognate of the Vedic eight-syllable *pāda*. The only form of subdivision of verses into constituent units attested for the fifth century is into 'measures', μέτρα. Thus Herodotus uses the adjectives 'six-measure' and 'three-measure' in reference to the standard epic and iambic verses. 'Measure', as we have seen above, also corresponds to a Vedic concept of versification, and the Greek noun comes from the same root as the Vedic verb.

If the earliest use of 'foot' was for a colon or verse of up to twelve syllables, what was the imagery? Indian scholars explained it from a conception of the stanza as a four-footed creature. But this does not suit the three-line stanza very well. If we look for something that may stand equally well on three feet or four, the best examples are the products of the carpenter, the three- or four-legged stool or table. The ordinary Greek word for table, τράπεζα, means 'four-footer', and comedians could make jokes about four-footed tripods and three-footed τράπεζαι.[94] This explanation of 'foot' as a metrical term is speculative, but it would fit very neatly with the idea of the poet as a carpenter.

Once invented, the term was open to wider interpretation. Feet are good for standing on, but also for walking on, and it was easy to envisage the verse as a step in the forward progress of the poem or song. Hence besides *pādaḥ* and πούς we have in Vedic *padám* and in Greek βάσις. At the completion of a verse or stanza one might be thought of as making a turn, and we can find some terminology that accords with this. In RV 8. 76. 12, quoted above, the poem was described as having nine corners or turnings, because of its nine-line structures. Another Sanskrit word for a metrical clausula, or a line containing a fixed number of syllables, was *vṛttam*, 'turn'. From the same root comes Latin *uersus*, 'verse', clearly a traditional term, and Greek has a semantic equivalent in στροφή, 'strophe', literally 'turning'.

[94] Epicharmus fr. 147, Aristophanes fr. 545 Kassel–Austin.

Poetic prose

At the outset of the chapter I gave a broad definition of poetry that (for the purposes of the present inquiry) identified its essence not in the use of metre but in the adoption of high style, 'a style which diverges from the ordinary by using elevated or archaic vocabulary, ornamental epithets, figures of speech, a contrived word order, or other artificial features'. I flagged the possibility that Indo-European practice might have recognized the use of such a style for certain sorts of composition that were not in verse.

Something of the kind is in fact found in several branches of the tradition.[95] It appears especially in prayers and religious ritual, where correct and lofty wording was called for. From India Watkins cites the liturgy of the Aśvamedha, the great horse sacrifice associated with the installation of a king. Some of the mantras are in regular verse, others are 'held together more by grammatical parallelism than by metre'. Avestan examples include the *Gāthā* of the Seven Chapters (Y. 35–41), which is divided into lines and strophes or periods, but is stylized prose, not metrical. Early Latin and Umbrian litanies show the same characteristics, and so do formulae prescribed for utterance in Hittite ritual texts. Greek priests intoned non-metrical but formally structured prayers, as evidenced by the parodies in Aristophanes' *Birds* (864–88) and *Thesmophoriazousai* (295–311).

Similar stylistic features could appear in secular use in formal rhetoric or high-flown narrative. One may refer to the fragments of the earliest Greek and Roman orators, who were no doubt continuing and developing long-standing traditions. Their too conspicuous artifice was found unsuited to the serious art of persuasion and was toned down by their successors, yet it left a permanent mark on ancient oratory. In Ireland there was a form of writing called *rosc* or *roscad*, associated with legal and narrative texts. It embraced both syllabic verse in the older, non-rhyming style and a sort of poetic prose marked by alliteration, balancing clauses with grammatical parallelism, strained syntax, perturbed word order, and 'strophic' organization.

Verse in a prose setting

A different form of marriage between prose and poetry, sometimes given the dismal and inept name of prosimetrum, consists of text alternating between prose and verse. The prose provides the narrative or explanatory frame. The

[95] Watkins (1995), 229–40 (Italic, Avestan), 249–51 (Anatolian), 255–64 (Irish), 267–76 (Indian).

verse passages are the more fixed or traditional elements, capable of being sung or recited on their own, but needing to be put in context at least by oral exposition, which then takes prose form in a written text.

This is an ancient and widespread format. An early non-Indo-European example is the Hebrew saga incorporated in the historical books of the Old Testament, which intermittently quotes songs that were sung at certain critical moments. At least some of these appear to be much older than the prose narrative, but they must always have been accompanied by some account of the circumstances in which they were sung.[96]

A pertinent Greek example is the pseudo-Herodotean *Life of Homer*, in the course of which are quoted some seventeen short poems, the so-called Homeric Epigrams, that Homer is supposed to have improvised in response to various situations. Again, the poems must be centuries older than the narrative in which they appear, much of which is constructed to support them. But most of them only make sense with the story to explain them, and they must always have been transmitted in the framework of some such account.

We see comparable narrative forms in the Indian *Brāhmaṇas* and *Jātakas*, the Irish and Norse sagas, and Snorri's *Gylfaginning*. The songs or poetic speeches represent the dramatic high points at which the characters give vent to their emotions, as in the arias of opera. They tended to be handed down with little change, whereas the prose narration that threads them together could be reformulated by every storyteller. Many of the Eddic poems are of this category, and in the Codex Regius that preserves them they are mostly introduced and interlaced with explanatory prose passages. In earlier ages when poetry was entirely oral it must have been quite common for poets to supplement their recitals with accessory information given informally.[97]

[96] Cf. West (1997), 91 f.

[97] Cf. Hermann Oldenberg, *Die Literatur des alten Indien* (Stuttgart–Berlin 1903), 44–7; Ernst Windisch, *Die altirische Heldensage Táin bó Cúalnge* (Leipzig 1905), xlviii f.; id., *Geschichte der Sanskritphilologie* (Strasbourg 1920), ii. 404–14; H. M. and N. K. Chadwick, *The Growth of Literature* (Cambridge 1932–40), ii. 478 n. 2, 506; Dillon (1948), 2; (1975), 70–94, 147–53; Winternitz (1959), 88 f., 184; L. Alsdorf, *Journal of the Oriental Institute of Baroda* 13 (1974), 195–207; Dillon (1975), 70–9, 147–53; Durante (1976), 68 n. 10; McCone (1990), 37 f. (sceptical); W. Meid, *Die keltischen Sprachen und Literatur* (Innsbruck 1997), 48. It has been argued that the Welsh saga *englynion* are relics of verse–prose narrative: Sir Ifor Williams, *The Beginnings of Welsh Poetry* (2nd edn., Cardiff 1980), 126–42, cf. Chadwick–Chadwick, i. 44; criticism in Rowland (1990), 260–75.

OCCASIONS AND GENRES

Hymns and praise poetry

The Homeric singer existed to tell forth 'the doings of men and gods' (*Od.* 1. 338). Having listened to the bard Lomaharṣaṇa, the chieftain Śaunaka knew 'the celestial tales, the tales of gods and Asuras, all the tales of men and snakes and Gandharvas' (*MBh.* 1. 4. 4). Whether or not these phrases represent a Graeco-Aryan formula, the celebration of gods and men is not a bad summary of the Indo-European poet's principal obligations. The gods had to be addressed and hymned in worthy style, and it was naturally for the professional exponent of the verbal arts to compose the words. But it was not the gods who gave him his daily bread and his gifts of horses and cows. It was the mortal king or noble at whose court he performed, and he too required the poet's praises.

As this king or noble was usually the patron of the sacrifice as well as of the poet, it often happened that he and the gods received their eulogies on the same occasion. Many of the Vedic hymns include praise of the patron. At the Aśvamedha, as described in the *Śatapatha Brāhmaṇa* (13. 1. 5. 6, 4. 2–3), priestly singers performed during the sacrifice and lauded the prince's sacrifices and liberality, and later in the evening the royal bard, accompanied on a zither or lute, 'sings three stanzas composed by himself (on such topics as) "Such war he waged,—Such battle he won" '(13. 4. 3. 5, trs. J. Eggeling). The Homeric *Hymn to Aphrodite*, like the other hymns in the collection, contains no explicit reference to living persons, but it is generally inferred, from the narrative of the goddess's seduction of Anchises and the prediction of unending rule for his descendants in the Troad, that it was composed to glorify and please these claimed descendants; it may have been performed at an Aphrodite festival instituted by them.

The hymn to the god or gods was typically of an invocatory nature. The poet invited him or them to come and participate in the ceremony, and prayed for blessings. We shall consider the characteristic ingredients of hymnic poetry in more detail in Chapter 8. For the moment let us note only that it could contain a narrative element, a recital of the deity's mythical exploits or of some particular exploit. This is something found in the Rigveda, especially in hymns to Indra and to the Aśvins, and in more extended form in all the longer Homeric Hymns.

There is an intrinsic connection between praise poetry and narrative, and this applies also to the eulogy of mortals. It is not enough just to list the honorand's virtues. He wants to be famed for specific achievements, especially the most recent, if they have not been sung of before; or if not his own, then those of his forefathers, for his ancestry is essential to his identity, and the praise poet typically refers to it.[98] He also wants to be ranked with other famous heroes of the past, and for his deeds to be set beside theirs. A commentator on the *Taittirīya Brāhmaṇa* (3. 9. 14. 4) says that the bard in praising the king's prowess in battle likened him to past heroes such as Pṛthu, Bharata, Bhagīratha, and Yudhiṣṭhira. To be able to compose such eulogies the poet needed to be learned in the ancient legends. As it is stated in one of the Welsh bardic grammars: 'The appropriate activity of the *prydydd* is approbation, and praise, and generating fame . . . It is not appropriate for the *prydydd* to concern himself with charms, and divination . . . [but rather with] ancient poetry, and written legends'.[99]

This is well illustrated by a passage in *Beowulf* (867–915). After the hero had killed the monster Grendel, a poet of Hrothgar's company, a man with a memory stocked with many old legends, composed and sang a new poem about the exploit; he paralleled it with the tale of the earlier dragon-slayer Sigemund, and told the latter's story at some length. This must reflect the methods of actual praise-poets of the time. The tales they told of great deeds of the past were of interest not only to the descendants of the persons involved. They could engage a wider audience, and so heroic narrative poetry could maintain an independent existence.

As an example of Greek praise poetry linked to heroic episodes from the past we may cite Ibycus' ode to Polycrates of Samos. After recalling the Trojan War at some length, it promises the prince unfading glory, so far as Ibycus' own artistry and reputation can achieve it. Then there are the odes of Pindar and Bacchylides celebrating various kings and nobles on the occasion of their sporting victories, with regular reference to their families' past glories. These poems may represent a last, luxuriant outgrowth from a Greek tradition of royal praise poetry, but we can still recognize in them elements of an ancient inheritance.

From Rome we have the testimony of Cato (sometimes questioned for no good reason) that banqueters used to sing the praises of outstanding men; or, according to Varro, boys at banquets, accompanied by a piper, sang traditional songs (*carmina antiqua*) containing *laudes maiorum*.[100]

For the ancient Celts we have the reports of classical writers. Posidonius defined the *bardoi* as poets who sang praises: ποιηταὶ δὲ οὗτοι τυγχάνουσι μετ' ᾠδῆς ἐπαίνους λέγοντες. He wrote that the chiefs had them in their entourage

[98] Cf. Schramm (1957), 110; Campanile–Orlandi–Sani (1974), 235 f.; Campanile (1988), 9.

[99] G. J. Williams, *Gramadegau'r Penceirddiaid* (Cardiff 1934), 35. 12 ff., trs. A. T. Matonis, *ZCP* 47 (1995), 222 n. 39.

[100] Above, n. 23; cf. Schmitt (1967), 56 n. 356.

even when they went to war, and that they recited encomia of them before the assembled company. One who was late for a feast and missed out on the chief's hospitality sang a eulogy of him, lamenting his own misfortune, and was rewarded with a bag of gold, whereupon he produced yet more extravagant praises, trotting along beside the chariot of the departing potentate. In 121 BCE Domitius Ahenobarbus, campaigning in Gaul, received an envoy from the Arvernian king Bituitus, in whose entourage was a poet who 'with barbarian music' exalted the pedigree, bravery, and wealth of Bituitus, his people, and the envoy.[101]

At the court of Attila the Hun, which seems to have been more Germanic than Mongolian in its cultural character, poems were recited in the evenings, celebrating the king's victories and his prowess in battle and moving some of his old warriors to tears.[102] In India the tradition of royal eulogies in verse was carried on under the Gupta kings of the third to fourth century; we have texts of them from inscriptions.[103] Less florid examples, more archaic-looking and more personal in tone, are preserved from sixth-century Ireland and Britain.[104] From medieval Russia we have the recollection in the *Lay of Igor* (5) of the famous poet Boyan, whose strings used to 'throb out praise (*slavu*) for the princes'.

Having praised his patron in life, and having in many cases, no doubt, become bound to him by real ties of affection, the poet would lament him also in death. Jordanes (*Getica* 257) gives a Latin paraphrase of the praise-song performed at Attila's funeral. It recalled his achievements, and dealt diplomatically with the fact that he died ignobly of a nosebleed while slumbering in a drunken stupor. It was easier if the man died heroically in battle. We have examples in the moving laments for the British kings Urien of Rheged, Cynddylan of Powys, and others. When Hector's body is brought back to Troy in the *Iliad*, the poet relates that they laid him on a bed and set singers beside him to sing dirges. He then puts formal laments in the mouths of Andromache, Hecuba, and Helen, as if in lieu of those of the professional singers. There is a parallel substitution in the Irish saga *Cath Finntrága*, where

101 Posidonius ap. Ath. 246cd, 152e (F 172, 170 Theiler); Diod. 5. 31. 2 (F 169); Appian, *Celt.* fr. 12. There is an Irish tale that begins, 'Once Diarmait mac Cerbaill's panegyrists were praising the king and his peace and his good conduct' (Koch–Carey (2000), 212).

102 Priscus, *Hist.* 67bc (*Corp. Script. Hist. Byz.* i. 204).

103 Edited and translated in D. R. Bhandarkar, B. Ch. Chhabra, G. S. Gai, *Corpus Inscriptionum Indicarum*, iii (revised edn., New Delhi 1981).

104 Campanile (1988), nos. 10, 12–13, 16–19; Koch–Carey (2000), 52, 58, 301, 342–51 (praise-poems for Urien), 360; *Y Gododdin* 30–8, 553–60, 608–16, 730–5. The Irish verses are compared with the Gupta inscriptions by Myles Dillon, *The Archaism of Irish Tradition* (London 1947), 15–18; Campanile–Orlandi–Sani (1974), 231–6.

Gelges laments her husband Cael, and in the *Táin bó Cúailnge*, where Cú Chulainn produces a series of laments for his foster-brother Fer Diad, whom he himself has killed in single combat.[105] In the *Battle of the Goths and Huns* the victorious king Angantýr recites a lament for his fallen brother Hlǫðr.[106]

Lament for the dead may naturally be accompanied by consolation of the bereaved. There is a particular consolatory technique that occurs in Greek, Old English, and Norse poetry (though only in the last case actually in the context of bereavement). It consists in the recital of other bad things that have happened in the past to other people and that were overcome. The aim is to persuade the one being consoled to put things in proportion. Dione uses the technique in comforting Aphrodite over her maltreatment by Diomedes in the *Iliad* (5. 382–404): she rehearses a series of tales of gods who suffered at the hands of mortals and yet endured. 'Ares endured, when . . . And Hera endured, when . . . And Hades endured, when . . .' The Norse parallel comes in the first *Guðrúnarkviða*, 3–11, where Gudrun sits dumb with grief over Sigurd's body and other warriors' wives come in turn and try to rouse her by relating their own past woes. In the Old English *Deor* the exiled bard consoles himself by recalling a series of five legendary tales of suffering, rounding off each one with the refrain 'That passed by: this may likewise'. This type of consolation may go back to Indo-European tradition, particularly as the technique of referring to a series of separate stories shows an affinity with the practice of listing a god's or hero's major exploits.

Narrative poetry

We have noted that hymnic and praise poetry both have a natural tendency towards narrative, towards telling of the accomplishments of the deity or of the mortal patron and his forebears. The Indo-European chieftain, as will appear more fully in Chapter 10, did not simply want to be flattered with praise of his good qualities: he wanted to be famed, remembered in future generations, and fame was won above all by battle. The deeds of great warriors were celebrated after their deaths in poems that found acclamation not only with their families but with a wider public.

Of the Gaulish Bards we are told that they 'sang the brave deeds of outstanding men in heroic verses to the sweet notes of the lyre'. Lucan writes that

105 Rowland (1990), 419, 422, 429–35 ~ 477–86, = Koch–Carey (2000), 352 f., 364, 367–9; *Il.* 24. 719–76; *Cath Finntrága* (ed. K. Meyer, Oxford 1885), 995–1034; *Táin* (L) 3440–63, 3470–85, 3491–550, 3556–95, cf. (I) 3106–42. See also the laments for kings of Leinster in Campanile (1988), nos. 5, 11, 14–15.

106 *Hervarar saga* 14 = *Hunnenschlacht* 33 Neckel–Kuhn.

by their praises they send down the ages the brave souls of those killed in war; Aelian, that they take as the subject of their songs the men who have died nobly in battle. The Goths 'used to sing of their forefathers' deeds with melody and lyres'. The sixth-century Lombard king Alboin's liberality, bravery, and success in war were celebrated in song throughout Bavaria and Saxony. In the late eighth century the blind Frisian bard Bernlêf 'knew well how to tell forth with music the deeds of the ancients and the battles of kings'. An Irish Saint's Life records that Aengus king of Munster had fine musicians who would sing before him to the lyre 'the deeds of heroes'.[107]

Heroic narratives were recited to armies before battle to spur them to valour. Tacitus says that the Germans, when going to fight, would sing of 'Hercules' first of all brave warriors; the implication is that the bards recalled a series of past heroes. They no doubt included the illustrious Arminius, who died in 19 CE and according to another passage of the same historian 'is still sung of among the barbarians'. Of the Coralli too, a Thracian–Danubian people, it is related that they roused their men to battle by singing of their ancient leaders' deeds, and we hear the same of the Visigoths before the battle of Hadrianople in 378. There is evidence for the like practice among the British.[108] In Ireland prose sagas took the place of verse narratives. Fergal, on the eve of battle in 722, bade a musician entertain the company with harps and pipes and poems and talk and royal stories of Ireland; he declined, but another was called on and 'set about telling the battles and combats of Leth Cuinn and the Leinstermen, from the destruction of Dind Ríg, in which Cobthach Cóel Breg was killed, up until that time'.[109]

Such lays would be accurately described by the Homeric–Hesiodic phrase *κλέα ἀνδρῶν* or *κλεία προτέρων ἀνθρώπων* 'renowns of (former) men'. Achilles is found singing these in his cabin (*Il.* 9. 189, cf. 524), and Demodocus sings them to the Phaeacians (*Od.* 8. 73). In Vedic the cognate word *śrávāṃsi* 'renowns' is similarly used meaning 'deeds of renown' (of Indra, RV 3. 37. 7; 8. 99. 2), while *śáṃsa-* 'appreciation' is combined with *narām* 'of

[107] Timagenes ap. Amm. Marc. 15. 9. 8 (*FGrHist* 88 F 2); Luc. 1. 447–9; Ael. *Var. hist.* 12. 23; Jordanes, *Getica* 43; Paulus Diaconus, *Hist. Langobard.* 1. 27; *Vita Liudgeri* (*MGH* Scriptores ii. 412); *Vita S. Ciarani de Saigir* 14 (Charles Plummer, *Vitae Sanctorum Hiberniae* (Oxford 1910), i. 222).

[108] Tac. *Germ.* 3. 1, *Ann.* 2. 88 (for German battle songs cf. also Tac. *Ann.* 4. 47, *Hist.* 2. 22, 4. 18); Val. Flacc. 6. 93 f.; Amm. Marc. 31. 7. 11; A. O. H. Jarman, *Y Gododdin* (Landysul 1988), lxxxi, xcv.

[109] J. N. Radner, *Fragmentary Annals of Ireland* (Dublin 1978), 68/9 f. (§178); cf. J. de Vries, *Beiträge zur Geschichte der deutschen Sprache und Literatur* 75 (1953), 246 f. In the *Cath Finntrága* the poet Fergus Finnbel repeatedly raises a hero's spirits during combat by praising him and reminding him of his previous victories (351 ff., 637 ff., etc.).

men' both phrasally and as a compound noun (*nárāśáṃsa*, 'praise-song') or adjective.[110]

It is a reasonable supposition that narrative poems about past warriors were an Indo-European institution, going back at least to Level 2 (MIE). But on what scale? Can we posit an Indo-European epic genre, that is, a tradition of narratives extending over hundreds or thousands of lines? Such traditions exist in early Greece, in classical India, in early medieval England and Germany (if we may take the Hildebrand fragment as evidence), and among the South Slavs and Albanians. On the other hand, in large parts of the Indo-European territories there is no sign of them. It is quite conceivable that they evolved independently in different lands from small beginnings. Once heroic narrative existed at all, there was nothing to stop poets expanding it to any length that their audiences would bear. However, if we ever reach Chapter 12 we shall see that different epic traditions—particularly the Greek and the Indian, but not only these—show numerous parallel features that are most naturally explained as common heritage and that would seem to presuppose an archetypal tradition of narrative in an ample style, requiring some hundreds of lines at least for the relation of a coherent story.

Personation

One of these typical 'epic' features is the inclusion of speeches exchanged by characters in the action. I referred earlier to a genre of literature in which only the characters' speeches or songs are in verse, with a prose narrative constructed around them. There is another genre in which they stand alone, or with a short introduction. The background events are taken as known, and the poet's aim is to see them through the eyes and hearts of those involved. It might be, for example, the lament of someone condemned to tragic suffering. Such compositions are typically songs in strophic form.

It is often an exchange between two people that marks a dramatic high point in the story, and dialogue songs are found widely. There may be a regular alternation of voices in alternate stanzas, or a longer series of stanzas may be given to one or both. The tone and content of each stanza make it clear enough who is speaking in each case, and it is not necessary to specify this in the text (though in manuscripts, for example of the Eddic poems, the information tends to be interpolated in prose). We are familiar with the convention in ballads, and we might designate this as 'ballad style', except that its applicability is wider than that term would suggest. A number of the Vedic

[110] It is listed among poetic genres at AV 15. 6. 4; ŚB 11. 5. 6. 8. Cf. Dumézil (1943), 70–98; Schmitt (1967), 29 f., 96–101; Durante (1976), 50–3.

hymns are in dialogue form, and there are elements of dialogue in some of the *Gāthās*. Most of these early Indo-Iranian examples are theological rather than narrative in essence, but several have a mythological setting (RV 3. 33; 4. 18; 10. 10, 95, 108), and this use of dialogue poetry is evidently as old as any. The tradition continues in the *Mahābhārata* and *Purāṇas*. More instances can be cited from Irish saga and from early Welsh poetry.[111]

One recurrent type is the dialogue of a man and a woman, or a boy and girl, in some sort of erotic situation. The setting may be mythological or ideal. Examples occur already in the Rigveda, and we find them also in archaic Greece and in Lithuanian folk song. The type is not exclusively Indo-European, as it appears also in Sumerian and Akkadian poetry, in the Song of Solomon, and in Egypt.[112]

Invectives?

The Gaulish Bards, wielding their lyres, 'eulogize some, but abuse others'.[113] The poet with the skill to praise and bless has also the skill to denounce and mock and curse, if his enmity is aroused, and woe betide the one who arouses it, because the hostile song can exercise a magical force and bring him to perdition. This is at any rate the belief in ancient Ireland, illustrated by many stories, for example of an inimical poet whose song brought a king's face out in boils, or made his land sterile. Similar properties are ascribed in Norse saga to 'hate stanzas', *níðvísur*.

Some have argued that this dual potency of the northern bard should be regarded as a feature of the Indo-European poet.[114] They can cite the stories of how the Greek iambographers Archilochus and Hipponax drove their victims to suicide with their invectives; the stories are no doubt apocryphal, and seem to be somehow grounded in a ritual institution,[115] but it is possible none the less that they are echoes of a serious belief in the harmful powers of satire. Certainly it is a very ancient notion that a malevolent poem has a dangerous potency. The old Roman Laws of the Twelve Tables prescribed penalties for anyone *qui malum carmen occentassit*. This probably referred

[111] *Táin* (I) 2754–97, 2835–58, 3017–80, (L) 1413–28, 1433–60, 2638–714, 3187–222, 3386–413; Rowland (1990), 461 f./506 f., 463 f./507 f. See further Winternitz (1959), 89 f. with literature; R. Ambrosini, *Bollettino del Centro di Studi Filologici e Linguistici Siciliani* 11 (1970), 53–87; Watkins (1995), 141–4.

[112] RV 1. 179; 10. 10, 95; Sappho fr. 137; Rhesa (1825), 268–70; West (1997), 530 f.

[113] Diodorus 5. 31. 2 (Posidonius F 169 Theiler).

[114] Dumézil (1943), 235–8; D. Ward, *JIES* 1 (1973), 127–44; Campanile–Orlandi–Sani (1974), 237 f.; questioned by Campanile (1990b), 79.

[115] M. L. West, *Studies in Greek Elegy and Iambus* (Berlin–New York 1974), 22–39.

to injurious spells and incantations of all kinds, obtainable from mountebanks and unsavoury old women. But there may have been a time when they belonged in the province of the professional poet, the master of words, and when it was not a private piece of hocus-pocus that was feared so much as a public verbal assault.

Codifications

Another use of verse was for the codification of knowledge or principles that it was thought important to preserve from the past and transmit to the future. By being versified they made a deeper impression and were more easily remembered. More than that, the language of poetry invested them with a certain solemnity and a relative fixity.

In general, verse could be used for listing names or things and for ordering them, for example the details of genealogies, or catalogues of places and peoples. There is much material of this kind in the Indian *Purāṇas*. It forms the basis of the Greek tradition of catalogue poetry as exemplified in the Homeric Catalogue of Ships and the Hesiodic *Theogony* and *Catalogue of Women*. It bulks large in early Irish poetry: genealogies, lists of local kings, lists of battles fought by a king or a tribe, heroes who took part in an expedition, and so on. And it is present in several of the Eddic poems, such as *Vǫluspá*, *Grímnismál*, *Vafþrúðnismál*, and *Hyndluljóð*. Many such catalogues, technically called *þulur*, are preserved in manuscripts; we have over 700 lines of them, making up a kind of poetic thesaurus, catalogues of kings, dwarfs, giants, titles of Odin and other gods, terms for battle and weapons, the sea, rivers, fishes and whales, ships and parts of ships, earth, trees, plants, animals, birds, islands, and so on.[116] There is no doubt some truth in the view that poets maintained these lists and catalogues primarily as raw material for their own use, to draw on the information contained in them as and when it came to be needed.[117]

Verse was also a convenient medium for the transmission of laws and precepts. The Solonic law-code once existed in a poetic version; the two opening lines are preserved as a quotation. The Spartan and Cretan laws were taught as songs, and the laws of Charondas too circulated in verse form. The

[116] *CPB* ii. 422–46. There was a type of official orator called *þulr*, Old English *þyle*, whose function may originally have been to memorize and recite such lists; cf. de Vries (1956), i. 402 f.; Lorenz (1984), 280.

[117] Cf. Thurneysen (1921), 56 f.; Campanile (1981), 53–74; (1988), 16; (1990b), 64 f., 66, 108–10.

Agathyrsi of Transylvania, perhaps a Dacian people, sang or chanted their laws 'so as not to forget them'. In Gaul the administration of justice, according to Caesar, lay in the hands of the Druids, the custodians of all tradition and poetic wisdom. Law-tracts in verse are among the oldest documents of Irish literature, law being the speciality of one class of *fili*.[118]

Gnomic verse is well attested in Indic, Greek, Latin, Irish, Old English, and Norse.[119] In the case of Hesiod's *Works and Days*, the prime representative of the Greek tradition, we must certainly admit the influence of parallel traditions in the Near East.[120] On the other hand, his formula 'I am going to tell you . . . Put it in your heart' (σὺ δ' ἐνὶ φρεσὶ βάλλεο σῇσιν) has close parallels in the *Gāthās* and Old Norse that may suggest common inheritance:

> sāxᵛənī . . . mraomī . . . : mə̄ṇcā ī [mąz]dazdūm.
>
> These prescriptions I speak . . . Commit them to mind.
>
> móður orð ber þú, mǫgr, heðan,
> ok lát þér í brióstí búa.
>
> Take away your mother's words, lad,
> and let them dwell in your breast.[121]

The similar Homeric formula ἄλλο δέ τοι ἐρέω, σὺ δ' ἐνὶ φρεσὶ βάλλεο σῇσιν, 'I will tell you another thing, and do you put it in your heart', may have originated in gnomic poetry of the type where successive sections began with the same formula, as in the maxims of Phocylides each section began καὶ τόδε Φωκυλίδεω. An Old English gnomic poem in the Exeter Book is presented as being the wisdom that a wise father taught his son, and the sections are introduced by 'The experienced father again addressed his son another time', 'A third time the wise man with his breast-thoughts taught his child', and so on until ten lessons have been reported. In the twelfth-century *Proverbs of Alfred* each of twenty-eight sections is introduced with the formula *þus quað Alfred*.[122] In Odin's instructions to Loddfáfnir in the *Hávamál* (112–37) each stanza begins

> Ráðomc þér, Loddfáfnir, at þú ráð nemir:
> nióta mundo, ef þú nemr,
> þér muno góð, ef þú getr.

[118] Solon fr. 31; Clem. *Strom.* 1. 16 78 = Terpander test. 40 Gostoli; Ael. *Var. hist.* 2. 39; Hermippus fr. 88 Wehrli; [Arist.] *Probl.* 19. 28; Caesar, *Bell. Gall.* 6. 13. 5; Dillon (1948), 172 n. 31; (1975), 114; Campanile–Orlandi–Sani (1974), 239–41.

[119] See West (1978), 15–20. Cf. Campanile–Orlandi–Sani (1974), 241 f.; Campanile (1977), 86–8.

[120] West (1997), 306 f.

[121] Hes. *Op.* 106 f., cf. 10/27, 274, 688; Y. 53. 5; *Gróugaldr* 16, cf. *Hugsvinnsmál* 129.

[122] M. L. West, *JHS* 98 (1978), 164 f., where a Sumerian parallel for this format is also cited.

I counsel thee, Loddfáfnir, and take thou my counsel:
profit shalt thou, if thou takest it,
good thy gain, if thou learnest.

The first line here very much resembles the Homeric formula, which may have served a similar purpose in pre-Homeric gnomic poetry.

Assemblies and contests

For all the importance of the poet's relationship to his patron, he was not a closeted courtier but a public figure. The subject of encomiastic poetry, after all, wanted his praises to be heard as widely as possible. He sought fame and prestige by the liberality of his sacrifices, which meant feasts for crowds and a captive audience for his eulogies. And the tales of past heroes that the poet had to tell were interesting and beguiling to all.

It was a feature of Indo-European societies that the people, or the body of fighting men, 'came together' at intervals for assemblies at which judicial and other decisions were made.[123] Caesar (*Bell. Gall.* 6. 13. 10) tells of the annual conventions in central Gaul to which all the Druids came and dispensed justice to everyone who needed it. At all such events, one may suppose, poets were in evidence and entertained the company with their songs. Pseudo-Scymnus (186) notes of the Celts: *σὺν μουσικῆι δ' ἄγουσι τὰς ἐκκλησίας*, 'they hold their assemblies with music'. These are what became the Welsh *eisteddfodau*, still noted today (after their revival in the nineteenth century) as festivals at which bards and minstrels compete for prizes. The most famous of the Irish conventions, those at Tailtiu (Teltown), 'seem to have been a combination of political decision-making assembly, market, and poetic and musical entertainment'.[124]

Contests between rival poets are an ancient feature of such gatherings. Some allusions in the Rigveda imply competition among Rishis, represented figuratively as a chariot-race or a fight.[125] In some passages the term *samaryám* is used, meaning a 'sending together' in the sense of a contest; Durante has argued for a Greek cognate **ὅμᾱρος* to account for the Achaean

[123] Sergent (1995), 302 f., 314 f. The 'coming together' is expressed in the Sanskrit *sám-iti-* (meeting, council, assembly) and the parallel Latin *com-itia*; cf. Tac. *Germ.* 11. 1, *coeunt . . . certis diebus, cum aut incohatur luna aut impletur.*

[124] Dooley–Roe (1999), 228.

[125] e.g. RV 1. 157. 2, 167. 10, 178. 4; 2. 16. 7; 3. 8. 5; 4. 16. 21; 5. 44. 7; 6. 34. 1, 66. 11; 7. 23. 1 f., 34. 1; 9. 110. 2; 10. 128. 1; F. B. J. Kuiper, *IIJ* 4 (1960), 217–80; G. Dunkel, *JIES* 7 (1979), 249–72.

Zeus Homarios and for the designation of epic poets as Homeridai.[126] Certainly Greek poets competed at festivals. Hesiod won a tripod at the funeral games for Amphidamas of Chalcis, and the author of the sixth Homeric Hymn prays explicitly for 'victory in this competition'.

There was a more intense kind of contest in which seers or poets did not just perform separately before a judge but engaged in verse dialogue with each other, asking difficult questions or setting each other challenges. This is what lies behind the *brahmódyam* of the earlier *Upanishads*, a trial between Brahmans involving an exchange of questions and answers about the Veda. The Hesiodic poem *Melampodia* related a contest between the seers Calchas and Mopsus. The motif continued to be productive in Greece: Aristophanes has a contest between Aeschylus and Euripides in his *Frogs*, and the sophist Alcidamas invented one between Homer and Hesiod, which later became the basis for the extant *Certamen Homeri et Hesiodi*. In Irish there is the *Colloquy of the Two Sages* (*Immacaldam in dá thuarad*), in which the *filid* Néde and Ferchertne contest for the supreme title of *ollam*. A poetic contest with riddles is also described in the *Tromdám Guaire*. The genre is represented in Norse literature in the *Vafþrúðnismál*, where Odin contests with the giant Vafthrudnir, setting him a series of tests of his mythological knowledge, and in the *Hervarar saga*, where king Heiðrek engages in a riddle contest with a man who has incurred his enmity and whom he will spare if he wins.[127]

As the examples indicate, the emphasis varies between depth of mythological learning, the insight needed for solving riddles, which is akin to decoding poetic periphrases, and artistic quality. All of these formed parts of the Indo-European poet's expertise. One particular agonistic test that links India, Greece, and Ireland is the completion of a half-finished poetic utterance. In India, since at least the time of the *Kāmasūtra* (1. 3. 15), poets have challenged each other by presenting a verse or half a quatrain with a deliberately paradoxical sense, which the other poet has to complete; this remains a popular literary diversion among pandits (*samasyāpūraṇa, samasyāpūrti*). In one section of the *Certamen* (8–9) Hesiod recites a series of apparently absurd verses which Homer has to restore to sense by supplying suitable continuations, and he succeeds in doing so. There is evidence that at least some of these verses were already current in older tradition before

[126] 'Homeros' was invented as their legendary eponym. See Durante (1976), 185–203; M. L. West, *CQ* 49 (1999), 375 f.

[127] *Colloquy*: Thurneysen (1921), 520–2; *Tromdám Guaire*: ibid. 263 f., Dillon (1946), 94 f. Heiðrek's riddles: *Hervarar saga* 10 (*Edd. min.* 106–20; translation in *CPB* i. 87 ff.).

Alcidamas.[128] In Irish saga too we find the motif of the contest in which one poet sets a half-quatrain and another completes it.[129]

Finally, it is a recurrent story motif that the loser in a contest of wisdom does not merely suffer chagrin but forfeits his life. In the *Bṛhadāraṇyaka Upaniṣad* (3. 9. 26) the interlocutor unable to answer the question has his head explode. In the *Melampodia* the defeated seer dies, as do Homer in the biographical tradition when he fails to solve the fisherboys' riddle and the Sphinx when Oedipus answers hers. In the *Vafþrúðnismál* the giant in proposing the contest declares that 'we shall wager our heads on our wisdom' (19, cf. 7), and at the end he acknowledges his doom.

We can hardly suppose that Indo-European poets normally competed for such stakes. The motif may be entirely mythical. Or perhaps some early king, beleaguered by importunate poets, set the condition to discourage them. Perhaps Indo-European poetry evolved, in more than one sense, by survival of the fittest.

[128] M. L. West, *CQ* 17 (1967), 440 f.

[129] So in the story of Senchán in Cormac's *Glossary* s.v. *prúll* (J. O'Donovan, *Cormac's Glossary* (Calcutta 1868), 137), and in a tale of a contest between St Columbcille and the Devil (ibid. 138); also in the *Tromdám Guaire* (Thurneysen (1921), 266; Dillon (1946), 96) and the *Colloquy* (Dooley–Roe (1999), 99). Dillon (1975), 65, notes the Indian and Irish parallelism but not the Greek.

2

Phrase and Figure

'So with the Soma-offering I bring to birth for you, Indra and Agni, a new praise-poem' (RV 1. 109. 2). This is one of nearly sixty places in the Rigveda where the Rishi refers to his song as new or the newest.[1] Zarathushtra sings 'I who will hymn You, Truth, and Good Thought as never before' (*apaourvīm*, Y. 28. 3). In the *Odyssey* Telemachus justifies the bard Phemius' singing of a recent event on the ground that 'men set in higher repute that song which falls newest on the listeners' ears'. Alcman calls upon the Muse to sing 'a new song' for the girls' chorus to sing. 'Praise old wine,' says Pindar, 'but the flowering of new songs'; and another of his odes too he characterizes as a 'new wingèd song'.[2]

There may seem something paradoxical about this insistence on newness by poets writing in traditional genres and availing themselves of many linguistic and other archaisms. It is not as if the old was scorned and tradition seen as something to be repudiated. 'Ancient songs' was an honourable term in several Indo-European cultures. Varro wrote of the old Roman praise-songs as *carmina antiqua*, and Tacitus uses the same phrase of the Germans' mythological poetry, surely echoing a native claim. Slavonic narrative poetry was referred to similarly. The Russian poems now generally called *byliny* were until the early nineteenth century known as *staríny* or *stáriny*, and likewise the Serbo-Croat epics as *starìnskē pjesme*, 'ancient songs'.[3]

The point about the 'new song' is not that it is novel or breaks with tradition, but on the contrary that it is an addition to the body of older poetry. This is made explicit in many of the Vedic hymns: 'I would guide him here for new praise, (him) who has been fortified by former praise-songs, by

[1] e.g. 1. 27. 4, 60. 3, 105. 12, 130. 10, 143. 1; 2. 17. 1, 24. 1, 31. 5; 5. 42. 13; 6. 49. 1; 7. 53. 2, 61. 6; 8. 20. 19, 25. 24, 51. 3, 95. 5; 9. 91. 5; 10. 4. 6. Cf. Campanile (1977), 51 f.; B. W. Fortson IV, '*návaṃ vácaḥ* in the Rigveda', in *Mír Curad* 127–38.

[2] *Od.* 1. 350–2; Alcman, *PMGF* 14, cf. 4 fr. 1. 6; Pind. *Ol.* 9. 48, *Isth.* 5. 63; cf. perhaps Simonides(?) in *PMG* 932. 3. The motif is familiar also from the Hebrew Psalms (33. 3, 40. 3, 96. 1, 98. 1, etc.; Isa. 42. 10).

[3] Jakobson (1962–88), iv. 443.

more recent and by present ones' (3. 32. 13); (Indra) 'who has been fortified by former and present songs of the praise-singing Rishis' (6. 44. 13); 'thus for Indra and Agni has an ancestral, new (song) . . . been voiced' (8. 40. 12); 'him (I praise) alike with (my) song and with the fathers' poems' (8. 41. 2).[4] In the passages from Greek poets cited above the word used for 'new' is *νέος* or *νεοχμός*, that is, new in the sense of young, newly appeared, not *καινός* 'novel'; Timotheos (*PMG* 736) is the first to boast of his *καινότης*. The traditional poet can advertise his new song while at the same time acknowledging his older models, as the twelfth-century Welsh poet Hywel ab Owain Gwynedd does when he writes (6. 45 f.) 'I compose an original song, music of praise such as Myrddin sang'.

Poets who write in a tradition, having been trained in the style and techniques proper to that tradition, do not strive for novelty of manner. They take over vocabulary, formulaic phrases, and typical expressions from older poets, and their language in general tends to have a more archaic appearance than that of contemporary speech. Archaism and formularity are conspicuous attributes of most of the older Indo-European poetic traditions: Indic, Iranian, Greek, Celtic, Germanic, Slavonic.[5] The poet of the *Lay of Igor* asks at the outset if it is not fitting to tell his story 'in ancient diction', *starymi slovesy*.

Two further features characteristic of Indo-European poetry, both of them favoured by the nature of the ancient language, are modification of word order and the use of formal figures of speech of various kinds. The figures will be studied in the latter part of this chapter. As to word order, it was not a matter of licence to arrange the words in any scrambled sequence, but of a greater freedom than in 'unmarked' speech to move a word into a position of emphasis: the verb, perhaps, or an adjective separated by the verb from its noun. Watkins has collected some illuminating material on this topic, but it would certainly repay a more systematic, large-scale study.[6]

Wackernagel drew attention to a particular type of modified word order in which, by an inversion of the normal Indo-European naming pattern 'X the son (or descendant) of Y', we have 'the son of Y, X'. He cited only Greek and Latin examples: the Homeric *Πηληϊάδεω Ἀχιλῆος*, *Τυδεΐδην Διομήδεα*, *Τελαμώνιος Αἴας*, and the Scipionic epitaph *CIL* i.[2] 7 (Saturnian

[4] Cf. also 1. 62. 11, 13; 3. 31. 19; 6. 22. 7; 8. 95. 5; Fortson (as n. 1), 131.

[5] Numerous formulae common to Vedic and Avestan are identified by Schlerath (1968). For the *Mahābhārata* and *Rāmāyaṇa* see Brockington (1998), 103–15 and 365–73. On linguistic archaism as a poetic feature cf. Campanile–Orlandi–Sani (1974), 236; Campanile (1990b), 156–61.

[6] See Watkins (1995), 36 f., 40 f., 128 f., 132 f., 146, 191, 280, 319; id. in H. Hettrich (ed.), *Indogermanische Syntax: Fragen und Perspektiven* (Wiesbaden 2002), 319–37.

verse), *Cornelius Lucius Scipio Barbatus.*[7] But they can be found in many other poetic traditions: in the Rigveda, as 5. 33. 8 *Paurukutsyásya . . . Trasádasyoḥ* 'of Purukutsa's son Trasadasyu'; 10. 14. 1 *Vaivasvatám . . . Yamáṃ rā́jānam* 'the son of Vivasvat, Yama the king', with the Avestan parallel at Y. 32. 8 *Vīvaŋhušō . . . Yimascīṯ*; in Lydian, inscr. 12. 1 *Sivāmlλ Saroλ* 'of Sivamś's son Saroś'; in Venetic, text 232 *Lavskos Kuges* 'L's son K.', 239A *[I]nijo Kapros* 'I.'s son K.';[8] in Old Irish, Campanile (1988), no. 1. 2 *hua Luircc Labraid* 'the grandson of Lorc, Labraid', and similarly in K. Meyer (1913), 40, lines 22, 24, 26, 30; in Old English, *Waldere* B 9 *Welandes bearn Widia*; *Battle of Maldon* 155 *Wulfstānes bearn Wulfmǣr*; in Serbo-Croat epic, *SCHS* ii, no. 7, lines 20, 26, 45, etc., *Kraljevića Marka*, 'of Marko Kraljević'.

Archaic vocabulary, disturbed word order, and, above all, metaphors and periphrases that reveal the identity of a thing only with the application of some intellectual effort, present a challenge to the hearer, which he may be able to meet only with difficulty or after acquiring familiarity with the style. It was not just a matter of using obscure vocabulary, but also of hiding meanings in symbolisms. Such verbal techniques were part and parcel of the Indo-European poet's stock-in-trade, of what gave him his claim to special status. His obscurities were not necessarily perceived as faults; what is not fully understood may seem more impressive than what is. In some branches of the tradition the poet seems to have positively gloried in his mastery of a language beyond common comprehension. I have elsewhere quoted Pindar's lofty lines (*Ol.* 2. 83–6):

> Many are the swift shafts under my elbow, within the quiver,
> that speak to those who understand, but for the generality
> require interpreters.

An Indian poet centuries earlier had stated (RV 1. 164. 45):

> Language (*vā́c*) is measured out (*párimitā*) in four steps (*padā́ni*),
> known to the Brahmans who are mindful (*manīṣíṇaḥ*).
> Three, stored in secret, they do not put about;
> the quarter of language humankind speaks.

This antithesis between the Brahmans' secret language and the language that 'humankind speaks' resembles that sometimes made between the language of the gods and the language of men. The gods' language, which will be discussed in the next chapter, is in fact a special vocabulary deployed by the poet; as in the Vedic passage, it is a poetic language that is contrasted with that of human beings. In this context Toporov aptly quotes Encolpius' remark to the

[7] Wackernagel (1943), 13 f.

[8] Lejeune (1974), 292, 296, cf. 45. For poetic word order in Lydian cf. Gusmani (1975), 266–8.

poet Eumolpus in Petronius, *saepius poetice quam humane locutus es.* Watkins cites a Middle Irish treatise on grammar and poetics, the *Auraicept ne n-Éces,* in which 'arcane language of the poets' and 'language of the Irish' are recognized as two of the five varieties of the Gaelic tongue.[9]

VOCABULARY AND PHRASEOLOGY

The first intimation of Indo-European poetry as a possible object of study came from Adalbert Kuhn's discovery in 1853 of a phrase common to Vedic and Homeric poetry: *ákṣiti śrávaḥ* or *śrávas . . . ákṣitam,* κλέος ἄφθιτον. The constituent words were cognate, and the concept they expressed, 'unfading glory', was clearly not so much at home in everyday speech as in poetry, or at any rate in elevated discourse. It seemed a reasonable hypothesis that this collocation of words was traditional both in Indic and in Greek poetry, and that the tradition went back to the time of a common language.

This particular formula, and others relating to glory, will be considered more closely in Chapter 10. Here we shall undertake a general survey of poetic vocabulary, phraseology, and verbal idioms that may plausibly be inferred for Indo-European from comparisons between the different traditions.

First it is important to make the point that while etymological correspondence, as in *śrávas . . . ákṣitam* = κλέος ἄφθιτον, is a satisfying and telling element in such comparisons, it is not a *sine qua non.* We have to allow for a phenomenon universal in the history of languages, namely *lexical renewal.*[10] An old word fades away and is replaced by a more modern synonym. This can happen even to the most basic and common vocables. One would not have thought that such essential everyday words in Latin as *caput* and *equus* could ever fall out of use; and yet in the Romance languages the words for 'head' and 'horse' derive from *testa* and *caballus,* slang words that came to prevail in vulgar Latin. In an ancient poetic formula one or more of the words might come to be replaced by younger equivalents, without the phrase losing its historical identity.

Sometimes we can see the process happening before our eyes. For instance, an early Indic formula **urú śrávas* 'wide glory', corresponding to Homeric κλέος εὐρύ, is reflected in the personal name Uruśravas, which occurs in the

[9] Petr. *Sat.* 90. 3; V. N. Toporov, *Poetica* 13 (1981), 209; Watkins (1994), 467. On the hermeticism of the Indo-European poet cf. Watkins's whole paper, 456–72; id. (1995), 179–93.

[10] Cf. Campanile (1977), 21–3; id., *Diachronica* 10 (1993), 1–12; Meid (1978), 13; Watkins (1995), 10, 15.

Purāṇas, and in the expanded phrase *urugāyám śrávaḥ* 'wide-going glory' (RV 6. 65. 6); but the old word *urú-* was giving way already in the Veda to the near-synonym *pṛthú-* (= Greek *πλατύς*), and hence we find in RV 1. 9. 7 *pṛthú śrávo ... ákṣitam*, and in 1. 116. 21 the name Pṛthuśrávas. Later *śrávas-* itself yielded ground to *kīrtí-* (which appears only once in the Rigveda) and *yáśas-*, so that in the *Mahābhārata* we find people's *kīrti-* or *yaśas-* declared to be *akṣaya-* (= the Vedic *ákṣiti-* or *ákṣita-*) or *mahat-* (as Vedic *máhi śrávaḥ*, Greek *μέγα κλέος*).[11]

Here is another example that involves more languages. There was evidently in MIE an expression 'both in word and in deed' or 'neither in word nor in deed', based on the alliterating instrumentals **wek^{w}esh$_1$ ... *wergoh$_1$*. Both words survive in the archaic Greek poetic version of the idiom, *ἢ ἔπει ἢ ἔργωι* (*Il.* 1. 504, cf. 395); *οὔτ' ἔπεϊ ... οὔτέ τι ἔργωι* (5. 879); *ἠμὲν ἔπει ἠδὲ καὶ ἔργωι* (*Hymn. Dem.* 117). In classical prose *ἔπος* has been replaced by *λόγος*, and so for example Lysias (9. 14) writes *οὔτε λόγωι οὔτε ἔργωι*. Gathic Avestan preserves the original root for 'word', but has a different one for 'deed': *vacaŋhā śyaoθanācā*.[12] Contrariwise, Old English and Norse have a different root for 'word' but the primary one for 'deed': in Norse, *orð ok verk* 'word and deed' (*Grāgās* i. 162, ii. 336); *orð mér af orði orðz leitaði, verc mér af verki vercs leitaði*, 'word found me word from word, deed found me deed from deed' (*Hávamál* 141); in Old English, *wordum nē worcum* 'by words nor deeds' (*Beowulf* 1100).[13] In modern English 'work' has come to have a more restricted sense, and instead of 'in word and work' we now say 'in word and deed'. Both of the original lexical terms have thus been replaced, but the five-thousand-year-old phrase retains its identity.

In looking for Indo-European idioms, therefore, it is not necessary to limit ourselves to comparisons where all the terms stand in etymological relationship. It is legitimate to adduce expressions that are semantically parallel, even if the vocabulary diverges, provided that they are distinctive enough to suggest a common origin.

Compound words

Where do 'poetic' words come from? They may be archaisms repeated from older poets, words that were once in general use but are no longer. Or they may be poetic coinages that never were part of ordinary speech. Much the

[11] *akṣaya-*, *MBh.* 3. 42. 22, 77. 26; 8. 738*. 3; *mahatiṃ kīrtim* 3. 83. 106.

[12] Y. 31. 22, cf. 34. 1, 47. 1, 48. 4; with a different form of the *vac* root, *uxδāiš*, *śyaoθnā*, 44. 10, 51. 21.

[13] Cf. *Beowulf* 289, 1833; *Christ III* 918, 1237; *Christ and Satan* 48, 223; *Guthlac* 581.

most numerous class of these in the Indo-European traditions consists of compound adjectives and nouns.

Nominal composition was a characteristic feature of Indo-European, and the language provided its users with a set of templates according to which new compounds could be formed whenever required, just as in modern English we can freely improvise new compounds on the patterns of 'dish-washer', 'mind-bending', 'kitchen-cum-diner', 'pro-hunting', or 'ex-convict'. In the ancient languages many compounds came into being to serve commonplace needs. Early examples can be reconstructed from Sanskrit *durmanas-* = Avestan *dušmanah-* = Greek δυσμενής, all meaning 'ill-spirited' in one sense or another, or from Vedic *sudína-* = Greek εὐδία, εὐδιεινός, 'good sky, fine day', with its antonym surviving in Old Church Slavonic *dŭždĭ*, Russian дождь 'rain'. There is nothing intrinsically poetic about these.

Poets, on the other hand, create and recycle compounds for decorative rather than pragmatic purposes. In Vedic, Greek, and Germanic verse we constantly encounter compounds which cannot have been current in normal speech and which serve to enrich the utterance with a condensation of associated ideas. In a limited number of cases parallel formations in different languages (with the same roots but sometimes a different stem) may point to common inheritance. The Homeric ἀνδροφόνος 'man-slaying', an epithet of heroes and of the war-god, is composed of the same elements as Vedic *nṛhán-*, which is applied to Rudra and to the Maruts' lightning-weapon. They appear in inverse order in the Avestan hapax *jənara-*.[14] In Hesiod's ὠκυπέτης ἴρηξ 'swift-flying hawk' the epithet corresponds to that in RV 4. 26. 4 *śyenáḥ . . . āśupátvā* 'swift-flying eagle (or falcon)'.[15] Homeric beds are ἔὔστρωτα, which corresponds to Avestan *hustarəta-* (of the couches of the righteous, Yt. 17. 9). Birds of prey are ὠμησταί 'raw-eaters' in Homer, *āmā́d-* in the Vedas (RV 10. 87. 7, AV 11. 10. 8), both from **ōmó- + *ed.*[16] When Empedocles calls the gods δολιχαίωνες (B 21. 12, 23. 8; P. Strasb. a(ii) 2), he may have known the word from older poetry, or put it together himself; in any case it is matched by Vedic *dīrghā́yu-* (of Indra, RV 4. 15. 9) and *-ā́yuṣ-*, Avestan *darəgāyu-* (Y. 28. 6, 41. 4).[17]

There are several examples of a curious type of compound in which a modifying prefix is attached to a proper name. In the Atharvaveda (13. 4. 2, 17. 1. 18) we find *Mahendrá*, that is, *maha-Indra*, 'Great Indra'. In the *Iliad* we

[14] Schmitt (1967), 123–7; H. Schmeja in Mayrhofer et al. (1974), 385–8; Durante (1976), 97; Campanile (1977), 118 f.; (1990b), 60.

[15] Hes. *Op.* 212; cf. Schmitt (1967), 236 f.; Campanile (1990b), 155; Gamkrelidze–Ivanov (1995), 455.

[16] Gamkrelidze–Ivanov (1995), 603.

[17] Schmitt (1967), 161 f.; Schlerath (1968), ii. 164.

have *Δύσπαρις* 'Ill-Paris', in the *Odyssey* *Κακοΐλιος* 'evil Troy', in Alcman *Αἰνόπαρις*, in Euripides (*Or.* 1387, *Iph. Aul.* 1316) *Δυσελένα*, and in Alexandrian poets *Αἰνελένη* 'Bane-Helen'. In west and north Germanic tradition the Goths were sometimes called *Hreiþgotar*, 'the glorious Goths'.[18] Thor appears in the Eddas with various prefixes: Vingþórr, Ásaþórr 'Thor of the Æsir', Ǫkuþórr 'driving Thor'. Instances are common in Irish poetry.[19] The individual examples are clearly not of Indo-European antiquity, but the type may be, providing poets with a traditional means of enhancing a name.

Kennings

The term *kenning* comes from Old Norse (where the plural is *kenningar*). It denotes a poetic periphrasis, usually made up of two elements, used in lieu of the proper name of a person or thing. It may be riddling, picturesque, or simply a trite alternative to the ordinary designation. The density of kennings, often elaborate and artificial, is the dominant stylistic feature of skaldic verse, which is intelligible only to those with the knowledge to decode them. But they are to some extent a general phenomenon in Germanic and Celtic poetry. Examples can also be quoted from early Indic and Greek, and a few may have a claim to be in some sense Indo-European.[20]

The simplest kind of kenning appears when a poet, instead of saying 'X the son of Y', says simply 'the son of Y'. This is common in many branches of the tradition, for example RV 1. 92. 5 'Dyaus' daughter' = Dawn; *MBh.* 7. 15. 9 (and often) 'Droṇa's son' = Aśvatthaman; in Homer, *Λητοῦς καὶ Διὸς υἱός* = Apollo, *Τυδέος υἱός* or *Τυδείδης* = Diomedes, and so on; in Welsh, *Y Gododdin* 1217 'Wolstan's son' = Yrfai; in English, *Beowulf* 268 et al. 'Healfdene's son' = Hrothgar, 1076 'Hoc's daughter' = Hildeburh; in Norse, *Vǫluspá* 56 'Hlóðyn's son' and 'Fiǫrgyn's child' = Thor. Or another relationship may be specified: RV 1. 114. 6 'the Maruts' father' = Rudra; *Αἰακίδης* 'the descendant of Aiakos' = Achilles; *ἐρίγδουπος πόσις Ἥρης* 'Hera's loud-crashing husband' = Zeus; *Hymiskviða* 3. 5 'Sif's husband', 24. 1 'Móði's father', both = Thor; *Vǫluspá* 32. 5 'Baldr's brother' = Váli; *Y Gododdin* 975

[18] First on the Rök stone (E. V. Gordon, *Introduction to Old Norse*, 2nd edn. (Oxford 1957), 188); *Vafþrúðnismál* 12. 3 with the commentary of Sijmons and Gering; *Widsith* 57; *Elene* 20.

[19] Campanile (1988), 39; (1990b), 161 f.

[20] On kennings see Wolfgang Krause, 'Die Kenning als typische Stilfigur der germanischen und keltischen Dichtersprache', *Schriften der Königsberger Gelehrten Gesellschaft* (Geisteswissenschaftliche Klasse, 7(1); Halle 1930); Ingrid Wærn, *ΓΗΣ ΟΣΤΕΑ. The Kenning in pre-Christian Greek Poetry* (Uppsala 1951); Schmitt (1967), 277–82; Campanile (1977), 108–10; Watkins (1995), 44 f., 153. For a bibliography, especially on Germanic kennings, see Bader (1989), 15 n. 5.

'the grandson of Neithon' = Domnall Brecc.[21] One such circumlocution, 'Grandson of the Waters', became at least for Indo-Iranian theology, and perhaps more widely, the proper name of a divinity.[22]

In principle any appositional phrase or characteristic epithet attached to a name or thing can become a kenning when used by itself, as happens with divine epithets in Homer such as *Γλαυκῶπις*, *Ἰοχέαιρα*, *Ἀμφιγυήεις*, *Ἐννοσίγαιος*. A specific type found in the Indo-European traditions is that by which a god or hero is identified by reference to the famous adversary that he killed. Thus in the Rigveda *Vṛtrahán-* 'the slayer of Vṛtra' = Indra, while in Avestan the cognate Vərəθraγna- is the god's primary name; he became the popular national deity of Armenia, Vahagn. Hermes in Homer is often called *Ἀργειφόντης*, understood as 'slayer of Argos', though the original sense may have been 'dog-killer'. The name of Bellerophon (*Βελλεροφόντης*) clearly means 'slayer of Bellero-', presumably an obsolete designation of the Chimaera. In *Beowulf* 1968 'the slayer of Ongentheow' identifies Hygelac. In the Edda we find 'the slayer of Beli' = Freyr, 'sole slayer of the serpent' = Thor, 'the slayer of Fafnir' and 'the slayer of Gothorm' = Sigurd, 'the slayer of Hogni' = Vilmund, 'the slayer of Isung' = Hodbrodd.[23]

In the Rigveda (10. 137. 7 = AV 4. 13. 7) *dáśaśākha-* 'ten-branched' is employed as an epithet of the hands, and in the *Rāmāyaṇa* (6. 47. 54) *pañcaśākha-* 'five-branched'. In Hesiod (*Op.* 742) 'the five-branched' (*πέντοζος*) appears as a kenning for 'the hand' in an injunction couched in oracular style: 'Do not from the five-branched, at the prosperous feast shared with the gods, cut the sere from the green with gleaming iron' (that is, do not cut your nails). In Norse poetry we meet *tiálgur* 'branches' for arms, *handar tiálgur* 'hand-branches' for fingers, and *ilkvistir* 'sole-twigs' for toes.[24] It looks as if we have here an ancient Indo-European metaphor capable of conversion into a kenning.

In the *Odyssey* (4. 707–9) Penelope, on learning that her son has gone away by ship, complains that he had no call to board ships, *αἵ θ' ἁλὸς ἵπποι | ἀνδράσι γίνονται* 'which serve men as horses of the sea'. This seems a strange conceit; but 'sea-horse', expressed with numerous different words for 'sea' and for 'horse', is a frequent kenning for 'ship' in Old English and Norse

[21] Some of this material is collected by Vittoria Grazi in *Poetry in the Scandinavian Middle Ages* (Seventh International Saga Conference, Spoleto 1990), 550–3.

[22] Vedic *Apā́m nápāt* = Avestan *Apąm napå*. We shall examine this god in Chapter 6.

[23] *Vǫluspá* 53. 5; *Hymiskviða* 22. 3; *Grípisspá* 15. 8; *Guðrúnarkviða B* 7. 7; *Oddrúnargrátr* 8. 4; *Helgakviða Hundingsbana A* 20. 2.

[24] *Víkarsbálkr* 4. 2, 24. 6 (*Edd. min.* 38 ff.); Sighvat, *Óláfsdrápa* 95 (*CPB* ii. 142); *Atlamál* 66. 2; other medieval material is cited in West (1978), 339. Cf. H. Humbach, *MSS* 21 (1967), 27; Schmitt (1967), 281 f.; Bader (1989), 106.

poetry.[25] Stephanie West in her note on the Homeric passage says that 'here ἵπποι is almost equivalent to "chariots" (Homeric heroes do not ride)', and she cites later classical poets who liken ships metaphorically to chariots. The Phaeacians' ship breasting the waves is likened to a chariot at *Od.* 13. 81–5. But perhaps the phrase goes back to a phase of Indo-European culture when the horse was men's normal means of travelling about, as it remained in many parts of Europe. For travel by water, the ship then appeared as a replacement for the horse, and poets might easily arrive at 'horse of the sea' as a decorative appositional phrase or kenning for a ship.

Another kenning shared by classical and Germanic verse is the 'iron shower', meaning the rain of spears or arrows in battle. It first appears in just this form in Ennius, *Annals* 266 Skutsch, *hastati spargunt hastas: fit ferreus imber*; the phrase was later borrowed by Virgil (*Aen.* 12. 284). Perhaps Ennius followed a lost Greek model, as σιδήρεος or χάλκεος ὄμβρος would sit very neatly in a hexameter. Pindar (*Isth.* 5. 49) has ἐν πολυφθόρωι ... Διὸς ὄμβρωι (... χαλαζάεντι φόνωι) in referring to the battle of Salamis, and a bombardment of stones is compared in a Homeric simile to a snowstorm (*Il.* 12. 278–87). The Ennian phrase has an exact counterpart in *Beowulf* 3115 *īsernscūre*, and a less exact one in *Guthlac* 1116 *hildescūr* 'battle-shower'. The skald Torf-Einar (quoted in Snorri's *Háttatal*, st. 55) used *stála skúrar* ... *Gautr* 'the Geat of the steel shower' as a compound kenning for 'warrior'. Other skalds offer *álmskúr* 'elm-shower' (sc. of missiles from bows), *skotskúr* 'shot-shower', *mélskúr* 'biting shower', *naddskúr* 'shield(-battering)-shower', *nadd-regn* 'shield-rain', while the Eddic *Grípisspá* (23. 7) has *nadd-él* 'shield-snowstorm'. Hiltibrant and Hadubrant discharge their spears at each other *scarpen scurim*, probably 'in sharp showers', a not very apt use of the formula (*Hildebrandslied* 64). If an Indo-European prototype lies behind all this, it could not, of course, have contained a reference to iron, but it might have referred to bronze, or at an earlier stage to wood or stone; the material would naturally be updated by later poets.

Epitheta ornantia

A recurring feature of the various poetic traditions is the use of noun–epithet phrases in which the epithet adds nothing essential to the sense or especially relevant to the context, but expresses a permanent or ideal characteristic of

[25] *Faroþ-hengestas* ... *sǣ-mēaras*, *Elene* 226/8; *wæg-hengest*, 236; *sǣ-mearh*, *Andreas* 267; *sǣ-hengest*, 488; *brim-hengest*, 513, *Rune Poem* 47, 66; *vágmarar*, *Reginsmál* 16. 7; *giálfrmarar*, *Waking of Angantyr* 26. 2 (*Edd. min.* 19); *Skáldsk.* 51; expressions collected in *CPB* ii. 458. Cf. Schmitt (1967), 282.

the thing. A number are shared by different branches of the tradition and may represent a common inheritance. Several of them will come into view in other contexts, for example 'immortal gods' in Chapter 3, 'broad earth' and 'dark earth' in Chapter 4, 'swift horses', 'prizewinning horses', 'well-wheeled chariot' in Chapter 12. Here are some others.[26]

A messenger is 'swift': RV 3. 9. 8, 4. 7. 4 *āśúṃ dūtám*; *Od.* 16. 468 ἄγγελος ὠκύς, *Il.* 24. 292 ταχὺν ἄγγελον, etc. *āśú-* and ὠκύς are etymologically identical.

A woman is 'well-clothed': RV 1. 124. 7, 4. 3. 2, al. *jāyā́* (married woman) . . . *suvā́sāḥ*; *Il.* 1. 429 ἐϋζώνοιο γυναικός, *Od.* 6. 49 Ναυσικάαν εὔπεπλον, etc. The prefixes *su-* and εὐ- are cognate. We can also compare the Homeric λευκώλενος 'white-armed' (applied to Hera, Helen, Andromache, and others; also *Od.* 6. 239 ἀμφίπολοι λευκώλενοι, 19. 60 δμωιαὶ λευκώλενοι) with *Hávamál* 161. 5 *hvítarmri konu*, 'a white-armed woman'. Here there is no etymological correspondence, but the compound adjective is formed in the same way (*bahuvrīhi*).

Clothes are 'bright, shining'. RV 1. 134. 4, 9. 97. 2 *bhadrā́ vástrā* 'shining garments' matches *Od.* 6. 74 ἐσθῆτα φαεινήν in sense, and there is a double etymological relationship, with the root **bha* in both adjectives and **wes* in both nouns. It becomes a triple one in RV 3. 39. 2 *bhadrā́ vástrāṇi árjunā* 'shining bright garments' ~ *Il.* 3. 419 ἑανῶι ἀργῆτι φαεινῶι, as ἑανόν also contains **wes*, while *árjuna-* and ἀργής are both from the root **h₂r̥ĝ*.

So is ἀργός 'swift', a Homeric epithet of dogs and the name of Odysseus' dog. The antiquity of the association is shown by the Vedic personal name Ṛjíśvan (= *Ἀργι-κύων). This does not show that the noun-epithet phrase was a poetic formula outside Greek, but certainly ἀργός is an archaism in Greek. *árjuna-* as a colour word is applied to a dog in RV 7. 55. 2.[27]

Wolves are embellished with a colour epithet, generally 'grey', though in RV 1. 105.18 we have *aruṇó vŕ̥kaḥ* 'a ruddy wolf'. In Homer it is πολιοῖο λύκοιο, πολιοί τε λύκοι; in the Exeter Gnomes (151) *wulf se græga*; in the Edda, *úlf grá(a)n* (*Helgakviða Hundingsbana B* 1. 5); Fenrir in the *Eiríksmál* (26, *CPB* i. 261) is *úlfr inn hǫsvi*. A warrior in *Y Gododdin* 740 has the nickname *glasvleid* (Greywolf). 'Grey wolf/wolves' is also a formula in Russian heroic poetry.[28]

The Vedic phrase *svādór . . . mádhvaḥ* 'of the sweet mead' has its etymological counterpart in the Homeric μέθυ ἡδύ, though the Greeks had

[26] Cf. the material collected in Schmitt (1967), 221–60; Durante (1976), 91–8.

[27] Cf. Durante (1976), 94; Watkins (1995), 172.

[28] *Igor* 3, 25, 42, 189; Chadwick (1932), 41, line 168; 45, line 9. Cf. Gering–Sijmons (1927–31), ii. 106; Wüst (1969), 28 f., 46–8.

abandoned mead for the Mediterranean intoxicant, wine, and μέθυ had undergone a corresponding change of meaning.

The sea is 'broad', as in the Homeric εὐρέα πόντον, etc.; in Old English, *Andreas* 283 *ofer wīdne mere*; in Serbo-Croat, *SCHS* ii, no. 17, line 347 *u more široko*, 'to the broad sea'. The comparisons may seem banal, but it is typical of traditional ornamental epithets that they express the most obvious properties of the thing described. A more detailed Greek–English parallel may be observed between *Il.* 18. 140 (et al.) θαλάσσης εὐρέα κόλπον, 21. 125 ἁλὸς εὐρέα κόλπον, and *Elene* 728 *sǣs sīdne fæðm*, 'the sea's wide embrace'.

The Homeric formula 'black ships' is paralleled in Russian *byliny*, and 'sea-going ship(s)' (ποντοπόρος) in Serbo-Croat epic.[29] Hesiod and Ibycus use the phrase νῆες πολύγομφοι, 'many-dowelled ships', and this may be compared with expressions used in Old English verse: *naca nægelbord* 'ship of nailed planks' (Exeter Riddles 59. 5, cf. *Genesis* 1418); *nægled-cnearrum* 'nailed ships' (*Battle of Brunanburh* 53).

Various idioms

The sun had a prominent place in Indo-European poetry and myth, as we shall see in Chapter 5, and it plays a part in a number of traditional expressions. As it traverses and surveys the whole earth, the idea 'the world from end to end' can be expressed by 'as far as the sun looks about' (AV 10. 10. 34 *yāvát sū́ryo vipáśyati*) or some equivalent. So in Greek, *Il.* 7. 451, 458 'its/your fame shall be known ὅσον τ' ἐπικίδναται ἠώς, as far as the daylight spreads'; in Welsh, *hyt yr etil heul*, 'as far as the sun wanders'.[30]

The sun, heaven, and other cosmic entities are also symbols of eternity. A Hittite curse on a conquered city condemns it to remain uninhabited 'so long as heaven, earth, and mankind (exist)' (*CTH* 423). The great Luwian and Phoenician bilingual inscription from Karatepe contains the prayer that Azitiwada's name 'may be for ever, like the name of the sun and moon'.[31] Indian expressions of 'for ever and ever' include 'so long as the sun shall be in the sky' (*yāvát sū́ryo ásad diví*, AV 6. 75. 3); 'as long as moon and sun shine' (*Rm.* 7. 1464*); 'as long as mountains stand and rivers flow' (*MBh.* 5. 139. 55); 'as long as earth endures' (*MBh.* 12. 54. 28). Similarly in Greek: 'as long as

[29] Chadwick (1932), 169, lines 13, 24, etc.; *SCHS* ii, no. 17, line 368 *na morsku demiju*, 'to the sea(-going) ship'.

[30] *Culhwch and Olwen*, ed. R. Bromwich and D. S. Evans (Cardiff 1992), line 158.

[31] H. Donner–W. Röllig, *Kanaanäische und aramäische Inschriften*, 3rd edn. (Wiesbaden 1966–9), no. 26 A iv 2 f. = C v 5–7.

earth and sun endure' (Theognis 252); 'so long as waters flow and trees grow tall, and the sun rises and shines, and the radiant moon' (Hom. *Epigr.* 3). And in the Celtic literatures: 'as long as the sun shall cross the sky' (*oiret rabh grian ar deiseal*, verse in *Acallam na Senórach* 520 Stokes); 'as long as heaven remains above earth' (*Moliant Cadwallon* 21).[32] I have collected a few similar expressions from Hebrew and Assyrian texts, but they are no older than the first millennium BCE.[33]

The world we live in can be equated with the world under the sun. Indeed the Baltic word for 'world', Lithuanian *pasaulis*, Latvian *pasaule*, means literally 'under the sun'. 'There are many birds flying about under the sun's beams' (*Od.* 2. 181) means no more than 'in the world'. In an early British poem we already meet the expression 'everyone under the sun'.[34] The phrase is especially used to emphasize uniqueness in respect of some quality. The horses that Zeus gave to Tros were 'the best of all the horses that there are under the day's light and the sun' (*Il.* 5. 266 f., ὑπ' ἠῶ τ' ἠέλιόν τε; cf. 4. 44). Euripides' Alcestis is declared to be 'by far the finest woman of those under the sun' (*Alc.* 151). In an early Irish poem we read that 'under heaven (*fo nimib*) there was none so strong as the son of Áine'.[35] In the Edda Helgi Hjorvardsson is proclaimed 'the prince who was best under the sun'. Sigurd is told 'a mightier man will not come on the earth, under the sun's seat, than you are deemed'. Hervor's dead father tells her that she will bear a son who will be 'the most glorious raised under the sun's tent'.[36]

To be here under the sun, to be able to see the sun, is synonymous with being alive. 'Do not give us over to death, O Soma; may we yet see the sun going up' (RV 10. 59. 4); 'let this man be here with his life, in the portion of the sun (*sū́ryasya bhāgé*), in the world of non-dying' (AV 8. 1. 1). *svàr* or *sū́ryam dṛśé* 'see the sun' stands for being alive (RV 1. 23. 21, al.), as does the simple 'seeing' (*páśyan*, 1. 116. 25). Similarly in the *Gāthās*, *astvaṯ aṣ̌əm x́yāṯ*, 'may Truth be there corporeal' (i.e. in the corporeal world), is parallel to *xᵛə̄ṇg darəsōi xšaθrōi x́yāṯ ārmaitiš*, 'may Rightmindedness be there in the realm in the sight of the sun'.[37] In Greek we have, for instance, 'while I am alive and

[32] Ed. R. G. Gruffydd in R. Bromwich and R. B. Jones, *Astudiethau ar yr Hengredd* (Cardiff 1978), 27 ff. On this poem cf. Jarman, *Y Gododdin*, xxiii.

[33] West (1997), 515.

[34] *Trawsganu Kynan Garwyn* 95–8 (*Book of Taliesin* 45; Koch–Carey (2000), 303). Some Semitic parallels (none earlier than the seventh century BCE) in West (1997), 235.

[35] Campanile (1988), 27 no. 4. 2; a parallel in Kuno Meyer, *Bruchstücke der älteren Lyrik Irlands* (Berlin 1919), 115.

[36] *Helgakviða Hiǫrvarðzsonar* 39. 4, cf. 43. 8; *Grípisspá* 52. 5–8, cf. 7. 2; *Waking of Angantyr* 17 (*Edd. min.* 17).

[37] Y. 43. 16. Cf. Y. 32. 10, 'that man corrupts the Message, who declares that the worst thing to behold with the eyes is the cow and the sun.'

seeing upon the earth'; 'this man . . . who has hit me and boasts of it and claims that I will not see the sun's bright light for much longer'; 'leave the light of the sun'; 'she is no longer under the sun'.[38] Old Norse has the expression *sjá sik* 'see oneself' (*Gylf.* 45).

To be born is to come into the light, πρὸ φόωσδε (*Il.* 16. 188, cf. 19. 103, 118), ἐς φάος (Pind. *Ol.* 6. 44), *in luminis oras* (Enn. *Ann.* 135 et al.), *an thit lioht* (*Hêliand* 626). An alternative expression, shared by Greek and Norse, is 'come to one's mother's knees': Hes. *Th.* 460 μητρὸς πρὸς γούναθ' ἵκοιτο; *Sigurðarkviða* 45 *of komz fyr kné móður.* It reflects the widespread and ancient practice of giving birth in a kneeling position.

The father's role as begetter is sometimes emphasized by coupling the two words. In the Rigveda (1. 164. 33 and often) we find the pairing *pitā́ janitā́* 'father begetter', just like the etymological counterparts in Avestan (Y. 44. 3 *ząθā ptā*), Greek (Eur. *Ion* 136 γενέτωρ πατήρ; elsewhere ὁ γεννήσας πατήρ and similar phrases), and Latin (Enn. *Ann.* 108 *o pater o genitor*).

Instead of saying 'you are a congenital so-and-so', Indic and Greek poets may say 'your father (or mother) bore you to be a . . .': RV 1. 129. 11 *ádhā hí tvā janitā́ . . . rakṣohánaṃ tvā jījanad*, 'for that is why your sire sired you as a gremlin-slayer'; *Il.* 13. 777 ἐπεὶ οὐδέ με πάμπαν ἀνάλκιδα γείνατο μήτηρ, 'for my mother did not give birth to me as a coward', cf. 6. 24, *Od.* 1. 223, 6. 25, 21. 172; *Hymn. Herm.* 160 f. 'your father has begotten you to be a great nuisance to mortal men and the immortal gods'. An analogous idiom is 'the gods made' (someone to be what he is): RV 7. 16. 12, 'him the gods made the sacrifice-priest, the observant, the conveyor of offerings', cf. 1. 31. 11; 7. 17. 6; 8. 23. 18; *Od.* 17. 271 (the lyre), 'which the gods made to be the companion of the feast'; 23. 166 f. 'the dwellers in Olympus made your heart hard beyond all women'; Hes. *Th.* 600 f.; Enn. *Ann.* 107 *qualem te patriae custodem di genuerunt!*

Where human emotions are described, we find a good deal of common ground in the kind of language used in different branches of the tradition, and this may to some extent reflect Indo-European idiom. On the other hand there is little that points to its being peculiarly Indo-European, and similar phraseology sometimes appears in Near Eastern literatures. Emotions tend to be represented as external forces that come to one, enter one, or seize one.[39]

[38] *Il.* 1. 88, 5. 119, 18. 11; Eur. *Alc.* 393 f. More in Durante (1976), 116 f. Naturally these associations are not exclusively Indo-European. In the Old Babylonian Gilgamesh epic (Meissner fr. i 12′–15′, p. 276 George) the hero, addressing the Sun-god, says 'I shall sleep for all time: let my eyes (now) look on the sun, let me have my fill of light . . . When might a dead man see the sun's radiance?'

[39] See the material collected by Durante (1976), 138–40, and for Semitic parallels West (1997), 234.

The idea that the heart is 'eaten' by cares or by the person who suffers from them appears in Greek and Old Norse, as well as in Sumerian and Egyptian.[40] Love's arrow that pierces the heart is known to the Atharvaveda (3. 25. 1–3) as well as to Greek poets and artists from the fifth century BCE on.[41] The Hittite king Hattusili III, writing in Akkadian to the Babylonian king Kadašman-Enlil II, uses the expression 'he chilled my heart (*libbī uktessi*) with the words he wrote to me', which corresponds to a phrase found in Hesiod and Homer.[42] But this might have been an areal idiom, at home in Anatolia, and in general these sporadic parallels provide no solid basis for reconstruction.

We are on firmer ground with phrases that are etymologically related. The Homeric word μένος, although it has become somewhat specialized in the sense of 'fighting spirit', 'consciousness of strength', is the exact counterpart of Vedic *mánas-*, Avestan *manah-* 'mind', 'disposition', and it appears in various lexical collocations that have Indo-Iranian parallels.[43] The compounds εὐμενής and δυσμενής, 'well/ill disposed', corresponding to Vedic *sumánas-* and epic *durmanas-*, Avestan *humanah-*, *dušmanah-*, preserve the original sense of μένος. On the other hand μένος ἠΰ means 'good courage'; it is something that a god 'sends' or 'blows' into men or animals (*Il.* 17. 456 ἐνέπνευσεν μένος ἠΰ, 20. 80, 24. 442), and so resembles the *bhadrám mánaḥ* 'bright disposition' which is appropriate for overcoming enemies (RV 2. 26. 2, 8. 19. 20) and which a god may blow into one: 10. 20. 1 = 25. 1 *bhadráṃ no ápi vātaya mánaḥ* 'blow at us a bright disposition'. A god may also inject μένος πολυθαρσές (*Il.* 17. 156, 19. 37; *Od.* 13. 387) or impart μένος καὶ θάρσος (*Il.* 5. 2; *Od.* 1. 321), '*menos* and boldness'. These formulae have their cognates in *dhṛṣán mánaḥ* 'bold spirit', which is an attribute of the war-god Indra (RV 1. 54. 2; 5. 35. 4; 8. 62. 5), and in the compound *dhṛṣanmánas-* (1. 52. 12; 8. 89. 4; epithet of Indra). We recall the Greek personal names Thersimenes and Thrasymenes, which may have been first coined at a much earlier date than that of their historical bearers. The same elements are perhaps contained in the Homeric adjective θρασυμέμνων, if it is from **-men-mon-*.[44]

Andromenes too may be an old name, paralleled as it is by the Avestan name Nərəmanah- (Yt. 5. 50, 19. 77) and the Vedic adjective *nṛmáṇas-*, 'man-spirited', 'having a hero's spirit'; they can all be derived from **$h_2$nr̥-menes-*. In the Avestan epithet *naire.manah-*, of the same meaning, the first

[40] See West (1978), 358; *Hávamál* 121. 8 *sorg etr hiarta*, 'care eats the heart'.

[41] Durante (1958), 8 = (1976), 128. It is possible that the idea is already expressed in Swedish Bronze Age rock drawings, where an archer, perhaps female, aims an arrow at a copulating couple, or leads an ithyphallic man ashore from a ship: de Vries (1956), i. 106 f., Abb. 2c and 3a.

[42] *CTH* 172 obv. 23, ed. A. Hagenbuchner, *Die Korrespondenz der Hethiter*, ii (Stuttgart 1989), 282/289; Beckman (1999), 140 §4; Hes. *Op.* 360 with my note.

[43] Schmitt (1967), 103–21.

[44] R. Schmitt, *ZVS* 83 (1969), 227–9.

element has taken adjectival form (**neryo-*). In the Vedas we find also the noun *nṛmṇám* 'heroism, heroic deed', and in Homer the phrase μένος or μένε' ἀνδρῶν.[45]

The strangest of the Greek formulae involving this noun is ἱερὸν μένος, used periphrastically with a hero's name in the genitive, ἱερὸν μένος Ἀλκινόοιο = Alcinous and the like. As in Ὀδυσσῆος ἱερὴ ἴς, ἱερὴ ἴς Τηλεμάχοιο, ἱερῶι ἐνὶ δίφρωι, ἱερός does not (or did not originally) mean 'holy' but had a sense corresponding to that of Vedic *iṣirá-*, 'strong, impetuous'. The antiquity of the phrase is confirmed by the parallel of RV 8. 48. 7 *iṣiréṇa . . . mánasā* 'with vigorous spirit', as Kuhn already noticed in 1853.[46]

An implacable or unyielding person is said in Homer to have a heart of bronze or iron, χάλκεον ἦτορ *Il.* 2. 490; σιδήρεος θυμός 22. 357, ἦτορ 24. 205, 521, κραδίη *Od.* 4. 293; ἀδάμαντος θυμός Hes. *Op.* 147; ἐξ ἀδάμαντος ἢ σιδάρου κεχάλκευται μέλαιναν καρδίαν Pind. fr. 123. 4. Similar images are common in the Indian epics: *MBh.* 3. 28. 5 'he must have a heart of iron (*āyasaṃ hṛdayam*), that man of evil deeds', cf. *Rm.* 2. 17. 30, 35. 20. In *MBh.* 6. 15. 53 and 10. 1. 10 the adjective is *adrisāramaya-* 'of rocky nature', in 6. 115. 4, 7. 8. 10 et al. *aśmasāramaya-* 'of stony nature', in 12. 171. 23 and *Rm.* 2. 55. 9 *vajrasāramaya-* 'of adamantine nature'.

The striking Homeric expression ἐγέλασσε δέ οἱ φίλον ἦτορ (*Il.* 21. 389), ἐμὸν δ' ἐγέλασσε φίλον κῆρ (*Od.* 9. 413), 'and his/my dear heart laughed', is used of someone who laughs internally on perceiving that things have turned out as he hoped. It has a series of parallels in Germanic poetry. In the *Þrymskviða* (31. 1–2), when Thor's stolen hammer is laid in his lap as he sits disguised as a bride, *hló Hlórriða hugr í brjósti*, 'Hlorridi's (Thor's) mind laughed in his breast'. Attila's does likewise when Gudrun's chastity is proved by ordeal (*Guðrúnarkviða C* 10. 1–2). So too in Old English: *Beowulf* 730 *þā his mōd āhlōg*, 'then his mind laughed'; *Andreas* 454 *ūre mōd āhlōh* 'our mind(s) laughed'; *Solomon and Saturn B* 336 *nǣfre ǣr his ferhð āhlōg* 'never before (had) his spirit laughed'.

In the last chapter we met the ancient root **wekʷ* 'speak' and the Graeco-Aryan noun **wekʷes-* (*vácas-*, ἔπος), used with particular reference to poetry. Both in Vedic and in early Greek it can be characterized as 'sweet', and by the same word, *svādú-* = ἡδύς, whose primary application is to sweet-tasting things such as honey and mead. RV 1. 114. 6 *idám . . . vácaḥ svādóḥ svā́dīyaḥ*, 'this utterance, sweeter than sweet'; 8. 24. 20 *vácaḥ ghṛtā́t svā́dīyo mádhunaś*

[45] Schmitt (1967), 105–8; Durante (1976), 158.

[46] Pisani (1969), 362; Schmitt (1967), 109–14; Durante (1976), 94 f. (with other parallel uses of *iṣirá-* and ἱερός); Watkins (1995), 13.

ca, 'utterance sweeter than ghee and honey'; with the feminine noun *vāc*-, 2. 21. 6 *svādmā́naṃ vācáḥ*, 'sweetness of utterance'. In Greek epic the compound ἡδυεπής is used of Nestor as a persuasive orator, of a singer, and of the Muses.[47]

Of Nestor the poet goes on to say that his speech used to run from his tongue sweeter than honey, μέλιτος γλυκίων, a semantic if not a lexical parallel to RV 8. 24. 20 just quoted. Compounds such as μελίγηρυς 'honey-voiced', μελιβόας 'honey-toned', μελιηδής 'honey-sweet', μελίγλωσσος 'honey-tongued', and others are routinely used of poetry and song in archaic and classical Greek verse. Similarly in the Vedas we have *mádhumattamaṃ vácaḥ* 'most honeyed speech', RV 5. 11. 5; *jihvā́ mádhumatī* 'honeyed tongue', 3. 57. 5; *óṣṭhāv iva mádhu āsné vádantā* 'like lips speaking honey to the mouth', 2. 39. 6; *vācó mádhu* 'honey of speech', AV 12. 1. 16, cf. 58; TS 3. 3. 2.[48] In Nordic myth the gift of poesy is conferred by a mead made from honey and the blood of a sage called Kvasir, who was created from the gods' spittle, and in skaldic verse poetry is referred to by such terms as dwarfs' mead, giants' mead, Odin's mead, etc.[49]

Certain Greek poets speak of 'ambrosial' song.[50] It is difficult to say how definite a meaning should be attached to the epithet, but some connotation of ambrosia, the delicious, honey-like food of the gods, can hardly have been absent. It is tempting to compare *MBh.* 12. 279. 1 *na tṛpyāmy amṛtasyeva vacasas te pitāmaha*, 'of your utterance, grandfather, as of *amṛtam*, I cannot get my fill', where *amṛtam* corresponds to the Greek 'ambrosia'. Its collocation with *vacas*- recalls Pindar's ἀμβροσίων ἐπέων.

The idea of song as something that runs liquidly finds further expression in the use of the verb 'pour' (Vedic *hu*, Greek χέω, Latin *fundo*, < *$\hat{g}^h$*u*) with prayers, hymns, and the like as the object. At the same time there may be an association with pouring out liquid offerings, and the metaphor may have been especially at home in sacral language. So RV 1. 110. 6 *ā́ manīṣā́m antárikṣasya nṛ́bhyaḥ srucéva ghṛtáṃ juhavāma vidmánā*, 'let us expertly pour a remembrancing for the heroes of the air [the Ṛbhus] like ghee with the spoon'; 2. 27. 1, 41. 18; 8. 39. 6; *Od.* 19. 521 χέει πολυηχέα φωνήν; Hymn. Hom. 19. 18; Pind. *Isth.* 8. 58; Aesch. *Supp.* 631 εὐκταῖα γένει χεούσας,

[47] *Il.* 1. 248; Hymn. Hom. 21. 4, 32. 2; ἡδυέπειαι Μοῦσαι Hes. *Th.* 965 f., fr. 1. 1 f.; Schmitt (1967), 255.

[48] Durante (1960), 233 n. 10; (1976), 113. For a couple of Semitic parallels see West (1997), 230.

[49] *Gylf.* 57 = *Skáldsk.* p. 3. 10 ff. Faulkes; *Skáldsk.* 3.

[50] Hes. *Th.* 69 ἀμβροσίῃι μολπῆι (cf. 43 ἄμβροτον ὄσσαν); Hymn. Hom. 27. 18 ἀμβροσίην ὄπα; Pind. *Pyth.* 4. 299 ἀμβροσίων ἐπέων; Bacchyl. 19. 2 ἀμβροσίων μελέων; cf. Soph. *Ant.* 1134 ἀμβρότων ἐπέων.

Cho. 449; Hor. *Epod.* 17. 53 *quid obseratis auribus fundis preces?*; Virg. *Aen.* 5. 234, 6. 55.[51]

Where we would say 'for two days', 'for three days', it is typical of Indo-European narrative to say 'for *n* nights and *n* days', or 'for *n* days and *n* nights'.[52] It is remarkable, moreover, how often the number is three; this is a formulaic period in Indo-Iranian, Celtic, and Slavonic. Thus RV 1. 116. 4 *tisráḥ kṣápas trír áhā* 'for three nights (and) three days'; *MBh.* 3. 12. 4 *tribhir ahorātraiḥ*, 3. 61. 57 *trīn ahorātrān*;[53] in Avestan, Yt. 5. 62, 10. 122 *θri.ayarəm θri.xšapanəm* (at 10. 122 also *bi.ayarəm bi.xšapanəm*); in Greek, *Od.* 17. 515 τρεῖς ... νύκτας ... τρία δ' ἤματα (with other numbers: 9. 74, 10. 142, Hes. *Op.* 612); in Armenian, *Sassountsy David* 130, 136 'they fought for three days and three nights' (cf., with other numbers, 13, 28, 59, al.); in Old Irish, *Erchoitmed ingine Gulidi* 10 *trí lá 7 teora aidhchi*,[54] cf. *Táin* (I) 1009, 2112/2136, 3297, *Táin bó Fraích* 124, 135 Meid, *Aislinge Áenguso* pp. 52, 63 Shaw, etc.; in a Welsh chronicle, *Annales Cambriae* sub anno 516, *tribus diebus et tribus noctibus*; in a Russian *bylina*, Chadwick (1932), 38 lines 28, 33, 53, etc.; in Serbo-Croat epic, *pa tri dana i tri noći ravne* 'for three days and three whole nights'.[55]

Another noteworthy idiom relating to time is 'all days', meaning 'day after day', often with the connotation of 'for ever'. So in RV 1. 52. 11, 171. 3 *áhāni víśvā*, cf. 3. 54. 22, 5. 41. 4, al.; Y. 43. 2 *vīspā ayārə̄*; *Il.* 8. 539 (and often) ἤματα πάντα; *Heiðreks gátur* 19 (*Edd. min.* 113, *Hervarar saga* 10) *of alla daga*.[56]

The noise and shouting of the Homeric battle is described as reaching up to heaven: *Il.* 12. 338 ἀϋτὴ δ' οὐρανὸν ἷκεν, cf. 14. 60; 13. 837 ἠχὴ δ' ἀμφοτέρων ἵκετ' αἰθέρα καὶ Διὸς αὐγάς; so of Ajax by himself, 15. 686 φωνὴ δέ οἱ αἰθέρ' ἵκανεν. Similarly in the Indian epics: *MBh.* 5. 197. 8 *divam ivāspṛśat*, the noise 'touched the sky as it were', cf. 6. 52. 22; 8. 7. 6; 'rose up to highest heaven', *Rm.* 2. 83. 15. In Irish saga too cries are 'heard even to the clouds of heaven', and it is the same in Serbo-Croat epic: *ljuto pisnu, do neba se ćuje*, 'she screamed in anger, and her cry reached the heavens'; *ode huka ispod oblakova*, 'the sound rose to the clouds'.[57]

51 L. Kurke, *JIES* 17 (1989), 113–25.

52 So too in Hebrew, cf. West (1997), 241.

53 *Ahorātra-* is a compound meaning 'day + night'.

54 Ed. Kuno Meyer, *Hibernica Minora* (Oxford 1894), 67.

55 Salih Ugljanin, *SCHS* ii, no. 10. 30, cf. no. 13. 287. As I shall cite Salih elsewhere, it may be noted here that he was originally trained as a singer in the Albanian tradition; he only learned Serbo-Croat at the age of 30.

56 There is a similar expression in Hebrew: *kol-hayyāmîm*, 'all the days'.

57 *Aided Con Chulainn* (version 2) 20 p. 88. 28 van Hamel; Salih Ugljanin, *Song of Baghdad* (*SCHS* ii, no. 1) 1239; ibid. no. 18. 347.

The root **wes* 'clothe' has similar metaphorical applications in the Rigveda and in Homer.[58] An unseen divinity may be clothed in a cloud. Soma in RV 9. 83. 5 is *nábho vásānaḥ*, where *nábhas-* and *vas-* are the exact cognates of Greek *νέφος* and *ἑσ-*. In other cases the 'garment' is a mist or storm (*míh-*, *abhrá-*) that is an actual part of the weather, clothing the storm-demon Vṛtra (2. 30. 3), the Maruts (5. 63. 6), or the mountains (5. 85. 4). This naturistic interpretation is not excluded in *Il.* 14. 350 f., where Zeus and Hera lie on Ida, *ἐπὶ δὲ νεφέλην ἕσσαντο | καλὴν χρυσείην, στιλπναὶ δ' ἀπέπιπτον ἐέρσαι*, 'clothed themselves in a cloud, a lovely golden one, and a glistening precipitation fell from it', though there is nothing to suggest it in 15. 308 *εἱμένος ὤμοιϊν νεφέλην* or 20. 150 *ἀμφὶ δ' ἄρ' ἄρρηκτον νεφέλην ὤμοισιν ἕσαντο*. In other Homeric passages *ἕννυσθαι* is constructed with *ἠέρα* 'air, mist', or *νεφέλη* and *νέφος* are combined with different verbs for 'wrap in, conceal in'.

The two Ajaxes are three times described as *θοῦριν ἐπιειμένοι ἀλκήν*, 'clad in furious valour', and a similar phrase is used of Achilles (*Il.* 20. 381). Durante has compared RV 4. 16. 14 (of Indra) *mṛgó ná hastī́ táviṣīm uṣāṇáḥ*, 'clothing yourself with strength like an elephant'; 9. 7. 4 *pári . . . kā́viyā . . . nṛmṇā́ vásānaḥ*, (a seer) 'clothing himself about with seerdom and manhood'; 9. 80. 3 *ū́rjaṃ vásānaḥ*, (Soma) 'clothed with invigoration'.[59]

NARRATIVE GAMBITS

Under this heading I collect some typical programmatic expressions used at the outset of a poem or story. One thing that naturally has its place there is the call to attention. Franz Specht observed the similarity between the openings of two Vedic hymns and of the Eddic *Vǫluspá*:

> idáṃ janāso vidata: mahád bráhma vadiṣyate.
> Know this, peoples: a great song will be uttered. (AV 1. 32. 1)
>
> idáṃ janā úpa śruta: nárāśáṃsa staviṣyate.
> Hear this, peoples: a heroic eulogy will be proclaimed. (AV 20. 127. 1)
>
> Hlióðs bið ec allar helgar kindir,
> meiri oc minni mǫgo Heimdalar:
> vildo at ec, Valfǫðr, vel fyrtelia
> forn spiǫll fira, þau er fremst um man.

[58] Durante (1976), 96 n. 15, 114.
[59] Durante (1976), 114. For Semitic parallels see West (1997), 239.

Hearing I ask from all holy-born,
the greater and lesser sons of Heimdall!
You desired me, Odin, to tell forth well
the old tales of men, those earliest that I recall. (*Vǫluspá* 1)

Many skaldic poems too begin with a call for attention.[60] Specht inferred an Indo-European opening formula, which he tried to reconstruct as *idém, ĝonōses, úpo ḱlute*, 'Hear this, men!' Schaeder added from the *Gāthās*

at̰ fravaxšyā: nū gūšōdūm, nū sraotā,
yaēcā asnāt̰ yaēcā dūrāt̰ išaθā.

I will tell forth—now listen ye, now hear ye,
who come seeking from near and from far, (Y. 45. 1)

and also Y. 30. 1–2, 'Now I will proclaim, O seekers . . . Hear (*sraotā*) with your ears the best message'.[61] Schaeder's further claim that all these poems were cosmogonic is questionable, but the parallelism in the form of *incipit* seems real. One might recognize the same pattern in Helen's interpretation of an omen in *Od.* 15. 172, κλῦτέ μοι, αὐτὰρ ἐγὼ μαντεύσομαι, 'Hearken ye, I am going to prophesy'. It is to be noted that *hlióð, sruta, sraotā*, κλῦτε are all from the same root.

A narrative very often begins with the verb 'to be' in the present or past tense and in initial position: 'There is . . .', 'There was . . .'.[62] The present tense is appropriate for specifying a place where the story is set. There are several Homeric examples, such as *Il.* 6. 152 ἔστι πόλις Ἐφύρη μυχῶι Ἄργεος ἱπποβότοιο κτλ., 'there is a city Ephyra in a nook of horse-pasturing Argos, and there Sisyphus dwelt, most cunning of men'. In the Hittite story of Appu the verb is omitted: 'A city, its name Sudul, and it is in the land Lulluwa on the sea coast. Up there lived a man named Appu.'[63] So in the *Rāmāyaṇa* (1. 5. 5), *Kosalo nāma*, '(There is a land), Kosala its name . . .'.

The pattern 'There was a king, *N* his name' has been widely traced, from *MBh.* 3. 50. 1 *āsīd rājā Nalo nāma*, 'There was a king, Nala (was his) name', to the Old Irish *Scéla mucce Meic Dathó* (*Story of Mac Datho's Pigs*), *boí rí amrae for Lagnaib, Mac Dathó a ainm*, 'There was a famous king in Leinster, Mac

[60] See Gering–Sijmons (1927–31), i. 2.

[61] F. Specht, *ZVS* 64 (1937), 1–3 = Schmitt (1968), 50 f.; H. H. Schaeder, *ZDMG* 94 (1940), 399–408 = Schmitt (1968), 61–71. Cf. Schmitt (1967), 30–2, 201–4.

[62] Briefly noted by Wackernagel (1943), 18; cf. K. H. Schmidt, *ZCP* 28 (1960/1), 224; Schmitt (1967), 274 f.; W. Euler in W. Meid, H. Ölberg, H. Schmeja, *Sprachwissenschaft in Innsbruck* (Innsbruck 1982), 53–68; Watkins (1994), 681; (1995), 25.

[63] J. Siegelová, *Appu-Märchen und Hedammu-Mythos* (Studien zu den Bogazköy-Texten 14; Wiesbaden 1971), 4. For an Akkadian parallel cf. West (1997), 259.

Dathó his name'.[64] The subject need not of course be a king; the same structure appears in *Od.* 20. 287 f. ἦν δέ τις ἐν μνηστῆρσιν ἀνὴρ ἀθεμίστια εἰδώς, Κτήσιππος δ' ὄνομ' ἔσκε, 'There was among the suitors a man of lawless character, and Ctesippus was his name'. But stories about kings are universal, and the pattern is recurrent, subject naturally to slight variations. Thus in Greek, Alcman, *PMGF* 74 ἦσκέ τις Καφεὺς Ϝανάσσων; Xenophon of Ephesus 1. 1 ἦν ἐν Ἐφέσωι ἀνὴρ τῶν τὰ πρῶτα ἐκεῖ δυναμένων, Λυκομήδης ὄνομα; in Latin, Ovid, *Met.* 14. 320 f. *Picus in Ausoniis, proles Saturnia, terris* ‖ *rex fuit*; Apuleius, *Met.* 4. 28. 1 *erant in quadam ciuitate rex et regina*; in Lithuanian, *bùvo karãlius*; in Russian жил (or был) король (or царь); in the Armenian oral epic, *Sassountsy David* 5 'There was an Armenian king named Cakig', cf. 113.

What is the narrator's authority for the tale? As we saw in the last chapter, he must 'recall' it to mind; but as it is always represented as true and not a fiction, what he recalls must be knowledge derived either from sight or from hearing. The Greek poet claims to have it from the Muses, and in *Il.* 2. 485 f. the rationale is given: they are always present and witness events, whereas the poets 'only hear the fame of them' (κλέος). Other Indo-European traditions have nothing corresponding to the Muses, but the poet sometimes says 'I have heard . . .': Vedic *śr̥ṇomi, aśravam, śuśrava*, Old Irish *ro-cúala*, all from the root **ḱlu*: RV 5. 32. 11 'I hear that you alone (Indra) were born as true lord of the five peoples'; 10. 88. 15 'I have heard from the fathers that there are two paths, of gods and mortals'; cf. 1. 109. 2, 5; 2. 33. 4; 8. 2. 11; 10. 38. 5, 42. 3. The *Hildebrandslied* begins 'I have heard it said that (two) challengers met in single combat . . .', and similarly in the apocalyptic poem *Muspilli* (37) we read 'I heard it told by those learned in worldly wisdom, that the Antichrist was to fight with Elias'. The ninth-century Norse poet Thiodolf in his *Haustlǫng* (12) says 'I have heard thus, that afterwards the trier of Hœnir's mind [Loki] by trickery won back the Æsir's darling . . .'.[65]

Occasionally the poet introduces a subject by asking a factual question, which is immediately followed by the answer.

kás te jāmír jánānaam, | Ágne? kó dāśúadhvaraḥ? | kó ha, kásminn asi śritáḥ?
tuváṃ jāmír jánānaam, | Ágne, mitró asi priyáḥ, | sákhā sákhibhya ī́diyaḥ.

Who of men is your kinsman, Agni? Who your sacrificer? Who is it, to whom do you lean?

[64] Similarly in *Togail bruidne Da Derga: buí rí amra airegda for Érinn, Eochaid Feidleach a ainm*, 'There was a king, famous (and) noble in Erin, Echu Feidlech his name'. For the nominative interpretation of *nāma* in the Sanskrit formula see Euler (as n. 62), 63, and compare the Hittite text quoted above.

[65] Cf. Watkins (1995), 187.

You are men's kinsman, Agni, you are their dear partner, a friend for friends to call upon. (RV 1. 75. 3–4)

The question is addressed to Agni, but it is not Agni who answers, it is the Rishi himself. At the outset of the *Iliad* the poet, having requested the Muse to sing of the quarrel between Agamemnon and Achilles, proceeds by asking (1. 8),

> Which of the gods was it that set them at each other in strife?
> The son of Leto and Zeus: for he, wroth with the king . . .

Here we must take the question to be directed to the Muse,[66] but formally there is no difference from the Vedic example. We find the same technique in Serbo-Croat epic, which knows no Muses: 'Who was the leader of the raiding band? The leader was Mujo . . .' (*SCHS* ii, no. 31. 12 f.).

SIMILES

Similes are perhaps a universal feature of poetry and colourful discourse. It is reasonable to expect that they occurred in Indo-European poetry. Certainly they are common enough in the literatures that concern us. A very few are common to several traditions, and may perhaps represent remnants of a shared heritage. A further series is shared by Greek and Indic (mainly the epics), and these might be Graeco-Aryan. Finally I note two similes in Sappho that are paralleled in Celtic and Germanic.

The great majority of similes are short, with the term of comparison not elaborated by more than a single clause. The long simile that is such a familiar ornament of the Homeric poems, where the picture is developed by successive clauses and a whole situation is sketched, is very rare elsewhere. In *The East Face of Helicon* (218 f.) I was able to cite a bare handful of Near Eastern examples. In the Indo-European literatures apart from Greek (and Latin) the only example I have noted is *Beowulf* 2444–62.[67]

Perhaps the most international of similes are the comparisons of a multitude to grains of sand or the stars of the sky. Both of these are found in Homer and in Near Eastern literatures.[68] In the *Mahābhārata* (3. 121. 9) King Gaya's wealth is said to have been 'as countless as are the grains of sand on

[66] As explicitly in 2. 761, and with indirect questions in 2. 484–7, Hes. *Th.* 114 f., Bacchyl. 15. 47. For the question technique cf. also Pind. *Ol.* 13. 18–22, *Pyth.* 4. 70 f., *Isth.* 5. 39–42, 7. 1–15.

[67] Durante (1976), 119 f., considers the long simile to be a Greek innovation. On similes in the Indian epics see Brockington (1998), 99–102 (*Mahābhārata*), 361–3 (*Rāmāyaṇa*).

[68] West (1997), 245 f.

earth and stars in the sky and drops in the rain'. In the Armenian oral epic armies are described as being as numerous as the stars in heaven, or as more uncountable than the sand of the sea, the stars in the sky, and the grass on the ground. In Irish saga it is related that the slain Fomori on the Mag Tuired were as numerous as the stars of heaven, the sands of the sea, the snowflakes, the dewdrops on a lawn, (etc.). When Cú Chulainn fought on the Mag Muirthemne, 'as many as the sands of the sea, and the stars of heaven, and the dew of May, and snowflakes and hailstones . . . were their cloven heads and cloven skulls and severed hands and their red bones'.[69]

'Swift as (or swifter than) thought' appears to be a more distinctively Indo-European idea.[70] It is common in the Rigveda: *mánojava-* or *mánojavas-* or *manojúv-* 'thought-swift' is a recurrent epithet of the gods' cars or of the animals that draw them (1. 85. 4, 117. 15, 119. 1, etc.); the Aśvins' car is 'swifter than a mortal's thought' (1. 118. 1, cf. 117. 2, 183. 1; 10. 39. 12). Thought (*mánas-*) is called the swiftest among things that fly (6. 9. 5). In the *Iliad* (15. 80–3) the speed of Hera's journey from Ida to Olympus is conveyed by saying that it was 'as when a much-travelled man darts about in imagination from one place to another, thinking "I should like to be there, or there".' The Phaeacian ships are 'swift as a wing or a thought' (*Od.* 7. 36), and Apollo can travel 'like a thought'.[71] An Irish warrior 'made a direct run at him . . . as an arrow from a bow, or as the swiftness of a man's thought'.[72] In the Welsh story of *Culhwch and Olwen* (330) there appear two servants of Gwenhwyfar, Ysgyrdaf and Ysgudydd, whose 'feet were as swift on their errand as their thought'. In Snorri's *Gylfaginning* (46) Thor's servant Thialfi, the fastest of runners, challenges the inhabitants of Utgard in Giantland to a race, and finds himself far outrun by a small person called Hugi, 'Thought'; the king, Utgarda-Loki, explains afterwards that it was his own thought, which Thialfi had no hope of matching in fleetness.

Another simile for speed is 'quick as/quicker than a blink'. In one Vedic passage (RV 8. 73. 2) the Aśvins are invited *nimíṣaś cij jávīyasā ráthenā́ yātam*, 'come on your car that is swifter even than a blink'. Similarly in the *Rāmāyaṇa* (4. 66. 21), 'in no more time than it takes to wink an eye, I shall rush swiftly across the self-supporting sky'. The expression was perhaps felt to be too homely for Greek epic, but it appears in Sophocles' *Inachus*, fr. 269c. 24 πρὶν μύσαι, 'before having time to blink', and in Euripides' *Bacchae*, 746 f.

[69] *Sassountsy David* 7, 101, 270, 314; *Cath Maige Tuired* 742–6 Gray; *Aided Con Chulainn*, trs. J. Carey in Koch–Carey (2000), 137. Further examples in *Togail bruidne Da Derga* 860, 986, 1092 Knott; *Aislinge Meic Con Glinne* pp. 9 f. Meyer.

[70] Cf. Durante (1976), 121, who, however, notes only the Vedic and Greek material.

[71] *Hymn. Ap.* 186, 448. Cf. also *Hymn. Herm.* 43–6; [Hes.] *Scut.* 222; Theognidea 985.

[72] *Acallam na Senórach*, trs. Dooley–Roe (1999), 170.

θᾶσσον . . . ἢ σὲ ξυνάψαι βλέφαρα βασιλείοις κόραις, 'quicker than you could close the lids of your kingly eyes'. A number of parallels from Old and Middle High German are collected by Grimm (1883–8), 791 f., cf. 1534. Sanasar in the Armenian oral epic rides to his mother's house and arrives 'in the wink of an eye' (*Sassountsy David* 57).

In Greek epic good-looking men and women are often described as looking like gods or goddesses.[73] So they are in the Indian epics. Śaṃtanu begot 'eight sons who resembled immortals'; Bhīmasena is 'like the offspring of a god'; the Pāṇḍavas had 'sons like children of gods'.[74] Damayantī is 'a woman with the form of a goddess'; Sītā is like a goddess, or like a daughter of the gods.[75] When Telemachus, and later his father and grandfather, come out of the bath 'like the immortals in bodily appearance', this is strikingly paralleled in the Rāmāyaṇa, where 'after bathing . . . Rāma resembled the blessed lord Rudra after his bath'.[76] It is not surprising that similes of this type are absent from literatures such as the Celtic and Germanic, produced in Christian times.

Another formula for female beauty appears in the pseudo-Hesiodic *Catalogue of Women*, where a woman is described as ἰκέλη φαέεσσι σελήνης, 'like the moon's beams'. So in the *Rāmāyaṇa* we read of women 'with a face like the moon'.[77] A woman's necklace can also shine like the moon (3. 50. 31), which recalls how, when Aphrodite went to seduce Anchises, 'it shone like the moon' about her breasts, upon which elaborate gold necklaces reposed (*Hymn. Aphr.* 88–90). In Armenian oral epic too we find 'a maiden lovely as the moon' (*Sassountsy David* 94).

The palaces of Menelaus and Alcinous in the *Odyssey* are built with bronze, gold, and silver, and shine with 'a splendour like that of the sun or moon'. Likewise the assembly hall built for the Pāṇḍavas, which had gold pillars and gem-encrusted walls, was 'radiant and divine; it had a superb colour like the fire, or the sun, or the moon'.[78] One may doubt whether any such opulent edifices were known even by repute in Graeco-Aryan antiquity, in the second half of the third millennium. Yet it is imaginable that the simile could have been applied at that period to some chieftain's hall that blazed in the night with torches, gold cups and ornaments, bronze weapons, and so forth.

No such doubt on cultural-historical grounds need attach to the simile used of one who stands out from a crowd 'like a bull among the herd'; it is

[73] For Near Eastern parallels see West (1997), 242 f.

[74] *MBh.* 1. 92. 43, 139. 23, 213. 82; cf. 3. 73. 25, 112. 1; 4. 67. 8; 8. 21. 7.

[75] *MBh.* 3. 65. 36; *Rm.* 5. 28. 2, 22. 42; cf. 2. 86. 20.

[76] *Od.* 3. 468, 23. 163, 24. 370 f.; *Rm.* 3. 15. 39.

[77] [Hes.] fr. 23a. 8, 252. 4; *Rm.* 3. 50. 2; 5. 12. 50, 13. 27. The male hero Rāma is praised in the same terms, 5. 29. 5, al., which a Greek hero would probably not have appreciated.

[78] *Od.* 4. 45; 7. 84; *MBh.* 2. 3. 20 f., cf. 11. 12. For neo-Assyrian and neo-Babylonian parallels see West (1997), 251 f., 419 f.

one that would have occurred naturally to the earliest pastoralists. It is found already in the Rigveda (9. 110. 9), of Soma: 'as in greatness, Clarified One, (you are) above these two worlds and all beings, you stand forth outstanding like a bull in the herd'. The reader of Homer will recall the picture of Agamemnon in *Il.* 2. 480–3:

> As a bull in the herd stands out far above all,
> for he is conspicuous among the gathering of the cows,
> that is how Zeus made Atreus' son that day,
> conspicuous and outstanding among the many warriors.

Another simile from the animal world, shared by Indians and Greeks, is perhaps much less ancient. Duryodhana, denouncing Vidura, says 'like a snake we took you into our embrace' (*MBh.* 2. 57. 3). The same image is found in the *Rāmāyaṇa* (2. 7. 23): 'he is like a viper, child, whom you have taken to your bosom and lovingly mothered'. In Greek it appears in the Theognidea (601 f.), though not quite in the true form:

> ἔρρε θεοῖσίν τ' ἐχθρὲ καὶ ἀνθρώποισιν ἄπιστε,
> ψυχρὸν ὃς ἐν κόλπωι ποικίλον εἶχες ὄφιν.
>
> To hell with you, whom gods abhor and men can't trust,
> who held in your bosom a cold and cunning snake.

Sintenis plausibly proposed reading ψυχρὸν ὃν . . . εἶχον, so that the sense becomes 'whom I held in my bosom as a cold and cunning snake'. This brings the verse into line with the logical sense and with the Aesopic fable of a man who found a viper that was nearly dead with cold and warmed it in his bosom; once revived, it bit him and he died.[79] Now, it seems quite possible that a version of the fable, like many other animal fables, came to India from the west at a comparatively late date. A form of it appears in the *Pañcatantra* (2 st. 17, trs. P. Olivelle): 'Yet a bad man inspires no confidence, because of his evil disposition, like a snake asleep in one's own bosom.' If so, the fable, rather than a common Graeco-Aryan tradition, may have been the source of the image in the Indian epics.

When Penelope is at last persuaded that it is Odysseus who stands before her, she is overcome by tears;

> and as when the land is welcome when it comes into view of swimmers
> whose sturdy ship Poseidon has smashed in the sea . . .
> and gladly they make land and escape hardship,
> so welcome was her husband to her as she looked on him.

[79] Aesop. *Fab.* 176 Perry; Babrius 143.

Again the Indian epic supplies a parallel: 'Like a tired swimmer in water when he reaches the land, Yuyudhāna became comforted on obtaining the sight of Dhananjaya (Arjuna)'.[80]

In my two remaining examples a simile in Sappho finds a parallel in the north-west. In a song about a friend who has married a Lydian and left her circle, Sappho says (fr. 96. 6–9), 'and now she shines among the women of Lydia, as after sunset the rose-fingered moon, surpassing all the stars'. In an Irish narrative we read: 'such was that warrior that, as the moon in her great fifteenth surpasses the stars of heaven, that warrior, in his form and shape, surpassed the sons of kings and chieftains of this world.'[81]

In a wedding song Sappho anticipates that the girls participating in the all-night celebration will 'see less sleep than the melodious bird', that is, than the nightingale, which had the reputation of never sleeping. In an Eddic poem King Frodi sets two doughty slave-women to work at a magic mill that grinds out whatever the grinder wants. He demands that they work non-stop, saying 'You'll sleep no longer than the cuckoo above the hall'. Snorri writes that the watchman of the gods, Heimdallr, 'needs less sleep than a bird'.[82] What we have in these passages is not, I imagine, a traditional poetic simile, but an ancient popular saying based on the observation that some birds seem to insist on singing when all good folk are in bed.

FIGURES

If I have not placed similes under this heading, it is because I am reserving the term 'figure' for the arrangement of words in specific patterns. Some such patternings, like anaphora and epanalepsis, can be found in non-Indo-European poetries. Others appear to be distinctively Indo-European. To some extent they were facilitated by features of the language such as inflection, flexible word order, and the principles of nominal composition.

Polar expressions ('merisms')

Especially characteristic is the use of polar expressions, that is, pairings of contrasted terms, as an emphatic expression of the totality that they make

[80] *Od.* 23. 233–9; *MBh.* 7. 116. 12.

[81] *Acallam na Senórach* 3733–6 Stokes, trs. Dooley–Roe (1999), 113.

[82] Sappho fr. 30. 7–9; *Grottasǫngr* 7. 3–4; *Gylf.* 27, cf. Lorenz (1984), 374.

up.[83] One may say that bipolarity (not trifunctionality) is the fundamental structuring principle of Indo-European thought.

For example, the concept of 'all intelligent beings' is expressed by 'gods and men' or 'immortals and mortals': RV 1. 35. 2 *amṛ́tam mártiyaṃ ca*; 6. 15. 8 *devā́saś ca mártiyāsaś ca*; Y. 29. 4 = 48. 1 *daēvāiščā mašyāiščā*; *Il.* 2. 1 *θεοί τε καὶ ἀνέρες*; 20. 64 *θνητοῖσι καὶ ἀθανάτοισι*; *Lokasenna* 45. 3, 55. 6 *goð ǫll ok gumar*; *Gylf.* 21 *guðanna ok manna*.[84]

Where the focus is not on the gods but on the animal world, the phrase is 'creatures two-footed and four-footed': RV 4. 51. 5 (and often) *dvipā́c cátuṣpāt*; Y. 9. 18 *bizaṇgranąm . . . caθβarəzaṇgranąm*, cf. 19. 8, Yt. 1. 10; Vd. 15. 19 *bipaitištanaca caθβarəpaitištanaca*; on the Iguvine tablets, VIb. 10 *dupursus peturpursus*; Cicero, *De domo* 48 *ministro omnium non bipedum solum sed etiam quadrupedum impurissimo*.[85] The same classification is implicit in the Hittite tale of the cow that gives birth to a human child after being impregnated by the Sun-god. She remonstrates: 'Now I ask you please: [a calf] should have four legs. Why have I borne this two-legged thing?'[86] It also underlies Aeschylus' kenning-like expressions *δίπους ὄφις* and *δίπους λέαινα*, 'two-legged snake', 'two-legged lioness' (*Supp.* 895, *Ag.* 1258): in each case the beast is a metaphor, and the epithet identifies its reference as a human one.[87]

It may be noted that in some of these examples there is no 'and' joining the words for four-footed and two-footed. Further instances of such asyndeton will appear in the following paragraphs. It is no doubt an ancient traditional feature of these pairings.[88]

The estate-owner's livestock is summed up as 'herds and men' (i.e. slaves): RV 5. 20. 4 *góbhiḥ . . . vīráiḥ*; Y. 31. 15 *pasə̄uš vīrāatcā*, 45. 9 *pasū̆š vīrə̄ṇg*, cf. Yt. 10. 112; Tab. Iguv. VIa. 32 (and often) *ueiro pequo*; Ovid, *Met.* 1. 286 *pecudesque uirosque*.[89] In most of these the original words **péḱu-* and **wī́ro* have survived, and in that order; the Umbrian *ueiro pequo*, though it has the inverse order, seems to be a dual *dvandva*, a remarkable archaism of a type known from the Rigveda, by which two terms forming a pair are both

[83] Gonda (1959), 337–47; Campanile (1977), 98–104; Watkins (1995), 44–7, 250 ('merisms').

[84] Many other passages could be quoted, and some will be in the next chapter.

[85] Further material in Schmitt (1967), 210–13; cf. R. Lazzeroni, *SSL* 15 (1975), 1–19; Watkins (1994), 650; Gamkrelidze–Ivanov (1995), 394 f., 398.

[86] *CTH* 363 iii 20 ff., trs. Hoffner (1998), 86.

[87] Campanile (1990b), 29, refers to Y. 9. 18 and Vd. 18. 38, where he says that the four-legged wolf is distinguished from the two-legged wolf; but no two-legged wolf appears in those texts.

[88] Cf. P. Chantraine, *Revue de philologie* 27 (1953), 16–20; B. K. Braswell, *A Commentary on the Fourth Pythian Ode of Pindar* (Berlin–New York 1988), 300.

[89] More in J. Wackernagel, *ZVS* 43 (1910), 295–8 (= *Kl. Schr.* 280–3; Schmitt (1968), 30–3); cf. Schmitt (1967), 16 f., 213–16; É. Benveniste in Cardona et al. (1970), 308 f.; Watkins (1994), 649 f.

put in the dual number. In Greek both words have been replaced by younger synonyms: Hes. *Op.* 558 προβάτοις ... ἀνθρώποις, cf. Hdt. 1. 203. 2; Hippocr. *De carnibus* 6.

The biosphere as a whole is covered in Vedic idiom by the merism *jágatas tasthúṣaḥ* (1. 89. 5, cf. 1. 115. 1, 4. 53. 6, etc.), 'what moves or stands still', that is, animals and plants. A trace of this categorization appears in the Greek word πρόβατα 'sheep, livestock', literally 'what moves forward' as opposed to the stockholder's stationary property.[90] The -βα- is the etymological equivalent of the -*ga*- in *jágataḥ*. But the opposition 'walking: stationary' was more widely applicable. Indra is king of 'the one travelling and the one at ease (*yātó ávasitasya*), of the domesticated (animal) and the horned' (RV 1. 32. 15).[91] The seer Theoclymenus declares to Penelope that Odysseus is already back in his native land, ἥμενος ἢ ἕρπων, 'sitting (still) or walking' (*Od.* 17. 158). The two original verbal roots reappear in tandem in the tragedians: Soph. *Aj.* 1237 ποῦ βάντος ἢ ποῦ στάντος οὗπερ οὐκ ἐγώ; 'where did he step, where stand, that I did not?'; *Phil.* 833 ὅρα ποῦ στάσῃ, ποῖ δὲ βάσῃ, 'consider where you will stand, where step'; Eur. *Alc.* 863 ποῖ βῶ; ποῖ στῶ; *Hec.* 1057 πᾷ βῶ; πᾷ στῶ; A more comprehensive formula appears in the *Mahābhārata*, 12. 161. 21 *āsīnaś ca śayānaś ca vicarann api ca sthitaḥ*, 'sitting and lying, walking and standing'. The phrase in Y. 68. 6 *vīspåsca āpō yazamaide yå zəmā, armaēštå frātat̰.caratasca*, 'and all the waters of the earth we worship, the stagnant and the forward-moving', may be regarded as a variation on the basic idea.

The Indo-European ability to create negative compounds with the prefix *n̥ made it easy to form polar expressions of the type 'X and non-X': *amṛ́tam mártiyaṃ ca* 'immortal and mortal' (RV 1. 35. 2); *yā́mann áyāman* 'whether moving or not' (RV 1. 181. 7); *dūnā́ ádūnā . . . śiṣṭā́n áśiṣṭān* 'burnt or unburnt . . . left or not left' (AV 2. 31. 3); *dāsyánn ádāsyann utá* 'whether he is going to give or not' (AV 6. 71. 3); *akāmo vā sakāmo vā* 'willy nilly' (*MBh.* 3. 289. 18), which corresponds in sense to Avestan *yezi zaoša yezi azaoša* (Y. 1. 21), Greek θέλεος ἀθέλεος (Aesch. *Supp.* 862), Latin *uolens nolens*; *yé ca ihá pitáro yé ca néhá* 'both those fathers who are here and those who are not here' (RV 10. 15. 13), corresponding to Greek οἵ τ' ὄντες οἵ τ' ἀπόντες (Soph. *Ant.* 1109), cf. Latin *quod fuit quod non fuit* (Plaut. *Trin.* 360); *yadacā anyadacā* 'here and not here' (Y. 35. 2); *srunvatascā asrunvatascā xšayaṇtascā axšayaṇtascā* 'hearers and non-hearers, rulers and non-rulers' (Y. 35. 4); *spə̄ṇcā aspə̄ṇcā* 'fortune and misfortune' (Y. 45. 9); ἄφατοί τε φατοί τε ῥητοί τ' ἄρρητοί τε

[90] On this term cf. Benveniste (1973), 32–9, 49–51; R. Lazzeroni, *SSL* 15 (1975), 20–35.

[91] With this latter merism compare Hes. *Op.* 529 κεραοὶ καὶ νήκεροι ὑληκοῖται, 'the horned and hornless forest-couchers', though the reference is not quite the same.

'unmentioned and mentioned, spoken and unspoken of' (Hes. *Op.* 3–4); καὶ δίκαια κἄδικα 'through right or wrong' (Solon fr. 30 and related texts), paralleled in Latin by *per omne fas ac nefas secuturi* (Livy 6. 14. 10), *honesta atque inhonesta* (Tac. *Ann.* 2. 38); *pennatas inpennatasque agnas* 'bearded and beardless ears of corn' (Carmen Saliare ap. Fest. p. 211 M.); *nerf śihitu anśihitu, iouie hostatu anhostatu* 'principes cinctos incinctos, iuuenes hastatos inhastatos' (Tab. Iguv. VIb. 59, cf. VIIa. 13 f., 28, al.); *snata asnata* 'umecta non umecta' IIa.19, cf. 34; *bennacht dé 7 andé fort* 'the blessing of gods and non-gods on you' (*Táin* (I) 2043), which recalls RV 6. 22. 11 *ná yā́ ádevo . . . ná deváḥ*, 'neither a non-god nor a god'.

An especially widespread and long-lasting formula is 'seen and unseen'. It occurs in several incantations of the Atharvaveda, as for example in 2. 31. 2 *dṛṣṭám adṛ́ṣṭam atṛham*, 'the seen, the unseen one [worm] I have crushed' (cf. 5. 23. 6–7; 8. 8. 15); the intention was to leave no loophole by which an undetected worm might escape. So in the Roman prayer given by Cato (*De agricultura* 141. 2), *uti tu morbos uisos inuisosque . . . prohibessis defendas auerruncesque*, 'that thou mayest ward off, repel, and avert distempers seen and unseen'. In the Umbrian ritual regulations expiation is offered to Jupiter Grabovius *persei . . . tuer perscler uirseto auirseto uas est* 'if in your sacrifice there is any seen or unseen imperfection' (Tab. Iguv. VIa. 28, 38, 48, al.). We read of an Irish oath sworn 'by all elements visible and invisible, in heaven and on earth'.[92]

Such apparently catch-all formulae were especially suited to legal or other prescriptive language where the intention was to exclude any transgression or oversight. It is in this spirit that Hesiod enjoins that we should not urinate while walking, 'neither on the road nor off the road' (*Op.* 729). Sometimes it is deemed advisable to provide for both male and female. The Hittites make a practice of invoking 'all gods and goddesses'; in the great prayer of Muwatalli, after a lengthy list of deities, the Storm-god is addressed, and then 'gods and goddesses of the king and queen, those named and those not named, those in whose temples the king and queen officiate and those in whose temples they do not officiate'.[93] In RV 6. 68. 4 the phrase 'all the gods' is reinforced by *gnā́ś ca náraś ca*, 'females and males'. Zeus in the *Iliad* calls on 'all gods and all goddesses' to hear him, and a similar phrase was traditional in Greek prayers and treaties.[94] In another of Cato's prayers for farmers (*De agric.* 139) the

[92] *Fled Dúin na nGéd* p. 1. 5 Lehmann: *rátha na n-uile dúl aicsige 7 nemaicsigi 7 nách dúil fil a nim 7 a talmain.*

[93] *CTH* 381 rev. iii 5–8; Lebrun (1980), 265/280. Further examples in Beckman (1999), 40, 47, 52, 58, 63, 68, 82, 86, 92, 112, 121. For a seventh-century Assyrian example see West (1997), 222.

[94] *Il.* 8. 5 = 19. 101; Ar. *Av.* 866 f. with Nan Dunbar's commentary. In two Eddic poems (*Þrymskviða* 14. 1–4 = *Baldrs draumar* 1. 1–4) we find the couplet 'All the gods were together at assembly, and all the goddesses at the debate'.

man thinning out a clump of trees is directed to say *si deus si dea es quoium illud sacrum sit*, 'be you god or goddess to whom this place is sacred'.[95] In a Vedic spell we read *śalabhasya śalabhiyās . . . api nahyāma āsyam* 'of the he-locust, of the she-locust . . . we tie up the mouth' (AV Paipp. 5. 20. 5).[96]

Sometimes the effort is made to stop a possible loophole by adding the middle term to the pair of opposites; the opposites are regularly placed first, with the intermediate term following. So in RV 4. 25. 8 *páre ávare madhyamā́saḥ* 'the higher, the lower, the middle-ranking';[97] Theognis 3, 'I will always sing of thee first and last and in the middle'; [Aeschylus], *Prom.* 115, 'what sound, what invisible fragrance floats upon me—godsent, or mortal, or a blend of the two?' Aeschylus' Eteocles demands obedience from every citizen of Thebes, ἀνὴρ γυνή τε χὤτι τῶν μεταίχμιον, 'man and woman and whatever is in the area between' (*Sept.* 197); and similarly in the *Mahābhārata* (12. 250. 30), 'among men you will become a man in form, among women a female, among the third class a neuter' (*napuṃsakam*, literally 'a non-male, an unmannikin').

In another idiom universality is expressed as the sum of past and future, or of past, present, and future, or rather 'what has been, what is, and what is to be'.[98] 'Purusha is this universe, *yád bhūtáṃ yác ca bháviyam*, the one that has been and the one that is to be' (RV 10. 90. 2, cf. AV 10. 7. 22, 8. 1); *bhūtasyeśānā bhuvanasya devī* 'goddess who has power over what has been (and) what is' (AV Paipp. 11. 1. 5); *vīspås tå hujītayō yå zī åŋharə̄ yåscā həṇtī* | *yåscā, Mazdā, buvaiṇtī* 'all those good lives that have been and those that are and those, Wise One, that shall be' (Y. 33. 10, cf. 45. 7, 51. 22); πάνθ' ὅσα τ' ἦν ὅσα τ' ἐστὶ καὶ ἔσται 'everything that was and that is and will be' (Empedocles B 21. 9).

These expressions appear particularly in connection with divine or vatic knowledge. Varuna in RV 1. 25. 11 sees *kṛtā́ni yā́ ca kártuvā*, 'things done and yet to be done'. The sage Mārkaṇḍeya knows past, present, and future (*MBh.* 3. 186. 85; cf. 9. 62. 38; 12. 47. 65, 50. 18, 82. 30, 275). The wise queen Vidurā is *bhaviṣyad-bhūta-darśinī*, a 'future-and-past-beholder' (*MBh.* 5. 134. 12). Calchas knew τά τ' ἐόντα τά τ' ἐσσόμενα πρό τ' ἐόντα, 'what is and what will be and what was before' (*Il.* 1. 70). Hesiod uses the same words of the songs that the Muses sing on Olympus, and claims a similar power for himself

[95] Cf. also *CIL* i.[2] 801 *sei deo sei deiuae sacrum*; 1485 *sei deus sei dea*; 2644 *sei deo sei deae*; and the early *evocatio* reported by Furius Philus ap. Macr. *Sat.* 3. 9. 7.

[96] Cf. also AV 1. 8. 1 *yá idáṃ strī́ púmān ákar ihá*, 'whoever—woman, man—has done this here'; *Od.* 4. 142; Gonda (1959), 342.

[97] Similarly in RV 10. 81. 5; AV 1. 17. 2; 6. 103. 2; 7. 83. 3; 10. 7. 8; 18. 4. 69.

[98] Cf. Schmitt (1967), 252–4; Schlerath (1968), ii. 159.

thanks to the wondrous voice that they have breathed into him (*Th.* 32, 38). The Nart hero Syrdon 'could not only relate what had already happened, but also predict the future'.[99] In a fifteenth-century Polish sermon the Christian is admonished that he will have no need of dream-interpreters, astrologers, incantation-mongers, or 'divinatores *badaczye*, qui futura ac eventus fortuitos et preterita occulta et presencia suis supersticionibus prenosticant':[100] the Slavonic seers of the time evidently still canvassed the old formula.

Past and future are also brought together in expressions of uniqueness: RV 1. 81. 5 *ná tvā́vām̐ Indra káś caná | ná jātó ná janiṣyate*, 'none like thee, Indra, has ever been born nor ever will be' (cf. 7. 32. 23, 99. 2); *MBh.* 10. 5. 26 'that man has not been born, nor will be, who . . .'; Sappho fr. 56, '[. . . ,] nor do I think that there will ever (again) be any girl of such musical skill born to the light of day'; in Armenian, *Sassountsy David* 303 'David, in all the world there has never been one as brave as you, and there never will be one as brave as you'; in Welsh, 'of all who were and will be, there is not your equal'; 'there does not come and will not come anything more grievous';[101] in Norse, *Gylf.* 47 *engi hefir sá orðit ok engi mun verða . . . at eigi komi ellin ǫllum til falls*, 'no such man has existed and none will exist, that old age will not bring them all down'.

The unique weapon or piece of armour is the subject of an interesting little group of parallels. Heracles appears to Odysseus in the underworld wearing an elaborately ornamented sword-belt, of which the poet exclaims, almost untranslatably (*Od.* 11. 613 f.),

> μὴ τεχνησάμενος μηδ' ἄλλό τι τεχνήσαιτο,
> ὃς κεῖνον τελαμῶνα ἑῇ ἐγκάτθετο τέχνῃ.
>
> He need have crafted nothing else before or since,
> the man who compassed that sword-belt in his craft.

There is nothing else like this in Homer. But in a little-known Norse saga the dying Hildibrand sings of his sword, now broken, which 'dwarfs now dead had forged, such as no one (else) can, before or hereafter'. And in a Serbo-Croat heroic song Marko Kraljević, after establishing that the craftsman of his sword has never made a better one, cuts off his right arm to ensure that he never will.[102]

[99] Sikojev (1985), 250.

[100] C. H. Meyer (1931), 71.

[101] *Uryen Erechwydd* 42 f. (*Book of Taliesin* 57), trs. Koch–Carey (2000), 344; *Y Gododdin* 1119.

[102] *Edd. min.* 53, 2. 5–8, from *Ásmundarsaga Kappabana*; *SCHS* ii, no. 7. 71–83.

Positive reinforced by negated opposite

Modern politicians often emphasize a concept by adding 'not (the opposite)': 'the many, not the few'; 'the future, not the past'. This is an ancient figure that can be documented especially, though not exclusively, from the Graeco-Aryan traditions.[103] I give a selection from many examples.

From Vedic: RV 7. 59. 12 *mṛtyór mukṣīya, mā́mṛ́tāt,* 'may I free myself from death, not from non-dying'; 8. 62. 12 *satyám . . . Índraṃ stavāma, nā́nṛtam,* 'let us praise Indra in truth, not in falsehood'; AV 5. 13. 4 *áhe mriyásva, mā́ jīvīḥ,* 'die, snake, do not live'.

From Avestan: Y. 30. 3 *åscā hudåŋhō ərəš vīšyātā, nōiṯ duždåŋhō,* 'and between them well-doers discriminate rightly, not ill-doers'; 46. 8 *yā īm hujyātōiš pāyāṯ, nōiṯ dužjyātōiš,* 'such as to keep him from good living, not from bad living'; 48. 5 *huxšaθrā xšə̄ṇtąm, mā nə̄ dušxšaθrā xšə̄ṇtā,* 'let good rulers rule, do not let bad rulers rule us'.

From Old Persian: DB iv 44 *hašiyam, naiy duruxtam,* 'true, not false'; DNb 7 *rāstam dauštā amiy, miθa naiy dauštā amiy,* 'I am a friend of right, I am not a friend of wrong'.

From Greek: Hes. *Th.* 551 γνῶ ῥ' οὐδ' ἠγνοίησε δόλον, 'he recognized the trick and did not fail to recognize it'; *Il.* 1. 416 μίνυνθά περ, οὔ τι μάλα δήν, 'for a short time, not for very long'; 5. 816 ἐρέω ἔπος οὐδ' ἐπικεύσω, 'I will say my word and not withhold it'.

In an old Dutch juridical formula: *ic ghebiede lust ende ic verbiede onlust,* 'I demand attention, and I forbid inattention'. From an Old Irish prayer: *do·m-thí áes, ní·m-thí bás,* 'may life come to me, may death not come to me'. From a Gaelic song: 'I lie down with God, and God will lie down with me; I will not lie down with Satan, nor shall Satan lie down with me.'[104]

In certain cases the instinct to create a figure of this type has provoked the coining of an irregular negative substantive: Y. 31. 10 *aṯ hī ayå fravarətā vāstrīm . . . nōiṯ, Mazdā, avāstryō . . . humərətōiš baxštā,* 'of these two (the cow) chose the herdsman . . . The non-herdsman, Wise One, . . . enjoys no good regard'; 31. 17 *vīdvå vīdušē mraotū, mā əvīdvå aipi də̄bāvayaṯ,* 'let the knowing one speak to the knowing, let the unknowing delude no longer'; Hes. *Op.* 355 δώτῃ μέν τις ἔδωκεν, ἀδώτῃ δ' οὔ τις ἔδωκεν, 'to the giver one gives, to the non-giver none gives'.

[103] H. Humbach, *MSS* 14 (1959), 23–33; Gonda (1959), 87–108; Schmitt (1967), 266–9; Campanile (1977), 104–7.

[104] Dutch formula adduced by E. Schwyzer, *Zeitschrift für Indologie und Iranistik* 7 (1929), 105; Irish text edited by Campanile, *SSL* 6 (1966), 161, 10 f.; Gaelic song in Carmichael (1928–59), i. 80 f.

Epanadiplosis

We now come to a series of figures involving repeated words. The first and simplest is iteration: an urgent or emotive word is uttered twice (or more) in succession. This is really an elementary tactic of language, not intrinsically a feature of the high style, though it can be employed deliberately for poetic purposes.[105]

Two particular uses may be mentioned here. One may be called liturgical-magical, where a word or formula is repeated to enhance its potency, as in AV 17. 6. 7 *úd ihy úd ihi Sūrya*, 'rise, rise, O Sun'; Y. 10. 20 *gave nəmō, gave nəmō*, 'homage to the bull, homage to the bull'; *Hænsa-Þóris saga* 8 *brenni, brenni Blundketill inni* 'let burn, burn, Blundketill within'; or in the Valkyries' song in *Njáls saga* 157 (*Edd. min.* 59) *vindum, vindum vef darraðar*, 'wind we, wind we the web of spears'.

The other may be called mimetic repetition. It expresses repeating or protracted action.[106] So in RV 1. 12. 2 *Agním-Agnim hávīmabhiḥ sádā havanta*, 'they keep invoking "Agni, Agni" with invocations'; 8. 12. 19 *devám̥-devam̥ vo ávasa, Índram-Indram̥ gr̥ṇīṣáṇi*, 'laud the god, the god for your aid, (laud) Indra, Indra'. Very similar is Aeschylus, *Ag.* 1144 Ἴτυν Ἴτυν στένουσα, of the nightingale who is always lamenting 'Itys, Itys', and the parallel passages in later poets. A different example in the same broad category is Euripides, *Bacch.* 1065 κατῆγεν ἦγεν ἦγεν ἐς μέλαν πέδον, 'he bent it down, down, down to the earth'; *Iph. Taur.* 1406 μᾶλλον δὲ μᾶλλον πρὸς πέτρας ᾔει σκάφος, 'further and further towards the rocks went the vessel'; Arist. *Nub.* 1288 πλέον πλέον τἀργύριον αἰεὶ γίγνεται, 'the money keeps getting more and more'. Similar expressions are commonplace in other languages, as in Old Irish *móo assa móo* 'more and more', *messa assa-mmessa* 'worse and worse'; Norse *meirr oc meirr* 'more and more', *ey ok ey* 'for ever and ever', etc.

Epanalepsis

Epanalepsis is the figure in which a word or a whole phrase from one verse is picked up in the next. RV 1. 133. 7 *sunvānó hi ṣmā yájati áva dvíṣo*, | *devā́naam áva dvíṣaḥ*, 'for the soma-presser turns away enmity, | (turns) away the gods' enmity'; 5. 85. 3 f. *téna víśvasya bhúvanasya . . . ví unatti bhū́ma*, | *unátti bhū́mim pr̥thivī́m utá dyā́m*, 'with it, of the whole world he waters the ground,

[105] Cf. Hofmann (1930), 12–48; Gonda (1959), 325–32; Campanile (1977), 112 f.; for Greek, E. Schwyzer–A. Debrunner, *Griechische Grammatik*, ii (Munich 1950), 699 f.; for Norse, Detter–Heinzel (1903), ii. 14, 41.

[106] Cf. Hofmann (1930), 26–35.

| he waters the ground, earth and sky'; AV 6. 42. 1 f. There are several examples in Homer, for instance:

> Ἀνδρομάχη, θυγάτηρ μεγαλήτορος Ἠετίωνος,
> Ἠετίων, ὃς ἔναιεν ὑπὸ Πλάκωι ὑλήέσσηι.
>
> Andromache, daughter of great-hearted Eetion,
> Eetion, who dwelt below wooded Plakos.
>
> ὃ μὲν ἔμπεδον ἡνιόχευεν,
> ἔμπεδον ἡνιόχευ', ὃ δ' ἄρα μάστιγι κέλευεν.
>
> He steered the chariot steadily on,
> steered the chariot steadily on, while his twin urged with the goad.[107]

Further instances can be gathered from other Indo-European poetries. From Old Irish: *fo chen Chet,* | *Cet mac Mágach,* 'Welcome Cet, | Cet son of Maga'.[108] From Norse: *Þrymskviða* 29. 8–9 *ef þú ǫðlaz vill ástir mínar,* | *ástir mínar, alla hylli,* 'if you want to earn my love, | my love (and) all (my) favour'; *Rígsþula* 36. 2–3 *kom þar ór runni Rígr gangandi,* | *Rígr gangandi, rúnar kendi,* 'there came from the thicket Ríg walking, | Ríg walking, (and) taught him runes'.[109] From Russian *byliny*: 'This is your only gift; God has given you no others, | God has given you no others; He has not endowed you further.'[110] From Balkan epic: 'From the cave he has never again emerged; | he has never emerged, nor has anyone seen him.'[111]

Questioner's suggestions negated in turn

A device widely used in narrative is that someone asks a question and suggests possible answers to it, and the respondent negates them one by one before giving the true answer. When Hector goes home and finds that his wife is not there, he asks the servants:

> Has she gone to one of her sisters-in-law or mine,
> or to the temple of Athena, where the other
> women of Troy propitiate the dread goddess?

And the answer comes:

[107] *Il.* 6. 395 f., cf. 2. 672 f., 21. 85 f., *Od.* 1. 22 f.; *Il.* 23. 641 f., cf. 20. 371 f., 22. 127 f. The figure also appears in Semitic poetry (Akkadian, Ugaritic, Hebrew); see West (1997), 256 f.

[108] *Scéla muicce Maic Dathó*, line 197 Thurneysen.

[109] Cf. 36. 8–9. More in Detter–Heinzel (1903), ii. 275.

[110] Chadwick (1932), 82, lines 25 f.; cf. 88, lines 253 f., 262 f.; 120, lines 149 f., 151 f.; 164, lines 1–4.

[111] *SCHS* i. 364. 169 f.; cf. 177 f., 180 f.; ii, no. 1. 2–3; no. 4. 296 f., 1202 f. Further Slavonic and Baltic examples in Hofmann (1930), 39–42.

She has not gone to one of her sisters-in-law or yours,
or to the temple of Athena, where the other
women of Troy propitiate the dread goddess:
she has gone to the great wall of Ilios . . .

I could fill several pages with examples from Hittite, from the Indian epics, from Old English and Norse, from Armenian, Russian and Serbo-Croat heroic poems, and from Lithuanian ballads, but it is sufficient to note the fact and to cite references.[112]

Anaphora

Perhaps the commonest of all figures is simple anaphora, the repetition of an important word in successive phrases or clauses. This word is normally placed in the emphatic initial position, and it is noteworthy that the verb, whose 'normal' or default position in Indo-European was after the subject and object, happily stands initially in anaphora, as well as in other situations where it carries some thematic weight.[113]

The repetition may be just twofold, but it is quite commonly threefold, as in Y. 36. 4 *vohū θβā manaŋhā, vohū θβā aṣ̌ā, vaŋhuyå θβā cistōiš ś̌yaoθanāiščā vacəbīščā*, '(thee) with good mind, with good truth, with good thoughts, deeds, and words', cf. 36. 5, 39. 5; *Il.* 5. 385–95 τλῆ μὲν . . . τλῆ δὲ . . . τλῆ δὲ . . . ; *Vafþrúðnismál* 4. 1–3 *heill þú farir, heill þú aptr komir, heill þú á sinnom sér*, 'safe go thou, safe come thou back, safe be thou on the way'; or fourfold, as in RV 4. 25. 5 *priyáḥ sukṛ́t, priyá Índre manāyúḥ, priyáḥ suprāvíḥ, priyó asya somī́*, 'dear is the doer of good, dear to Indra the pious, dear the attentive, dear to him the soma-bringer'; of εὖ, *Il.* 2. 382–4 εὖ μέν τις . . . εὖ δὲ . . . εὖ δέ τις . . . εὖ δέ τις . . . ; *Táin* (I) 2936–8 *Cú na hEmna Macha, Cú co ndelb cach datha, Cú chreichi, Cú chatha*, 'the Hound of Emain Macha, the Hound with beauty of every colour, the Hound of spoils, the Hound of battle'.

One characteristic use of anaphora is to emphasize quantity, as in *Il.* 11. 494 f., 'many the withered oaks, many the pines that it bears off, and much the débris that it casts in the sea' (cf. 20. 326, 23. 30, *Od.* 1. 3, 9. 45, 22. 47, 23.

[112] *Il.* 6. 374–86, cf. 1. 65/93, 16. 36 f./50 f.; *Od.* 2. 30–45, 11. 397–410; myth of Wasitta, J. Friedrich, *Jahrbuch für kleinasiatische Forschung* 2 (1952/3), 150–2 (*CTH* 346); *MBh.* 3. 61. 69 f.; *Rm.* 2. 10. 6/14; 5. 48. 6–11; *Finnesburh* 1–4; *Helgakviða Hundingsbana B* 40 f.; *Sassountsy David* 158 f.; Chadwick (1932), 119, lines 79 ff.; 147, lines 117 ff.; Sulejman Fortić, *The Capture of Budapest*, in *SCHS* i. 227; Alija Fjuljanin, *The Captivity of Osmanbey*, ibid. 315; Avdo Međedović, *The Wedding of Smailagić Meho*, ibid. iii. 94; Rhesa (1825), 94/5 f., 114/15 f., 158/9, 176/7. There are several instances also in Ugaritic: West (1997), 198.

[113] Cf. Gonda (1959), 128–65; Watkins (1995), 88, 107, 305, 502, 510 f.

304); *Vafþrúðnismál* 3. 1–3 *fiǫlð ec fór, fiǫlð ec freistaða, fiǫlð ec reynda regin*, 'much I have travelled, much have I experienced, much have I tried the gods'; *Þrymskviða* 23. 5–6 *fiǫlð á ec meiðma, fiǫlð á ec menia*, 'many treasures I have, many necklaces I have'.

Another is to underline the importance of a particular quality or possession: RV 4. 3. 10–12 *ṛténa . . . ṛténa . . . ṛténa* . . . 'through right', with which Watkins has aptly juxtaposed a passage from an Irish wisdom text, *is tre fír flathemon . . . is tre fír flathemon . . . is tre fír flathemon* . . . , 'it is through the ruler's truth that . . .';[114] RV 6. 75. 2 *dhánvanā . . . dhánvanā . . . dhánvanā* . . . 'with the bow', with which the same scholar compares Archilochus fr. 2 ἐν δορὶ . . . ἐν δορὶ . . . ἐν δορὶ . . . , 'in my spear';[115] *Il.* 23. 315–18 μήτι . . . μήτι . . . μήτι . . . , 'through cleverness'.

In Indo-Iranian and Greek we find a form of anaphora in which a preverb is repeated in subsequent clauses with ellipse of the verb that it modified in the initial one: RV 1. 123. 6 *úd īratāṃ sūnṛ́tā, út púraṃdhīḥ*, 'forth let come the bounties, forth the riches';[116] Y. 57. 24 = Yt. 10. 92 *aya daēnaya fraorəṇta* | *Ahurō Mazdå aṣ̌ava*, | *frā Vohu Manō, frā Aṣ̌əm vahištəm, frā Xšaθrəm vairīm, frā spəṇta Ārmaiti*, etc.; *Il.* 18. 483 ἐν μὲν γαῖαν ἔτευξ', ἐν δ' οὐρανόν, ἐν δὲ θάλασσαν.

Anaphora of first element of compounds

A kind of anaphora within the phrase occurs with the juxtaposition of two or more adjectives compounded with the same fore-element.[117] We find it especially often with words formed with the prefixes *h_1*su*- 'good-', **dus*- 'ill-', **n̥*- 'not', and **pl̥hu*- 'much-'.

With *h_1*su*-: RV 1. 35. 10 *sunīthá̄ḥ sumṛḷīká̄ḥ suávān*, cf. 1. 42. 7, 47. 8, 49. 2, 92. 3, 116. 25, 118. 1, 159. 3, 185. 7; 2. 2. 1, 32. 7; 3. 7. 10, 61. 4; 6. 51. 11, 64. 1, 4; 8. 5. 10, 22. 18; Y. 35. 2 *humatanąm hūxtanąm huvarštanąm*; 38. 3; Yt. 10. 76 *hvaspō ahi, hurāθyō*; in Old Persian, AmH 6 *huaspā humartiyā*; AsH 9 f. *hukāram huaspam*; DSp 3 *huraθaram huaspam humartiyam*; DPd 8 *huaspā humartiyā*; DSf 11 = DZc 4 *huaspam humartiyam*; DSs 5 *huaspā huraθācā*; *Od.* 15. 406 εὔβοτος εὔμηλος; *Táin* (I) 2710 *sogabáltaich sodaim*, 2952 *súaithinte sogabálta sodain*.

[114] *Audacht Morainn* 12 ff.; Watkins (1995), 261.

[115] Watkins (1995), 21 f. Cf. also the Tocharian example that he quotes on p. 66, 'the strong . . . the strong . . .', etc.

[116] Cf. 1. 118. 6; 3. 61. 4; 5. 76. 5; 8. 70. 9; 10. 15. 1, 127. 5, 141. 2.

[117] Cf. Gonda (1959), 266–70; Durante (1976), 151 f.

With *dus-: AV 4. 17. 5 = 7. 23. 1 *daúṣvapnyaṃ daúrjīvityam*; 9. 2. 3 *duṣváp-nyam ... duritám ca*; Y. 49. 11 *dušxšaθrə̄ṇg duššyaoθnə̄ṇg dužvacaŋhō duždaēnə̄ṇg dušmanaŋhō*; Aesch. *Ag.* 746 δύσεδρος καὶ δυσόμιλος.

With *n̥-: RV 1. 32. 7 *apā́d ahastó*, cf. 1. 116. 5; 7. 6. 3; 8. 70. 11; 10. 37. 7, 39. 5; AV Paipp. 11. 1. 8; *Il.* 9. 63 ἀφρήτωρ ἀθέμιστος ἀνέστιος; *Od.* 1. 242 ἄϊστος ἄπυστος, 4. 788 ἄσιτος ἄπαστος; Hes. *Th.* 489 ἀνίκητος καὶ ἀκηδής; *Sigrdrífumál* 19. 5–6 *óviltar oc óspiltar*. The paired epithets applied to Dawn in RV 1. 113. 13 *ajárāmŕ̥tā* (that is, *ajárā amŕ̥tā*), 'unageing, immortal', correspond in sense, and partly in etymology, to the Homeric ἀθάνατος καὶ ἀγήραος (*Il.* 2. 447 ἀγήραον ἀθανάτην τε).

With *pl̥hu-: RV 7. 73. 1 *purudáṃsā purutámā purājā́*, cf. 6. 34. 2; 8. 5. 4, 8. 12, 93. 17; Yt. 13. 65 *paoirīš pourusatå, paoirīš pouruhazaŋrå, paoirīš pouru-baēvanō*; *Il.* 5. 613 πολυκτήμων πολυλήϊος; 9. 154 πολύρρηνες πολυβοῦται, cf. *Hymn. Dem.* 31, Hes. fr. 70. 6; in Irish, *ilchrothach ilgnúisech ilbrechtach*, 'of many forms, many faces, many spells'.[118]

Other Vedic and Avestan examples include: RV 1. 47. 2 *trivandhuréṇa trivŕ̥tā* 'three-', cf. 118. 2; 10. 94. 7 *dáśāvanibhyo dáśakakṣiyebhiyo dáśayok-trebhyo dáśayojanebhiyaḥ dáśābhīśubhyaḥ* 'ten-'; 8. 22. 12 *viśvápsuṃ viśvávāriyam* 'all-'; 1. 113. 12 *r̥tapā́ r̥tejā́ḥ* 'right-', cf. 7. 66. 13; 2. 21. 3 *janabhakṣó janaṃsaháḥ* 'people-'; 8. 81. 2 *tuvikūrmíṃ tuvídeṣṇaṃ tuvī́magham tuvimātrám* 'strongly'; Y. 39. 3 *yavaējyō yavaēsvō* 'of eternal life, of eternal benefit', cf. 4. 4, Yt. 19. 11.

Juxtaposition of opposed terms

In the collocations surveyed above, the words juxtaposed are grammatically parallel and the ordering of syntactic elements in the sentence is not affected. In what follows we shall be dealing largely with juxtapositions of words that have different syntactic roles, especially of nouns or adjectives in different cases. In unmarked discourse they would not necessarily stand side by side. Their juxtaposition, which serves to emphasize the relationship between them, is a stylistic choice; it is part of what makes the thing into a figure.

In the most basic type, two opposed terms—often from the same root, but one with the negative prefix—are set together in different cases. Interaction between immortals and mortals is often so pointed up in the pagan literatures: RV 1. 90. 3 *amŕ̥tā mártiyebhiyaḥ*, '(you) immortals to (us) mortals', cf. 1. 138. 2; 4. 1. 1, 2. 1; 5. 18. 1; 6. 5. 5, 9. 4; 8. 48. 12; 10. 91. 11, 95. 9; 3. 9. 1

[118] Watkins (1995), 262 with references. The phoneme [p] was lost in Celtic, and *il-* is in fact the Irish cognate of *puru-*, *pouru-*, πολυ-.

devám mártāsaḥ, '(we have chosen you,) mortals a god', cf. 4. 2. 10, 5. 2, 11. 5; 5. 17. 1; *Il.* 2. 821 θεὰ βροτῶι εὐνηθεῖσα, 'goddess bedded with mortal'; 22. 9 θνητὸς ἐὼν θεὸν ἄμβροτον, '(why do you pursue me,) a mortal (pursuing) a god?'; Hes. *Th.* 942 ἀθάνατον θνητή; epitaph of Naevius, *immortales mortales si foret fas flere*, 'if it were proper for immortals to weep for mortals'. To the same category belong RV 1. 33. 5 *áyajvāno yájvabhiḥ* 'the impious (contending) with the pious'; Y. 49. 4 *fšuyasū afšuyaṇtō*, 'non-stockraisers among stockraisers'; Hes. *Op.* 490 ὀψαρότης πρωιηρότηι, 'the late-plougher (might rival) the early-plougher'.

This last example opposes two compounds, both probably coined *ad hoc*, with the same second element and contrasted fore-elements.[119] We may compare the two that appear in a disjunctive phrase at Y. 31. 12, *miθahvacå vā ərəšvacå vā*, 'one of false words or one of straight words'. Elsewhere (*Op.* 471 f.) Hesiod opposes εὐθημοσύνη to κακοθημοσύνη, and the poet of the *Odyssey* (22. 374) εὐεργίη to κακοεργίη. The phrase quoted above from Y. 49. 4 is continued by *yaēšąm nōiṯ huvarštāiš vąs dužvarštā*, 'through whose not (doing) good works the ill works prevail'.

Juxtaposition of like terms (polyptoton)

Common as such antithetical combinations are, they are less abundant than collocations of like terms. In the great majority of cases it is a noun or adjective that is juxtaposed with the same word in a different case (governed perhaps by a preposition). But there are also instances with verb forms, especially with an opposition of active and passive action, as in RV 8. 84. 9 *nákir yáṃ ghnánti, hánti yáḥ*, 'whom none slay, (but) who slays'; *Il.* 4. 451 ὀλλύντων τε καὶ ὀλλυμένων, 'killing and being killed' (cf. 11. 83); 18. 309 καί τε κτανέοντα κατέκτα, 'and he slays him who would slay'; Aesch. *Sept.* 961 παιθεὶς ἔπαισας·—σὺ δ' ἔθανες κατακτανών, 'stabbed, you stabbed.—And you were killed, that killed'; *Y Gododdin* 1128 *cyd ryladded wy, wy lladdasant*, 'before they were slain, they slew'; *Llawsgrif Henregadredd* 60a4 *ef wanei wanwyd*, 'he who would slay was slain'; *Togail Bruidne Dá Derga* 783 *génait 7 ní génaiter*, 'they will kill and not be killed'.[120]

With nouns and adjectives we may use the term polyptoton, which also covers the rarer instances where three or four cases of the same word are employed in a single sentence. Three principal uses of the figure may be

[119] For this type cf. Gonda (1959), 270–2.

[120] Cf. Gonda (1959), 246, and for further Irish and other material Watkins (1995), 258, 260, 262, 326–9.

distinguished: in elative expressions; to express accumulation or continuity; and to express the matching status or reciprocal relationship of the referents.

(a) Elative expressions. A superlative may be combined with a genitive plural of the same word: RV 2. 33. 3 *tavástamas tavásām* 'strongest of the strong', cf. 1. 5. 2, 11. 1; 2. 24. 3 *devā́nāṃ devátamāya*, 'most godly of the gods'; 3. 51. 4 *nṝṇā́m . . . nŕ̥tamam*, 'most manly of men', cf. 4. 25. 4; Yt. 10. 141 *aojištanąm asti aojištəm, taṇcištanąm asti taṇcištəm*, 'of the mightiest he is the mightiest, of the strongest he is the strongest'; Aesch. *Supp.* 524 μακάρων μακάρτατε καὶ τελέων τελειότατον κράτος, 'most blessed of blessed ones and most powerful of powers'; Soph. *OT* 334 ὦ κακῶν κάκιστε, 'most villainous of villains'; *Phil.* 65 ἔσχατ' ἐσχάτων κακά, 'utmost of utmost ills'; *CIL* i.² 9 *duonoro(m) optumo(m)*; Plaut. *Cas.* 793 *pessumarum pessuma, Men.* 817 *miserorum miserrimus*; Martial 1. 100. 2 *mammarum maxima mamma*; Lithuanian *gerių̃ geriáusiasis*, 'best of the good'.

A comparative may be used with an ablative of the same word: RV 6. 47. 29 *dūrā́d dávīyaḥ*, 'further than far'; 1. 114. 6 *svādóḥ svā́dīyaḥ*, 'sweeter than sweet'; 10. 176. 4 *sáhasaś cid sáhīyān*, 'stronger even than the strong'; Y. 43. 3 *vaŋhə̄uš vahyō*, 'better than the good'; 51. 6 *vaŋhə̄uš vahyō . . . akāṯ aśyō*, 'better than the good . . . worse than the bad'; Sappho 156 χρύσω χρυσοτέρα, 'golder than gold'; Aesch. fr. 391 σοφοῦ σοφώτερος, 'cleverer than clever'(?); Soph. *OT* 1301 μείζονα (μάσσονα Blaydes) . . . τῶν μακίστων, 'further than the furthest'; Plaut. *Asin.* 614 *melle dulci dulcior*, 'sweeter than sweet honey', cf. *Truc.* 371; *Amph.* 907 *stultior stultissumo*, 'a bigger fool than the biggest'; English 'whiter than white'.[121]

An elative phrase is occasionally formed from a simple adjective or noun with its own genitive plural: RV 10. 128. 7 *dhātā́ dhātṝṇā́m*, 'the creator of creators'; *Taittirīya Brāhmaṇa* 2. 6. 8. 3 *devānāṃ devam*, 'the god of gods' (of Indra); Aesch. *Pers.* 681 ὦ πιστὰ πιστῶν '(most) trusty among the trusty'; Soph. *OT* 465 ἄρρητ' ἀρρήτων; *OC* 1238 κακὰ κακῶν; in the Carmen Saliare, *diuom deo supplicate* 'pray to the god of gods'; Plaut. *Truc.* 25 *summa summarum, Curc.* 388 *reliquiarum reliquias*; Petr. *Sat.* 37. 8 *nummorum nummos*; Florus 1. 22 *urbem urbium*, 2. 26 *barbari barbarorum*; *Hyndlulióð* 1. 1 *mær meyia . . . rǫcr rǫcra*, 'maid of maids . . . darkness of darknesses'.[122]

(b) Expressions of accumulation or continuity: *CHLI* i. 49 Karatepe 1. 41 ff., 'and I made horse upon horse, and I made army upon army, and

[121] Cf. Gonda (1959), 261 f.

[122] Cf. Hofmann (1930), 49–61 (with abundant Norse and Baltic material); Gonda (1959), 263–5; Brigitte Gygli-Wyss, *Das nominale Polyptoton im älteren Griechisch* (Göttingen 1966), 30. Aeschylus' ἄναξ ἀνάκτων (*Supp.* 524) imitates Near Eastern divine titles, see West (1997), 557 f.

I made shield upon shield'; RV 1. 53. 7 *yudhā́ yúdham . . . purā́ púram*, 'fight after fight . . . citadel after citadel'; 2. 24. 15 *vīréṣu vīrā́m̐ úpa*, 'sons upon sons'; *Il.* 14. 130 ἐφ' ἕλκεϊ ἕλκος, 'wound upon wound'; 19. 290 δέχεται κακὸν ἐκ κακοῦ, 'trouble succeeds trouble'; Hes. *Op.* 361 σμικρὸν ἐπὶ σμικρῶι, 'a little upon a little', 644 ἐπὶ κέρδεϊ κέρδος, 'profit upon profit'; in Umbrian, Iguv. VIa. 20 *pir pureto*, 'fire from fire'; IV. 16 *asa asam-a*, 'from altar to altar'; *Y Gododdin* 246 *ar beithing beithing*, 'destruction upon destruction'; 645 *a lychwr y lychwr*, 'from light to light', i.e. from dusk to dawn; poem in *Fled Bricrenn* 48 (cf. 52) 'battle on battle, exploit upon exploit, head upon head he heaps'; poem in *Acallam na Senórach* 3368, 3375 Stokes *glind do glind . . . a hor and-or*, 'from glen to glen . . . from border to border'; *Beow.* 931 *wunder æfter wundre*; *Hávamál* 141. 4–7 *orð mér af orði orðz leitaði, verc mér af verki vercs leitaði*, 'word found me word from word, deed found me deed from deed'; Salih Ugljanin, *The Song of Baghdad* (*SCHS* ii, no. 1) 975 *zub po zubu*, 'tooth upon tooth'; Đemail Zogić, *Alija Rescues the Children of Alibey* (*SCHS* ii, no. 24) 754 *dan po danu, konak po konaku*, 'day followed day, night's rest followed night's rest'; Sulejman Makić, *The Battle of Temišvar* (*SCHS* ii, no. 27) 290 *dan po danu, zeman od zemana*, 'day followed day, week followed week'.

(c) Expressing matching status or reciprocal relationship.[123] Here are some of the commonest categories:

God to god, a god among gods, etc.: RV 1. 1. 5 *devó devébhiḥ*, cf. 1. 13. 11, 31. 1, 9, 136. 4, 160. 1, 169. 8, and often; 1. 123. 10 *éṣi devi devám*, 'you go, goddess, to god', cf. Hes. *Th.* 380 θεὰ θεῶι εὐνηθεῖσα, 'goddess bedded with god'; 405 θεὰ θεοῦ ἐν φιλότητι; *Od.* 5. 97 θεὰ θεόν; Campanile (1988), 25 no. 1. 8 *deeib dia*, 'a god among gods'.

Mortal to mortal, man to man, etc.: RV 1. 147. 5 *márto mártam*; [Hes.] *Scut.* 6 θνηταὶ θνητοῖς; *Il.* 15. 328, 16. 306 ἀνὴρ ἕλεν ἄνδρα; *Hávamál* 47. 6 *maðr er mannz gaman*, 'man is a man's pleasure'.

Men of a particular trade or condition: RV 6. 32. 3 *kavíbhiḥ kavíḥ sán*, 'with the seers himself a seer'; *Od.* 10. 82 ποιμένα ποιμήν, 'shepherd to shepherd'; *Il.* 23. 318 ἡνίοχος περιγίνεται ἡνιόχοιο; Hes. *Op.* 23 γείτονα γείτων, 25 f. κεραμεὺς κεραμεῖ, τέκτονι τέκτων, πτωχὸς πτωχῶι, ἀοιδὸς ἀοιδῶι.

Brother to brother: *MBh.* 6. 44. 2 *bhrātā bhrātaram*; Aesch. *Sept.* 674 κασιγνήτωι κάσις; *Vǫlundarkviða* 23. 3 *bróðir á bróður*; *Igor* 77 *rekosta bo bratŭ bratu*, 'brother spoke to brother'; *SCHS* ii, no. 24. 1299 *da brat brata poznat' ne mogaše*, 'brother could not recognize brother'. Cf. *Beowulf* 1978 *mǣð wið mǣge*, 'kinsman beside kinsman'.

[123] Cf. Gonda (1959), 285–91.

Friend to friend:[124] RV 1. 26. 3 *sákhā sákhye*, cf. 1. 53. 2, 75. 4; 3. 4. 1, etc.; Y. 62. 8 *haxa hašē*, cf. Vd. 18. 26; Hes. *Op.* 183 ἑταῖρος ἑταίρωι; Pind. *Nem.* 4. 22 φίλοισι γὰρ φίλος ἐλθών; Aesch. *Cho.* 89 παρὰ φίλης φίλωι, cf. *Eum.* 999, etc.; *Hávamál* 42. 1–3 *vin sínom scal maðr vinr vera, oc gialda giǫf við giǫf*, 'a man shall be friend to his friend and repay gift with gift'.

All with all: RV 4. 1. 18 *víśve víśvāsu dúriyāsu devā́ḥ*, 'all the gods in all houses'; Heraclitus B 41 πάντα διὰ πάντων, 'all things through all things'; Oscan inscr. no. 40. 12 Buck *eisunk uhftis sullum sullas* 'all the wishes of all of them'.

Willing with the willing: RV 10. 15. 8 *uśánn uśádbhiḥ*; *Od.* 3. 272 ἐθέλων ἐθέλουσαν, cf. 5. 155; Aesch. *Supp.* 144 θέλουσα δ' αὖ θέλουσαν; [Aesch.] *Prom.* 218 ἑκὼν ἑκόντι. ἑκών is cognate with the Vedic word.

One to another: RV 7. 103. 3 *anyó anyám*, cf. 2. 18. 2; 3. 33. 2; 10. 97. 14; Y. 53. 5 *anyō ainīm*; Greek ἄλλος ἄλλου, Latin *alius aliud*, etc.

Miscellaneous (selection): RV 1. 102. 1 *mahó mahī́m*, 'of the great (god) a great one (song)', cf. 2. 33. 8, 15. 1, etc., beside *Il.* 16. 776, 18. 26 μέγας μεγαλωστί; RV 1. 173. 2 *vṛ́ṣā vṛ́ṣabhiḥ*, 'the bull with the bulls'; 5. 68. 4 *ṛtám ṛténa*, 'truth with the truth'; Y. 53. 4 *aṣ̌āunī aṣ̌avabyō*, 'as a truthful woman the truthful'; 43. 5 *akəm akāi, vaŋvhīm aṣ̌īm vaŋhaovē*, 'evil for the evil one, a good reward for the good'; Faliscan vase inscription, no. 152 Pisani (sixth century) *Titias duenom duenas*, 'nice thing of nice Titia'; *Hávamál* 31. 3 *gestr at gest*, 'guest at guest', cf. 32. 6; *Helgakviða Hundingsbana A* 5. 5 *hrafn kvað at hrafni*, 'quoth raven to raven'; *Vafþrúðnismál* 33. 4 *fótr við fóti*, 'foot with foot'; *Heiðreks gátur* 18 (*Edd. min.* 113, *Hervarar saga* 10) *elr við kván kona, mær við meyiu mǫg of getr*, 'woman begets with woman, girl with girl bears a son'; ibid. 24 *á sat nár á nái, blindr reið blindum*, 'a corpse sat on a corpse, the blind rode the blind'.

The figure is much favoured for the decription of close order or confrontation in battle: Tyrt. 19. 15 ἀσπίδας εὐκύκλους ἀσπίσι τυπτ[, 'round shields against shields'; *Hildebrandslied* 38 *ort widar orte*, 'spear-point against spear-point'; *Beowulf* 440 *lāð wið lāðum*, 'foe against foe'; *Maxims B* 53 f. *fyrd wið fyrde . . . lāð wið lāðe*, 'army against army, foe against foe'; *Elene* 1181 *wrāð wið wrāðum*, 'enemy against enemy'; *Edd. min.* 87. 2. 1 *bǫrðumk einn við einn*, 'we fought one to one', cf. *Hervarar saga* 3; *Vǫlundarkviða* 27. 3 *brast rǫnd við rǫnd*, 'shield smashed against shield'.

In this context of urgent action on the battlefield there is a tendency, common to the Indian epics, Greek and Latin, Old Irish, and Serbo-Croatian heroic poetry, to pile up a series of polyptota. In two passages of the *Iliad* this compound figure is used of a battle line in close order: 13. 130 f. φράξαντες

[124] Cf. Schlerath (1968), ii. 160.

δόρυ δουρί, σάκος σάκεϊ προθελύμνωι 'covering spear with spear, shield with layered shield'; 16. 215 ἀσπὶς ἄρ' ἀσπὶς ἔρειδε, κόρυς κόρυν, ἀνέρα δ' ἀνήρ, 'shield pressed shield, helmet helmet, and man man'. Tyrtaeus employs similar language where the two front lines are clashing (11. 31–3):

> *καὶ πόδα πὰρ ποδὶ θεὶς καὶ ἐπ' ἀσπίδος ἀσπίδ' ἐρείσας,*
> *ἐν δὲ λόφον τε λόφωι καὶ κυνέην κυνέηι*
> *καὶ στέρνον στέρνωι πεπλημένος.*
>
> And planting foot by foot, and pressing shield on shield,
> bringing crest close to crest and helm to helm
> and breast to breast.

The Iliadic example at 11. 150,

> *πεζοὶ μὲν πεζοὺς ὄλεκον φεύγοντας ἀνάγκηι,*
> *ἱππῆς δ' ἱππῆας,*
> foot-soldiers were destroying foot-soldiers as they fled,
> and chariot-fighters chariot-fighters,

has many striking parallels in the *Mahābhārata*, for example at 4. 31. 8,

> rathā rathaiḥ samājanmuḥ pādātaiś ca padātayaḥ,
> sādibhiḥ sādinaś caiva gajaiś cāpi mahāgajāḥ,
>
> chariots engaged chariots, foot soldiers other foot soldiers,
> riders attacked riders, elephants elephants.[125]

In Latin epic there are several examples, beginning with Ennius, *Ann.* 584 *premitur pede pes atque armis arma teruntur,* who is no doubt following Greek models rather than a native Italic tradition.[126] It is less certain that Classical influence must be invoked to account for Irish instances such as

> I mbíat fáebra fri fáebra | ocus findne fri findne.
>
> When edges shall be against edges | and shields against shields.
>
> Wrist to wrist and palm to palm, tunic to tunic they stand,
> shield to shield and frame to frame [*etc.*][127]

[125] See also 6. 43. 79, 111. 41; 7. 19. 37, 31. 73, 72. 19, 139. 6; 8. 8. 9, 16. 32, 33. 56, 36. 5; 9. 8. 10, 22. 58; 10. 8. 92; *Rm.* 5. 44. 37. Battles involving chariots were a development of the early second millennium, so this component in the parallel must be due either to independent evolution from a common original pattern or to Mycenaean contact with Indo-Iranian poetry (a possibility I have adverted to elsewhere).

[126] See Otto Skutsch, *The* Annals *of Q. Ennius* (Oxford 1985), 724–6.

[127] *Cath Cairnn Conaill* ed. W. Stokes, *ZCP* 3 (1901), 208; poem in *Fled Bricrenn* 53. Cf also *Táin* (I) 2308 *dobert fóbairt bidbad fo bidbadaib forro co torchratár bond fri bond ⁊ méde fri méde*, 'he made upon them the attack of a foe upon his foes so that they fell, sole of foot to sole of foot, and headless neck to headless neck'.

Nor does it come into question for the verse employed more than once by the *guslar* Salih Ugljanin:

> konj do konja, junak do junaka.
> horse by horse and hero by hero.[128]

The priamel

The 'priamel' (*praeambulum*) is a figure familiar to classicists from archaic elegy and lyric, whereby a series of parallel statements serves to throw the last into relief.[129] Solon fr. 9 may serve as an illustration: 'From the cloud comes the fury of snow and hail, | from the bright lightning comes thunder, | and from big men a city is destroyed.' When Achilles says to Hector 'As there are no treaties between lions and men, nor do wolves and lambs maintain concord, . . . so there is no friendship for me and you' (*Il.* 22. 262–5), it is from the formal point of view a simile, but otherwise it much resembles a priamel.

Occasional Indic examples can be found. Watkins has adduced RV 8. 3. 24, 'The soul is food, the body clothing, | unguent gives strength; | as the fourth I have named Pākasthāman, | generous giver of the bay.'[130] The poet's patron, Pākasthāman, has given him a horse, and the priamel serves to praise him by setting him in parallel with those things that give food, clothing, and strength.

Another Vedic passage seems an astonishing pre-echo of Pindar's most famous priamel. RV 1. 161. 9:

> ā́po bhū́yiṣṭhā, íti éko abravīd;
> agnír bhū́yiṣṭa, íti anyó abravīt;
> vadharyántīm bahúbhyaḥ praíko abravīd;
> ṛtā́ vádantaś camasā́m apiṃśata.
>
> 'The waters are best', said one;
> 'fire is best', said another;
> one commended the thunderbolt(?) to many;
> (but) speaking the truth, you (Ṛbhus) carved the (gods') chalice.

This is how Pindar exalts the Olympic Games:

[128] *SCHS* ii, no. 1. 805; no. 18. 1070.

[129] W. Kröhling, *Die Priamel (Beispielreihung) als Stilmittel in der griechisch-römischen Dichtung* (Diss. Greifswald 1935); Franz Dornseiff, *Antike und alter Orient* (Leipzig 1956), 379–93. In West (1997), 509 f., 526, I have noted some Hebrew examples.

[130] Watkins (1995), 115; his translation.

The best thing is water; gold shines like a blazing fire
in the night above all proud wealth;
but if you yearn to sing of games, my heart . . .[131]

The *Rāmāyaṇa* provides a couple of fine examples: 2. 34. 25, 'Without strings a lute cannot be played, without wheels a chariot cannot move, and without her husband a woman finds no happiness, though she have a hundred sons'; 2. 98. 6, 'An ass cannot match the pace of a horse, birds cannot match Tārkṣya's pace, nor have I the power to match yours, lord of the land.'

From Old Norse and Old English we may adduce *Hávamál* 53 *lítil lá sanda, lítil lá sæva, lítil ero geð guma*, 'narrow the sands' edge, narrow the seas' edge, narrow are the minds of men'; *Maxims B* 16–20, 'The hawk belongs on the glove . . . ; the wolf belongs in the forest . . . ; the boar belongs in the wood . . . ; a good man belongs in his native land, forging his reputation'; 21–8, 'The javelin belongs in the hand . . . ; the gem belongs on the ring . . . ; the stream belongs among the waves . . . ; [four more items, then] the king belongs in his hall, sharing out rings' (trs. S. A. J. Bradley).

This evidence is perhaps rather too scant and scattered to allow us at present to claim the priamel as an Indo-European figure. But future observation may augment it.

Behaghel's Law; the Augmented Triad

The priamel is an end-weighted structure, the final component forming a climax. To this extent, at least, it fits a pattern widely attested for Indo-European. The principle underlies what is known as Behaghel's Law, or the 'Gesetz der wachsenden Glieder'. This is the rule that shorter phrases tend to be placed before longer ones, both in prose and in verse, so that the sentence gains rather than loses weight as it develops.[132]

A special case of Behaghel's Law that is distinct and easily recognizable is what I call the Augmented Triad. It consists of the construction of a verse from three names (or occasionally other substantives), of which the third is furnished with an epithet or other qualification. I have devoted a paper to this topic and collected there numerous examples from the Vedas, the Indian epics, the Avesta, Hesiod and Homer, and the Germanic and Celtic literatures (West 2004). A few will suffice here by way of illustration. I can now add one from Hittite and a couple from Latvian.

[131] Pind. *Ol.* 1. 1 f., cf. 3. 42–4; Bacchyl. 3. 85–92. For the Vedic comparison see Wüst (1969), 70–108.

[132] O. Behaghel, *IF* 25 (1909), 110–42; cf. Hermann Hirt, *Indogermanische Grammatik* (Heidelberg 1927–37), i. 126, vii. 232 f.; Gonda (1959), 61–4, 69–71, 142–4; Schmitt (1967), 272–4.

If he has seen something with his eyes,
or taken something with his hand,
or trodden something with his powerful foot. (*CTH* 760 V iv 1 ff.)[133]

Diyaúr, Vánā, Giráyo vṛkṣákeśāḥ.

The Sky, the Forests, the Mountains tree-tressed. (RV 5. 41. 11)

Tváṣṭā, Savitā́, suyámā Sárasvatī

Tvaṣṭṛ, Savitṛ, easy-guided Sarasvatī. (RV 9. 81. 4)

Daityānāṃ Dānavānaṃ ca Yakṣāṇāṃ ca mahaujasām.

Daityāna and Dānavāna and Yakṣāṇā of great might. (*MBh.* 1. 2. 76)

Βῆσσάν τε Σκάρφην τε καὶ Αὐγείας ἐρατεινάς.

Bessa and Skarphe and lovely Augeae. (*Il.* 2. 532)

Heorogār ond Hrōðgar ond Hālga til.

Heorogar, Hrothgar, and Halga the good. (*Beowulf* 61)

Vara sandr né sær né svalar unnir.

There was not sand nor sea nor the cool waves. (*Vǫluspá* 3)

Nōe, Ladru Lergnaid, luath Cuar.

Nóe, Ladru Lergnaid, the swift Cuar. (Campanile (1988), 29 no. 6. 3)

Simtiem dzina govis, vēršus, | simtiem bērus kumeliņus.

Par centaines elle menait les vaches, les taureaux,
par centaines les bruns chevaux. (*LD* 33957; Jonval (1929), no. 144)

Līgo bite, līgo saule, | līgo mana līgaviņa.

Sing, bee, sing, sun, | sing, O my bride. (*LD* 53542)

In the Indian, Greek, Germanic, and Celtic traditions we often find such triadic lines within longer catalogues of names. Catalogues are typical of heroic poetry, as they are of genealogical and other antiquarian verse. They may have been a feature of Indo-European heroic poetry, and the augmented triad a traditional device in them.

But triads also appear where there is no longer list but just a trio of names. Sometimes it is explicitly noted that the last name is the third: *Il.* 14. 117 'Agrios and Melas, and horseman Oineus was the third', cf. 15. 188; Campanile (1988), 33 no. 17. 3 f. 'from a branch of Galian's line (came) Find fer Umaill (i.e. Find and his father Umall); an active hero was Trénmór as third';[134] *Grípisspá* 37. 3–4 'Gunnarr and Hǫgni and you, prince, as third'.

[133] Quoted by Watkins (1995), 251.

[134] So emended by Campanile, 57.

Sometimes the trio of names is preceded by the announcement that they are three. There is one especially common type, where three sons are recorded as sprung from one father, for example:

> *Τρωὸς δ' αὖ τρεῖς παῖδες ἀμύμονες ἐξεγένοντο,*
> *Ἶλός τ' Ἀσσάρακός τε καὶ ἀντίθεος Γανυμήδης.*
>
> From Tros three fine sons were born:
> Ilos and Assarakos and godlike Ganymedes. (*Il.* 20. 231 f.)
>
> trayas tv Aṅgirasaḥ putrā loke sarvatra viśrutāḥ:
> Bṛhaspatir Utathyaś ca Saṃvartaś ca dhṛtavratāḥ.
>
> But of Angiras, three sons renowned everywhere in the world:
> Bṛhaspati and Utathya and Samvarta the resolute. (*MBh.* 1. 60. 5)
>
> Tri meib Giluaethwy ennwir,
> tri chenryssedat kywir:
> Bleidwn, Hydwn, Hychdwn hir.
>
> The three sons of false Gilfaethwy,
> three champions true:
> Bleiddwn, Hyddwn, Hychdwn the tall. (*Math vab Mathonwy* 281–3 Ford)
>
> trī meic Nōe nair cech neirt:
> Sem, Cam, Iafet aurdairc.
>
> Three sons of Noah, of every (kind of) strength:
> Shem, Ham, Japheth the glorious. (*Lebor Gabála Érenn* 189 f.)

In these and in many other cases we have a more or less identical pattern: the words 'three sons', with the father's name in the genitive, with or without a verb such as 'were born'; a general qualification of the sons as 'fine', 'renowned', etc.; and then their individual names in an Augmented Triad.[135]

It is hard to avoid the inference that this was a traditional formula from the common poetic inheritance. Here we seem to find a remnant of the Indo-European storyteller's building work: a recognizable structural component, with the lineaments of its verbal patterning still in place.

[135] To the examples quoted in my 2004 paper, 46 f., may be added a further Irish one from *The Fort of Árd Ruide* (E. Gwynn, *The Metrical Dindshenchas*, iv (Dublin 1924), 368–71), 'Three sons did Lugaid leave; | whither are gone their riches?— | Ruide, son of broad-built Lugaid, | Eochaid and manly Fiachu'.

3

Gods and Goddesses

The Indo-Europeans, it is clear, spoke both about 'the gods' collectively and about gods as individuals. They perhaps had their different words for different categories of supernatural being. But the most important term, one that has left representatives in nearly all branches of the Indo-European family, was based on the root **diw/dyu*, which denoted the bright sky or the light of day. In MIE it took the form **deiwós*, plural **deiwṓs*. From this come Vedic *devá-*, Avestan *daēva-*, Old Phrygian *devos* (Neo-Phrygian dative-locative plural δεως), Oscan *deívā-*, Messapic *deiva*, *dīva* 'goddess', Venetic *deivos* 'gods', Latin *deus*, proto-Germanic **tīwaz*,[1] Old Irish *día*, Old Church Slavonic *divŭ* 'demon', Old Prussian *deiws/deywis*, Lithuanian *Diẽvas*, Latvian *Dievs*. A derivative *deiwios* seems to be attested in Mycenaean *de-wi-jo*, *de-u-jo-i*.[2] In Anatolian we find forms derived from **dyeus*: Hittite *siūs*, *siūn-* 'god', a declension built on the old accusative **siūn*; similarly, with thematic stem, Palaic *tiuna-* 'divine'.[3]

The gods, then, or at any rate those designated by this word, were literally 'the celestials'; they belonged in the sky. Although Greek had long abandoned **deiwṓs* in favour of a different word, the concept of the heavenly location survived: the Homeric gods are portrayed as dwelling in heaven, and they are designated in formulaic phrases as 'the heavenly ones' (*οὐρανίωνες*) or as 'the gods who occupy the broad heaven' (*τοὶ οὐρανὸν εὐρὺν ἔχουσιν*).

Certain other terms for 'god' current in particular areas can be explained on the basis of Indo-European cognates. A proto-Germanic word **guða-* is represented in Gothic *guþ*, Old Norse *goð*, Old High German *got*, English 'god'. This has the peculiarity of being neuter, perhaps, as Schulze argued,

[1] The plural *tívar* survives in Norse as a poetic word for 'the gods', and the singular *týr* occurs in kennings for Odin and Thor. Otherwise in Germanic the singular appears as the name of a different deity: Norse *Týr*, West Germanic **Tīwaz*, whose name was chosen in translating *Martis dies* 'Tuesday'. See de Vries (1956), ii. 4 f., 11, 25 f.

[2] M. S. Ruipérez and E. Risch in A. Heubeck–G. Neumann (edd.), *Res Mycenaeae* (Akten des VII. Internationalen Mykenologischen Colloquiums, 1983), 411 f.

[3] Cf. Melchert (1994), 150, 209. For **dyeus* (> Greek *Ζεύς*, etc.) see Chapter 4.

because it originated as a plural collective term for 'gods and goddesses'; in Germanic the neuter was used for groups including both males and females.[4] The word is evidently a participial formation, **g^hu-to-*, the underlying verb corresponding to Vedic *hu* 'pour out, make libation'; the chief priest in the Vedic ritual was called the *hótar*. The **guðō*, then, were 'those worshipped (with libations etc.)'.[5]

Another Germanic term is more difficult to relate to extra-Germanic roots. The standard word for the pagan deities in Norse literature is *áss*, plural *æsir*. It corresponds to Old English *ōs* and to the title *anseis* (= *semidei*) with which the Goths, according to Jordanes (*Getica* 78), exalted their victorious kings. A proto-Germanic form **ansuz* has usually been reconstructed, and connected on the one hand with Hittite *ḫassu-* 'king' and on the other with Vedic *ásura-*, Avestan *ahura-*, a title applied to divinities. However, recent work has cast doubt on this construction.[6]

In Iranian and Slavonic we find a different word again: Old Persian *baga-*, Younger Avestan *baγa-*; Old Church Slavonic *bogŭ*, Russian бог, Polish *bóg*, Czech *bůh*, etc. In Vedic India Bhaga is the name of an individual god, listed together with Mitra, Varuna, Aryaman, and others as one of the Ādityas, the sons of Aditi. There is no mystery here: *bhaj* means 'dispense', and *bhága-* is the fortune dispensed by the gods, or the divine dispenser, like Greek δαίμων.

Finally, Greek θεός, a word already attested in the Mycenaean tablets. Compounds such as θέσ-φατος 'god-spoken', which must have been created even earlier, before the loss of intervocalic [s], show that it goes back to **d^hes-ós*. It has a cognate in Armenian *dikʿ* (< **d^hēses*) 'gods', and perhaps in the *desa-*, *disa-*, *diza-* that appears as an element in some Thracian personal names.[7] The same root can be traced in certain Italic words with a religious connotation: Oscan *fíísnú* 'temple', Latin *fānum* (< **fas-nom*); Latin *fēriae* (< **fēs-yā*), *fēstus diēs* 'holy day'.

It is not probable that the Indo-Europeans had a fixed canon of deities or assigned a specific number to them. The Hittites spoke of a thousand, the

[4] Schulze (1966), 853 f.

[5] Cf. Meid (1991), 17 f.; *EIEC* 231; M. E. Huld, *SIGL* 2 (1999), 135 f.; differently C. Watkins in Mayrhofer et al. (1974), 102 n. 5. The same root probably appears in *gutuater*, a type of Gaulish priest (*CIL* xiii. 1577, 2585, al.); *-ater* is Celtic for *pater*, so 'father of the sacrifice' or something of the kind.

[6] M. E. Huld, *SIGL* 2 (1999), 136–9, argues that the proto-Germanic form was **ansa-*, an *o*-stem with a heteroclite *i*-stem plural; he relates this to the root **$h_2en(h_1)$* 'breathe'. J. Puhvel, *Hittite Etymological Dictionary*, iii (Berlin–New York 1991), 245 f., shows that *ḫassu-* was 'the (true)born one' and not cognate with the other words. P. Moisson, *Études Indo-Européennes* 11 (1992), 113–41, persuasively explains *ásura-* as a derivative of *ásu-*, the vital spirit that animates the living and exists independently after death. Cf. also Watkins (1995), 8.

[7] I. Duridanov in Meid (1998), 562.

Vedic poets of thirty-three, or in one passage 3,339. Boards of twelve make sporadic appearances in various cultures, but they look like products of secondary systematization, not continuations of any ancestral tradition.[8] What is more likely to be ancient, at least Graeco-Aryan, is the practice of invoking 'all the gods', without there being a definite notion of all their individual identities. Some forty Vedic hymns are addressed to 'all the gods', *víśve devā́ḥ*, and this phrase occurs frequently in the text. Zarathushtra (Y. 32. 3) uses the etymologically corresponding phrase *daēvā vīspåŋhō*, though in a less ingratiating way: for him the Daevas are demons unworthy of worship, and he is telling them that they are all born of Evil Thought. In Homer, again, 'all the gods' or 'all the immortals' is a common formula. Dedications to 'all the gods' are documented from Mycenaean times on, and they are often cited as witnesses to oaths and treaties.[9]

Sometimes, instead of '(all) the gods', one major deity is picked out and the rest are attached as a collectivity, so that we get the formula 'X and the other gods'. Zarathushtra twice uses the expression *Mazdåscā ahuråŋhō*, 'Mazdā and Lords', that is, all the others (Y. 30. 9, 31. 4). In the Younger Avestan hymn to Mithra we find a similar coupling, with Mithra appended in addition: Yt. 10. 139 'neither Ahura Mazdā nor the other Bounteous Immortals nor Mithra of the broad pastures'. Darius in the great Behistun inscription declares (DB iv. 60) *Auramazdā-maiy upastām abara utā aniyāha bagāha tyaiy hatiy*, 'Ahuramazda brought me aid, and the other gods that exist'. The early Greek poets often refer to 'Zeus and the other immortals'.[10] In Livy (24. 38. 8) we find an invocation in the form *uos, Ceres mater ac Proserpina, precor, ceteri superi infernique di.*

Upper and lower gods

The **deiwṓs*, as we have seen, were originally and by etymology the celestial ones. When the gods are spoken of in a general way, they tend to be located in

[8] The Hittites recognized 'twelve gods of the crossroads': Gurney (1977), 23, 41. Hesiod lists twelve Titans, and 'the Twelve (Olympian) Gods' had a cult at Olympia and other places (O. Weinreich in Roscher, vi. 764–848; D. Wachsmuth in *Der Kleine Pauly*, v. 1567–9), but they were never central to Greek religious thought. They have their counterparts in the twelve Di Consentes at Rome. Snorri (*Gylf.* 14, 20, 55) speaks of twelve ruler gods under Odin; cf. Gering–Sijmons (1927–31), i. 390 f.; A. Faulkes, *Snorri Sturluson*, Edda: *Prologue and* Gylfaginning (Oxford 1982), 62 f.; Lorenz (1984), 213. Jocelin of Furness in his Life of St. Patrick (6. 50 p. 552D) gives a similar picture of the great oracular god Keancroithi, *caput omnium deorum*, encircled by twelve *deiculi aerei* (Zwicker (1934–6), 161 f., cf. 213).

[9] KN Fp 1 + 31. 7 et al. *pa-si-te-oi* (= πάνσι θεοῖhι); Usener (1896), 344 f.; Durante (1976), 91. Sometimes, as mentioned in the last chapter, it is expanded to 'all gods and all goddesses'.

[10] Hes. *Th.* 624, *Op.* 725, fr. 75. 19 f.; *Il.* 2. 49, 3. 298, 308, etc.

heaven. Indra is said to be *prathamé víyomani, devā́nām sádane*, 'in the foremost heaven, the seat of the gods' (RV 8. 13. 2). Only the gods' lowest seats (*sádāṃsi*, plural of *sádas-*) are said to be visible to us.[11] The same expression, 'seat of the gods', *θεῶν* or *ἀθανάτων ἕδος*, is used in Hesiod of the heaven (*οὐρανός*) and in Homer of Olympus.[12] *ἕδος* and *sádas-* are the same word, while *sádanam* and *sádman-* show the same root with different suffixes. It appears also in Irish *síd*, literally 'seat', the term used for the hills or mounds within which the old pagan gods were imagined to be dwelling.

Heaven, however, could not be thought of as the home of all the supernatural powers whose activity impinges on our awareness. Some belong on the earth, or under it. If one makes a distinction between the pure heaven above the clouds and the lower air, there are clearly powers whose sphere of operation is the latter. So it is not surprising if a division is made between upper and lower gods.

In Hittite treaties the lengthy lists of divine witnesses often conclude with 'the gods of heaven and the gods of the earth'.[13] The same dichotomy can be found in Greek, for example in Aeschylus, *Supp.* 24 *ὕπατοί τε θεοὶ καὶ βαρύτιμοι χθόνιοι θήκας κατέχοντες*, 'both highest gods and chthonian ones of heavy office who occupy tombs'; *Ag.* 90 *ὑπάτων, χθονίων*; Euripides, *Hec.* 146 *θεοὺς τούς τ' Οὐρανίδας* (v.l. *οὐρανίους*) *τούς θ' ὑπὸ γαίας*, 'both the heavenly gods and those below the earth'. Likewise in Latin, Livius Andronicus refictus fr. 3 Courtney (rendering *Od.* 10. 64 *τίς τοι κακὸς ἔχραε δαίμων*) *inferus an superus tibi fert deus funera, Vlixes?*, Pacuvius Trag. 212 *quis deos infernos quibus caelestis dignet decorare hostiis?; CIL* i.² 2525 *di superi et inferi*; Livy 24. 38. 8 as quoted above; and by implication in the Oscan inscription no. 19. 7 Buck, *nip huntruis nip supruis aisusis* 'nec inferis nec superis sacrificiis' (where *hun-* is related to Greek *χθον-*). In the first line of the Gaulish *defixio* from Chamalières, *andedíon . . . diíiuion risunartiu* appears to mean 'by the virtue of the Lower Gods'; these gods are referred to again in line 3 *anderon* 'inferorum', *ander-* being etymologically identical with Latin *infer-* (< **n̥dʰer-*).

The Indians made a threefold division. The most exact statement in the Rigveda is at 1. 139. 11, where the gods addressed are said to be eleven in heaven (*diví*), eleven on the earth (*pr̥thiviyā́m ádhi*), and eleven dwelling in the waters (*apsukṣítaḥ*). Several other hymns mention the tally of thirty-three

[11] RV 3. 54. 5. For the divine seat cf. also 9. 83. 5 *máhi sádma daíviyam*; 10. 96. 2 *diviyáṃ . . . sádaḥ*.

[12] Hes. *Th.* 128; *Il.* 5. 360, 367, 868, cf. 24. 144; *Od.* 6. 42; *Hymn. Ap.* 109, cf. *Hymn. Dem.* 341, Hymn. Hom. 15. 7; Pind. *Nem.* 6. 3 f.

[13] Beckman (1999), 14, 29, 47, 53.

gods (3. 6. 9; 8. 28. 1, 35. 3) or the three cohorts (6. 51. 2, 52. 15; 7. 35. 11; 10. 49. 2, 63. 2, 65. 9). In the Atharvaveda the three groups have their 'seats' in heaven, in the lower air (*antárikṣam*, literally the in-between domicile), and on the earth:

> yé devā́ diviṣádo, | antarikṣasádaśca yé, | yé cemé bhū́miyām ádhi.
>
> The gods who are heaven-seated,
> and those who are interzone-seated,
> and these who are on the earth.

(10. 9. 12, cf. 11. 6. 12.) The same classification is given by the early Vedic commentator Yāska (*Nirukta* 7. 5) and in TS 2. 4. 8. 2. The gods of the *antárikṣam* are alternatively described as *madhyamasthāna-*, of the middle station. We might be tempted to compare Plautus, *Cistellaria* 512, where Alcesimarchus exclaims *at ita me di deaeque, superi atque inferi et medioxumi*, except that this has all the appearance of a comic invention. In the solemn prayer reported by Livy 1. 32. 10 we find a threefold division that does not correspond to the Indian: *audi Iuppiter et tu Iane Quirine diique omnes caelestes uosque terrestres uosque inferni.*

The Indo-Europeans perhaps had no clear-cut doctrine of a division of gods between two or three levels of the cosmos. But in certain circumstances it was natural to draw such distinctions, and they may have been drawn informally and inconsistently to suit the occasion.

Gods and men: two races

The opposition of celestial and terrestrial did, however, play a fundamental role in Indo-European thought and language: not in contrasting different orders of supernatural being, but in contrasting the gods with humankind. As the gods were **deiwṓs*, the heavenly ones, man was 'the earthly', designated by a derivative of the old word for earth, *$d^h\acute{e}\hat{g}^hom$-/$d^h\hat{g}^hm$-.[14] This is the source of words for 'man, human being' in various languages: Phrygian *zemelos*; Latin *homo* (cf. *humus* 'earth'), Oscan *humuf*, Umbrian *homu*; old Lithuanian *žmuõ*, plural *žmónės*; Gothic and Old English *guma*, Old Norse *gumi*, Old High German *gomo* (< proto-Germanic **guman*);[15] Old Irish *duine*, Welsh *dyn*, Breton *den* (< **gdon-yo-*).[16] In Greek the inherited word was replaced by

[14] Schulze (1966), 146.

[15] This survives in modern German Bräuti-*gam*, English bride-*groom* (with intrusive r by false association).

[16] Cf. Feist (1939), 225 f.; Gamkrelidze–Ivanov (1995), 720.

ἄνθρωπος (of obscure etymology), but in the poetic language mortals can be referred to as ἐπι-χθόνιοι, literally 'those on earth'. The meaning is spelt out more fully in the formula χαμαὶ ἐρχομένων ἀνθρώπων, 'men who go on the earth', or for example in the Eddic *Fáfnismál* (23. 4–6), *manna þeira er mold troða | þic qveð ec óblauðastan alinn*, 'of those men who tread the earth, I say you are the most intrepid'. The modern Lithuanian word for 'man' in the sense of 'human being' is *žmõgus*, in origin a compound, 'earth-goer', combining the roots seen in Greek χαμαί and βαίνω.

In Indic, Phrygian, Italic, and Celtic tradition the ancient pairing of 'heavenly' (divine) and 'earthly' (human) was maintained with the original lexical roots. In RV 7. 46. 2 Rudra is said to have concern for both the earthly race and the heavenly: *kṣámyasya jánmanas ... divyásya*. In the Phrygian inscriptions there is much use of the formula με δεως κε ζεμελως κε and variants, understood to mean 'among both gods and men'.[17] Ennius has *diuomque hominumque* several times, and not only in adapting the Homeric πατὴρ ἀνδρῶν τε θεῶν τε (*Ann.* 284, 591, 592, cf. 203 Skutsch). A Gaulish boundary stone of the second or first century BCE designates a piece of land with the remarkable compound adjective TEUOXTONION, rendered in the Latin version of the inscription as *co(m)munem deis et hominibus*.[18] In Insular Celtic the derivative of proto-Celtic **gdonyo-* had lost its inital velar and come to alliterate with the word for 'god', and so in early Irish texts we find *for doíne domnaib scéo déib* 'over worlds of men and (over) gods'; *sech bid día, bid duine* 'he will be both god and man'; *arddu deeib dóen* 'a man more exalted than the gods'; in an early Welsh poem *as clywo a duw a dyn*, 'let both God and man hear it'.[19] In Germanic the two terms would have been **teiwōz* and **gumanez*, but in this coupling, at least, **teiwōz* was replaced by **guðō*, probably for the sake of alliteration;[20] hence in the Edda we find *goð ǫll ok gumar* for 'all gods and men' (*Lokasenna* 45. 3, 55. 6). In Snorri's prose the poetic *gumar* is also replaced, and he writes *guðanna ok manna* (genitive plural, *Gylf.* 21, al.).

17 W. M. Ramsay, *Jahreshefte des Österreichischen Archäologischen Instituts in Wien* 8 (1905), Beiblatt, 107 f.; C. Brixhe in Gusmani et al. (1997), 45; A. Lubotsky in *Mír Curad* 419 f. with a Luvian parallel.

18 **Dēvoχdonion* (masculine or neuter, agreeing with *atom* or *atoś* = *campum*). M. Lejeune, *Recueil des inscriptions gauloises*, ii. 1 (Paris 1988), 36, no. E-2; Meid (1994), 22; Lambert (2003), 78–80; K. T. Witczak, *SIGL* 4 (2002), 103–5; J. N. Adams, *Bilingualism and the Latin Language* (Cambridge 2003), 188 f. X. Delamarre in his *Dictionnaire de la langue gauloise* (2nd edn., Paris 2003) takes the word as the genitive plural of a *dvandva* compound, 'gods-and-men'.

19 K. Meyer (1914), 10; *Imran Brain* 48; Campanile (1988), 28 no. 4. 3; Rowland (1990), 441 st. 88a.

20 Meid (1991), 17.

In Greek the old Indo-European words had both given way to alternative vocables, but 'gods and men' (θεοί τε καὶ ἀνέρες, etc.) is still a formulaic pairing in Homer. And the traditional antithesis between *heavenly* gods and *terrestrial* humans still appears, as when Odysseus says to Nausicaa,

εἰ μέν τις θεός ἐσσι, τοὶ οὐρανὸν εὐρὺν ἔχουσιν . . .
εἰ δέ τίς ἐσσι βροτῶν, τοὶ ἐπὶ χθονὶ ναιετάουσιν . . .

'If you are one of the gods who dwell in the broad heaven, I reckon you are most like Artemis . . . but if you are of the mortals who live on earth, then thrice fortunate are your parents and brothers' (*Od.* 6. 150/3; cf. Hes. *Th.* 372 f.).

There are many references in the Rigveda to the 'race' or 'breed' of the gods: 10. 57. 5 *daíviyo jánaḥ*, cf. 1. 31. 17, 44. 6, 45. 9 f., etc.; 6. 22. 9 *diviyó jánaḥ*, cf. 9. 91. 2; 10. 63. 17 = 64. 17; 1. 71. 3 *devā́ñ jánma*, cf. 6. 11. 3; 10. 64. 13—the only survival of an old genitive plural ending; 7. 42. 2 *devā́nāṃ jánimani*, etc. We also hear of 'the race of gods and mortals' (1. 70. 6 *devā́nāṃ jánma mártāṃś ca*), or 'the earthly race and the heavenly' (7. 46. 2, quoted above). Sometimes the phrase 'both races' is used, meaning gods and men (1. 31. 7; 2. 2. 4, 6. 7; 8. 52. 7). The words that I have rendered as 'race' are *jána-*, *jánas-*, and *ján(i)man-*. The second of these corresponds exactly to Greek γένος, and in Greek epic we find several times the expression θεῶν (μακάρων, ἀθανάτων) or ἀνθρώπων γένος, with the same meaning as in the Veda.[21] Pindar famously declared (*Nem.* 6. 1):

ἓν ἀνδρῶν, ἓν θεῶν γένος· ἐκ μιᾶς δὲ πνέομεν
ματρὸς ἀμφότεροι.

The race of men is one, and of gods one; from one mother
we both draw breath.

Here are the 'both races' of the Vedic poets.

The words γένος, *jána-*, etc. have Germanic cognates in Old High German *chunni*, Norse *kyn*, Old English *cyn(n)* (modern 'kin') and *gecynd(e), cynd* ('kind'). Corresponding to γένος ἀνδρῶν we have Old Saxon *manno cunni*, Old English *manna cyn(n)* (*Beowulf* 701, 712, al.), Norse *mannkind* (*Gylf.* 9), our 'mankind'. The idiom was applicable to other orders of being too. Hesiod's Muses sang to Zeus of 'the race of men and of the powerful Giants' (*Th.* 50), and the poet of *Beowulf* speaks similarly of 'the race of Giants': 883 *eotena cyn*, 1690 *gīganta cyn*.

[21] Hes. *Th.* 21, 33, 44, 50, etc.; fr. 204. 98; *Hymn. Dem.* 320; 'Eumelus' fr. 13. 1 West; Asius fr. 8. 2 W.; cf. *Il.* 6. 180 ἣ δ' ἄρ' ἔην θεῖον γένος, οὐδ' ἀνθρώπων; 12. 23 ἡμιθέων γένος ἀνδρῶν.

Characteristics of divinity

Despite the occasional myth of a god such as Baldr who was killed, it is a basic feature of the gods that they are immortal.[22] In Vedic as in Greek, they are often referred to as 'the immortal gods', or simply 'the immortals': *devā́ amṛ́tāḥ* RV 3. 4. 11, cf. 5. 69. 4; 6. 15. 18, 18. 15; 7. 2. 11; *amṛ́tāḥ* 7. 63. 5; *Il.* 1. 520 ἐν ἀθανάτοισι θεοῖσιν, etc.; 9. 110 ἀθάνατοι, etc. The synonym ἄμβροτος, which corresponds exactly to Vedic *amṛ́ta-* (**n̥-mr̥-to-*), is used in the singular formula θεὸς ἄμβροτος (22. 9, 358, al.), but for the gods in the plural the inherited word had been displaced by the newer ἀθάνατοι. The old lexeme appears in Avestan as *aməṣ̌a-*, and in Zoroastrian theology the divine entities that Zarathushtra had associated with Ahura Mazdā are called the *Aməṣ̌a Spəṇta*, 'Bounteous Immortals'. In Latin, the expected **immortus* is replaced by the extended form *immortalis*. The gods are the *di immortales*, or occasionally *immortales* alone.

Just as we have seen the phrase 'all the gods' in Vedic and Greek, so we find 'all the immortals' in a parallel series: RV 1. 59. 1, 72. 2, etc. *víśve amṛ́tāḥ*; Y. 42. 6 *vīspą̄sca aməšą̄ spəṇtą̄*, cf. 71. 4;[23] *Il.* 10. 463 πάντων ἀθανάτων, 20. 314, etc.

As human beings are 'terrestrials' by contrast with the celestial gods, so they are 'mortals' by contrast with the immortal deities: in Vedic, RV 1. 35. 2 *amṛ́tam mártiyaṃ ca* 'immortal and mortal'; 6. 15. 8 *devā́saś ca mártiyāsaś cā* 'gods and mortals', cf. 13; in Avestan, Y. 29. 4 = 48. 1 *daēvāiščā maṣ̌yāiščā*, cf. 34. 5, Yt. 10. 34, 13. 89;[24] Pahlavi *dēwān ud mardōmān*; in Greek, *Il.* 11. 2 = 19. 2 ἀθανάτοισι . . . ἠδὲ βροτοῖσιν; 12. 242, 20. 64 θνητοῖσι καὶ ἀθανάτοισι; 14. 199 ἀθανάτους ἠδὲ θνητοὺς ἀνθρώπους, etc. From Latin one might add the Naevius epitaph that I have quoted elsewhere, *immortales mortales si foret fas flere.*

In Iranian generally 'mortal' became an ordinary word for 'man': Old Persian *martiya-*, Sogdian *mrtyy*, modern Persian *mard*. Similarly in Armenian, *mard*, though this may be a loan or calque from Iranian.[25] One has the impression that the mortal–immortal antithesis is characteristic of the Graeco-Aryan family rather than of Indo-European overall, though it may be noted that a Tocharian word for 'man' (as opposed to woman), in the A

[22] Cf. P. Thieme in Schmitt (1968), 122 f.; Durante (1962), 28 = (1976), 91; Schmitt (1967), 193 f.

[23] See the following note.

[24] The traditional Indo-Iranian formula lives on, although *daēva-* in general in the Avesta has changed its meaning to 'demon'. Cf. É. Benveniste, 'Hommes et dieux dans l'Avesta', *Festschrift für Wilhelm Eilers* (Wiesbaden 1967), 144–7.

[25] Durante (1976), 43 f.

dialect *oṅk*, in B *eṅkwe*, is held to derive from **n̥ku̯-ó-* 'subject to death, mortal'.[26]

Readers of Homer will remember that the gods there are not only immortal but also unageing. We tend to associate old age and death together, as major inconveniences of our existence, and it was natural enough to conceive the gods as being exempt from both. The two ideas are coupled in the recurrent formula ἀθάνατος καὶ ἀγήραος, with that anaphora of the negative prefix ἀ- (< *n̥-) that was illustrated in the last chapter. It is paralleled in the Veda and Avesta.[27] The goddess Dawn in RV 1. 113. 13 is *ajárā amŕ̥tā*, where *ajárā* contains a root cognate with that of Greek γέρων, γῆρας. Similar phrases are used of other entities with divine status: 3. 53. 15 *amŕ̥tam ajuryám*, 10. 94. 11 *ámr̥tavaḥ | anāturā́* (unimpaired) *ajárāḥ*; AV 10. 8. 26 *ajárā mártiyasyāmŕ̥tā gr̥hé*, 'unageing, an immortal in a mortal's house'. The men formed by Ahura Mazdā will, under his sovereignty, reshape the world to be *azarəšəntəm amərəšəntəm afriθyantəm apuyantəm*, 'unageing, undying, undecaying, unrotting' (Yt. 19. 11). In the Old English *Maxims A* (9–12) similar attributes are predicated of the Christian God: 'nor does sickness or age trouble the Almighty in any way; he does not grow old in heart, but is still as he was, the patient Lord'.

Cosmic divinities such as the Sun and the Earth impress us with their untiring stamina.[28] Vedic *ámr̥dhra-* 'unwearying, unfailing' is applied to the Dawns (RV 5. 37. 1), Heaven and Earth (5. 43. 2), Agni (ibid. 13), Indra (8. 80. 2). Fire is *ájasra-* 'untiring' (2. 35. 8; 3. 1. 21, al.), and so are the Sun and Moon (10. 12. 7). In Greek the similar-meaning (though not cognate) ἀκάματος is formulaically applied to fire (*Il.* 5. 4, 15. 598, etc.). The Sun is ἀκάμας (18. 239, 484, etc.), as is the river Spercheios (16. 176). Earth, 'highest of the gods', is ἄφθιτος ἀκαμάτα (Soph. *Ant.* 339). The winds are also ἀκάματοι (Empedocles B 111), and the sea (Bacchyl. 5. 25, cf. Pind. *Nem.* 6. 39).

Of certain gods who watch over the world it is said that they never sleep. Aryaman, Varuna, and Mitra are *ásvapnajo animiṣā́ ádabdhāḥ*, 'unsleeping, unblinking, undeceived' (RV 2. 27. 9; cf. 4. 4. 12). *ásvapna(j)-* corresponds to Avestan *axᵛafna-* (Yt. 10. 7 of Mithra; Vd. 19. 20 of Ahura Mazdā) and Greek ἄυπνος.[29] One of the tragedians wrote that 'the eye of Zeus does not sleep' (Trag. Adesp. 485); another, that his power never falls victim to sleep (Soph. *Ant.* 606).

[26] Cf. Greek νέκυς, Avestan *nasu-*, 'dead person, corpse', Old Irish *ēc* < *n̥kú- 'death', etc.; Gamkrelidze–Ivanov (1995), 396; D. Q. Adams in *EIEC* 150b.

[27] Durante (1976), 98, cf. 101. On the Greek formula cf. West (1966), 246.

[28] Cf. Durante (1976), 93.

[29] Euler (1979), 99.

Gods often have many names and titles. 'Many-named' (*puruṇā́man-*, πολυώνυμος) in fact appears as a divine epithet in both Vedic and Greek: RV 8. 93. 17, AV 6. 99. 1, of Indra; *Hymn. Dem.* 18 and 32, of Hades; *Hymn. Ap.* 82, of Apollo; Soph. *Ant.* 1115, of Dionysus; Ar. *Thesm.* 320, of Artemis, etc.[30] At the same time there was uncertainty about which of his names the deity was to be called by in order for prayers to be effective; there was the notion that he had one true name, which might in some circumstances be kept secret.[31] The Soma, pressed, poured out, and imbibed, 'reveals the secret names of the gods for proclamation on the sacrificial floor' (RV 9. 95. 2). Indra has a secret name as creator of the world (10. 55. 1 f.). In Euripides' *Phaethon* (225 f. = fr. 781. 12 f.) Clymene cries to the Sun-god

> ὦ καλλιφεγγὲς Ἥλι', ὥς μ' ἀπώλεσας
> καὶ τόνδ'. Ἀπόλλων δ' ἐν βροτοῖς ὀρθῶς καλῇ,
> ὅστις τὰ σιγῶντ' ὀνόματ' οἶδε δαιμόνων.
>
> O fair-beamed Sun, how you have destroyed me
> and him here. You are rightly called *Apollon* ('Destroyer') among mortals,
> (by) whoever knows the divine powers' unspoken names.

The Romans held their city to be under the protection of a deity whose name was a closely guarded secret, and Rome itself had an alternative name that was uttered only in secret rites, in case an enemy should learn it and so acquire power to harm the city.[32] Nordic gods' names such as Freyr and Freyja, which mean (the) Lord and Lady, may have been substitutes for these divinities' 'real' names.

Some gods are called 'celebrated', with an adjective formed on the old **k̑lu* root. The Maruts are *práśravas-* (RV 5. 41. 16); Mithra is *frasrūta-* (Yt. 10. 47), as are the Fravashis (Yt. 13. 29, 30, 35), the divinized spirits of the faithful; Poseidon and Hephaestus are familiar in Homer as κλυτὸς Ἐννοσίγαιος and περικλυτὸς Ἀμφιγυήεις respectively. There is a Gaulish dedication 'to the Renowned Ones', Ροκλοισιαβο, where the *Ro-* (< **pro-*) corresponds to the *pra-/fra-* of the Vedic and Avestan passages.[33]

Divine epithets often take the superlative form.[34] Indra is 'the highest' (RV 10. 159. 4 *uttamá*), as is Zeus (ὕπατος in Homer; ὕψιστος in Pindar, *Nem.* 1. 60, 11. 2, and Aeschylus, *Eum.* 28). The Yasna liturgy is performed (Y. 1. 1)

[30] Usener (1896), 334–7; Schmitt (1967), 183 f.; Campanile (1977), 55–7, 76.

[31] Cf. de Vries (1956), i. 299 f.; Campanile (1977), 59–61.

[32] Plin. *HN* 3. 65, 28. 18; Macr. *Sat.* 3. 9. 3–5; Serv. ad *Aen.* 1. 277.

[33] E. Campanile, *Le lingue indoeuropee di frammentaria attestazione* (Pisa 1983), 215; Meid (1994), 25; inscr. G-65.

[34] Usener (1896), 50–4, 343; C. Watkins in *Mélanges Linguistiques offerts à Émile Benveniste* (Paris 1975), 531 f. = (1994), 510 f.; id. (1995), 485 n. 4.

Ahurahe Mazdå ... mazištaheca vahištaheca sraēštaheca xraoždištaheca xraθβištaheca hukərəptəmaheca aṣ̌āt̰ apanōtəmaheca, 'for Ahura Mazdā the greatest and best and most beautiful and firmest and wisest and best-formed from truth and highest'. More modest aggregations appear in RV 1. 161. 1 *śréṣṭhaḥ ... yáviṣṭhaḥ*, 'the most beautiful ... the youngest' (Agni); 2. 6. 6 *yáviṣṭha ... yájiṣṭha*, '(O Agni) youngest ... most reverent'; *Il.* 2. 412 Ζεῦ κύδιστε μέγιστε, '(O) Zeus most glorious (and) greatest', where μέγιστος corresponds to the Avestan *mazišta-*; 19. 258 θεῶν ὕπατος καὶ ἄριστος, '(Zeus) the highest and best of the gods' and in the Romans' Iuppiter Optimus Maximus. Artemis is καλλίστη (Eur. *Hipp.* 66, 70), and so is Aphrodite (Eur. *Hel.* 1348, al.).

Relations with mankind

Although certain individual deities are charged with the supervision of justice, contracts, and so on, in general the Indo-European gods do not have an ethical character. The essential thing about them is their power, which they can exercise at their pleasure. It is therefore important to have them as friends.[35] In Hittite ritual the priest prayed 'May the Tabarna, the king, be dear to the gods!'[36] The Indian prayer *priyó devā́nāṃ bhūyāsam*, 'may I be the gods' friend' (AV 17. 1. 2), or *priyám mā kṛṇu devéṣu*, 'make me a friend among the gods' (19. 62. 1), would have seemed quite normal to the Greeks. Compare Theognis 653, 'May I be of good fortune (εὐ-δαίμων) and dear to the immortal gods'; Pindar fr. 155, 'What can I do to be dear to you, strong-thundering son of Kronos, and dear to the Muses?'; Euripides fr. 800. 2, 'may I never be anything but dear to the gods'. In the epics Hector and others are characterized as 'dear to the gods'; kings are 'dear to Zeus', warriors 'dear to Ares'. People were given names such as Diphilos and Herophilos, 'dear to Zeus', 'dear to Hera'. These have parallels in Germanic and Slavonic names such as Oswini 'God's friend', Serbian Bogoljub, Polish Bogumil, etc.[37] In the *Sigurðarkviða* (24. 7) Sigurd is called *Freys vinr*, 'Freyr's friend'. Conversely certain persons were held to be hated by a god or the gods, or temporarily to be the object of their anger, and to suffer in consequence.[38]

[35] Cf. Oldenberg (1917), 292, of the Vedic picture, 'das Bild der Götter im allgemeinen trägt ethische Züge doch nur oberflächlich an sich. Für das religiöse Bewußtsein ist es das Wesentliche, daß der Gott ein starker Freund ist.'

[36] *CTH* 537. 1 obv. 2 f. Near Eastern kings regularly styled themselves 'beloved of the gods', or more often of a particular god: West (1997), 130 f.

[37] Cf. Grimm (1883–8), 93, 211; Schramm (1957), 32 f., 71.

[38] Grimm (1883–8), 18–20 and 137, collects Germanic examples; see also West (1997), 124–8.

The relationship of god to people was expressed using terms taken from the human world: king, father, herdsman. In the Rigveda gods are frequently addressed or described as *rā́jan-*, 'king', or *samrā́j-*, 'great king': Varuna (1. 24. 7–9, 12–14, 156. 4, etc.), Indra (1. 63. 7, 178. 2, etc.), Soma (1. 91. 4, 8, etc.), Agni (1. 79. 6; 3. 1. 18, etc.), Mitra (3. 59. 4). The Greek deities are similarly titled *ἄναξ* or *ἄνασσα*; a Wanax appears as a deity in the Pylos tablets. *βασιλεύς* and *βασίλεια* are used especially of Zeus and Hera, but sporadically of others, and as an independent divine name (*Βασιλεύς*, *Βασίλη*) in several places.[39]

The titles 'father' and 'mother' cleave especially to Heaven and Earth, as will be shown in the next chapter. But other Vedic gods besides Dyaus are called 'our father' or 'the father': Agni (RV 1. 31. 10; 2. 1. 9), Tvaṣṭṛ (2. 17. 6; 10. 64. 10), Bṛhaspati (6. 73. 1), Varuna (7. 52. 3). In Greece the practice is rare, but Ion of Chios addresses Dionysus as *πάτερ* (fr. 26. 13; cf. Aesch. fr. 382). At Rome it was well established. Cato quotes prayers containing the vocatives *Iane pater* and *Mars pater* (*De agric.* 134. 2 f., 141. 2–4). Aeneas in Ennius (*Ann.* 26) prays to *pater Tiberine*, as does Cocles in Livy (2. 10. 11). Gellius (5. 12. 5) records a Neptunus pater and Saturnus pater, and inscriptions attest Marspiter, Dis pater, Vediovis pater, Liber pater, and others.[40] Divine 'mothers' are especially common in northern and western Europe; I shall come to them presently.

In the Hittite treaty between Muwatalli and Alaksandu of Wilusa (*CTH* 76 iv 1) one of the gods invoked is 'the Sun-god of heaven, king of the lands, shepherd of mankind'. The shepherd metaphor may in this case be a Semitic borrowing, as it is commonly used of gods in Babylonian and Hebrew poetry.[41] But it could equally be Indo-European inheritance; it was natural in any pastoralist society, and we shall see in Chapter 11 that its application to human rulers was common to Indo-European and Near Eastern peoples. In the Rigveda *gopā́ḥ* 'cowherd' is widely used in the general sense of protector of anyone or anything, and often applied to gods. For example, Vishnu in RV 1. 22. 18 is called *gopā́ ádābhiyah*, 'undeceived cowherd', that is, protector of men; cf. 2. 9. 6. Agni in 1. 96. 4 is *viśā́ṃ gopā́ḥ*, cowherd of human settlements. Bṛhaspati in 2. 23. 6 is told *tuváṃ no gopā́ḥ pathikṛ́d, vicakṣaṇáḥ*, 'you are our pathmaking, observant cowherd'. From Greek poetry we can quote Anacreon's prayer to Artemis (*PMG* 348), in which he uses the verb *ποιμαίνειν* 'shepherd' of her power over the people of Magnesia on the Maeander.

[39] Cf. Usener (1896), 226–31; Campanile (1977), 67–71. For Near Eastern gods as kings see West (1997), 108, 557 f.

[40] *CIL* i.^{2} 970, 1012, 1439, 2290, etc.; Campanile (1977), 68, 71–3, 76.

[41] West (1997), 533.

Gods are givers. We saw at the beginning of the chapter that a word meaning 'dispenser' became the common term for 'god' in Iran and the Slavonic countries. In prayers the gods are constantly being asked to give things. As Theodor Benfey first observed in 1872, a more specific predicate 'giver(s) of good things' can be inferred (at least for Graeco-Aryan) from parallel expressions in the Veda, Avesta, and Greek epic.[42] In Indo-Iranian they are based on the roots *dā* 'give' and *vasu-* 'good'. Indra is *vasudā́* (RV 8. 99. 4; so of Earth, AV 12. 1. 44); *dā́tā vásu* 'giver (of) good' (2. 22. 3; 6. 23. 3; 7. 20. 2; 10. 55. 6); *dātā́ vásūnaam* 'giver of good things' (8. 51. 5; so of Aryaman in TS 2. 3. 14. 4); Agni is *vasudā́van-* (2. 6. 4). Similarly in the Avesta Ahura Mazdā is *vaŋhudå* (Y. 38. 4) or *dāta vaŋhuuąm* (Vd. 22. 1, 8, 14, cf. 19. 17), while the Holy Immortals are *vohunąm dātārō*, 'givers of good things' (Y. 65. 12, *Visprat* 11. 12). This corresponds quite closely to the Hesiodic and Homeric formula which calls the gods δωτῆρες ἐάων. The vocative singular δῶτορ ἐάων is used in addressing Hermes in the *Odyssey* (8. 335) and twice in the Homeric Hymns. It looks as if the Greek and Vedic phrases must go back to a common prototype, though ἐάων—evidently an archaic word—is difficult to analyse.[43] The 'giving' root reappears in the Old Russian Dažĭbogŭ, Church Slavonic Daždĭbogŭ, 'Giver of Wealth', while a Lithuanian god written as Datanus and glossed as *donator bonorum seu largitor* is attested in a sixteenth-century source.[44]

It is a common idea, not confined to Indo-European peoples, that gods sometimes roam the earth disguised in human form.[45] 'Of old, in the Aeon of the Gods, O king, the blessed Lord Āditya came down from heaven, unwearied, in order to see the world of men' (*MBh.* 2. 11. 1). The Aśvins 'are healers and servants, and, taking any form they please, they walk in the world of the mortals' (ibid. 3. 124. 12). 'Even gods, taking the likeness of strangers from elsewhere and assuming every kind of aspect, go from one community to another, monitoring men's unrighteous or orderly conduct' (*Od.* 17. 485–7). Several Greek and Roman myths tell how a god, or two or three gods together, travelled about and received hospitality from someone who did not know

[42] Durante (1962), 28 ~ (1976), 92; Schmitt (1967), 142–8; cf. Schlerath (1968), ii. 149.

[43] Karl Hoffmann, *Aufsätze zur Indoiranistik*, ii (Wiesbaden 1976), 600–4, explains it as a replacement for *ϵϝέϝων < **ewéhwōn* < **h₁wéswōm*.

[44] R. Jakobson (1962–88), vii. 29 f.; Usener (1896), 89 ~ Mannhardt (1936), 356. The Germanic and Celtic word for 'give' (in Celtic 'take') seems to have given names to the Gabiae and Alagabiae, beneficent goddesses recorded from the northern provinces of the Roman empire, and to some individuals such as Ollogabia, Garmangabi, Friagabi, and the later attested Scandinavian Gefjon, Gefn: de Vries (1956), ii. 293, cf. 317, 319 f., 329; Olmsted (1994), 412–14. There is no connection with the Lithuanian Gabia, Gabjauja, Matergabia, and Polengabia listed by Usener (1896), 90, 95, 98; see Biezais–Balys (1973), 407.

[45] For Sumerian and Old Testament evidence see West (1997), 123 f.

what they were and who impressed them with his goodness and piety, or his lack of it. In Nordic mythology Odin goes about similarly, accompanied by Loki and Hœnir.[46] A Lithuanian legend explains why horses graze continuously while oxen chew the cud: it is because a horse was too busy eating to show the god Perkunas the way when he was walking the earth, but an ox helped him.[47]

The gods' disguise is not always perfect. Their divine nature may betray itself in certain visible clues. Helen recognizes Aphrodite by her beautiful neck and breast and her sparkling eyes (*Il.* 3. 396 f.; cf. *Hymn. Aphr.* 181); the Locrian Ajax recognizes Poseidon by the movements of his lower legs as he departs (13. 71 f.). According to a passage in the *Mahābhārata* (3. 54. 23) the gods are distinguished by absence of sweat and dust, unblinking eyes, and by their feet not touching the ground. Pisani found a remarkable parallel in Heliodorus' *Aethiopica* (3. 13. 2), where Calasiris tells Cnemon that while a layman would be taken in by gods in human form, the expert can recognize them by their steady, unblinking gaze and even more by their gait, as they glide smoothly along off the ground without parting their legs.[48] There is no great likelihood that coincident details attested only in such late texts represent independent transmission of Graeco-Aryan heritage rather than post-Alexandrian diffusion. But as the Homeric passages already refer specifically to eyes and gait, the basic idea may be ancient.

Another curious parallel concerning a sign that manifests a god's presence may be mentioned in passing. In the *Iliad* (5. 838 f.), when Athena steps into Diomedes' chariot beside him, the poet remarks that the wooden axle groaned at the weight, because it was carrying a formidable goddess and a hero. This Athena is no incorporeal phantom; she has mass. A Norse narrative tells how the Swedish king Eric, wanting to consult an oracular deity called Lýtir, took the god's wagon to a certain place and waited till it became heavy. That meant that Lýtir was in it.[49]

The disguised deity may at a certain point declare his or her own identity, as Poseidon does to Tyro, *αὐτὰρ ἐγώ τοί εἰμι Ποσειδάων ἐνοσίχθων* (*Od.* 11. 252), or Dionysus to the Tyrrhenian helmsman, *εἶμι δ' ἐγὼ Διόνυσος ἐρίβρομος*, or Indra in the *Mahābhārata*, *Indro'ham asmi*, where *aham asmi* = *ἐγώ εἰμι*.[50]

[46] *Vǫluspá* 17 f.; *Reginsmál*, introductory prose; *Skáldsk.* G56, 39.

[47] Grimm (1883–8), iii. xxxviii–xliii and iv. 1702–4, collects this and further material, much of it featuring Christ and Peter; the old story pattern survived in Christian dress.

[48] V. Pisani, *ZDMG* 103 (1953), 137 f. (= Schmitt (1968), 169 f.); id. (1969), 64.

[49] *Flateyjarbók* i. 467; Davidson (1964), 94. Davidson suggests that this was also the sign by which the priest of Nerthus ascertained that the goddess was present at her sacred wagon, which was then led in procession (Tac. *Germ.* 40. 3, *is adesse penetrali deam intellegit*).

[50] *Od.* 11. 252; *Hymn. Dion.* 56; *MBh.* 13. 12. 36. Further Greek (and Biblical) examples in West (1997), 183 f.

Animals such as dogs are better than humans at sensing the presence of gods and spirits.[51] But a human being may be temporarily granted the special kind of vision that enables him to see the gods in their true form and know them for what they are. In the fifth book of the *Iliad* (127 f.) Athena tells Diomedes that she has removed the 'fog' (ἀχλύς) that has hitherto lain upon his eyes, so that he will be able to distinguish between god and mortal and identify any deity that he may encounter in the battle. In the *Mahābhārata* (3. 42. 16 f.) Arjuna, before being given divine weapons, is visited by the gods, and Yama bellows 'Arjuna, Arjuna, behold us! The World Guardians have assembled. We bestow on you eyesight, for you are worthy of seeing us.'

GODS' NAMES

Of the many individual gods that the Indo-Europeans must have known by name, very few can now be identified. In principle divine names, no less than ordinary vocabulary items, could appear in recognizably related forms in different language branches. In a small number of cases they do, or may do, and these will be discussed in due course. But for the most part the different pantheons have very little in common, at least in terms of shared names. Sometimes a god's essence survived under a different name, or his functions were taken over by another deity.

More than one factor contributed to the replacement of names. A god's primary name might be avoided for taboo reasons. It might be displaced by familiar epithets or titles, rather as the Christian deity is no longer known as Yahweh or Jehovah but is mostly just called God, or alternatively the Almighty, the Heavenly Father, the Lord, and so forth.[52]

Scholars have often found that divine names in different traditions looked as if they should be the same, but showed anomalies of form, and did not quite correspond in the way that the laws of phonology would predict. There is a school of thought that admits some licence in the matter. Jan de Vries wrote that 'the research of recent years has shown that especially in religious nomenclature the sound laws do not need to be followed in their unconditional strictness'. No less a philologist than Roman Jakobson opined

[51] Eumaeus' dogs whimper and cower as Athena comes to talk to Odysseus (*Od.* 16. 162 f.; see A. Hoekstra's note on 161). Grimm (1883–8), 667, 1484, collects material from Germanic folk-tales. Dogs howl at the approach of the Lithuanian death goddess Giltinė: Biezais–Balys (1973), 408.

[52] Cf. Usener (1896), 324 f.; Vendryès (1948), 264 f.; G. Dumézil, *Les dieux des Indo-Européens* (Paris 1952), 5 f.; M. Gimbutas, *JIES* 1 (1973), 469 f.; Sergent (1995), 390.

that 'a rigorous, pedantic application of current phonetic and grammatical rules to such a highly specialized field of language as hieratic onomastics would be sheer fallacy'. Freedom of treatment was 'quite a typical feature of mythological nomenclature, prompted in part by the severe rules of taboo and partly by the vital needs of ecstatic expressivity'.[53] It is widely accepted that the force of taboo can operate by deforming rather than suppressing the supernatural being's proper name.[54] That might explain some of the anomalies that confront us. It might, for example, have played a role in the irregular dialect variations found in the names of many Greek gods—Poseidon, Athena, Hermes, Apollo, Ares, Dionysus.[55] At any rate it is a convenient theory.

Gods' names are not invented arbitrarily, like those of aliens in science fiction. Originally they have a meaning, they express some concept, and sometimes this is still apparent or discoverable.

In PIE, before the development of the three-gender system characteristic of MIE, there was a two-gender system which simply distinguished between animate and inanimate. In some cases there were pairs of words, one of either gender, for what we would think of as the same thing. For instance, Fire considered as an active principle was **hn̥gʷnis* (animate), but as a mere physical entity **péh$_2$u̯r̥* (inanimate); the first gave the Latin masculine *ignis*, the second the Greek neuter πῦρ, English *fire*, etc. Water as a living, moving thing was **h$_2$ĕ̄p-* (animate), as an inert element **u̯ódr̥* (inanimate). If either was to be accorded divine status, it was naturally the animate, and in Vedic we duly find Agni 'Fire' and Āpaḥ 'the Waters' as the recipients of hymns.

On a similar principle other things could be made into deities by transferring them to the animate gender.[56] Thus the Indo-Iranian god of the contract, *Mitráḥ/Miθrō*, is the masculinized form of the neuter *mitrám/miθrəm* 'contract'. Indra's monstrous enemy *Vr̥tráḥ*, who blocked the waters, is the masculinized form of the neuter *vr̥trám* 'blockage'. What is in Vedic the neuter noun *vánaḥ*, genitive *vánasaḥ* (< **vénos*, **vénesos*), 'loveliness', appears in Latin as the female deity *Venus*, genitive *Veneris*. Zarathushtra very frequently sings of *Aša-* 'Truth' as a divine principle, mostly as a neuter (*aṣ̌əm*, = Vedic *r̥tám*), but when he wants to address him directly, or represent him as a

[53] de Vries (1956), ii. 275; Jakobson (1962–88), vii. 44 f., cf. 13.

[54] The phenomenon can be illustrated from English exclamations of an earlier generation: 'by Gum', 'Golly', 'Gosh' for (by) God, 'O Lor' for Lord, 'Jeepers Creepers', 'Cripes', 'Crikey' for (Jesus) Christ, 'Heck' for Hell, 'well, I'll be darned' (or dashed, danged) for damned.

[55] As noted by Müller (1897), 399 f.

[56] Cf. Paul Thieme, *Mitra und Aryaman* (New Haven 1957), 20–6, 38, 81 f.; id., *Paideuma* 7 (1960), 135–46; Pisani (1969), 257 f., 264; Johanna Narten, *Die Aməṣ̌a Spəṇtas im Awesta* (Wiesbaden 1982), 64.

speaking figure, he becomes masculine (Y. 28. 5, 29. 3, etc.). In Greek the god of war and destruction, Ares, is a masculine related to the feminine ἀρή 'ruin, destruction' and the neuter ἄρος 'damage'. In the *Iliad* he is attended by two figures representing fear and panic, Deimos and Phobos; Phobos is the personification of a noun that is masculine already, while Deimos is masculinized from the neuter δεῖμα.

Sometimes male gods are made out of feminine nouns. The Avestan feminine *mazdā* 'wisdom' (Y. 40. 1, = Vedic *medhā́*) was deified as the masculine Ahura Mazdā, 'Lord Wisdom'. The gods who according to Hesiod make Zeus' thunder and lightning, Brontes and Steropes, are masculines made from the feminine nouns βροντή and στεροπή. Latin *cupido* fluctuates in gender as a common noun, but as a god Cupido is male.

Many gods were created for specialized roles and named accordingly, whether by the above method or by attaching a suffix to the operative word or forming a compound with it. It has even been maintained that the Indo-Europeans had only deities of this sort.[57] We cannot go as far as that, but the type is certainly early, and we can recognize some pervasive patterns of nomenclature.

Some names have the form of agent nouns built on verbal roots. In the Veda we have Savitṛ, 'Arouser, Stimulator', a deity hard to distinguish from the Sun; Dhātṛ, 'Creator'; Tvaṣṭṛ, 'Artificer', the maker of Indra's weapon and other articles (= Avestan *Θβōrəštar*, Y. 29. 6); and a few other minor figures.[58] In Greece we have Alastor, probably 'Unforgetter', the demon that pursues those tainted by blood-guilt, and many titles of Zeus that focus on a single function, such as Ἀγήτωρ, Αὑαντήρ, Ἀστραπάτας (Homeric ἀστεροπητής), Ἀφίκτωρ, Γεννήτωρ, Ἕκτωρ, Μαιμακτήρ, Σωτήρ.[59] Jupiter too has such titles in plenty: Cultor, Defensor, Depulsor, Inventor, Iutor, Monitor, Pistor, Stator, Victor, and others. There are many Roman godlets of comparable form. When the Flamen performed the *sacrum cereale* for Tellus and Ceres, he invoked Vervactor, Reparator, Imporcitor, Insitor, Obarator, Occator, Sarritor, Subruncinator, Messor, Convector, Conditor, and Promitor, all controlling different stages of the agricultural cycle.[60] There is no single name among all the above that can be attributed even to a late phase of Indo-European. But we may assume that this method of creating divine names goes back to early times.

[57] Usener (1896), 279; Schrader (1909), 35–7. On such 'Sondergötter' see Usener, 75–9 (Roman), 108–15 (Baltic), 122–77 (Greek); Oldenberg (1917), 63, 258 (Indian).

[58] On all of them see Macdonell (1898), 115–18.

[59] For these and others see the catalogue of Zeus' titles in *RE* xA. 253–376.

[60] Fabius Pictor fr. 6 in E. Seckel–B. Kuebler, *Iurisprudentiae Anteiustinianae Reliquiae*, i.[6] (Leipzig 1908); Usener (1896), 76.

Many gods' names contain the suffix *-*nos* or (feminine) *-neh_2 > -*nā*. They include deities attested in the second millennium BCE, the Hittite storm-god Tarḫunna (from *tarḫ-* 'overcome, vanquish') and the Indic Varuna (from *var(-u-)* 'cover, protect'). In the European languages the suffix was added to existing nouns to signify 'controller of', 'lord of'. It made not only divine names but also human titles like Greek *κοίρανος* 'army leader' (see p. 449), Latin *domi-nus, tribū-nus*, Gothic *þiudans* 'king' (< **teuto-nos*: **teutā* 'people'), Old English *dryhten*, Old Norse *drottinn* 'lord' (< **drukti-nos*: **drukti-* 'armed retinue').[61] As for deities, we may refer to the Greek Ouranos < **Worsanos*, 'lord of rain', and Helena < **Swelenā*, 'mistress of sunlight' (p. 231); the Illyrian Menzanas, 'lord of horses'; the Roman Neptūnus, 'lord of waters' (p. 276), Volcānus, 'lord of fire-glare' (p. 268), Silvānus, 'lord of woods', Portūnus, 'lord of ports', Tiberīnus, 'lord of the Tiber', and goddesses such as Fortūna, Bellōna, Pōmōna; the Germanic Woden/Odin < **Wōðanaz*, 'lord of frenzy'; the Gallic Epona, goddess of horses, Nemetona, goddess of groves, Ritona Pritona, goddess of buying and selling, and many others;[62] the Lithuanian thunder-god Perkunas, 'lord of oaks', Vēlinas, 'lord of the dead' (modern Vélnias, the Devil), and Žemýna, Žemýnė, 'mistress of the Earth'. Perkunas, as we shall see in Chapter 6, has some claim to Indo-European antiquity, but for the rest, as in the case of the agent-noun formations, it is the type that is inherited rather than the individual representatives of it.

In the more easterly parts of the Indo-European area the idea 'lord/lady of' could be expressed more explicitly through the use of the word **potis*, feminine *$potnih_2$*. This too was applicable in either the human or the divine sphere. The master of the house (Latin *domi-nus*) was in Vedic *dáṃpatiḥ*, in Avestan *dəṇg paitiš*, in Greek δεσπότης; the master of the clan or settlement (**woiḱos*) was in Vedic *viśpátiḥ*, in Lithuanian *viẽšpat(i)s*.

As for gods, we meet in the Rigveda a deity Bṛhas-pati or Brahmaṇas-pati, 'Lord of Prayer', to whom eleven hymns are addressed. Both parts of the name are accented, showing that they were still felt as independent elements. In Prajāpati, on the other hand, the 'Lord of Generation', they are integrated into one word with a single accent. The common noun *páti-* is frequently coupled with a genitive to make an attributive phrase describing a god's province. It can also have the sense of 'husband', like its Greek equivalent

[61] Cf. Meid (1957); Benveniste (1973), 89–94, 245–8; B. Schlerath in *Sprache und Kultur der Indogermanen* (Akten der X. Fachtagung der Indogermanischen Gesellschaft (1996); Innsbruck 1998), 91.

[62] Cf. Duval (1957), 56 f.; Olmsted (1994), 356 f., 360, 374 f., 409 f.; Lambert (2003), 29. Note that in Gaulish *-ona*, unlike Latin *-ōna*, the [o] is short.

πόσις, and in the *Mahābhārata* we find titles such as Umāpati 'husband of Umā' = Rudra (5. 49. 24), Śacīpati 'husband of Śacī' = Indra (5. 158. 13).

These recall the Homeric designation of Zeus as ἐρίγδουπος πόσις Ἥρης, 'the loud-thundering husband of Hera'. Poseidon (in dialects Poteidaon, Potidas, etc.) has often been explained as 'Husband of Earth'; this is linguistically problematic (apart from the fact that he was not the husband of Earth) but it is plausible enough that the name should contain the **poti-* element and that its original meaning was 'Master of (something)'. On a Linear B tablet from Pylos (PY Tn 316) that lists various deities receiving offerings, there is one spelled *do-po-ta*, perhaps to be read as Dospotās, 'Master of the House', like the classical δεσπότης but with a more specific reference.

The Vedic Dawn goddess is *bhúvanasya pátnī*, 'mistress of creation' (RV 7. 75. 4), and the same phrase is used of the Waters (10. 30. 10). The plural *pátnīḥ* is used as a collective name for the gods' wives (1. 103. 7; 5. 41. 6, 50. 3). The corresponding Greek word, πότνια, is commonly used of goddesses, sometimes with a defining qualification, as in the Mycenaean Potnia Daburinthoio 'Mistress of the Labyrinth', Potnia Ikk^{w}eiā 'Mistress of Horses', etc., and the Homeric πότνια θηρῶν, 'Mistress of Animals'. Potnia by itself serves as a goddess's name at Pylos, and plural Potniai were worshipped in several places.

The ancient pattern remained productive in Baltic. A series of Lithuanian gods' names are compounds formed with *-patis*: Dimstipatis 'Master of the House', Laũkpatis 'Master of the Fields', Raugupatis 'Master of the Sour Dough', Vėjopatis 'Master of the Wind', Žemėpatis, fem. Žempati, 'Master/Mistress of the Earth'.[63] Apart from such names, the *patis* element survives in Lithuanian only in the very old compound *viẽšpatis* mentioned above: an indication of their archaic character.

FEMALE DEITIES

As far back as we can see, Indo-European gods are conceived anthropomorphically. So even at the stage when the language did not make formal distinctions between masculine and feminine, it is likely that each deity was thought of as male or female. In the Greek or the Norse pantheon we take it for granted that some are males and others females, as if by the random play

[63] Usener (1896), 89, 94, 100, 104 f., 110 f. 115; cf. Clemen (1936), 109, 110; V. Blažek, *JIES* 29 (2001), 352.

of chromosomes. In Indo-European theology, however, it would seem that goddesses played only a minor part. In those areas where they are most prominent, in southern and western Europe, it may be due to the influence of earlier, pre-Indo-European populations.[64]

We cannot reconstruct a feminine counterpart of **deiwós*. Different languages created feminine forms in divergent ways. The Vedic *devī́* is matched by Avestan *daēvī*, but not by Lithuanian *diẽvė* or Latin *dea*. Although the Greek θεός is a different word, it is noteworthy that originally the same form was used for masculine and feminine: in Attic ἡ θεός remained normal, while θεά and θέαινα were essentially poetic. They must have been secondary creations, and the same applies to the distinct feminine forms in the other languages.

In the Vedic pantheon, which in this regard may be considered our best indicator of the Indo-European situation, such goddesses as there are play little part in ruling the world, and they have no special connection with mortal women.[65] They fall into the following categories:

(i) Natural entities with feminine names, such as Pṛthivī = Earth, Uṣas = Dawn, Rātrī = Night, Āpaḥ = the Waters; the river Sarasvatī.

(ii) Personified abstractions of feminine gender, such as Aditi (Freedom from Bondage), Vāc (Utterance), Śraddhā (Trust), Lakṣmī (Happiness).[66]

(iii) Spouses or associates of male gods, named after their husbands by means of a suffix, such as Sūryā (cf. p. 227), Rudrāṇī, Varuṇānī, Agnā̆yī.[67]

(iv) Terrestrial goddesses such as the Apsaras nymphs and Araṇyānī the Lady of the Forest (pp. 281, 284).

The first and fourth of these categories may certainly be taken as Indo-European. The second is probably a later development, though paralleled and extensively exploited in Greek and Latin.[68] The third is sufficiently paralleled outside India to suggest that it is an inherited type. In the Younger Avesta there is an Ahurānī who is wife or daughter of Ahura Mazdā, and the Waters are Ahurānīs, while the stellar god Tištrya (Sirius) is accompanied by

[64] Cf. M. Robbins, *JIES* 8 (1980), 19–29.

[65] Cf. Usener (1896), 29–33; Macdonell (1898), 124 f.; Oldenberg (1917), 240 f.; Hillebrandt (1927–9), ii. 398–401; Campanile (1977), 68 f., 73; id. in E. C. Polomé (ed.), *Indo-European Religion after Dumézil* (*JIESM* 16; Washington 1996), 74.

[66] Cf. Macdonell (1898), 119 f.; Hillebrandt (1927–9), ii. 394–8.

[67] Cf. Schrader (1909), 38; Oldenberg (1917), 244; Oberlies (1998), 230 n. 390.

[68] Cf. Usener (1896), 364–75; West (1966), 33 f.

Tištryaēnīs, who represent the lesser stars surrounding him. In the Pylos tablets there are both Poseidaon and Posidaeia, both Zeus and Diwya. In Homeric mythology and in Dodonaean cult one of Zeus' wives is Dione, again a name formed from his by adding a standard feminine suffix. In some cases the same divine title is used in the masculine and the feminine for different (but related) deities: there is a Phoibos and a Phoibe, a Hekatos and a Hekate. Many such pairs are attested at Rome: Janus and Jana, Liber and Libera, Faunus and Fauna, and others.[69] In Nordic myth we have the pairs Freyr and Freyja (in origin 'Lord and Lady'), Fjǫrgynn and Fjǫrgyn, and a male god Njǫrðr whose name, apart from its masculine declension, corresponds to that of the goddess Nerthus that Tacitus knew in Germany. Of some four hundred divine names recorded from Gaul, the great majority—some eighty per cent—are males, and the females are mostly their consorts.[70]

'Mothers'

As male gods are in certain cases called Father, so are goddesses called Mother. In the Graeco-Aryan area, however, this is quite rare. The river Sarasvatī in RV 2. 41. 16 is addressed as *ámbitame, nádītame, dévitame,* 'most motherly, most torrently, most goddessly', and in the next line as *amba,* 'mother'. In post-Vedic popular religion a Mother (Mātā or Ambā) appears as the protecting goddess of a village. In Greece there is a Mother or Great Mother, but she is the Mother of the Gods, a deity of Near Eastern provenance,[71] though she suffered syncretism with the Indo-European figure of Mother Earth. Demeter, whose name incorporates 'mother', was perhaps originally a form of Mother Earth (see p. 176), but in classical times she is a separate goddess, and her motherhood is understood in relation to her daughter Persephone, not to her human worshippers.

In the greater part of Europe, especially the west and north, Mothers are much commoner. It seems likely that this reflects the influence of a pre-Indo-European substrate population for whom female deities had a far greater importance than in Indo-European religion. The archaeologist Marija Gimbutas saw the Indo-Europeans as bringing a male-oriented religion into a goddess-worshipping 'Old Europe', and this reconstruction, based largely on iconic evidence, seems essentially sound.

Certain Illyrian and Messapic goddesses (some borrowed from Greek) have the title Ana or Anna, which is plausibly interpreted as 'Mother'.[72] In Italy we

[69] Usener (1896), 33–5.
[70] Vendryès (1948), 266–71.
[71] West (1997), 109.
[72] Mayer (1957–9), ii. 6.

meet the Umbrian Cubra Mater and the Roman Mater Matuta, Mater Mursina, Luna Mater, Stata Mater, Iuno Mater, etc.[73] Celtic and Germanic Matres, Matrae, or Matronae, as individuals or groups (especially groups of three), are extremely common.[74] Many of the names attached to them are non-Indo-European.

In the Baltic lands too, especially in Latvia, we find many Mothers, but here they are *Sondergöttinnen*, individuals each presiding over a specific area or function. In the Latvian folk-songs they proliferate: there is the Mother of wind, the Mother of fog, of forest, of flowers, of death, of the tomb, of the sea, of silver, of bees, and so on. It is evident that this was a secondary, local development. Usener notes that where the Lithuanians have Laũkpatis 'Master of the Fields' and Vėjopatis 'Master of the Wind', adhering to the old Indo-European **poti-* formula, the Latvians have Lauka māte and Vēja māte.[75]

We must conclude that there was a scarcity of divine Mothers in the Indo-European pantheon. Perhaps Mother Earth was the only one.

SOME INDIVIDUALS

How many individual members of that pantheon can we identify? Certainly not as many as some savants have claimed.[76] The clearest cases are the cosmic and elemental deities: the Sky-god, his partner Earth, and his twin sons; the Sun, the Sun Maiden, and the Dawn; gods of storm, wind, water, fire; and terrestrial presences such as the Rivers, spring and forest nymphs, and a god of the wild who guards roads and herds. All these will be investigated in the next four chapters. Here we will try to round up a few other suspects.

[73] Umbrian inscr. 83 Buck; Campanile (1977), 72.

[74] F. Heichelheim, *RE* xiv. 2213–50, xvi. 946–78; Vendryès (1948), 275–8; Duval (1957), 52–5; de Vries (1956), ii. 288–302; id. (1961), 120–3; Campanile (1981), 75–82; M. Green (1986), 74–91, 165 f.; colloquium volume *Matronen und verwandte Gottheiten* (*Bonner Jahrbücher* Beiheft 44, Köln 1987); Davidson (1988), 108–11; W. Meid, *JIES* 17 (1989), 305 f.; id. (1991), 41; Olmsted (1994), 287–96, 414–25; E. Campanile in E. C. Polomé (ed.) (as n. 65), 74–6; Polomé, ibid. 132–4; F. Battaglia in Dexter–Polomé (1997), 48–82.

[75] Paul Einhorn, *Wiederlegunge der Abgötterey* (1627) in Mannhardt (1936), 464 f.; id., *Reformatio gentis Lettiae* (1636) in Mannhardt, 472; Usener (1896), 106–8, 115; Jonval (1929), 15–18 and nos. 464–741; Biezais–Balys (1973), 384 f., 423. The land of the dead is ruled by Veļu māte, the Mother of Ghosts (ibid. 448 f.).

[76] K. T. Witczak and I. Kaczor, 'Linguistic evidence for the Indo-European pantheon', in J. Rybowska–K. T. Witczak (edd.), *In honorem Annae Mariae Komornicka* (*Collectanea Philologica* ii, Łódź 1995), 267–77, list fifty-one items, but few of them stand up to scrutiny.

There are two ways of hunting them. If possible, we find names in different branches of the tradition that appear to correspond and that denote figures who have features in common. Otherwise we can look for common features distinctive enough to suggest historical identity even in the absence of a shared name.

A whole series of divine names in the Rigveda can also be found in the Avesta, even if only as reviled *daēvas*: Mitra, Aryaman, Apām napāt, Tvaṣṭṛ, Indra, Nāsatya, Śarva, Narāśaṃsa, correspond to Avestan Miθra, Airyaman, Apąm napå, Θβōrəštar, Indra, Nåŋhaiθya, Saurva, Nairyō.saŋha. The inference is that these go back to the Indo-Iranian period, sometime in the first half of the second millennium BCE. But we know from the similarity of the languages that early Indic and early Iranian were closely related, so this does not get us very far towards Indo-European.

*Aryomen

One of those names, however, may have a cognate at the other end of the Indo-European world. Aryaman/Airyaman has long been equated with the Irish Éremón. All three names appear to go back to **Aryo-men-*, nominative **-mēn*, a masculine counterpart of neuter **aryo-men-*, nominative **-mn̥*, 'Aryan-ness', just as the god Brahmā (< **-mēn*) is the deified Prayer (*bráhma* neuter, < **-mn̥*). It is no longer politically correct to call the Indo-Europeans Aryans, but the name was conferred on them in the nineteenth century because it was a term that they, or at least their ruling classes, used of themselves. It is reflected in Sanskrit *aryá-*, *ā́rya-* 'trusty, honourable, worthy, Aryan' and Irish *aire* 'a noble, chief'; it has given its name to Iran and perhaps to Eire. A god *Aryomen might be expected to embody the social ideals of the people and its rulers.[77]

Aryaman is a god frequently mentioned in the Veda, usually in company with Mitra and Varuna, the gods of justice and order. He is rather lacking in distinctive profile, but he is associated with social and marital ties; as a common noun *aryamán-* means 'comrade'.[78] His association with marriage comes to the fore in the Atharvaveda (2. 36. 2; 6. 60; 14. 1. 17, 34, 39, 50; 14. 2. 13, 40; cf. RV 10. 85. 23, 36, 43). He provides the girl with a husband and the man with a wife.

In the *Gāthās* (Y. 32. 1, 33. 3–4, 46. 1, 49. 7) *airyaman-* stands in a hierarchy of social units, above *x*ᵛ*aētu-* (family, clan) and *vərəzāna-* (local community);

[77] Cf. J. Puhvel in Cardona et al. (1970), 376–8; id. (1987), 49, 'the deified embodiment of social self-identification'; 182; Oberlies (1998), 183–5.

[78] Macdonell (1898), 45; von Schroeder (1914–16), i. 384–8.

it seems to denote the wider tribal network or alliance. In a famous prayer that perhaps goes back to the prophet's time Airyaman is invoked as a god to the aid of Zarathushtra's men and women (Y. 27. 5 = 54. 1 = Vd. 20. 11). This prayer, regarded as a general defence against illness, magic, and evil (Y. 54. 2; Yt. 3. 5; Gāh 1. 6; Vd. 20. 12, cf. 22. 6–20), has traditionally been used in the Zoroastrian marriage ritual, and perhaps was so from the start.

As for Éremón, he is not a god, indeed he was the man who drove the Tuatha Dé Danann, the people who stand for the old gods in Irish mythology, underground. He was the legendary first king of the sons of Míl, the Goidelic Celts, that is, in our terms, of the first Indo-Europeans in Ireland (unless the earlier Fir Bolg represent a prior settlement of 'Belgic' P-Celts). It is appropriate, therefore, that his name should mark him as the eponymous representative of Aryanness. No doubt he originally had divine status but, like the rest of the pagan pantheon, was euhemerized in Christian times. A trace of his old connection with marriage may survive in the story that he provided wives to the Cruithnig (Picts). Perhaps this means that he sanctioned a measure of intermarriage.

It has been conjectured that *Aryomen's name is further to be recognized in the Germanic **ermina-* or **ermana-* that appears as a name of Odin (*iǫrmunr*) and in a number of compounds in various languages: Gothic *Ermanareiks* 'Ermanaric'; Old Norse *Iǫrmungandr*, the world serpent, *iǫrmungrund* 'the whole vast earth'; Old English *eormengrund, eormencyn* 'mighty race', *eormenþeod* 'mighty people'; Old Saxon *irminman, irminthiod; Irminsûl*, a pillar revered in Saxon cult; Old High German *Irmingot*, a god called to witness in the *Hildebrandslied* (30).[79] It seems to have existed as a god's name, and in the compounds it appears to have a cosmic or universal connotation. One can see how this might relate to *Aryomen's sphere.

Some Western goddesses

We have seen that the gods were celebrated as givers of good things, these being denoted in Indo-Iranian with the word *vásu-*, *vaŋhu-* (**wesu-*). Combined with **poti-* it gives *vásupati-* 'lord of good things', which occurs some fifteen times in the Rigveda as an attribute of Indra or other gods. There is also a class of deities, headed by Indra, known as the Vasus (*Vásavaḥ*), the Good Ones. One might say that just as certain neuter singulars turn into gods

[79] Cf. von Schroeder (1914–16), i. 500–2; J. de Vries, *Cahiers du Sud* 36 (1952), 18–27; id. (1956), ii. 14–16; Puhvel in Cardona et al. (1970), 382 n. 26. On the sources for the Irminsûl see Grimm (1883–8), 115–19; Clemen (1928), 48, 54, 61, 67–9; de Vries (1956), ii. 386.

by being given the masculine (or animate) form, here the neuter plural *vásūni* that the gods bestow are transformed into the masculine plural *Vásavaḥ*, representing the active principle of good-giving: instead of benefits, Benefactors.

The **wesu-* stem is attested in central Europe by personal names such as the Illyrian Vescleves and the Gaulish Bellovesus. It is almost certainly to be recognized in the name of the Italo-Celtic goddess who appears in central Italy as Vesuna, at Périgueux as Vesunna, and perhaps at Baden-Baden as Visuna.[80] She is surely the 'Mistress of good things', with the familiar nasal suffix. She stands in the same relationship to the Vedic *vásupati-* as the Lithuanian Earth goddess Žemyna to the male Žemėpatis. She probably owes her sex to the European substrate that favoured goddesses. She might have replaced an Indo-European *Wesunos, though there is no necessity to postulate one. Given the continued productivity of the *-no-* suffix, a *Wesupotis or *Wesus would have been a sufficient model.

Our Fridays are named after an old goddess Frīg, corresponding to Norse Frigg, Old Saxon Frî, Old High German Frîja, who was taken for calendrical purposes as the northern equivalent of Venus. A Langobardic form Frea appears in Paulus Diaconus' *Historia Langobardorum* (1. 8). The proto-Germanic form is reconstructed as **Friyō*, and it is from Indo-European **priyā* 'dear, loved, own'.[81] In RV 1. 46. 1 the beautiful Dawn goddess is called *priyā́ Diváḥ*, 'the beloved (daughter) of Dyaus'. The Germanic goddess was the adulterous wife of Odin/Woden.

Was there an Indo-European goddess *Priyā, or was *Friyō a local creation from an epithet which, as the Vedic evidence shows, could be applied to goddesses? That she had a wider currency than the Germanic lands might follow if an alleged Old Czech *Prije* = Aphrodite were better accredited.[82] It is equally doubtful whether she can be recognized in *Wanassa*(?) *Preiia*, named on early coins of Perge in Pamphylia, as that must be the city goddess elsewhere called (Artemis) Pergaia.

It is generally accepted that the Greek Hestia, eponymous goddess of the hearth, is cognate with the Roman Vesta, despite the absence of an initial

[80] S. Weinstock, *RE* viiiA. 1798 f.; F. Heichelheim, ibid. 1800 f.; Meid (1957), 106–8; Olmsted (1994), 429.

[81] Lorenz (1984), 177; Meid (1991), 28. On the Germanic deity see de Vries (1956), ii. 302–7. From the fact that in part of Germany Fridays are particularly favoured for weddings he infers that she was originally the goddess of marriage. In view of her mythical infidelity as a wife it might be preferable to say love and marriage.

[82] Grimm (1883–8), 303, probably from the *Mater verborum* of the notorious forger Václav Hanka. The **priy-* root is well represented in Slavonic words for friend, pleasant, agreeable, etc.

digamma in dialect inscriptions where it would be expected.[83] The name may relate to a root **wes* 'burn', seen in Old High German *wasal* 'fire'. In India and Iran the sacred hearth-flame falls in the province of the god Fire (Agni, Ātar: Chapter 6). The Greek and Roman hearth cults must have contained elements going back to Indo-European times. But the specialized goddess was a regional creation of south central Europe.

One of the local titles under which Dionysus was worshipped was Eleuthereus. It does not mean 'liberating' (from social constraint, psychological repression, sin, etc.), it means 'of (the town) Eleutherai'. Like other old Greek towns that have a feminine plural form—Athenai, Plataiai, Potniai, and, it may be conjectured, others such as Mykenai, Kleonai, Thebai, Thespiai—Eleutherai will have had its name from a local goddess or group of goddesses. It points to an ancient goddess Eleuthera.[84] She would correspond etymologically to the Roman couple Līber (Pater) and Lībera. There was also a Jupiter Līber, matching Oscan *Iúveís Lúvfreís* (genitive; inscr. 5 Rix). Līber and Lībera, at least, had to do with agrarian and human fertility; Varro attests phallic processions *pro eventibus seminum*. If the Greek *Eleuthera had a similar character, it is not surprising that she should have been replaced by Dionysus, or that his local cult should have retained some distinctive features that caused him to be titled after Eleuthera's town.

Greek ἐλεύθερος and Latin *līber* both mean 'free'. Why should a god or goddess or divine couple be so designated? Perhaps it is necessary to dig deeper into the word's past. According to current opinion it is a derivative from the old word for 'people' seen in Old High German *liut*, Old English *lēod*, Lithuanian *liáudis*, Russian люд, etc., related to a root **$h_1$leud^h* 'increase'.[85] For a divinity concerned with increase of produce and people, this makes good enough sense.

With Līber–Lībera and Vesta we are clearly not dealing with Greek deities transferred to Italy under the influence of Greek culture, like Apollo and Bacchus. They are old established Italic gods. The parallelism with Greek divinities is to be explained by common tradition from a time when the ancestors of both Italics and Greeks lived in central Europe and the north Balkans.

Another case where a male god of classical Greece has a title that may be taken over from an earlier goddess is that of Poseidon Hippios, 'Poseidon god of horses'. The Pylos tablets attest a *po-*]*ti-ni-ya i-qe-ya* = Potnia Ikk^{w}eiā,

[83] See Ernout–Meillet (1959), 1288; Chantraine (1968–80), 379.

[84] Usener (1896), 233 f. Eleuthera appears in a late source as a title of Artemis in Lycia, but this may be unconnected.

[85] E. C. Polomé in *EIEC* 416 f.

'Mistress of horses'.[86] This figure may be directly compared with the well-known Celtic horse-goddess Epona: *epo-* = Latin *equus*, Greek ἵππος, and *-nā*, as we have seen before, is equivalent to a **poti-* compound.

Naturally it is impossible to prove that the Mycenaean–Celtic parallel rests on a historical continuity rather than independent development among peoples for whom the horse was important. But they have to be seen against a wider Indo-European background of divinities linked with the horse. In the Rigveda the compound *áśvapati-*, which contains the same elements as Potnia Ikkʷeiā, is an epithet of Indra. The same word, as a divine name, perhaps underlies the Irish Echaid, a title of the god known as the Dagda.[87] The twin sons of *Dyeus (pp. 186–91) in their Indic, Greek, and Baltic manifestations have a strong association with horses, and their Indian name is the Aśvins, which means 'having horses'. There was also an Illyrian god Menzanas, formed with the *-no-* suffix from *mendyo-*, denoting a type of small horse.[88]

Velesŭ, Vēlinas, and others: a dubious equation

Old Russian sources attest an important divinity Velesŭ or Volosŭ, described as a god of cattle; he also had to do with the harvest. The famous poet Boyan is said in the *Lay of Igor* (17) to have been his grandson. There is evidence for the name in Czech, as a devil somewhere beyond the sea. This Slavonic deity has been brought into connection with the Lithuanian Vēlinas (Latvian Vȩ̄lns), the Vedic Varuna, the Gaulish Vellaunos, the Nordic Ullr or Ullinn, and a Hittite Walis, all supposedly from the root **wel* 'see'.[89] If this could all be substantiated, it would add a significant member to our Indo-European pantheon.

We met the **wel* root in Chapter 1 in connection with the Irish *fili* and the German prophetess Veleda, where it referred to vatic 'seeing'. None of the gods in question, however, is connected with prophecy. Varuna is noted for being all-seeing (see pp. 171 f.), but this is not expressed with the **wel* root (which is unknown to Indo-Iranian), and his name is more convincingly

[86] PY An 1281. 1. There is also a *po-ti-ni-ya a-si-wi-ya* = Potnia Aswiā (PY Fr 1206), usually interpreted as 'of Asia (Assuwa)', but it has been suggested that *aswiā* is an Anatolian (Luwian?) equivalent of the Greek *ikkʷeiā*: K. T. Witczak ap. V. Blažek, *SIGL* 2 (1999), 22. In theory it could equally be an Indic form from Mitanni, with Potnia Aswiā = Indic *áśvapatnī*. There is also a man's name *a-si-wi-yo* = Aswios.

[87] Dillon (1975), 138.

[88] Meid (1957), 124 f.

[89] See especially F. de Saussure in *Cahiers F. de Saussure* 21 (1964), 115 f.; R. Jakobson in *Studi Linguistici in onore di Vittore Pisani* (Brescia 1969), 579–99 = id. (1962–88), vii. 33–48; Puhvel (1987), 234; Bader (1989), 46–8. On Velesŭ see also Váňa (1992), 76–8.

explained, as the Vedic poets and commentators understood it, from *var*(*-u-*) 'cover, protect'.[90] Vēlinas is primarily the god of the dead, and located below the earth; hence forest pools are said to be his eyes. But this does not justify the **wel* etymology. His name (with the **-no-* suffix) relates directly to the Vėlės, the spirits of the dead.

Both Vēlinas and Varuna had connections with cattle, and this is the one thing that they have in common with Velesŭ. It is hardly sufficient to establish an underlying identity. As for Vellaunos and Walis, they are mere names to us. Ullr is usually etymologized as **Wulþuz* 'glory, splendour' and this is favoured by what appears to be a theophoric name Wlþuþewaʀ on an early runic inscription. His essential nature is hard to make out. He carried a bow and travelled on skis, and was invoked by warriors in single combat. In place-names his name is often attached to fields and pastures, but there is no evidence for any specific connection with cattle.[91] All in all, there is nothing in this whole ragtag assemblage that we can trace back with any confidence to the Indo-European past.

Heteronymous homologues

It remains to ask whether we can find gods in different countries who, while not having names that hint at any relationship, nevertheless overlap sufficiently in their functions to suggest that they share some common heritage.

Of course, many of the purposes for which people require gods are universal. If we find a god of healing here, there, and everywhere, we cannot assume them to be historically connected unless they show more distinctive identifying features. Nor is it remarkable if many peoples have a god of war to help them to victory or defend them against defeat; war is a critical event, and success must depend on divine support as well as military prowess. We find war-gods, for instance, among the Indians (Indra), Greeks (Enyalios, Ares), Scythians ('Ares', Herodotus 4. 62), Romans (Mars), Gauls ('Mars', Caes. *Bell. Gall.* 6. 17. 2–5), Germans ('Mars', Tac. *Germ.* 9. 1, *Ann.* 13. 57, *Hist.* 4. 64), and Goths ('Mars', Jordanes, *Getica* 41). Perhaps it is more noteworthy when the war-god is also an agrarian deity, a protector of the fields, as is the case with the Roman Mars, the Celtic 'Mars' Teutates, and the Slavonic Svętovit.[92] Enemy action is of course one thing that the fields need to be saved from, but

90 Cf. Macdonell (1898), 28; Puhvel (1987), 49; enlarged stem *varu-* as in *varūtṛ́* 'protector', *várūtham* 'protection', cf. Greek ἔρυμαι.

91 On Ullr cf. de Vries (1956), ii. 153–63; Puhvel (1987), 208.

92 Cf. Gimbutas (1971), 160; Puhvel (1987), 172.

these gods are also concerned with successful harvests and with protection from blight.

As for healing gods, they do occur everywhere, but again there are sometimes other coincident features. The Greek Apollo, a rather complex figure, has probably taken over the characteristics of more than one older divinity, including the healer Paiawon (Paieon, Paion, Paian). He has points of contact on the one hand with the Indian Rudra, on the other with Celtic and Germanic deities. His power over sickness and health is dramatically portrayed in the first book of the *Iliad*, where he first shoots his arrows to bring plague upon cattle and men, and then relieves it in response to prayer. The image has striking parallels in Ugaritic and the Old Testament.[93] But Rudra too is pictured in the Veda as an archer whose missiles send disease and death upon humans, cattle, and horses. Prayers are directed to him imploring him to spare his worshippers and their animals. He is said to have a thousand remedies at his disposal, and a healing hand.[94]

Caesar (*Bell. Gall.* 6. 17. 2) reports that the Gauls had an 'Apollo' who dispelled diseases. In fact, as the later inscriptions indicate, they had many local healing gods, the more important of whom will have been identified with Apollo. The Celtic divine healer who shows the strongest point of contact with him is Dían Cécht, who appears in Irish legend as the healer of the Tuatha Dé Danann, that is, of the gods. In the *Cath Maige Tuired* (lines 133–46 Gray), after Núadu's hand has been cut off in battle, Dían Cécht provides him with an artificial silver hand that works just as well. But Dían's son Míach improves on this by re-attaching Núadu's original hand. Dían is indignant and hurls a sword at his son's head four times. The first three wounds Míach is able to heal, but the fourth penetrates his brain and he dies. The story recalls that of Apollo's son Asclepius, whom Zeus (not Apollo) killed with the thunderbolt for being too expert a healer and raising men from the dead.

In the Greek myth Apollo reacts by killing the makers of the thunderbolt, the Cyclopes, and is punished by being exiled from the gods for a year, or nine years, and being forced to serve a mortal man, Admetus. In this he can be compared with Odin, of whom Saxo Grammaticus tells that he was exiled from the gods and reduced to servile estate for nine years.[95] In itself this would not count for much, especially as the transfer of a motif from Classical myth cannot be ruled out. But Odin/Woden has other links with Apollo, not so much *qua* healer—though it is he who cures Baldr's lamed horse in the

[93] West (1997), 348 f.

[94] References in Macdonell (1898), 75 f.; cf. Puhvel in Cardona et al. (1970), 372 f.; id. (1987), 58, 134 f.

[95] Saxo 3. 4. 9–11 p. 72, cf. 1. 7. 1 p. 25.

Merseburg spell (pp. 336 f.)—but rather as a kind of shamanic figure. He presides over the poetic art, and he is associated with the wolf and the raven. Just as Apollo's raven reports to him the lovemaking of Ischys and Coronis, so Odin's two ravens fly about the world all day and then return to perch on his shoulders and speak into his ears of all they have seen or heard.[96]

The affinity between the two gods extends to the Celtic Lugus, Irish Lug. He, like Odin, is a chief among gods, a leader in battle who fights with a great spear, a master of poetry and magic; he has two ravens who warn him when the enemy Fomoire are approaching.[97] Neither deity does much healing, but Lug heals his wounded son Cú Chulainn and Odin heals the Danish prince Sivard.[98]

However, to the extent that these gods have significant points in common with Apollo, I should be inclined to ascribe them not to (Indo-)European inheritance but to the diffusion of shamanistic motifs from the Finno-Ugric peoples, from the east to Scandinavia and from the north, across Scythia and Thrace, to the Greeks.

MYTHICAL THEMES

The mighty infant; the typical weapon

A god, like a hero, grows up with extraordinary rapidity: both estates are defined by competence, and helpless infancy does not suit them.[99] Indra was a warrior as soon as he was born (RV 1. 102. 8; 3. 51. 8); heaven and earth trembled, and all the gods were afraid (1. 61. 14; 4. 17. 2, 22. 4; 5. 30. 5); he put his opponents to flight, and looked for further deeds of heroism (10. 113. 4). Hesiod (*Th.* 492–6) relates how the baby Zeus' body and strength grew swiftly, and within a year he was able to overthrow his father Kronos. In the Homeric Hymns (3. 127–34; 4. 17 f.) we read how Apollo, as soon as he had had a feed of nectar and ambrosia, burst out of his swaddling, announced what sort of a god he was going to be, and began walking; and how Hermes on the first day of his life invented the lyre and stole Apollo's cattle. Nordic

[96] 'Hesiod', fr. 60; *Gylf.* 38; cf. Grimm (1883–8), 147, 671, 1333. For the raven's association with Apollo cf. Hdt. 4. 15. 2; Ael. *HA* 1. 48. There are Gaulish monuments representing a god and goddess with birds (doves or ravens?) on their shoulders, their beaks facing inwards as if speaking into their ears: Duval (1957), 51; de Vries (1961), 166 f.

[97] Cf. de Vries (1961), 54; Davidson (1988), 90 f.; B. Sergent, *Lug et Apollon* (Brussels 1995).

[98] *Táin* (I) 2088–115; Saxo 9. 4. 12 p. 254.

[99] Grimm (1883–8), 320 f. We shall examine the motif in relation to heroes in Chapter 11.

neonates are no less precocious. Váli avenges Baldr at one day old (*Vǫluspá* 32; *Baldrs draumar* 11). When Thor is pinned down by the leg of a giant he has felled, his son Magni, three nights old, is the only one of the gods strong enough to shift it off him (*Skáldsk.* 17).

The newborn Indra at once reached for his bow and asked who were his rivals (RV 8. 45. 4). Apollo's first words are 'May the lyre be dear to me, and the crooked bow'. Certain gods are firmly associated with a particular weapon, and are imagined with it in their hand. Indra is frequently called *vájrahasta-* or *vájrabāhu-*, '*vájra*-handed, *vájra*-forearmed'; the *vájra-* is his characteristic thunderbolt-weapon. In one passage (RV 10. 103. 2) he is *íṣuhasta-*, 'arrow-handed'. Rudra-Śiva in the *Mahābhārata* and elsewhere is *śūlapāṇi-*, 'lance-handed'. These compounds have a parallel, though a less than obvious one, in Artemis' ancient formulaic epithet in Greek epic, ἰοχέαιρα. Its first element, ἰός 'arrow', is the same word as Vedic *íṣu-*; its second element was anciently understood as being from χέω 'pour out', but the formation is anomalous, and most modern scholars derive it from **-kʰésari̯a* < **kʰésr̥-i̯a*, the root being **ĝʰésr-* (> χείρ) 'hand'. The Vedic *hásta-* is from a by-form **ĝʰésto-*.[100] Artemis was accordingly, like Indra, 'arrow-handed'. She is also called τοξοφόρος 'bow-carrying', as is her brother Apollo. There are other formulaic epithets in Homer that refer to characteristic objects that gods carry, such as Hermes χρυσόρραπις 'of the gold rod', Apollo χρυσάορος 'of the gold sword', Artemis χρυσηλάκατος 'of the gold distaff'.

While on the subject of gods' special weapons, we may notice that the Irish Dagda wielded a great club (*lorg mor*) which had 'a smooth end and a rough end: the one end kills the living and the other end brings to life the dead'.[101] We cannot but recall the rod that Hermes carries in his hands (*Il.* 24. 343–5 = *Od.* 5. 47–9), 'with which he charms (to sleep) the eyes of men, those he wishes to, and wakes others from sleep'.

The gods' assembly

The gods are imagined as meeting and debating in assembly. The motif, familiar from the Homeric poems, was very well established in the Semitic

[100] V. Pisani, *Crestomazia Indeuropea* (2nd edn., Turin 1947), 142; A. Heubeck, *Beiträge zur Namenforschung* 7 (1956), 275–9 = *Kl. Schr.* 275–9; Schmitt (1967), 177–81. J. Puhvel, however, *HS* 105 (1992), 4–6, defends the traditional etymology, 'arrow-shedding'.

[101] *Mesca Ulad* 623–38; Yellow Book of Leinster 789, ed. O. Bergin in *Medieval Studies in Memory of Gertrude Schoepperle Loomis* (New York 1927), 402–6.

literatures of the Near East.[102] But it also appears in a number of other Indo-European traditions. In the *Mahābhārata* the gods assemble for debate on the mythical Mt Meru (1. 15. 5–10), which is where they dwell (3. 160. 16, cf. 247. 8). On other occasions they meet on Himālaya (3. 40. 31), or on Mt Kailāsa (3. 140. 10). When Indra joins them, they stand up for him (3. 89. 2), just as the Olympians do for Zeus in the *Iliad* (1. 533–5). Similarly in a Hittite fragment all the gods stand up before Ea.[103]

That the gods are located on the highest and most inaccessible mountains is typical. The Homeric gods live and meet on Olympus, the highest mountain in Greece. In Caucasian story the gods live on the summit of Wiriwsh Yiqimghwa, on Mt Elbruz; in Albanian folk-tale, on Mt Tomor(r), near Berat in south Albania.[104]

The Norse gods have their stronghold of Ásgarð, which means 'god-enclosure'. In the Eddic poems they meet to deliberate on weighty matters.

> Þá gengo regin ǫll á rǫcstóla,
> ginnheilog goð, oc um þat gættuz.
>
> Then all the Governors went to the destiny seats,
> the most holy gods, and took counsel about it.
> (*Vǫluspá* 6, 9, 23, 25)
>
> Senn vóro æsir allir á þingi
> oc ásynior allar á máli.
>
> All the gods were together at assembly,
> and all the goddesses at the debate.

(*Þrymskviða* 14 = *Baldrs draumar* 1; cf. *Vǫluspá* 48. 4.) According to another passage they meet every day at Yggdrasil's Ash (*Grímnismál* 30). An Irish saga tells of the Dé Danann meeting in council to judge a woman taken in sin.[105]

The reference in the *Vǫluspá* to the gods' individual seats recalls the ἕδεα from which the Olympians spring up when Zeus arrives. In *Gylfaginning* (14, cf. 17) it is related that after Ásgarð was made, the gods built the hall that their seats (*sæti*) stand in, twelve of them plus a high seat (*hásæti*) for Odin. They set themselves up on their seats and made their decisions (*réttu dóma sína*).[106]

102 West (1997), 177–80.
103 See West (1997), 354, where a second-millennium Babylonian parallel is also cited.
104 Colarusso (2002), 266; Lambertz (1973), 504.
105 *Echtrae Airt meic Cuinn* 3 in R. I. Best, *Ériu* 3 (1907), 150.
106 The Babylonian and Ugaritic gods also sit on seats in their assemblies: West (1997), 179.

Getting about

Gods often travel long distances, and they do so swiftly and efficiently, even as pedestrians. In several of the Hittite mythological texts gods are said to complete a journey *1-anki*, an adverb formed from the numeral 1 and in such contexts understood to mean 'at one go', as if with one enormous step.[107] In Vedic literature Vishnu is celebrated for the three cosmic strides with which he traverses the universe, the third taking him to a transcendental region.[108] In Homer Poseidon crosses the sea from Samothrace to Aigai in four giant strides, and Hera springs from peak to peak to reach Lemnos from Olympus. Pindar lets Apollo get from Delphi to Thessaly in a single step.[109]

Some gods have special footwear that makes it even easier. Several times in the *Song of Ullikummi*, and in at least one other Hittite text, a god or his messenger, on starting a journey, puts the swift winds on his feet as shoes. Zeus' messenger Hermes puts on ambrosial, golden sandals that carry him over earth and sea with the speed of the winds, and so does Athena on one occasion.[110] Snorri (*Skáldsk.* 35) relates that Loki too had shoes that enabled him to run over air and water.

More often gods ride horses, or travel in vehicles drawn by horses or by some other creature.[111] Indra, Varuna, and other Vedic deities go in chariots, as in the *Iliad* do Hera with Athena, Iris with Aphrodite, Zeus, and Poseidon, and in the *Hymn to Demeter* Hades. Odin and other Norse gods ride horses; Thor drives in a car drawn by goats. The Irish Lug has his horse Aenbarr, who is as swift as the wind and crosses the sea as easily as the land. The Slavonic Svętovit rides a horse, as do the Latvian Sons of God.

Or again, as gods generally have the ability to transform themselves into bird or animal form,[112] they sometimes fly down from heaven, or back up to

[107] Hoffner (1998), 50, 53, 58, 86, translated as 'in one stage'.

[108] Macdonell (1898), 37–30; Oldenberg (1917), 229–33; Hillebrandt (1927–9), ii. 316–20; Oberlies (1998), 219 f.

[109] *Il.* 13. 20 f.; 14. 225–30; Pind. *Pyth.* 3. 43. Cf. also [Hes.] *Scut.* 30–3, and West (1997), 113, where two Ugaritic texts are also cited.

[110] Hoffner (1998), 57–62, 86; *Il.* 24. 340–2 = *Od.* 5. 44–6; *Od.* 1. 96–8.

[111] Cf. Grimm (1883–8), 328 f., 1381 f. Lists of Indian and Nordic gods' steeds are given in *Bṛhaddevatā* 4. 140–2, *Grímnismál* 30 (which is the source of *Gylf.* 15), and the fragment from *Þórgrímsþula* quoted in *Skáldsk.* 58.

[112] Cf. Grimm (1883–8), 1380 f., 1385 f.; J. A. MacCulloch, *Celtic Mythology* ((Boston 1918) London 1992), 56 f. Animal transformations play a particular role in myths where a deity has sexual congress: Prajāpati and his daughter have intercourse as a stag and doe (*Aitareya Brāhmaṇa* 3. 33); Vivasvat and Saraṇyū as a horse and mare (Yāska, *Nirukta* 12. 10); Boreas became a horse to impregnate the mares of Erichthonios (*Il.* 20. 224); Kronos mated with Philyra as a horse, as did Poseidon with Demeter Erinys; Zeus made love to Europa as a bull, to Leda as a swan, to Nemesis as a goose; Loki took the form of a mare to seduce the stallion Svaðilfœri (*Gylf.* 42).

it, as birds. In the Rigveda, where the approach of deities is not a mythical datum but a liturgical desideratum, there is, I think, no reference to their taking the bodily form of birds, but there are a number of similes in which their coming is likened to the descent of birds.[113] In Homer Poseidon, Apollo, and Athena do fly up from or down to earth as birds,[114] and on other occasions gods perch in trees in bird form so as not to be observed (*Il.* 7. 58–60, 14. 289–91). In some of these passages the god has been conversing with a mortal in human guise and then flies away as a bird. This has an exact parallel in the *Hervarar saga* (10 ad fin.). At the end of his riddle contest with Heiðrek, during which he has maintained the identity of a stranger called Gestumblindi, Odin *viðbrast í vals líki*, 'made off in the form of a falcon'. However, it seems that this faculty was not automatically available to all the Norse gods, as Loki, in order to go flying, has to borrow a special 'feathered form' or 'falcon form' (*fiaðrhamr, valhamr*) from Freyja or Frigg (*Þrymskviða* 3–5; *Skáldsk.* 18).

El Dorado

The gods' accoutrements, and even aspects of their persons, are often described as being of gold.[115] Indra and the Maruts are 'golden' (*hiraṇyáya-*, *hírīmat-*) or 'gold-coloured' (*híraṇyavarṇa-*) (RV 1. 7. 2; 2. 34. 11; 5. 38. 1, 87. 5; 10. 105. 7). Indra is also *híraṇyabāhu-* 'gold-armed' (7. 34. 4) and *háriśmaśārur hárikeśaḥ* '(gold-)yellow-bearded and -haired' (10. 96. 8). Varuna's messenger Vena is *híraṇyapakṣa-* 'gold-winged', just as Zeus' messenger Iris is χρυσόπτερος. Aphrodite has χρυσῆ 'golden' as a formulaic epithet, while Apollo, Dionysus, and Demeter are χρυσοκόμης or χρυσοέθειρ, 'gold-haired'. These adjectives are not applied to mortals, and surely mean more than the 'golden-haired' which we can apply in English to children or glamorous young adults. Thor's wife Sif had hair that was made out of gold by elves (*Skáldsk.* 35).

Indra's horses have gold manes (RV 8. 32. 29, 93. 24), as do those of Zeus (*Il.* 8. 42) and Poseidon (13. 24); the Norse gods have a horse called Gullfaxi, 'Goldmane' (*Skáldsk.* 17). The chariots that the gods ride in are of gold (RV 1. 35. 2, 56. 1, 139. 3, etc.; Yt. 10. 124; *Hymn. Dem.* 19, 431, Hymn. Hom.

[113] RV 1. 118. 11; 2. 34. 5; 5. 59. 7, 74. 9, 78. 4; 7. 59. 7; 8. 35. 7, 73. 4; 9. 38. 4; Durante (1976), 120 f.

[114] *Il.* 13. 62, 15. 237 f., 19. 350 f.; *Od.* 1. 320, 3. 372, 22. 240. For Semitic parallels see West (1997), 185.

[115] Cf. Campanile (1977), 125 f.; G. Costa, *Archivio Glottologico Italiano* 69 (1984), 26–52; West (1997), 112 (sparse Babylonian and Ugaritic parallels).

9. 4, Pind. *Ol.* 1. 41); the compound *híraṇyaratha* 'gold-charioted' (of Agni, RV 4. 1. 8) has equivalents in Avestan *zaranyō.vāṣ̌a* (of Vayu, Yt. 15. 57) and Greek χρυσάρματος (of Athena, Bacchyl. 12. 194). Gold too are the vehicle's parts:

> Mount your car with the golden seat and the golden reins, O Aśvins . . .
> Golden are your handgrips(?), the shaft, the axle is golden,
> both the wheels are golden. (RV 8. 5. 28 f.)

The Iranian Vayu too has golden wheels (Yt. 15. 57). The axle of Hera's chariot is of iron, and the wheels of bronze, but

> they have a rim of gold . . .
> The car is strapped fast with gold and silver thongs,
> and there are two rails running round it.
> From it extended a silver shaft; on its end
> she fastened the fair golden yoke, and put in
> the fair golden yoke-straps. (*Il.* 5. 724–31)

Artemis and other deities are χρυσήνιος, 'of the golden reins'. Both Indra and Zeus wield a golden goad (RV 8. 33. 11; *Il.* 8. 44 = 13. 26).

Of gold too are the gods' armour and weapons. Pūṣan wields a golden axe (RV 1. 42. 6), as do Bṛhaspati (7. 97. 7) and the Maruts (8. 7. 32). Mithra is *zaranyō.vārəθman-*, 'gold-armoured' (Yt. 10. 112). Vayu is celebrated in Yt. 15. 57 with a long series of compounds in *zaranyō-*: he has a gold helmet, diadem, collar, chariot, wheels, weapons, garment, footwear, girdle. Athena too has a golden helmet (*Il.* 5. 743 f.). Indeed she was born in armour of shining gold (Hymn. Hom. 28. 5 f.). Apollo has a golden sword (*Il.* 5. 509, etc.), a golden bow (Pind. *Ol.* 14. 10), and a golden lyre (*Pyth.* 1. 1).

The gods' houses are of gold (*Il.* 13. 21 f.; Hes. *Th.* 933; Pind. *Nem.* 10. 88, *Isth.* 3/4. 78; cf. *Od.* 4. 74), as are their thrones (*Il.* 1. 611, etc.; Pind. *Pyth.* 3. 94). The hall in Ásgarð where the Nordic gods have their thrones 'is the best built on earth and the biggest. Outside and inside it is all like gold and nothing else . . . they had all their household effects and all their utensils of gold' (*Gylf.* 14).

The divine smith

The Æsir constructed this edifice without the help of a specialist craftsman. Snorri says that they set up forges and made all their own tools, with which they then shaped metal, stone, and wood. The Greek gods' houses on Olympus, on the other hand, were built for them by Hephaestus (*Il.* 1. 607 f.). He is their regular smith and general artificer. He is the idealized projection of a human craftsman: although he makes things that no mortal could, such as robots to serve in the house, they are all such things as could be used in the human world. It is not he but the Cyclopes who make Zeus' thunderbolt.

The Homeric Hephaestus has much in common with the Ugaritic craftsman god Kothar, and the descriptions of his activity may show the influence of Canaanite poetic traditions.[116] But craftsman gods appear in several other Indo-European mythologies, and we should consider whether they reflect a common prototype.

In Hittite and Palaic texts there are references to a divine smith Hasammili, often in the context of underworld gods. He is either taken over from the non-Indo-European Hattic pantheon, or the Hattic name was adopted for a divine smith figure that the Indo-European Anatolians had.[117]

The Vedic figures who come into consideration are Tvaṣṭṛ and the three Ṛbhus.[118] Tvaṣṭṛ's name is the agent noun from the obsolescent verb *tvakṣ*, 'exercise strength'. He wields a metal axe; he fashioned Indra's thunder-weapon, and the gods' drinking vessel. He is also the shaper of all human and animal forms, and he develops the embryo in the womb. The Ṛbhus were originally mortals, but they attained divine status on account of their marvellous skills. The verb *takṣ* (~ Greek τέκτων, etc.) is generally used of their work. They are associated with Indra, whose steeds they fashioned. They also made a self-propelled flying car for the Aśvins, and a cow that yields the divine drink *sabar*. Their most famous accomplishment was to improve on Tvaṣṭṛ's work by dividing the gods' drinking vessel into four.

In the Ossetic tales there figures repeatedly a divine artificer Kurdalagon who makes things in the heavenly smithy. Like Hephaestus, he makes things on request to meet the special needs of human heroes: a cradle for the new-born Soslan, armour, weapons, a plough, a flute that plays melodies by itself. There are references to his anvil and to the fierce fire of his forge, maintained by twelve bellows.[119]

The Roman Volcanus is best left out of the picture, as he was essentially the god of volcanic and other fire, not a smith. His literary appearances in this role are the consequence of his identification with Hephaestus.

The Irish gods were served by three craftsman deities, the brothers Credne, a metal-worker, Luchta, a carpenter, and the smith Goibniu. These made the weapons with which the Dé Danann defeated the Fomoire. The most prominent was Goibniu, who made Lug's great spear and who was also thought of as a healer. His forge was located in various parts of Ireland. He

[116] See West (1997), 57, 384, 388 f.

[117] On Hasammili see E. von Weiher in the *Reallexikon der Assyriologie*, iv. 127 f.

[118] On these see Macdonell (1898), 116–18 and 131–4, where all source-references are given.

[119] Sikojev (1985), 10, 70 f., 76, 132, 145, 169 f., 209, 296.

is especially associated with the hosting of a feast at which the Dé Danann drank an ale that made them immortal and exempt from old age and disease.[120] This recalls Tvaṣṭṛ's and the Ṛbhus' intimate connection with the vessel or vessels that held the gods' drink. In the *Iliad* (1. 597 f.) Hephaestus appears as the cupbearer who plies the gods with draughts of nectar. We cannot but suspect a common background to these stories.

Although there is no smith among the Æsir, the Edda does know of a legendary smith Volund, of Lappish descent, not a god, but called *álfa lióði* or *vísi álfa*, 'prince of elves' (*Vǫlundarkviða* 10. 3, 13. 4, 32. 2). He appears in Old English poetry as Wēland, and since the tenth century, at least, megalithic barrows in southern England have been identified as Wayland's Smithy. He made famous weapons for heroes, such as Waldere's sword Mimming and Beowulf's coat of mail.[121] In the *Vǫlundarkviða* he is enslaved to a Swedish king, kept on an island, and lamed to prevent his escape, but he overcomes his master by cunning and escapes by flying. The story was well known in England, as artistic evidence and literary allusions show.[122] The laming recalls Hephaestus, while the escape from an island by flying is paralleled in another Greek myth about an outstanding artificer: Daedalus, whom Minos detained in Crete.[123]

According to a Russian text of 1261, the gods to whom the Lithuanian pagans sacrifice include 'Telyavelik, the smith (кузнец) who forges the sun . . . and sets it up in the sky'.[124] This seems to have been conceived as a daily event. A series of Latvian folk songs refer to a celestial smith, working at his forge in heaven, or sometimes in or beside the sea; the sparks fly, the cinders fall to earth. He is making a crown for his sister, a crown, a gold belt, or a ring for the Daughter of the Sun, spurs for the Sons of God, etc.[125]

There is considerable diversity among these myths, and none of the smiths' names is related to any other. The argument for a single mythical prototype is not strong. As J. P. Mallory observes in a judicious entry in *EIEC* (139 f.), 'deities specifically concerned with particular craft specializations may be expected in any ideological system whose people have achieved an appropriate level of social complexity'. On the other hand, craft specialization goes

[120] *Altram Tige Dá Medar* in E. O'Curry, *Atlantis* 3 (1865), 385, 387 f.; W. Stokes, *RC* 12 (1891), 61 ff. §§96, 122; *Book of Fermoy* 111 f.; *Acallam na Senórach* pp. 180 and 191 Dooley–Roe.

[121] *Waldere* A 2, cf. *Waltharius* 965 *Wielandia fabrica*; *Beowulf* 455.

[122] See Dronke (1997), 269–71, 276–80.

[123] On these motifs see Dronke (1997), 265–8. She points out that mythical smiths often have some physical disability or deformity, and she sees the magical flight as a shamanistic element, to which Volund's Lappish origins are relevant. But the influence of the Daedalus myth (by way of Ovid) is also possible.

[124] Mannhardt (1936), 58–60, cf. 65–8.

[125] Jonval (1929), nos. 453–63.

back at least to the Neolithic period, and may be assumed in some degree for the Indo-Europeans. They pictured their gods anthropomorphically, and if they pictured them in dwellings and with material possessions, they may well have told of a particular god who made these things for them. Two motifs that recur in different branches of the tradition stand out as potentially significant: the making by a special artificer of the chief god's distinctive weapon (Indra's and Zeus' bolt; Lug's spear), and the craftsman god's association with the immortals' drinking. This brings us on to our next topic.

The food of the gods

Our mortal life and death, our health and sickness, are bound up with what we eat and drink. If the gods are exempt from death and disease, it is because they are nourished by special aliments not available to us. That they do not eat or drink human food is stated explicitly in Greek and Indian texts. 'For they do not eat cereals, they do not drink red wine; that is why they are without blood, and known as the Deathless Ones' (*Il.* 5. 341 f.). 'The gods, of course, neither eat nor drink. They become sated by just looking at this nectar' (*Chāndogya Upaniṣad* 3. 6. 1, trs. P. Olivelle). The doctrine is partially preserved in the Edda: 'on wine alone the weapon-lord Odin ever lives' (*Grímnismál* 19); 'he needs no food; wine is to him both drink and meat' (*Gylf.* 38).

The Vedic gods, as we have seen, are *amṛ́tāḥ*, literally 'non-dying', and their food is designated by the neuter of the same word, *amṛ́tam* (e.g. RV 3. 26. 7; 6. 44. 16; 9. 70. 2, 110. 4; 10. 123. 3). It was secondarily identified with *soma*, the intoxicating yellow juice offered to the gods in Indo-Iranian cult; but *soma* was a material reality, present on earth as well as in the world of the gods, whereas *amṛ́tam* was a mythical entity. There is a rarefied echo of its status as divine food in the *Gāthās*, where Zarathushtra says to Ahura Mazdā 'Thou hast both wholeness [i.e. perfect health] and deathlessness (*amərətatåh*) for nourishment' (Y. 34. 11).

The Greek word that corresponds exactly to *amṛ́tam* (**n̥-mr̥-to-m*) is ἄμβροτον. We do not find this used by itself of the divine food, but we find ἄμβροτον εἶδαρ (*Hymn. Ap.* 127, *Aphr.* 260), which should not be understood as 'immortal food' but as 'food of non-dying'.[126] It is alternatively called ἀμβρόσιον . . . εἶδαρ or ἀμβροσίη, 'ambrosia'. It is a nice detail that it can

[126] In the same way the phrase ἄμβροτα τεύχεα, used of the armour that the gods gave to Peleus (*Il.* 17. 194, 202), must originally have meant 'armour of non-dying, invincible armour'. Apollo in 16. 680 anoints Sarpedon's body with ambrosia and wraps it in ἄμβροτα εἵματα, a relic of a version in which he was granted immortality.

be fed to the gods' horses; they too need to be immortal. Mithra's steeds likewise 'are immortal, having been reared on supernatural food (*mainyuš.xᵛarəθa*)'.[127]

Ambrosia is often coupled with νέκταρ 'nectar', which in Homer is consistently liquid, though other poets occasionally speak of the gods eating it.[128] According to a widely (though not universally) accepted etymology, the word is to be analysed as **neḱ-tr̥h₂*, 'getting across (i.e. overcoming) (premature) death'. This has some support in Vedic idiom, where the verb *tar* is used of overcoming obstacles and opponents, including in one passage death: AV 4. 35. 1 *tarāṇi mr̥tyúm*, 'I will overcome death'.[129]

Where do the gods obtain their wonderful food that is inaccessible to us? Circe tells Odysseus that ambrosia is brought to Zeus by a flight of doves from a remote source beyond the Clashing Rocks. One of the birds is always caught by the rocks as they slam together, but Zeus supplies another to make up the number.[130] We recognize here a version of the widespread folk-tale motif that the elixir of life is located on the far side of a narrow portal that closes behind the traveller to prevent his return, so that one might get to the elixir but not bring it back to the world of men.[131]

According to Indian texts too the divine Soma was difficult to get at. It was 'enclosed between two golden bowls. At every twinkling of the eye they closed shut with sharp edges' (ŚB 3. 6. 2. 9). In another account it had in front of it 'an iron wheel with a honed edge and sharp blades, which ran incessantly, bright like fire and sun, the murderous cutting edge for the robbers of the Elixir'; and behind the wheel were two large and fearsome snakes keeping guard over the precious fluid (*MBh.* 1. 29. 2–6).

In the Rigveda there are many allusions to the story that the Soma was brought to Indra from the furthest heaven by an eagle or falcon. In the most

[127] *Il.* 5. 369, 777, 13. 35; Yt. 10. 125, trs. Gershevitch; the parallel noted by Durante (1976), 55.

[128] The texts are inconsistent about whether ambrosia is eaten or drunk. See West (1966), 342.

[129] P. Thieme in Schmitt (1968), 102–12; Schmitt (1967), 46–8, 186–92; id. in Mayrhofer et al. (1974), 155–63; Gamkrelidze–Ivanov (1995), 721 f.; Watkins (1995), 391–3; Bader (1989), 192 n. 5; R. Lazzeroni, *La cultura indoeuropea* (Rome–Bari 1998), 9, 65–8, 70–5. Criticized by E. Risch, *Gnomon* 41 (1969), 325.

[130] *Od.* 12. 62–5. There are traces of related ideas elsewhere in Greek poetry. Euripides, *Hipp.* 748, imagines 'ambrosial springs' in the far west, by Atlas and the Hesperides; *pace* Barrett, he surely means something more than divine water-springs. Moiro, fr. 1. 3–6 Powell, describes the infant Zeus being nourished in the Cretan cave on ambrosia that doves brought to him from Oceanus and on nectar that an eagle brought him from a rocky source.

[131] E. B. Tylor, *Primitive Culture* (4th edn., London 1903), i. 347–50; P. Friedländer, *Rh. Mus.* 69 (1914), 302 n. 2; A. B. Cook, *Zeus* (Cambridge 1914–40), iii(2). 976–9; Stith Thompson, *Motif-Index of Folk-Literature* (Helsinki 1932–4), F 91. 1, 152. 2, 156. 4.

explicit account the Soma's guardian Kṛśānu shot an arrow at the bird and sheared off one of its tail feathers—an analogue of the one dove from the flight that gets caught in the Homeric myth.[132] According to the Avesta (Y. 10. 10–12) the Haoma (which corresponds to the Indian Soma) was first planted on the cosmic mountain Haraitī and then carried by birds to other more accessible mountains.

In other countries the divine nourishment was conceived in different forms. I have quoted the testimony that Odin did not eat but only drank wine (*vín*); in earlier tradition his beverage was probably called ale or mead. I have referred also to Goibniu's ale, clearly a different brew from any obtainable at your regular Irish Pub, that made the Dé Danann immortal and exempt from old age and disease.

In other Irish sources these blessings are conferred by certain berries that grow in the Land of Promise, or on an island in a loch, guarded by a dragon.[133] In Nordic myth the gods keep themselves from ageing by eating certain apples which are in the custody of the goddess Idunn.[134] These fruits recall the golden apples of Greek myth that grow in the garden of the Hesperides in the far west (where Euripides locates the ambrosia springs) and are guarded by a great serpent. Heracles' acquisition of them may once have been an essential step in his attainment of immortality.[135]

There is a further parallel in Ossetic legend, which tells of a tree on which golden life-giving apples grew. They were regularly stolen by three doves that carried them overseas. The tree's guardian shot an arrow at them, and succeeded in wounding one of them, but it escaped all the same.[136] This is clearly another version of the Indic and Greek myth of the bird or birds that fetch the ambrosia for the chief god but suffer loss in the process.

There are various stories of how the elixir was stolen from the gods by some interloper and then recovered. Here again the bird motif plays a recurrent part. Near the start of the *Mahābhārata* (1. 23–30, cf. *Rm.* 3. 33. 33 f.) there is

[132] RV 4. 27. 3 f., cf. 9. 77. 2; Hillebrandt (1927–9), i. 289–93. Other Vedic passages: RV 1. 80. 2, 93. 6; 3. 43. 7; 4. 18. 13, 26. 4–7; 5. 45. 9; 6. 20. 6; 8. 82. 9, 100. 8; 9. 68. 6, 86. 24; 10. 11. 4, 144. 4. In Apollonius Rhodius (2. 571–3, 601, following Asclepiades of Tragilos, *FGrHist* 12 F 2, 31) the Argonauts release a dove to test the state of the Clashing Rocks, and it has its tail feathers cut off as it passes through; the ship itself loses the tip of its stern.

[133] S. H. O'Grady, *Transactions of the Ossianic Society* 3 (1855), 113 f.; ballad from the *Dean of Lismore's Book*, ed. T. McLauchlan (Edinburgh 1862), 54 f.; J. A. MacCulloch (as n. 112), 54 f., 131.

[134] Thiodolf, *Haustlǫng* 1–13; *Gylf.* 26; *Skáldsk.* G56, 22. In *Skírnismál* 19/20, where Skirnir offers a giant's daughter 'eleven' golden apples, Grundtvig attractively emended the pointless *ellifo* into *ellilyfs*, 'of medicine for age', a word used of Idunn's apples in *Haustlǫng* 9 and *Skáldsk.* 22.

[135] See M. P. Nilsson, *The Mycenaean Origin of Greek Mythology* (Berkeley 1932), 214.

[136] Sikojev (1985), 12; cf. Colarusso (2002), 13–15, 50 f., 183.

an elaborate narrative telling how Garuḍa, the mighty king of birds, captured the Soma on behalf of the Snakes, but Indra got it back before the Snakes could drink more than a little of it. In the Norse myth the giant Thiazi, taking the form of an eagle, carries Idunn off, apples and all. The gods begin to grow old and grey, until she is recaptured by Loki, flying in the form of a falcon. Another tale (*Skáldsk.* G58) concerns 'Odrœri's Drink', the special mead, made from honey and the blood of the omniscient Kvásir, which inspires poets: not an elixir of life or youth, but still a divine, magical tipple. The dwarfs who created it were forced to surrender it to the giant Suttung. Odin inveigled his way into Suttung's daughter's bed; she allowed him to drink up the stored liquor, and he then escaped in the form of an eagle. Here the bird who obtains the precious fluid is the chief god himself. This in turn recalls a story related in the Yajurveda (*Kāṭhaka* 37. 14). The *amṛtam* was in the possession of the demon Śuṣṇa and the Asuras, so that when death came to the Asuras they revived, but when it came to the Devas they died. This unsatisfactory state of affairs was put right when Indra, in the form of a falcon, stole the vital juice.[137]

The language of the gods

In narratives about the gods there is no difference between their speech, when they are represented as speaking, and that of men. On occasion, however, certain persons or things are said to have a different name among the gods (and sometimes among other orders of being) from the one familiar to mankind.[138]

The oldest examples are found in Hittite and proto-Hattic ritual texts.[139] For example (*CTH* 733 ii 1), 'When he speaks prayers to his (the god's) wife, the singer [says]: "(Among mankind) you (are) Tahatanuitis, among the gods [you] (are) the fountain mother, the Queen" ', and so on. These formulae perhaps come from Hattic rather than Indo-European tradition. But there are parallels in Indic, Greek, Germanic, and Celtic.

Early in the last chapter I quoted a verse of the Rigveda about the division of language into four parts, three of which were stored in secret, known only

[137] Compared with the myth of Odrœri's mead by Kuhn (1859), 144–61. On the opposition between Asuras and Devas see below.

[138] On this topic cf. H. Güntert, *Von der Sprache der Götter und Geister* (Halle 1921); de Vries (1956), i. 299; R. Lazzeroni, *Annali della Scuola Normale di Pisa* ser. 2: 26 (1957), 1–25; West (1966), 387 f.; id. (1997), 352 f.; V. N. Toporov, *Poetica* 13 (1981), 201–14; Watkins (1994), 456–72.

[139] E. Laroche, *JCS* 1 (1947), 187; J. Friedrich in *Sprachgeschichte und Wortbedeutung* (Festschrift für A. Debrunner, Bern 1954), 135–9.

to the Brahman poets. This esoteric knowledge must have included the 'hidden names of the gods' (RV 5. 5. 10, *devā́nām gúhyā nā́māni*), needed for successful ritual; the expression implies that the gods had names for themselves that differed from those in common use but were not unknown to the learned Rishi. Whatever other poetic or cultic vocabulary he had at his disposal might, if it suited him, be classified as gods' language. In 4. 58. 1 'the secret name of the ghee', understood to be the holy Soma, is called 'the tongue of the gods', apparently because it causes the sacral vocabulary to be uttered at the sacrifice.

ŚB 1. 1. 4. 4 describes a ritual in which the priest takes a black antelope skin (*carman-*) with the words 'You are a defence (*śarman-*)', and it is explained that while *carman-* is its human name, 'it is *śarman-* among the gods'. Grammarians faced with Vedic forms that differed from those expected put them down as 'gods' words'. *Aitareya Brāhmaṇa* 7. 18. 13 explains how the officiating priest, the *adhvaryu*, responds to the *hotar*'s mantras: ' "*Om*" is the response to an *ṛc*, "*evaṃ tathā*" to a *gāthā*. For "*om*" is divine (*daivam*), "*tathā*" is human (*mānuṣam*).' *Om* is a sacred word, more or less 'amen', while *evaṃ tathā* is a pedestrian 'just so'.

In the ritual of the Aśvamedha, the great royal horse sacrifice, the horse was ceremonially addressed with its four names, *áśva-*, *háya-*, *árvan-*, *vājín-*, of which the last three are elevated synonyms of the ordinary word for 'horse'; as it were, steed, courser, racer. The four terms are assigned to four distinct cosmic orders: 'As *háya-* it carried the gods (Devas), as *árvan-* the Asuras, as *vājín-* the Gandharvas, as *áśva-* men'.[140] This is virtually saying that these four races each have their own language, to which the respective words belong.

In many places in Homer and later Greek poetry the gods' name for a person, place, or thing is stated, usually contrasted with the human name.[141] It is a means by which poets can present alternative, elevated or 'marked' names and vocables and acknowledge their special status.

The Greeks never go beyond a pair of names and the binary opposition of gods and men. On the other hand, the fourfold division made in the Indian text is outbid in the Eddic poem *Alvíssmál* (9–34), where the dwarf Alvíss (Know-all) systematically recites the names of various things—earth, heaven, moon, sun, cloud, wind, etc.—in the languages of six orders of being: they are usually humankind, the Æsir, the Vanir, the giants, the elves, and the dwarfs, but in some stanzas one or other of these is replaced by another term. It is

[140] TS 7. 5. 25. 2; Güntert (as n. 138), 160; Watkins (1995), 269. For the Asuras see below.

[141] *Il.* 1. 403 f., 2. 813 f., 14. 290 f., 20. 74; *Od.* 10. 305, 12. 61, etc.; a full collection in West (1966), 387.

in effect a poetic thesaurus cast in literary form; the Know-all is the poet himself.

The compiler of the Irish bardic grammar *Auraicept na n-Éces*, apropos of grammatical gender, cites three different ways of expressing the distinction of masculine, feminine, and neuter, and says that 'according to some' the first (the plainest and simplest) is the idiom of the sons of Míl, that is, of the ordinary Irish people; the second, which uses artificial terms, is that of an earlier race, the Fir Bolg; the third, an old set of technical words, is that of the Tuatha Dé Danann. These last are in a sense the gods (see below).[142]

Indo-European poets no doubt had at their disposal a professional vocabulary that included rare, choice, archaic, or artificial words. On the evidence cited above, it may be inferred that they also had the concept (or conceit) that some such words, not current in the speech of men, belonged to that of the gods.

Predecessors and antagonists

According to several of the mythic traditions that concern us, before the present gods ruled in heaven there was a different set, still known as gods but no longer active in the world. In Greek myth they are identified as the Titans. Hesiod applies to them the expression 'the former gods', θεοὶ πρότεροι (*Th.* 424, 486). The Rigveda too knows of 'former gods', *pū́rve devā́ḥ* (1. 164. 50, identified as the 'Sādhyas'; 7. 21. 7; 10. 90. 16, 109. 4, 191. 2). They dwelt in heaven before the present gods arrived there, and they submitted their powers to the supreme dominion of Indra. Both gods and Sādhyas are ruled by Indra (AV 7. 79. 2).

There are equally old or older allusions to 'former gods' (*karuilies siunes*) in Hittite texts. The Hittites identified them with the infernal gods of the Babylonian pantheon, the Anunnaki, and their image is strongly coloured by Mesopotamian myth mediated through Hurrian culture.[143] The title Former Gods, however, seems to be specifically Hittite, and may therefore be inherited. Like Hesiod's Titans, the *karuilies siunes* are confined in the underworld by gates which they cannot open. They are sometimes said to be seven or nine in number, but most often twelve, like the Titans.

According to a ritual text they were driven down to the lower world by the Storm-god, the chief deity of the ruling pantheon. In Hesiod's account the Titans are imprisoned at the instance of Zeus following their defeat in a war

[142] *Auraicept* 1493–6 ~ 4554–6; see Watkins (1994), 463–6.
[143] Cf. Gurney (1977), 15.

which they fought against the Olympian gods; a Homeric allusion (*Il.* 14. 203 f.) refers to Zeus' setting Kronos below earth and sea. The agreement with the Hittite myth points to an ancient mythical prototype. But the question is complicated. On the one hand, Babylonian myth, at least from the time of *Enūma eliš* (late second millennium), presents a parallel story, that the Anunnaki were confined below the earth by the chief god, Marduk. It could be argued that both the Hittite and the Greek myths derive from the Babylonian.[144] On the other hand, other Indo-European traditions tell of a conflict in which the dominant gods defeated a rival set, and we must entertain the possibility of an Indo-European origin for the motif. It is *a priori* likely that people who recognized an order of Former Gods had some account of the events that caused them to be deposed.

In Indian texts, though not in the older body of the Rigveda, the gods are pitted against the Asuras. The word *ásura-* was an old divine title, probably meaning 'lord'; it was applied especially to Varuna or Mitra–Varuna. But it came to have a bad sense, 'demon', in opposition to *devá-* 'god'.[145] The Asuras are associated with sorcery and the night. They are nowhere identified with the Former Gods. But there are references to the gods having defeated them:

> When the gods, having struck the Asuras, went off guarding their godhead,
> they brought the sunlight back by their arts. (RV 10. 157. 4, cf. 124. 5 f.)
>
> (Earth,) on whom the gods overturned the Asuras. (AV 12. 1. 5)

However, it was also possible to speak of a continuing struggle:

> Today may I meditate, as the beginning of my utterance,
> that by which the gods may overcome the Asuras. (RV 10. 53. 4)

According to the Black Yajurveda (TS 5. 7. 3. 1) the Asuras tried to evict the gods from heaven, but were repulsed with arrows and thunderbolts.

There are further references to the conflict in the epics. We hear of a terrific cosmic battle, at the end of which the Asuras (or Dānavas) took refuge below earth and sea (*MBh.* 1. 17). The Asuras, elder brothers of the gods, were defeated by them with trickery (3. 34. 58). In olden times they had frequent battles, and the Asuras/Dānavas always had the upper hand until the champion Skanda took command (3. 213. 3–6, 221. 32–69; cf. 269. 10; 4. 31. 4). The gods always sought the hero Bhīṣma's aid against them (6. 15. 38). Varuna fettered the Dānavas and keeps them under guard in the ocean

[144] Cf. West (1997), 298 f.

[145] In Avestan the opposite development occurred. Mazdā and his associates were Ahuras, while the Daēvas were the 'heathen' gods that Zarathushtra discarded and his followers abhorred. Cf. Macdonell (1898), 156 f. On *ásura-/ahura-* cf. above, n. 6.

(5. 126. 40–6; cf. 8. 24. 120). Daśaratha helped the gods in their war against the Asuras (*Rm.* 2. 9. 9–12).

Norse myth told of a war between the Æsir and the Vanir, a separate group of gods who seem to have had associations with sorcery, fertility, and the earth.[146] The Vanir were initially successful and broke into Ásgarð. Peace was concluded with an exchange of hostages, after which the distinction between Æsir and Vanir appears to have lost definition and importance. The gods collectively are known as the Æsir; the Vanir are as it were absorbed in them.

In Irish mythical history, as systematized in the *Lebor Gabála Érenn*, the pagan deities are euhemerized as a people who occupied Ireland before the arrival of the Goidelic Celts. They are the Tuatha Dé Danann, 'people of the gods of Danu(?)'. They succeeded a series of earlier populations, among them the brutish, misshapen Fomoire, who, when not in possession of Ireland, were given to raiding it from the sea. Bres, a son of one of their kings, ruled over the Dé Danann for a time, but so tyrannically that he was deposed. A great battle between the two peoples followed, in which the Fomoire were decisively routed. The event is described in a work of the ninth or tenth century, the *Cath Maige Tuired* or *Battle of the Plain of Pillars*; the location gives the encounter a megalithic setting. Buried in the story it is perhaps possible to discern the myth of a war between the gods and a prior race of demons, in which the latter were overthrown.

These Greek, Indian, Nordic, and Irish myths of wars between different orders of gods are not linked togther by such strong similarities as to make the hypothesis of a common Indo-European archetype irresistible. If there was one, considerable modifications must have taken place in the different branches of the tradition. The parallelisms are nevertheless suggestive.

Assaults on heaven

The heavenly gods live in regions that no one can reach from earth. But according to the mythologies of various peoples they have on occasion had to take action against attempts to climb to heaven. The Rigveda mentions one Rauhiṇa who was struck down by Indra the thunderbolt-armed as he was climbing to the sky (2. 12. 12, cf. 1. 103. 2). In another hymn Rauhiṇa's place is taken by the Dasyus, the dark-skinned Dravidian people who preceded the Aryans in northern India and were subjected by them:

[146] *Ynglinga saga* 1 f., 4 f.; *Skáldsk.* [G]57; allusions in *Vǫluspá* 21–4; *Vafþrúðnismál* 38 f.; *Lokasenna* 34; de Vries (1956), ii. 174 f., 208–14; Lorenz (1984), 329–32. On the nature of the Vanir cf. de Vries (1956), ii. 203; Meid (1991), 23; M. E. Huld, *SIGL* 2 (1999), 139–46.

Those ones seeking by magic arts to creep up, Indra, and mount to heaven, the Dasyus, thou didst shake down. (8. 14. 14; cf. 1. 78. 4)

The *Taittirīya Brāhmaṇa* (1. 1. 2. 4–6) relates that the Kālakañja demons tried to reach heaven by piling up bricks in a great altar. Indra put in a brick of his own, and when their work was nearly complete he withdrew it so that it all collapsed.

In Greek myth Otos and Ephialtes, the colossal sons of Poseidon and Aloeus' wife Iphimedeia, tried to pile Ossa upon Olympus and Pelion upon Ossa so that they could climb to heaven and attack the gods. Apollo killed them before they could grow to their full size and strength.[147] Latin poets transfer the mountain-stacking to the Giants.

The motif of piling things up to reach the sky, which may remind us of the Biblical Tower of Babel (Genesis 11: 4), appears again in a West Circassian story about the Narts, perhaps an offshoot of the Iranian tradition represented by the Nart sagas of Ossetia. The Narts tried to reach the sky by going to a mountain-top and standing on one another. As that did not suffice, they added other people, dwarfs, animals, birds, trees, and stones to the pile, whatever they could lay their hands on. The hero Pataraz climbed on top of the heap, and he would have been able to reach the sky if only he had had one more cat's tail at his disposal.[148]

The Norse gods have Giants as their perpetual enemies: not the Gigantes of Classical myth, but *hrímþursar* and *bergrisar*, Frost Giants and Mountain Giants. Thor is always decimating them with his flying hammer. Snorri (*Gylf.* 15) avers that they would climb up to heaven across the Rainbow Bridge if the way were not barred by fire.

Once again we must wonder if this is not ultimately an Indo-European myth, whatever its original form. It would have a clear purpose: to emphasize, by means of a paradigmatic story, that the division separating the Celestials from the Terrestrials is unbridgeable.[149]

[147] *Od.* 11. 309–20; cf. 'Hes.' fr. 19–21, Pind. fr. 162, Apollod. 1. 7. 4.
[148] Colarusso (2002), 153.
[149] For more on this theme see West (1997), 121 f.

4

Sky and Earth

THE DIVINE SKY

There is one Indo-European god whose name we can trace across a vast area, from India to Italy. Its original form is reconstructed as *D(i)yéus. Its archaic system of declension is reflected most clearly in the parallel case-forms of Vedic and Greek:

	MIE	Vedic	Greek
Nom.	*D(i)yéus	D(i)yáus	*Ζεύς*
Voc.	*D(í)yeu	D(í)yaus	*Ζεῦ*
Acc.	*D(i)yḗm	D(i)yā́m (Dívam)	*Ζῆν* (*ΔίϜα*)
Gen.	*Diwós	Divás	*ΔιϜός*
Dat.	*Diwéi	Divé	*ΔιϜεί* (Myc. *di-we*)
Loc.	*Dyéwi/Diwí	Dyávi/Diví	*ΔιϜί*

Various forms of the name are recognizable in Phrygian *Tiy-*,[1] Thracian *Zi-*, *Diu-*, *Dias-*, etc. (in personal names),[2] Messapic *Zis* or *Dis*.[3] In Latin the simple form is almost restricted to the oblique cases *Iouis* (older *Diouis*), etc., but the old nominative is preserved in the name of the specialized deity *Diūs Fidius*. The usual nominative is supplied by the originally vocative compound *Iup(p)iter*, 'father (D)iūs', but another nominative form, *Diespiter*, survived beside it in old and poetic Latin.[4] Other Italic languages too have agglutinations of the ancient name with 'father'; compare the genitive *Dipoteres* on a fifth-century BCE Sabellian amphora, Marrucinian *Ioues patres*

[1] Haas (1966), 67, 86, 143; A. Lubotsky, *Kadmos* 28 (1989), 84 f.; id. in Gusmani et al. (1997), 127; C. Brixhe, ibid. 42–7.

[2] Kretschmer (1896), 241; I. Duridanov in Meid (1998), 562.

[3] Krahe (1955–64), i. 86; Haas (1962), 16, 171, 177.

[4] On the relationship of the forms see K. Strunk in *Serta Indogermanica* (Festschr. für G. Neumann; Innsbruck 1982), 427–38.

(also genitive), Oscan *Dípatír*, and Umbrian *Iupater* and *Iuve patre.*[5] A similar compound appears also in Illyrian *Deipaturos*, recorded by Hesychius as a god among the Stymphaioi.[6]

The name *Dyeus originated as one of a number of words built on the root **di* /*dei* 'give off light' and located in the semantic sphere 'brightness of heaven, heaven, daylight, day'.[7] Latin *dies* 'day' is in origin the same word as *Iu(piter)*, though it developed a quite separate declension, starting from the old accusative *diēm*. The old nominative still survives in the phrase *nū-diūs tertius* 'the day before yesterday', literally 'now (it is) the third day'. The sense of 'day' also appears in Vedic *divé-dive* 'day by day', Greek ἔνδῖος (< *ἐν–διϜyος) 'in the mid part of the day', Armenian *tiw* 'bright day', Old Irish *die* 'day', Welsh *heddyw* 'today', etc. In some forms relating to 'day' the **di* root is extended by -*n*- instead of -*w*-, as in Vedic *dínam* 'day', Latin *n(o)undinum*, Old Irish *noenden* 'nine-day period', Old Church Slavonic *dĭnĭ*, Lithuanian *diena* 'day', etc.

The -*w*- forms are more typically associated with the (bright diurnal) sky. Vedic *dyáu*-, besides being the name of a god, is the common word for 'heaven'. The word occurs once in the Avesta, in reference to Angra Mainyu's falling from heaven (Yt. 3. 13), and we may recall Herodotus' statement (1. 131. 2) that the Persians call the whole circle of the sky 'Zeus'. Greek εὔδιος, εὐδία refer to a 'good sky', that is, fine, calm weather; they have their counterpart in Church Slavonic *dŭždĭ*, Russian дождь (< **dus-dyu*-), 'rain'.

Besides **dyéw*-/**diw*- MIE had the adjectival form **deiwó*- 'celestial', which, as we saw in the last chapter, was the common term for 'god'. In part of the Indo-European area it may have been used as a synonym of **dyéw*-, as **deiwós* was the source of the Finnish loan-word *taivas*, Estonian *taevas*, 'sky', and also of the Lithuanian Diẽvas, Latvian Dievs, whose role in the mythological songs, as we shall see later, parallels that of the Vedic Dyaus and Greek Zeus.[8]

[5] E. Vetter, *Handbuch der italischen Dialekte* (Heidelberg 1953), 186, 218; H. Rix in D. Q. Adams (ed.), *Festschrift for Eric P. Hamp*, ii (*JIESM* 25, Washington 1997), 144–9; id. in *Per Aspera ad Asteriscos: Studia Indogermanica in honorem Jens Elmegård Rasmussen* (Innsbruck 2004), 491–505; Tab. Iguv. IIa. 7, 18, 22, IIb. 24.

[6] Hesych. δ 521. The Stymphaioi or Tymphaioi were a mountain people of Epirus, on the borders of Thessaly and Macedonia. *Δει-* perhaps represents **Dē* from a vocative **Di̯ē*. Cf. Krahe (1955–64), i. 54, 64; Mayer (1957–9), ii. 39; C. de Simone, *JIES* 4 (1976), 361 f.

[7] On the whole complex cf. C. Watkins in Mayrhofer et al. (1974), 101–10; J. Schindler, *RE* Supp. xv. 999–1001; Haudry (1987), 29 f., 36–8, 40–4; Gamkrelidze–Ivanov (1995), 196, cf. 211; E. Seebold, *HS* 104 (1991), 29–45; S. Vanséveren, ibid. 111 (1998), 31–41; B. Schlerath in Meid (1998), 91–3.

[8] Cf. von Schroeder (1914–16), i. 528; Haudry (1987), 44. The Germanic **Tīwaz* (Norse Týr, etc.) also goes back to **deiwós* (cf. Chapter 3, n. 1). But he does not seem to be the old Sky-god, and it is preferable to suppose that he once had another name, which came to be supplanted by the title 'God'.

But in general we may say that MIE had **dyéus* (*Dyéus*) for 'heaven (Heaven)', whether considered as a cosmic entity or as a divine figure, and **deiwós* for 'heavenly one, god'.

In Anatolian the picture is a little different. The thematic stem **deiwo-* is not found. The reflex of **dyeus* (Hittite *sius*) does not mean 'heaven' but either 'god' in general or the Sun-god. In an Old Hittite text, the Proclamation of Anitta, there is a deity Sius-summi, 'Our God', who has been shown to be the Sun-god.[9] There is also a set of forms with a dental extension, Hittite *siwat-* 'day', Luwian *Tīwat-*, Palaic *Tīyat-*, 'Sun, day', going back to a proto-Anatolian **díwot-*.[10] The underlying sense of 'heavenly brilliance' is still recognizable; the identification with the sun must be secondary, not inherited from PIE.

The Greek Zeus is king of the gods and the supreme power in the world, his influence extending everywhere and into most spheres of life. There is little reason, however, to think that the Indo-European Dyeus had any such importance. He was the Sky or Day conceived as a divine entity. He was the father of the gods (see below), but not their ruler. In the world of the Rigveda Dyaus has no prominence. Not one of the 1028 hymns in the corpus is addressed to him alone, though six are addressed to him and Earth as a pair. He has no mythical deeds to his credit. He can do what the sky does: he roars and thunders (RV 5. 58. 6; 10. 44. 8, 45. 4, 67. 5); the rain is his seed (1. 100. 3; 5. 17. 3). But he is not even the major storm-god. That is Indra. We shall see in Chapter 6 that the god of thunder and lightning was a distinct figure in the Indo-European pantheon, not identified with the deified Sky.

In Greece this storm-god's functions have been taken over by Zeus. The poetic attributes of Zeus as the storm-god, as well as some other features of his image as exalted ruler, show the influence of Near Eastern poetry and theology.[11] But the starting-point was his celestial nature. Most of the formulaic epithets applied to him in epic verse refer to this: cloud-gatherer, thundering on high, god of lightning, delighting in the thunderbolt, he of the dark clouds. In other texts he appears as the source of rain (Ζεὺς ὄμβριος, Ζεὺς ὕει), and he is equally the god of the unclouded sky (Ζεὺς αἴθριος) or of the fair wind (Ζεὺς οὔριος).

[9] E. Neu, *Der Anitta-Text* (Studien zu den Boğazköy-Texten 18, 1974), 116–31; Gurney (1977), 9–11. In later Hittite texts *sius, siun-* has the general sense 'god', as does Lydian *civs, civ-*. On the Hittite forms see E. Laroche, *JCS* 24 (1967), 174–7; C. Watkins (as n. 7), 103–9.

[10] Melchert (1994), 209, 214, 231, al. A Luwian theophoric name Tiwazidi occurs on a tablet of the sixteenth century from Inandık: Neu (as n. 9), 54 n. 51. The Urartian Sun-god ^{d}Ši-u-ini is evidently a loan from Hittite: Gamkrelidze–Ivanov (1995), 793; I. M. Diakonov, *JIES* 13 (1985), 136 with 171 n. 52.

[11] West (1997), 114–16, 557–60.

At Rome Jupiter likewise enjoyed sovereign status, but his original connection with the sky has left traces, especially in the poetic language. *Iuppiter* is used with some freedom to mean the sky, especially in the phrase *sub Ioue* 'in the open air', for which the prose equivalent is *sub diuo*.[12]

The most obvious characteristic of the sky, apart from its brightness, is its vastness. In the Rigveda 'big, great' (*máh*) is a frequent epithet of *dyáu-* 'heaven', and in a few places it attaches to Dyaus as a divine figure:[13]

> mahī́ Dyáuḥ Pṛthivī́ ca na | imáṃ yajñám mimikṣatām.
>
> May great Heaven and Earth water this sacrifice for us. (1. 22. 13)
>
> mahé yát pitrá īṃ rásaṃ Divé kár . . .
>
> When he had made seed for great Father Heaven. (1. 71. 5)
>
> máhi mahé Divé arcā Pṛthivyái.
>
> I will sing a great (song) for great Heaven (and) Earth. (3. 54. 2)

The related word μέγας is often applied to Zeus in Homer and elsewhere, as well as to οὐρανός, the lexical replacement for 'sky', and to Ouranos as a god (Hes. *Th.* 176, 208). It is not a standard epithet of gods.

Another Homeric formula is Διὸς ὄμβρος, 'Zeus' rain', that is, the rain that comes from the sky (*Il.* 5. 91, 11. 493, etc.). There is a parallel formula in the Rigveda, *Divó vṛṣṭí-*, 'Dyaus' rain' (2. 27. 15; 5. 63. 1, 83. 6, 84. 3; 6. 13. 1).[14] The Vedic cognate of ὄμβρος, *abhrám*, appears in close association with this phrase at 5. 84. 3, *yát te abhrásya vidyúto | Divó várṣanti vṛṣṭáyaḥ*, 'when the rain-cloud's lightnings (and) Dyaus' rains rain on you'. Compare also 9. 87. 8, *Divó ná vidyút stanáyanti abhráiḥ*, 'like Dyaus' lightning thundering with the rain-clouds', or perhaps 'like the lightning thundering with Dyaus' rain-clouds'.

The genitive Διός can also be attached to the clouds: *Il.* 2. 146 πατρὸς Διὸς ἐκ νεφελάων. A similar collocation occurs in the Latvian mythological songs, but with a slightly different sense, as *debes-*, the Latvian cognate of Greek νέφος, means 'heaven' (though Lithuanian *debesis* = 'cloud'). There we find the phrase *Dieva debesīm*, 'to God's heaven'.[15]

Several times in the *Iliad* there is reference to the house of Zeus, Διὸς δόμος or Διὸς . . . δῶ or δῶμα Διός, where the gods regularly gather. There is no corresponding **Divó dáma-* in Vedic, but one of the Latvian songs (*LD*

[12] See the passages quoted in the *Oxford Latin Dictionary* s.v. Iuppiter, §2.
[13] Schmitt (1967), 155 f.
[14] Compared by Durante (1976), 97.
[15] *LD* 25804 (Jonval no. 78); cf. 34042 (Jonval no. 130). I owe this and the following comparisons to an uncompleted dissertation by Mr Didier Calin, made available to me by the kindness of Michael Meier-Brügger.

34127, Jonval no. 7) tells of an oak growing from the top of God's house (*Dieva nama*) that not even the stroke of Perkōn (the thunder-god) causes to tremble; *nams* 'house' is the same word as δόμος. In another song a girl is told that her deceased mother is sitting in God's house (*pošâ Dìva nameņâ*) and embroidering (*LD* 4993 var. 4, Jonval no. 948).

The Vedic Dawn is said to open the doors of heaven (*dvā̆rau diváḥ*) with her brilliance (RV 1. 48. 15; cf. 113. 4). Several of the Latvian songs mention the *Dieva durvis* (door) or *namdurvis* (house-door). In some cases it is where the souls of the dead go, but one song has the door in a cosmological context analogous to that of the Vedic passage:

> A qui les chevaux, à qui la voiture
> auprès de la porte de la maison de Dieu (*pie Dieviņa namdurēm*)?
> Ce sont les chevaux de Dieu, la voiture de Dieu,
> ils attendent que Saule (the Sun) s'y asseye.[16]

Father Sky

The most constant title of the gods who inherit *Dyeus' name is 'father'. Scholars long ago noted the striking agreement of the vocatives *Díauṣ pítar* (RV 6. 51. 5, al.), Ζεῦ πάτερ, and the agglutinated *Iupater* or *Iuppiter* of the Italic peoples. The phrase is used equally in the nominative (RV 4. 1. 10 *Diáuṣ pitā́*, 1. 89. 4 *pitā́ Dyáuḥ*; *Il.* 11. 201 Ζεύς (με) πατήρ, 4. 235 πατὴρ Ζεύς; Illyrian *Deipaturos*; Latin *Diespiter, Iuppiter*), and to some extent in other cases too (RV 1. 71. 5 *pitré . . . Divé*; Homeric πατρὸς Διός, Διὶ πατρί; Italic *Dipoteres, Ioues patres, Iuve patre*).

Herodotus (4. 59. 2) reports that the Scythians, 'most correctly in my opinion', call Zeus 'Papaios'. He must have understood the name to mean 'father' or 'fatherly', and he was very likely right. This looks like another reflex of Father Dyeus. The same is assumed for the Bithynian Zeus Παπίας or Παππῷος.[17] The 'father' title may perhaps also survive in the name of the Old Russian deity Stribogŭ, if *stri-* is from **ptr-*.[18] In the Latvian songs we find the declinable formula *Dievs debess tēvs*, 'God, father of heaven' (*LD* 31167, 9291, 269 = Jonval nos. 79–81). An ecclesiastical source dating from 1604 records that the Letts believed in a supreme deity whom they called

[16] *LD* 33799, Jonval no. 139. Other references are *LD* 12238, 19491 (Jonval no. 10), 27601, 27690 var. 2, 27378, 27850. There is no lexically equivalent phrase in Homer, but one may refer to the πύλαι οὐρανοῦ, 'gates of heaven', of *Il.* 5. 749 = 8. 393. For Semitic parallels see West (1997), 141–3.

[17] Kretschmer (1896), 241 f.; *RE* xviii(2). 934, 977, 1083 f., and Supp. xv. 1471.

[18] Cf. Puhvel (1987), 233.

'Tebo Deves'; this may represent *debess Dievs* 'God of heaven' or *tēvs Dievs* 'father God'.[19]

The title of 'father' was not confined to MIE. We have seen that in Anatolian *Dyeus, as a specific deity, became identified with the Sun. But the divine name and its variants continued to be associated with the term 'father'. In the Hittite phrase *attaš* ᵈUTU-*uš*, *attaš* is 'father', ᵈUTU is a Sumerogram denoting a Sun-god, and -*uš* is a phonetic complement helping the reader to identify the Hittite name and case-ending. Here it is possibly to be read as *Sius*, though *Istanus*, a solar name borrowed from Hattic, may be a stronger candidate. Also attested, however, are a Luwian *tatiš* ᵈ*Tiwaz* and a Palaic *Tiyaz* . . . *papaz*. The words for 'father' are not the same as Vedic *pitā́*, Greek πατήρ, Latin *pater*; they are hypocoristic forms, related to them as 'dad' or 'papa' to 'father'. We can infer nevertheless that the combination 'Father *Dyeus' goes back to PIE.

The all-seeing, all-knowing god

Another Homeric epithet of Zeus is εὐρύοπα, since antiquity often interpreted as 'with far-reaching voice', but originally probably 'with wide vision', referring to his ability to survey the world from his lofty station. Hesiod warns unjust rulers that 'the eye of Zeus sees everything and notices everything'. 'Thrice countless are they on the rich-pastured earth, Zeus' immortal watchers of mortal men, who watch over judgments and wickedness, clothed in darkness, travelling about the land on every road.' In the *Iliad* it is the Sun who 'oversees everything and overhears everything', and for that reason he is invoked, together with Zeus, as a witness to oaths. But in tragedy it is more often Zeus who is called 'all-seeing'.[20]

These appear to be fragmented survivals of an Indo-European complex of ideas. The Indic Dyaus is 'all-knowing' (AV 1. 32. 4 *viśvávedas*-, cf. RV 6. 70. 6), and this is doubtless because of his celestial nature. As Raffaele Pettazzoni showed in a wide-ranging study,[21] omniscience is not an automatic privilege of gods. It is predicated primarily of sky and astral deities, because they are in a position to see all that happens on earth. In India it is another god of celestial nature, Varuna, or the pair Mitra–Varuna, that supervises justice,

[19] W. Euler in Meid (1987), 38 f., 54 n. 27, citing H. Biezais, 'Baltische Religion' in C. M. Schröder, *Die Religionen der Menschheit*, 19.1 (Stuttgart 1975), 323.

[20] Hes. *Op.* 267–9, 249–55; *Il.* 3. 276 f., 19. 258 f.; Aesch. *Supp.* 139, *Cho.* 985 (986 is interpolated), *Eum.* 1045; Soph. *Ant.* 184, *El.* 175 (cf. 659), *OC* 1085; Eur. *El.* 1177; Achaeus *TrGF* 20 F 53; Trag. adesp. 485; cf. Ar. *Ach.* 435; Usener (1896), 59, 196 f. We shall return in the next chapter to the topic of oaths by the Sun.

[21] Pettazzoni (1955).

oaths, and contracts. Varuna too is *viśvávedas-* (RV 8. 42. 1) and wide of eye (*urucákṣas-*, 1. 25. 5, al.). He has watchers who 'come hither from heaven; with a thousand eyes they watch over the earth'.[22] The all-seeing Sun is sometimes identified as the eye of Varuna or of Mitra–Varuna.[23]

In the *Gāthās* Varuna's place is taken by Ahura Mazdā. He too is addressed as 'wide of eye' (*vourucašānē*, Y. 33. 13). He witnesses everything, watchful with his eye's beam (31. 13); 'he is not to be deceived, the Lord who observes all' (45. 4). In the Younger Avesta the sun is called his eye. At the same time Mithra, who corresponds to the Indian Mitra, emerges in a parallel role. He has ten thousand spies (or in other passages a thousand ears and ten thousand eyes), he is all-knowing, and he cannot be deceived.[24]

How does all this hang together? The eye, the wide vision, and the myriad spies that the Greeks ascribe to Zeus are ascribed in the Indo-Iranian tradition not to Dyaus[25] but to Mitra and Varuna, or in Zoroastrian doctrine to Mithra and Ahura Mazdā. The critical factor is the allocation of responsibility for the supervision of justice and righteousness. Whichever god assumes this function is furnished with the appropriate apparatus of eyes or spies.

It is hard to say which was original. Mitra–Varuna are certainly an old-established firm, already attested in the fourteenth-century treaty between Hatti and Mitanni. It would not be difficult to suppose that as Zeus grew in importance among the Greeks he took over the supervision of justice from another celestial god or gods who faded out of sight. On the other hand the deified Sky, *Dyeus, was from the beginning suited to serve at least as a witness to oaths and treaties. He appears in the role at Rome under the name of Dius Fidius (*Diūs* < **Dyéus*); this god's temple on the Quirinal had an opening in the roof, because oaths had to be taken under the open sky (*sub Ioue*). The Luwians had a Tiwaz of the Oath, *ḫīrutallis* ᵈUTU-*waza*: this is the Sun-god, but the name, as we have noted, is a derivative of **Diw-*. We see how easily Heaven and its dazzling focal point, the Sun, can take on similar functions.

The commonest Greek form of asseveration is 'by Zeus', *νὴ Δία*, or in a negative sentence *μὰ Δία*. A more emphatic expression is *ἴστω Ζεύς*, 'let Zeus know it', that is, let him take note of my affirmation and hold me

[22] AV 4. 16. 4, cf. RV 1. 25. 13; 6. 67. 5; 7. 34. 10, 61. 3, 87. 3; 10. 10. 8; Schmitt (1967), 157–9.

[23] See below, p. 198.

[24] Yt. 10. 7, 24, 35, 82, 91; Nyāyišn 1. 6, 2. 10; Gāh 1. 2, al.; Pettazzoni (1956), 132–6.

[25] The sun and moon, however, are called the eyes of Dyaus, RV 1. 72. 10; cf. AV 10. 7. 33; 11. 3. 2; ŚB 7. 1. 2. 7. The dual phrase used in the Rigveda passage, *Divó . . . akṣī́*, corresponds etymologically, though not semantically, to *Διὸς ὄσσε* in *Il.* 14. 286, and in part to the Latvian *Dieva actiņa* 'the eye of God' (*LD* 8682 var. 5).

responsible for it. It is as the all-seeing one that he is thus invoked: Soph. *Ant.* 184 ἴστω Ζεὺς ὁ πάνθ' ὁρῶν ἀεί, 'let Zeus know it, he who sees all things at all times'.[26] There is perhaps a Germanic parallel in the *Hildebrandslied* (30), where Hiltibrant begins a speech with the words *wettu Irmingot obana ab heuene*. One of the more attractive of many interpretations proposed for *wettu* is that it is an old third-person imperative (< **wētidu*), so that the sense would be 'let Irmingot know it from above in heaven'.[27]

A Germanic reflex of the god *Dyeus is not readily identified, since (as already noted) the Nordic Týr and his continental cognates seem to derive their names from the generic title **deiwós* and do not resemble *Dyeus in character. It is possible, however, that Wodan-Odin (proto-Germanic **Wōðanaz*), while not being a direct continuation of *Dyeus, took over certain of his features. In Lombardic myth as retailed by Paulus Diaconus (1. 8), Wodan was imagined habitually surveying the earth from his window, beginning at sunrise. This corresponds to the position of Odin in the Eddas. He has the highest seat among the gods, and from it he surveys all the worlds, rather as Zeus, sitting on the peak of Mt Ida, can survey not only the Troad but Thrace and Scythia too.[28] Odin also has the distinctive title of Father. In the poems he is called *Alfǫðr*, 'All-father'. Snorri uses of him the phrase *faðir allra goðanna ok manna*, 'father of all gods and men', just as Zeus is πατὴρ ἀνδρῶν τε θεῶν τε, though here we may perhaps suspect the influence of Classical learning, for example from Virgil's *hominum sator atque deorum*.[29]

THE DIVINE EARTH

The principal Indo-European name for the earth is represented by forms in many languages. The story of its development is complicated and cannot be explained here in detail.[30] The original form is reconstructed as **d^hé$\hat{g}^h$om-/ $d^h\hat{g}^h$m-*, with a 'holodynamic' accentual pattern by which the accented [é] moves between root, suffix, and ending in different case-forms, with vowel

[26] For ἴστω Ζεύς cf. also *Il.* 7. 411, Soph. *Tr.* 399, Ar. *Ach.* 911, Eur. *IT* 1077, Pl. *Phaed.* 62a.

[27] See W. Braune–K. Helm, *Althochdeutsches Lesebuch* (13th edn., Tübingen 1958), 154 (not later editions). On Irmingot as the possible equivalent of the Indo-Iranian Aryaman cf. above, p. 143.

[28] *Gylf.* 9, 17; prose introduction to *Grímnismál*; *Il.* 13. 3–6. Cf. Grimm (1883–8), 135–7.

[29] *Grímnismál* 48. 3, *Helgakviða Hundingsbana A* 38. 4; *Gylf.* 9, cf. 20; Virg. *Aen.* 1. 254, 11. 725.

[30] The best exposition is that of J. Schindler, *Die Sprache* 13 (1967), 191–205, cf. 23 (1977), 31, whom most modern scholars follow; cf. Ernout–Meillet (1959), s.v. *humus*. A divergent view recently in C. Rico, *IF* 109 (2004), 61–111.

loss ('zero grade') in unaccented syllables: nominative **dʰéĝʰōm*, locative *dʰĝʰém*, genitive *dʰĝʰmés*. Forms with the full grade of the root (**dʰéĝʰ-*) are found only in Anatolian, as in Hittite *dḗgan* (written *te-e-kan*). In MIE, it seems, only forms with the zero grade of the root were continued, with the awkward initial cluster [dʰĝʰ] generally suffering metathesis and/or simplification:

1. Without metathesis: (a) unsimplified, Tocharian A *tkaṃ*; (b) simplified, Tocharian B *keṃ*, Avestan *zå* (locative *zemi*, genitive *zəmō*), Greek *γαῖα* (< **gm̥-ya*),[31] *χαμαί* 'on the earth', Phrygian *zem-elo-* 'earthling, human', Old Church Slavonic *zemlya* (< proto-Slavonic **zem-yā*), Old Prussian *same*, *semmē*, Lithuanian *žẽmė*, Latin *hum-us*, Albanian *dhe*.[32]
2. With metathesis: (a) unsimplified, Vedic *kṣám-*, Greek *χθών*, Pisidian(?) *Γδαν*, Gaulish (*Dēvo*)*χdon-ion*; (b) simplified, Old Irish *dú* (genitive *don*).

In the MIE languages the word is regularly feminine. In Hittite it is neuter, but this is explained by its assimilation to the class of neuter *n*-stems.[33] Originally we may assume that it belonged to the animate gender and was capable of being treated as an active being, a divinity. Historically the goddess Earth is well attested. Sometimes she is named with a direct reflex of *Dʰeĝʰōm, sometimes this is extended by means of a personalizing suffix, and sometimes it is replaced by a different appellation.

In Hittite the neuter *dḗgan* is personalized as Daganzipas. The added element comes from a proto-Hattic suffix *šepa* or *šipa*, denoting *genius*.[34] In the Rigveda *kṣám-* is normally used only for the physical earth, while the goddess is called Pṛthivī or Pṛthvī, the Broad One. But the *dvandva* compound *dyā́vākṣā́mā* 'heaven and earth' is sometimes used in passages where the pair are personified (1. 121. 11, 140. 13; 3. 8. 8; 8. 18. 16; 10. 36. 1).

In Greece the goddess Earth is usually Gaia or Ge, but she can also be referred to as *Χθών* (Aesch. *Eum.* 6, fr. 44. 1; [Aesch.] *Prom.* 205; Eur. *Hel.* 40). The suffixed form *Χθον-ίη* was used by Pherecydes of Syros to denote the primal goddess who later became Ge, and by a poet writing under the name of Musaeus (2 B 11 Diels–Kranz) for the oracular goddess at Delphi, otherwise identified as Ge. The fertility goddess Damia who had a cult in parts of the Peloponnese, Aegina, and Thera possibly represents another form of the name, taken from a substrate language, with a similar suffix,

[31] L. Hertzenberg in Mayrhofer et al. (1974), 96, who supposes the Greeks to have taken this over from a substrate or adstrate language, the inherited Greek form being *χθών*.

[32] From *ĝʰō-, according to E. Hamp, *Minos* 9 (1968), 199.

[33] Schindler (as n. 30), 195. Luwian *tiyammi-* and Hieroglyphic Luwian *takami-* are animate.

[34] J. Tischler in W. Meid–H. Ölberg–H. Schmeja, *Sprachwissenschaft in Innsbruck* (Innsbruck 1982), 223, 230 n. 10.

**(ĝ)dom-ya* or the like.[35] The Earth-goddess is also recognizable under the name of Plataia, the eponymous nymph of Plataiai in Boeotia and a consort of Zeus (Paus. 9. 3. 1), for this is again the Broad One, like the Indic Pṛthivī.

A better known consort of Zeus in Greek myth is Semele, mother of Dionysus. This seems to be a Thracian name of the Earth-goddess, from **g^hem-elā*.[36] The Thracian pronunciation was probably Zemelā.

At Rome there was an ancient goddess Tellūs who had a place in certain agrarian rituals. Her name is unexplained, but she was always understood to be the Earth. From the second century BCE on we meet references to Terra Mater, who is not distinguished from Tellus, though this does not seem to be a traditional name.[37]

In the Norse tradition Earth (Iǫrð, also called Fiǫrgyn or Hlóðyn) is named as the wife of Odin and mother of Thor, but is not otherwise a figure to be reckoned with.

The Lithuanian Earth-goddess is Żemýna, celebrated as the bringer of flowers, and a recipient of prayers and sacrifices.[38] As with the Thracian Zemela, we recognize the old Indo-European name for the earth, extended by means of a suffix.

Among the Slavs the Earth appears as a deity in various popular usages and superstitions, especially under the title of *mat' syra Zemlya*, 'Mother Moist Earth'. This is a formulaic phrase in the Russian *byliny*, and *sura zemya* 'the moist earth' also in Bulgarian folk songs.[39] Oaths were sworn by Earth, and she was called to witness in land disputes.[40] This prompts us to wonder whether Solon, when he put the goddess Earth to similar use (fr. 36. 3–5), was doing something more than indulging in a rhetorical conceit.

Mother Earth

The Earth-goddess is widely celebrated with the title of 'mother'. In Hittite we find Mother Earth(-spirit) (*annas Daganzipas*) paired with the Storm-god of

[35] Hertzenberg (as n. 31). For Damia cf. Hdt. 5. 82 f.; O. Kern, *RE* iv. 2054.

[36] Detschew (1957), 429; U. Dukova, *Orpheus* 4 (1994), 7 f. The formation resembles the Phrygian *zemelo-*. The dialect variations in the first element of Dionysus' name (Διω–, Διο–, Δεο–, Ζο–) resemble the variants in Thracian personal names (Διο–, Δεο–, Ζι–, Ζου–, etc.).

[37] Cf. S. Weinstock, *RE* vA. 791–806.

[38] Rhesa (1825), 300; Schleicher (1857), 220 no. 10, cf. 221 no. 11; Usener (1896), 105; Mannhardt (1936), 357, 402, 532, etc.; Gimbutas (1963), 192; Biezais–Balys (1973), 454.

[39] Chadwick (1932), 37. 8, 50. 4, 60. 39, 63. 64, etc.; 237. 12 (recorded in 1619); D. and K. Miladinovi, *Bălgarski narodni pesni* (Sofia 1981), 201, 568. U. Dukova, *Orpheus* 4 (1994), 10, compares the Iranian goddess Arədvī Sūrā Anāhitā.

[40] Gimbutas (1971), 169.

heaven (*nebisas* ^dU-*as*) (*KBo* xi. 32. 31). The Vedic Pṛthivī often has the epithet 'mother', especially when she is mentioned together with Dyaus the father. Greek poets call Ge 'the mother of all', 'mother of the gods', 'the all-mother' (παμμήτωρ, παμμήτειρα) and the like, or simply 'the mother'.[41]

There is another Greek goddess who has 'mother' incorporated into her name, much as 'father' is in the name of Jupiter. This is Demeter, in the older form of her name *Δᾱμάτηρ*, with a Lesbian variant *Δωμάτηρ*. As the mistress of cereal crops she clearly had a close association with the earth, and some in antiquity made the equation *Δημήτηρ* = *Γῆ μήτηρ*.[42] The *Δᾱ-*, however, cannot be explained from Greek. But there is a Messapic *Damatura* or *Damatira*, and she need not be dismissed as a borrowing from Greek; she matches the Illyrian *Deipaturos* both in the agglutination and in the transfer to the thematic declension (*-os*, *-a*). (It is noteworthy that sporadic examples of a thematically declined *Δημήτρα* are found in inscriptions.) Damater/Demeter could therefore be a borrowing from Illyrian.[43] An Illyrian *Dā-* may possibly be derived from *$*D^h\hat{g}^h(e)m$-*.

In Asia Minor, to the north of Konya, there was a village with the remarkable name Gdanmaa or Gdammaua.[44] It is generally seen as a compound, with the first element, Gdan-, representing a version of the Earth-goddess's name. It is surprising to encounter such a form in Anatolia, as it resembles neither the Hittite and Luwian nor the Phrygian reflexes of *$*d^he\hat{g}^h\bar{o}m$*. It may perhaps be Pisidian, since there are several Pisidian personal names beginning with Gda-. *Gdan could derive from earlier Anatolian *Dgan by a local metathesis. The second part of the compound may represent 'mother'.

In Armenian folklore the earth is the maternal element from which we are born. The supernatural Divs of legend, who represent the old gods, often refer to men as 'earth-born'.[45]

The Roman evidence for the idea of Earth as a mother is of doubtful weight. Where it occurs, it usually attaches to the name Terra, not Tellus, and it may be due to Greek influence.[46]

[41] Hes. *Op.* 563, Hymn. Hom. 30. 1, 17, Solon fr. 36. 4, Aesch. *Sept.* 16, [Aesch.] *Prom.* 90, Soph. fr. 269a. 51, Eur. *Hipp.* 601, *Hel.* 40 (*Χθών*), fr. 182a, 839. 7, etc.; Dieterich (1925), 37–42.

[42] Eur. *Phoen.* 685 f., cf. *Bacch.* 275 f.; Orph. fr. 302 K. = (398), 399 B.; E. Fraenkel on Aesch. *Ag.* 1072.

[43] Hertzenberg (as n. 31), 96. The Lesbian *Dō-* may simply reflect a different dialectal pronunciation of the non-Greek name; cf. Messapian *Domatriax* = *Damatrias* (Haas (1962), 180). The gemination of *μ* in Thessalian *Δαμμάτειρ* is merely a regional peculiarity; see A. Thumb–A. Scherer, *Handbuch der griechischen Dialekte*, ii (2nd edn., Heidelberg 1959), 62.

[44] *MAMA* 1. 339, 7. 589. It appears as *Ἐκδαύμαυα* in Ptol. *Geogr.* 5. 4. 10, as *Egdaua* on the Tabula Peutingeriana. Cf. O. Masson in *Florilegium Anatolicum. Mélanges . . . E. Laroche* (Paris 1979), 245–7.

[45] I take this from Dieterich (1925), 14, who had it from an Armenianist colleague.

[46] Cf. Dieterich (1925), 74 f.

Tacitus reports that the German tribes in general worship 'Nerthum, id est Terram matrem' (*Germ.* 40. 2). The clearest traces of Mother Earth in a Germanic source appear in an Anglo-Saxon ritual to be performed on ploughland that is unfruitful (*ASPR* vi. 117 f.). It contains four metrical prayers, superficially Christian but pagan in substance. The first contains the line 'I pray to Earth and Heaven above'. The second begins:

Erce Erce Erce,   Eorþan mōdor,
geunne þē se alwalda   ēce drihten
æcera wexendra   and wrīdendra.

Erce Erce Erce,   Earth's mother,
may the Almighty,   the Eternal Lord,
grant thee growing   fields and flourishing.

Erce is evidently an old goddess; she is here titled the mother of Earth, but the following lines suggest identification with Mother Earth herself. The name may mean 'Bright' or 'Pure'.[47] The third prayer, to be uttered as one ploughs the first furrow, runs:

Hāl wes þū, Folde   fīra mōdor:
bēo þū grōwende   on Godes fæþme,
fōdre gefylled   fīrum tō nytte.

Hail, Earth,   mother of men!
Be thou fertile   in God's embrace,
filled with fodder   for men's benefit.

Folde, which has a counterpart in Old Norse *fǫld*, goes back to *pl̥th$_2$wī, 'the Broad One', and so is cognate with Pṛthivī and Plataia. Cædmon in his famous hymn praises God who created heaven as a roof for the children of men, *ælda barnum*, or according to a variant that has the air of authenticity, for the children of Earth, *eorðan bearnum*.

In his account of the development of religion in the Prologue to the *Prose Edda*, Snorri writes that from the properties of the earth men reasoned that she was alive, 'and they realized that she was extremely old in years and mighty in nature. She fed all living things, and took to herself everything that died. For this reason they gave her a name, and traced their lineages to her.'

There is some scattered Celtic evidence. The Gaulish divine name Litavi- is perhaps, as Thurneysen suggested, a further example of *Pl̥th$_2$wī, 'the Broad One'.[48] A goddess Ana is listed in Cormac's *Glossary* and explained as 'mater deorum Hibernensium'; she is said to feed the gods well. That she was the

[47] Cf. Old High German *ërchan*, Gothic *airkns*, Greek ἀργός.
[48] Olmsted (1994), 421.

Earth is suggested by the name of a pair of hills east of Killarney, Dá Chích Anann, 'the Two Breasts of Ana'.[49]

In Slavonic lore too Mother Earth is a well-established concept. I have referred above to her standing title of 'Mother Moist Earth'. It may be added that peasants of Volhynia and the forests of Belarus held it sinful to dig before 25 March, because at that period the earth is pregnant. She 'gives birth' to the trees and plants that grow on her.[50]

According to a Latvian song (*LD* 1224 = Jonval no. 835),

> vienas mātes mēs bērniņi,
> ne visiem viena laime.
>
> Of one mother we are (all) the children;
> not for all is there one fortune.

This strikingly recalls Pindar (*Nem.* 6. 1): 'The race of men is one, and of gods one; from one mother we both draw breath; but we are divided by totally differentiated ability'. The common mother is of course Earth. 'Mother Earth' does not appear as such in the Latvian material. In accord with the preference for the 'Mother-of' title (above, p. 141), we find instead the 'Mother of Earth', *Zemes māte.* Her principal roles are controlling the fertility of the fields and presiding over the dead.[51]

Attributes of Earth

The commonest epithet applied to the earth in Indo-European poetic traditions is 'broad'.[52] The Homeric εὐρεῖα χθών finds its etymological counterpart in RV 6. 17. 7 *kṣā́m . . . urvī́m,* while at 1. 67. 5 and 10. 31. 9 we have *kṣā́m . . . pṛth(i)vī́m,* with the adjective that is related to Greek πλατύς. This is exactly paralleled in Avestan *zą̄m pərəθβīm* (Y. 10. 4, Yt. 13. 9, cf. Vd. 9. 2), and presumably reflects an old Indo-Iranian formula. As we have seen, *pṛthivī́* or *pṛthvī́,* used as a feminine substantive, is the commonest Vedic word for the earth or the Earth-goddess, and a cognate kenning appears in Greek Platai(w)a, Old Norse *fǫld,* Old English *folde,* and perhaps Gaulish Litavi-.

Analogous expressions with different vocabulary occur in Germanic verse. In the Old High German *Muspilli* (58) we find *daz preita wasal,* 'the broad

[49] Cf. de Vries (1961), 119 f.

[50] Gimbutas (1971), 169; U. Dukova, *Orpheus* 4 (1994), 10.

[51] *LD* 27340, 27406, 27519–21, 27699 = Jonval no. 1205–10; Usener (1896), 108; Biezais–Balys (1973), 453.

[52] Durante (1962), 29 = (1976), 92 f.; Schmitt (1967), 181–3. It is also formulaic in Akkadian: West (1997), 221.

wetland'; in Old English poems, *wīdre eorþan, Genesis* 1348; *geond ginne grund, Widsith* 51, cf. *Judith* 2, *Judgment Day A* 12.

We saw that Vedic and Greek agree in speaking of heaven as the 'seat' of the gods (*sádas-*, *sádman-*, ἕδος). The term is used of the earth too. In RV 1. 185. 6 Heaven and Earth, the recipients of the hymn, are called *urvī́ sádmanī*, the two broad seats, that is, the dwelling-places for gods and mortals. Hesiod (*Th.* 117 f.) speaks of Γαῖ' εὐρύστερνος, πάντων ἕδος ἀσφαλὲς αἰεί | ἀθανάτων, 'Earth the broad-breasted, ever the sure seat of all the immortals'. The association of 'broad' and 'seat' in relation to the earth is clearer in Simonides' phrase εὐρυεδέος . . . χθονός, 'the broad-seated earth' (*PMG* 542. 24), and it may well underlie the Homeric formula χθονὸς εὐρυοδείης, where the irregularly formed epithet is suspected of having taken the place of an older *εὐρυεδείης.[53]

In the Atharvaveda Earth is characterized as 'bearing all (things or creatures)': *viśvabhṛ́t* (5. 28. 5), *viśvaṃbharā́* (12. 1. 6). Similarly the *Gāthā* of the Seven Chapters speaks of *imąm . . . ząm . . . yā nå baraitī*, 'this earth that bears us' (Y. 38. 1). The same verb is often used in Greek of the earth 'bearing' its produce; one of its traditional epithets is φερέσβιος, 'bearing (bringing forth) (the means of) life', and Aeschylus calls flowers παμφόρου Γαίας τέκνα, 'the offspring of all-bearing Earth' (*Pers.* 618). The universality expressed in the Vedic *viśva-* and Greek παν- compounds is a typical theme. So too, for instance, in RV 2. 17. 5 *pṛthivī́ṃ viśvádhāyasam*, 'the all-nurturing earth'; *Cypria* fr. 1. 4 παμβώτορα γαῖαν, Soph. *Phil.* 391 παμβῶτι Γᾶ, with the same meaning; Hymn. Hom. 30. 1 f. Γαῖαν παμμήτειραν . . . ἣ φέρβει ἐπὶ χθονὶ πάνθ' ὁπόσ' ἐστίν, 'Earth the all-mother . . . who nourishes everything there is'. The common epic formula, with the original word for 'earth', is χθόνα πουλυβότειραν, 'much-nurturing'.

In many traditions the earth is characterized as 'dark' or 'black'. In Hittite literature *dankui degan*, 'the dark earth', is a frequent formula, used especially of the underworld, but sometimes also of the earth's surface. The adjective, like the noun, is Indo-European; it is related to German *dunkel*. It is possible to imagine a PIE alliterative phrase **dʰegʰōm dʰn̥gu-/dʰengwo-*.[54] Outside Hittite, however, other adjectives are current. The Greek epic formula is γαῖα μέλαινα. In Old Irish it is *domun donn*, properly 'brown earth'.[55] In Slavonic poetries we find the reflexes of a proto-Slavonic **čr̥nā(yā) zemyā*: *Igor* 67 *črŭna zemlya*; *SCHS* ii, no. 4. 12 *zemlje crne*, 1562 *crne zemlje*; no. 11. 477

[53] See Schmitt (1967), 246–8.

[54] Cf. N. Oettinger, *Die Welt des Orients* 20/21 (1989/90), 83–98; Meid (1978), 9 f. with 22 n. 30; Bader (1989), 230.

[55] Examples are quoted by Meid (1978), 21 n. 28.

zemlju crnu, 478 *s crnom zemljom*. In Serbian the phrase is employed especially in connection with death or burial.[56] A Lithuanian affirmation takes the form 'may the black earth not support me'.[57]

Earth and the dead

The Indo-Europeans in all probability disposed of their dead by inhumation. This was the normal practice in the fourth millennium, which is when the latest phase of undivided Indo-European has to be dated, in all the lands that come into serious question as the original habitat. The deceased terrestrial returned to his Mother Earth. She had therefore a connection with the dead as well as with life and growth. In a famous funeral hymn in the Rigveda, in verses used in later funerary ritual, the dead man is advised:

> úpa sarpa mātáram Bhū́mim etā́m, | uruvyácasam Pṛthivī́ṃ suśévām,
>
> Slip in to this Mother Earth, the wide-extending Broad One, the friendly,

and she is asked

> mātā́ putráṃ yáthā sicā́, | abhy ènam Bhūma ūrṇuhi.
>
> As a mother her son with her hem, wrap him round, O Earth. (10. 18. 10 f.)

In Greek epitaphs from the fourth century BCE and later, Earth is said to conceal the deceased's body, or to have received him lovingly, in her *κόλποι*, a word suggesting the folds of a garment: *CEG* 551. 1 *σῶμα σὸν ἐν κόλποις, Καλλιστοῖ, γαῖα καλύπτει*, cf. 606. 9; 611. 1 *σ]ῶμα μὲν ἐν κόλποισι κατὰ χθὼν ἥδε καλ[ύπτει*; 633. 2 *ἦ μάλα δή σε φίλως ὑπεδέξατο γαῖ᾽ ὑπὸ κόλποις*.[58] On one of the 'Orphic' gold leaves from Thurii, from the same period, the dead man declares *δεσποίνας δ᾽ ὑπὸ κόλπον ἔδυν χθονίας βασιλείας*, 'I have ducked down into the *κόλπος* of the Mistress, the Queen of Earth'.[59] In some Roman *devotiones* and curses the Di Manes are associated with Tellus or with Terra Mater.[60] She is evidently conceived as an underworld power in concert with the spirits of the dead. As mentioned above, the Latvian Mother of Earth, Zemes māte, had a similar role and presided over the dead. So did the Old Prussian Zemynele (Mannhardt (1936), 577, 603 f.).

[56] Cf. U. Dukova, *Orpheus* 4 (1994), 9.

[57] Schleicher (1857), 189, 'die schwarze Erde soll mich nicht tragen'.

[58] Similarly, doubtless under Greek influence, in the epitaph of P. Cornelius P. f. Scipio, *CIL* i.[2] 10. 6 (*c.*170 BCE), *quare lubens te in gremiu(m), Scipio, recipit | Terra.*

[59] A1. 7 Zuntz. On other leaves (those of the B series) the deceased announces to the guardians of the Water of Recollection that he is a child of Earth and Heaven and therefore entitled to pass.

[60] Cf. Livy 8. 9. 8; 10. 28. 13, 29. 4; Suet. *Tib.* 75. 1; *CIL* vi. 16398.

SKY AND EARTH AS A PAIR

In the lengthy lists of deities invoked as witnesses to Hittite treaties, 'Heaven and Earth' regularly appear as a pair. They do not, to be sure, stand in a position of any prominence but in the middle of the closing sequence of cosmic entities: 'Mountains, Rivers, Springs, the Great Sea, Heaven and Earth, Winds and Clouds'.[61]

The Vedic evidence is of much greater mythological interest. Here Dyaus the father is frequently paired with Pṛthivī the mother.

> Díyauṣ pítaḥ, Pŕthivi mātar ádhrug.
>
> O Heaven (our) father, Earth (our) guileless mother. (RV 6. 51. 5)
>
> Dyáuś ca naḥ pitā́ Pṛthivī́ ca mātā́.
>
> Heaven is our father and Earth our mother. (AV Paipp. 5. 21. 1)

Cf. RV 1. 89. 4, 164. 33, 191. 6; 6. 70. 6; AV Paipp. 2. 64. 3. They are called 'parents of the gods' (*deváputre*, literally 'having gods for sons', RV 1. 106. 3, 159. 1, al.), 'the former-born parents' (*pūrvajé pitárā*, 7. 53. 2), 'the parents good of seed' (*surétasā pitárā*, 1. 159. 2, cf. 6. 70. 1). They are good of seed because from their union all things grow. Dyaus' seed is more specifically the rain (1. 100. 3; 5. 17. 3), with which he fertilizes the earth.

In Greek epic formula Zeus is 'the father of gods and men'; Earth, as we have seen, is celebrated as 'the mother of the gods' or 'mother of all'. However, the two of them do not make a couple as Dyaus and Pṛthivī do. The ancient pairing has been broken up. We see why. As Zeus developed into something much more than the deified Sky, his place as primeval father of the gods and consort of Earth was transferred to Ouranos, a new personification made from the ordinary classical word for 'sky'. A theogonic scheme was worked out (as in Hesiod) in which Ouranos and Gaia, Heaven and Earth, are the primeval parents, while Zeus is born only in the third generation. His traditional title 'father of gods and men' survived in spite of this. The old designation of the gods as Celestials was also maintained (or reinvented) after the loss of the word **deiwōs*, by calling them the *Οὐρανίωνες* (*Il.* 1. 570, 5. 373, etc.).

In Hesiod the union of Ouranos and Gaia is put in the distant past. The amputation of Ouranos' genitals by Kronos put a stop to it. The oriental myth of the castration is incompatible with the Vedic picture of Heaven's impregnation of Earth as a continuing process whose effects we witness. But

[61] Gurney (1977), 5; Beckman (1999), 29, 52, 58, 63, 68, 92, 121.

this picture reappears in the tragedians. In a famous fragment from Aeschylus' *Danaids* (44) Aphrodite describes how, under her influence, Ouranos and Chthon/Gaia are seized by mutual desire for sexual intercourse; the rain falls, Earth conceives, and brings forth pasture, cereal crops, and foliage. The passage is echoed more than once by Euripides (frs. 839, 898, 941). But in fr. 839 he replaces Ouranos by *Διὸς Αἰθήρ*, Zeus' Air, whom he then calls 'progenitor of men and gods', giving Zeus' title back to the Sky-god; and in fr. 941 the speaker instructs that the boundless *αἰθήρ* that holds earth in its moist embrace is actually identical with Zeus.

If Zeus is not Gaia's standard consort, he is Demeter's and Semele's. We have seen that both of these are likely to have been in origin manifestations of the Indo-European Mother Earth, adopted by the Greeks from neighbour peoples. Demeter in union with Zeus gives birth to Persephone, who is intimately associated with the growth of crops. Semele has a more electrifying encounter with the Sky-god: she is struck by lightning. Her child, Dionysus, is again a deity much involved with fertility and growth.

Pherecydes of Syros in his idiosyncratic, half-mythical, half-philosophical cosmogony described a wedding between two primal deities, Zas and Chthonie. Chthonie changed her name to Ge when Zas married her and clothed her in a robe embroidered with a map of the world. 'Zas' seems to be a conflation of Zeus and the Anatolian weather-god Santa or Sandon. Pherecydes had a father with the Anatolian name of Babys, and he may perhaps have drawn on Anatolian as well as Greek myth for his inspiration.

The Scythians, according to Herodotus (4. 59), considered Earth to be the wife of Zeus. Their name for Zeus was Papaios, meaning perhaps 'Father' (see above), and for Earth Apia (variant reading: Api). It would be nice if this meant 'Mother', but we have no ground for thinking so. We can only guess at its etymology. One possibility may be 'Kindly One', a cognate of Vedic *āpí-* 'friend' and Greek *ἤπιος* 'gentle, kindly'.

The formal parallelism between the names of the Illyrian Deipaturos and the Messapic (Illyrian) Damatura may favour their having been a pair, but evidence of the liaison is lacking.[62]

Tellus Mater is invoked together with Jupiter in a consecration-prayer recorded by Macrobius (3. 9. 11), and for literary purposes by Varro (*De re rustica* 1. 1. 5):

> Primum (inuocabo), qui omnis fructos agri culturae caelo et terra continent, Iouem et Tellurem: itaque, quod ii parentes magni dicuntur, Iuppiter pater appellatur, Tellus {terra} mater.

[62] Cf. C. de Simone, *JIES* 4 (1976), 361–6.

First (I will invoke) the ones who delimit all the fruits of agriculture with sky and earth, Jupiter and Tellus—and so, as they are said to be the great parents, Jupiter is called Father and Tellus Mother.

It is doubtful whether this coupling has genuine ancient roots in Roman religion.[63]

Snorri, in the passage cited earlier where he calls Odin 'father of all gods and men', states that Iǫrð, Earth, was his daughter and his wife. As we have said, Odin cannot be directly identified as a sky-god: rather he has stepped into an older scheme in which the Sky became father of gods and men in marriage to the Earth.

Another Germanic echo of the myth is to be seen in that Old English ploughing prayer, also cited earlier, where Earth, addressed as mother of men, is exhorted to become fertile—that is, pregnant—*on Godes fæþme*, in God's embrace. The Christian God here takes the place of the old Sky-god. The prayer may have an Indo-European pedigree, as the association of ploughing with magical-religious ritual must go back to its very beginnings.[64] As the farmer ploughed his first furrow he would utter the simple prayer that Mother Earth with the aid of Father Sky might bring forth a heavy crop. The Greek version is recorded by Hesiod (*Op.* 465–9):

> Pray to Zeus of the Earth and pure Demeter
> for Demeter's holy grain to ripen heavy,
> at the beginning of ploughing when you take the stilt
> in your hand and come down with a stick on the oxen's back
> as they pull the yoke-peg by the strapping.

Here again the earth-goddess is coupled with the sky-god, even if he is now understood as a Zeus of the Earth (Chthonios), that is, Zeus operating in the earth.[65]

[63] Cf. S. Weinstock, *RE* vA. 800.

[64] I note in passing that nakedness once had a ritual potency in connection with ploughing and sowing. According to Hesiod (*Op.* 388–93), 'this is the rule of the land . . .: naked sow and naked drive the oxen, and naked reap, if you want to bring in Demeter's works all in due season, so that you have each crop grow in season'. Pliny (*HN* 18. 131) reports a belief that one should sow turnips naked, with a ritual prayer. 'Aus Deutschland ist an mehreren Stellen die Sitte bezeugt, daß der Bauer nackt die Saat bestellen muß. Um das Ackerfeld gegen die Vögel zu schützen, begab sich in Siebenbürgen der Bauer vor Sonnenaufgang aufs Feld, und schritt, nachdem er sich nackt ausgezogen hatte, das Vaterunser betend, dreimal um das Feld herum; dasselbe tat auch der dänische Bauer auf der Insel Fünen' (de Vries (1956), i. 290). In times of drought Hindu women still perform a naked ploughing: Frazer (1911–36), i. 282–4; reported from Uttar Pradesh, the *Guardian*, 27 August 1979; from Nepal, *Daily Telegraph*, 12 August 2002 (the husbands were shut indoors with the windows closed).

[65] For Indic ploughing prayers, which are not so similar, cf. AV 3. 17, 24; 6. 142; TS 4. 2. 5. 5 f.; 5. 2. 5. 1–4; Oldenberg (1917), 258; Hillebrandt (1927–9), ii. 199–202.

Bull and cow

Cattle were of high importance to the early Indo-European pastoralists and provided them with a ready point of reference in many aspects of life. Among a man's possessions his cattle stood on a level with his wife (RV 10. 34. 13; Hes. *Op.* 405). Terms like 'cow', 'bull', 'heifer', were often applied metaphorically to human family members.[66] A god or ruler was a 'cowherd', or a herdsman of some other variety (pp. 131 and 421). The cow served as a unit of value.[67] Times of day were designated as 'the cow-gathering' (the morning milking: *sáṃgatiṃ góḥ*, RV 4. 44. 1; *saṃgavé*, 5. 76. 3), 'the yoking of oxen' (Old Irish *im-búarach*), 'the unharnessing of oxen' (*govisarga-*, *Rm.* 7. 1523*.1; *βουλυτός*, *Il.* 16. 779, al.). The measure of a small puddle was 'a cow's hoofprint' (*góṣpadam*, *MBh.* 1. 27. 9; 9. 23. 18; *Rm.* 6. 77. 11; cf. Hes. *Op.* 488 f.).

In the Rigveda the reader is struck by the proliferation of bovine imagery. The stars are herds of cattle, Dawn's rays are cows, or steers drawing her car, the rain-clouds are cows, and so on. As for Heaven and Earth, Dyaus and Pṛthivī, they too are occasionally represented as a bull and cow. 'From the brinded cow and the bull good of seed he (the Sun) milks every day the glistening juice' (RV 1. 160. 3; the hymn is to Dyaus and Pṛthivī, and they have been mentioned in the same verse as 'the parents'). 'Let the bull Dyaus strengthen you (Indra) the bull' (5. 36. 5). 'When you ride out, Maruts (storm deities), . . . the waters rise, the forests flood; let the red bull Dyaus bellow down' (5. 58. 6). When the rain is called Dyaus' seed (1. 100. 3; 5. 17. 3), it is perhaps in his bovine form that we should think of him. Indra, who has in general appropriated the functions of the storm-god, is praised in bullish terms:

> vṛ́ṣāsi divó, vṛṣabháḥ pṛthivyā́,
> vṛ́ṣā síndhūnāṃ, vṛṣabhá stíyānām.
>
> You are the steer of heaven, the bull of earth,
> the steer of the rivers, the bull of the pools. (RV 6. 44. 21)

The Hittite Storm-god too is represented as a bull.[68]

[66] E. Campanile, *JIES* 2 (1973), 249–54; id. (1977), 21 f.; (1981), 19 f.; O. Szemerényi, *Acta Iranica* 7 (1977), 22. Armenian *ordi, ordvo-* 'son' comes from **portiyo-*, cognate with Greek *πόρτις*.

[67] Cf. Thurneysen (1921), 82; J. Vendryès, *RC* 42 (1925), 391–4; V. M. Apte in R. C. Majumdar (ed.), *The Vedic Age* (*The History and Culture of the Indian People*, i, London 1951), 396; Dillon (1975), 121. Vedic *śatagvín-* 'worth 100 cows' corresponds to Homeric *ἑκατόμβοιος*, cf. Euler (1979), 165.

[68] Gurney (1977), 25 f.

The passage about Dyaus 'bellowing down' (*áva krad*) may recall one of the formulaic epithets applied to Zeus: ὑψιβρεμέτης, 'roaring on high' (also once ἐριβρεμέτης). The verb on which this is formed, βρέμω, has no particular association with bulls. On the other hand, there are several Greek myths in which Zeus takes the form of a bull, or his partner that of a cow.

It is as a bull that he seduces Europa. She appears in the story simply as a girl, but her name, 'the broad of aspect', is appropriate to the Earth-goddess, εὐρεῖα χθών: we have seen that 'the Broad One' (Pṛthivī, Folde, etc.) is a typical name of hers. Εὐρώπη is used in early poetry as a name for central and northern Greece (*Hymn. Ap.* 251, 291); from that it developed into the term for the continent of Europe as opposed to Asia.

Then there was Io, who was turned into a cow by Hera, or according to others by Zeus himself. He metamorphosed into a bull and mated with her (Aesch. *Supp.* 301), in consequence of which she gave birth to Epaphos. Io appears in the myth as a mortal, but she has a close connection with Zeus' regular consort, Hera: she is her priestess. It may be that she was an old goddess whose cult was taken over by Hera. Hera herself has in Homer the strange formulaic epithet βοῶπις, 'cow-faced'.

One of the Latvian songs, recorded in several variants, runs:

> Where have they gone, the great rains?
> —They have all run into the river.
> Where has it gone, this river?
> —God's bulls (*Dieva vērši*) have drunk it up.
> Where have they gone, God's bulls?
> —They have gone a long way away.[69]

In place of *Dieva vērši* another version has *melni vērši*, 'black bulls'. These bulls seem to be the rain-clouds.

Finally, a Russian riddle: *dva byka bodutsja, vmeste ne sojdutsja*, 'two bulls are butting, they do not come together'. The solution is Sky and Earth.[70]

CHILDREN OF *DYEUS

The Vedic Dyaus is not explicitly called 'father of gods and men', as Zeus is, but it would have been an appropriate title, as he and Pṛthivī are the universal

[69] *LD* 2221, quoted by D. Calin (as n. 15); my translation is based on his German version. He draws attention to the verbal parallel between *Dieva vērši* and *vṛ́ṣā divó* in RV 6. 44. 21 quoted above. Latvian *vērsis* and Vedic *vṛ́ṣan-* come from the same root with different stems. The same word is used of Dyaus in RV 5. 36. 5 (also quoted above).

[70] Krek (1887), 812.

parents. At the same time (as with Zeus) certain individual deities are called his progeny. They are generally gods that have a connection with the sky: Agni, the god of fire; Sūrya, the Sun; the storm-gods Indra, Parjanya, and the Maruts. But labelling these as children of Dyaus seems to be little more than a casual acknowledgement of their celestial affinities. It is not a distinctive means of identifying them.

It is different in the case of one who is called his child more often than all the rest: Uṣas, the goddess of the dawn. She is *duhitā́ Diváḥ* or *Divó duhitā́* in over thirty places in the Rigveda, and the phrase is uniquely hers.[71] She is also *duhitā́ divojā́ḥ*, 'the daughter born of Dyaus/heaven' (6. 65. 1), and *divijā́ḥ*, 'born in heaven' (7. 75. 1). This goddess will occupy us in the next chapter. Here it is enough to note that she corresponds in name and nature to the Greek Eos, and that while Eos does not appears as a daughter of Zeus—he has become one of the younger gods, and she must clearly have existed before him—one of her most constant Homeric epithets is δῖα < **díw-ya*, originally 'belonging to Zeus' or 'heavenly'. When we add that in Lithuanian folk-song the (feminine) Sun is addressed as *Diẽvo dukrýtė*,[72] it seems reasonable to assign at least to Graeco-Aryan theology, and probably to MIE, the idea that the Dawn-goddess was the daughter of *Dyeus.

In Greek epic *Διὸς θυγάτηρ*, or less often *θυγάτηρ Διός*, is used of several goddesses, especially the Muse, Athena, and Aphrodite, and also of Helen. In the case of Aphrodite, a deity of oriental provenance who probably did not enter the epic tradition until the Sub-Mycenaean period at earliest, it has been suggested that certain of her attributes, including perhaps *Διὸς θυγάτηρ*, may have been taken over from Dawn, the existing goddess outstanding for beauty and desirability.[73] Helen, as we shall see later, has a more intimate connection with the Dawn-goddess.

The divine Twins

Scholars were long ago struck by the similarities between the Vedic Aśvins, the Greek Dioskouroi, and the 'Sons of God' who often appear in the Lithuanian

[71] It is applied to her and Night as sisters at 10. 70. 6, and to Night alone at AV 19. 47. 5. Cf. Schmitt (1967), 169–75.

[72] Rhesa (1825), no. 78; G. H. F. Nesselmann, *Litauische Volkslieder* (Berlin 1853), no. 1; cf. W. Euler in Meid (1987), 44 f.

[73] G. E. Dunkel, *Die Sprache* 34 (1988–90), 8 f. If Dawn could still be called *ΔιϜὸς θυγάτηρ* in the Sub-Mycenaean period, this has the interesting implication that Zeus had not yet been firmly redefined as one of the younger gods, the sons of the Titans.

and Latvian songs.[74] The common features are clear and the inference obvious. Three separate poetic traditions have preserved in recognizable form a pair of figures from MIE mythology or religion. There is a rare consensus among comparativists on this conclusion.

The Aśvins are the subject of more than fifty hymns of the Rigveda. They are always referred to in the dual, *Aśvínā* or *Aśvínau*, and do not have individual names. The word *aśvín-* means 'having (to do with) horses', and these gods are notable for their constant travelling in a car drawn by horses that never weary (RV 7. 67. 8). They are also known as the *Nā́satyā* (or *-au*), which may mean 'Saviours', though this is disputed. The appellation goes back to Indo-Iranian times, as the *Na-ša-at-ti-yas* are among the treaty-gods of Mitanni, and the related form *Nåŋhaiθya* appears as the name of a demon in the Avesta (Vd. 10. 9, 19. 43).

They are youthful gods (*yúvānā*, RV 1. 117. 14; 3. 58. 7; 6. 62. 4; 7. 67. 10), even the youngest (TS 7. 2. 7. 2). They are *Divó nápātā* (1. 117. 12, 182. 1, 184. 1; 4. 44. 2; 10. 61. 4), which turns easily into Latin as *Iouis nepotes*. *Nápāt-* is 'grandson', or more generally 'progeny'; it is used in metaphorical expressions, as when gods are described as the *nápātaḥ* of abstract qualities such as force or strength. So it is not necessary to look for an intermediate generation between Dyaus and the Aśvins, even if 'sons' would normally be expressed by *sūnávaḥ* or *putrā́saḥ*. In fact in one passage (1. 181. 4) one of the Aśvins is said to be *Divó . . . putráḥ* and the other the son of *Súmakha-*, 'Good Warrior'. It is not clear whether this Sumakha is a god such as Indra, to whom the epithet is sometimes applied, or a mortal king.[75]

The Greek pair are usually called the Diosko(u)roi, meaning the Sons of Zeus, but sometimes the Tyndaridai, understood to mean 'sons of Tyndareos'. Tyndareos was a mortal king, the husband of Leda. Zeus visited her. According to some, the two boys, Castor and Polydeuces, were both fathered by Zeus, while others say that Polydeuces was Zeus' son and Castor Tyndareos'. They appear to mortals in the form of young men (*iuuenes*, Cic. *De orat.* 2. 353, *De nat. deorum* 2. 6).

Like the Aśvins, they are much associated with horses. Castor has the

[74] Cf. (among others) F. G. Welcker, *Griechische Götterlehre*, i (Göttingen 1857), 607; Mannhardt (1875), 309–14; L. Myriantheus, *Die Açvins oder arischen Dioskuren* (Munich 1876), 46–53, 108–14, 118 f., 154, 175–80; von Schroeder (1914–16), ii. 438–58; Güntert (1923), 253–76; Ward (1968); Puhvel (1987), 59, 141–3, 228 f.; S. O'Brien in *EIEC* 161–5.

[75] There are other references to their separate origins. At RV 5. 73. 4 they are said to have been born in different places, and the early Vedic commentator Yāska, *Nirukta* 12. 2, quotes a verse according to which they had different mothers, one of them being the son of Vasāti ('Gloaming'?), the other of Uṣas. At RV 1. 46. 2 their mother is Sindhu, 'Stream'. On *nápāt-* cf. L. Renou, *Études védiques et pāṇiniennes* 7 (1960), 68; Dumézil (1968–73), iii. 21 n. 1, 23 f., 36.

formulaic epithet ἱππόδαμος 'horse-taming', and in the two Homeric Hymns addressed to the Dioskouroi they are ταχέων ἐπιβήτορες ἵππων 'riders on swift steeds'.[76] They 'travel over the broad earth and the whole sea on their swift-footed horses' (Alcaeus fr. 34. 5). Pindar (*Ol.* 3. 39) uses of them the epithet εὔιπποι, 'having good horses', which matches the *suáśvā* predicated of the Aśvins (RV 7. 68. 1, cf. 69. 3). Their horses are always described as white; and the Aśvins famously gave a white horse to the hero Pedu, who won ninety-nine victories with it.[77] In another place (*Pyth.* 5. 10) Pindar speaks of 'gold-charioted Castor'. The Aśvins' car too is golden (RV 4. 44. 4, 5; 5. 77. 3; 7. 69. 1; 8. 5. 35).

The Dioskouroi are celebrated and prayed to as saviours and rescuers from danger, especially at sea and in battle. In an anonymous verse they are invoked as ὦ Ζηνὸς καὶ Λήδας κάλλιστοι σωτῆρες, 'O (sons of) Zeus and Leda, finest saviours' (*PMG* 1027(c); cf. Trag. adesp. 14). The longer of the two Homeric Hymns (33) describes how sailors in a rough sea pray and sacrifice to them, and they come darting through the air on their wings (ξουθῇσι πτερύγεσσι) and calm the winds and waves. Alcaeus' prayer to them is very similar. Easily they come and rescue men from death, 'leaping from afar in brightness upon the masts of well-thwarted ships, in arduous night bringing light to the dark ship'.[78] Legends tell of their appearing on battlefields to assist armies, for example for the Locrians at the river Sagra in the battle against Croton, and for the Romans at Lake Regillus.

The Aśvins act in similar fashion. They are bright with fire, *dī́diyagnī* (RV 1. 15. 11; 8. 57. 2). They bring light to men (1. 92. 17, 182. 3). 'That sustaining light, O Aśvins, which brings us across the darkness, grant to us!' (1. 46. 6). They are *púruścandrā*, 'much-gleaming' (8. 5. 32), as is their chariot (7. 72. 1); the attribute has been compared with the name of Polydeuces, interpreted as by dissimilation from Πολυλεύκης, 'very lucent'.[79] They are winged (*suparṇā́*, 4. 43. 3).

They are rescuers (1. 112. 5–8, 116. 3–24, 117. 3–18), most prompt to come against misfortune (3. 58. 3). The hymnists list many legendary instances in which they saved persons from diverse predicaments. They have brought, and can yet bring, help in battle (1. 112. 14, 22; 116. 20 f.; 8. 8. 21, 35. 12). They

[76] Hymn. Hom. 17. 5, 33. 18; cf. Alcman *PMGF* 2, Simon. eleg. 11. 30, Pind. *Isth.* 1. 17.

[77] Pind. *Pyth.* 1. 66, Eur. *Hel.* 639, Cic. *De nat. deorum* 2. 6, Ov. *Met.* 8. 373; RV 1. 116. 6, 118. 9, 119. 10; 7. 71. 5; 10. 39. 10.

[78] Alc. 34. 7–12. Cf. also Eur. *El.* 992 f., 1241 f., 1347–53, *Hel.* 1495–1505, 1664 f.; *PMG* 998 (= Pind. fr. 140c), 1004; Theoc. 22. 6–22, etc.

[79] Durante (1976), 164 n. 7. For a different etymology of Polydeuces' name see R. Janko, *Glotta* 65 (1987), 69–72.

saved Bhujyu from drowning when he was abandoned in the sea at the ends of the earth (1. 116. 3–5, 117. 14 f., 119. 4, 8, 182. 5–7, etc.), and also Rebha, whom evil men had attacked and thrown into water. Their car comes from the ocean (*samudrā́d*, literally 'the gathered waters', 4. 43. 5); their horses were born in the waters (1. 184. 3).

The Baltic figures in whom we are interested are referred to as the Sons of God: in Lithuanian *Dievo sunẽliai*, in Latvian *Dieva dēli*. Their similarities to the Aśvins and Dioskouroi appear initially in this title, and in the frequent references to their horses. Their number, where specified, fluctuates. They are two in *LD* 33766 and 34023 (Jonval nos. 413 and 102), but in certain other songs four or five, or only one; in the last case we may suspect the influence of Christianity. And because of Christianity it is not surprising that they do not have a religious but only a mythological status. They do not perform services for mankind or rescue them from perils. There may, however, be an echo of their ancient function in a song where they are urged to save the Daughter of the Sun from sinking in the sea:

> La Fille de Saule traversait la mer,
> on ne voyait que sa couronne.
> Ramez la barque, Fils de Dieu,
> sauvez l'âme [*var.* la vie] de Saule!
> (*LD* 33969, Jonval no. 402, trans. Jonval.)

They ride every morning to see the Sun (*LD* 33977, Jonval no. 390). The Aśvins too are associated with the dawn: they (and their car) are *prātaryā́vāṇa*, 'early-morning-going' (RV 2. 39. 2; 5. 77. 1; 10. 40. 1, 41. 2), or *prātaryújā*, 'early-morning-yoked' (1. 22. 1; 10. 41. 2). They accompany Uṣas, the Dawn goddess (1. 183. 2; 8. 5. 2); she is their sister (1. 180. 2) or friend (4. 52. 2 f.), born at the yoking of their car (10. 39. 12).

The Dioskouroi have no obvious connection with dawn or sunrise. But we shall see in the next chapter that their sister Helen corresponds in a most interesting way both to the Baltic Daughter of the Sun and to a Vedic Daughter of the Sun with whom the Aśvins have much to do. We shall find that these figures are bound together in a mythical complex that confirms the identity of the Aśvins, the Dioskouroi, and the Dieva dēli beyond peradventure.

Dimmer traces of these Sons of *Dyeus may be recognized elsewhere with varying degrees of probability. In Greek myth, besides the Dioskouroi, who are particularly associated with Laconia, we can find other pairs of twins who have some of the right features. There are the Thebans Amphion and Zethos, who were sons of Zeus, had a local cult as divinities, and are called λευκόπωλοι 'white-colt', 'Zeus' white colts', or even 'the white-colt

Dioskouroi'.[80] There are also the famous Siamese twins Kteatos and Eurytos, the Molione: they too are λεύκιπποι κόροι, 'white-horse youths', and they were born from an egg, like Helen.[81] Their divine father, however, was Poseidon, not Zeus. The same is true of the Apharetidai, Idas and Lynkeus, who appear in legend as rivals of the Tyndaridai and have been dubbed 'the Messenian Dioskouroi'.

Timaeus wrote that the Celts who lived by the Ocean venerated the Dioskouroi above all other gods, having an ancient tradition of their having visited them from the Ocean.[82] This was taken as evidence that the Argonauts (with whom the Dioskouroi sailed) had passed that way. But to us it recalls the Vedic conception of the Aśvins' coming from the *samudrá-*. Tacitus (*Germ.* 43. 3) reports that the Nahanarvali in Silesia had a grove sacred to two gods called the Alcis: they were brothers, and *iuuenes*, and identified with the Roman Castor and Pollux.[83]

Jan de Vries drew attention in this context to a number of Germanic legends of migrations and conquests led by pairs of princely brothers (and also to the danger of seeing Dioskouroi in every pair of brothers occurring in saga). One pair stands out among these: Hengist and Horsa, the fabled leaders of the Anglo-Saxon invasion of England, who came over the sea in response to a plea from the beleaguered British king Vortigern.[84] They were descendants of Woden. Their names mean Stallion and Horse, and it seems significant that the same names, Hengist and Hors, were given to pairs of horses' heads that used to adorn farmhouse gables in Lower Saxony and Schleswig-Holstein, perhaps a relic of pagan cult.

Further echoes of 'Dioskouric' myth have been sought in Irish and Welsh saga. Some of the material is certainly suggestive, but as it can hardly be said to add weight to the argument for the Indo-European myth, I will pass over the details, which the curious may explore elsewhere.[85]

[80] Eur. *HF* 29 f., *Antiope* fr. 223. 127 f., *Phoen.* 606; sch. *Od.* 19. 518 (Pherec. fr. 124 Fowler); cf. Hesych. δ 1929.

[81] Ibycus *PMGF* 285. 1. In late sources the Dioskouroi themselves are born from the egg with Helen: see Gantz (1993), 321.

[82] *FGrHist* 566 F 85 §4; de Vries (1956), ii. 247, thinks that the notice relates to Germans on the North Sea.

[83] Tac. *Germ.* 43. 3. Cf. Grimm (1883–8), 66 f., 366, 1390; Schrader (1909), 39; Güntert (1923), 262 f.; R. Much, 'Wandalische Götter', *Mitteilungen der Schlesischen Gesellschaft für Volkskunde* 27 (1926), 20–9; id., *Die Germania des Tacitus* (Heidelberg 1937), 380 f.; de Vries (1956), ii. 247–55; Ward (1968), 42–5; bibliography, ibid. 122 f.

[84] Principal sources in Clemen (1928), 40 f. (Bede), 55 (Nennius), 73 f. (William of Malmesbury); cf. de Vries (1956), ii. 252 f.; Ward (1968), 54–6. For fuller discussion of other Germanic legends see Ward, 50–84; id. in Cardona (1970), 405–20.

[85] See especially S. O'Brien, *JIES* 10 (1982), 117–36; id. in *EIEC* 161 f.

There are many artistic representations of twinned figures who might be interpreted as Dioskouric. They come from diverse countries and periods. From the third-millennium Cycladic civilization of the Aegean, which has Anatolian affinities, there is a figurine of two males closely conjoined in an embrace that seems mutually supportive, not erotic; they are presumably a significant pair of brothers. From the second and first millennia BCE there are rock drawings and decorated bronze objects from Scandinavia, some of which show two figures in association with horses, a ship, and/or the sun.[86] Artefacts from Luristan in western Iran from the first half of the first millennium depict the birth of twin deities from a sky- or sun-god.[87] Urns from the La Tène period in east Silesia show riders of horses or stags linked in pairs by a crossbar; some have connected this with the ancient Spartan *dokana*, an arrangement of two parallel wooden beams joined by two crossbars, which represented the Dioskouroi and was supposed to symbolize their indissoluble fraternal love.[88] A west Slavonic wooden effigy of the eleventh or twelfth century, from an island on the Tollense-See near Neubrandenburg, shows two conjoined male figures.[89] And so forth.

Even without this penumbral evidence we have sufficient grounds for belief in a pair of MIE divine twins, the Sons of *Dyeus, who rode horses through the sky and rescued men from mortal peril in battle and at sea. If it be asked what sea the worshippers of these prehistoric divinities went down to in **nāwes* and sailed on and foundered in, the likely answer is the northern Black Sea or the Sea of Azov.

A one-parent family?

We have identified a father Heaven, a mother Earth, a daughter Dawn, and twin sons. A nice happy family, it might seem. But the sons and the daughter have nothing to do with Mother Earth. Their affinity is strictly with the sky. The union of Heaven and Earth, with his fertilization of her by means of his rain, is all to do with the production and sustenance of terrestrial plant and animal life. They may be celebrated in general terms as the parents of the gods as well as of mankind, but in the few cases where they are the parents of a

[86] Güntert (1923), 272 f.; Ward (1968), 46 f.; Gelling–Davidson (1969), 126–8, 176–9.

[87] See illustrations in R. Ghirshman, *Artibus Asiae* 21 (1958), 37–42. He interprets them in terms of the later-attested myth of the birth of Ohrmazd and Ahriman from Zurvan (Time).

[88] E. Krüger, *Trierer Zeitschrift* 15 (1940), 8–27; 16/17 (1941/2), 1–66, esp. 44–7; de Vries (1956), ii. 248–50. *Dokana*: Plut. *De fraterno amore* 478a.

[89] Váňa (1992), 182 Abb. 26. The twin gods Lel and Lelpol (or Polel) reported from a sixteenth-century Polish chronicle seem to be spurious (Váňa, 204).

specific god, it is one connected with earthly fertility, like Dionysus the son of Zeus and Semele, or Persephone the daugher of Zeus and Demeter.

If Earth is not the mother of Dawn and the Twins, who is? The answer is that there need not be one. This is mythology, not biology. In Hesiodic myth Chaos, Gaia, and Hera all achieve parthenogenesis, and Zeus fathers Athena by himself, out of his cranium. The birth of Dawn is a natural daily event: she appears in or out of the sky. It is impertinent even to ask how *Dyeus fathered the Twins. It is enough that they are his children. There need not have been any story about their births.

G. E. Dunkel, in an elegant but tenuous argument expounded in an inaugural lecture, has sought to identify the missing mother as *Diwōnā.[90] This would be a spouse-goddess of a type discussed in the last chapter, with a name formed from her husband's by suffixation. Dunkel suggests that she survives in Dione, Zeus' consort at Dodona, and in myth the mother of an Aphrodite who might have usurped the place of the Dawn-goddess. In Vedic one might expect the remodelled form **Divānī́*. It does not occur, but Dunkel thinks that, as Indra has become the chief god, *Divānī's personality has been taken over by Indra's wife Indrāṇī. In RV 10. 86, a humorous dialogue poem, Indrāṇī displays (under provocation) something of a jealous and quarrelsome disposition, reminiscent of Hera's in Homer. Dunkel hypothesizes that this was a traditional feature of *Diwōnā, transferred from *Divānī to Indrāṇī in India and from Dione to Hera in Greece.

Evidence for *Diwōnā does not extend further, for as Dunkel acknowledges, the Roman goddesses Iūnō and Dīāna are not relevant. In Greek, however, besides Dione, there are traces of another consort of Zeus with a name formed from his, in the Mycenaean *di-u-ja*, *di-wi-ja*, Pamphylian *Διϝια*. A goddess Dia (*Δῖα* < **Díw-ya*), identified with Hebe, was worshipped in classical times in Phleious and Sicyon (Strabo 8. 6. 24). There was also a Dia, represented as a mortal, to whom Zeus made love in the form of a horse, resulting in the birth of Peirithoos.[91] Dia then married Ixion, whom Zeus befriended and received in heaven. There Ixion was overcome with a desire for Hera. He was deluded with a phantom Hera made from cloud, and from their union the first Centaur was born, half horse, half man.

This strange story shows beguiling similarities with the Indian myth of Saraṇyū. Her father, the god Tvaṣṭṛ, offered her in marriage. She was given to the mortal Vivasvat, but after becoming pregnant with the Aśvins she assumed the form of a mare and ran away, leaving Vivasvat with a facsimile of herself. Or according to a later version she was not yet pregnant, and Vivasvat

[90] 'Vater Himmels Gattin', *Die Sprache* 34 (1988–90), 1–26.

[91] Sch. Oxy. 421 and D on *Il.* 1. 263; Nonn. *Dion.* 7. 125; Eust. in Hom. 101. 1.

(now interpreted as the sun) took the form of a horse and pursued her, and it was then that she conceived.[92] Common to the Indian and the Greek myth are the union of immortal bride and mortal bridegroom, the substitution of a facsimile for the wife, the motif of horse-metamorphosis, and the birth of a son or sons with equine characteristics.

Finally, we should consider the Homeric epithet δῖα, meaning originally 'belonging to Zeus'. We have noted that this is applied in epic formula to Eos, the Dawn, originally the daughter of *Dyeus. It is also applied to χθών, the earth.[93] It is possible to speculate that this goes back to a time when *$D^{h}\hat{g}^{h}$ōm was still the consort of *Dyeus, and that from this collocation χθὼν δῖα the adjective came to seem appropriate to other major constituents of the cosmos, hence ἅλα δῖαν, αἰθέρα δῖαν. It may also be suggested that the formulae δῖα θεάων and δῖα γυναικῶν, in extant epic applied freely to any goddess, nymph, or respectable woman, originally designated consorts of Zeus.

[92] RV 10. 17. 1 f.; AV 18. 2. 33; Yāska, *Nirukta* 12. 10; *Bṛhaddevatā* 6. 162–7. 7; Wendy D. O'Flaherty, *Hindu Myths* (Harmondsworth 1975), 60 f., 69, 318.

[93] *Il.* 14. 347 χθὼν δῖα, 24. 532 χθόνα δῖαν, etc.

5

Sun and Daughter

THE DIVINE SUN

The words for 'sun' in nearly all branches of the Indo-European family, or at least of MIE, are related. Quite how they are related is a problem of great complexity that has not yet been resolved to everyone's satisfaction.[1] The most widely favoured approach is to postulate a prototype *$s.h_2w.l$*, a neuter noun with variable vowel gradation in either syllable, a susceptibility to laryngeal metathesis (*h_2w > *wh_2), and a heteroclite declension in which the final *-l* of the nominative/accusative alternated with *-n-* in oblique cases. No other such *l/n* heteroclite is found, though *r/n* heteroclites form a well-established class. This neuter prototype is continued in one way or another by Vedic *súvar/svàr*, Avestan *hvarə* (Gāthic genitive *x^vəng* < **swens*), Gothic *sauil* (all neuters), and Latin *sōl* (masculine). Other masculine or feminine forms were created by adding the suffix *-(i)yos/-yā*: *suh_2l-iyos* > Vedic *sū́r(i)ya-* (also *sū́ra-*); *seh_2wel-iyos* > Greek **hāweliyos*, ἀ(Ϝ)έλιος, ἥλιος; *seh_2ul-yā* > Lithuanian *saulė*. The oblique stem in *-n-* gave rise to Germanic **sun-(n)ōn* (feminine), from which German *Sonne*, English *sun*, etc.

Solar deities are often mentioned in Hittite texts, their names largely concealed under the Sumerogram ᵈUTU, sometimes with a phonetic complement indicating the Hittite ending; this generally has the form *-uš*. We saw in the last chapter that one name for the Sun-god in Old Hittite times was Sius-summi, and that Luwian and Palaic had the cognate names Tiwat-, Tiyat-. The usual later Hittite name for the Sun-god of heaven seems to have been Istanus, adapted from a native Hattic goddess Estān, and ᵈUTU-*uš* may represent this. In just one text (*KUB* xvii. 19. 9) we find a ᵈUTU-*li-i-aš*, which, it has been thought, might represent something like **Sahhulias*. That would be an isolated Anatolian instance of the name derived from *$s.h_2w.l$*.

[1] For some recent discussions see R. P. Beekes, *MSS* 43 (1984), 5–8 (and in *EIEC* 556); A. Bammesberger, *ZVS* 98 (1985), 111–13; M. E. Huld, *ZVS* 99 (1986), 194–202, who is criticized briefly by E. Hamp, *HS* 103 (1990), 193 f.; R. Wachter, *HS* 110 (1997), 4–20.

On the other hand, there is a Luwian neuter noun written *še-ḫu-wa-a-a[l]* or *ši-wa-al*; it denotes a source of artificial illumination, in one place it is accompanied by a determinative indicating a metal object, and it evidently meant 'lamp', 'brazier', or something of the kind.[2] This puts a different complexion on the lexical question. That a word originally meaning 'sun' was applied to a lamp seems altogether less likely than the alternative, that a word meaning 'lamp' was applied to the sun. In a Hittite prayer to the Sun-goddess of Arinna she is called 'the land of Hatti's torch (*zupparu*)', and in a narrative text the Sun and Moon say, 'we are the torches of what [lands] you [govern]'.[3] Greek poets speak of 'the pure lamp (λαμπάς) of the sun' (Parmenides B 10. 3; cf. Eur. *Ion* 1467), 'the god's lamp' (Eur. *Med.* 352), or simply 'the λαμπάς' (Soph. *Ant.* 879). In Old English verse the sun is referred to in a variety of similar phrases: *rodores candel* 'heaven's candle' (*Beow.* 1572), *woruldcandel* (ibid. 1965), *heofoncandel* (*Andreas* 243), *wedercandel* (ibid. 372), *Godes candel* (*Battle of Brunanburh* 15, *Phoenix* 91).

This suggests that MIE *$^{*}s.h_2w.l$* 'sun' may go back to some such expression as 'the lamp of *Dyeus'. It is then easier to understand why the oldest recoverable word for the sun is a neuter. As we have noted, the oldest 'gender' distinction in Indo-European was between animate and inanimate, between active principles and mere physical entities. A lamp is naturally assigned to the latter class, but we should have expected the sun to be assigned from the beginning to the former. Historically we observe a general tendency to personalize the original neuter and to make the sun and the Sun-god masculine or feminine. We have seen that Indo-European deities are on the whole male, except for certain categories. In the case of the Sun we find a geographical division. In Vedic the neuter *súvar/svàr* remains in the less personal sense of 'sunshine, sunlight', while beside it there is the more personalized masculine derivative *Sū́rya-*, as it were 'the god of the sunlight'.[4] The Greek ἥλιος and the Latin *sol* are likewise masculine, as are Middle Welsh *heul*, Cornish *heu(u)l*, Breton *heol*. In Slavonic the word has a different suffix and remains neuter, Old Church Slavonic *slŭnĭce*, etc. Gothic has neuter *sauil* besides feminine (but sometimes neuter) *sunno*. Across northern Europe the feminine

[2] F. Starke, *ZVS* 95 (1981), 152–7; id., *Untersuchung zur Stammbildung des keilschrift-luwischen Nomens* (Wiesbaden 1990), 342 f. The forms may go back to *$^{*}seh_2wṓl$*; cf. Melchert (1994), 264. Pretonic *[e] gave [i] in Luwian (ibid. 240).

[3] *CTH* 383 i 4 = Lebrun (1980), 310; *CTH* 364 (*The Song of Silver*) 7. 3, trs. Hoffner (1998), 50.

[4] But *sū́rya-* can equally be used of the sun as a celestial body. Cf. B. Schlerath in Meid (1998), 96, on the development ' "Sonne"—"der" oder "die sonnenhafte"—"Gott Sonne", wobei dann unter Umständen "Gott Sonne" auch wieder das Gestirn bezeichnen konnte'. As for *svàr*, it sometimes appears in lists of divinities and divine cosmic elements, as in RV 5. 46. 3; 7. 44. 1; 10. 36. 1, 65. 1, 14.

gender prevails: Baltic *saule*, Germanic **sunnōn* and derivatives, Old Norse *sól*, and Irish *súil* 'eye', which is generally thought to be the same word;[5] the Irish word for 'sun', *grían*, is also feminine. This northerly feminine zone is perhaps to be accounted for in terms of influence from the substrate population(s).

Finally, as a lamp is an item of material culture, we must reckon with the possibility that the old Indo-European word was originally a loan from another language. That might explain its unusual morphology.

The Sun as a deity

There is extensive evidence for the recognition of the Sun as a deity among Indo-European peoples. The solar gods mentioned in Hittite texts include one or more of probably non-Indo-European pedigree, such as the Sun-goddess of Arinna, but others, like the above-mentioned Sius-summi and Tiwat/Tiyat, are securely Indo-European. It is also worth noting that in taking over the name of the Hattic Sun-goddess Estān, the Hittites applied it to a male god. 'The goddess took on the personality of an ancient Indo-European god.'[6]

The Indic gods listed in Suppiluliuma's treaty with Mitanni do not include the Sun. But the (non-Indo-European) Kassites had a Sun-god whose name, Šur(i)yaš-, closely resembles Vedic *Sū́r(i)ya-* and may be a borrowing from those western Indics. In the Amarna letters there appears a north Syrian prince Šuwardata, which looks very much like a theophoric name, 'given by Suwar', parallel to the Sūryadatta attested in post-Vedic India.[7] Sūrya is the recipient of ten hymns of the Rigveda, and eleven more are addressed to Savitṛ, the Arouser, who is also in some sense the god of the Sun.

In Greek myth Helios appears as a god with a genealogy and progeny. He is invoked as a witness to oaths (see below). He can be portrayed as a speaking character interacting with other gods (*Od.* 8. 302, 12. 374–88, *Hymn. Dem.* 26–9, 62–89). He is not prominent in public cult except in Rhodes, but there he had an important festival.

Greek writers observed what they took to be Sun-worship among some other Indo-European peoples: the Persians (Hdt. 1. 131), the Thracians

[5] O. Szemerényi, however, *Akten der 2. Fachtagung der Indogermanischen Gesellschaft* (1962), 191 f., derives it from **sokʷ-li-* ~ **sekʷ* 'see'.

[6] Gurney (1977), 11. On Sun-gods in Hittite texts cf. Daisuke Yoshida, *Untersuchungen zu den Sonnengottheiten bei den Hethitern* (Heidelberg 1996).

[7] Cf. T. Burrow, *The Sanskrit Language* (London, n.d.), 28; Kammenhuber (1968), 48–51, 173 (sceptical).

(Soph. fr. 582), or more vaguely 'the barbarians' (Ar. *Pax* 406–11). At Rome the cult of the Sun was regarded as native to the Sabines (Varro, *De lingua Latina* 5. 68, 74; Festus p. 22. 5 L.). As Sol Indiges, he had annual festivals, and a sacred grove at Lavinium. There was an old temple of Sol and Luna at the Circus Maximus.

The Germans, according to Caesar (*Bell. Gall.* 6. 21. 2), 'class as gods only those whom they can see and by whose offices they evidently benefit, the Sun, Vulcan, and the Moon'. This is clearly a very reductionist and superficial view of German religion. However, Tacitus (*Ann.* 13. 55) represents the German noble Boiocalus as invoking the Sun *et cetera sidera* in a rhetorical appeal, and many centuries later the goddess Sunna makes her appearance in a little mythological narrative in the second Merseburg spell. Snorri (*Gylf.* 35) says that Sól was counted among goddesses, and she appears occasionally in personified form (*Vǫluspá* 5; *Gylf.* 11).

Cormac's *Glossary* s.v. Indelba records that the Irish set images of the Sun on their altars, and St Patrick (*Confessio* 60) speaks of Irish heathen worship of sun and moon. This corresponds, to be sure, with a conventional Christian notion of paganism, but in some cases there is circumstantial detail that adds credibility to the reports. A fourteenth-century chronicler, Peter of Duisburg, writes that the Prussians, having no knowledge of God, 'omnem creaturam pro deo coluerunt, scilicet solem, lunam et stellas, tonitrua, volatilia, quadrupedia eciam, usque ad bufonem'.[8] In the following century Jerome of Prague encountered a Lithuanian community who worshipped the sun and venerated a huge mallet; the priests explained that with this mallet the signs of the Zodiac had liberated and restored to mankind the Sun, who for several months had been held captive in a strong fortress by a most powerful king.[9] There must once have been a springtime ritual of breaking up the earth with mallets, associated with this myth of the return of the Sun-goddess.

The Slavs too are regularly credited with sun- and moon-worship by chroniclers and clerics. But we are not dependent only on such vague notices. There is record of a god Dažbog who was identified with the Greek Helios and called Солнце Царь, 'Tsar Sun'—the neuter 'sun' being personified by means of the royal title. He was the son of Svarog, who was equated with the Greek Hephaestus; probably we should understand 'Fire'. The Sun also appears in Russian folklore in female persona as Матушка красное Солнце, 'Mother red Sun'.[10]

[8] Mannhardt (1936), 87 = Clemen (1936), 97.

[9] Recounted by Jerome to Enea de' Piccolomini (Pope Pius II): Mannhardt (1936), 135 = Clemen (1936), 104.

[10] See further von Schroeder (1914–16), ii. 39–41; Váňa (1992), 68–71. The identifications with Greek deities are in glosses on Malalas' chronicle in the twelfth-century *Ipateev Annals*.

The literary testimony to the Sun's divine status may be supplemented by the evidence of prehistoric art. Starting from the third millennium BCE, and across much of Europe as well as further east, there are numerous examples of what are clearly solar symbols, in some cases the object of adoration by human figures. We shall return to this later.

Attributes; the all-seeing god

In Vedic and Greek poetry the Sun, like Dyaus/Zeus, has the epithet 'great': RV 2. 23. 2 *Sū́riyo . . . mahó*, 3. 2. 7 *súvar mahát*; Hes. *Th.* 19 and 371 Ἠέλιόν τε μέγαν. He is also 'swift': AV 13. 2. 2 *āśúm . . . Sū́ryam*; Mimnermus fr. 11a. 1 and 14. 11 ὠκέος Ἠελίοιο.[11] In both cases the Vedic and Greek adjectives are cognate. And as Savitṛ in the early morning raises up his banner *jyótir víśvasmai bhúvanāya kṛṇván*, 'making light for all creatures' (RV 4. 14. 2), so Helios goes up into the sky 'to shine for the immortals and for mortal men' (*Od.* 3. 1–3, cf. 12. 385 f.).

The most widely noted attribute of the Sun-god is that he (or she, as the case may be) surveys the whole world and sees everything that goes on. Sūrya is *urucákṣas-*, 'wide of vision' (RV 7. 35. 8, 63. 4), and indeed *viśvácakṣas-*, 'all-seeing' (1. 50. 2; 7. 63. 1), just as Helios πάντ' ἐφορᾶι (*Il.* 3. 277, *Od.* 11. 109) and is παν(τ)όπτης ([Aesch.] *Prom.* 91, fr. 192. 5). The Indian Sun is also *nṛcákṣas-*, 'men-watching' (1. 22. 7; 7. 60. 2): he sees *ṛjú márteṣu vṛjinā́ ca*, '(what is) straight among mortals and crooked' (4. 1. 17; 6. 51. 2; 7. 60. 2). Sometimes he is identified as the eye of the god or gods who supervise justice: of Varuna (1. 50. 6), of Mitra–Varuna (1. 115. 1; 6. 51. 1; 7. 63. 1; 10. 37. 1), or in the Younger Avesta of Ahura Mazdā (Y. 1. 11, 3. 13, 7. 13, al.). In other passages he is just 'the eye of the gods' (RV 7. 76. 1, 77. 3).

He is the spy or watcher of all that lives and moves (*spáś- víśvasya jágataḥ*, RV 4. 13. 3, cf. AV 7. 81. 1). In the Homeric *Hymn to Demeter* (62) Helios is θεῶν σκοπὸς ἠδὲ καὶ ἀνδρῶν, 'watcher of gods and men', where σκοπός has the same root as *spáś-*, the word used in the Vedic verse.[12] Derivatives of it are similarly used in connection with the Sun at *Od.* 8. 302 Ἠέλιος γάρ οἱ σκοπιὴν ἔχεν 'for Helios had been keeping watch on his behalf', and Pindar, *Pae.* 9. 1 (A1. 1 Rutherford) ἀκτὶς Ἀελίου, τί πολύσκοπ' ἐμήσαο; 'Ray of the Sun, what, O far-sighted one, have you done?'[13]

[11] Schmitt (1967), 164 f.

[12] First noted by Kuhn (1859), 103; cf. Schmitt (1967), 163.

[13] πολύσκοπος may be an old compound; cf. the Avestan noun *pouruspaxšti-* 'extensive vision' (Yt. 9. 1, 10. 11, al.), implying the adjective **pouruspas-*.

We need not confine ourselves entirely to Graeco-Aryan. In the Old English poem *Phoenix* (210 f.) the sun 'performs its appointed task and *woruld geondwliteð*, 'surveys the world'. The Latvian Sun-goddess Saule is represented as seeing all that happens in different parts of the earth (*LD* 33830, 33901, 33991 = Jonval nos. 252–4). In a Scots Gaelic song to the Sun recorded from old men in the Western Isles in the nineteenth century the luminary is addressed as *sùil Dhé mhóir*, 'eye of great God', where *sùil* is (probably) the same word as the MIE word for 'sun', and the name of God, though actually from **deiwós*, here in effect covers the Sky-god *Dyeus, one of whose oldest epithets was 'great'.[14]

The analogy of sun and eye finds various expression in Indo-European languages. Greek dramatists call the sun 'eyelid of golden day', 'this holy eye of the lamp', 'the tireless eye of the air'. In Ovid the Sun-god calls himself 'the eye of the world'. Macrobius says that 'antiquity' called the sun *Iouis oculus*.[15] Vedic poets refer to Sūrya's own eye, and Firdawsi too speaks of 'the eye of the sun'.[16] The Armenian *aregakn* 'sun' means literally 'eye of the sun', a compound of the genitive of *arew* 'sun' with *akn* 'eye'.

Contrariwise, the human eye is sometimes seen as an analogue of the sun. Euripides in Aristophanes' *Thesmophoriazousai* (13–18) propounds a cosmogonic theory by which the divine Aither created living creatures, and to endow them with sight contrived the eye in imitation of 'the wheel of the sun'. In the old Armenian mythological verses about the birth of the hero Vahagn his eyes are described as 'little suns'. In Norse skaldic verse 'suns of the forehead' (*ennis sólir*) is a kenning for the eyes, and in Old Irish, as we have seen, *súil* (feminine) is the word for 'eye'.

Oaths by the Sun

The Sun's capacity for seeing everything that people do qualifies him as a supervisor of justice, or at least gives him a valuable role as the god of justice's eye and as a trusty witness. His credentials are reinforced by his own strict observance of cosmic law: *díśaḥ Sū́ryo ná mināti prádiṣṭāḥ*, 'Sūrya does not infringe the directions prescribed' (RV 3. 30. 12), where *diś-* is cognate with Greek δίκη 'justice, right' and Latin *con-dicio*. The verse might be converted

[14] Carmichael (1928–59), iii. 306, quoted in full later in this chapter.

[15] Soph. *Ant.* 103 χρυσέας ἁμέρας βλέφαρον, 879 τόδε λαμπάδος ἱερὸν ὄμμα; Ar. *Nub.* 285 ὄμμα αἰθέρος ἀκάματον; Ov. *Met.* 4. 228 *mundi oculus*; Macr. *Sat.* 1. 21. 12.

[16] RV 1. 113. 9; 5. 59. 5; 7. 98. 6; 9. 10. 9; 10. 10. 9; *Shāh-nāma*, Levy (1967), 185. Savitṛ is *híraṇyākṣa-* 'golden-eyed' (RV 1. 35. 8), much as Helios is χρυσωπός (Eur. *El.* 740 with Denniston's commentary); cf. G. Costa, *Archivio Glottologico Italiano* 69 (1984), 35.

root for root into Greek: δίκας Ἥλιος οὐ μινύθει προδείκτους, and the idea in fact recurs in the early Greek philosophers. Heraclitus (B 94) wrote that 'Helios will not overstep his measures; otherwise the Erinyes, Dike's police, will track him down'. Parmenides (B 1. 14) stations Dike at the gates of Day and Night, holding the keys and controlling their alternation.

The practice of invoking the Sun as a witness to oaths is attested widely and over millennia. In Hittite treaties the Sun-god of heaven, the Sun-goddess of Arinna, and the Storm-god of heaven head the lengthy list of gods named. Agamemnon in the *Iliad* (3. 276 f.), in making a treaty with Priam, calls upon 'Father Zeus who rulest from Ida, greatest and most glorious, and Helios, who overseest everything and overhearest everything'. In a later oath (19. 258) he testifies by Zeus, Ge, Helios, and the Erinyes. When the infant Hermes denies to Zeus that he has stolen Apollo's cattle, he insists that he is telling the truth, saying 'I am in awe of Helios and the other gods' (*Hymn. Herm.* 381). The chorus in Sophocles' *Oedipus Tyrannus* (660) swears to Oedipus by Helios that they wish him no harm. 'By Helios' appears frequently as a colloquial asseveration in New Comedy, and a more explicit 'I swear by Helios' a couple of times. Helios continues to be named in treaties in inscriptions.[17]

The Bithynians, as Arrian recorded (ap. Eust. 414. 30), 'judged cases seated facing the Sun, so that the god should oversee them'. Movses Xorenac'i relates in his Armenian history (2. 19) that 'when Hyrcanus sought an oath from Barzap'ran, he swore to him by the sun and moon and all their cults in heaven and earth and by the sun of Artashēs and Tigran'.[18] Rostam in the *Shāh-nāma* 'swore by his soul and by the king's head, by the sun and the sword and the field of battle'.[19]

The Franks in the seventh century, although converted to Christianity, still had the habit of swearing by the Sun.[20] In one of the Norse heroic ballads Gudrun reproaches Atli (Attila) with 'the oaths you swore often to Gunnar and pledged long ago by the Sun southward-curving and by Odin's crag'.[21]

[17] Cf. L. Preller and C. Robert, *Griechische Mythologie*, i (4th edn., Berlin 1894), 433 n. 2; West (1997), 20 f., where some Near Eastern evidence is also cited.

[18] Trs. R. W. Thomson, *Moses Khorenats'i. History of the Armenians* (Cambridge, Mass. 1978). Cf. 2. 81, 'my father had sworn to him by the light of the sun'.

[19] *Shāh-nāma*, Levy (1967), 205; cf. 106, '[Key Khosrow] swore an oath by the all-possessing Lord, by white day and azure night, by sun and moon, by throne and crown, by seal and sword and royal diadem'.

[20] *Vita S. Eligii* in *MGH* Scriptores Meroving. iv. 708, *nullus dominos solem aut lunam vocet neque per eos iuret.*

[21] *Atlakviða* 30. For further Germanic material see J. Grimm, *Deutsche Rechtsaltertümer* (4th edn., Leipzig 1899), i. 73, 354, ii. 438–43, 545. Unbegaun (1948), 425, writes of a similar practice among the west Slavs: 'La fameuse prestation de serment sur le soleil des nobles polonais et tchèques, au Moyen Age, semble n'être qu'une coutume d'origine germanique.'

Oaths by the Sun and Moon, Sun and Wind, etc., are also mentioned in Old Irish literature.[22]

THE SUN'S MOTION CONCEPTUALIZED

Saying that the Sun is an all-seeing god, or the eye of a god, is satisfying to morality but leaves an obvious question unanswered. The luminary's smooth and regular daily transit from east to west, and its reappearance in the east the next morning, call for further exegesis. There is much evidence, both literary and iconographic, for the sun being conceived as a wheel. A wheel—more than an eye—is perfectly circular, and it runs easily along. But one can hardly say that a god is a wheel, and the solar wheel needs a moving cause, as its path is not all downhill. So the Sun-god may be said, not to be, but to have a wheel, which he drives or rolls along. Or the wheel is drawn along by a horse. Or it becomes a one-wheeled chariot in which the god rides; or a regular chariot, drawn by two horses or even four. Another concept is that of a boat that carries the solar disc across the sky. Or again the two ideas are combined, with the horse or horses taking the sun across the sky during the day and the boat conveying him on the ocean through the night.

The solar wheel

In the Rigveda there are eleven references to the wheel (*cakrám*) of Sūrya or Suvar.[23] In Greek tragedy ἡλίου κύκλος is something of a formulaic phrase (Aesch. *Pers.* 504, [Aesch.] *Prom.* 91; Soph. *Ant.* 416; Eur. *Hec.* 412, *El.* 465), and Empedocles (B 47) has ἄνακτος . . . ἁγέα κύκλον 'the lord's pure wheel' in the same sense. We also find ἡλίου τροχός (Ar. *Thesm.* 17). But κύκλος is evidently the traditional word. It corresponds etymologically to the Vedic word (which is usually neuter, but occasionally masculine), both going back to *k^w(*e*)-k^w*l-o-*, a reduplicated formation from the root *k^w*el* 'turn'. This is also the source of Old Norse *hvél*, which is likewise found in poetic expressions for the sun and sometimes the moon. In *Alvíssmál* 14. 3

[22] *Fled Dúin na nGéd* p. 1. 5 Lehmann (Dublin 1964); a poem attributed to Cinæd ua h-Artacáin, ed. L. Gwynn, *Ériu* 7 (1914), 227/235 st. 61; further references in O'Rahilly (1946), 298.

[23] RV 1. 130. 9, 174. 5, 175. 4; 2. 11. 20; 4. 16. 12, 17. 14, 28. 2, 30. 4; 5. 29. 10; 6. 31. 3, 56. 3. The passages are set out by Schmitt (1967), 166 f. There are others referring simply to 'the wheel' in a solar context.

and 16. 5 *hverfandi hvél* 'the roaming wheel' is given as a name for the moon, and *fagrahvél* 'the beautiful wheel' for the sun. The phrases *sunno hvél* and *mána hvél* appear in the non-Eddic poems *Harmsól* 36. 7 and *Líknarbraut* 7. 3.[24]

Another old Indo-European word for 'wheel' is represented in Latin *rota*, Old Irish *roth*, Lithuanian *rãtas*, etc.; it provides an Indo-Iranian word for 'chariot' (Vedic *rátha-*, Avestan *raθa-*). We should expect it to appear in Italic or Celtic reflexes of an inherited formula 'wheel of the sun'. Such phrases occur in Latin poetry from Ennius onwards. He called the sun *rota candida*, and *solis rota* is found in Lucretius and others. In Old Irish we have *roth gréine*, 'wheel of the sun', or in one place just 'the wheel', and in Welsh *rhod tes*, 'wheel of heat'.[25]

In RV 2. 11. 20 Indra is said to have felled the demon Arbuda and set him rolling (*ávartayat*) as Sūrya does his wheel. Here we have the simple picture of a god rolling his wheel forward. If the sun's daily path is seen as climbing up to its high point and then descending, the wheel would need pushing, one might suppose, only for the upward part, and then it would roll down of its own accord. We cannot but recall the Greek myth of Sisyphus' underworld labour: he is forever rolling a stone up to the top of a hill, from which it runs down again. It does not make sense to say, in the manner of the old nature-mythologists, that Sisyphus' stone 'is' the sun.[26] But it might well be that an old solar myth provided the model for Sisyphus' cruel and unusual punishment.

As a pictorial device the solar wheel is abundantly attested. A simple circle, or a circle with a central point, need not be a wheel, but when it has spokes it clearly is. The connection with the sun is sometimes demonstrable.[27] For example, on early pottery from the hill fort of Vučedol on the middle Danube the sun is depicted either by a series of concentric circles, with stylized flames shooting from the outer rim, or by a cross inscribed within circles (again with flames).[28] The cross characterizes the disc as a four-spoked wheel. Achaemenian cylinder seals show a four-winged solar figure hovering

[24] Old English *sunnan hweogul*, sometimes cited in this connection, should not be. It occurs only in a word-for-word translation of a Latin hymn that uses the phrase *Solis rotam*: Joseph Stevenson, *Latin Hymns of the Anglo-Saxon Church* (Durham 1851), 22.

[25] Enn. *Ann.* 572 (with Skutsch's note, pp. 712 f.); O'Rahilly (1946), 304, cf. 519–22; *Saltair na Rann* 1077 *ardRuiri ind roith*, 2385 *ardRī grēne*; Bader (1989), 242.

[26] So interpreted by V. Henry, *Revue des études grecques* 5 (1892), 289.

[27] For methodological considerations in the identification of solar symbols see M. Green (1991), 24 f., 34, 40, 44; Lucy Goodison, *Death, Women and the Sun* (Institute of Classical Studies, *Bulletin* Supplement 53; London 1989), 11–15, 78–80.

[28] M. Gimbutas in Cardona et al. (1970), 184.

over a large, upright eight-spoked wheel with a milled edge.[29] On certain early coins from Latium and Campania we find the device of a six- or eight-spoked wheel alternating with the solar disc or with the radiate head of the personified Sun.[30] Model wheels, whether ritually significant or for personal ornament, are common in Romano-Celtic Europe, and some of them have clearly solar decoration or are associated with lunar crescents.[31]

Another very widespread artistic motif, especially in Iron Age Europe, is the swastika. This seems to be a variant of the spoked wheel, giving a clearer suggestion of rotary movement, and again its religious and specifically solar significance is often contextually apparent.[32]

The solar steed(s)

The solar wheel must be travelling at some speed, as it traverses the whole earth within a day. The idea that it is drawn by a horse became current at an early date.

> úd ū eti prasavitā́ jánānām, | mahā́n ketúr arṇaváḥ Sū́riyasya,
> samānám̐ cakrám pariyāvívṛtsan | yád Etaśó váhati dhūrṣú yuktáḥ.
>
> Up goes the arouser of peoples, the great waving banner of Sūrya,
> to set rolling forward the common Wheel that Etaśa conveys, yoked in harness.
> (RV 7. 63. 2)

Etaśa 'Swift' is often mentioned as the steed who draws the sun or the Sun's wheel.[33] Dawn is said to bring with her the eye of the gods and to guide the fair white horse (7. 77. 3).

Among the many rock carvings from Scandinavia, dating from between 1500 and 400 BCE, are a number depicting a horse or a pair of horses pulling a wheel or disc. One from Kalleby in Bohuslän, Sweden, shows a horse pulling a large four-spoked wheel and hovering over a longship.[34] Another from Balken in the same region shows a horse with a band running back from its head to a disc that flies above its back. Further designs of a horse pulling the sun, here represented by concentric and/or radiate circles, appear on several

[29] David Stronach, *Pasargadae* (Oxford 1978), 178 f. and pl. 162a.

[30] Pettazzoni (1956), 167; cf. 197 (Hallstatt culture), 240.

[31] M. Green (1986), 46 f. Cf. the same author's study, *The Wheel as a Cult Symbol in the Romano-Celtic World* (Brussels 1984).

[32] Cf. de Vries (1956), i. 139 f.; M. Green (1986), 55 f.; (1991), 46–8.

[33] RV 1. 121. 13; 4. 17. 14; 5. 31. 11; 7. 66. 14; 8. 1. 11; 9. 63. 8; cf. 1. 61. 15; 4. 30. 6; 5. 81. 3; Macdonell (1898), 149 f.; Hillebrandt (1927–9), ii. 161–4.

[34] Glob (1974), 103, 151 fig. 61; M. Green (1991), 78, 79 fig. 61.

bronze razors from different sites in Denmark.[35] In all of the above except the Kalleby carving the horse is facing to the right, in other words pulling the sun in the direction in which it is seen to cross the sky.

The most spectacular of Scandinavian representations is the famous Trundholm sun-horse, discovered in 1902 in a bog in north-west Zealand. This is a bronze model horse about 25 cm. long, drawing behind it a bronze disc taller than itself, 26 cm. in diameter. The whole group measures about 60 cm. in length. The disc has a bright side, covered with gold leaf, and a dull side; the bright side is displayed when the group is viewed with the horse facing to the right. The set was mounted on three pairs of wheels, two for the horse and one for the sun-disc, each wheel having four slender spokes and actually able to turn.[36] This remarkable artefact, now in the National Museum in Copenhagen, is dated to about the fourteenth century BCE. It is not unique: fragments of a similar assembly, but with two horses, had been found a few years earlier near Hälsingborg on the other side of the sound. Sun-discs comparable to the one in the Trundholm group have been found in Ireland, the Isle of Man, and near Bath.[37]

When one knows these second- and first-millennium depictions of the horse pulling the solar disc, it is tempting to recognize an analogous theme on certain Aegean objects from a much earlier period. They are from Troy and the Cyclades, from the mid-part of the third millennium; we do not know that the populations in question were Indo-European, but there is no historical implausibility in it, seeing that Anatolia had probably been colonized by Indo-European-speakers well before 3000.

The first item in question is an Early Cycladic II silver diadem from Syros, on the preserved section of which we see a male quadruped facing left, with a band of some sort round his neck, and behind him a large sun-disc with flames radiating from centre to rim. The animal is more like a dog than a horse, and one would not expect the horse to be known in the Aegean at this period. It is not possible to see if the band round his neck was continued as a link to the disc. Behind the sun is a standing figure with a bird's head and outspread wings. Left of the animal, on the broken edge, is another sun-disc, which probably occupied the centre of the whole design. Symmetry suggests

[35] F. Kaul in Meller (2004), 57, 61 (fig. centre right; first millennium BCE).

[36] J. Déchelette, *Revue archéologique* [4]13 (1909), 308 f.; de Vries (1956), i. 112 f.; Glob (1974), 99–103; Gelling–Davidson (1969), 14–16, 19–21; M. Green (1991), 64–6; F. Kaul in Meller (2004), 54–7.

[37] Déchelette (as n. 36), 309 f.; Gelling–Davidson (1969), 16.

that the animal–sun–bird sequence was repeated in reverse on the lost half of the diadem.[38]

Among the many crudely decorated spindle-whorls from Troy II there are some on which the swastika symbol seems to be associated with a many-legged animal.[39] The many legs (six to ten) were perhaps a mythical expression of speed and stamina. Slovak and Russian folklore tells of an eight-legged horse that draws the sun, and although he has no apparent solar associations we think also of Odin's famous eight-legged steed Sleipnir.

A god is not a wheel, as someone recently observed, and a god is not a horse. So with the horse pulling the wheel, what becomes of the Sun-god? He is provided for by making the wheel into a chariot—initially a one-wheeled chariot.

saptá yuñjanti rátham ékacakram; | éko áśvo vahati saptánāmā.
trinā́bhi cakrám, ajáram, anarvám̥, | yátremā́ víśvā bhúvanā́dhi tasthúḥ.

Seven yoke the one-wheeled car; one horse with seven names draws it.
Three-naved is the wheel, unageing, unstoppable, on which all these creatures stand.
(RV 1. 164. 2 = AV 13. 3. 18)

Indian art of the first century BCE to the second CE shows Sūrya riding his one-wheeled chariot, now drawn by four horses.[40] The solar vehicle must be the model for the one-wheeled, golden chariot, drawn by immortal white horses, that Mithra rides in the Avestan hymn to him, even if he is not yet identified with the Sun.[41]

The number of horses varies. Sūrya's (or Savitṛ's) are often mentioned in the plural. Sometimes they are two (RV 1. 35. 3), or seven (1. 50. 8 f.; 4. 13. 3; 5. 45. 9; 7. 60. 3), seven or a hundred (AV 13. 2. 6 f.), even a thousand (RV 5. 62. 1); in other places the number is indefinite (1. 115. 4; 4. 45. 6; 5. 29. 5; 7. 45. 1; 10. 37. 3, 49. 7; AV 13. 1. 24, al.).

In the Avesta the Sun has the formulaic epithet 'possessing swift horses' (Y. 3. 13, Yt. 6. 0, 1, 4, 10. 90, etc., *hvarə aurvaṭ.aspəm*). At Hasanlu in north-west Iran, a site associated with early Aryan migrations, a gold bowl of the twelfth to eleventh century BCE was found with mythological scenes in which the Weather-god in a bull-chariot is followed by solar and lunar deities in

[38] Illustrated in Emily Vermeule, *Greece in the Bronze Age* (Chicago 1964), 53 f.; Goodison (as n. 27), 16 and fig. 27.

[39] See Heinrich Schliemann, *Ilios* (London 1880), figs. 1872, 1947, 1991.

[40] Sukumari Bhattacharji, *The Indian Theogony* (Cambridge 1970), 226.

[41] Yt. 10. 125, 136; see Gershevitch (1959), 35 f., 281 f., 330 f. The Irish saint Aed mac Bricc (*aed* = 'fire') rode through the air in a one-wheeled chariot: *Acta sanctorum Hibern. ex cod. Salmant.*, ed. C. de Smedt–J. de Backer (Edinburgh 1888), 337, 339, 352, 354, 358; O'Rahilly (1946), 472.

chariots drawn by equids.[42] Later Iranian ideology may be reflected in Xenophon's account of a procession of Cyrus in which there appeared a white chariot with golden yoke, consecrated to Zeus, and another belonging to the Sun (*Cyrop.* 8. 3. 12; cf. Curt. 3. 3. 11).

There is no allusion in the *Iliad* or *Odyssey* to Helios' horses or chariot, though Dawn is given horses in one passage (*Od.* 23. 244–6). But they appear in several of the Homeric Hymns, in Mimnermus and other archaic poets, and in art perhaps from the first half of the seventh century.[43] In Hymn. Hom. 31. 15 the chariot is χρυσόζυγον, 'golden-yoked', as in the Rigveda (1. 35. 2–5) Savitṛ's is a golden car with golden yoke-pegs and pole. When Euripides describes a shield-device of 'the Sun's shining wheel on the winged mares' (or 'chariot': *El.* 464–6 φάεθων κύκλος Ἀλίοιο | ἵπποις ἂμ πτεροέσσαις), we almost seem to be back with the horse-drawn wheel, but perhaps he is just combining traditional images in a careless way.

An association of the Sun-god with horses is attested for other ancient peoples. Herodotus (1. 216. 4) records that the Massagetai worship only the Sun, and that they sacrifice horses to him, assigning the swiftest of mortal creatures to the swiftest of gods. In Sophocles' *Tereus* (fr. 582) someone, perhaps Tereus himself, addressed 'Helios, highest object of reverence for the horse-loving Thracians'. Xenophon in Armenia found himself in possession of an elderly horse that was sacred to the Sun (*Anab.* 4. 5. 35). Sun, wheel, and horse are variously associated on Celtic Iron Age coins.[44] An Irish legend tells of one Eochaid Mairccend 'Horsehead' who had Wind and Sun (Gaeth, Grian) as his steeds. Grian outran the fastest horses of the Ulstermen.[45] In Norse myth the Sun has two horses, Árvakr (Earlywake) and Alsviðr (Allswift) (*Grímnismál* 37; *Sigrdrífumál* 15; *Gylf.* 11).

Tacitus knew the rumour of a Baltic region where the sun did not sink far enough beneath the semi-frozen sea to allow the stars to shine (*Germ.* 45. 1). When it rose, the sound was audible, so people believed, and the outlines of horses (*equorum*: v.l. *deorum, eorum*) and the rays emanating from the god's head could be discerned.

Certainly the myth of the Sun's horse or horses persists in the folklore of Baltic and Slavonic peoples. In the Latvian songs the Sun travels on horseback or in a horse-drawn carriage; the number of horses varies between one and six (Jonval nos. 123–4, 168, 171–3, 179, 186). They are yellow (*dzeltens*, 123,

[42] M. J. Mellink, *Iranica Antiqua* 6 (1966), 72–87; *EIEC* 258 f.

[43] Mimn. 12; *Hymn. Dem.* 63, 88, *Herm.* 69, Hymn. Hom. 28. 14, 31. 9, 15; 'Eumelus' fr. 11 West; *LIMC* v (add.) Helios.

[44] M. Green (1991), 57 f., 117 f.

[45] Edward J. Gwynne, *The Metrical Dindshenchas*, iv (Dublin 1924), 182, 126; O'Rahilly (1946), 291.

171–3), or grey (179), or brown (124). Slavonic folk traditions tell of a golden car and two white horses, or three (gold, silver, and diamond), or twelve (yellow-brown).[46]

In RV 4. 53. 4 the phrase *mahó ájmasya*, 'the great drive', is apparently used of the path of the solar horses (cf. 1. 163. 10). It has an exact equivalent in Greek *μέγας ὄγμος*, which in one of the later Homeric Hymns (32. 11) designates the moon's orbit and in Aratus (749) the sun's path through the zodiac. The word *ὄγμος* generally means a furrow or row; it perhaps refers to wheel-ruts in a passage of Nicander.[47]

The solar boat

The idea of a ship, boat, or other floating vessel as transport for the Sun is less widely attested, but certainly old. It is not, of course, exclusively Indo-European; it is well known as a feature of the Egyptian solar mythology.

In RV 5. 45. 10 Sūrya is said to have risen into the shining flood (*árṇas-*; i.e. the air), after harnessing his straight-backed mares; these intelligent creatures have guided him like a ship through the water. This is only a simile, but in the Atharvaveda (17. 1. 25 f.) the risen Sun is twice told 'O Āditya, thou hast boarded a ship of a hundred oars for well-being'. The oars perhaps represent the rays of light.

As with the horse-drawn wheel, the Vedic image finds graphic expression in Bronze Age Scandinavia. Ships are a favourite subject of the rock artists, and in a number of cases there is a solar wheel—or sometimes two—riding just above them, or attached to the vessel by means of one or two ropes or posts. Some of these may be depictions of a ritual in which a solar emblem was carried in a ship, though others can hardly be understood in this way. At Nors in Jutland a clay jar was found containing about a hundred tiny model ships made of bronze and gold leaf and decorated with solar symbols. Again some ritual use seems likely.[48]

Three representations are of particular interest, because the solar horse appears as well as the ship, in such a way as to suggest that the horse is supposed to take the sun across the sky by day and then rendezvous with the ship. One is the carving from Kalleby already mentioned. The horse and sun-wheel are just above the ship, but clearly not in it; they could be

[46] Mannhardt (1875), 93–6; Váňa (1992), 61.

[47] Nic. *Th.* 371. Cf. Watkins (1995), 16.

[48] J. Déchelette (as n. 36), 329 fig. 14, 330–7, 338–40; de Vries (1956), i. 108 f., 122; Gelling–Davidson (1969), 11–15, 64; M. Green (1991), 77–9; Meller (2004), 31, 52 f.; F. Kaul, ibid. 58–63, 66–8, 72.

taken as just landing in it or taking off from it. Such an interpretation seems irresistible in the case of two of the bronze razors from Denmark.[49] On one the ship sits at the left, and the flying horse with the sun attached is just ahead of its prow, as if having just taken off. On the other, both the prow and the stern of the ship are crowned with haloes of rays. Behind the prow a horse, outlined with stippling to suggest radiance, is landing from above, his fore legs already on the deck, his hind legs still high in the air. The radiant sun-disc, unattached, hangs low over the after deck.

A sensational find was made recently at Nebra in central Germany. It is dated to around 1600 BCE.[50] It is a bronze disc, 31–32 cm. in diameter, with gold embellishments representing the sun, the crescent moon, and about thirty stars, including a cluster suggestive of the Pleiades. Two arcs were later added on opposite sides of the rim (one of them is now lost): they subtended angles of 82° from the centre, and evidently represented the range of sunrise and sunset points on the horizon between midwinter and midsummer. A separate arc, touching the rim of the sky at the southern horizon, was added later still. It is divided by lines into three bands and outlined with a bristle pattern that has been compared to the lines of oars on some Bronze Age representations of ships. But the ends of the arc are cut off square with no suggestion of a prow or stern, and if it is meant for a solar vessel, as some have argued, it would seem to be a plain round bowl rather than a regular ship. If the bristles stand for oars, we are reminded of the hundred-oared ship of the Atharvaveda and the implication that a powerful driving force is required.

A round bowl or cup, not a ship, is the form that the Sun's vessel takes in Greek poetry and usually in Greek art. Like the horses and chariot, it finds no mention in the *Iliad* or *Odyssey* but appears in other seventh- and sixth-century poets. It conveys Helios at night along the river Oceanus that encircles the earth, and needs no rowers:

> A wondrous couch (εὐνή) bears him across the waves—
> winged, by Hephaestus intricately wrought
> in precious gold—as he in grateful sleep
> skims o'er the water from the Hesperides
> to Aethiopia, where a chariot
> and steeds await the early birth of Dawn;
> and there the god mounts his new equipage,
> Hyperion's son. (Mimnermus fr. 12. 5–11)

[49] F. Kaul in Meller (2004), 61 (centre and bottom right), 62 f.; cf. Gelling–Davidson (1969), 133 fig. 58b.

[50] M. Kerner, *Helvetia Archaeologica* 34 (2003), no. 134; Meller (2004).

Stesichorus and others called it a δέπας, 'goblet'. Vase painters from the late sixth century onward show Helios in it with his horses, or Heracles using it to cross the Ocean to Erythea; the part that shows above the water-line sometimes looks like the top of a large jar.[51]

The integrated transport system, wheeled vehicle for the day connecting with night ferry, recurs in the Latvian folk tradition.

> Qui l'a dit, il en a menti,
> que Saule court à pied:
> par-dessus la forêt, dans une voiture,
> par-dessus la mer, dans une barque. (*LD* 33811, trs. Jonval no. 167)

The word rendered 'voiture', *rati*, is from the previously mentioned root that gives Vedic *rátha*- and Latin *rota*. In other songs we hear that Saule sleeps through the night in the golden boat (*laiva*). She brings it to the shore in the morning when she gets up, and it stays there rocking on the water.[52]

The dark side of the sun

Several passages in the Rigveda and Atharvaveda hint more or less riddlingly at a doctrine stated more explicitly in the Yajurveda and *Brāhmaṇas*, namely that the sun has a bright and a dark side: he never sets, but on reaching the western horizon turns his bright side away from us and returns invisibly across the sky to the east in the course of the night.[53] In post-Vedic cosmology this curious theory was replaced by the idea that the sun and stars disappear behind the mythical Mt Meru when they set, and pass behind it to reach the east again.

The Trundholm sun-disc too has a bright and a dark side. One side was gold-plated, on the other the dull bronze was left uncovered. This might be accounted for by saying that the group was intended to be displayed somewhere where it would be seen from only the one side, with the horse to the right, as it were pulling the sun westwards. But the dark side of the disc is covered with the same fine, elaborate pattern of ornamentation as the bright

[51] Stes. *PMGF* S17 = 185; Aesch. fr. 69; Pherecydes fr. 18a Fowler; Antim. fr. 86 Matthews. Cf. 'Eumelus' fr. 10 West, Pisander fr. 5 W., Panyassis fr. 12 W. (φιάλη in Athenaeus' paraphrase), Theolytus *FGrHist* 471 F 1 (λέβης); *LIMC* ii Astra 61, v Herakles 2546, v (add.) Helios 2. A late fourth-century Apulian volute krater, *LIMC* iv (add.) Demeter 459, shows Helios with Demeter in his quadriga, springing out of a ship.

[52] *LD* 33860, 33910, 33908, 33878 = Jonval nos. 221–4. According to Biezais–Balys (1973), 450 f., its nocturnal voyage takes it by the land of the dead.

[53] E. Sieg, *NGG* 1923, 1–23; cf. Gershevitch (1959), 38 f.

side, with concentric circles and spirals; it only lacks the outer ring of radial lines that encircles the gold side and suggests rays of light going out in all directions. It is therefore tempting to explain the design by reference to the old Indian theory, and to suppose that the bright face, displayed when the horse was going to the right, represented the daytime sun, and the dark face, shown when the horse was going to the left, represented the night-time sun that travels unseen across the sky from west to east.

How old is all this?

The myth of the Sun's boat could be of any antiquity, as seagoing vessels had existed for thousands of years before the break-up of the proto-Indo-European unity. On the other hand, as noted in the Introduction, the myth of the horse-drawn chariot, as we have it in the Rigveda, the Greek poets, and elsewhere, cannot be proto-Indo-European, because such a vehicle only became possible with the invention of the spoked wheel, which first appears near the close of the third millennium. Of course, the sun might have been pictured before that as a block wheel, or the god as driving a block-wheeled cart, drawn by a stronger animal such as a bull; or he might have ridden on horseback. But whether the horse and chariot version represents the modernization of an older myth or a completely new concept, we have to suppose that it spread like a wave, together with the techniques of chariot construction and warfare, across Indo-European territories that were already well on the way towards developing separate languages and cultures.

It was probably spread primarily by the fast-moving, chariot-borne warrior bands that roamed widely in the mid-part of the second millennium and by the poets who followed in their wake. The Scandinavian rock-carvings and the Trundholm sun-horse are products of the Bronze Age culture that flourished in southern Sweden and Norway, Denmark, and north Germany contemporaneously with the Mycenaean civilization in Greece, and archaeological links with south-eastern Europe can in fact be traced.[54] There can be no doubt that the people who brought it to the north, warriors with horses, chariots, and battle-axes who had themselves interred in great round tumuli, were Indo-Europeans. We have noted elsewhere that the early Mycenaean civilization may itself have received input from Iranian-speaking invaders from the steppes.

The notion that the Sun-god commands a yoked team of animals of some

[54] Gelling–Davidson (1969), 102 f., 122, 128 f.; Glob (1974), 101, 109–11, 129, 158; cf. H. Genz and others in Meller (2004), 186–93.

kind is not exclusively Indo-European.[55] But where the horse or team of horses is found in connection with the sun in non-Indo-European settings, as in Egypt in the Amarna period and in China, it may be assumed to be a borrowing from an Indo-European source.[56]

FURTHER MYTHICAL MOTIFS

Contemplating the Sun-god's daily round, poets embellished it with imaginative anthropomorphic and domestic detail. In Indic, Greek, and Baltic tradition its tireless continuity is remarked on. Everything else that moves rests, but the waters and Sūrya always keep coming forth (RV 10. 37. 2). The sun comes unceasing, *arámati-*, 2. 38. 4; unflagging, *ájasra-*, 10. 12. 7; *atandrita-*, *MBh.* 3. 160. 35; 5. 29. 8. Similarly in Homer he is ἀκάμας, unwearying. Mimnermus in the poem quoted above writes:

> For Helios must toil day after day:
> there's never any break or rest for him
> or for his horses, once rosefinger Dawn
> leaves Ocean's stream and climbs into the sky. (fr. 12. 1–4)

Some of the Latvian songs deny that Saule ever sleeps (*LD* 6702, 33812 f. = Jonval nos. 218–20). Her horses do not sweat or tire, and she does not let them rest (*LD* 33914 f. = Jonval nos. 172 f.). They cross the world without eating or drinking, but she takes them to the sea to drink at morning and night (*LD* 33994, 33944 f. = Jonval nos. 27, 174 f.).

Sūrya keeps strictly to his appointed daily programme, but when he has completed his journey he rests with his horses (RV 3. 30. 12). Mimnermus describes how the golden bowl carries Helios on his nocturnal voyage εὕδονθ' ἁρπαλέως, 'sleeping pleasantly'. In Stesichorus he crosses Oceanus in it 'to the holy deeps of Night, to his mother, his wedded wife, his dear children' (*PMGF* S17 = 185). In the Old English poem *Guthlac* (1214) the Sun, sinking in the west at evening, is *setlgonges fús*, 'eager to settle'. In medieval German verse too the Sun is portrayed as being tired and going to rest, to bed, etc.[57]

[55] I have cited Sumerian and other Near Eastern material in West (1997), 507. On the Hittite hymn there mentioned see G. Wilhelm in W. Burkert–F. Stolz (edd.), *Hymnen der alten Welt im Kulturvergleich* (Freiburg/Schweiz–Göttingen 1994), 65 f. Add a reference to Shamash's swift mules in *Gilgamesh* III 96 with A. R. George's note, *The Babylonian Gilgamesh Epic* (Oxford 2003), 814.

[56] Egypt: Gamkrelidze–Ivanov (1995), 638 n. 41. China (from the Tocharians): E. G. Pulleyblank, *JRAS* 1966, 31–6.

[57] Grimm (1883–8), 739 f., 1514.

A simile in the *Iliad* implies that Sirius shines brightest when he comes up λελουμένος Ὠκεανοῖο, 'washed in Oceanus' (5. 6). Another passage refers to the 'baths of Oceanus' that most of the stars pass through (18. 489 = *Od.* 5. 275). That the Sun takes this bath is not explicitly mentioned. But at *Od.* 3. 1 he is said to rise from a beautiful λίμνη (body of water, usually a lake or lagoon), and a tragedian wrote of a Red Sea and an Aethiopian λίμνη, 'where Helios the all-seeing ever relieves his immortal body and his horses' fatigue in warm springs of gentle water'.[58] The idea recurs in Baltic tradition. A sixteenth-century investigator of Lithuanian beliefs recorded that '*Perkuna tete* [Perkunas' mother] is the mother of lightning and thunder; she bathes the tired and dusty Sun and sends him out the next day clean and shining'. A Latvian song has Mary heating the bathwater for 'the orphan girls', that is, the stars, the children abandoned by the Sun and Moon after their separation.[59] The Sun's cleansing bath is also a Slavonic motif.[60] The notion that the sun actually plunges into the sea is presupposed in Posidonius' report of a belief that the Celts living by the western ocean, being closer to it, see it larger when it sets and hear a hissing sound as its fire is put out. The audible sound has its counterpart in the one heard at sunrise in the Baltic east according to the report of Tacitus cited earlier.[61]

CULTIC OBSERVANCE

The Sun is a god of regular habits, which he does not vary in response to human intercession. He can inspire joy and admiration, but no real anxiety. It is the moody gods, the ones liable to tantrums, the ones who rollick about and do not know their own strength, who are greater promoters of religious activity. When Helios in the *Odyssey* (12. 376–88) is outraged by the violation of his cattle, he can threaten to go and operate in the lower instead of the upper world, but he cannot send a storm upon the miscreants; he has to persuade Zeus to do that for him.

[58] [Aesch.] fr. 192. From later classical verse cf. Stat. *Theb.* 3. 407–14; Nonn. *Dion.* 12. 6–14.

[59] J. Lasicius (Łasicki), *De diis Samagitarum* in Mannhardt (1936), 356, cf. 392 'was er von der Perkuna tete erzählt, sieht ganz so aus, als sei es aus einer Daina oder einer Pasaka (Märchen) geschöpft'; Usener (1896), 97; von Schroeder (1914–16), ii. 247; Mannhardt (1875), 76 no. 6, 303 f., 307.

[60] Grimm (1883–8), 742 f.; von Schroeder (1914–16), ii. 245–7; Váňa (1992), 62.

[61] Posid. fr. 16 Theiler ap. Strab. 3. 1. 5; Tac. *Germ.* 45. 1. I doubt if von Schroeder (1914–16), ii. 9, is justified in connecting this with the 'wake-up call' (*ślóka-*) delivered by Savitṛ in RV 3. 54. 11; 4. 53. 3; 5. 82. 9; 7. 82. 10.

Solar festivals, accordingly, are in general of a calendrical nature, celebrating significant dates such as the first day of spring/summer, or the longest or shortest day. They are characterized by activities that in some way imitate the behaviour of the sun. Solar symbols are displayed, fires lit on hilltops, fiery wheels rolled down slopes.

The oldest palpable evidence comes from Scandinavia, from those Bronze Age rock drawings found especially in western Sweden but also in parts of Norway and Denmark.[62] Some of them show a large solar disc being set upon a stand, held aloft by men, adored, mounted on two wheels and drawn along by a horse or a pair of horses, or conveyed in a ship. One has the impression of rites in which the emblem of the sun was carried in procession or taken on a symbolic journey. The Trundholm sun-disc perhaps belongs in this context. It seems too small to have played a role in a public festival, but it might be seen as a model imitating a larger disc that was set on wheels and pulled by a real horse. One of the rock drawings shows a large wheel mounted on two smaller wheels with a shaft attached to its right-hand side, ready for a horse to pull it in that direction, and in Gotland a bronze disc was found together with bridle-pieces of two horses.[63]

In certain Indian rituals the sun was represented by a wheel, a gold plate, or a round white skin. At the winter solstice festival (Mahāvrata) there was a struggle for the skin between an Aryan and a Śūdra, who had to surrender it. A priest sat on a swing, facing east, and measured with his hand the small gap between its seat and the ground. Amid other mantras and ritual actions he whispered to the swing-seat 'you are the Sun!' The swing clearly symbolized the sun's seasonal change of declination, and the measuring indicated that it had reached its lowest point.[64]

Swinging is a recurrent feature of Indo-European springtime and midsummer festivities. In India, besides the Mahāvrata, it had a role in the springtime Dolayātrā festival, at which an image of Krishna was swung to and fro on a swing three times a day. In Europe we find it in ancient Athens (the Aiorai, incorporated as part of the spring Anthesteria), Latium (the Feriae Latinae, April), modern Greece (around Easter), Russia and the Balkans (Easter), and Latvia (Easter and midsummer). A South Slavonic myth relates that as Grosdanka was swinging on Easter Day the Sun came down on his own invisible swing and carried her away up to heaven to make her his

[62] de Vries (1956), i. 101–15; Gelling–Davidson (1969), 9–14; M. Green (1991), 43, 74–83; F. Kaul and C. Sommerfeld in Meller (2004), 58–63, 66–9, 82.

[63] de Vries (1956), i. 111 fig. 5d, 113.

[64] Oldenberg (1917), 85 f., 443 f.; von Schroeder (1914–16), ii. 137–40; Oberlies (1998), 395, 423 n. 130. The sun is Varuṇa's 'golden swing' in RV 7. 87. 5.

wife.[65] Here the ritual swinging performed by mortal girls is put in direct contact with the cosmic swinging of the Sun.

Hopping, jumping, and dancing are also characteristic of the spring and midsummer festivals.[66] It is not so clear that these are meant as an imitation of something the Sun does. Yet there was a belief that the Sun does dance at certain times or on certain days. Lucian (*De saltatione* 17) says that the Indians greeted the Sun at daybreak with a silent dance in imitation of the god's dancing. In Germany and England the Sun was supposed to dance and leap on Easter morning, and people would go out early to observe the phenomenon. In the Baltic and Slavonic countries it was associated rather with Midsummer Day.[67]

Ring-dances, where the executants form a circle that rotates as they dance and sing, have a potential reference to the sun's movement, and it may be significant that in parts of Latvia such dances by women and girls, accompanied by cries of *rōtō!* ('turn, circle'), were customary at the beginning of spring. An association of ring-dances with the sun is also suggested by designs on Minoan seals.[68] We think further of the 'circular dances' (*κύκλιοι χοροί*) that provided the Athenians with a traditional show at the spring Dionysia.

Bonfires are a typical feature of all the season-marking festivals: the beginning of summer, midsummer, the beginning of winter, and midwinter.[69] Their analogy with the fire of the sun has often been noted. It becomes more pointed with the (mainly midsummer) custom, observed across Europe from Russia to Wales, of rolling a burning wheel or barrel down a hill, sometimes all the way to a river or lake in which it is extinguished. Records of the practice go back to the fourth century.[70]

Buns or cakes used in ritual may also symbolize the sun. In the Indian Vājapeya sacrifice the animal victim was tied to a post, on top of which a wheel-shaped cake of grain was placed. Steps were set against the post, and the royal sacrificer climbed up, saying to his wife, 'Come, wife, let us go up to

[65] von Schroeder (1914–16), ii. 44, 129–50, 343–6, cf. 434 (a Greek version of the Grosdanka story); Frazer (1911–36), iv. 277–85.

[66] von Schroeder (1914–16), ii. 114–29.

[67] Grimm (1883–8), 291, cf. 741; von Schroeder (1914–16), ii. 37, 43 f., 48 f., 104, cf. 109 f.; de Vries (1956), i. 358.

[68] von Schroeder (1914–16), ii. 124–8; Goodison (as n. 27), 138–40.

[69] Grimm (1883–8), 612–28, 1466–8; von Schroeder (1914–16), ii. 201, 204 f., 211, 220–2, 225–40; Frazer (1911–36), x. 106–269; de Vries (1956), i. 461–3; Unbegaun (1948), 431 f., 440; Gimbutas (1971), 162; Váňa (1992), 118, 241–4.

[70] *Acta S. Vincenti* 1 in Zwicker (1934–6), 302 f. (Aquitania), cf. M. Green (1991), 59, 108; Grimm (1883–8), 619 f., 623, 627 f., 1467; Mannhardt (1905), i. 455, 463, 500 f., 507–11, 518–21, 537; von Schroeder (1914–16), ii. 155–9, 229 f., 234; Frazer (1911–36), x. 116–19, 141, 143, 161–4, 166, 173 f., 201, 334, 337 f.; Gelling–Davidson (1969), 143–5; Váňa (1992), 62.

the sun'. At the top he took hold of the cake and said 'We have reached the sun, O gods!' Among some of the western Slavs in Upper Silesia round cakes called 'little suns' would be baked for Midsummer Day, offered to the Sun, and danced round in the fields. In Anglo-Saxon times, as Bede records, the offering of cakes to gods was the principal feature of *Solmonath* or 'Sun month' (February).[71] Probably the hot cross buns that we associate especially with Easter perpetuate the ancient solar symbol of the cross-in-circle or four-spoked wheel.

Salutation of the rising and setting sun

Besides these seasonal activities there is a simple daily observance that can be documented over thousands of years and over most of the Indo-European area, as well as in other parts of the world: the salutation of the Sun at its rising, and to a lesser extent also at its setting.[72] In India it has been practised since ancient times. Brahmins have long used for this purpose the so-called Gāyatrī or Sāvitrī prayer, RV 3. 62. 10, 'This desirable light of the god Savitṛ we apprehend: may he sharpen our thoughts'. Such morning and evening prayers, facing east and west respectively, are mentioned occasionally in the *Mahābhārata*.[73]

Hesiod (*Op.* 338–40) enjoins that we should propitiate the gods with libations and oblations 'both when you go to bed and when the divine light returns, so that they may have a favourable mind towards you'. The sun appears here only as a time marker, but Plato (*Laws* 887e) refers to prostrations and hand-kissings at the rising and setting of the sun and moon among Greeks and all barbarians. He also mentions that Socrates prayed to the sun at sunrise after concluding a prolonged meditation (*Symp.* 220d). Orpheus was portrayed in Aeschylus' *Bassarai* as going up Mt Pangaion to greet Helios-Apollo at sunrise. Lucian (cited above) says that whereas the Indians faced the east and performed dance movements, the Greeks contented themselves with a hand-kissing salutation.

Xerxes, according to Herodotus (7. 54), prayed and made libation to the Sun at sunrise before crossing the Hellespont. There are also later references to sunrise prayers among Persians and Parthians.[74]

[71] Oldenberg (1917), 85; von Schroeder (1914–16), ii. 43 (104, 115, 365), cf. 378–81; Bede, *De temporum ratione* 15, *Solmonath potest dici mensis placentarum quas in eo diis suis offerebant.*

[72] von Schroeder (1914–16), ii. 97–106; West (1978), 241.

[73] Oldenberg (1917), 431 f., cf. 597; von Schroeder (1914–16), ii. 8 f.; *MBh.* 5. 92. 6; 7. 1268*; 12. 186. 5.

[74] Procop. *Bell. Pers.* 1. 3. 20; Herodian, *Hist.* 4. 15. 1.

There is one medieval Nordic allusion to the practice: *Sólarlióð* 41, 'I saw the Sun; it seemed to me as if I saw the magnificent God. To her I bowed for the last time in this mortal world.' Bavarian farmers in the Oberpfalz were observed in the nineteenth century to raise their hats to the rising sun. Greetings and prayers to the rising and setting sun are attested also from the Baltic lands, Belarus, the Ukraine, and southern Poland.[75]

Remarkable survivals of the custom, including some actual chants in Scots Gaelic, are recorded from the Western Isles.

The people addressed invocations to the sun, moon, and stars. Men and women saluted the morning sun and hailed the new moon. . . . The reciter, Mór MacNeill of Barra, said:—[Gaelic version]—'In the time of my father and of my mother there was no man in Barra who would not take off his bonnet to the white sun of power . . . And old persons will be doing this still, and I will be doing it myself sometimes. Children mock at me, but if they do, what of that?'[76]

Old men in the Isles still uncover their heads when they first see the sun on coming out in the morning. They hum a hymn not easily caught up and not easily got from them. The following fragments were obtained from a man of ninety-nine years in the south end of South Uist, and from another in Mingulay, one of the outer isles of Barra.

Sùil Dhé mhóir,	The eye of the great God,
Sùil Dhé na glòir,	the eye of the God of glory,
Sùil Rìgh nan slògh,	the eye of the King of hosts,
Sùil Rìgh nam beò.	the eye of the King of the living,
Dòrtadh oirnne	pouring upon us
gach òil agus ial,	at each time and season,
Dòrtadh oirnne	pouring upon us
gu fòill agus gu fial.	gently and generously.
Glòir dhuit fhéin,	Glory to thee,
a ghréin an àigh.	thou glorious sun.
Glòir dhuit fhéin, a ghréin,	Glory to thee, thou sun,
a ghnùis Dhé nan dùl.	face of the God of life.[77]

I commented earlier on the Indo-European lexical character of the phrase *sùil Dhé*. One might perhaps recognize further in *sùil Rìgh nam beò* a title akin to one predicated of Indra and Varuna in the Rigveda (3. 46. 2 = 6. 36. 4; 5. 85. 3): *viśvasya bhúvanasya rā́jā*, 'king of all existence', that is, of all creatures.

[75] C. F. A. Wuttke, *Der deutsche Volksaberglaube* (2nd edn., Berlin 1869), 12; Gimbutas (1963), 201; ead. (1971), 165.
[76] Carmichael (1928–59), iii. 274, cf. 287.
[77] Ibid. 306 f.; further examples ibid. 309, 311.

A taboo

μηδ' ἄντ' ἠελίου τετραμμένος ὀρθὸς ὀμείχειν.

And do not urinate upright facing the sun. (Hes. *Op.* 727)

The prohibition on urinating towards the sun was also a Pythagorean rule. Pliny (*HN* 28. 69) attributes it to the Magi. It is paralleled in a number of Indian texts.[78] Some of them add as separate injunctions that one must not urinate while standing up, or while walking or on the road (also prohibited by Hesiod, 729).

DAWN (AND NIGHT)

Dawn, like the sun, has names in many languages that continue an Indo-European prototype. It is based on a verbal root **h₂us*/**h₂eus* meaning 'glow (red), flame' (also seen in Latin *aurum* < **ausom*, Old Prussian *ausis*, 'gold'), extended by a suffix *-ós-* or alternatively *-ró-*.[79] From these come Vedic *uṣás-* and *usrā́*, Avestan *uš́ah-*, Greek ἀώς, αὔως, ἠώς, ἕως, Latin *aurora* (**ausōs-ā*), Lithuanian *aušrà*, Old Church Slavonic *za ustra* 'in the morning', Welsh *gwawr*, and so on.

Dawn appears as a goddess in several branches of the tradition. As Uṣas she is the subject of twenty-one hymns in the Rigveda, including some of the most beautiful. As Ušå she is honoured in one passage of the Avesta (Gāh 5. 5). As Eos she plays a role in Greek poetry and myth. At Rome the personified Aurora is no more than a reflection of Greek literature, but the old Dawn goddess perhaps retained a position in cult under the name of Mater Matuta (see below). In Anglo-Saxon England she lived on as Eostre: her springtime festival gave its name to a month and to the Christian feast of Easter that displaced it.[80] As the month and the festival have similar names in Old

[78] AV 13. 1. 56; *MBh.* 12. 186. 23; 13. 107. 28, 41–3; *Harivaṃśa* 1. 13; *Rm.* 2. 69. 15; *Laws of Manu* 4. 48–52. Hesiod's phrase ὀρθὸς ὀμείχειν, 'urinate upright', has been compared with AV 7. 102. 1 *mekṣyā́my ūrdhvás tiṣthán*, 'I will urinate standing upright', which contains the same lexical elements and similar syntax. But the conjunction of words is too natural to be claimed as a poetic or ritual formula.

[79] Recent discussions: Mayrhofer (1986–2001), i. 236; M. E. Huld in Dexter–Polomé (1997), 178; K. T. Witczak, *SIGL* 2 (1999), 172; M. Nassivera, *HS* 113 (2000), 64 f.

[80] Bede, *De temporum ratione* 15 *Aprilis, Eosturmonath . . . Eosturmonath, qui nunc paschalis mensis interpretatur, quondam a dea illorum quae Eostre vocabatur et cui in illo festa celebrabant nomen habuit; a cuius nomine nunc paschale tempus cognominant, consueto antiquae observationis vocabulo gaudia novae solemnitatis vocantes.*

High German, *Ôstarmânôth*, *Ôst(a)rûn*, it has been inferred that the goddess too was once recognized in southern German lands.[81] In sixteenth-century Lithuania the personified Aušra was still acknowledged, for hers is the name that must be identified in the statement, 'Ausca dea est radiorum solis vel occumbentis vel supra horizontem ascendentis'.[82]

The mistress of the Dawn may be detected under a heavier disguise in the British Brigantia, the goddess of the Brigantes, and the Irish saint Brigit, both going back to a Celtic **Brigantī* < IE $^{*}b^{h}r̥g^{h}n̥tih_2$, 'Great, Lofty'. The corresponding Vedic form, *bṛhatī́*, is several times used as a title of Uṣas (RV 1. 113. 19, 123. 2; 5. 80. 1, 2). This does not in itself justify an equation, but it becomes significant when we take account of St Brigit's peculiar features. She was born at sunrise on the threshold of the house, her mother having one foot inside, one outside. She was the daughter of the Dagda, the 'Good God', or of Dubthach (Dark) son of Dallbrónach (Dark and gloomy). She would only drink milk of a white cow with red ears; reddish cows, as we shall see, are a typical Vedic image of the dawns. She filled the house with a flame that went up to heaven; the neighbours ran to put the fire out, but found that it had vanished. All of this is singularly appropriate to the Dawn goddess.[83]

Attributes; imagery

Even more than the Sun, the Dawn was a deity not so much to be propitiated and appealed to as simply admired and celebrated in poetic images. The imagery is very similar in Vedic and Greek, and implies a common tradition at least from the Graeco-Aryan era.

The appearance of dawn is sometimes represented as a birth. (This really implies that each day's dawn is a different one, and in fact the Vedic poets speak indifferently of Dawn or of the Dawns as an indefinite series.)

> śukrā́ kṛṣṇā́d ajaniṣṭa śvitīcī́.
>
> The shining one has been born bright-beaming from the dark. (RV 1. 123. 9)
>
> ávantu mā́m uṣáso jā́yamānāḥ.
>
> Let the Dawns as they are born help me. (6. 52. 4)

[81] Grimm (1883–8), 290 f., cf. 1371 f.; de Vries (1956), i. 357; D. H. Green (1998), 352 f. A contrary view in J. Knobloch, *Die Sprache* 5 (1959), 27–45.

[82] Lasicius in Mannhardt (1936), 356. If the report is accurate, Aušra had taken possession of sunset as well as dawn, but more probably the Polish writer has got things a bit wrong.

[83] Campanile (1990b), 130–5.

The Aśvins are asked to come with the chariot *yásya yóge duhitā́ jā́yate Diváḥ*, 'at whose harnessing the daughter of Dyaus is born' (10. 39. 12). As noted in the last chapter, 'daughter of Dyaus' (or if one prefers, 'of Heaven') is a frequent and distinctive title of Uṣas, paralleled by Lithuanian *Diẽvo dukrýtė* as a title of the Sun-goddess and in pre-Homeric Greek, quite probably, by *Diwós tʰugátēr* as a title of *Hāwōs. All that remains in Homer of Eos' relationship to Zeus is her formulaic epithet δῖα.[84] All that remains of her being 'born' is her epithet ἠριγένεια 'early-born'. But a welcome parallel from the West is supplied by the story of the birth of St Brigit, related above.

Though born and reborn, Dawn never dies. She partakes of the general divine condition of being unageing and immortal: *ajárā amṛ́tā* (RV 1. 113. 13); *ámartiyā* (1. 30. 20; 3. 61. 2). The cognate ἄμβροτος is used of her by Bacchylides (17. 42) and an anonymous epic poet (Choerilus fr. °23. 12 Bernabé = *SH* 904. 12).

Her most obvious characteristic is that she gives light. In *Od.* 14. 502 φάε δὲ χρυσόθρονος Ἠώς (and also in Hesychius φ 146 φάντα· λάμποντα) we have an old root verb whose Vedic cognate *bhā* is regularly used of Uṣas or the Uṣasaḥ: RV 3. 6. 7 *Uṣó vibhātī́r ánu bhāsi pūrvī́ḥ* 'you shine in accord with the many shining Dawns'; 3. 61. 2 *ví bhāhi* 'shine forth'; 6. 65. 2 *bhā́nty Uṣásaḥ* 'the Dawns shine', etc. Similarly in Avestan, Vd. 19. 28 *uši . . . bāmya* 'shining dawn'; hence Manichaean Middle Persian *'wšyb'm*, Pahlavi *ušbām* 'daybreak, morning'.[85] Various adjectives derived from this root are applied to Dawn in Greek: φαεινή, φαινόλις, φαεσίμβροτος, etc.

In one of the Homeric Hymns (31. 2) an otherwise unknown Euryphaessa appears as the mother of the Dawn, the Moon, and the Sun. As Campanile has pointed out, the name may reflect an old poetic formula, for in RV 1. 92. 9 (cf. 6. 64. 2) it is said of Uṣas that she *urviyā́ ví bhāti*, 'shines out widely': here we have the same lexical elements as in εὐρὺ φα-. Campanile postulates a pre-Homeric formula *Ἀὼς εὐρυφάασσα (< *b^heh_2-*n̥t-ih*$_2$), from which Euryphaassa or -phaessa became an independent name in the same way as Erigeneia does. The Dawn could be said to be mother of the Sun, as in RV 7. 78. 3 *Uṣáso vibhātī́ḥ | ájījanan Sū́riyam*, 'the shining Dawns have given birth to Sūrya'.[86] But then, we must suppose, it was forgotten that Euryphaessa was Dawn, and she became her mother too.

Hesiod (*Th.* 451, cf. 755) uses the phrase φάος πολυδερκέος Ἠοῦς, 'the

[84] The corresponding Vedic word is used of Night and Dawn together when they are called *yóṣaṇe diviyé* or *divyé yóṣaṇe*, 'the two heavenly maidens' (RV 7. 2. 6; 10. 110. 6). Because of their equal alternation they are often treated as sisters (1. 113. 3, 124. 8; 7. 71. 1, etc.), although Night would not be called daughter of Dyaus.

[85] Gershevitch (1959), 291.

[86] E. Campanile, *Études Indo-Européennes* 6 (1987), 17–24.

light of much-seeing Dawn'. The adjective may mean that Dawn herself sees far and wide, like the Sun-god, or that she enables much seeing to be done. In the Rigveda the root *dṛś*, the cognate of Greek δερκ-, is often used in connection with Dawn. She herself is *darśatā́*, a sight to behold (5. 80. 2; 6. 64. 5; 7. 75. 3). She is beheld when she appears: *dṛśānā́*, 1. 92. 12; *práty adarśi*, 1. 113. 7, cf. 124. 3; 4. 52. 1, etc. She displays herself for seeing, *dṛśé kám*, 1. 123. 11, 124. 6, cf. 5. 80. 5.

Every reader of Homer is delighted by the formula *ῥοδοδάκτυλος Ἠώς*, 'rose-fingered Dawn'. It refers, of course, to her spreading rays of reddish light. The 'rose' part is probably a Greek refinement. But the spread hand as an image of the sun's rays may be inherited from older poetic tradition. The Vedic *suaṅgurí-* 'with good fingers' is a complimentary epithet of goddesses, but when it is applied to the solar god Savitṛ (RV 4. 54. 4) it is surely to be understood in terms of rays. In other hymns he is called 'golden-handed' (*híraṇyapāṇi-*, *híraṇyahasta-*) and 'broad-handed' (*pṛthúpāṇi-*). In a Latvian song the gold on the Sun's fingers is made into rings:

> Saule, ma marraine,
> tendait la main au-dessus du fleuve;
> les doigts de ses deux mains étaient couverts
> d'anneaux d'or en spirale.

(*LD* 33932 = Jonval no. 159, cf. 33933–4 = 158, 157.) Large spread hands, attached to human figures or on their own, are a recurrent motif in the rock art of Bronze Age Scandinavia, where they have been suspected of embodying solar symbolism.[87]

A variant on 'rose-fingered' is 'rose-armed', *ῥοδόπηχυς*, applied to Dawn by Sappho (58. 19 *βροδόπαχυν Αὔων*) and in a Homeric Hymn (31. 6). In the Hesiodic corpus this compound is used more generally as an ornamental epithet for nymphs and mortal women, but in relation to Dawn we naturally interpret the rosiness with reference to the glow of the sky.

Likewise with Bacchylides' 'gold-armed Dawn' (5. 40). Savitṛ too has golden arms, *hiraṇyáyā bāhū́* (RV 6. 71. 1, 5; 7. 45. 2; *bāhúḥ* = *πῆχυς*); and to his arms the light of the Dawns is compared (7. 79. 2). Uṣas herself is *híraṇya-varṇā*, 'gold-coloured' (3. 61. 2; 7. 77. 2). Ovid calls the personified Aurora *flaua*, 'the golden-yellow one' (*Amores* 1. 13. 2). The Latvian Sun-goddess Saule or her daughter can be called a *zelta jumpraviņa*, 'golden maid' (*LD* 33971 var. 6, 33989 var. 6 = Jonval nos. 309, 176).

Other passages refer not to Dawn's skin but to her dress. She is clothed in light, *jyótir vásānā* (1. 124. 3); she wears a bright shining garment (7. 77. 2,

[87] Gelling–Davidson (1969), 56–8; M. Green (1991), 50–2.

cf. 1. 113. 7); the Dawns spread out their lovely garments to the wind (1. 134. 4). In Homer Dawn is called κροκόπεπλος, 'saffron-robed', and in a later poet ἑανηφόρος, 'wearing fine raiment' (Antimachus fr. 152 Matthews). In the Latvian songs Saule and her daughter(s) are dressed in fabrics of silk, silver, or gold.[88] Saule also wears shoes of gold (*LD* 33951, 33992 = Jonval nos. 226, 155), which parallels Sappho's χρυσοπέδιλος Αὔως, 'gold-sandalled Dawn' (fr. 103. 10, 123).

Uṣas is not shy of displaying her beauty. She comes before men like a girl with no brothers, like one who goes on stage, and she uncovers her bosom like a courtesan (RV 1. 124. 7, cf. 92. 4; 5. 80. 6; 6. 64. 2).

Like a girl proud of her body you go, goddess, to the god who desires (you);[89]
a smiling (*saṃsmáyamānā*) young woman, shining forth from the east you bare your breasts.
Good-looking, like a young woman adorned by her mother, you bare your body for beholding. (1. 123. 10 f.)

The verb *smayate* 'smiles' is used of her also at 1. 92. 6, and of 'the two Uṣasā' (i.e. Uṣas and her sister, = Dawn and Night) at 3. 4. 6. In the former passage, as in 1. 123. 10, the smile is clearly erotic, enticing. It has been suspected that this seductive smiling was once a feature of the Greek Dawn goddess too, and that Aphrodite took over from her the epithet φιλομμειδής, as she may have taken over the title Διὸς θυγάτηρ.[90] The Greek μειδιάω is from the same root as the Vedic *smi*.

Uṣas throws on embroidered garments *nṛtū́r iva*, like a dancer (RV 1. 92. 4). Eos has χοροί, dancing places, in the east where she has her house and where the sun rises (*Od.* 12. 4). This must allude to dance performances witnessed by mankind. Saule is described dancing in her gilded shoes on a silver hill.[91]

Eos' house (οἰκία, neuter plural) may be put beside the mythical eastern mountain of the Avesta called Ušidam-, 'Dawn-house' (Yt. 1. 28, 31; 19. 2,

[88] Jonval nos. 137, 157, 298, 307, 349 = *LD* 33783, 33934, 33866, 33948, 33891; compared with the Homeric Ἠὼς κροκόπεπλος by Mannhardt (1875), 219. The counterpart of Dawn's bright garment is Night's dark mantle (RV 4. 13. 4, cf. 1. 115. 4; Eur. *Ion* 1150), sometimes pictured as embroidered with the stars (AV 19. 49. 8, reading *nákṣatrāṇy* with Whitney; [Aesch.] *Prom.* 24). Cf. West (1997), 579 f.

[89] This is the Sun, cf. 1. 69. 1, 9, 92. 11, 115. 2; 4. 5. 13; 7. 9. 1, 10. 1, 75. 5, 76. 3; 10. 3. 3.

[90] D. D. Boedeker, *Aphrodite's Entry into Greek Epic* (Leiden 1974), 23–6, 30–42; cf. W. Sonne, *ZVS* 10 (1861), 351, 361 n. 1. Perhaps the strange 'golden Aphrodite' (χρυσῆ) is to be explained on the same lines; cf. above on Dawn's golden colouring, and Boedeker, 22 f. In Homeric formula Eos is χρυσόθρονος, 'gold-throned'. It is conceivable that this originally meant 'gold-patterned' (from θρόνα), referring to Dawn's robe, and that after reinterpretation as 'gold-throned' the epithet was then extended to other goddesses such as Hera. Saule and her daughter wear shawls woven with gold thread (*LD* 33790 = Jonval no. 513).

[91] *LD* 33992 = Jonval no. 155. These comparisons were drawn by Mannhardt (1875), 99.

66). Saule too has a house; by its doors may be seen the horses of the Son(s) of God, who court Saule's daughter (*LD* 33801, 34000 = Jonval nos. 351, 350). Saule is urged to hurry and open the door to the suitors (34014 = J. 138 var. 1). In other versions 'the house of Saule' is replaced by 'the house of God' (Dievs) (33799 f. = J. 139, 352). As already mentioned in the last chapter, the verse 'by the doors of the house of God', *pie Dieviņa namdurēm* or *nama durīm,* is lexically comparable with the Vedic *dvā́rau Divā́ḥ,* 'doors of Heaven', which Uṣas opens with her light (RV 1. 48. 15, cf. 113. 4). Later Classical poets also have Dawn opening heavenly doors or gates.[92]

In another hymn the Dawns are said to have opened the doors of the cow-pen of darkness (4. 51. 2). Dawn and Night in the Rigveda are sisters (n. 84), and the poets celebrate their alternation (1. 62. 8, 95. 1, 96. 5). Dawn drives her sister away (1. 92. 11, cf. 123. 7; 10. 172. 4); Night in turn does likewise (10. 127. 3).

Bright with bright calf the white one has come; the black one has vacated her seats for her.
Cognate, immortal, consecutive, Day and Night, alternating colour, move on.
The same road is the sisters', endless: in turn they travel it by divine ordinance.
They collide not, stay not, well-regulated, Night and Dawn, of one mind but divergent hue. (1. 113. 2; cf. 124. 8)

Hesiod has a strikingly similar passage about the house of Night,

where Night and Day approaching
greet one another as they cross the great threshold
of bronze: the one goes in, the other comes out,
and never the house holds both of them within,
but always one of them outside the house
is ranging over the earth, while the other inside the house
waits until the time comes for her to go,
the one carrying far-seeing light (*φάος πολυδερκές*) for men on earth,
the other with Sleep in her arms, the brother of Death—
Night the baleful, shrouded in clouds of mist. (*Th.* 748–57)

Parmenides claims personally to have journeyed out from the house of Night, riding in a chariot driven by the Daughters of the Sun (*Ἡλιάδες κοῦραι,* B 1. 9). As they left the house of Night they pushed the veils back from their faces, like Uṣas uncovering her bosom. 'There stand the gates of the paths of Night and Day, kept apart by a lintel and a stone threshold . . . Dike of the many atonements holds their keys of exchange.' As a further parallel for this imagery we may recall again the Irish story of St Brigit, born as her mother

[92] Ov. *Met.* 2. 112–14; Quint. Smyrn. 2. 666. Some earlier Greek source may lie behind these.

stood in the doorway of the house at sunrise with one foot on either side of the threshold. As for the two sisters who never meet, they reappear in similar guise in a Latvian riddle: 'Two sisters who are at odds; one appears, the other runs away; one is white, the other black'.[93]

The idea of the Sun's horses and chariot was easily transferred to Dawn, his harbinger who goes before him. Her steeds and chariot(s) are referred to several times in the Rigveda (1. 48. 7, 113. 14, 123. 7; 4. 14. 3; 7. 75. 6). In 7. 77. 3 she commands a fine-looking white horse. In the one Avestan passage where she is personified, *Gāh* 5. 5, she has the epithets *ranjaṯ.aspa-*, *ravaṯ.aspa-*, both explained by Bartholomae as 'making her horses run nimbly'; at any rate they mean something to do with horses. In the *Odyssey* (23. 246) Eos appears once as a charioteer, with two swift horses named Lampos and Phaethon. Bacchylides (fr. 20C. 22) calls her λεύκιππος Ἀώς, 'white-horsed Dawn', and tragedians use the similar phrase λευκόπωλος ἡμέρα, 'white-colt Day' (Aesch. *Pers.* 386, Soph. *Aj.* 673). Night, by contrast, has dark horses and a dark chariot (Aesch. fr. 69, *Cho.* 660 f.). In Norse myth we hear of two horses called Skinfaxi (Shine-mane) and Hrímfaxi (Soot-mane), who draw the cars of Day and Night respectively (*Vafþrúðnismál* 11–14; *Gylf.* 10, *Skáldsk.* 58).

The Dawns 'awaken the sleeper, two-legged and four-legged living things to go forth' (RV 4. 51. 5; cf. 1. 48. 5, 49. 3, 92. 9, 113. 4–6, 124. 12). Dawn comes 'rousing the people, making the roads easy to travel' (5. 80. 2, cf. 6. 64. 1; 7. 75. 1, 79. 1). Zarathushtra sings of 'morning, noon, and night, which prompt the prudent man to his endeavour' (Y. 44. 5). The obscure compounds *framən.nar-*, *framən.narō.vīra-* applied to Ušå in *Gāh* 5. 5 probably meant something of the same sort. Again we find something curiously similar in Hesiod, this time in the *Works and Days* (579–81):

> Dawn forwards the journey, forwards the task;
> Dawn, whose appearing puts many a man on the road,
> and sets the yoke on many an ox.

Mannhardt adduced a Russian riddle about Night and Day: 'The black cow has laid everyone low; the white cow has brought them back to life'.[94]

Uṣas too yokes oxen or cows (RV 1. 92. 2, 124. 11), but these are specified as red ones, and are certainly not our farm animals but pictorial metaphors for the red clouds or rays seen at morning light. Elsewhere the Dawns themselves are likened to cows (4. 51. 8, 52. 5; cf. also 1. 92. 4, 12). The sense may well be

[93] A. J. G. Bielenstein, *1000 lettische Rätsel* (Mitau 1881), no. 138.

[94] Mannhardt (1875), 308 n. 1 (with others from Ukraine and Slovakia); cf. Müller (1897), 98, 761–4; Aarne (1918–20), i. 147. The Vedic and Hesiodic passages are compared by Boedeker (as n. 90), 75.

the same when it is said that 'Sūrya with his rays has driven forth the cattle' (7. 36. 1, cf. 81. 2), though it could be read either way.

This bovine imagery is clearly very ancient. The Hittite Storm-god drives a chariot drawn by bulls named Day and Night.[95] In the *Gāthās* we find the poetic expression *uxšānō asnąm* 'bulls of days', which apparently means 'new dawns'.[96] The immortal cattle of the Sun in the *Odyssey*, 350 cows and 350 sheep, herded by two daughters of Helios, Phaethousa and Lampetie, must originally have represented the days and nights of the year.[97] Day and Night are symbolized by black and white cows in the Russian riddle quoted above.

I have cited a Vedic passage in which Uṣas arrays herself like a dancer (RV 1. 92. 4). The verse then takes a turn that we might not consider tasteful: 'she uncovers her breast as a cow her udder'. In other hymns we read that 'Dawn and Night are as a cow good for milking: in the course of one day I measure out my song, in different-coloured milk at that (one) udder', that is, in light and darkness (1. 186. 4); 'where mother and daughter, the two milch cows, together feed (their calf)' (3. 55. 12);[98] 'may the Dawns ever shine for us . . . being milked of ghee' (7. 41. 7). The archaic phrase νυκτὸς ἀμολγῶι 'at the milking(-time) of night', which in Homer seems to mean no more than 'in the dark of night' (*Il.* 11. 173, 15. 324, al.), must once have conveyed some more definite notion based on the idea of Night and Day as cows.

Dawn's lovers

In Greek myth Eos is a predatory goddess, falling in love with the handsomest young men such as Tithonos, Kleitos, Kephalos, and carrying them off. The Rigveda, as we have seen, portrays Uṣas as a beautiful and uninhibited young woman who smiles alluringly and is happy to display her bodily charms. The Sun, who is always tagging along after her, is sometimes represented as her lover (above, n. 89).

> The lover has woken from the Dawns' lap . . .
> He is giving the signal to both races. (7. 9. 1)

[95] Gurney (1977), 25 f.

[96] Y. 46. 3, cf. 4; 50. 10. Cf. Campanile (1977), 20, 25; id. (1990b), 138; R. Lazzeroni, *La cultura indoeuropea* (Rome–Bari 1998), 102 f. Campanile (1990b) argues that 'bulls' reflects the notion of an ox-cart carrying the sun. This would have preceded the image of the horse-drawn chariot.

[97] *Od.* 12. 127–36; E. Campanile, *Incontri Linguistici* 11 (1986), 25–30; (1990b), 136–9; below, pp. 370–2.

[98] The calf is Agni the morning altar-fire (cf. 1. 95. 1, 96. 5, 146. 3), and the mother and daughter Night and Day (despite their being called sisters in the preceding verse). For Night as mother of Dawn cf. Aesch. *Ag.* 265 with Fraenkel's note.

'Both races' means gods and men. We can hardly fail to be reminded of the Homeric lines:

> Dawn from her bed, from beside glorious Tithonos,
> sallied forth to bring light to immortals and mortals.[99]

Uṣas is not associated with a specific mortal lover. But there seems to be a suggestion that she might be tarrying with one in 1. 30. 20:

> Who is there for you, O whose-friend Dawn,
> to enjoy, (which) mortal, immortal one?
> Whom are you visiting, radiant one?

If there is no Indian Tithonos, growing ever older in the house of his perpetually young consort, there is at least an awareness of the tragic contrast between her and us. 'Bringing old age, thou hast come, O unageing Dawn . . . Unageing, thou dost make to age all else' (TS 4. 3. 11. 5; cf. RV 1. 124. 2).

The Dawn goddess and the spring festival

Dawn is not a goddess of cult. She was hymned at the Vedic morning sacrifice because it was that time of day, but she was not the object of the ceremony. The Agniṣṭoma, the springtime festival that began the year, opened with songs to her, and this led Alfred Hillebrandt to argue that Uṣas was especially a goddess of New Year.[100] The Vedic texts themselves make it abundantly clear that she appeared every day in the same way; they contain nothing that points to a special association with a particular time of year.

It seems nevertheless that the Dawn goddess did have such an association in some branches of the tradition. It is not too hard to understand how this could come about. Many Indo-European peoples had festivities to celebrate the beginning of spring or summer, the time when the sun began to shine more warmly after the winter months. The sun was the focus of interest on these occasions, and the custom of getting up at dawn or before dawn to greet the rising sun is widely attested. In these circumstances it was natural that the Dawn herself, appearing in the east in advance of the sun, should attract more attention than on other days of the year.

[99] *Il.* 11. 1–2 = *Od.* 5. 1–2; compared by Kretschmer (1896), 83 n. 1. Helios too shines for immortals and mortals (*Od.* 3. 2 f., 12. 385 f.); cf. RV 1. 50. 5.

[100] Hillebrandt (1927–9), i. 28–32; von Schroeder (1914–16), ii. 204–6. Hillebrandt's theory was rejected by many scholars, but defended with learning by F. B. J. Kuiper, *IIJ* 4 (1960), 223–42, who concludes, 'the hymns to Uṣas are unaccountable as documents of religious thought, unless we take Uṣas to be in the first place the Dawn of New Year'. He puts this at the winter solstice.

We have seen that the practice of swinging was characteristic of these solar festivals, and that it was a feature of the Greek springtime festival known as the Aiorai, 'Swings'. According to the aetiological myth, girls swung from trees because one Erigone had hanged herself from a tree. We have testimony from Aristotle (fr. 515) that women sang a traditional song about her at the Aiorai. Her hanging became attached to the story of Ikarios, the man who brought viticulture to Attica, and she was made his daughter. But her name is simply a variant of Erigeneia 'Early-born', the familiar title of the Dawn goddess.[101] Her hanging was probably invented as the mythical counterpart of a custom of hanging images in trees, and it was then used to explain the swinging as well.[102]

Alcman's first Partheneion (*PMGF* 1) is a song composed for a Spartan ceremony in which girls apparently carried a plough in procession. The time of year is uncertain, but there are indications that the activities began before sunrise. On one interpretation of lines 39–43 Agido, a girl who is located apart from the singers and whose 'light' they acclaim, 'is bearing witness to us that the sun is shining': this could mean that she is standing on an eminence, watching for the first appearance of the sun's disc above the horizon and signalling it by raising a torch. In lines 87–9 the chorus sings, 'my chief desire is to be pleasing to Aotis, for she has become our healer of toils'. Aotis is evidently a divinity, and her name can only be an extended form of Aos, Dawn. Here then is a dawn goddess celebrated on the occasion of what is presumably an annual festival. Perhaps her appearance on this day brings to an end the toils of winter.[103]

The Italic goddess Mater Matuta, 'Mother Morning', was considered, at least by some (Lucr. 5. 656; Prisc. *Inst.* 2. 53), to be none other than Aurora, though she evidently had other associations too. Her festival at Rome, the Matralia, fell on 11 June. It began at dawn with an offering of cakes that were *flaua*, the same colour as Aurora (Ovid, *Fasti* 6. 473–6, cf. *Amores* 1. 13. 2). Like the cakes previously mentioned, these may originally have been solar symbols.[104]

[101] von Schroeder (1914–16), ii. 144.

[102] For hanging images on the May-tree or Maypole in various parts of Europe see Mannhardt (1905), i. 156 (a doll in the form of a woman dressed in white), 173 (man and wife), 210, 408 f., 430 f. (young man and girl).

[103] Procopius, *Bell. Goth.* 2. 15. 13, reports that in 'Thule' (somewhere in Scandinavia?) the sun did not appear in midwinter for forty days. When thirty-five had elapsed, scouts were sent up to mountain peaks to watch for its first appearance, and they then announced to those below that it would shine for them in five days' time.

[104] Dumézil (1968–73), iii. 305–30, made an ingenious attempt to explain other features of the ritual in terms of the mythology of Dawn. He took the date, 11 June, to mark the approach of the solstice. It is certainly noteworthy that it falls exactly six months before the festival that Johannes Lydus (*De mensibus* 4. 155) associates with the Sun.

The plainest example of the Dawn goddess's becoming attached to a single festival, and that in the spring, is that of the Anglo-Saxon Eostre and her postulated German counterpart Ôstara, who have given us Easter and the *Ostertage*. Our source does not connect Eostre with dawn, but that is undoubtedly the meaning of her name.

THE DAUGHTER OF THE SUN

The Vedic evidence

Besides the Sun and the Dawn, the Rigveda makes frequent reference to a figure called *Sū́ryasya* (or *Sū́re, Sū́ro*) *duhitṛ́*, 'the daughter of the Sun', or *Sūryā́*, which is a feminine form corresponding to masculine *Sū́ryă-* (only with a shift of accent).[105] In most cases she appears in connection with the Aśvins, that youthful equestrian pair whom we met in the last chapter and found to be a close parallel to the Greek Dioskouroi. It is often mentioned that Sūryā joined them in their car. She chose it, or them (1. 117. 13; 4. 43. 2; 7. 69. 3 f.), and her beauty added to their lustre; all the gods approved (1. 116. 17; 6. 63. 5 f.). It was a bridal car: the Aśvins mounted it for her sake, and their swift riding made them her husbands (7. 69. 3; 8. 22. 1; 4. 43. 6; cf. 1. 184. 3).

In the wedding hymns RV 10. 85 and AV 14. 1–2 she has a special role as the divine model for the mortal bride. In RV 10. 85 (largely repeated in AV 14. 1) she has the Aśvins as groomsmen or suitors, but her marriage is to Soma, to whom Savitṛ gave her with her consent. Soma in this hymn (1–5) is identified with the moon. Sūryā appears in some of the Soma hymns of book 9 as somehow connected with the Soma ritual.

According to the *Aitareya Brāhmaṇa* (4. 7–9; cf. *Kauṣītaki Brāhmaṇa* 18. 1) Sūryā's father had intended to give her in marriage to Soma. But all the gods desired her, and to decide who should have her a race was arranged, from Agni (the house-fire) to the Sun. The Aśvins were the winners. Some of the Rigvedic allusions make sense in terms of this story, though we cannot be sure that it is not in part a later construction.

105 *Sūryā́* 1. 167. 5, 184. 3; 4. 43. 6, 44. 1; 5. 73. 5; 6. 58. 4, 63. 6; 7. 68. 3; 8. 22. 1; 10. 85. 6–17, 20, 34–8; *Sū́ryasya* (or *Sū́re, Sū́ro*) *duhitṛ́* 1. 34. 5, 116. 17, 117. 13, 118. 5; 3. 53. 15; 4. 43. 2; 6. 63. 5; 7. 69. 4; 9. 1. 6, 72. 3, 113. 3. She is alluded to also in 8. 8. 10 (as *yóṣaṇā*, 'the young woman') and 8. 29. 8.

The Baltic and Slavonic evidence

The Daughter of the Sun, Lithuanian *Sáulės dukrýtė*, Latvian *Saules meita* ('Sun's girl', presumably for older **Saulēs duktē*), is a figure who appears in many of the Baltic songs. In some cases she is just a variant of the personified (female) Sun herself. Sometimes there are two, three, or more *Saules meitas.* But there are never any sons of Saule.

Saules meita wears fine clothes and ornaments. She herds cows (*LD* 33971 = Jonval no. 309 var. 2), which may make us think of the motif of solar cattle, but this is only one of many homely activities which she is pictured as performing after the fashion of a domesticated young woman on earth. She is in fact a paragon, as illustrated by a Lithuanian saying recorded in the eighteenth century, applicable to someone who finds fault with everything: 'he wouldn't even be satisfied with the daughter of the Sun'.[106]

She is in constant relationship with the Sons of God (Jonval nos. 369–417) in a way that strikingly parallels Sūryā's relationship with the Aśvins, the *Divó nápātā.* On occasion they are at odds (370–4, 416), but more often they are on friendly terms (375 ff.). They greet her on Midsummer Day (404). She rides on a sleigh behind the Son of God's horse (417). She heats the bath for the two Sons of God, who arrive on sweating horses (381).

They are her suitors (405, 410–13; cf. 120, where her place is taken by the Virgin Mary). The Son of God is seen saddling his horse and riding to find a wife (128). The suit is associated with sunrise:

> Les coqs d'argent chantent
> au bord de la rivière d'or.
> Ils faisaient lever les Fils de Dieu,
> prétendants de la Fille de Saule. (*LD* 34008 = Jonval no. 405)
>
> Dieu a deux fils,
> prétendants de la Fille de Saule.
> Saule elle-même, mère des filles à marier,
> pare la chambre de ses filles,
> chaque matin en se levant,
> éparpillant les fleurs. (*LD* 33766 = Jonval no. 413)

Saule's daughter is indeed much sought after in marriage. Her suitors or bridegrooms in different songs include God, Mēnesis (the Moon), Mēnesis' son, Pērkons (the thunder-god), Pērkons' son, Auseklis (the Morning Star),

[106] Jakob Brodowski's manuscript Lithuanian–German dictionary (early eighteenth century) in Mannhardt (1936), 614, *nei Sáules dukte negál jám intikti.*

and Auseklis' son. The Sons of God appear in particular rivalry with Mēnesis or with Auseklis. In one song (346) Auseklis, or in a variant Mēnesis, has risen early, before Saule, wanting her daughter, and Saule is urged to get up herself and deny her to him. In another song (415) we read that the Sons of God and the Daughters of Saule were celebrating their wedding-feast in mid-air, when Mēnesis (or Auseklis) ran up and switched the rings. In another, Saule promised her daughter to the Son of God, but then gave her to Mēnesis instead.[107]

The wedding apparently takes place at the beginning of summer:

> Aujourd'hui Saule court chaudement
> plus que tous les autres jours.
> Aujourd'hui on emmène la Fille de Saule
> de la Daugava en Allemagne. (*LD* 33996 = Jonval no. 356)

It is attended by Pērkons, whose thunder shatters the golden oak-tree (J. 128, 359, cf. 349, 361; Schleicher (1857), 216 no. 4).

As in India, songs about the Sun's daughter were sung at weddings.[108] The celestial nuptials were evidently seen as a cosmic paradigm of terrestrial ones. Similarly, songs about the wedding of the Sun and the Morning Star were sung at weddings among the southern Slavs.[109] The Daughter of the Sun does not seem to have maintained her distinct identity in the Slavonic area, though I have found one reference to a Russian story about a daughter of the Sun and Moon who asks to be ferried over the water.[110] Her place appears to be partly taken by 'the sister of the Sun', who was sometimes identified with the Morning Star or the Dawn. Her limbs were golden-yellow, and she was referred to as a paradigm of beauty: 'as beautiful as the Sun's sister'.[111]

The Greek evidence

More than one individual in Greek mythology is said to be a daughter of Helios. There is Minos' wife Pasiphae 'Shining for all', whose name at least

[107] Mannhardt (1875), 82 no. 72, cf. no. 73. Note that although the Sons of God may appear as plural suitors of Saules meita, when a marriage is spoken of there is either only one Son of God or plural Daughters of the Sun. No *ménage à trois* is countenanced as in the Aśvins' joint possession of Sūryā.

[108] Mannhardt (1905), ii. xx n.

[109] F. S. Krauss, *Sitte und Brauch der Südslaven* (Vienna 1885), 351.

[110] Mannhardt (1875), 305.

[111] Gregor Krek, *Die Wichtigkeit der slavischen traditionellen Literatur* (Vienna 1869), 83; von Schroeder (1914–16), ii. 398.

suggests a bright celestial, though this has no obvious relevance to the story that she mated with a bull and gave birth to the Minotaur. In the *Odyssey* there is Circe, who lives close by the house and dancing-place of Dawn and the risings of the sun (12. 3 f.), and also the two nymphs who herd Helios' calendrical cattle, Phaethousa and Lampetie—lucent names again, and although they live on earth, they are able to go and visit their father (12. 132, 374 f.). Then there are those Heliad maidens mentioned earlier, who actually ride out in a chariot from the gates of the sunrise in company with a *kouros*—Parmenides—if not with a Dioskouros.[112] Another group of Heliades appeared as the chorus in Aeschylus' tragedy of that name: its subject was Phaethon, and they were his sisters who lamented his fiery death. Hyginus (*Fab.* 154. 4) serves up a list of their names, and it is interesting that one of them is Helie, which stands in the same relationship to Helios as Sūryā to Sūrya.

But if we ask who is the divine paragon of female beauty most intimately connected with the Dioskouroi, those Greek counterparts of the Aśvins and the Baltic Sons of God, there can only be one answer: Helen. She is not called the daughter of the Sun, except in one late and supremely disreputable source (Ptolemy Hephaestion ap. Phot. *Bibl.* 149a31): she is the daughter of Zeus (*Διὸς θυγάτηρ*, *Od.* 4. 227), as the Vedic Uṣas is of Dyaus (*Divó duhitā́*), the Lithuanian Sun-goddess of Dievas, and St Brigit of the Dagda. She is thus the sister of the Dioskouroi, and it follows that they cannot appear as her suitors. But she is much sought after in marriage, and although her suitors gather at the house of her mortal 'father' Tyndareos to bid for her, it is the Dioskouroi, not Tyndareos, who organize the event ('Hes.' frs. 196–9).

In the epic tradition Helen appears as a mortal queen at Sparta who by eloping with Paris caused a huge and disastrous war. But in Laconia she was worshipped as a goddess, and so she was on Rhodes, where Helios too was a major deity.[113] The cults can hardly have grown out of the epic myth; rather Helen was a goddess from the start. By blaming her for the Trojan War the poet Stesichorus, according to legend, offended her and she struck him blind, later restoring his sight after he had composed a palinode. In a variant of the story (Horace, *Epod.* 17. 42) it was the Dioskouroi who blinded and then healed him. In either case it is noteworthy that restoring sight to the blind is a typical accomplishment of the Aśvins.[114]

[112] Parmenides B 1. 24 *ὦ κοῦρ' ἀθανάτοισι συνάορος ἡνιόχοισιν.*

[113] The Rhodian Helios had a daughter Ālektrōnā, who died unmarried and was venerated as a heroine (*SIG* 338; Diod. 5. 56. 5).

[114] RV 1. 112. 8; 116. 14, 16; 117. 17 f.; 8. 5. 23; 10. 39. 3; *MBh.* 3. 121–5. The parallel was noted by Pisani (1969), 346.

In two early Laconian dedications to Helen her name is spelled with a digamma, Ϝελένα.[115] This rules out attempts to connect it with σέλας 'brightness', σελήνη 'moon', or the Indian Saraṇyū, the Aśvins' mare-mother mentioned at the end of the last chapter. The older form of the name must have been *Swelénā. We can recognize here the *-*no-/-nā* suffix that is so characteristic of Indo-European divine names (Chapter 3). As for **swel-*, it is hard not to see it as somehow related to the words for 'sun'. It resembles the Vedic and Avestan forms *súvar/svàr, hvarə*, 'sun, solar glare', the verb *svarati* 'shine, gleam', Albanian *diell* 'sun',[116] Old English *swelan* 'burn', German *schwelen*, Lithuanian *svìlti* 'grill'; in Greek itself we have ἕλη, εἵλη (< *ἐ-*h*Ϝέλᾱ), meaning 'sunshine, sun's heat'. These connections have long been noted.[117] They set Helen in etymological contact with Sūryā, and make her by origin something like the Mistress of Sunlight.

She can manifest herself as a luminous body. The Dioskouroi, who can appear to storm-tossed sailors bringing light and salvation, were identified in the electrical discharges that can play about ships' masts and are known as corposants or St Elmo's fire. Occasionally Helen too is associated with this phenomenon.[118]

Her birth from a goose-egg (*Cypria* fr. 11 W., cf. Sappho fr. 166) may perhaps reflect her solar affinities. Baltic myth furnishes a striking parallel. The Indo-European mythology of the Daughter of the Sun spread from Latvia to neighbouring Estonia and across the gulf to Finland.[119] *Saules meita* became in Estonia 'Salme', a maiden of outstanding beauty who was wooed by the Sun, the Moon, and the eldest son of the Stars (whom she chose). And she was born from a goose-egg.[120]

The Dioskouroi cannot be Helen's suitors, but they do pursue two other girls who seem to represent another version of the Daughter of the Sun. These

[115] *SEG* 457 (*c*.675–650), 458 (sixth century). The digamma is also attested by grammarians: Dion. Hal. *Ant.* 1. 20. 3; Marius Victorinus, *Gramm. Lat.* vi. 15. 6; Astyages ap. Prisc. *Inst.* 1. 20, who quoted a verse ὀψόμενος Ϝελέναν ἑλικώπιδα (*PMG* 1011a, perhaps Alcman). It is mostly neglected in Homer except in the formula (δῖος) Ἀλέξανδρος, Ἑλένης πόσις ἠϋκόμοιο.

[116] From **swel-*: E. Hamp in *Per Aspera ad Asteriscos* (as Chapter 4, n. 5), 207.

[117] At least since Mannhardt (1875), 310.

[118] Cf. Eur. *Or.* 1637, 1690. Later a double corposant was considered a good sign, a single one (= Helen) a bad one: Sosibius *FGrHist* 595 F 20; Pliny, *HN* 2. 101; Stat. *Theb.* 7. 792, *Silv.* 3. 2. 8–12; O. Skutsch, *JHS* 107 (1987), 191 f. One of the Latvian songs (*LD* 33776, Jonval no. 403) goes: 'Deux chandelles brûlaient sur la mer, | dans les flambeaux d'argent. | Elles sont allumées par les Fils de Dieu | attendant la Fille de Saule.'

[119] Mannhardt (1875), 314 f.; K. Krohn, *Finnisch-ugrische Forschungen* 3 (1903), 15–44; von Schroeder (1914–16), ii. 425–33.

[120] H. Neus, *Ehstnische Volkslieder* (Reval [Tallinn] 1850–2), i. 9–23; *Kalevipoeg* 1. 126–863. For the sun as an egg see F. Lukas, 'Das Ei als kosmologische Vorstellung', *Zeitschrift des Vereins für Volkskunde* 4 (1894), 227–43.

are the Leukippides, daughters of Apollo or of Leukippos 'Whitehorse'. They were called Phoibe 'Shining' and Hilaeira 'Genial' (a word applied by Empedocles to fire and the Moon). All these names look distinctly solar. If 'Whitehorse' stands for the Sun-god, the girls are daughters of the Sun; two rather than one, because it was felt (as in the Baltic tradition) that two males could not jointly possess one female. They were betrothed to Idas and Lynkeus, but the Dioskouroi carried them off from the wedding feast in their chariot. They were venerated at Sparta in conjunction with the Dioskouroi, and the egg from which Helen was born was to be seen (miraculously repaired) hanging from the roof of their shrine.[121]

Abduction of the Sun-maiden figure is a recurrent motif in this complex of legend. Helen as a young girl was abducted by Theseus and Peirithoos; the Dioskouroi pursued them to Aphidna in Attica and recovered her. Her more famous abduction, however, came about when she was already married. Her marriage, we have noted, was arranged by the Dioskouroi, her brothers. Since they cannot be suitors, they are replaced in that role by another pair of brothers, the two Atreidai, Agamemnon and Menelaus. The monogamy principle means that the Atreidai cannot both have her, but 'Hesiod' (fr. 197. 1–5) related that they made their suit jointly: Agamemnon was able to offer a bigger bride-price than anyone else in Greece, and the Dioskouroi would have awarded Helen to him, but he (being already married to her sister Clytaemestra) was bidding on behalf of his brother. She therefore became the wife of Menelaus. But when she was abducted by Paris, it was the Atreidai as a pair who led the expedition to retrieve her.[122]

This is the story of the Trojan War. Here we are in the realm of semi- or quasi-historical saga. Helen has become a mortal woman, if an exceptional one, and her celestial connections are forgotten. But the pattern of the old Indo-European myth has left its imprint.[123]

Daughters of the Sun in other traditions

Sporadic and somewhat heterogeneous references to a daughter of the Sun occur in several other branches of the Indo-European tradition. Some of

[121] *Cypria* fr. 15 W., Theoc. 22. 137–211, Ov. *Fast.* 5. 699–720, Hyg. *Fab.* 80, etc.; Carl Robert, *Die griechische Heldensage* (Berlin 1920–3), 314–19. The Dioskouroi's temple was in the temenos of Phoibe at Therapne: Paus. 3. 14. 9, 20. 2, cf. Hdt. 6. 61. 3.

[122] Late sources say that the Dioskouroi pursued Paris as far as Lesbos but there vanished from the earth (Dares 11), or that they seized Helen from him in Africa (St. Byz. p. 233. 20 s. v. *Διοσκούρων κώμη*).

[123] For a new attempt to disentangle myth from history in the story of Troy see my lecture 'Geschichte und Vorgeschichte: die Sage von Troia', printed in *Studia Troica* 14 (2004), xiii–xx.

them have no apparent relevance to the present context, as when in a Hittite narrative the Earth, 'daughter of the Sun-god', asks to be fed in the morning and is given groats(?) by the Sun; or when we hear in the Edda that the Sun will give birth to a daughter as fair as herself to take her place after Ragnarøk; or when Albanian legend tells of a daughter of the Sun and Moon who is the dew and who helps a hero in his fight against a female dragon of rain and drought.[124]

We find matter of greater interest among the Ossetic Nart legends. In one story the hero Soslan pursues a shining golden hart whom he sees at sunrise in a reed-bed. She is in fact Aziruxs ('this light'), the daughter of the Sun. He tracks her down, and after performing some difficult tasks he wins her in marriage. In another episode, while he is out hunting, she is abducted by the prince of the stronghold Xisa. When he finds out what has happened, he assembles the Nart army and goes and lays siege to the stronghold. They are unable to take it and return home downcast, but a second expedition is successful and Aziruxs is recaptured.[125]

Astronomical interpretations

Common threads in the traditions about the Daughter of the Sun are (*a*) her association with the Twin Horsemen, and (*b*) rivalry for her hand, which sometimes leads to vicissitudes: she is given to someone other than she was originally promised to, or the wedding feast is interrupted, or she is abducted afterwards. In the Indian and Baltic traditions the Moon is implicated in these contretemps, in the latter also the Morning Star. We have the sense that the stories are romantic interpretations of astronomical phenomena. At times when Venus or the moon is visible at dawn, their positions change from day to day, and an intrigue might easily be read into their movements.

The Baltic and Slavonic songsters are particularly given to putting the heavenly luminaries in personal and domestic relationships. The Morning and Evening Stars are the Moon's horses (Jonval nos. 280 f.). In Slovak fancy the Zori, or morning and evening twilights, daughters of God, with the Morning Star, serve the Sun and harness his white horses.[126] In Lithuanian songs the Morning Star lights the fire for the Sun, daughter of God, and the

[124] *KBo* iii. 38 recto 3′; H. Otten, *Eine althethitische Erzählung um die Stadt Zalpa* (*Studien zu den Boğazköy-Texten* 17; Wiesbaden 1973), 37; *Vafþrúðnismál* 47, *Gylf.* 53; M. Lambertz, *Albanesische Märchen* (*Sitz.-Ber. Wien. Ak.*, Linguistische Abteilung 12, 1922), 77; id. (1973), 471 f., 486 f.

[125] Sikojev (1985), 110–28, 187–9; cf. 184, 202–5, 286 f.

[126] Mannhardt (1875), 305.

Evening Star prepares her bed. The Moon married the Sun in the first springtime, but wandered off and fell in love with the Morning Star; Perkunas was angry, and clove him with his sword.[127]

But what does the Daughter of the Sun represent? In some of the Baltic songs she alternates in different versions with Saule herself, though in other songs they are separate individuals. In one Lithuanian song the Morning Star (Aušrinė, fem.) is called daughter of the Sun.[128] But this is clearly not a fixed equation. It is impossible in Latvian, where the Morning Star is masculine.

One Vedic passage suggests Sūryā's identification with the Dawn,[129] but otherwise there is no overlap between what is said about the one, the daughter of Sūrya, and the other, the daughter of Dyaus. She seems nevertheless to have a connection with the solar glow or glare. A post-Vedic systematizer says of Sūrya's wife, 'they call her Uṣas before sunrise, Sūryā when midday reigns, but Vṛṣākapāyī at the setting of the sun' (*Bṛhaddevatā* 2. 9–10, cf. 7. 120 f.). Such a formula is inapplicable to the Vedic material, but it implies a sense that Sūryā signified something like the sun's effulgence.

As a creature of surpassing beauty the Sun's daughter naturally aroused desire among the celestials. But we cannot attach any exact astronomical meaning to her liaisons, any more than we can to the journeyings of the Aśvins, whose chariot she joins, or of the Dioskouroi. The twin brothers have sometimes been identified with the Morning and Evening Stars.[130] But these can never appear at the same time, or on the same day, or even in the same month.

Ritual aspects

We have noted that the solar festivals are characterized by imitation on earth of what happens in heaven. The sun is held aloft, transported by horse or ship, rolled down from hilltop to water. Certain features of the mythology surrounding the Daughter of the Sun also have their counterpart in seasonal festive custom. But here, perhaps, it is not a matter of imitating phenomena observed in the sky, but rather of projecting earthly sports into the sky, with myth reflecting ritual.

[127] Rhesa (1825), 92, 282; Schleicher (1857), 215 nos. 1–2, cf. no. 3. Cf. Jonval no. 301: Saule (*var.*: Pērkons) clove the Moon with his sword because he had abducted Auseklis' fiancée.

[128] Rhesa (1825), 220–2; Schleicher (1857), 216 no. 4.

[129] RV 7. 75. 5, where *Sū́riyasya yóṣā* 'Sūrya's young woman' and Uṣas stand in parallel.

[130] Aśvins: von Schroeder (1914–16), ii. 445–7; Oldenberg (1917), 209–13; *contra*, Hillebrandt (1927–9), i. 39 f. Dioskouroi: Stat. *Silv.* 4. 6. 15 f.; Serv. *Aen.* 6. 121; F. G. Welcker, *Griechische Götterlehre* (Elberfeld 1857–63), i. 606; Mannhardt (1875), 309; von Schroeder (1914–16), ii. 451–3; Ward (1968), 15–18.

Several of the Latvian songs describe how, when the wedding of the Sun's Daughter is celebrated, the Sun or the Sons of God decorate the trees with green cloth, gold rings, and other ornaments.[131] This reflects the practice, widely attested across northern and eastern Europe,[132] of decorating the May-tree with coloured ribbons, garlands, eggshells, and trinkets at the beginning of summer—just when, as we have seen, the wedding of the Daughter of the Sun was supposed to take place. Another stanza runs: 'The Sun's children (or in variants the Sun's maidens, or maid, or Saule herself) have made a ring-dance at the edge of the forest: put a golden girdle on me, mother, so I can run and join the throng.' It is plausibly argued by von Schroeder that these Sun maidens are not mythical creatures but the mortal girls who take part in the sun-dances.[133] Other songs describe the Sons of God and the Daughters of Saule dancing hand in hand, or the Sons and Daughters of God (*var.*: the Sun's Daughters) dancing in the moonlight by a spring; again, perhaps, projections of, and sung at the time of, terrestrial dances.[134] The story of the birth and marriage of Salme, the Estonian version of Saules meita, was told in songs for swinging, an activity, as we saw earlier, associated with spring and midsummer and symbolic of the sun's cyclical changes of declination.[135] Here too myth is linked to ritual.

Helen's wedding was a recurring event at Sparta, celebrated by a company of girls who sang and danced before dawn, hung garlands on the goddess's holy plane-tree, and poured olive oil on the ground at its foot. This is securely inferred from Theocritus' eighteenth Idyll, which after a narrative introduction presents an epithalamium supposedly sung and danced by the original girl chorus. Helen will be Menelaos' bride 'from year to year' (15). Her beauty is compared with Dawn and spring (26 f.). The girls are going to the meadows before first light to gather flowers (39 f.); they will return at dawn, when the bridal pair are due to awake (55–7). The girls who celebrated the festival in historical times identified themselves with Helen's friends and coevals, much as the girl votaries of the Leukippides were themselves called Leukippides (Paus. 3. 16. 1), and the Latvian celebrants of the Sun maiden's wedding became Sun maidens themselves.

In Rhodes the story was told that Helen was seized there by a group of women dressed as Erinyes and hanged from a tree, in memory of which there

[131] Mannhardt (1875), 77 nos. 13–15, 85 no. 83; *LD* 33802 var. 1, 33804 = Jonval nos. 359, 358.

[132] Mannhardt (1905), i. 156–82; Frazer (1911–36), ii. 59–70.

[133] von Schroeder (1914–16), ii. 122–4. My rendering of the song is based on his German translations of versions communicated to him by 'Frau Direktor A. Feldt in Libau'; they are variants of *LD* 32865 = Jonval no. 165.

[134] *LD* 33758 = Jonval no. 375; Schleicher (1857), 221 no. 12.

[135] von Schroeder (1914–16), ii. 432 f.

was a shrine of Helena Dendritis, Helen of the Tree. We recall that Erigone, 'the Early-born', hanged herself from a tree, and we divined that this corresponded to the practice of hanging images from trees. The Rhodian myth is to be understood in the same way.

Another common decoration of the May-tree, May-branch, or Maypole consists of eggs or painted eggshells.[136] This is not the only part that eggs play in the springtime festivities. Often they are collected from householders by a begging procession.[137] We still associate Easter with eggs. They make an obvious symbol of rebirth or of the reborn sun. The births of Helen and of Salme from eggs make sense in the light of the seasonal customs.

The wedding of the Daughter of the Sun has its counterpart in the widespread custom of choosing a May Queen or May Bride and a young man to be her royal consort, the two being then celebrated as a newly-wedded pair.[138] In the story of Helen's wedding suitors come from all over Greece and offer what they can by way of a bride-price. She goes to the highest bidder—in fact to a pair of brothers, who, as we have seen, take the place of the ineligible Dioskouroi. This auctioning of the bride does not correspond to normal procedure for arranging a marriage. But in various rural parts of Germany it used to be the custom on May Day or Easter Monday to auction the girls, starting with the prettiest: each one in turn became the 'May-wife' of the young man who bid most for her, and she remained his dancing-partner throughout the summer.[139]

The Aśvins got Sūryā as their wife not in an auction but by winning a chariot-race, with the sun as its goal. This too makes sense as a reflection of seasonal custom. In Germany at Whitsun there were races on foot or on horseback to the Maypole, which was adorned with flowers, ribbons, a crown, etc., and the winner became King of the May. In some places he could then choose his queen, or was provided with one already selected.[140] The Maypole, about which circular dances take place, has often been seen as a representation of the world tree or world axis, and as connected with the sun. Mention was made earlier of an Indian ritual in which a wheel-shaped cake was fixed to the top of a sacrificial pole, and the sacrificer 'reached the sun' by climbing up and touching it.

[136] Mannhardt (1905), i. 156 f., 160, 165, 169, 177, 181, 241, 245, 271; A. Dieterich, *Kleine Schriften* (Berlin 1911), 324; Frazer (1911–36), ii. 63, 65, 69.

[137] Mannhardt (1905), i. 181, 256, 260, 263 f., 281, 353, 427, 429; Dieterich (as n. 136), 327 f.; Frazer (1911–36), ii. 81, 84 f., 92, 96.

[138] Mannhardt (1905), i. 422–5, 431–40; Dieterich (as n. 136), 331 f.; Frazer (1911–36), ii. 87–96; iv. 257 f.

[139] Mannhardt (1905), i. 449–54.

[140] Mannhardt (1905), i. 382–9; Frazer (1911–36), ii. 69, 84, 89, iv. 208.

Finally, there is some Celtic evidence for the ritual abduction of the May Queen. In the Isle of Man there used to be a mock battle between the Queen of the May, with her maids of honour and male supporters, and the Queen of Winter with her followers. If the May Queen was captured, her men had to ransom her. Arthurian legend tells of an ambush and abduction of Guinevere on the morning of 1 May, when according to custom she went into the woods to gather birch branches and bring the Summer in, attended by ten knights 'all rayed in grene for maiynge'. She was carried off by Mellyagaunce or Melwas to his castle, and rescued by her lover Lancelot. A. H. Krappe has plausibly argued that a parallel ritual lies behind the mythical abduction of Helen.[141]

CONCLUSION

There was a time when the very existence of solar and celestial mythology was denied, and when, as usual in the absence of knowledge and argument, it was ridiculed as drawn from that bank with unlimited liability, the inner consciousness of German professors.[142]

Müller's critics were right to castigate his excesses and those of the nature-myth school generally. But the reaction against that approach sometimes went too far. We have seen in this chapter that there was such a thing as solar mythology in Indo-European tradition, and a body of festive ritual associated with it. The poetic stories and imagery attaching to the Sun and to Dawn are for the most part directly intelligible in terms of diurnal experience. With figures such as the Daughter of the Sun and the Sons of Heaven, it is less clear how much has a meteorological or astronomical basis and how much is fanciful invention or the mythic reflection of seasonal rituals on earth. What is apparent in this context is that ancient Indic myth and more recent European folklore and custom are not to be studied exclusively as regional specialisms, but to be seen as patches remaining from one great historical tapestry for which 'Indo-European' is a singularly apt label.

[141] J. Train, *A Historical and Statistical Account of the Isle of Man* (Douglas 1845), ii. 118–20, retold by Frazer (1911–36), iv. 258; Sir Thomas Malory, *Le Morte Darthur*, book xix; G. O. Jones and William Owen (edd.), *Barddoniaeth Dafydd ab Gwilym* (Llundain 1789), 540; A. H. Krappe, *Rh. Mus.* 80 (1931), 126 f.

[142] Müller (1897), 165.

6

Storm and Stream

Sky and Earth, Sun, Dawn, Night: these make up the outer frame of the world we live in. We now come to the more energetic and unpredictable elemental powers that shape our environment, deities of rain and thunder, wind and fire, river and flood.

THE GOD OF THUNDER

Apart from earthquakes, tsunamis, and volcanic eruptions, which are liable to occur only in certain specific regions of the world, there is no more frightening manifestation of nature than the thunderstorm. Amazing flashes of light crackling out of darkened skies; menacing rumbles, building up to terrific crashes; trees stricken and scorched; on occasion even instantaneous death to humans. All this is readily ascribed to the fury of a supernatural being. In most of the ancient pantheons of Indo-European peoples we can identify a god whose province it was. The question is whether these storm-gods show shared characteristics, apart from their command of thunder and lightning, such as to mark them as heirs to a common Indo-European heritage.

For classicists it is natural to think of the storm function as belonging to the great god of the sky, as it does to Zeus in Greece and to Jupiter at Rome. But elsewhere we find a dedicated storm-god who is not identified with the sky or the sky-god: the Hittite Tarḫunna, the Indic Indra, the Slavonic Perun, the Baltic Perkunas, the Germanic Donar or Thor, the Celtic Taranus or Taranis. This is almost certainly the original situation. The Indo-European *Dyeus was essentially the bright sky of day. We saw in Chapter 4 that his Indic and Greek representatives could fertilize Earth with rain. But this peaceful conjugal relationship, of which we are the incidental offspring, is complete in itself. Thunderous electrical rages directed (in most mythologies) against demons or dragons cannot be considered an organic part of it. And the specialist storm-gods have a distinctive character of their own; they are more like each other than they are like the god of the sky, where he can still be made out. So it seems altogether more likely that Zeus and Jupiter have appropriated the functions of a separate storm-god who has faded from sight than that they alone preserve the integrity of *Dyeus' personality, the other traditions having conspired to create a separate thunderer.[1]

The storm-gods have diverse names. But there is one name whose cognates and variants appear over a wide area.[2] The Baltic Perkunas may be taken as its prime exponent. We will begin with him, trace the connections of the name in various directions, and then go on to gods unrelated in name but akin in character.

Perkunas

Perkūnas is the Lithuanian form of the name; the Latvian is Pērkons, and an Old Prussian *percunis*, meaning thunder, is recorded in the Elbing glossary, which dates from around 1300. From the thirteenth century onwards there are many records of Prussians, Lithuanians, or Letts worshipping a god of thunder and storm whose name is given as Percunus, Percunos, Pirchunos, Perkuns, Parcuns, or Pargnus (for -uns).[3] There is mention of sacrificing to him for rain, and of a perpetual sacred fire maintained for him in the forests or on hilltops. He appears as a mythical figure in the Lithuanian and Latvian folk songs and in popular imprecations such as 'God grant that Perkunas strike you', 'God grant that Perkunas lift you up and dash you ten fathoms deep in the earth'.[4] Countrymen prayed to him to pass by without harming their house and crops, or on the other hand to bring rain in time of drought.[5] In modern Lithuanian *perkúnas* and in Latvian *pērkons* are the ordinary words for 'thunder'.

[1] Cf. von Schroeder (1914–16), i. 455 f.

[2] Cf. Grimm (1883–8), 171 f., 1340; H. Hirt, *IF* 1 (1892), 480 f.; Kretschmer (1896), 81 f.; T. R. von Grienberger, *Archiv für slavische Philologie* 18 (1896), 9–15; R. Koegel, *GGA* 159 (1897), 653 f.; C. Watkins in Mayrhofer et al. (1974), 107; G. Nagy, ibid. 113–31 ≈ id. (1990), 182–201; Puhvel (1987), 226; Gamkrelidze–Ivanov (1995), 526–8; P. Friedrich in *EIEC* 407 f.; D. Q. Adams–J. P. Mallory, ibid. 582 f.

[3] T. R. von Grienberger (as n. 2), 9 f.; Mannhardt (1936), 58/60, 71, 139, 143, 192–8, 200, 207, 233–5, 246 f., 249, 280, 295 f., 356, 362 f., 402, 435 f., 438, 458, 513, 534–40, 627; the testimonies are summarized in Usener (1896), 97. On the god cf. also Grimm (1883–8), 171, 1340; von Schroeder (1914–16), i. 531–4, ii. 603–7; Gimbutas (1963), 202 f. and *JIES* 1 (1973), 466–78; Biezais–Balys (1973), 430–4; Nagy (1974), 113–15 ≈ (1990), 183–5.

[4] Schleicher (1857), 189; cf. M. Gimbutas, *JIES* 1 (1973), 474.

[5] Usener (1896), 97; T. R. von Grienberger (as n. 2), 10; von Schroeder (1914–16), ii. 603 f.; Mannhardt (1936), 197, 356, 382, 458; *LD* 33710 f. = Jonval nos. 446 f.

Perkunas appears as a bellowing bull in Lithuanian riddles, but is otherwise pictured in human form. Simon Grunau in his *Prussian Chronicle* (*c.*1520) says he was depicted as an angry-looking, middle-aged man with a fiery face and a dark crinkly beard. He spits fire, and hurls an axe or (less often) a hammer, which returns to his hand. He kills devils, or the Devil, or the goblin or dragon Áitvaras.[6] Pērkons too fights devils; his weapon is variously given as a mace (*milna*), a spear, a sword, an iron rod, arrows, or stone bullets.

Perkunas' car is sometimes said to be drawn by a he-goat (*ožys*) or goats.[7] This is connected with a belief that a coming storm is presaged by the flight of the snipe, a bird whose tail-feathers produce a goat-like bleating noise as it dives through the air. In German country lore it was called *Himmelsziege* or *Donnerziege*; in Lithuanian 'God's goat' or 'Perkunas' goat' (*Dievo* or *Perkūno ožys*), and likewise in Latvian *Pērkona ahsis* (he-goat) or *kasa* (she-goat).[8]

Perkunas/Pērkons has a special association with the oak tree. This is the tree that he typically strikes with lightning, and because of this it has fire stored up inside it which men can use. There were oaks sacred to him and containing his idol: *Perkūno ąžuolas*, *Pērkōna ōzōls*, 'P.'s oak'.[9]

This is relevant to the etymology of his name. It has the *-no-* suffix that we have seen to be a frequent element of Indo-European divine nomenclature, generally interpretable as 'master of'. What precedes the suffix, *Perku-*, has an exact counterpart in Latin *quercus*, 'oak'. A Roman deity *Quercūnus does not occur, but would not have been surprising. The underlying form is **perk^{w}u-*; in Italic **p—k^w-* became **k^w—k^w-* by retroactive assimilation, as in *quinque* 'five' from **penk^{w}e*. Related forms for 'oak' are preserved here and there in Germanic, with the regular change of [p] to [f].

In Celtic original [p] disappeared, probably with [h] as an intermediate

[6] Simon Grunau in Mannhardt (1936), 195, 'wie ein zorniger man und mittelmessigk alten, sein angesicht wie feuer und gekronet mit flammen, sein bart craus und schwarcz'; Schleicher (1857), 150, 182; Gimbutas (as n. 4), 471; ead. (1963), 202; Biezais–Balys (1973), 431 f.; Greimas (1992), 47, 61–3. On Áitvaras cf. Usener (1896), 85. Lithuanian folk-tale tells of a strong smith whose hammer fells trees. He teams up with an even stronger hero, Martin, who carries an iron club and kills three-, six-, and nine-headed dragons: Schleicher (1857), 128 f., 135–7. The nine-header snorts fire like lightning and roars so that the earth shakes, ibid. 137.

[7] J. Balys, *Tautosakos darbai*, iii (Kaunas 1937), nos. 316 f.; Gimbutas (1963), 202, and *JIES* 1 (1973), 466.

[8] Gimbutas (1963), 199, 202; C. Watkins in Cardona et al. (1970), 354 n. 43 = (1994), 455; Grimm (1883–8), 184, 1347; West (1978), 367; (1997), 115. For Perkunas himself as a goat (in a riddle), and the practice of hanging up a goatskin as a rain charm, cf. Gimbutas, *JIES* 1 (1973), 471.

[9] Mannhardt (1936), 196, 435, 438, 534; Jakobson (1962–88), vii. 17; Nagy (1974), 114 ≈ (1990), 184. Pērkons strikes an oak in many of the Latvian songs: *LD* 34127, 34047, 33802, 33713, 33715 f. = Jonval nos. 7, 128, 359, 438, 444 f. It is a fact that oaks are struck by lightning disproportionately often: Nagy (1974), 122 f. ≈ (1990), 195 f.

stage. In the 'Hercynian' mountains or forest in central Europe mentioned by classical writers we see the Celtic reflex of **perkʷun(i)yo-* or **perkʷun(i)yā-*.[10] Such a formation would be appropriate for 'the realm of *Perkʷūnos', i.e. the wooded mountains. Whether or not this is the correct analysis, we find a parallel Germanic form in the Gothic neuter *fairguni* (< **perkʷunyom*) 'mountain (range)', Old English *fi(e)rgen-* 'mountain' (only in compounds), and Färge- and the like in south Swedish place-names; also Latinized forms such as Fergunna, Virgunnia, of metalliferous mountains.[11] There is a similar Slavonic word for 'wooded hill', Old Church Slavonic *prĕgynja*, Old Russian *peregynja*.[12] But here the [g] is not (as in Germanic) the regular outcome of *[kʷ] or *[k], and we must either take it as an early borrowing from Germanic (with reversion of [f] to [p]) or assume a divergent form of the underlying word, with voiced instead of unvoiced labiovelar. This possibility will be relevant presently when we contemplate the Indian Parjanya.

Fiǫrgynn

The Norse pantheon includes a god Fiǫrgynn and a goddess Fiǫrgyn. These go back to **Perkʷún(i)yos*, **Perkʷunī*. Apart from having a stem in *-yo-* instead of *-o-*, the masculine name corresponds exactly to that of the Baltic thunder-god.[13] Fiǫrgynn is an obsolescent figure, mentioned only as the father of Frigg (*Lokasenna* 26. 1, *Gylf.* 9, *Skáldsk.* 19), and we cannot tell from the Nordic evidence what he originally stood for.

The position is a little better with his female counterpart Fiǫrgyn. She is the mother of Thor, the thunder-god (*Vǫluspá* 56. 10, *Hárbarðzlióð* 56. 7). Her name was used as a poetic synonym for 'land' or 'the earth' (*Oddrúnargrátr* 11. 6, *Skáldsk.* 57, 75). It is an easy hypothesis that she was properly the

[10] Arist. *Meteor.* 350b5 τῶν ὀρῶν τῶν Ἀρκυνίων; Caes. *Bell. Gall.* 6. 24. 2 *Hercyniam siluam, quam Eratostheni et quibusdam Graecis fama notam esse uideo, quam illi Orcyniam appellant*; Strabo 4. 6. 9, 7. 1. 3/5 Ἑρκύνιος δρυμός, cf. Dion. Per. 286; Plin. *HN* 3. 148 *Hercuniates*, Ptol. 2. 15. 2 Ἑρκουνιάτες. The quantity of the second syllable varies in Greek and Latin poets. Cf. H. Krahe, *Sprache und Vorzeit* (Heidelberg 1954), 42 f., 68 f.; R. Much, *Tacitus. Germania* (3rd edn., Heidelberg 1967), 351 f.; Jane Lightfoot, *Parthenius of Nicaea* (Oxford 1999), 193 f. We might have expected **kʷerk⁽ʷ⁾unyo-*, since Celtic shared the Italic change of **p—kʷ–* to **kʷ—kʷ–*. But the /kʷu/ may have become /ku/ before that could take effect (H. Hirt, *IF* 1 (1892), 480). Kretschmer (1896), 81 n. 1, infers that the word was not original in Celtic.

[11] Feist (1939), 137–9.

[12] Jakobson (1962–88), ii. 637; vii. 6, 21.

[13] There is actually a *-yo-* variant in Latvian: Nagy (1990), 188 n. 54. Meid (1957), 126, considers that Fiǫrgynn 'wohl nach dem *ī*-movierten Fem. . . . erst sekundär aus einem ursprünglichen **Fergunaz* umgestaltet worden ist'.

mistress of the wooded mountains, the personification of what appears in Gothic as *fairguni*.

Perún

In Slavonic lands the thunder-god was called Perún, Old Russian Perunŭ, Belorussian Piarun, Slovak Parom. The word also meant 'thunderbolt', and in this use it survives in the modern languages: Russian *perúny* (plural), Polish *piorun*, Czech *peraun*. There are Russian, Ukrainian, and Slovenian imprecations parallel to the Lithuanian ones featuring Perkunas: 'may Perun (or Perun's bolt) kill you (or take you)'. The importance of the god in tenth-century Kiev and Novgorod is attested by a series of documents, and already in the sixth century a Byzantine historian mentions the Slavs' worship of 'the maker of the lightning', considered to be the one in charge of everything.[14]

He is similar in character to Perkunas. He has a tawny beard. He is located high up, on a mountain or in the sky, and sends his axe or arrow down on his victim below.[15] He has a close association with the oak: he strikes it, he puts fire into it, and there are sacred trees called 'Perun's oak'.[16]

Scholars have naturally looked for a connection between his name and that of his Baltic neighbour Perkunas. One solution has been to treat it as a taboo variant: people avoided speaking the dread name by suppressing the velar consonant in the second syllable.[17] Taken on its own, Perunŭ can be satisfactorily explained as 'the Striker', from the Slavonic verb **per* 'strike' and the common agent suffix *-unŭ* (from **-ūnos* or **-aunos*). This is the commonly accepted etymology. To make the connection with Perkunas, it has been proposed that the **per* root had a by-form with radical extension, **per-k*^{w}*-*. Perkunas too would then be the Striker. But this conflicts with the more obvious derivation from **perk*^{w}*u-* 'oak' with the *-nos* suffix. The attempt has been made to square the circle by deriving the tree-name from the verb, the oak being the tree that gets smitten, the tree that is dedicated

[14] Procop. *Bell. Goth.* 3. 14. 23; S. Rożniecki, *Archiv für slavische Philologie* 23 (1901), 488–93, 503, 509. Cf. Grimm (1883–8), 171 f.; von Schroeder (1914–16), i. 550; Unbegaun (1948), 401 f.; Gimbutas (1971), 154–7, 166 f.; N. Reiter in *Wb. d. Myth.* i(2), 189–91; Puhvel (1987), 233–5; Nagy (1974), 113, 117–19 ≈ (1990), 183 f., 187–9; Váňa (1992), 71–5.

[15] Schrader (1909), 38; von Schroeder (1914–16), ii. 627; V. V. Ivanov–V. N. Toporov in Jean Pouillon–Pierre Maranda, *Échanges et communications. Mélanges offerts à Claude Lévi-Strauss* (The Hague–Paris 1970), ii. 1182–4.

[16] Grimm (1883–8), 172; Ivanov–Toporov (as n. 15), 1183 f.; Jakobson (1962–88), vii. 17; Nagy (1974), 115 ≈ (1990), 184.

[17] Watkins in Mayrhofer et al. (1974), 107. Perūnas is apparently attested in Lithuanian as a substitute for Perkūnas: Jakobson (1962–88), vii. 19. One might compare archaic English 'Odds-bobs' (= God's body), 'Ods-life', etc.

to the Smiter. This is not impossible, but it does not absolve us from the necessity of choosing between two incompatible analyses of Perkunas' name.[18]

Possible cognates in south-east Europe

Inscriptions from Bulgaria attest a hero-cult of one Perkos or Perkōn. He was presumably an old Thracian divinity of some kind, and the similarity of the name to those we have been considering has prompted the guess that he belonged in this context. It is not an implausible guess, but a guess it remains.[19]

The Albanian Perëndi 'Heaven', 'God', has been analysed as a compound of which the first element is related to Perunŭ and the second to **dyeus*.[20]

At Lebadea in Boeotia there was a cult of a divinity Herkyna or Herkynna, identified with Demeter, and a stream of the same name (Lycophron 153, Livy 45. 27, Paus. 9. 39. 2–3, Hesych. ε 5931). If she was originally a cognate of Fiǫrgyn, the goddess of the wooded landscape, it is understandable that she could be equated with Demeter. The problem is that *Herk-* for **Perk*$^{(w)}$- could only be a Celtic form, which would be very unexpected so far south. The Gauls who invaded Greece in 279 BCE can hardly have managed to leave a goddess behind. If the similarity of Herkyna's name to those we have been considering is not fortuitous, it is theoretically possible that at some earlier period a Celtic splinter group had found its way down there, perhaps in the late second or early first millennium when Illyrian and other tribes from the north-west were infiltrating. Feminine river-names are more typical of Celtic than of Greek or Illyrian.

The thunder-god's functions were taken over in Greece by the great sky-god, Zeus. What was his name when he still existed as an independent deity? It is tempting to conjecture that it was Keraunos, the name used in historical Greek for Zeus' thunderbolt. It is perfectly plausible that the obsolete god's name should come to be used in this way; we have seen that this is exactly what happened to the Baltic and the Slavonic thunder-gods. Heraclitus (B 64) spoke of Keraunos as a purposeful cosmic force, allied to Zeus and 'steering everything'. A Mantinean inscription of the mid-fifth century BCE, consisting of the two words *Διὸς Κεραυνô*, marked a place where lightning had

[18] See Jakobson (1962–88), ii. 636 f.; Nagy (1974), 115 f. ≈ (1990), 185 f.

[19] G. Mihailov, *Inscriptiones Graecae in Bulgaria repertae* (Serdica 1956), nos. 283–283 bis *Ἥρωει Περκωνει, Περκω(ι) Ἥρωι*. Cf. V. I. Georgiev, *Linguistique Balkanique* 18.1 (1975), 46; I. Duridanov in Meid (1998), 562.

[20] Pisani (1969), 242; Lambertz (1973), 496 f.

struck as '(sacred to) Zeus Keraunos' (*IG* v(2). 288): this looks like a case where, as often happened, an old deity's name survived locally as a surname of the national god who replaced him or her.[21]

κεραυνός is conventionally explained as a formation from the same root as κερα(Ϝ)ίζω 'devastate, slaughter, plunder'. But there have long been suspicions that it was somehow related to *Perun* and *Perkunas*. There is a Latvian variant form *pērkauns* 'thunderbolt', and *Perunŭ* may go back to **Peraunos*. It has been proposed that for taboo reasons **Peraunos* was replaced by the rhyming *Keraunos*, or that **Perkaunos* suffered first metathesis to **Kerpaunos* and then deletion of the initial consonant of the second syllable, on the same principle as suggested for Perunŭ.[22] Another hypothesis is that the anomalously formed Homeric epithet of Zeus τερπικέραυνος, traditionally understood as 'delighting in the thunderbolt', is derived by metathesis from **perkʷi-peraunos*, 'having a smiting bolt'; the simple κεραυνός was then abstracted from the compound.[23] I cannot solve these conundrums, but the structural similarity of *Keraunos* to **Per(k)aunos*—if that is a correct reconstruction—looks too great to be coincidental.

Parjanya, Indra

The major Vedic storm-god is Indra, though he also has other functions, especially as the giver of victory in battle. There are other deities whose energies are more closely focused on thunder, lightning, and rain: the Maruts, who very often appear in association with Indra, and Parjanya.

Parjanya[24] is called a son of Dyaus (RV 7. 102. 1), which expresses his natural relationship with the sky. Sometimes he takes the place of Dyaus as the consort of Earth who fertilizes her with his seed and so fathers living creatures (5. 83. 4; 7. 101. 3; AV 12. 1. 12, 42). He is especially associated with the rains, and *parjánya-* as a common noun means 'rain-cloud'. He is

[21] Seleucus I established a cult of Keraunos at Seleucia Pieria (App. *Syr.* 58). Cf. also *Inscriptions grecques et latines de la Syrie*, v. 2220 (Emesa); H. Usener, *Rh. Mus.* 60 (1905), 1–30 = *Kleine Schriften*, iv (Leipzig–Berlin 1913), 471–97; Prehn, *RE* xi. 270.

[22] Grimm (1883–8), 171 n. 3, 'might *perun* be connected with κεραυνός = περαυνός?'; H. Güntert, *Reimwortbildungen im Arischen und Altgriechischen* (Heidelberg 1914), 215 f., 221; Jacobson (1962–88), ii. 636; vii. 6, 20; C. Watkins in Cardona et al. (1970), 350); id. in Mayrhofer et al. (1974), 107; id. (1995), 343 n. 1.

[23] Nagy (1974), 126–8 ≈ (1990), 194 f.; Puhvel (1987), 235. But 'having a smiting bolt' would be as tautologous as 'having thunder that thunders'. G. Meyer, *Curtius' Studien* 7 (1875), 180 f., connected the τερπι- with Latin *torqueo*, as in Virg. *Aen.* 4. 208 *cum fulmina torques*, etc.

[24] On him cf. Macdonell (1898), 83–5; von Schroeder (1914–16), i. 413–23; Oberlies (1998), 200 f.

pictured as a bellowing bull who deposits his semen in the plants (RV 5. 83. 1; 7. 101. 6). But he is also a thunderer (5. 83. 2–9; 10. 66. 10) and dispenser of lightning (5. 83. 4; AV 19. 30. 5, TS 3. 4. 7. 2). In a simile in the *Rāmāyaṇa* (6. 45. 28) a drum-roll is compared to Parjanya's roaring. He smites demons and evildoers (RV 5. 83. 2, 9). In another hymn he is implored to direct his thunder and lightning at the snake or snakes, not at mankind.[25]

His name has long been felt to belong in the company of Perkunas, Fiǫrgynn, and the others. But **Perkʷū̆n(y)o-* would have come out in Vedic as **Parkū̆n(y)a-*. The *-jan-* that we actually have should come from **-ĝan-* or **ĝen-* or **-ĝon-*. The comparativists' response has been to postulate **per-ĝ* as another variant of the 'strike' root beside **per* and **per-kʷ*. An Armenian form is cited in support. The extended root is then furnished with a deverbative suffix *-áni-*, which makes an adjective 'striking' or an abstract noun, and finally we postulate conversion from an *-i*-stem into a *-yo*-stem.[26] Bravo! But even if we allow the concurrence of **per*, **perkʷ*, and **perĝ*, all meaning the same thing, the upshot is that Perkunas, Perun, and Parjanya are independent creations on this root, each fashioned with a different formant, and we fail to reconstruct a single prototype as the name of the Indo-European god. To achieve that, we have to invoke taboo deformation, a valid tactic in principle but unfortunately subject to no philological control.

We should not on this account abandon the idea of an Indo-European storm-god. There are sufficient common features among the historical storm-gods, whether or not they have related names, for that to remain a probable hypothesis. Let us move on to the ones whose names clearly have other origins, working our way back from India to Iceland.

Firstly Indra, an Indo-Iranian deity who goes back at least to the first half of the second millennium. His name is perhaps related to Slavonic **jędrŭ* 'virile, vigorous'. He is one of the gods named in Suppiluliuma's treaty with Mitanni, and the most prominent of all the deities of the Rigveda.

He is sometimes made a son of Dyaus (RV 4. 17. 4, cf. 10. 120. 1), sometimes of Tvaṣṭṛ. He is king of the gods (1. 174. 1, AV 19. 46. 4). Men pray to him in battle (RV 1. 63. 6, 81. 1, 100. 1, etc.). As god of the storm, he is 'equal in strength to the rain-bringing Parjanya' (8. 6. 1). However, there is a notable difference in the treatment of the two deities. Parjanya's operations are described with altogether more direct naturalism than Indra's.[27] There is pictorial imagery, he travels in a car, pours the water out of a skin bag, and so

[25] AV Paipp. 2. 70. 1–3, quoted and translated by Watkins (1995), 543.

[26] Nagy (1974), 115 f. ≈ (1990), 185 f. G. E. Dunkel, *Die Sprache* 34 (1988–90), 3 f., analyses as **per-g-n̥nyo-*.

[27] Oldenberg (1917), 137 f.; Nagy (1990), 192. On Indra generally see Macdonell (1898), 54–66.

on, but he is not credited with any mythical accomplishments. Indra, on the other hand, hardly ever causes rain; his activities are wrapped up in mythical language and often expressed as past achievements. It is recalled how with his bolt he killed Vṛtra or Vala or some other adversary and so released the blocked-up waters or the hidden cows. We shall see presently that these stories contain an Indo-European element. Indra may have taken them over from Parjanya.[28]

Like Parjanya, Indra is sometimes portrayed as a bull. At the Sākamedha sacrifice a real bull had to bellow as a signal that Indra was present to receive his offering and ready for the killing of Vṛtra.[29] Apart from the analogy between the bull's bellow and the thunder, the bull image is an expression of Indra's terrific strength, a property often emphasized.

As one might expect of such a champion, he is a mighty eater and drinker. He eats the flesh of twenty bulls or a hundred buffaloes, and drinks whole lakes of Soma.[30] He then shakes the excess liquid out of his beard, which is fiery or reddish in colour (*hárita*), and it comes down as rain (2. 11. 17; 10. 23. 1, 4, 96. 8).

He rejoices in the title *vṛtrahán-*, '*vṛtra*-smasher', applied to him over fifty times in the Rigveda. The word *vṛtrá-* denotes something or someone that blocks the way, an obstacle or enemy. As a masculine, *Vṛtráḥ*, it is usually the name of the demon or dragon that blocks the waters and is shattered by Indra's bolt. As a neuter plural, *vṛtrā́* or *vṛtrā́ṇi*, it has the general sense of 'opposing forces, enemies'. So *vṛtrahán-* may be understood either as a generic epithet appropriate to Indra as god of battle or as having specific reference to his defeat of Vṛtra in his capacity as storm-god. In the Avesta we find a god Vərəθraγna-, whose name corresponds to *vṛtrahán-* and presumably began as the by-name of an Iranian Indra, though he has developed into an independent figure.[31] He is unequivocally a god of battle, and his name means Victorious, with no reference to a storm demon. So this, we may presume, was the primary sense of the title, and Indra probably had it before he took over the storm-god's role. The monster Vṛtra, or at least his name, then looks like a secondary creation, abstracted from *vṛtrahán-*.[32] However, the Armenian national hero Vahagn, who developed from the Iranian Vərəθraγna-, was celebrated for fighting and slaying dragons, and he had the

[28] Cf. Müller (1897), 756; G. E. Dunkel, *Die Sprache* 34 (1988–90), 7 f.

[29] Oldenberg (1917), 74.

[30] Macdonell (1898), 56, with references; Oldenberg (1917), 165 f.

[31] Indra is mentioned only in the late Avestan *Vidēvdāt*, and there as a demon (*daēva*, 10. 9, 19. 43).

[32] Cf. R. C. Zaehner, *The Dawn and Twilight of Zoroastrianism* (London 1961), 103; Puhvel (1987), 51, 102; Watkins (1995), 298.

reddish beard that seems to be a distinguishing feature of the Indo-European thunder-god (Perkunas, Perun, Indra, Thor).[33]

Tarḫunna

One of the principal deities in the Anatolian pantheon was the storm-god whose Hittite name was Tarḫunna or Tarḫunta (Luwian Tarḫunza, Palaic Taru). The root here is the verb *tarḫ-* 'overcome, vanquish', but the formation with **-u-no-* is curiously parallel to that of Perkunas and Perun.[34]

The attested mythology of Tarḫunna contained in the so-called Kumarbi cycle is largely taken over from the Hurrian storm-god Teššub and does not reflect Indo-European myth. There is, however, one detail in the story of his birth that deserves notice. He is confined in Kumarbi's belly with two other gods, having grown there after Kumarbi swallowed the seed of Anu, that is, of the personified Heaven. There is discussion in the fragmentary text of how they might come out. One of the alternatives is 'the good place', which seems to be neither the mouth nor the skull, and it is by this route that the Storm-god is born. It involves a rupture of Kumarbi's body, which has to be stitched up.

There is an intriguing parallel in a dialogue hymn of the Rigveda which begins with the unborn Indra inside his mother (unnamed). She has held him there for a thousand months. She, or someone, calls for him to be born in the traditional, tried and tested way by which all gods have been born. But he declares, 'I will not go out this way, it is bad going (*durgáhā*) thus. Sideways from her ribs I will go out.' And so he does, without explaining why he regards this as a superior place of exit. Macdonell suggested that 'this trait may possibly be derived from the notion of lightning breaking from the side of the storm-cloud'.[35] That seems plausible enough, and if the Indo-European storm-god was said for this reason to have been born from his mother's side, designated as 'the good place', the motif might have been imported into the Hittite version of the Hurrian narrative.

Zeus, Jupiter, Heracles

I have suggested that Zeus, the original sky-god, took over the tempestuous functions of the more dedicated Keraunos. According to Hesiod (*Th.* 140 f.,

[33] Movses Xorenac'i 1. 31; Zaehner (as n. 32); J. R. Russell, *Zoroastrianism in Armenia* (Cambridge, Mass. 1987), 204 f.; Ishkol-Kerovpian (1986), 151.

[34] Cf. Watkins in Mayrhofer et al. (1974), 107; id. (1995), 343 f.; Bader (1989), 93 f.; Nagy (1990), 189 f.

[35] *CTH* 344 A ii, translated in Hoffner (1998), 43 f.; RV 4. 18. 1 f.; Macdonell (1898), 56.

501–6) he received the necessary equipment from three sons of the secondary sky-god Ouranos. Their names, Brontes, Steropes, and Arges, represent the thunder (βροντή), the lightning (στεροπή), and the shining bolt (ἀργὴς κεραυνός). They made these weapons for Zeus and gave them to him in gratitude when he released them from the prison in which Ouranos had shut them up—perhaps another expression of the eruption of lightning from the cloud in which it had been confined.

The three brothers reflect an analysis of the god's fulmination into three aspects: the thunder is what you hear, the lightning is what you see, and the thunderbolt is what hits you. There is an interesting parallel in one of the Latvian songs, where Pērkons is said to have nine sons:

> trois frappaient du pied, trois grondaient,
> trois étincelaient.[36]

Here too the three functions are separated and assigned to different brothers, while a superior figure, Pērkons himself, takes the credit for the whole production.

It was mentioned above that Perkunas rides behind a goat or goats, and that the goat is really the snipe that presages a storm. One of Zeus' commonest epithets in Homer is αἰγί(ϝ)οχος, which must originally have meant 'riding on a goat'; the traditional interpretation as 'aegis-bearing' does violence to the language. In one of the Orphic theogonies (fr. 236 (ii) Bernabé) Zeus rode to heaven on a goat after his birth. The feminine αἴξ presupposed in the Homeric word is cognate with the masculine *ožys* that denotes Perkunas' goat.

Perkunas' and Perun's special relationship with the oak tree is not foreign to Zeus. His holy oak at Dodona was famous from Homer on (*Od.* 14. 327 f. = 19. 296 f.), and he had another at Troy (*Il.* 5. 695, 7. 60). His partiality for oaks is implied by a joke in Aristophanes (*Av.* 480, cf. schol.; Eust. in Hom. 594. 35). His habit of striking them with lightning is noted (*Il.* 14. 414, Ar. *Nub.* 402, Lucian *Dial.* 20. 16).

In the absence of an independent Jupiter mythology we need not dwell on the Roman god except to note that he too is regularly associated with the oak (*quercus*). 'Quercus in tutela Iouis est', writes Servius (on Virg. *Ecl.* 1. 17). The ancient temple of Iuppiter Feretrius was sited by an oak on the Capitol (Livy 1. 10. 5). Many understood the title Feretrius as being from *ferire* 'strike', though this is probably wrong. The god of lightning had a separate shrine in the Campus Martius as Iuppiter Fulgur.[37]

[36] Mannhardt (1875), 317; *LD* 33704 = Jonval no. 437; von Schroeder (1914–16), ii. 628 f.

[37] C. Thulin, *RE* x. 1130 f. For Jupiter and the oak cf. also Virg. *G.* 3. 332, *Aen.* 3. 680 f.; Ov. *Met.* 1. 106; Phaedr. 3. 17. 2; Plut. *Coriol.* 3, *Quaest. Rom.* 286a; F. Olck, *RE* v. 2051 f.

Certain aspects of the Indo-European storm-god that might have seemed beneath Zeus' dignity appear to have been transferred to his son Heracles. Heracles, of course, made his reputation as a mortal hero, performing mighty deeds on earth (though partly in mythical regions of the earth, beyond ordinary people's ken). Whatever the first part of his name signifies, the second part, 'glory', marks it as a compound of a heroic, not a divine type (cf. pp. 400 f.). The story of his posthumous deification is late and inorganic. He is not a déclassé storm-god. But as a beefy, brawny, swaggering figure, always quick to resort to violence, a match for any monster, he had features in common with the storm-god and was able to attract other features. Like Indra, he is a prodigious eater; for example, in an eating contest with Lepreus he consumed a whole ox, and gluttony is one of his standing characteristics on the comic stage from Epicharmus on (fr. 18 K.–A.). Among his legendary feats there is one that deserves particular notice in regard to the mythology of the storm-god: his capture of Geryon's cattle. We shall give attention to this presently.[38]

Taranis, Thor

In Celtic Gaul and Britain the god of thunder was worshipped under the name of Taranis, Taranus, or Tanarus; compare Old Irish *torann*, Welsh *taran*, 'thunder'. The corresponding Germanic theonym, Old High German Donar or Thunar, Old Norse Þórr, goes back to **Þunaraz*, from which also English 'thunder'. These all seem to be cognate variants, related to Latin *tonare*, *tonitrus*, Vedic *(s)tan-*, 'thunder'. It may originally have been an onomatopoeic word for thunder that could be used also for the god.[39] But a connection has also been suggested with the Anatolian Tarḫunna-, and so with the verbal root *tarḫ*, by way of a metathesis, **tr̥h*$_2$*Vno-* > **tn̥h*$_2$*Vro-*.[40]

Thanks to the preservation of Old Norse literature Thor appears to us with a much clearer profile than Donar or Taranis.[41] He developed into something

[38] Comparisons have been drawn especially between Heracles and Indra: L. von Schroeder, *Herakles und Indra* (Denkschr. Wien. Ak. 58(3); 1914); Durante (1976), 58 f.; Watkins (1995), 375 f., cf. 507 f. The German thunder-god was rendered by the Romans as 'Hercules' (Tac. *Germ.* 9. 1, inscriptions); see de Vries (1956), ii. 107–9.

[39] Similarly Perkunas' name was often avoided in favour of Dundulis or other names meaning 'rumble': Gimbutas, *JIES* 1 (1973), 469 f.; Biezais–Balys (1973), 433; Jakobson (1962–88), vii. 7, 23. For the Celtic god cf. de Vries (1956), ii. 111 f.; M. Green (1986), 66 f.; Puhvel (1987), 169.

[40] Watkins (1995), 343 n. 1; cf. F. Bader (1989), 93 f.; ead. *BSL* 85 (1990), 12.

[41] On him cf. Grimm (1883–8), 166–92; von Schroeder (1914–16), ii. 609–15; de Vries (1956), ii. 113–53.

much more than the simple thunderer. He was the controller of the weather and hence of the fertility of the crops. He was man's friend and protector against demonic forces in general, one of the most popular and highly regarded of the gods.

In the Eddic poems, as mentioned earlier, he is the son of Fiǫrgyn, who was identified with Earth. Earth (Iǫrð) is explicitly given as his mother in other passages (*Lokasenna* 58, *Gylf.* 9). But we have seen that Fiǫrgyn and her male counterpart Fiǫrgynn are linked by their names to Perkunas. It is conjectured that the obscure Fiǫrgynn was once Thor's father and himself the old Germanic storm-god. That 'Thunder' should be his son would be analogous to Brontes, Steropes, and Arges as sons of Ouranos and assistants of Zeus, and to the thundering sons of Pērkons.[42]

Thor's connection with trees is shown by Danish and Swedish place-names such as Thorslund, Torslunde, 'Thor's grove'. An oak forest was dedicated to him at Dublin. The evidence goes back to antiquity. In 16 CE Germanicus crossed the Weser in the territory of the Cherusci and faced Arminius' army, which had gathered in a wood that was sacred to 'Hercules', i.e. *Þunaraz (Tac. *Ann.* 2. 12).

Thor's weapon is his great hammer Miǫllnir, which he hurls at his victims. His targets are creatures located outside our world, typically giants, some of whom have many heads.[43] He also overcame the cosmic monster known as Iǫrmungand or the Miðgarð Serpent. On account of this achievement he is called *orms einbani*, 'the slayer of the serpent' (*Hymiskviða* 22. 3). The title has been compared with Indra's *vṛtrahán-*,[44] though we have seen that this probably did not at first refer to a specific victim.

Thor has several of the other features that we have seen to be characteristic of the Indo-European storm-gods.[45] He rides in a car drawn by two goats, and the thunder is the rumbling of his vehicle.[46] He is a mighty eater and drinker.[47] He is known for his great red beard (*Óláfssaga Tryggvasonar* 213),

[42] R. Koegel, *GGA* 159 (1897), 653 n. 1; von Schroeder (1914–16), i. 518, ii. 629.

[43] On many-headed giants see pp. 299 f.

[44] Vittoria Grazi in *Poetry in the Scandinavian Middle Ages* (Seventh International Saga Conference, Spoleto 1990), 561.

[45] His similarities with Indra have long been the subject of comment, and sometimes Heracles too has been brought into the comparison. Cf. W. Mannhardt, *Germanische Mythen* (Berlin 1858), 1–242; Müller (1897), 744–9; von Schroeder (1914–16), ii. 625–8; Oldenberg (1917), 138; F. R. Schröder, *Zeitschrift für Deutsche Philologie* 76 (1957), 1–41; M. E. Huld in Dexter–Polomé (1997), 179; Oberlies (1998), 248 n. 484.

[46] Thiodolf, *Haustlǫng* 15. 3; *Gylf.* 21, 44. He is the 'lord of goats' (*Hymiskviða* 20. 2, 31. 2) or 'user of goats' (Bragi, *Ragnarsdrápa* 18). Cf. Grimm (1883–8), 166 f.; von Schroeder (1914–16), ii. 610 f. Some classical poets represented the thunder as the noise of Zeus' chariot: Pind. *Ol.* 4. 1 with sch., Hor. *Carm.* 1. 34. 8 with Porphyrio.

[47] *Hymiskviða* 15. 5–8, *Þrymskviða* 24, *Gylf.* 46; Grimm (1883–8), 189.

which he shakes when he becomes angry (*Þrymskviða* 1. 6). The verb employed here, *dýja*, corresponds to the *dhū* used of Indra's beard-shaking in RV 2. 11. 17 and 10. 23. 1 and 4.[48]

Snorri states that Ása-Thor is always victorious because *honum fylgði afl ok sterkleikr*, 'power and strength followed with him' (*Gylf.* 9). In the same way it is said that the goddess Strength (*devī́ Táviṣi*) follows (*siṣakti*) Indra like the sun the dawn (RV 1. 56. 4). Hesiod says that Zelos, Nike, Kratos, and Bia (Aspiration, Victory, Power, and Strength) do not dwell or sit or go anywhere but where Zeus leads the way, and he provides a mythical explanation for this (*Th.* 386–401). It may be going too far to postulate a common archetype for these parallel theological propositions, especially as analogies can be cited from Semitic hymns.[49] But they deserve notice.

There is one further feature that links Indra, Heracles, and Thor. In each case we find poetic recitals in which their famous achievements are listed. From the numerous hymns to Indra in the Rigveda one may cite, for example, 1. 33, 130; 2. 14, 15; 4. 16, 19, etc. In Greece whole epics were composed on Heracles' deeds, and Euripides in his tragedy on Heracles' killing of his children takes the opportunity to rehearse his previous accomplishments in a choral ode (359–435). Skaldic poets wrote praises of Thor with enumerations of his deeds.[50] See below, pp. 314–16.

The thunder-weapon

The thunder-god typically wields his own special weapon. It is generally conceived as a club, mace, or hammer, made of stone or metal. The Anatolian Tarḫunna is depicted with a club, a battle-axe, or a three-pronged lightning bolt.[51] Indra's weapon is most often called a *vájra-*, probably 'smasher', from the same root as Greek *Ϝάγνυμι* 'smash, break'. From the Sanskrit comes Tocharian A *waśir*, B *waśīr* 'thunderbolt'. This is a very old noun, represented not only in Avestan *vazra-* but in the second element of the Greek heroic name Mele(w)agros. It gives also, as a loan-word in Finno-Ugric, Finnish *vasara* 'hammer' and Mordvinian *užer* 'axe'.[52] It must originally have denoted an ordinary club or celt. Another term used for Indra's weapon is *vadhá-* (or

[48] Grimm (1883–8), 177; Güntert (1923), 12; F. Specht, *ZVS* 65 (1938), 208–10; F. R. Schröder (as n. 45), 40 f.; Schmitt (1967), 34 f., 185 f.

[49] West (1997), 305.

[50] de Vries (1956), i. 439 f.

[51] Gurney (1977), 22; Watkins (1995), 430.

[52] B. Schlerath, *Orbis* 24 (1975), 493–518, cf. 26 (1977), 133 f.; Watkins (1995), 332, 411–13; D. Q. Adams in *EIEC* 112; *aliter* Nagy (1974), 124 ≈ (1990), 197.

vádhar, vádhatram), which has a similar meaning, 'smasher, killer'. It is also denoted by various words meaning 'stone' (*aśáni-, áśman-, ádri-, párvata-*). The poet of RV 7. 104. 4 f. speaks of burning stone darts, forged from mountains.

The weapon is embellished with much imaginative detail. It was made for Indra by the divine artificer Tvaṣṭṛ (1. 32. 1, 85. 9). It is of metal, *āyasá-* (1. 52. 8, 80. 12, al.; *āyasá- . . . áśman-*, 1. 121. 9). It is bright (*árjuna-*, 3. 44. 5; *dyumánt-*, 5. 31. 4); hot (3. 30. 16); eager (2. 11. 6; 4. 22. 3; 6. 17. 10; 10. 96. 3); sharp (1. 54. 4; 2. 30. 3; 7. 18. 18; AV 12. 5. 66); Indra sharpens it like a carving-knife (RV 1. 130. 4, cf. 55. 1; 7. 104. 19 f.; 8. 76. 9). It is pronged (*bhṛṣṭimánt-*, 1. 52. 15); tripartite (*tríṣaṃdhi-*, AV 11. 10. 3); a four-edged rain-producer (RV 4. 22. 2); hard, six-cornered, made from seer's bones (*MBh.* 3. 98. 10, cf. RV 1. 84. 13); it has a hundred knots or joints (*śatáparvaṇ-*, RV 1. 80. 6; 8. 6. 6, 76. 2, 89. 3; AV 8. 5. 15; 12. 5. 66); a hundred edges (RV 6. 17. 10); a thousand spikes (1. 80. 12; 5. 34. 2; 6. 17. 10).

The *vazra-* appears with similar features in the Avesta, here as the weapon of Mithra, who swings it at the heads of Daēvas (*Nyāyišn* 1. 15 = Yt. 6. 5). It has a hundred bosses and a hundred 'mouths' (= blades), and is made of strong, yellow, gold-like iron (Yt. 10. 96 = 132).

The effect of the *vajra-* on Vṛtra is devastating. It breaks his head (RV 1. 52. 10, 15; 8. 6. 6, 76. 2; 10. 67. 12); burns or scorches him up (2. 11. 10, cf. 30. 5; 7. 104. 4); chops him down (2. 11. 18, 19. 2; 3. 33. 7; 4. 17. 7, 19. 3); blows him down from the air (8. 3. 20); lays him low (10. 111. 6); dismembers him (1. 32. 7; 8. 6. 13, 7. 23); hides him in darkness (1. 32. 10; 8. 6. 17).

The Greek poets' *keraunos* is made for Zeus by the Cyclopes, Brontes, Steropes, and Arges, as Indra's *vajra-* is made by Tvaṣṭṛ. It is 'bright', ἀργής (cf. Zeus ἀργικέραυνος); the adjective is a derivative of the same root as the *árjuna-* applied to Indra's weapon. It is fiery (Hes. *Th.* 692–700, 844–6, 859–67, Pind. *Pyth.* 3. 58, etc.), but also sooty (αἰθαλόεις, ψολόεις) and sulphurous (*Od.* 12. 417 = 14. 307). It is not said to be of metal or stone, though the phrase χάλκεος ἄκμων, 'a bronze anvil', which Hesiod imagines descending from heaven to earth and from earth to Tartarus (*Th.* 722–5), may once have referred to the divine missile, like the Vedic *āyasá- . . . áśman-* cited above.[53] When represented in art, the thunderbolt is shown held in Zeus' fist, typically with three spiky flames shooting out at each end.

[53] *áśman-* and ἄκμων are the same word, as is Lithuanian *akmuo*: *Perkūno akmuo* is used of belemnites or other stones supposed to have been hurled down in thunderstorms. In [Aesch.] fr. 192. 3 the Aethiopian λίμνη in which Helios bathes is called χαλκοκέραυνος; this presumably means 'flashing dazzlingly with coppery light', and has no bearing on the material that thunderbolts are made of.

However, this iconography derives from Near Eastern art and does not reflect Indo-European tradition.[54]

The *keraunos* affects its victim in much the same way as does the *vajra-*. Hesiod's description of the thunderbolting of Typhoeus (*Th.* 853–68) is sufficient illustration. The monster's multiple heads are comprehensively scorched. He collapses crippled on the earth, setting it on fire and melting it like tin or iron. Finally he is flung into Tartarus' dark prison.

Celtic myth does not deal in explicit thunderbolts. However, the Irish Dagda's iron club, with which he kills the living or revives the dead, has been seen as the counterpart of Indra's and Thor's weapons.[55] Thor's, at least, had the power of bring the dead back to life (see below).

Saxo Grammaticus describes Thor as wielding a mighty club whose handle was broken off (*clava*, 3. 2. 10 p. 66). In the Norse sources it is a *hamarr*, which we render as 'hammer', though we should not imagine something too much like a carpenter's hammer.[56] Thiodolf (*Haustlǫng* 18. 3) calls it 'sharp'. It was forged from iron by the dwarf Eitri with the help of his brother Brokk. When Brokk gave it to Thor he told him that 'he would be able to hit as hard as he wished, whatever was before him, and the hammer would not fail; and if he threw it, it would never miss and never fly so far that it would not find its way back to his hand. And if he wished, it was small enough for him to keep inside his shirt. But it had the defect that the handle was rather short' (*Skáldsk.* 35).

That Thor's weapon represents the thunderbolt follows from his own name and is acknowledged in the story of the giant Hrungnir, who saw lightning and heard thunder immediately before Thor appeared and hurled the hammer at him to fatal effect (*Skáldsk.* 17). The killing of giants and trolls is the hammer's principal occupation. Its effect is regularly described as breaking the victim's head (*Gylf.* 21, 48; *Skáldsk.* 17); there is no scorching or burning. But it can also restore to life, as appears from an episode where Thor kills his goats, feasts on them, and resurrects them the next morning, using the hammer to hallow the skins (*Gylf.* 44).

The name of the hammer was Miǫllnir, from a proto-Germanic **melðuniyaz*. Pērkons' mace has a similar designation in Latvian, *milna*, from Baltic **mildnā*. These terms relate on the one hand to a series of words in other languages meaning 'hammer' or 'mallet' (Luwian *maldani-*, Latin *malleus*, Russian *mólot*, Breton *mell*), and on the other to words meaning 'lightning'

[54] Paul Jacobsthal, *Der Blitz in der orientalischen und griechischen Kunst* (Berlin 1906).

[55] de Vries (1961), 38 f. In Chapter 3 (p. 150) I compared the implement with Hermes' rod as described in the *Iliad*.

[56] On Thor's hammer cf. Grimm (1883–8), 180–2, 1344 f.; de Vries (1956), ii. 124–8; Turville-Petre (1964), 81–5; Klaus von See et al., *Kommentar zu den Liedern der Edda*, ii (Heidelberg 1997), 529–31.

(Old Church Slavonic *mlŭnĭji*, Russian *mólnija*, Old Prussian *mealde*; Welsh *mellt*; cf. Icelandic *myln* 'fire'). The underlying notion is that of crushing or grinding, as in Greek μύλη 'mill' and the verbs Latin *molare*, Russian *molót*. The semantic steps are crush: crushing instrument: thunderbolt: lightning.[57]

The Baltic and Slavonic thunder-gods' weapons are not pictured so consistently. Perkunas and Perun usually hurl an axe. But Perkunas sometimes has a hammer, which returns to his hand when thrown; this is probably a Germanic borrowing. Perun sometimes shoots an arrow (*strelá*).[58] The Latvian Pērkons has his *milna*, but at other times a spear, a sword, an iron rod, arrows, or stone bullets. With all of these, as with Thor's hammer, the emphasis is on the physical impact of the thunderbolt and not on brightness or burning. But the Belorussian Piarun is said to make lightning flash out from between two stones. This is of some interest, as the same is said of Indra:[59]

> He who by killing the Serpent made the seven streams flow,
> he who drove forth the cows with the removal of Vala,
> he who generated fire between two stones,
> the contest victor—he, O peoples, is Indra!

As the damage caused by the thunderbolt is everywhere conceived as being due to the impact of a solid object, the question arises how the god responsible is able to repeat the performance indefinitely. There are two alternative answers, either or both of which may be of Indo-European antiquity. Either he gets his unique weapon back each time, or he has an inexhaustible supply of ammunition.

We have seen that Miǫllnir returns to Thor of its own accord, and that the same is sometimes said of Perkunas' hammer. It is also said of the Dagda's missile. It is not, so far as I know, ever said of Indra's *vajra*-, though in the *Mahābhārata* he has a spear with this property.[60] In Roman times there was a belief that the lightning goes back into the sky.[61] At the mythical level there was a story that it was taken back to Zeus by his bird, the eagle (Manil. 5. 489, 500 f.).

[57] Ernout–Meillet (1959) s.vv. *malleus*, *molo*; V. V. Ivanov–V. N. Toporov (as n. 15), 1195; Lorenz (1984), 312; Bader (1989), 89 n. 201; Gamkrelidze–Ivanov (1995), 619; Watkins (1995), 429.

[58] M. Gimbutas, *JIES* 1 (1973), 475; Váňa (1992), 72.

[59] RV 2. 12. 3; V. V. Ivanov–V. N. Toporov (as n. 15), 1195 f.; cf. Nagy (1990), 196.

[60] *Skáldsk.* 35 (quoted above); de Vries (1956), ii. 127; *MBh.* 3. 286. 16, 294. 24 (*śakti*-, explicitly distinguished from the *vajra*-). We shall see in Chapter 12 (p. 463) that the motif is not confined to divine weapons.

[61] Cic. *De div.* 2. 45; Lucr. 6. 87–9 = 383–5; Luc. 1. 155–7; Pliny, *HN* 2. 143 f.; Arrian ap. Stob. 1. 29. 2 (i. 238. 1 Wachsmuth).

On the other hand a popular belief is attested from end to end of Europe and Asia, as well as in parts of Africa, that certain types of stone found on the earth are thunderstones and have valuable magical properties, especally that of protecting a house against future strikes. It is widely believed that the thunderstone when first hurled or shot down from the sky penetrates the earth to a depth of several feet, and then gradually rises to the surface over a period of many days or years. The belief attaches particularly to wedge-shaped flints or stones that look like axes and are in fact, in many cases, prehistoric stone tools. Such are the objects known as 'Perkunas' stone', 'Perun's arrows', and the like. These ideas are already attested in Classical authors.[62]

The Water Dragon

The thunder-god is not after you and me. His wrath is directed against devils, demons, giants. Their identity varies from one country to another. But there is an adversary of a different order who lurks in Vedic, Greek, and Norse mythology and who seems to represent an Indo-European concept: a monstrous reptile associated with water, lying in it or blocking its flow. It is perhaps a cosmic version of the common mythical motif of the serpent who guards a spring, or some other desirable thing, and prevents access to it.

The defeat of this creature by the thunder-god is in essence a nature myth: thunderstorms release torrents of water that had previously been pent up. But whereas the god can always go on killing giants or demons, because there are always more of them, a unique dragon can only be slain once. There is therefore a dilemma. Is the killing of the monster a heroic deed that the god did sometime in the past, to be celebrated in his hymns of praise? Or is the monster not after all dead, so that the conflict is renewed again and again? On the whole the first approach prevails. The story is set in the past, weakening its connection with our weather. But we shall see that there is some ambivalence.

Indra is celebrated for many victories over different demons, for example Vala, Viśvarūpa, Śambara, Namuri, Śuṣna, Uraṇa, Pipru, Arbuda. However, his principal opponent is Vṛtra. Vṛtra's name, as we have seen, means 'resistance, blockage', and was abstracted from Indra's epithet *vṛtrahán-*. But it was abstracted to bestow on a mythical creature already conceptualized.

[62] Pliny, *HN* 2. 146; 37. 134 f., 150, 176; Lydus, *De ostentis* 45; Grimm (1883–8), 179 f., cf. 1221, 1686; Mannhardt (1875), 294; von Schroeder (1914–16), i. 546; most fully documented in C. Blinkenberg, *The Thunderweapon in Religion and Folklore* (Cambridge 1911).

Vṛtra is a huge serpent, *áhi-*. The same verb that appears in *vṛtrahán-* is used in the formula *áhann áhim*, '(Indra) smashed the serpent' (RV 1. 32. 1, 2, 103. 2, etc.). This has an almost exact counterpart in Avestan *janaṯ ažīm* (Y. 9. 8, Yt. 14. 40, of Θraētaona's defeat of a three-headed dragon), and Calvert Watkins has shown how cognates and variants of the phrase can be traced extensively in Hittite, Indo-Iranian, and Greek.[63]

A translation of part of RV 1. 32 will serve to convey the essential features of the Vṛtra myth.[64]

1 Of Indra's heroic deeds will I now tell,
the ones that the *vajra*-bearer did first.
He smashed the Serpent, pierced a path for the waters;
he split the innards of the mountains.

2 He smashed the Serpent that lay on the mountain;
Tvaṣṭṛ fashioned for him the roaring *vajra*.
Streaming like lowing cows,
the waters ran straight down to the sea. . . .

4 When, Indra, you smashed the firstborn of serpents
and shrivelled the magicians' magics,
then, bringing sun, sky, and dawn to birth—
since then you have truly found no antagonist.

5 He smashed Vṛtra the *vṛtra*-most, the wide-shouldered,
Indra with his *vajra*, his great weapon.
Like branches lopped off by an axe,
the Serpent lies flat on the earth. . . .

7 Without feet, without hands, he fought against Indra,
(but) he smashed his *vajra* into his shoulderblades.
A castrated ox matching himself with a bull,
Vṛtra lay shot to pieces all over the place.

8 As he lies thus like a broken reed,
Manu's rising waters go over him:
the very ones that Vṛtra had surrounded in his greatness,
at their feet the Serpent was prostrate . . .

10 In the unstaying, unresting
watercourses' midst his body is laid away.
Over Vṛtra's concealment the waters ride;
into long darkness he sank, Indra's antagonist.

11 Demon's wives, Serpent's herd they had stood
shut in, the waters, as the cows by Paṇi.

[63] Watkins (1995), 297–407. This is the basis of his splendid title, *How to Kill a Dragon*.

[64] Cf. also Macdonell (1898), 58–60, 158 f.; Oldenberg (1917), 133–41; Joseph Fontenrose, *Python* (Berkeley–Los Angeles 1959), 194–201.

The waters' cleft that had been blocked,
by smashing Vṛtra he opened it up.

12 . . . You won the cows, hero, you won the Soma,
you freed the seven streams to flow.

13 Nor lightning nor thunder availed him,
nor the rain and hail he poured forth.
As Indra and the Serpent have fought,
for the future too the Bounteous one is victorious.

That this is a nature myth is clear enough, though the consciousness that Indra's *vajra-* represents the thunderbolt has faded: the storm is interpreted in stanza 13 as Vṛtra's assault on Indra instead of vice versa (cf. 1. 80. 12). The conflict is mostly treated as a past event, but the tenses fluctuate between past and present, and it is recognized that Indra's victory is of continuing significance (4, 13). Vṛtra's body lies now in the waters, sunk in darkness (10).

There is in the Avesta a demon of drought Apaoša who fights against Tištrya (Sirius) and at first overcomes him, to the detriment of the waters and plants. But then he is defeated and driven away, whereupon the streams that water the crops flow forth unhindered. Apaoša fights in the form of a hairless black horse, Tištrya as a fine white one with golden ears (Yt. 8. 21–31, cf. 18. 2, 6). There is no thunder-god here; the role of victor over the demon is assigned to the stellar deity as seasonal power. But Apaoša's function is parallel to Vṛtra's, and his name is analysed as from **ap(a)-vṛt-*, 'water-blocker', with the second element as in Vṛtra.[65]

The Greek thunder-god's great mythical opponent is Typhoeus. The classic account of their conflict is to be found in Hesiod's *Theogony* (820 80). Typhoeus (or Typhaon, as Hesiod calls him elsewhere) is a monster with a hundred serpent heads that flash with fire and give out alarming animal noises of many kinds. He would have become master of gods and men if Zeus had not seen the danger and attacked him with his thunder. The world is plunged into tumult:

A conflagration held the violet-dark sea in its grip,
both from the thunder and lightning and from the fire of the monster,
from the tornado winds and the flaming bolt.
All the land was seething, and sky, and sea;
long waves raged to and fro about the headlands
from the onrush of the immortals, and an uncontrollable quaking arose. (844–9)

[65] J. Wackernagel in *Aufsätze Ernest Kuhn gewidmet* (Munich 1916), 158 f. = *Kl. Schr.* 448 f.; cf. Oldenberg (1917), 140.

Zeus' thunderbolt scorches all the monster's heads on every side. Lashed by Zeus' blows, Typhoeus collapses crippled on a remote mountain, flames shooting from his body and burning the earth. Finally he is flung into Tartarus. It is remarkable to what extent his afflictions match those of Vṛtra, whose head is broken, who is scorched and burnt about, lies broken on a mountain, and is hidden away in the darkness.

Hesiod then makes it clearer that Typhoeus is a figure of meteorological significance by explaining that he is the source of wild, squally winds (869–80). In a simile in the *Iliad* (2. 780–3) Zeus' 'lashing' of Typhoeus appears as something that still happens from time to time.

There is another famous encounter in which an Olympian god slays a dragon. Apollo kills the Python at Delphi. At first sight this does not seem to have much in common with the myths we have been comparing. Python is just a pestilential serpent dealing death to people and animals in the area. Apollo is no storm-god, and he kills the monster with arrows, not thunderbolts. But it is curious that in the *Hymn to Apollo* the creature is associated with a spring at Delphi (300), and that immediately after killing it Apollo goes back to the other spring where he had thought of establishing his shrine, Telphousa, and covers it over with rocks (375–83). The association of these motifs, blocking the flow of waters and killing the dragon, may be the fragmented relic of a myth similar to that of Indra and Vṛtra.[66]

Among Typhaon's offspring Hesiod numbers the Lernaean Hydra that Heracles slew with the help of Iolaos. Her name marks her as a water creature. According to other literary accounts and artistic evidence, she was a serpent with a huge body, many heads, and poisonous breath. There is no agreement in the sources on the weapon that Heracles used against her, whether it was a sword, a sickle, a club, a bow, or stones. But from the second half of the sixth century it is a feature of the story that the clubbed or severed heads had to be cauterized with fire to prevent their regrowth. Some say that one of the creature's heads was indestructible; Heracles cut it off and buried it under a heavy rock (Apollod. 2. 5. 2. 5).

In antiquity the Hydra's heads were interpreted as prolific water springs that kept bursting out and flooding the countryside; if one was blocked, others appeared, until Heracles burned the region and shut off the flow (Serv. *Aen.* 6. 287, sch. Stat. *Theb.* 1. 384). This is the converse of Indra's achievement in releasing the pent-up waters by his killing of Vṛtra. But there are enough common motifs—the great serpent occupying a watery site, the smashing and scorching of heads, the covering with rock—to suggest

[66] Cf. Durante (1976), 47 n. 4.

that here again some elements of an Indo-European myth have been preserved.[67]

Thor, a genuine thunder-god, killed (or perhaps only wounded) the Miðgarð Serpent 'which lies round all lands' (*Gylf.* 47). He went out in a boat with the giant Hymir on the outer sea and fished for the monster, using an ox's head as bait. He managed to pull its head out of the water and dealt it a smashing blow with his hammer, whereupon it sank back into the sea (*Hymiskviða* 20–4). The poem leaves it ambiguous whether the blow was fatal. Snorri, telling the story more fully (*Gylf.* 48), writes 'and men say that he struck its head off on the sea-bed. But I think the truth to tell you is that the Miðgarð Serpent still lives and lies in the surrounding sea.' In this Norse myth the great serpent is located outside our world and has nothing to do with our water supplies. But like Vṛtra he is struck on the head by the thunder-god's weapon and sinks into the waters, where he now lies hidden. The phrase that Snorri uses about him, that he 'lies round all lands' (*liggr um lǫnd ǫll*), is reminiscent of a formula repeatedly used of Vṛtra, *áhann áhim pariśáyānam árṇaḥ*, 'he smashed the Serpent who lay round the flood' (RV 3. 32. 11; 4. 19. 2; 6. 30. 4).

The more recently recorded mythologies of eastern Europe yield a few residual motifs that are relevant in this context. In Lithuania Perkunas' first spring thunderclap is said to 'unlock the earth' from its frozen winter state. The Slavonic Perun fought a dragon, a conflict later transferred to St Ilya (Elijah). According to a Ukrainian legend the divine smith Kuy, who assisted the thunder-god against the dragon, ploughed a furrow with its body, and this was the origin of the river Dnieper with its 'snake ramparts'. Albanian myth tells of a dragon called Kulshedra (from Greek/Latin *chersydros*, an amphibious serpent) or Ljubi, who grows huge in a mountain cave and often causes streams to dry up, though her approach also brings storms; she has nine tongues and spits fire. What is most to be feared is her lethal urine. She is fought by a Drangue, who uses meteoric stones or lightning-swords and protects mankind from storm by overwhelming her with piles of trees and rocks.[68]

Viśvarūpa and his cows

The waters imprisoned by Vṛtra are likened to cows pent up in a stall, cows being a standard Vedic metaphor for anything capable of giving nourishment.

[67] Vṛtra and the Hydra have been compared by L. von Schroeder, *Herakles und Indra* (as n. 38), 32–8; F. R. Schröder (as n. 45), 8.

[68] Greimas (1992), 31; Váňa (1992), 72, 283 f.; Lambertz (1973), 471 f., 473 f., 486 f., 488 f.

There is another Vedic myth in which a herd of cows is in the possession of a three-headed dragon (*áhi-*); the dragon is killed, his heads cut off, and the cows liberated. The dragon's name is Viśvarūpa, 'Omniform'. He was the son of Tvaṣṭṛ, and had a wealth of cows and horses (RV 10. 76. 3). His slayer was Trita Āptya, a figure associated with Indra and the Maruts. Indra delivered Viśvarūpa to Trita (2. 11. 19). Trita fought him, killed him, and let the cows out (10. 8. 8). Indra cut off his three heads and drove the cows home for Trita (10. 8. 9, 48. 2).[69]

A version of the same myth is alluded to in the Younger Avesta. The hero who corresponds to Trita Āptya is Θraētaona, son of Āθβya. He defeated the three-headed demon Aži Dahāka[70] and took away, not a herd of cows, but his two beautiful wives (Y. 9. 7–8, Yt. 5. 29–35, 9. 13–15, 14. 40, 15. 19–25, 19. 46–50, Vd. 1. 17). 'Θraētaona son of Āθβya' would seem to have replaced an earlier *Θrita Āθβya = Trita Āptya, perhaps signifying 'Third McWaters'.[71] At least in its Indic form the surname suggests that this deity was somehow associated with the waters. The inference is that the demon he slays is, like Vṛtra, a blocker of the waters.

This Indo-Iranian myth has long been compared with another of Heracles' exploits:[72] his journey across the western Ocean to the island of Erythea to capture the cattle of Geryoneus, also called Geryon. Geryon had three heads (Hes. *Th.* 287) and (at least from the time of Stesichorus) a triple body, with six arms and six legs. Heracles borrowed the Sun's cup in order to cross to Erythea, killed Geryon together with his herdsman Eurytion and his dog, and drove the cattle back to Greece. Geryon's name is presumably related to *γῆρυς*, *γηρύω*, which are elevated poetic words for 'voice, utter, sing',

[69] On Trita cf. Macdonell (1898), 67–9; Oldenberg (1917), 141 f.; K. Rönnow, *Trita Āptya. Eine vedische Gottheit*, i (Uppsala 1927); Hillebrandt (1927–9), ii. 307–11; Oberlies (1998), 195–9.

[70] *Aži-* = Vedic *áhi-*, 'serpent'; *Dahāka-* is related to Vedic *dāsá-*, 'devil'. The Iranian demon is described as 'three-headed, six-eyed' (Y. 9. 8, Yt. 9. 34, al.), as is Viśvarūpa ('six-eyed, three-headed', RV 10. 99. 6). In Yt. 5. 61 Θraētaona is called *vərəθrajå*, '*vərəθra*-smasher', which implies the same label for the dragon as gave Vṛtra his name; cf. Puhvel (1987), 102.

[71] Cf. Mary Boyce, *A History of Zoroastrianism*, i (Leiden–Köln 1975), 97–100; Puhvel (1987), 110 f.; Watkins (1995), 314; P. Jackson and N. Oettinger, *IIJ* 45 (2002), 221–9. The interpretation of both terms is disputed. Θrita appears elsewhere as a separate hero (Y. 9. 9–11, Yt. 13. 113, Vd. 20. 1–3; one of those who defeated the Turanian Dānavas, Yt. 5. 72–4). 'Third' as a mythical name has been compared with Zeus' title of Third Saviour (*τρίτος σωτήρ*); Athena *Τριτογένεια* (Third-born? Born of Tritos?); the Norse þriði 'Third' (*Grímnismál* 46. 4, *Gylf.* 2). Cf. Grimm (1883–8), 162; de Vries (1956), ii. 86 f.; F. R. Schröder (as n. 45), 26 f.; B. Lincoln, *History of Religions* 16 (1976), 43–53. One might add the mysterious Troyan of Russian and Serbian myth, cf. Váňa (1992), 83. Note that 'Third' would be a poetic or hieratic code-name, fully comprehensible only with specialized knowledge.

[72] M. Bréal, *Hercule et Cacus* (1850) = *Mélanges de mythologie et de linguistique* (Paris 1882), 1–162; Müller (1897), 766–8; Watkins (1995), 464–8.

though cognate with Old Irish *gáir* 'shout'; it is just possibly relevant that Viśvarūpa is described as *tuvīrávaḥ*, 'loud-roaring' (RV 10. 99. 6).[73]

Geryon's dog has a mythological dignity of his own, for Hesiod lists him as Typhaon's first offspring, before Cerberus and the Hydra, and he in turn fathers the Sphinx and the Nemean Lion (*Th.* 309, 326 f.). Some authors give him two heads. The name of this noteworthy hound is Orthos or Orthros, the first variant being the better attested.[74] This has been compared with *Vṛtra-*, Avestan *vərəθra-*.[75] We should have expected *Artros as the corresponding Greek form, but if certain allowances are made the equation is not impossible.

The location of Geryon and his cattle beyond the river that encircles the earth recalls another Vedic myth. Indra's cows are stolen by the demons known as Paṇis and taken and concealed in their stronghold on the far side of the world-encircling stream Rasā. They are tracked down by Indra's dog Saramā; the Paṇis are curious to know how she has managed to cross the Rasā. They suborn her, and on her return to Indra she denies that she has found the cows. But he discovers the truth, follows her back to the Paṇis, kills them, and recovers his cattle.[76] It is doubtful whether the imprisoned beasts here have anything to do with pent-up waters. The myth perhaps belongs with another series of texts in which the release of cows by rupturing a rock barrier represents the dawn (RV 1. 71. 1 f.; 2. 24. 2 f.; 3. 39. 4–7; 4. 1. 13–17, 3. 11; 10. 67. 4, 68. 2–12). We saw in the last chapter that Uṣas and Sūrya have their red cows that they drive out each morning.

Roman writers relate that Hercules stopped in Latium on his way back from Erythea with Geryon's cattle. A fire-breathing ogre called Cācus (three-headed according to Propertius) lived at that time in a cave on the Aventine. He abducted some of the cattle in the night and concealed them in his cave, the entrance of which he then blocked up with a massive rock. Hercules managed after some time to find out where the animals were and to break into the cave from above. He then clubbed Cacus to death and recovered the cows.[77]

According to the Augustan antiquarian Verrius Flaccus the hero of the story was not the Greek Heracles but a herdsman of outstanding strength

[73] Durante (1976), 58. Of the Italic Cacus (see below) it is obscurely mentioned that his mouth or mouths gave forth a noise (Prop. 4. 9. 10, Ov. *Fast.* 1. 572).

[74] See West (1966), 248 f.

[75] F. Max Müller, *Chips from a German Workshop* (3rd edn., London 1894–5), iv. 252–4; id. (1897), 421–5; Pisani (1969), 200 f.

[76] RV 10. 108; *Bṛhaddevatā* 8. 24–36; Oldenberg (1917), 143 f. For the Rasā cf. RV 9. 41. 6; 10. 121. 4.

[77] Virg. *Aen.* 8. 190–272; Livy 1. 7. 3–6; Prop. 4. 9. 1–20; Ov. *Fast.* 1. 543–82; Dion. Hal. *Ant.* 1. 39; Verrius Flaccus ap. Serv. auct. *Aen.* 8. 203.

named Garanus. Evidently a native Italic myth featuring this Garanus was assimilated into the Greek saga of Heracles. But who was he? Can he perhaps be related to the widely attested Celtic god Grannus, a god of water and watering places? In Propertius' version of the Cacus story Hercules, on recovering his cows, is assailed by parching thirst and finds the land waterless. Some distance away he finds the secluded sacred grove of the Bona Dea, with a temple and a stream, but it is closed to men. The priestess refuses him access. He breaks in nevertheless and slakes his thirst.

Triśiras, Ullikummi, Hrungnir

In post-Rigvedic myth Viśvarūpa appears under the name Triśiras, 'Three-head'. His father Tvaṣṭṛ created him out of resentment towards Indra. He grew so great that Indra was afraid he would ingest the whole universe. In an attempt to undo him Indra told the Nymphs (Apsarases) to dance before him, display their charms, and try to seduce him. But he proved too austere to be moved by the exhibition. So Indra hurled his fiery bolt and struck him dead. He fell like a mountaintop, but still blazed with ardour. Indra then persuaded a woodcutter to cut off his heads with his axe. When this was done, heathcocks, partridges, and sparrows flew out from the different heads.[78]

The Hittite *Song of Ullikummi* relates a story with noteworthy similarities to this. Kumarbi, the father of the gods, has hostile designs towards the Storm-god. He copulates with a cliff, which gives birth to a stone child, Ullikummi. Ullikummi grows rapidly to a prodigious size, threatening the gods. The Storm-god is downcast. The goddess of love and sex arrays herself seductively, goes before Ullikummi, and makes music and sings, but he is blind and deaf to her charms. The Storm-god then attacks him with lightning and tempest. But these too are ineffective. Ullikummi is bigger than ever, nine thousand leagues high and the same in width, blocking communications among the gods. Finally his feet are cut through with the saw that once separated heaven and earth. The Storm-god renews the battle and (we must suppose; the end is lost) brings the colossus crashing down.

This narrative is agreed to be translated or adapted from a Hurrian original.[79] Its Indo-European status is therefore doubtful. Certain motifs in it—the insemination of a rock that gives birth to a formidable god or hero, and his eventual undercutting from below—recur in Caucasian legend,

[78] TS 2. 5. 1; ŚB 1. 6. 3. 1; *MBh.* 5. 9. 3–38; *Bṛhaddevatā* 6. 149–51. The motif of the creatures springing forth from the severed heads has an indirect link with Geryon: his father Chrysaor and the winged horse Pegasus leapt out when Perseus decapitated Medusa (Hes. *Th.* 280 f.).

[79] Cf. West (1997), 102–5.

whether by diffusion from east Anatolia or by originally kindred tradition.[80] But these are not the features that it shares with the Indian myth, and it may be that we have to do with an Anatolian compound of Indo-European and non-Indo-European elements. We should not forget that an Indic dynasty had ruled over Hurrian Mitanni in about the sixteenth century.

The possibility of an Indo-European ingredient is strengthened by a Nordic parallel. The mightiest of the giants, Hrungnir, who had a head and heart of stone and a massive stone shield, got into Ásgarð and threatened to destroy it, carry off Freyja and Sif, and kill the rest of the gods. It was arranged that Thor would fight him. Hrungnir stood waiting with a great whetstone on his shoulder. As his second, the giants made a clay giant Mǫkkurkálfi, 'Fog-leg', who was nine *rasts* high and three wide. But he was a coward, and when he saw Thor he wet himself (which presumably dissolved his legs). Hrungnir was tricked into believing that Thor would attack him from below, and he put his shield under his feet. Then Thor came with thunder and lightning, hurled his hammer, and shattered Hrungnir's stone head.[81]

WIND GODS

In most branches of the tradition we find evidence for the personification of the wind or winds, and in some cases for their receipt of religious honours. The onomatopoeic PIE root **h_2weh_1* 'blow' was the basis for two words for 'wind', **h_2weh_1-yú-* and **$h_2w(e)h_1$-nt-* (MIE **h_2weh_1nt-o-*). Both were of the animate gender, implying active forces, and after the differentiation of a feminine gender both remained masculines. Hence Hittite *huwant-*, Vedic *vāyú-* and *vā́ta-*, Avestan *vayu-* and *vāta-*, Lithuanian *vė́jas*; Tocharian A *want* (B *yente*), Latin *uentus*, Germanic **windaz*, Welsh *gwynt*.

In the Hittite god-lists the Winds are often included among the cosmic powers that conclude the catalogue: Mountains, Rivers, Springs, the Great Sea, Heaven, Earth, Winds (IM^{MEŠ}-*uš* = *huwantus*), Clouds.[82] However, they are written without the divine determinative, the sign that normally accompanies a god's name.

[80] K. Wais in Hermann Schneider (ed.), *Edda, Skalden, Saga. Festschrift zum 70. Geburtstag von Felix Genzmer* (Heidelberg 1952), 229–34, 247–50; W. Burkert, *Würzburger Jahrbücher für die Altertumswissenschaft* 5 (1979), 253–61 = *Kleine Schriften*, ii (Göttingen 2003), 87–95.

[81] Thiodolf, *Haustlǫng* 14–20; *Hárbarðzlióð* 14 f. and other Eddic allusions; *Skáldsk.* 17; compared with the Ullikummi narrative by K. Wais (as n. 80), 211–29.

[82] Gurney (1977), 5; Beckman (1999), 47, 58, 63, 86, 92.

In the Rigveda both Vāyu and Vāta, but much more often the former, appear in personified form as divine powers, occasionally in the plural. A few hymns are devoted wholly to one or other of them (1. 134; 4. 48; 7. 92; 10. 168, 186). Vāyu is associated with Indra (e.g. 1. 2. 1–6; 4. 46 f.; 7. 90 f.), Vāta, who represents a more violent sort of wind, with Parjanya. Vāyu rides, sometimes with Indra, in a chariot drawn by red horses (1. 134. 1, 3, 135. 1–3, etc.).[83]

Both Vayu and Vāta are recognized also in the Younger Avesta. One or other or both tend to appear in litanies among objects of reverence.[84] They are associated with the bringing of victory or success. Vayu in this role is the recipient of one entire hymn (Yt. 15). In *Sīh rōcak* 1. 22 and 2. 22 Vāta is named and then detailed as '(coming) from below (i.e. from the lowlands), from above, from in front, from behind', in other words 'the westerly, the easterly, the southerly, the northerly'. These Iranian texts confirm Herodotus' statement (1. 131. 2) that the Persians 'sacrifice to Sun and Moon and Earth and Fire and Water and the Winds'.

In Greek the old words for 'wind' were lost, though the epic language still has the verb ἄ(ϝ)ημι and derivatives such as ἀήτη, ἄελλα. As the standard word for 'wind', ἄνεμος prevailed. Already in Mycenaean Knossos a cult of the Anemoi is attested (KN Fp 1 + 31). In the classical period there is sporadic evidence for cults of the Winds, some of them involving animal sacrifice, as well as for occasional offerings in time of need.[85] Hesiod (*Th.* 378–80, 870 f.) recognizes three divine winds, Zephyros, Boreas, and Notos, sons of Astraios and Dawn, contrasted with the evil, irregular, nameless winds that come from Typhoeus. Achilles prays to Boreas and Zephyros with libations and promise of sacrifice (*Il.* 23. 194–8), and they are represented as anthropomorphic figures who hear the prayers and respond. Elsewhere in the *Iliad* (16. 150, 20. 223) they are said to have fathered horses, and later Greek and Latin poets speak of them as riding through the air with horses or perhaps even in horse form.[86]

The old word did survive in Latin; poets personified the Venti, or individual winds, in the Greek manner. Evidence for any Roman cult, however, is scanty and not early. Seafarers traditionally propitiated the Tempestates.[87]

[83] For further particulars see Macdonell (1898), 81–3; Oldenberg (1917), 227 f.; Hillebrandt (1927–9), ii. 294–8; Oberlies (1998), 217–19.

[84] Y. 16. 5, 25. 5; *Sīh rōcak* 1. 21 f., 2. 21 f.; *Nyāyišn* 1. 8; cf. also Y. 70. 3, Yt. 10. 9, 11. 16, 21, 12. 4, 13. 47, 14. 2; Vd. 19. 13.

[85] R. Lantier in Daremberg–Saglio, *Dictionnaire des antiquités* s.v. Venti, 717 f.; H. Steuding in Roscher, vi. 513–15; M. P. Nilsson, *Geschichte der griechischen Religion* i.[3] (Munich 1967), 116 f.

[86] Cf. H. Lloyd-Jones, *CQ* 7 (1957), 24 = id., *Greek Epic, Lyric, and Tragedy* (Oxford 1990), 383 f.

[87] Venti: Lantier (as n. 85), 718 f.; J. B. Keune in Roscher, vi. 181–3. Tempestates: H. Steuding in Roscher, v. 360 f. Georg Wissowa, *Religion und Kultus der Römer* (2nd edn., Munich 1912), 228.

No wind-gods play a significant part in the mythology of the North, but the instinct to personify and systematize operated here too. Vindr 'Wind' appears in a twelfth-century verse catalogue of giants quoted by Snorri (*Skáldsk.* 75, verse 421. 7). One genealogy grouped Sea, Fire, and Wind (Kári) together as the three sons of the primal giant Forniótr.[88]

In medieval Russia too the Winds could boast a pedigree, for in *Igor* 48 we read of *Vĕtri Striboži vnutsi*, 'the Winds, Stribogŭ's grandsons', that blow (*vĕyutŭ*) from the sea against Igor's army. The god Stribogŭ is mentioned in two other texts; his name, as noted in Chapter 4, perhaps means 'Father God'. In Slavonic folklore the wind is variously pictured as an old man blowing through iron teeth, with a brother and sisters who also affect the weather, or as a white horse. Propitiatory offerings are sometimes appropriate. In Slovakia the ruler of the winds drives a cloud chariot drawn by fiery horses.[89]

Sixteenth- and seventeenth-century writers report that the Baltic heathens worshipped a god of the winds, or the winds themselves. The name Wejopat(t)is, Wejpons, or Wejdiews is given, and for the Letts Weja Maat; that is, in more modern spellings, Vėjopatis, Vėjpons 'Master of wind', Vėjdievs 'God of wind', Vēja māte 'Mother of wind'.[90] Praetorius met a fisherman who had made an image of Vėjopatis and set it up on his boat: it was winged, with two faces facing opposite ways, and the fisherman would raise his arms in homage to it. Vēja māte appears dozens of times in the Latvian songs. Sometimes she is addressed as if in prayer, though there is no longer a real sense of her as a divine power. One song speaks of the wind's horse.[91]

The Gaels of the Western Isles of Scotland, whose hymns to the Sun and Moon were noticed in the last chapter, are recorded as having had others addressed to gods of the sea, the wind, the storm, lightning, and thunder.[92]

FIRE GODS

We observed in an earlier chapter that PIE had both an animate and an inanimate word for fire, **hn̥g^wni-* and **péh$_2$u̯r̥*. The first was applicable to fire

[88] *Flateyjarbók* i. 219 (*Fundinn Nóregr*), *Orkneyinga saga* 1; cf. *Skáldsk.* 27.

[89] Váňa (1992), 115.

[90] Matthaeus Waissel, Paul Einhorn, Matthaeus Praetorius, in Mannhardt (1936), 243, 468 f., 472, 481, 542. We saw in Chapter 3 that Lithuanian gods' names are often made with *-patis* = IE **-potis*, and that Latvian tends to turn them into Mothers.

[91] Jonval (1929), 16 and nos. 464–98. There is also a Mother of the North Wind, Ziemeļa māmuliņa, *LD* 31724 = Jonval no. 500.

[92] Carmichael (1928–59), iii. 271.

considered as an active principle. This suggests, at least as a potentiality, the treatment of fire as a divinity.

In India he does indeed appear as a divinity, an important one, under the name Agni, which is the direct continuation of **h̥ngʷni-*. Elsewhere—even in lands where reflexes of **h̥ngʷni-* served as the ordinary word for fire—we find fire-gods under a variety of other names. The diversity makes it harder to argue for their original identity. But fire has always played a major role in cult and must always have retained its sacral character in that context. And in the case of such a dangerous entity it is only to be expected that its primary name should often have become taboo and alternative names substituted. So we should keep an open mind, and be alert for points of contact that go beyond the simple association with fire.

Agni is fire of all kinds, terrestrial and celestial: the fire of the sun and lightning, a forest fire, the fire of the domestic hearth and the sacrificial altar. Two of his attributes, 'seen from afar' and 'untiring', correspond in sense, though not etymologically, to epithets applied in Greek to the impersonal 'fire'.[93] It is the sacrificial fire that is of central importance for religion, and this is why Agni is celebrated in over two hundred hymns in the Rigveda. Lit anew every morning, this fire carries the oblation to the gods and also brings them to the sacrifice, thus linking heaven and earth. In looking for cognate fire-gods in other traditions we must keep the fires of altar and hearth, regulated as they are by ceremony and ritual, as a central point of reference.

Herodotus in the passage quoted above includes fire among the Persians' objects of worship. The Avestan word for it is *ātar-* (masculine). In its scope it is entirely comparable to Vedic *agní-*. It denotes fire generally, and especially the sacral and hearth fire, often personified and honoured as a god. Ātar is closely associated with Ahura Mazdā as his ally and agent; he is indeed constantly called his son (Y. 1. 12, 3. 2, 22. 3, etc.). It may be that this filiation was adapted from an Indo-Iranian tradition that Agni was the son of Dyaus, as he is in the Rigveda (4. 15. 6; 6. 49. 2; son of Dyaus and Pṛthivī, 3. 2. 2, 3. 11, al.).

In Yt. 19. 46–51 a mythical account is given of the contest for the sovereign glory (*xᵛarənah-*) between Spənta Mainyu and Aŋra Mainyu, the Bounteous Will and the Hostile Will. It is fought for by their respective champions Ātar and Aži Dahāka, the three-headed dragon. The latter threatens that he will extinguish Ātar, and Ātar is deterred. But then he counter-attacks, threatening to shoot a jet of flame through the monster from his rear end to his mouths,

[93] RV 7. 1. 1 *dūredṛ́śa*, cf. TS 4. 1. 3. 4 ~ Hes. *Th.* 566 *πυρὸς τηλέσκοπον αὐγήν*; RV 2. 35. 8; 3. 1. 21, 54. 1, al. *ájasra-* ~ *Il.* 5. 4, al. *ἀκάματον πῦρ*. The latter parallel is noted by Durante (1976), 93.

and faced with this prospect Aži prudently withdraws. The story is set in a framework of Zoroastrian theology, but it is evidently a version of the old myth in which the many-headed enemy of the storm-god was overcome with the help of fire.

Chief among the Scythian gods, according to Herodotus (4. 59, 127. 4), was Hestia, the goddess of the hearth, called in the Scythian language Tabiti. It is a natural conjecture that this contains the Indo-European root **tep* 'be hot, burn'.[94] Our Greek source perhaps gives us the name in a slightly distorted guise, but it might represent a feminine participial form corresponding to an Indo-Iranian **Tapatī́*, 'the Burning one'.

In view of the difference of gender we cannot say that this Scythian goddess is just Agni or Ātar under another name. But she must have had some of their most important functions. In Greece and Italy we again find the sacral or domestic hearth under the tutelage of a female deity, Hestia or Vesta; and these names too, as we saw in Chapter 3, may originally have meant 'Burning'. In cult terms they are the Greek and Roman counterparts of Agni. According to Ovid (*Fasti* 6. 291) the living flame was itself Vesta. Her shrine in the Forum, with its perpetual fire, was the civic hearth of Rome and its oldest temple. Its distinctive circular form recalls the use of round altars for the domestic fire in the Agni cult.[95] If the fire ever went out, a new flame had to be kindled by the same ancient ritual method as was employed in India for the regeneration of Agni, drilling with wood in wood.[96]

Both Greeks and Romans also had a male god of fire, though he appears somewhat marginalized. The Greek Hephaestus (a son of Zeus, as Agni is of Dyaus) has in the epic and mythological tradition the specialized role of divine smith and artificer. He has clearly been to some extent assimilated to the Canaanite smith-god.[97] On the other hand ἥφαιστος can also mean fire, especially the fire over which the flesh of sacrificial victims is cooked or in which a body is cremated, as in *Il.* 2. 426, 'they spitted the innards and held them over (the) ἥφαιστος'; cf. 9. 468 = 23. 33 'in the flame of Hephaestus', *Od.* 24. 71. In the battle of the gods in *Iliad* 21 Hephaestus creates a conflagration to counter the river Scamander, burning trees and vegetation and making the water boil (330–82; cf. *Hymn. Herm.* 115). The etymology of his name is obscure. From its bulk it looks like a compound, and this would point to a periphrastic title that replaced an original proper name. It may perhaps

94 Schrader (1909), 35.

95 G. Dumézil, *Archaic Roman Religion*, i (Chicago 1970), 313–17; A. Della Volpe, *JIES* 18 (1990), 166–70, who argues that it symbolized the sun; J. P. Mallory in *EIEC* 203.

96 On the technique and its Indo-European status see Kuhn (1859), 36–47. He notes the use of oak wood attested for this purpose in Greek, Roman, and Germanic sources.

97 Cf. West (1997), 57, 384, 388 f.

contain the 'burn' root that appears in Greek *αἴθω*, Latin *aestus* < **aid*[h]*-tus*. But the first element resists analysis.

The Roman Volcanus looks more perspicuous, to us if not to Cicero (*De nat. deorum* 3. 62). The *-no-* suffix is the typical appendage to a word indicating the god's domain. *Volca-* evidently represents an old word to do with fire, related to Vedic *ulkā́* 'darting flame' (RV 4. 4. 2 of Agni's flames; 10. 68. 4) and/or *várcas-* 'brilliance, glare'. Wolfgang Meid found a matching theonym in the Ossetic legendary smith Kurd-Alä-Wärgon, 'the Alan smith Wärgon', and postulated an original **wl̥kā-*.[98] In literature Volcanus is assimilated to Hephaestus and portrayed as a smith, but in essence he was the god of volcanic and other fire. A connection with the hearth fire is presupposed in the legends of Caeculus, the founder of Praeneste, and Servius Tullius: each of them was conceived as a result of his mother's contact with the hearth fire, and was said to be a son of Volcanus.[99]

The Germans, according to Caesar (*Bell. Gall.* 6. 21. 2), recognized as gods only those whom they could see and from whom they received manifest benefits, Sun, Moon, and 'Volcanus'. The reference is clearly not to a divine smith but to fire considered as a (male) deity. In late pre-Conquest England King Canute proscribed worship of 'heathen gods, Sun or Moon, fire or flood, water, wells or stones or trees of any kind'. It was mentioned above that a Nordic genealogy named Sea, Fire, and Wind as the three sons of a primal giant. 'Fire' is Logi, an ordinary word for a blaze, here personified. He makes another appearance in Snorri's story of Thor's adventures in Giantland, where—seen as a person and not recognized for what he is—he defeats his near-namesake Loki in an eating contest.[100] He is Wagner's Loge. But he scarcely exists as a mythical figure, let alone as an object of cult. There is more to be said for Loki as a god of the hearth fire and fire more generally, though this is not at all reflected in his mythology, only in certain popular sayings recorded from Scandinavia and Iceland.[101] German folklore provides a

[98] Kretschmer (1896), 133; Müller (1897), 799 f.; von Schroeder (1914–16), ii. 534 n. 1; Meid (1957), 95–7; id., *IF* 66 (1961), 125–31; Puhvel (1987), 150. Agni is *suvárcas-*, *pāvakávarcas-*, *śukrávarcas-*, 'of good/shining/bright brilliance'.

[99] Cato, *Origines* fr. 59 Peter; Serv. *Aen.* 7. 679; Dion. Hal. *Ant.* 4. 2. 1–3, cf. Ov. *Fast.* 6. 627; von Schroeder (1914–16), ii. 539.

[100] *Gylf.* 46 f. Agni too is a great eater, RV 4. 2. 7; 10. 79. 1–2; *MBh.* 1. 215. 5; TS 1. 1. 7. 1; he devours food, however much, in an instant, RV 7. 4. 2; he is omnivorous, 8. 44. 26; he has teeth and jaws, 1. 58. 5, 143. 5; 5. 2. 3; 8. 60. 13 f.; 10. 87. 2. Greek poets too speak of fire eating (*Il.* 23. 182), having jaws ([Aesch.] *Prom.* 368), being omnivorous (*πάμφαγον*, Eur. *Med.* 1187). The eating metaphor is paralleled in Germanic literature: *Beowulf* 1122, 3014 f., 3114; *Helgakviða Hiǫrvarðzsonar* 10. 5, *Alvíssmál* 26. 4; Grimm (1883–8), 601. Cf. Durante (1976), 142. It is also at home in Akkadian and Hebrew: West (1997), 254.

[101] von Schroeder (1914–16), ii. 549, 554; de Vries (1956), ii. 264.

quantity of evidence for prayers being addressed to the stove, and for the solemn provision of food offerings to the fire with the expectation of good will in return.[102]

In Lithuania, as fifteenth-century sources attest, priests maintained a perpetual holy fire, worshipped as 'Vulcanus', at which they practised divination.[103] Eighteenth-century lexica say that the heathens' Vulcanus was called Jagaubis or Ugnis szwenta ('holy Fire').[104] *Ugnis* 'fire', the cognate of *agníḥ*, *ignis*, Slavonic *ogonĭ*, is feminine in Lithuanian, and the fire was in fact venerated as a female deity. An archaic, elevated word or name for it/her was *gabè* or *gabija*, *šventa Gabija*. Jan Łasicki (Lasicius) in his *De Diis Samagitarum* (1580) records a prayer to be addressed to the house-fire, 'Gabie Deuaite', that is, 'Fire, daughter of God', if damp weather prevented the harvested grain from drying out. He also mentions a goddess Polengabia or Pelengabia, 'Hearth-fire'.[105] Another title by which the fire was addressed was *šventa Ponìkė*, 'holy Mistress'.[106] In Latvia, predictably, the goddess became Uguns māte, 'the Mother of Fire'.[107]

A tenth-century Persian geographer states that the Slavs (*Ṣaqlāb*) all venerate fire, and more recent literary sources and ethnographic evidence attest fire-worship or prayers to the fire among various Slavonic peoples.[108] The house fire was especially honoured in Ukraine and Belarus.[109]

It has often been assumed, and with reason, that the cult of the hearth goes back to Indo-European times.[110] The hearth fire was the indispensable centre and defining point of the home. It had to be tended with care and given offerings at appropriate times. If one moved to a new house, one carried fire there from the old one. New members of the household, such as a newborn child or a new bride, had to be introduced to the hearth fire by being led or carried round it. The custom that the bride circles the hearth three times is common to Indians, Ossetes, Slavs, Balts, and Germans.[111]

102 von Schroeder (1914–16), ii. 575–9; de Vries (1956), i. 176 f., 360 f.

103 Enea Silvio Piccolomini (Pope Pius II) and Johannes Długosz in Mannhardt (1936), 135, 139 = Clemen (1936), 104, 105.

104 Mannhardt (1936), 610 f., who takes Jagaubis to be a corrupt form of Gabjaujis, a god of crops who also protected against fire (cf. ibid. 572 f.).

105 Mannhardt (1936), 359, cf. 372, 389; 357, 'Polengabia diva est, cui foci lucentis administratio creditur'.

106 Ibid. 254, 546.

107 Ibid. 622.

108 C. H. Meyer (1931), 95. 3; 18. 21 (Cosmas of Prague), 21. 4, 69. 34; von Schroeder (1914–16), ii. 579; Unbegaun (1948), 426; Váňa (1992), 57 f., 69, 117–20, 231 (offerings).

109 Gimbutas (1971), 162; Váňa (1992), 118.

110 Cf. Kretschmer (1896), 91 f.; von Schroeder (1914–16), ii. 589–91; de Vries (1956), i. 176 f.; A. Della Volpe, *JIES* 18 (1990), 157–66.

111 Cf. von Schroeder (1914–16), ii. 574 f., 589–91; Mannhardt (1936), 254–6, 296 f., 363; de Vries (1956), i. 177; Biezais–Balys (1973), 410; N. Reiter in *Wb. d. Myth.* i(2), 180.

The god of the hearth fire is fitly called 'master of the house'. Agni has this title (*dáṃpati-*, RV 5. 22. 4; 8. 84. 7; *gṛhápati-*, 1. 12. 6, 36. 5, etc.), as does Ātar (Y. 17. 11 *Ātrəm vīspanąm nmānanąm nmānōpaitīm*, 'housemaster of all houses'), and a variant of the same compound survived in Lithuania. The Jesuit *Relatio* for 1604 records the cult there of a *deus domesticus* named Dimstapatis: some said he was a god of fire, and they would offer a cock to him, eating it themselves and committing the bones to the hearth, while others regarded him as the housewives' god.[112] In Chapter 3 we noticed the Mycenaean deity written as *do-po-ta*, perhaps standing for Dospotās (**doms-*). Here is the same title again; unfortunately we cannot tell whether this Housemaster too was a fire-god.

The Fire in the Waters

The Indo-Iranian pantheon includes a marvellous, mysterious being known as (Vedic) *Apā́ṃ nápāt-*, (Avestan) *Apąm nápāt-*, the *napāt-* of the Waters.[113] The Waters are themselves a holy quantity, to be considered below. As we noted in connection with the Divine Twins in Chapter 4, *napāt-*, the cognate of Latin *nepōs*, means literally 'grandson' or more vaguely 'progeny'.

This deity resides in the waters. He shines there in golden splendour, surrounded by the youthful, divine, female Waters, who nurture him (RV 2. 35. 3–5). He is the source of all life; plants and creatures propagate themselves as his branches (2. 35. 2, 8, cf. 7. 9. 3). He created mankind (Yt. 19. 52), and helps to distribute the waters to human settlements (Yt. 8. 34). He can be identified with Agni (RV 1. 143. 1; 3. 9. 1; 7. 9. 3), but also distinguished from him (6. 13. 3); he is somehow a form of fire, but not synonymous with fire. Agni too is often said to have his abode in the waters, or to have been discovered by the gods in concealment there. In 3. 1. 3–9 it is related that they found him 'in the activity of the sisters', that is, of the rivers: 'The seven streams nurtured his strength . . . They ran up to him like mares to a newborn foal; the gods admired Agni at his birth. . . . He went in to heaven's streams . . . There the old ones who are (ever) young, who share a common womb, . . . received the one embryo . . . Moving hidden from his good friends, from heaven's streams he was not hidden.'

[112] Mannhardt (1936), 432, cf. 435; F. Solmsen in Usener (1896), 89, 'Dimstipatis zu *dimstis* haus hof, also herr des hauses, hofs'.

[113] Cf. Macdonell (1898), 69 f., 92; Oldenberg (1917), 101, 117–20; Hillebrandt (1927–9), i. 349–57, ii. 304 f.; Dumézil (1968–73), iii. 21–4; Oberlies (1998), 176 f.; in Iran, von Schroeder (1914–16), ii. 490–2; Dumézil, 24–7. The Avestan references are Y. 1. 5, 2. 5, 65. 12, 71. 23; Yt. 5. 72, 8. 34, 13. 95, 19. 51 f.

There are a few possible traces of these motifs in Greece. The fiery god nurtured in the waters by their female embodiments recalls the Homeric myth that Hephaestus, having been thrown out of heaven at birth by his mother Hera, was reared in secret in Ocean's stream by Eurynome and Thetis, chief of the Oceanids and Nereids respectively, who received him in their bosom. For nine years he stayed with them, crafting lovely ornaments, with Ocean flowing all around (*Il.* 18. 395–405). As usual, Hephaestus is here portrayed as a smith. But if we think of him in his more basic identity as fire, a similarity to the Agni myth becomes apparent.

It has been suggested that the story related by Bacchylides in his *Ἠΐθεοι* (poem 17) is relevant.[114] Theseus, claiming to be a son of Poseidon, is challenged to recover a gold ring that Minos throws into the sea from the ship in which they are travelling. Theseus dives in and is carried by dolphins to his father's home beneath the waves. There he sees the Nereids dancing, their bodies shining like fire. The similarity with Apām napāt is somewhat indistinct, but the fiery apparition deep in the water, with the female spirits of the water circling about, may possibly owe something to the old myth. The dive for the gleaming gold ring, which might be taken as the concrete symbol of Minos' sovereignty, has an analogue in the Avestan myth that the Turanian warrior Fraŋrasyan dived three times into the lake Vourukaša in a misguided attempt to obtain the shining *x^{v}arənah-* (sovereign glory) which Apąm napāt held in the depths of its waters for the Aryans (Yt. 19. 51–64); there is evidently a close relationship here between the effulgent symbol of sovereignty and Apąm napāt himself.[115]

A poetic formula resembling *apā́ṃ nápāt-* seems to occur at *Od.* 4. 404, where Proteus' seals are called *νέποδες καλῆς Ἁλοσύδνης*, 'the *nepodes* of fair Halosydna'. *Nepodes* is apparently a Greek cognate of *nápāt-/nepos*, while Halosydna 'Sea-watery' is in another place a name or epithet of Thetis (*Il.* 20. 207; of Nereids collectively, Ap. Rhod. 4. 1599). We might hypothesize that there had once been a figure called **nepōs Hudnās*, 'Grandson of the Watery (goddess)', and that after his nature had been forgotten the phrase was adapted as a picturesque designation of other denizens of the deep.[116]

The old Armenian poem about the birth of the hero Vahagn may preserve another reflex of the motif of the fiery divine figure in the waters.[117] A little red reed in the sea bursts into flame, and from the flame a golden-haired youth leaps forth, with hair and beard of fire and eyes that are suns.

114 B. Louden, *JIES* 27 (1999), 57–78.

115 Yt. 19. 51–64. Cf 13. 95, where Apąm napāt appears as a guarantor of governmental authority; Gershevitch (1959), 27 f., 59 f.

116 Cf. Louden (as n. 114), 73 f.

117 Compared by Watkins (1995), 254.

Finally, the ninth-century Norwegian poet Thiodolf uses the phrase *sǽvar niþr* 'grandson/descendant of the sea' as a kenning for fire (*Ynglingatal* 4. 3). That so distinctive an expression, asserting a paradoxical kinship between fire and water, should have been created in the Nordic tradition independently of the Indo-Iranian parallel is difficult to credit. The Norse kenning may derive ultimately from a sacral formula of Indo-European hymnic poetry, based on a cosmological myth.[118]

The acquisition of fire

Fire is the most ostentatiously supernatural element in the world around us: spectacular, constantly changing, difficult to control, unstable. Peoples the world over have felt that it must have somehow been brought to earth from heaven, the home of the burning sun and the source of the lightning. There are sundry myths about how it was first obtained.[119] On the other hand it can be conjured out of stones and wood. The inference is often drawn that it lies hidden in these, and especially in the trees from which fire-sticks are made, having been lodged there by the god of lightning.

This is probably Indo-European. We saw earlier that Perkunas and Perun were believed to put fire into oaks. Hesiod must have a similar idea in mind when he says that Zeus, to withhold fire from mankind, 'would not give it to the ash-trees'.[120] In the Indian tradition, where Agni is treated as a god with a will of his own, he is said to have hidden from the gods, usually in the waters (as above) or in plants, and been sought and found.

> Thee, Agni, laid in concealment, the Angirases
> tracked down, that wert distributed tree by tree.
> As such thou art born through drilling, a great force;
> they call thee the son of Force, O Angiras.[121]

An extended narrative in the *Mahābhārata* tells how, after being betrayed in a series of hiding-places, Agni settled in a *śamī* tree. There the gods found him, 'and so they made that tree the sacred abode of fire, for all rituals. From that

[118] W. Krause, *NGG* 1925, 140; Schmitt (1967), 280 f.; Campanile (1977), 109 f.

[119] Cf. J. G. Frazer, *Apollodorus. The Library* (Cambridge, Mass.–London 1921), ii. 326–50; id., *Myths of the Origin of Fire* (London 1930).

[120] Hes. *Th.* 563; see West (1966), 323 f., where a reference to Soph. *Phil.* 296 f. may be added for the idea that fire is latent in stones.

[121] RV 5. 11. 6; cf. 3. 9. 4 f.; *Bṛhaddevatā* 7. 61–7, 73–80; Macdonell (1898), 92; Hillebrandt (1927–9), i. 149–55. The Angirases are prototypical Brahman priests.

time forth, Agni is considered to be within the interiors of *śamī* trees, and men use it as a means of producing fire.'[122]

The verb for 'drill' in the Vedic verse and elsewhere is *manth*. In a later Sutra the fire-drill is called a *pramantha-*. Kuhn proposed to find here the origin of Promātheus, Prometheus, the god who in Greek myth stole fire from heaven and gave it to mankind.[123] According to a later construction he actually invented fire-sticks (Diod. 5. 67. 2). The Greeks understood his name to mean 'foresighted', in line with the verb *προμηθέομαι* and noun *προμηθεία*. Kuhn supposed that it had originally meant 'the Fire-driller', and was reinterpreted when the related words fell out of use.

When Kuhn wrote, *manth* (with zero grade *math*) had not been distinguished from the similar-looking verb *math* 'seize', which is used, *inter alia*, of the eagle seizing the Soma (RV 1. 93. 6; 9. 77. 2) and of Mātariśvan's capture of fire from heaven (1. 71. 4 = 148. 1; 141. 3; 3. 9. 5; cf. 1. 93. 6). Unlike *manth*, this verb is found compounded with *pra*, meaning then 'forcibly snatch to oneself'. Johanna Narten, who clarified all this, suggested that while Prometheus could not be explained from *pra-manth-* (Kuhn's idea had long since been abandoned), he might perhaps be related to *pra-math-*, as the Seizer of fire; the long vowel in his second syllable is somewhat problematic, but not an insuperable obstacle. This has been accepted by Durante and Watkins.[124] Snatch-thief seems indeed an apter sobriquet for Prometheus than Foresighted, and the lexical link with the Vedic firebringer myth is striking.

It remains to explain how *προμηθέομαι/προμηθεία* fit in. Volkmar Schmidt has shown how these can be related to *μᾰθ*, the root of *μανθάνω*.[125] As words meaning 'grasp, apprehend' are readily transferred to the mental sphere, why should this *μαθ* not be the same in origin as the Vedic *math*? As its meaning changed, the mythical Snatcher might well be reinterpreted as Sharpwit, and his name might influence the formation of *προμᾱθέομαι* etc., even though they bear a rather different sense.

The Mātariśvan who brings fire from heaven in the Indian myth is identified as the emissary of Vivasvat.[126] Vivasvat was the first sacrificer and, as father of Manu, the ancestor of the human race. It was for Manu as sacrificer

[122] *MBh.* 13. 84. 42 f., trs. W. D. O'Flaherty, *Hindu Myths* (Harmondsworth 1975), 103. Sometimes the wood from a tree struck by lightning was sought out for generating the ritual fire, cf. Oldenberg (1917), 111 n. 5.

[123] A. Kuhn, *ZVS* 4 (1855), 124; id. (1859), 12–18.

[124] J. Narten, *IIJ* 4 (1960), 121–35; on Prometheus, 135 n. 40; Durante (1976), 57 f., who notes that in later Sanskrit there is a noun *pramātha-* 'seizing, violent abduction', with the long vowel; Watkins (1995), 256 n. 0.

[125] *ZPE* 19 (1975), 183–90.

[126] RV 6. 8. 4. On Mātariśvan cf. Macdonell (1898), 71 f.; Oldenberg (1917), 121–3; Watkins (as n. 124).

that the gods sent Agni down (RV 1. 36. 10, cf. 10. 63. 7). The bringing of fire is thus connected with the beginnings of sacrificial ritual and of mankind. The Prometheus myth, though dissimilar in detail, likewise associates the theft of fire with the institution of sacrifice, when gods and men were first coming to a settlement and defining their relations (Hes. *Th.* 535–70). It is further bound up in Hesiod, not with the creation of mankind, but with that of the first woman. In other sources Prometheus is the father of Deucalion who, as the only male survivor of the Flood, became the progenitor of mankind, or at any rate of a major division of it; or Prometheus fashions mankind out of clay. In Argive myth Phoroneus was both the bringer of fire and 'the father of mortal men' (*Phoronis* fr. 1). So there is a similar nexus in India and Greece. We seem to be dealing with remnants of a Graeco-Aryan fire myth that had its place within a larger construct.[127]

THE WATERS

A wide range of evidence attests the holy status of terrestrial (potable) waters among Indo-European peoples. Sometimes they are venerated collectively, as 'the Waters' or divided into 'Rivers and Springs'; sometimes individual rivers or fountains are worshipped under their own names.

The Indo-European animate word for water, **āp-*, became assigned to the feminine gender, probably because of water's fostering properties. In the Indo-Iranian tradition we find it developed as an individualizing (non-collective) plural, 'the Waters', Vedic *Āpaḥ*, Avestan *Āpō*. In the case of rivers the assignation of gender was not straightforward. As fosterers they might be considered female; as fructifiers and fertilizers they might be seen as male. If they were large and fast-flowing, their strong and forceful nature might also favour this choice. In south-eastern Europe (Greece, the Balkans, Italy) rivers are generally masculine, but in Iran and India they are generally feminine. Elsewhere the picture is more mixed. In the Germanic and Celtic areas feminine names have come to predominate more widely than they did in antiquity.[128] Some names fluctuate; for example, the Danube is masculine in Latin and Slavonic, but feminine in German and Romanian (and in Dante, *Inferno* 32. 26), while the Rhine is masculine in Latin and German, feminine in Old Norse.

[127] Cf. Müller (1897), 810–13.

[128] On the gender of rivers see P. Kretschmer in *Mélanges linguistiques offerts à M. Holger Pedersen* (Acta Jutlandica 9, Copenhagen 1937), 76–87; P. Arumaa, *Annales Societatis Litterarum Estonicae in Svecia* 5 (1965–9), 16–34; Schramm (1973), 26 f.

In the lists of divine witnesses to Hittite treaties the Rivers and Springs, like the Winds, appear repeatedly. In Suppiluliuma's treaty with Mitanni the Tigris and Euphrates are named specifically.[129]

Four hymns of the Rigveda are devoted to the Waters, and there are many references to them in other hymns. Several more are addressed to particular rivers, sometimes invoked as mothers (RV 2. 41. 16; 10. 64. 9). The Vipaṣ and Śutudrī are said to speed their waters down 'like two bright mother cows who lick their calves' (3. 33. 1), and at the end of the same hymn they are called bulls.[130]

In the Avesta water is frequently mentioned as a holy element, and the Waters are sometimes paid homage in direct addresses and prayers, as for example in Y. 38. 3–5 (from the *Gāthā* of the Seven Chapters), 65, 68. 6–12. In mythical cosmology they are all held to derive from the celestial river Ardvī, which flows down into the lake Vourukaša. The fifth Yašt is a lengthy hymn to this river, pictured in the form of a beautiful maiden. She is a source of human fertility, perfecting men's seed and helping women to give birth (2, 5).

Herodotus in the passage cited earlier (1. 131. 2) correctly includes the Waters among the divinities that the Persians worship. He has to use the word *ὕδατα*, as Greek had lost the word corresponding to *ā́paḥ/āpō* (**āpes*).[131] But Durante has well noted that in Homer *ὕδωρ* is still essentially a passive element and does not normally occur as the subject of active verbs. Instead it is words like *ποταμός* 'river', *ῥόος* 'stream', *κρήνη* 'spring', that have intrinsic energy and send out their *ὕδωρ*.[132] These are the live forces that are capable of personification and may have divine status. Hesiod's divine genealogies include a section devoted to the Rivers, who are collectively the sons of Oceanus and Tethys (*Th.* 337–45). This leads on to the same couple's daughters, the Oceanid nymphs, who are associated especially with springs. At the beginning of *Iliad* 20 Zeus summons all the gods to assembly, 'and none of the Rivers was absent apart from Oceanus, nor of the Nymphs who inhabit the fair woods and the sources of rivers and the grassy meads' (7–9). Agamemnon includes the Rivers in the divine witnesses to his treaty with Priam (*Il.* 3. 278), as in the Hittite treaties, and 'Springs and Rivers' or 'Rivers, Daimones(?), and Waters' recur in a similar role in certain Hellenistic oaths and treaties.[133]

[129] Gurney (1977), 5 f.; Beckman (1999), 40, 47, 53, 58, etc.

[130] On the Waters and rivers cf. Macdonell (1898), 85–8; Oldenberg (1917), 246–8.

[131] It may be seen in Āpiā, an old poetic name for well-watered Argos, and the Thessalian river name Āpidanos.

[132] Durante (1976), 142 f.

[133] Like other features of Greek treaties, however, this probably reflects oriental cultural influence, not Indo-European inheritance; see West (1997), 19–23.

Individual rivers are personified in Greek myth and honoured in cult.[134] Poets and artists represent them with the head or at least the horns of a bull. Scamander, who plays a lively role in the narrative of *Iliad* 21, bellows like a bull (237). Achelous fought with Heracles. These and other rivers fathered heroes by impregnating nymphs or mortal women.[135] Rivers and nymphs are often associated with the nurture of young people to adulthood.[136] They could be prayed to as appropriate. Odysseus prays to the river he is trying to swim into (*Od.* 5. 445), and Hesiod advises never crossing a river without a purificatory hand-wash and a prayer uttered while gazing into the water (*Op.* 737–41).

In Italy too rivers could have divine status. The cult of Father Tiber (Tiberinus) is well attested. The Augurs' prayer included him with a number of other rivers (Cic. *De nat. deorum* 3. 52). There were also goddesses of springs such as Egeria and Iuturna, to whom we shall return in the next chapter.

But the water god who chiefly interests the comparativist is Neptūnus. Originally he was the god of rivers, lakes, and springs. (If we think of him primarily as god of the sea, that is because he was assimilated to the Greek Poseidon.) His name invites analysis as 'Master of the **neptu-*', and **nep-tu-* (**nebh-*) is a plausible word for 'wetness', with presumptive cognates in Avestan *nap-ta-* 'wet', Vedic *nabh-anú-* 'spring'.[137]

Against this conventional etymology there stands a rival one which relates Neptune to the Indo-Iranian Apām napāt and the Irish Nechtan.[138] Nechtan was the inhabitant of a *síd*, which marks him as one of the old pagan gods. Near by he had a well from which only he and his three servants could draw water with impunity: anyone else would suffer burst eyes or some other harm. Nechtan's wife Bóand, thinking her beauty would protect her, approached the well. Three great surges of water erupted, depriving her of a thigh, a hand, and an eye. The flood then pursued her all the way to the sea, thus creating the river Bóand (the Boyne). This river continues under the sea, reappearing as other rivers in other countries, finally finding its way back to Nechtan's *síd*.

[134] For a full treatment see O. Waser, 'Flußgötter', *RE* vi. 2774–815.

[135] Similarly in an Ossetic legend a river-god impregnates a girl and she gives birth to the hero Syrdon: Sikojev (1985), 250.

[136] West (1966), 263 f., where a reference to Pind. *Pyth.* 9. 88 may be added.

[137] Kretschmer (1896), 133; S. Weinstock, *RE* xvi. 2516; Meid (1957), 103 f.; *IEW* 316; Dumézil (1968–73), iii. 41. Umbrian *nepitu* (Tab. Iguv. VIb. 60, VIIa. 49) has been interpreted as 'let him flood', but this is a guess based on Neptune's name.

[138] The connection with Nechtan was first suggested in the nineteenth century, that with Apām napāt by Ernout–Meillet; the larger hypothesis was developed in stages by Dumézil, cf. *Celtica* 6 (1963), 50–61; id. (1968–73), iii. 27–85; J. Puhvel, *JIES* 1 (1973), 379–86; id. (1987), 65, 277–82; Olmsted (1994), 398–400; *EIEC* 203 f.

Dumézil argues dashingly that the well, as it was so injurious to eyesight, must have contained something fiery, analogous to Apām napāt. With its inundation he compares on the one hand the Roman legend of the miraculous overflow of the Lacus Albanus early in the fourth century BCE,[139] and on the other the Avestan myth of Fraŋrasyan, cited earlier, in which the Turanian dived three times into Vourukaša in quest of the sovereign glory that Apąm napāt guarded there: each time it eluded him, and the lake developed a new 'outflow'.

As for the names Neptunus and Nechtan, Dumézil suggests that **nept-*, an Ablaut form of the 'grandson' word, was furnished in proto-Celtic with the individualizing suffix *-ono-* which appears in certain other divine names, including a couple formed from names of family relationships.[140] **Neptonos* would have developed regularly into Irish Nechtan. For Neptune Dumézil has to assume some more Italic suffix such as **-īno-*, and then deformation on the analogy of Portūnus.

This is all ingenious and beguiling. Puhvel and others have taken it over wholesale. But even allowing that the Grandson of the Waters could be abbreviated to the Grandson, it is hard to see why this title should devolve upon a Roman god who does not represent a fiery element nurtured by the waters but the waters themselves; and the argument that there was something fiery about Nechtan is a dubious inference from the circumstance that his well was damaging to eyes. We shall see below that the same was true of a stream in another country, where there is no suggestion that fire or brightness was involved. Satisfactory alternative etymologies exist both for Neptunus (as above) and for Nechtan.[141]

There were of course other Celtic water deities. Many local cults are attested by inscriptions in Roman Gaul, where their names are often rendered as Neptunus, confirming that he represented water of all kinds and is not to be relegated to the sea.[142] The Life of St Patrick records that in Ireland a *rex aquarum* was worshipped 'ad fontem Findmaige qui dicitur Slan'.[143]

It is not surprising if the Rhine was considered a god, though the evidence is scanty. Propertius (4. 10. 41) refers to a Belgic chieftain who boasted that he was descended from it, just as Asteropaios claims to be a son of the Axios in

[139] The sources do not connect this with anything fiery, or with Neptune. However, Dionysius of Halicarnassus (*Ant.* 12. 10. 1) says that the prodigy occurred 'about the rising of the Dog star' (as against Plutarch, *Camillus* 3. 2, who puts it in the autumn), and Dumézil connects this with the date of the Neptunalia, 23 July.

[140] Mātronā 'the Mother (par excellence)', = the river Marne; Maponos 'the Son'; Dumézil (1968–73), iii. 38.

[141] Either **nig^{w}-to-* 'washed, pure, bright', or **nebh-tu-*: W. Meid ap. Olmsted (1994), 399.

[142] Vendryès (1948), 279 f.; Duval (1957), 59; de Vries (1961), 85, 114–16.

[143] *Vita Patricii* i. 122 (ii. 323 Stokes).

Homer. In one of the Eddic poems Gunnar says that the Rhine 'will rule over' the Niflungs' treasure, and he appears to call the river 'of the race of the gods' (*Rín . . . in áskunna, Atlakviða* 27). Rivers and springs were no doubt venerated in Germanic lands from the earliest times. Agathias reports that the Alemanni worshipped rivers (ῥεῖθρα ποταμῶν) as well as trees, hills, etc., and that they made sacrifices of horses, bulls, and much else to such divinities. Christian writers in the following centuries routinely refer to Germanic cults of rivers and springs.[144] Canute's edict quoted earlier shows that 'flood, water, wells' were still objects of reverence to some in eleventh-century England.

Of the Slavs Procopius (*Bell. Goth.* 3. 14. 24) writes that they 'revere rivers and nymphs and various other heathen powers' (ἄλλα ἄττα δαιμόνια); and they sacrifice to them all, and practise their divinations at these sacrifices'. Again, this is a commonplace that recurs in many later sources, both Latin and vernacular.[145] In the Russian *byliny* rivers are affectionately referred to as Mother Dniepr, Mother Volkh, Papa Don. A princess anxious to escape from captivity prays 'O you river, Mother Darya! Grant me to ford you and go to my husband.' 'And the river gave ear to Marya, it let her ford it and go to her husband.'[146]

Among the Balts too the worship of springs and streams is attested by many writers from the Middle Ages on. Some sources provide circumstantial detail, like the sixteenth-century report of a holy stream Golbe near Chernyakhovsk in east Prussia which, as a sign of special favour, sometimes deprived its devotees of the sight of one eye, which they regarded as a great honour; or the account from the Jesuit *Relatio* for 1600 of a rustic who made an annual sacrifice of a hen to a river in which he had once nearly drowned while crossing.[147] Another sixteenth-century source names a god Upinis, 'who had rivers in his power; and to him they sacrificed white piglets, so that the water should flow clear and transparent'. His name is equally transparent, being formed from *ùpė* 'river' (IE **apā*). So are those of 'Ezernis, lacuum deus', from *ežeras* 'lake', and 'Szullinnys, der den Brunnen vorsteht', from *šulinys* 'spring'. The great god Potrimpo is sometimes identified as the god of flowing waters, or of rivers and springs; he was invoked in a form of divination that involved dropping wax into water and observing the images formed. In Latvia

144 Grimm (1883–8), 100–2; Agath. *Hist.* 1. 7; Clemen (1928), 38. 36, 42. 3, 45. 8, 46. 3, 18, 37, 51. 13, 61. 11, 68. 12–21, 72. 24; de Vries (1956), i. 349 f.

145 C. H. Meyer (1931), 15. 23, 20. 27, 21. 3, 22. 23, 23. 21, 26. 37, 43. 38, 46. 15, 58. 15; Váňa (1992), 109.

146 Chadwick (1932), 112 lines 309, 327, 332, 352, etc.; 140 line 148; 171 lines 104–9.

147 Mannhardt (1936), 313, 433. The loss of an eye recalls the Irish legend of Nechtan and Bóand, as well as the Norse myth that Odin deposited one of his eyes in Mimir's well. More general references to holy rivers and springs: Mannhardt, 12, 28, 39, 87, 107, 280, 443, 464, 511.

these male gods give way to Mothers: a Mother of Water, Ūdens māte; a Mother of the River, Upes māte.[148]

Everywhere the picture is similar. These cults of fountains and rivers cannot have developed independently all over Europe and the Middle East. No doubt the Indo-Europeans had no monopoly in religious feeling and observance of this type; it may go back tens of thousands of years. But it must have been part of their religion, and its prevalence among their linguistic and cultural heirs must be due at least in some degree to the power of Indo-European tradition.

[148] Upinis: Mannhardt (1936), 331, 340. Ezernis: Mannhardt, 356, 369 f.; Usener (1896), 90. Szullinnys: Mannhardt, 545; Usener, 102. Potrimpo: Mannhardt, 245, 295 f. ~ 362 f.; Usener, 98 f. Ūdens māte: Mannhardt, 622; *LD* 30731, 9549 = Jonval nos. 521 f. Upes māte: *LD* 30890 = Jonval no. 519.

7

Nymphs and Gnomes

The last chapter has brought us down to earth. Now we shall round off our theological tour by surveying a miscellany of deities and supernatural beings who, while not constituent elements of our terrestrial environment like the Waters or the Earth-goddess herself, inhabit some part of it.

If Indo-European religious experience was in part a response to the orderly beauties of the heavens and the tumultuous dramas of the troposphere, another part of it was prompted by the more numinous aspects of the natural landscape. Away from human settlements, out in the wild where we do not feel at home, the encounter with forest or mountain may arouse exultation, awe, or unease. The oldest Indo-European holy places seem to have been situated amid nature, associated with trees, groves, or springs. Hittite gods had their stelai set up in such places, and numerous writers from antiquity on tell of the sacred trees and groves of the Celtic, Germanic, Baltic, and Slavonic peoples.[1] We have seen that rivers and springs were themselves objects of veneration. There are many records too of worship directed towards holy trees.[2]

But here we are concerned with the more personal beings that live Out There, in trees or caves or underground, not fixed in one spot but seen unpredictably in different places, or not seen but manifested in mocking voices or mischievous pranks. They are for the most part not unique individuals but pluralities such as nymphs, elves, dwarfs, or giants. They have only occasional dealings with humankind, and contact with them is best avoided.

[1] Gurney (1977), 27, 35 f.; Tac. *Germ.* 7. 2, 9. 2, 39. 1, 40. 3, 43. 3, *Ann.* 1. 59, 61, 2. 12, etc.; Clemen (1928), 15. 27, 26. 23, 46. 3, 72. 13; id. (1936), 93. 3, 95. 2, 96. 8, 97. 9, etc.; C. H. Meyer (1931), 20. 23, 22. 23, 23. 20, 43. 38, 44. 5, 45. 16, 58. 15, 59. 21. Cf. Grimm (1883–8), 66–87, 1309–12, 1454; Feist (1913), 353 f.; Unbegaun (1948), 422, 429; de Vries (1956), i. 351–3; M. Green (1986), 21; Váňa (1992), 177–9.

[2] Max. Tyr. 2. 8, 'the Celts revere Zeus, but the Celtic effigy of Zeus is a tall oak', cf. Val. Fl. 6. 90; Grimm (1883–8), 75 n. 1, 648–54; Mannhardt (1905), i. 9–70; id. (1936), 442 f. = Clemen (1936), 112; C. H. Meyer (1931), 6. 21, 26. 37, 30. 35; Vendryès (1948), 281; de Vries (1956), i. 350 f.; id. (1961), 187–90; Biezais–Balys (1973), 413, 424; Váňa (1992), 140–2.

Though basically similar to us in form, they are often differentiated from the human race by their larger or smaller size, or by having some admixture of animal features, or extra heads or limbs, or some other peculiarity.

In the case of sylvan deities there is some fluctuation between plural and singular. Are the woods, after all, one domain or many? In Indic mythology we have on the one hand the nymphs called Apsarases (on whom more below), on the other Araṇyānī 'Mrs Forest', who is praised in a late hymn of the Rigveda and called 'mother of wild creatures' (*mṛgā́ṇām mātáram*, 10. 146. 6). In Greece we have Silenus and Sileni, Pan and Panes; in Italy Faunus and Fauni, Silvanus and Silvani, Silvana and Silvanae; in Lithuania Medeine 'Wood-girl' and Medeines.[3]

Some of these have appellations derived directly from words for 'forest', 'wood'. There may be one such name with a wider than regional attestation, remaining from a late Indo-European stratum. An Illyrian god Vidasus, known from a group of inscriptions from Croatia and corresponding to Silvanus in other Balkan inscriptions, appears to be derived from **widʰu-* 'tree, forest', a word represented in Celtic and Germanic. It has been argued that he has a counterpart in the Norse god Víðarr, whose name (apart from the long first vowel) recalls *viðr* 'tree, forest' and who is said to live amid long grass and brushwood (*Grímnismál* 17). Nothing else is recorded about him, however, except that he will avenge his father Odin at Ragnarøk by killing the wolf Fenrir.[4]

A god of ways and byways

A longer-standing equation that many philologists have looked on with favour is that of the Vedic god Pūṣan with the Greek Pan.[5] Pan is absent from Homer and other early poetry: he became famous only in the fifth century, his cult having previously, as it seems, been confined to Arcadia. There,

[3] Mannhardt (1936), 356, 371, 402; Usener (1896), 95.

[4] A. Mayer, *Glotta* 31 (1951), 238–43, cf. id. (1957–9), ii. 125 f.; F. M. Heichelheim, *RE* viiiA. 2095 f. On Víðarr cf. de Vries (1956), ii. 275–7.

[5] P. von Bradke, *Theologische Literaturzeitung* 20 (1895), 581; A. Döhring, *Etymologische Beiträge zur griechischen und deutschen Mythologie* (Progr. Königsberg 1907), 11; W. Schulze, *ZVS* 42 (1909), 81, 374 = id. (1966), 217 f.; cf. Pisani (1969), 315 n. 3; Puhvel (1987), 63, 132; F. Bader, *Revue de Philologie* 63 (1989), 7–46; E. C. Polomé in *EIEC* 415; M. S. Rodríguez, *JIES* 23 (1995), 209–11; N. Oettinger in *Mír Curad*, 539–48; id. in B. Forssman–R. Plath (edd.), *Indoarisch, Iranisch und die Indogermanistik* (Wiesbaden 2000), 393–400; T. Oberlies, ibid. 380. On Pūṣan see Macdonell (1898), 35–7; Oldenberg (1917), 234–7; Hillebrandt (1927–9), ii. 326–35; Oberlies (1998), 201–4.

however, he may have been an old survival. The familiar form of his name is contracted from earlier *Παων*, genitive *Παονος*, which is attested on a sixth-century dedication (*IG* v(2). 556). The prototype reconstructed is a derivative from the root **peh*$_2$ 'guard, watch over' (cf. Hittite *paḫs-*, Vedic and Avestan *pā-*, Latin *pās-tor*): perhaps **Péh*$_2$*ush*$_3$*ō*(*n*) and (by laryngeal metathesis) genitive **Puh*$_2$*s*(*h*$_3$)*nés.* Partial generalization of the different Ablaut grades could have led on the one hand to *Pūṣán-*, genitive *Pūṣṇáḥ*, on the other to **Pā*(*u*)*son-* > *Πᾱ*(*h*)*ον-* > *Πᾱ́ν-*.[6]

The probability of the identification depends on the degree of similarity obtaining between the functions of the two deities. They have in fact enough in common to encourage the equation. Both are pastoral gods, with a special affinity with the goat. Pūṣan has goats to pull his car (RV 1. 138. 4; 6. 55. 3–4, cf. 6; 58. 2; 9. 67. 10; 10. 26. 8), and goats were sacrificed to him on occasion; Pan has goat's legs (Hymn. Hom. 19. 2, 37; Anon. mel. P. Oxy. 2624 fr. 1. 4 = *SLG* 387). Both have bushy beards (RV 10. 26. 7; Hymn. Hom. 19. 39, *PMG* 936. 11) and keen sight: Pūṣan goes about surveying everything (RV 2. 40. 5; 3. 62. 9; 6. 58. 2); Pan roams the mountains and climbs the peaks to view the flocks.[7] Pūṣan follows and protects the cattle (RV 6. 54. 5–10, 58. 2, 53. 9; a producer of cattle, TS 2. 1. 1. 6; 2. 4. 4. 3). He is a guardian of roads who protects the wayfarer from wolves and brigands (RV 1. 42. 1–3, 7; 6. 49. 8, 53. 1, 54. 9). Pan's province includes 'the rocky tracks' (Hymn. Hom. 19. 7), and in Hellenistic Egypt he was worshipped as *εὔοδος*, 'of good journeying' (*OGIS* 38, 70–2, al.).

Some of Pūṣan's functions parallel those for which Hermes is noted rather than Pan.[8] Hermes too is a good lookout (*ἐΰσκοπος Ἀργειφόντης*), a god of roads (*ὅδιος, ἐνόδιος, πομπαῖος*) and a guardian of flocks and herds. As *ψυχοπομπός* he guides the dead on the path that they must go, and similarly Pūṣan conducts the dead to join their ancestors (RV 10. 17. 3–6; AV 18. 2. 53–5, cf. 16. 9. 2). Both gods also lead the bride to the groom.[9] With his knowledge of ways and byways, Hermes can spirit away cattle or other property; he is the patron god of the sneak-thief. But by the same token he is good at finding things that are hidden, he knows where animals have strayed, and he gets the credit if someone makes a lucky discovery (*ἕρμαιον*). As *μαστήριος* (Aesch. *Supp.* 920) he helps people to track down their stolen

[6] On the linguistic analysis see especially N. Oettinger (as n. 5, 2000), 394–400.

[7] Hymn. Hom. 19. 10 f. (cf. 14 for his sharp eyes); Leonidas epigr. 29. 3, *Inscriptiones Creticae* i. xvi. 7. 2, Philip epigr. 20. 1, 'forest-watcher'; Babr. 3. 7 'Pan who watches over the glens'; Orph. *Hymn.* 11. 9.

[8] Cf. Oldenberg (1917), 237 n. 1; C. Watkins in Cardona et al. (1970), 345–50 = id. (1994), 446–51; Oberlies (1998), 202 f.

[9] Watkins (as n. 8), 348 f. = 449 f.

property. Pūṣan for his part is the patron of professional trackers, and can bring lost, hidden, or stolen goods to light.[10] In general he is a god of gain (RV 1. 89. 5; 6. 54. 4, 8; TS 1. 2. 3. 2; 2. 4. 5. 1), and the same can be said of Hermes.

So the Arcadian Pan and the Panhellenic Hermes overlap, and both have many features in common with Pūṣan. Pan was held to be Hermes' son. It seems likely that they were originally the same. Paon-Pan in the mountain fastnesses of Arcadia preserved the old Graeco-Aryan name, which elsewhere in Greece, already in the Mycenaean period, was replaced by the title '*herma*-god'.[11] *Herma* seems to have had the basic meaning of an upright stone or pile of stones; hence it is used of a prop for a beached ship, an underwater reef, a foundation stone. It was no doubt used of the occasional stone pillars which marked out the way through the mountains, and to which every passing traveller added a stone to build up a cairn. These erections once belonged to Pan, but in time he was remembered only as the *herma*-god. The pillar itself became a Hermes, a herm.

The Roman Mercury was primarily a god of commerce. He was equated with Hermes, who also had this function, but he is not (except in consequence of this equation) notable for the features that link Hermes with Pan and Pūṣan, and I am not inclined to identify him with them. However, among the various Celtic gods that the Romans equated with Mercury there was perhaps one who does belong here. Caesar (*Bell. Gall.* 6. 17. 1) names Mercury as the Gauls' principal god and says that they regard him as, among other things, the patron of roads and journeys, *uiarum atque itinerum ducem*. The god of roads appears again, without a name, in a dedication of 191 CE from Thornbrough, North Yorkshire, *deo qui uias et semitas commentus est* (*CIL* vii. 271).

In Lithuania too there is record of such a figure. The sixteenth-century chronicler Matys Stryjkowski lists 'Kielu Dziewos der Reisegott' (i.e. *Keliũ diẽvas*, 'god of roads'). He describes the sacrifice and prayer made to him by those setting out on a journey. Something over a century later, Matthaeus Praetorius knows him as 'Kellukis, der auf die Wege Achtung hat'.[12]

[10] RV 1. 23. 13; 6. 48. 15, 54. 1–2, 8, 10; AV 7. 9. 4; Macdonell (1898), 36; Hillebrandt (1927–9), ii. 328–30; Oberlies (1998), 202.

[11] Mycenaean Hermāhās, later Ἑρμείας, Ἑρμάων, Ἑρμῆς, etc. For this interpretation of Hermes' name cf. M. P. Nilsson, *Griechische Feste von religiöser Bedeutung* (Leipzig 1906), 388–90; id., *Geschichte der griechischen Religion* (3rd edn., Munich 1967), i. 503–5.

[12] Mannhardt (1936), 331, 545; Usener (1896), 93, 114.

NYMPHS

Over almost all the Indo-European area we find the belief in a breed of supernatural females who haunt the lonelier parts of the land, especially the waters, the trees, and the mountains. They go by different names in every country, but they can conveniently be summed up by the Greek appellation 'Nymphs'.

Indian nymphs

The Indian term is *Apsarás*-, or less often *Apsarā́*. The name was taken, rightly or wrongly, to contain *ap*- 'water', and this association is sometimes apparent, as in a verse where the *samudríyā Apsarásaḥ*, the Apsarases of the vat, represent the waters ritually mixed with the Soma.[13] Outside the Rigveda they are represented as frequenting forest lakes, rivers, trees, and mountains (cf. AV 4. 37. 4; 14. 2. 9; TS 3. 4. 8. 4; *MBh.* 1. 16. 2, 111. 6; 3. 107. 10). They love to sing, dance, and play (ŚB 11. 6. 1; *MBh.* 1. 114. 43, 49; 2. 4. 31, 7. 21, etc.). They have swings in the branches of trees (AV 4. 37. 5, al.).

They are of outstanding beauty (ŚB 13. 4. 3. 7 f.); women in the epic are praised as being 'as beautiful as an Apsaras' (*MBh.* 1. 96. 3, 100. 23). They are accordingly very attractive to men. Indra sends them to tempt ascetics whose power he fears (1. 65. 21 ff., 120. 5 ff.; 5. 9. 9 ff.). Sometimes the mere sight of one makes a holy man ejaculate. On encountering a lovely woman a hero is liable to ask, 'Are you a goddess . . . or perhaps an Apsaras?' (1. 92. 31, cf. 142. 4; 3. 248. 10; 4. 8. 13). But they are to be feared, being liable to cause mental derangement. They are *manomúhaḥ*, 'mind-bewildering' (AV 2. 2. 5); 'it is the Gandharva and the Apsarases who madden him who is mad' (TS 3. 4. 8. 4).

They do occasionally have liaisons with mortals, and some royal and priestly families traced their descent from such unions. The Bhāratas, for example, were descended from the Apsaras Śakuntalā. The most famous legend of a marriage between a mortal king and an Apsaras is the story of Purūravas and Urvaśī. This involved the folk-tale motif that the unequal syzygy could only last so long as the mortal partner observed a taboo, which

[13] RV 9. 78. 3, cf. AV 2. 2. 3. There is a remarkable parallel in the Greek elegist Euenus (fr. 2. 3), who with reference to the proportionate mixing of wine and water says that Bacchus 'loves being mixed as fourth with three Nymphs'. On the Apsarases in general cf. Macdonell (1898), 134 f.; Oldenberg (1917), 254–7; Oberlies (1998), 229 n. 384.

he was eventually induced to break. Purūravas was not to let his wife see him naked, but the jealous Gandharvas tricked him into doing so.[14]

Iranian, Lycian, Armenian

In the last chapter some passages of the Avestan Yasna were cited in which the Waters were addressed. In the oldest of these texts (38. 3) they are called *Ahurānīš Ahurahyā*, 'Ahura's Ahura-wives'. In pre-Zoroastrian times, before the elevation of Ahura Mazdā to supremacy, they were probably Ahurānīs in the sense of 'the Asuras' wives'. In any case the term suggests a high degree of personification, and it will not be inappropriate to consider them as nymphs. In Y. 66. 1 and 68. 1–14 a singular 'Ahurānī of Ahura' is revered.

There is other scattered evidence for water nymphs among Iranian peoples. That the Ahurānīs were known in the western parts of the Persian empire as well as the north-east is indicated by the great trilingual inscription at Xanthos in Lycia, where *Νυμφῶν* in the Greek version is matched in the Aramaic version, if H. Humbach's reading is correct, by *'ḥwrnyš*: Aramaic having no term for nymphs, the translator used an Iranian one familiar to him.

The Lycian version has *Eliyãna*; this seems to be related to Luwian *ali*(*ya*), 'qui désigne un élément liquide: lac, étang ou rivière . . . les *Eliyãna* seraient, au propre, des Naïades.'[15] Water nymphs are perhaps also to be recognized, together with the Indo-European word for 'water', in the *wedri* of another Lycian inscription.[16]

Herodotus (4. 5. 1) relates a Scythian myth that the Scythians were descended from a union between 'Zeus' and a daughter of the river Borysthenes (the Dnieper). This daughter of a river was evidently not herself a mortal woman, and she must be classed as a nymph.

In Ossetic legend the waters are ruled by Donbettyr, 'Water-Peter'. He has daughters of extraordinary beauty, with long golden hair. One story tells of

[14] RV 10. 95; ŚB 11. 5. 1; *Bṛhaddevatā* 7. 146–52; Kuhn (1859), 78–94; Oldenberg (1917), 256 f., who observes that in the original version it was probably the Apsaras who was not to be seen in her true form. The Gandharvas are another class of supernatural, male, often coupled with the Apsarases. The name (usually singular in the Rigveda) is the same as that of the Avestan yellow monster Gandarəβa who was defeated by Kərəsāspa (Yt. 19. 38–41, al.). In the latter half of the nineteenth century it was held to be one of the clearest results of comparative mythology that the Gandharvas were the same as the Greek Centaurs (*kéntauroi*). But the names do not correspond by the rules of phonology, and the creatures have virtually nothing in common mythologically.

[15] E. Laroche in H. Metzger et al., *Fouilles de Xanthos*, vi: *La stèle trilingue du Létôon* (Paris 1979), 114.

[16] *Tituli Lyciae* 56; D. Schürr, *Kadmos* 36 (1997), 127–40.

the unlucky marriage of one of them to the Nart hero Axsartag. She turned them both into fishes, and so they spent a year together in the sea, but after they went to live in his homeland disaster struck, Axsartag killed himself, and she returned to the waters. But she was pregnant with twins, and had to go back to the Narts to give birth to them; they were the heroes Uryzmæg and Hæmyts. Uryzmæg was later taken to visit his relatives under the sea. In the nineteenth century Ossete girls went to river banks on the Saturday after Easter to pay their respects to Donbettyr's daughters.[17]

Armenian folklore knows of good fairies, the *Parik*, who often take the form of beautiful women and dance amid nature. The forest is inhabited by the *Mayrekin*, the mistress of the cedars or of the wood. There is also a collectivity called the *Yaveržaharsunk'*, the 'eternal brides', who are protectors of young life and assist brides and young mothers.[18] Hellenists will recall that the Greek word *νύμφη*, besides meaning 'nymph', also means 'bride', both in the sense of a woman shortly to be married and of one newly married.

Greek, Roman

Nymphs play a major role in Greek myth, religion, and folklore.[19] They are associated with the sea, rivers and springs, trees, caves, and mountains.

The sea nymphs, the Nereids, are a class apart; the others are less clearly differentiated. In early epic there are references to Naiad nymphs, that is, nymphs of flowing water (*Il.* 6. 21 f., *Od.* 13. 356, al., cf. 17. 240), tree nymphs (Meliai, Hes. *Th.* 187), and mountain nymphs (*Il.* 6. 420, 'Hes.' fr. 10a. 17, cf. *Th.* 130). The divine assembly in *Il.* 20. 4 ff. is attended by all the nymphs 'who inhabit the fair groves and the river waters and the grassy meadows'. Circe (herself called a nymph) is attended by female servants who 'come from springs and groves and holy rivers' (*Od.* 10. 350 f.). Hesiod includes two catalogues of nymphs in his *Theogony*; one is of the Nereids (240–64), the other is of the daughters of Oceanus, 'who nurture men on earth with the lord Apollo and the Rivers . . . widely scattered they haunt the earth and the

[17] Sikojev (1985), 15–24, 40–2; G. Dumézil, *Le livre des héros* (Paris 1965), 14, 'Au siècle dernier, le samedi qui suit Pâques, les jeunes filles célébraient sur le bord des rivières le culte gracieux des filles de Donbettyr, assurant ainsi aux maisons et aux écuries les vertus que recèle l'essence puissante des eaux.'

[18] Ishkol-Kerovpian (1986), 100, 134 f., 159.

[19] H. Herter, *RE* xvii. 1527–81; Jennifer Larson, *Greek Nymphs* (Oxford 2001); Fátima Díez Platas in J. C. Bermejo Barrera and F. D. P., *Lecturas del mito griego* (Madrid 2002), 169–328. On the Nymphs (*Νεράϊδες*) in modern Greek folklore see Bernhard Schmidt, *Das Volksleben der Neugriechen* (Leipzig 1871), 98–131; J. C. Lawson, *Modern Greek Folklore and Ancient Greek Religion* (Cambridge 1910), 130–73.

depths of the waters everywhere alike, shining goddess-children' (346–66). Elsewhere nymphs are identified as daughters of particular rivers such as the Achelous or Asopus.

Mountain nymphs have an intimate connection with mountain trees. They cause them to grow (*Il.* 6. 419 f.), or, according to the poet of the *Hymn to Aphrodite*, they themselves are born and die with the trees (260–72; cf. Pind. fr. 165, Call. *Hymn.* 4. 82–5). So they are not immortal, but they enjoy very long lives. In a Hesiodic fragment it is reckoned that the crow lives nine human generations, the stag four times as long as a crow, the raven three times as long as a stag, the date-palm nine times as long as a raven, and the Nymphs ten times as long as the date-palm.[20] A similar concept is found in the Buddhist *Jātakas*: there is a deity living in the tree and closely identified with it. The deity of a tree that has stood and been revered for sixty thousand years sees that his end is approaching when the tree is about to be felled.[21]

The Nymphs are outstandingly beautiful, and typically occupy themselves with singing and dancing (*Od.* 6. 105–8, 122 f., 12. 318; *Hymn. Aphr.* 261; *Hymn. Pan.* 3, 19–21; *Cypria* fr. 6. 6). Just as in the *Mahābhārata*, a man encountering an exceptionally beautiful female may suspect her of being a goddess or a nymph: 'Hail, Lady, whichever of the blessed ones you are that arrive at this dwelling, Artemis or Leto or golden Aphrodite . . . or perhaps you are one of the Graces . . . or one of the Nymphs who haunt the fair groves and the waters of rivers and the grassy meads' (*Hymn. Aphr.* 92–9). A century ago Greek brides were praised as being 'as lovely as a Neráïs', or as singing or dancing like one.[22]

It was the water nymphs in particular who were honoured with cults. They were on the whole considered friendly and beneficent, promoting fertility and growth, nurturing the young. But they could carry off children or handsome youths for themselves, or afflict a person with a frenzy that might be perceived either as inspiration or insanity. One so possessed was νυμφόληπτος 'Nymph-seized', in Latin *lymphatus, lymphaticus* (Varro, *De lingua Latina* 7. 87; Festus p. 107. 17 L.).

There are many stories of sexual unions between nymphs and mortal men, resulting in the birth of a child or twins, or the origin of a whole family. Sometimes it is herdsmen alone in the countryside who have such encounters (*Il.* 6. 21–6, 14. 444 f.), sometimes others (20. 384; 'Hes.' fr. 235, al.), but in any case it is the rural nymphs, those of mountains and streams, who are generally involved. The Aeacidae, on the other hand, were descended from

20 'Hes.' fr. 304. J. C. Lawson heard an abbreviated version of this piece of popular wisdom from 'an unlettered peasant in Arcadia' (as n. 19, 156–8). On the Nymphs' longevity cf. H. Herter, *RE* xvii. 1530.

21 Oldenberg (1917), 262 f.

22 Lawson (as n. 19), 133.

Aeacus' liaison with a Nereid, Psamathe, while her sister Thetis, not from choice but by Zeus' ordinance, was joined to Peleus in holy matrimony. She did not stay with him, however, after giving birth to Achilles. Such couplings are never stable.[23]

The cult of the Greek Nymphs, together with the name, spread to Italy at an early date, and their mythology and ideology were happily absorbed by the Roman poets. We must be cautious, therefore, in using Latin documents as evidence for native Italian conceptions. There were certainly individual goddesses of springs such as Numa's lover Egeria, to whom pregnant women sacrificed for an easy delivery (Festus p. 67. 25 L.), and Iuturna, *stagnis quae fluminibusque sonoris praesidet* (Virg. *Aen.* 12. 139 f.). Egeria is associated with the group called the Camenae, identified by poets with the Greek Muses but in reality the divinities of a spring, meadow, and grove below the Mons Caelius. Here we seem to have genuine Italic nymphs.

Another name is Silvanae, the feminine plural corresponding to Silvanus, god of the forest. Most of the dedications to them, however, come not from Italy but from Pannonia,[24] and they may represent Illyrian rather than Italian nymphs.

Albanian

Ancient Illyrian religion is perhaps one of the underlying sources from which Albanian legend and folklore have drawn nourishment. Albania harbours several classes of nymph-like being. There are the Jashtēshme, who live in the wooded mountains; they abduct children, who must then dance with them by night until they drop dead. There are mountain nymphs, Peris or Zânas, paradigms of beauty but dangerous creatures; they sing and dance round springs by night. There are the Shtojzvalet, male and female sprites of mountain, wood, and meadow, who have sometimes been known to marry mortals. There are also sea nymphs, and one of these too married a young man.[25]

[23] Cf. Lawson (as n. 19), 134, 'The marriage of men with Nereids not only forms the theme of many folk-stories current in Greece, but in the more remote districts is still regarded as a credible occurrence. Even at the present day the traveller may hear of families in whose ancestry of more or less remote date is numbered a Nereid. A Thessalian peasant whom I once met claimed a Nereid-grandmother, and little as his looks warranted the assumption of any grace or beauty in so near an ancestor—he happened to have a squint—his claim appeared to be admitted by his fellow-villagers, and a certain prestige attached to him.'

[24] Keune, *RE* iiiA. 116 f.

[25] For all this I am dependent on Lambertz (1973), 479, 481 f., 493 f., 497, 500, 508 f.

Germanic

Writers from the sixth century on, as noted in the last chapter, testify to the Germanic reverence for rivers, springs, and trees. Procopius (*Bell. Goth.* 2. 15. 23) reports that the people of Thule, by which is meant some part of Scandinavia, 'worship many gods and demons, celestial, aerial, terrestrial, and marine, as well as certain powers said to exist in the waters of springs and rivers'. His wording is too vague to reveal whether these powers manifested themselves in female human form. In later Germanic folklore there are water sprites of both sexes, the males being apparently more prominent.[26]

A tenth-century German source attests belief in 'agrestes feminae quas Silvaticas vocant'; they are said to show themselves at will to their lovers and take their pleasure with them, and again, as the fancy takes them, to vanish.[27] These are clearly wood nymphs, with the same erotic proclivities as we have noted in nymphs of other nationalities. There are many later stories of wood spirits forming unions with mortal men.[28]

In north Germany and Scandinavia different types of tree were under the protection of different 'mothers' or 'ladies', who received offerings and prayers and whose permission had to be asked if a tree was to be cut: the Elder-Mother or Lady, the Ash Lady, the Alder Lady. In central Germany there were tree-spirits known as Holzfräulein, Waldfräulein, Moosweiblein, and the like.[29] Their life was bound up with the life of the trees, and they could die in consequence of a woodcutter's assault.[30]

From the mass of material collected by Grimm and Mannhardt on women of the wild in Germanic lore I pick out a few further points. They can befuddle people's wits, making them lose their way in the forest or impairing their long-term sanity.[31] They can be paragons of beauty, as implied by the Old Norse phrase *fríð sem álfkona*, 'lovely as an elf-woman'. On the other hand they are sometimes hairy all over, or covered with moss or foliage. In Unter Engadin (eastern Switzerland) the sprites known as Dialen were conceived to be good-looking and amiable but to have goat's legs, like Pan.[32] In Danish legend the elf-women, who dance on the grass by moonlight, look

[26] Grimm (1883–8), 433–5, 487–99.

[27] Burchard of Worms, *Decreta* 19. 5 (*Patrologia Latina* cxl. 971c); cf. Mannhardt (1905), i. 113.

[28] Cf. Mannhardt (1905), i. 79, 88, 102 f., 109, 112, 135, 152 f.

[29] Grimm (1883–8), 432, 651 f.; Mannhardt (1905), i. 10 f., 74–86. Burchard's 'Silvaticae' may represent a vernacular name of this sort.

[30] Mannhardt (1905), i. 75, cf. 69 (a Bohemian meadow spirit), 89, 91 n. 1 (Tirol), 124; an analogous story of an elf who resided in a tree-stump, 62 f.

[31] Ibid. 108 f., 112, 126, 129.

[32] Ibid. 95 n. 1.

young and attractive from the front, but seen from behind they are hollow like kneading-troughs.[33]

Celtic

Dedicatory inscriptions from Roman Spain and Gaul bear witness to many indigenous nymph cults, the Latin *Nymphae* being qualified by various local names. Probably no sharp distinction was made between these and the collectivities of Mothers whose popularity in these countries was noted in Chapter 3.[34]

In any case we must turn to later evidence before any clearer profile emerges. Guillaume d'Auvergne, Archbishop of Paris from 1228 to 1249, wrote of people being deluded by evil spirits who appeared sometimes in the likeness of girls or women, dressed in white, in groves and among leafy trees; sometimes they visited houses and stables, carrying wax tapers, and left drops of wax on horses' manes.[35]

French folklore tells of Green Women (Dames vertes) who dwell in the woods and may sometimes be heard there singing and calling out. They appear, singly or in groups, to travellers and lead them astray, enticing them into the deepest thickets, where they persecute them without mercy and lead them a merry dance.[36]

The korrigans of Breton lore are irresistibly beautiful creatures with golden hair, living in the ancient forest of Brocéliande around wells, fountains, dolmens, and menhirs. They seduce mortal men and cause them to perish for love. The Manx *lhiannan-shee* likewise haunts wells and springs. She appears before a man, devastatingly beautiful, but unless he resists her charms she drains him body and soul. There are many Irish and Welsh stories of such supernatural females who take a mortal lover, perhaps marry him, but then leave him, often because he has broken an agreed condition, as in the Indian story of Purūruvas and Urvaśī.[37]

The Welsh fairies known as the Fair Folk (*y tylwyth teg*) are often associated with lakes, especially Llyn y Fan Fach in south Wales. They have fair hair, and are liable to claim fair-haired children as their own.[38]

[33] Ibid. 125.

[34] Vendryès (1948), 278; cf. F. Heichelheim, *RE* xvii. 1581–99.

[35] Guilielmus Alvernus, *Opera Omnia*, i (Paris 1674), 1066G, quoted by Grimm (1883–8), 287.

[36] Mannhardt (1905), i. 117–20.

[37] James MacKillop, *Dictionary of Celtic Mythology* (Oxford–New York 1998), 256, 179 f.

[38] MacKillop (as n. 37), 368

Slavonic

Slavonic reverence for 'rivers and nymphs and various other heathen powers' is already noted by Procopius (*Bell. Goth.* 3. 14. 24). Cosmas of Prague (1046–1125) wrote of the foolish people's adoration of mountain and tree nymphs (Oreades, Driades, Amadriades).[39] Mountain nymphs were widely known throughout the Balkan peninsula as *víle planinkinje* or *samovile samogorske*. Tree nymphs danced in the woods and lived in certain trees designated by the southern Slavs as *sjenovite drveta*, 'sprite-trees', which could not be cut down. These were generally oaks or limes, and they received cult attention.[40]

Water nymphs are widely attested in Slavonic lands, generally under the name of *víly* or *rusalky* or terms meaning 'goddess'.[41] They are said to be the souls of girls who died before their time. They are described as beautiful maidens with long golden or green hair, dressed in white. They sing and dance in a circle, which leaves its imprint in the long grass or as a ring of fungi. At night they make swings in the trees. They are widely thought to live in, on, or beside lakes, rivers, springs, and marshes. Some of them possess springs with curative properties, and these have prophetic powers. People bring offerings to their springs, and girls pray to them for beauty. They like young men, and may help them and protect them in battle. But they can also do harm if offended. They can send sickness, confuse men's wits, lead them away from the path, inflict heatstroke, or cause them to drown; they may also steal children.[42]

Baltic

Oliver of Paderborn, writing in about 1220, says that the Baltic peoples, before their conversion in the time of Pope Innocent III, walked in darkness and worshipped the pagan deities, 'Driades, Amadriades, Oreadas, Napeas, †Humides (Semideos?), Satiros, et Faunos'; their holy places were groves untouched by any axe, springs and trees, mountains and hills, rocks and valleys.[43] The classicizing list of rustic gods is conventional, the first three being the same as those which Cosmas (above) ascribes to the Slavs, and we

[39] *Chronica Boemorum* 1. 4; C. H. Meyer (1931), 18.

[40] Váňa (1992), 107, 122.

[41] South Slavonic **divā*; Ukrainian *bohyna*, Polish *boginka*, Czech *bohyňka*; Váňa (1992), 110 f.; U. Dukova, *Orpheus* 4 (1994), 6 f.

[42] Grimm (1883–8), 436, 492, 1406, 1595; Unbegaun (1948), 427 f.; N. Reiter in *Wb. d. Myth.* i(2). 193, 203 f.; Váňa (1992), 111 f.; E. J. W. Barber in Dexter–Polomé (1997), 6–19.

[43] Mannhardt (1936), 39; Clemen (1936), 94 f.

cannot trust it as being an accurate typology of Baltic nymphs. But it is not to be doubted that the Balts recognized beings of this character. Among the pagan deities that Jakob Brodowski enumerates under 'Götze' in his German–Lithuanian dictionary, compiled in the first half of the eighteenth century, are 'Najades: Deiwaites, Göttinnen der Brünnen und Flüssen' (*sic*).[44] *Deivâitės* means literally '(little) goddesses'. There were evidently female water-sprites to whom the term was applied in Lithuania.

Another appellation of nymph-like creatures is *Laũmės*. They are beautiful, with long fair hair, and good at spinning and weaving. They live in forests or near expanses of water and stones. They like bathing, and when sighted are usually naked. They sometimes have sexual relations with men, or even marry them, though the marriage never lasts. They can be malicious when offended. They are also in the habit of stealing children or substituting a changeling.[45]

A few of the Latvian songs refer to 'Daughters of the Sea', Jūŗas meitas, who sit on the waves and weave bright and dark shawls that represent the visual effects seen from the shore.[46] We might class them as sea nymphs, but they may be local poetic creations rather than Indo-European heritage.

ELVES, DWARFS, AND SATYRS

We turn now to the male or mixed populations of the woods and mountains. Naturally there is a wide variety of these in the folklore and mythology of different peoples. A general account of all of them would not be profitable and cannot be attempted here. We are concerned to identify distinctive motifs such as may point to genetic relationships.

Beings with elements of animal physique

One such motif is the combination of a basically anthropomorphic physique with animal features. The notion seems to be that in the half-way zone between the human and the animal worlds there exist creatures endowed with elements of both. Such are the Kiṃpuruṣas or Kiṃnaras of the *Rāmāyaṇa*

[44] Mannhardt (1936), 612; cf. Usener (1896), 89.

[45] M. Praetorius in Mannhardt (1936), 532; Usener (1896), 94; Gimbutas (1963), 197; Biezais–Balys (1973), 421 f.

[46] *LD* 30686, 34028, 30733, 30865 = Jonval nos. 513–16.

(7. 79. 22 ff.). They are half human, half animal beings who live in the mountains and attend Kubera, the ruler of the north; their name might be rendered as 'Query-humans'.

In a Greek setting we immediately think of the goat-shanked god Pan, whom we have already discussed, of the Satyrs and Sileni, and of the Centaurs. Satyrs and Sileni, who are hard to distinguish from each other, live in the wild and have the ears and tails (and sometimes legs) of horses. Sileni make love to the Nymphs in caves, as does Hermes (*Hymn. Aphr.* 262 f.). In the *Catalogue of Women* the birth of the mountain Nymphs occurs together with that of the 'good-for-nothing, prankster Satyrs' and the 'divine Kouretes, dancers who love to sport':

>]οὔρειαι Νύμφαι θεαὶ ἐξεγένοντο
> καὶ γένος οὐτιδανῶν Σατύρων καὶ ἀμηχανοέργων
> Κουρῆτές τε θεοὶ φιλοπαίγμονες ὀρχηστῆρες. ('Hes.' fr. 10a. 17–19)

The Satyrs evidently had a reputation for playing tricks on people and interfering with their property; this is in accord with their character as portrayed in the satyric drama of fifth-century Athens. The Centaurs of myth, four-legged mountain-dwellers compounded from man and horse, are also liable to be unruly, and in the poem *Kaminos* (Hom. *Epigr.* 14 = 'Hes.' fr. 302) they appear as potential wreckers of human constructions.[47]

On the other hand some such creatures possess wisdom and knowledge that is useful to mankind if they can be induced to impart it. Midas was said to have captured a Silenus who gave him a philosophical insight (Aristotle fr. 44, cf. Hdt. 8. 138). Virgil in his sixth *Eclogue* describes how two boys tied Silenus up as he lay in a drunken slumber and made him sing a cosmogony. The Centaur Chiron educated Achilles and several other heroes, and one of the Hesiodic wisdom poems purported to convey his teachings. There is a parallel story from the Tirol that can hardly be explained as an echo of Classical learning. There people told of a Wild Man who lived in a cave and who, once made drunk and so captured, taught woodcutters how to make cheese.[48]

A corrupt entry in Hesychius (σ 259) gives *Sauadai* (?) as the Macedonian name for Sileni. Whatever the true reading, the inference is that silenus-like figures existed also in Macedonian lore. Another entry (δ 713), unintelligible

[47] They gave their names to the Kallikántzari of modern Greek folklore, who have a similar destructive character, though in other respects they are more like the Satyrs or Sileni. See Lawson (as n. 19), 190–235.

[48] Mannhardt (1905), i. 112.

as transmitted, has been emended to yield an Illyrian name for Satyrs, *Deuadai*.[49] It looks like a diminutive of the inherited word for 'god'.

Augustine and others refer to hairy Gallic demons called *Dusii*, who would take human form and seduce women. The name survives in Breton *duz*, *duzik*.[50] Several figures of later Celtic folklore have goaty features: the Irish *bocánach*, a demon of the battlefield; the Manx *goayr heddagh*, a ghostly goat; the Scottish *ùruisg*, half man and half goat, and *glaistig*, half woman and half goat, a malevolent seducer who haunted lonely pools.[51]

The *lešiy* of Russian folklore is a forest goblin who can change his size at will. His head and body are covered with rough green hair; he has goat's horns, ears, and feet, and long, clawlike fingernails. Often he has only one eye. He makes his presence known by whirlwind and storm, or by his loud laughter and other strange noises. He tricks travellers in the forest into losing their way or blundering into a bog. He is also a stealer of children.[52]

Dancers and mischief-makers

There is a wider class of denizens of the wild who, without being distinguished by animal features, behave in similar ways to some who are. Dancing is one pursuit often attributed to them. Another is playing pranks on country-dwellers, stealing from them, damaging or befouling their property, upsetting churns, deluding them.

The poet of the Hesiodic *Catalogue*, as mentioned above, associated the mountain Nymphs and Satyrs with 'the divine Kouretes, dancers who love to sport'. The 'sporting' that they love (*φιλοπαίγμων*) may just be the dance, or there may be a hint of tomfoolery. Their name means simply 'Young men', and corresponds to Kourai 'Maids', a name sometimes used of the Nymphs. They faded out of the general Greek consciousness at an early date except in Crete, where they were held to live in the wooded mountain glens and protect livestock. Their rowdy dancing was on the one hand incorporated in the myth of Zeus' birth, on the other hand imitated in cult.[53]

[49] Krahe (1955–64), i. 82; Mayer (1957–9), i. 120. Note that neither *Σάτυρος* nor *Σειληνός* is a native Greek word. Krahe, *Die Sprache* 1 (1947), 37–42, argued that the former was of Illyrian origin.

[50] Augustin, *De civitate Dei* 15. 23, followed by Isid. *Etym.* 8. 103; Hincmar of Rheims, *Patr. Lat.* lxxxii. 326; Grimm (1883–8), 481 n. 2. A thirteenth-century writer, Thomas of Chantimpré, says that groves were consecrated to the *Dusii* by Prussians among other pagans: Mannhardt (1936), 48.

[51] J. MacKillop (as n. 37), 226 and under the above lemmata.

[52] Mannhardt (1905), i. 138–43; Váňa (1992), 122 f.

[53] M. L. West, *JHS* 85 (1965), 149–59, esp. 155.

More definitely mischievous and knavish, though in classical times no longer part of living folklore, were the Kerkopes and Kobaloi. The Kerkopes figured in a story about Heracles. They were brothers (two or more) who tormented people in their neighbourhood—variously located—with their monkey tricks, until Heracles caught them and carried them away. According to another legend they were turned into the apes of Pithecusae. It seems likely that they were originally a species of goblin rather than rascally humans. As for the Kobaloi, they are said to be *daimones* in the entourage of Dionysus, which suggests something like the Satyrs or Sileni. There are no particular myths about them, but in colloquial Attic κόβαλος meant an impudent rogue or trickster.

The Armenian dancing nymphs, the Parik, had male counterparts called Pay(n).[54] Having no more detailed information, I cannot say how far they are comparable to any of the Greek male sprites or to the northern Elves.

The word 'elf' is common Germanic: Norse *álfr*, Old English *ælf*, Old and Middle High German *alp* ('incubus'). A possible Indic cognate will be discussed below. In the Edda the Elves appear as one of the major categories of intelligent being beside gods (Æsir) and men, and an Old English charm against the stitch promises help *gif hit wære esa gescot, oððe hit wære ylfa gescot*, 'whether it be god-shot or elf-shot' (*ASPR* vi. 122 no. 4. 23). Snorri (*Gylf.* 17) distinguishes between *liósálfar* and *døkkálfar*, Light and Dark Elves, but this seems to be a scholarly move to resolve the contradictions in their character. They are more beautiful than humankind, and live very much longer. They are given to music and dancing, the evidence of which is to be seen in fairy rings.[55] But they play tricks, put tangles in people's hair and that of their horses, steal children and substitute changelings. They can cause physical illnesses, or turn people into halfwits.[56]

Dwarfs and manufacturers

'Dwarf' too is a Germanic word: Norse *dvergr*, Old English *dweorh*, Old High German *twerg*. In principle the Dwarfs and the Elves are separate peoples. In the *Alvíssmál*, for example, each item listed is assigned a different term in their two vocabularies. But in practice the boundary is fluid. Snorri's Dark Elves in

[54] Ishkol-Kerovpian (1986), 135.

[55] Grimm (1883–8), 449, 469, 1421 f.; Mannhardt (1905), i. 62.

[56] Grimm (1883–8), 443, 463–9, 1418–22; Mannhardt (1905), i. 62 f.; Turville-Petre (1964), 232. On elves in general cf. Grimm, 442–72; de Vries (1956), i. 257–60; Turville-Petre, 230–2.

particular are not distinguished from dwarfs (*Gylf.* 34, *Skáldsk.* 35). Dwarfs are often credited with the same kinds of antisocial behaviour as elves.

Dwarfs, however, are more especially associated with living underground, beneath rocks, and with magical craftsmanship. In Nordic myth they make all kinds of wonderful things, sometimes commissioned by the gods.[57] They can make things for men too. German legends tell of a dwarf smith or smiths who would work by night under his hill and leave finished ploughshares or other articles to be found in the morning.[58] A parallel story from the Mediterranean was recorded by Pytheas of Massalia in the fourth century BCE: Hephaestus was believed to live under Stromboli, where the roar of his furnace and the clanging of his hammers could be heard; in former days a man could leave unworked iron at the place, and the next day he would collect the sword or whatever it was that he required, and pay for the work (sch. Ap. Rhod. 4. 761–5a).

'Hephaestus' here must stand for a local smith figure, who may or may not have been a dwarf in the sense of being small of physique. Certainly there is a wider association between dwarfs and secret manufacturing or creative labour. In Latvian folklore there is a dwarf Rūķis who lives under mountains or tree roots and who comes out at night to advance the works of men.[59] The Idaean Dactyls of Greek myth were conceived as wizards who lived on the Phrygian or Cretan Mt Ida and invented iron-working ('Hes.' fr. 282, *Phoronis* fr. 2). But these mountains took their name from a word for 'timber forest', and the *ἴδαῖοι Δάκτυλοι* must originally have been the 'forest Finger-people', dwarfs no bigger than a finger who lived in the wooded hills and worked with metals.[60] Analogous names are borne by the Pygmaioi, 'Fist-sized folk', and by the Tom Thumb and Däumling of folk-tale. The Lithuanian *Barzdùkai*, dwarfs who lived underground or under elders, were according to Praetorius 'about a finger tall'.[61]

The artificer function is not altogether foreign to elves. Snorri, as we saw, regarded the dwarfs as a category of elf. The mythical smith Volund (Weland) is called 'prince of elves', as noted in Chapter 3, and the fact that one of the

[57] *Alvíssmál* 3, cf. *Vǫluspá* 48; *Ynglinga saga* 12; *Gylf.* 34, *Skáldsk.* 35; de Vries (1956), i. 254; Turville-Petre (1964), 233–5.

[58] A. Kuhn, *ZVS* 4 (1855), 96–8. A similar legend, cited by Kuhn, attached to Wayland's Smithy on the Ridgeway above the Vale of the White Horse. Someone whose horse had lost a shoe would take it there, put down some money, and withdraw for a while. When he returned the money would be gone and the horse re-shod.

[59] Biezais–Balys (1973), 438.

[60] U. von Wilamowitz, *Kl. Schr.* v(2) (Berlin 1937), 31.

[61] Cf. Grimm (1883–8), 449–51, 1412; Mannhardt (1936), 542. Albanian dwarfs too live under mountains: Lambertz (1973), 507 f.

poetic terms for the sun is *álfrǫðull*, 'elf-halo', could be taken to imply that elves made it. There is a long-standing theory that the name of the Vedic Ṛbhus, whose marvellous craftsmanship was also mentioned in Chapter 3, is cognate with *elf*.[62] The phonological equivalence is not perfect, however, as the Germanic word is an *o*-stem, not a *u*-stem, and different Ablaut grades have to be assumed in the root, **h₂elbʰ-*/**h₂l̥bʰ-*. The alternative connection of *Ṛbhú-* with Greek *Orpheus* is easier linguistically (if we posit dialect transmission), though the figures have next to nothing in common.[63]

GIANTS

The remaining category of articulate creature recognized in the *Alvíssmál* and the Edda generally, besides the Æsir, Vanir, mankind, Elves, and Dwarfs, is that of the Giants (*Iǫtnar*). Giants appear as a class also in Greek and Ossetic mythology, and individual giants in Celtic, Baltic, and Slavonic. Great size is hardly a significant unifying feature in itself, but perhaps we can identify other motifs that may suggest elements of a shared heritage.

Giants differ from nymphs, elves, and other groups that we have been considering in that they do not live in the countryside around us but in a remoter, separate region: the sprites that we are liable to see in the wild are our own size or smaller. Giants are essentially figures of story, not objects of superstitious fear, and they do not receive offerings, as nymphs and other sprites often do. They are often treated as extinct. In the stories they are always worsted, or at any rate kept in their place. They have tremendous physical strength in proportion to their size, and an aggressive, bullying nature, but no subtlety of mind.

The Nart heroes of Caucasian legend fought various enemies, among them the giants who formerly dwelt in the mountains. The land where the giants lived, according to one Abkhaz account, was encircled by a massive stone wall. They were generally conceived to be one-eyed, like the Greek Cyclopes, and indeed one of the Nart stories closely parallels Odysseus' adventure with Polyphemus.[64] This is, of course, a folk-tale with a wide distribution and not a

[62] A. Kuhn, *ZVS* 4 (1855), 109 f.; E. H. Meyer, *Anzeiger für deutsches Altertum* 13 (1887), 31–6; id., *Germanische Mythologie* (Berlin 1891), 124; Dronke (1997), 261–3; E. C. Polomé in *EIEC* 177b. Meyer compares the Ṛbhus' feat in dividing the gods' cup into four with the dwarf Eitri's forging of the gold ring Draupnir, which became nine rings every ninth night (*Skáldsk.* 35).

[63] Cf. A. Kuhn, *ZVS* 4 (1855), 114; M. Estell, *JIES* 27 (1999), 327–33.

[64] Sikojev (1985), 54–60, 322; Colarusso (2002), 163, 170 n. 1, 200 f., 362.

strong candidate for Indo-European status.[65] One-eyed giants also occur in Irish and Lithuanian tales.[66]

Hesiod (*Th.* 185) associates the birth of 'the great Gigantes' with that of the tree nymphs and the Erinyes, all sprung from the drops of blood that fell on the earth when Ouranos was castrated by Kronos. The Gigantes' bellicose nature was at once apparent, as they were in shining armour and brandishing spears. In the *Odyssey* (7. 59, 206) they are mentioned as an uncivilized and overbearing folk who belong to the same world as the Cyclopes and the peace-loving Phaeacians, dwelling somewhere in the outer regions of the earth (cf. 6. 4 f.). Later sources refer to their conflict with the gods, in which Heracles' assistance gave the gods the victory.

There are others in Greek epic myth besides the Gigantes that we must class as giants: the Cyclopes, who for Hesiod are the artificers of Zeus' thunder; the Hundred-Handers, who assisted the Olympians against the Titans (Hes. *Th.* 147–53, 617–75, 713–35); and the Laestrygones, who lived far away, close to the paths of Night and Day, and were 'not like men but like Gigantes' (*Od.* 10. 86, 120). One thing that unites these three groups, apart from their body mass, is that they all hurl huge boulders. Polyphemus hurls a couple at Odysseus' departing ship; the Laestrygonians hurl a large number down on the ships moored in their harbour; and it is with a hail of mighty rocks that the Hundred-Handers overwhelm the Titans. At Cyzicus in the Propontis there was a local legend that the massive stone blocks which formed the wall of one of the harbours had been thrown there by six-armed giants from the hills (Ap. Rhod. 1. 942–5, 989–1002).

The motif appears also in Ossetic, Celtic, Germanic, and Baltic tradition. A group of Narts on a long expedition, overtaken by night, bed down in what they take to be a cave. In the morning they find that it was the shoulderblade (or in another version the skull) of an enormous giant from a past age. They pray to God for the owner of the skeleton to come back to life, only blind so that he cannot harm them. The prayer is granted. The Narts enquire of the resuscitated ogre how the giants used to compete with one another. He invites one of them to stand on one side of the valley, and he will throw a rock at him from the other side. Soslan sets his cloak on the hillside, shouts that he is ready, and makes himself scarce. The blind giant hurls a large rock at the voice

[65] Cf. D. L. Page, *The Homeric Odyssey* (Oxford 1955), 1–20; id., *Folktales in Homer's* Odyssey (Cambridge Mass. 1973), 23–48; J. Glenn, *TAPA* 102 (1971), 133–81; R. Mondi, ibid. 113 (1983), 17–38; J. N. O'Sullivan, *Symbolae Osloenses* 62 (1987), 5–24.

[66] Dillon (1948), 46 n. 19; O'Rahilly (1946), 330 f. (the Polyphemus theme); Greimas (1992), 139. Grimm (1883–8), 1440, refers to a Norwegian folk-tale in which three trolls share a single eye, just like the Greek Graiai. Here one may suspect direct Classical influence, perhaps from Ov. *Met.* 4. 775.

and flattens the cloak. The Narts tell him that he has killed a man, which pleases him greatly.[67]

The Foawr of Manx legend are another group of stone-throwing giants. In an Eddic poem Thor recalls how he was in the east (where Giantland was located) and was pelted with stones by the sons of Svárang. The giant Hrungnir, whose story was mentioned in the last chapter, used a whetstone as a missile. In certain German and Lithuanian folk-tales giants throw stones and stone tools over great distances.[68] Many of these stories presumably served to account for particular rocks and boulders lying about in the landscape.

The Germanic giants are known to us largely from Eddic mythology, though the Norse words *iǫtunn* and *þurs* have cognates in Old English and continental German, so that the concepts they denoted must once have been common to the whole or a large part of the Germanic area.[69] The *iǫtnar* live in their own province, Iǫtunheim. They appear as a somewhat backward people, physically powerful, insensitive, and unruly. They are the prime target of Thor's hammer, which kills them off at a sufficient rate to prevent their taking over the world.

Multiple heads and limbs

Sometimes the giants are represented as having three or more heads. In the cosmogonic account in *Vafþrúðnismál* (33) their ancestor is a six-headed son of Ymir. In *Hymiskviða* Týr is disconcerted on meeting his giantess grandmother, who has nine hundred heads (8), and later in the poem (35) a crowd of giants is called 'an army of many-headed ones'. Thor slew these, and in another episode the nine-headed Thrivaldi (Bragi, *Ragnarsdrápa* 20). When the giantess Gerðr refuses Freyr's suit, his page Skírnir pronounces a series of choice curses on her, including 'with a three-headed *þurs* you shall ever live on, or else be husbandless' (*Skírnismál* 31). A *þurs* is basically a demon rather than a giant, but the distinction is not sharp.[70]

Multiple heads are a characteristic of grotesque beings in many traditions. In the last chapter we passed safely by the three-headed Indo-Iranian dragon

[67] G. Dumézil, *Légendes sur les Nartes* (Paris 1930), 146; a variant version in Sikojev (1985), 282–4.

[68] J. MacKillop (as n. 37), 211; *Hárbarðzlióð* 29. 5; *Skáldsk.* 17; Grimm (1883–8), 543–6, 1443; Greimas (1992), 139 (two giants, sometimes identified as Perkunas and his brother).

[69] See Grimm (1883–8), 519–22 (and for other Germanic terms 524–6, 1438 f.); de Vries (1956), i. 243, 252. On the Germanic giants cf. Grimm, 518–57, 1436–48; de Vries, i. 241–52.

[70] See further Grimm (1883–8), 527 f., 1440.

Viśvarūpa–Aži Dahāka and his Greek analogue Geryoneus, the many-headed Hydra, and the hundred-headed Typhoeus. The giant-like Hundred-Handers had fifty heads apiece. The Fomoire of Irish legend, who preceded the Tuatha Dé Danann, were sometimes conceived as three-headed.[71] Slavonic paganism gave a prominent place to Triglav 'Three-head' and other polycephalic figures.[72]

Such over-endowment is not limited to heads but sometimes extended to arms and trunks. Multiple arms in particular make for a more formidable antagonist, as he can wield a corresponding plethora of weapons. The Hundred-Handers' value in the Titanomachy is that the three of them can hurl three hundred rocks at once (Hes. *Th.* 715). The six-armed, rock-throwing Cyzican giants have been mentioned above. The Molione, the Siamese twins of Greek myth, are spoken of as two men, but they fought as one and were fearsome because of their double equipment ('Hes.' frs. 17a–18). Geryoneus is called 'three-headed' by Hesiod, but later poets and vase-painters gave him a triple body with six arms and legs. Saxo relates that the Danish king Fridlef berated a giant who had assumed human shape and abducted a boy, beginning 'As you are a giant, three-bodied and most invincible, and you almost reach the sky with the top of your head, . . .'. Shortly afterwards the same author recounts that the hero Starcatherus (Starkaðr), born of giant stock, had six arms until Thor tore off the supernumerary ones to make him more normal.[73] The eight-legged horse Sleipnir was sired by a stallion from Giantland (*Gylf.* 42).

By their works shall ye know them

The size and strength of giants is not deployed solely for aggressive purposes. They sometimes appear in the role of builders of mighty structures. This is the mythical explanation of striking geological features, such as the Giants' Causeway in Ireland, or of massive ancient ruins. In classical Greece the mighty walls of Mycenae and Tiryns were attributed to the Cyclopes (Pind. fr. 169a. 7, Bacchyl. 11. 77, Soph. fr. 227, Eur. *HF* 15, etc.). In Old English poems we read of *enta geweorc, enta ærgeweorc*, or *eald enta geweorc*, 'the

[71] *Togail bruidne Da Derga* 902–9 Knott.

[72] C. H. Meyer (1931), 26. 24, 33. 15, 35. 35, 41. 9, 45. 36, 49. 17, 56. 2, 62. 1; Unbegaun (1948), 411, 416, 423; Gimbutas (1971), 153 f., 160; Váňa (1992), 93 f.

[73] Saxo 6. 4. 6 p. 148 *cum sis gigas tricorpor invictissimus, | tuoque caelum paene exaeques vertice*; 6. 5. 2 p. 151; cf. Davidson (1979–80), ii. 99. Saxo's *gigas tricorpor* recalls Naevius' *bicorpores Gigantes* (fr. 8 Büchner), but Naevius probably meant 'half human, half serpent', cf. Accius, *Trag.* 307 *Pallas bicorpor anguium spiras trahit.*

(ancient) work of giants'.[74] A champion builder engaged by the Norse gods to build their fortifications turned out to be a giant (*Gylf.* 42).

In Baltic and Slavonic legend giants of a past age are cited in explanation of outsize skeletal remains and of geological features such as lakes and mountains. Latvian has the expressions *milzeņu kauli* 'giant's bones', *milžu kapi* 'giants' graveyard'. The east Slavs told of giants called *asilki* or *osilki* who uprooted trees, smashed rocks, and shaped the hills and rivers.[75]

Strange meeting

Let us return briefly to the Ossetic story of how certain wandering Narts bedded down in a giant's shoulderblade or skull, which in the dark they had taken to be a cave. I have described how they then encountered the giant himself and questioned him about giants' sports. After the rock-throwing episode they ask him further about what giants used to eat. He takes a huge fistful of earth and squeezes the juice out of it: that was the giants' food. He then rubs some of it on their brows and those of their horses, whereupon they fall into a deep sleep. On waking they pray to God to turn the giant back into a skeleton, and the Deity obliges.[76]

The tale bears a curious similarity to part of Snorri's narrative in *Gylfaginning* (45–7). Thor and Loki, with two human attendants, travel to the country of the Giants, which seems to be located in Finland. They walk all day through a great forest, and when night falls they occupy what appears to be an oddly designed hall, open at one end and with a side-chamber halfway down. In the morning Thor goes out and finds a huge giant lying asleep. He realizes that they have been sleeping in the giant's mitten. The giant, Skrýmir, wakes up and they converse. First they all have breakfast, Skrýmir from his own food and the others from theirs. They travel on together through the day and pass another night. Then Skrýmir sends Thor and his companions on to the castle Útgarðr, where the giant king Útgarða-loki has his court. (It is later revealed that Skrýmir was Útgarða-loki in disguise.) Útgarða-loki greets them and enquires what feats they can perform. A series of contests takes place, in all of which the visitors find themselves unexpectedly outclassed. The next day they

[74] *Beowulf* 2717, 2774, *Andreas* 1237, 1497, *The Wanderer* 87, *The Ruin* 2; cf. Grimm (1883–8), 534, 547–52, 1020 f., 1444, 1446; J. de Vries, *The Problem of Loki* (*FF* [= *Folklore Fellows*] *Communications* 110; Helsinki 1933), 66–78.

[75] Mannhardt (1936), 629; Biezais–Balys (1973), 428; Váňa (1992), 60, 107.

[76] In the version translated by Sikojev (cf. n. 67) the discussion of diet precedes that about sports. The giant lets Soslan drink some of the juice, and he immediately feels sated and invigorated. 'Now you won't need to eat so often', the giant remarks.

leave the castle, escorted by Útgarða-loki, who now explains that the contests were not what they seemed and that they had in fact performed frighteningly well; he is glad to see the back of them. At this, he and the castle vanish from sight.

The Norse story is much the more detailed, and it contains much that is absent from the Ossetic. But there is a common scheme. A party of adventurers from 'our' world enters Giantland, is benighted, and takes shelter in what they think to be a cave or building. In the morning they discover that it is a part or appurtenance of a giant, of a quite different order of magnitude from what the corresponding thing would be among us. The giant to whom it belongs is roused from death or slumber and dialogue ensues. The parties are curious about each other's habits and competitive abilities, which are put to the test. Finally the giant disappears and the travellers return home to tell the tale.

The story of Thor's encounter with Skrýmir also shows significant similarities with the north Russian legend of Ilya Murometz and the giant Svyatogor. These, however, are almost certainly to be explained from first-millennium contacts between the Vikings and Russia.[77] The kinship between the Nordic and Ossetic narratives seems to lie at a deeper level. It reflects, I suggest, a late, regional Indo-European tale illustrating the nature of giants.

CONCLUSION

We must now take stock and ask how much of the comparative material surveyed in this chapter can be projected back to atavistic mythologies. Do these nymphs, satyrs, giants, etc., all represent inherited concepts, or must we reckon extensively with secondary diffusion by folk-tale? If these beings had a place in the Indo-European world-view from the beginning, what was their social or poetic status? Did they rank beside the heavenly gods as recipients of cults and hymns? Did they play an equal role in stories of heroes? Or was there always a dichotomy between 'higher' and 'lower' mythology, the one sustained by bards, the other by grandmothers?

Not for the first or last time in this book, there are more questions than answers. But unanswered questions are better than unasked ones.

Pūṣan and Pan agree well enough in name and nature—especially when Hermes is seen as a hypostasis of Pan—to make it a reasonable conclusion that they are parallel reflexes of a prototypical god of ways and byways, a

[77] See N. K. Chadwick, *Folklore* 75 (1964), 243–59.

guide on the journey, a protector of flocks, a watcher of who and what goes where, one who can scamper up any slope with the ease of a goat. We do not know enough about the north European gods of roads to tell whether they were the same god in origin. If they were, that would put him back from the Graeco-Aryan to the MIE level.

With the nymphs we cannot trace any one name across linguistic boundaries. But they show such a remarkable uniformity of conception from India to the Celtic West that the hypothesis of a common Indo-European background seems unavoidable. Neither independent development nor diffusion has any plausibility as an explanation. If the Lycian Eliyãna and Wedri are genuine Luwian survivals, nymphs can be assumed not just for MIE but for PIE, though confirmation from Bronze Age evidence would be welcome.

Our elves and satyrs, goblins and giants are a more motley crew, and while we can recognize many recurrent traits, it is difficult to see so coherent an overall pattern as with the nymphs. It is unlikely that the Indo-Europeans had no concept of such creatures, but we cannot define with any sharpness of outline what their conceptions were.

One thing that does seem clear is that these were not gods to whom one prayed, sang hymns, or made offerings. One might recite spells to ward them off, as in the Atharvaveda (e.g. 1. 16; 2. 14; 4. 36 f.; 8. 6) we find incantations to banish demons and injurious spirits (*rakṣásaḥ*). They are thus in a different category from the god of ways: there are regular hymns to Pūṣan in the Rigveda and to Pan and Hermes in Greek, celebrating the deity and seeking his favour. Nymphs come somewhere in between. There are no hymns to the Apsarases in the Rigveda, and those addressed to them in the Atharvaveda are of an apotropaic character. In Greek I think there are none to the Nymphs until we come to the late, intellectual corpus of Orphic Hymns, composed in the Imperial period. On the other hand there were genuine popular cults in Greece and other countries, reflecting the belief that nymphs were resident in certain places and had a generally beneficent interest in their human neighbours.

The distinction between 'regular' hymns, crafted by professional poets on traditional metrical and formal principles, and spells and incantations, which have their own distinctive rhetoric, will be explored in the following pages.

8

Hymns and Spells

INVOCATORY HYMNS

Something was said in the first chapter about the invocatory hymn as one of the genres in which the Indo-European poet was called upon to exercise his skills. The occasion for its performance was a public ceremony, in most cases no doubt involving a sacrifice or other offering. The poet was not conducting a private devotional colloquy with the deity but engaging his or her attention on behalf of the king or patron and his family and retainers, or a wider community, and petitioning for blessings for them.

The textual evidence from which we must work is rather unbalanced in its distribution. We are fortunate in having a large corpus of early hymns in the Rigveda. It is easy to distinguish what is typical and formulaic in them from what is not. Hittite hymns are not nearly so abundant, and they seem to owe more to Mesopotamian than to Indo-European traditions, but they provide some useful points of comparison all the same.

The Avesta shows a fascinating interplay of old Iranian religious tradition and Zoroastrian renovation. The *Gāthās*, Zarathushtra's own compositions, are not hymns in the Vedic mould but songs or poems that he sang or recited at gatherings of his family and/or his followers, and in which he voiced his devotional and other aspirations. They contain nevertheless some typical hymnic elements. The Younger Avesta, less firmly imprinted with the master's personality, is also less purified of older residues.

In pre-Hellenistic Greek we have a range of material, from the Homeric Hymns, which rhapsodes used as prefaces to epic recitations and which have little religious content, to society poetry in hymn form by the elegiac and lyric poets, hymns put in the mouths of dramatic choruses, and hymns composed for local religious events and recorded in inscriptions. Later poets and prose writers had a sure ear for the old formal features of hymns and prayers and continued to echo them in appropriate contexts. Such features often appear in Latin too, clearly not as independent inheritance but taken over from

Greek.[1] Certain early Latin texts such as the Saliar Hymn, however, may represent native Italic tradition.

For the rest, the evidence that once existed is almost wholly lost. The oral literatures of ancient Europe have perished, and only the occasional scrap can be gleaned from inscriptions. It is no better with the later Celtic, Germanic, Baltic, and Slavonic traditions. There are some records of their pagan gods and mythologies, but very little information about the structures and formulae of their hymns and prayers.

Our picture, therefore, will be largely based on the Indo-Iranian and Greek evidence, with sporadic contributions from elsewhere. If it were not for these latter, our conclusions would be valid only for the Graeco-Aryan level. As it is, there are hints of wider and deeper vistas.

Calling the god

If one wishes to communicate with a distant person by telephone or e-mail, it is first necessary to enter the number or address that will direct the message to the recipient and catch his or her attention. So in a polytheist's hymn or prayer it is important at the outset to identify the deity being addressed. Often the name appears as the first word, as in RV 1. 1. 1 *Agním īḻe puróhitam*, 'Agni I invoke, the house priest'; 1. 2. 1 *Vā́yav ā́ yāhi darśata*, 'Vayu, come, beautiful one'; Y. 16. 1 *Ahurəm Mazdą̄m aṣ̌avanəm aṣ̌ahe ratūm yazamaide*, 'Ahura Mazdā the truthful, the judge of truth, we venerate'; Yt. 6. 1 *Hvarəxṣ̌aētəm aməṣ̌əm raēm aurvaṯ.aspəm yazamaide*, 'the Sun, the immortal splendour, the swift-horsed, we venerate'; *Hymn. Dem.* 1 *Δήμητρ' ἠΰκομον σεμνὴν θεὸν ἄρχομ' ἀείδειν*, 'Of Demeter the lovely-haired, the august goddess first I sing'; Cato, *De agric.* 141 *Mars pater, te precor quaesoque uti sies . . .*, 'Father Mars, I pray and request that you be . . .'.[2]

In these examples the god's name in the accusative, or an accusative second-person pronoun accompanied by the name in the vocative, is governed by a first-person verb meaning 'I (or we) call upon', or 'venerate', 'celebrate', etc., and constituting a performative utterance. There are many more examples of this pattern, with the accusative not necessarily being the

[1] Norden (1913), 145, 157. The central part of Norden's book (143–308) is the classic study of stylistic features in Greek and Latin hymns and prayers in comparison with Jewish and oriental tradition. He is not interested in the Indo-European dimension and makes no reference to the Rigveda.

[2] Cf. Hes. *Th.* 1, *Hymn. Ap.* 1, Hymn. Hom. 6. 1, 7. 1, etc.; Durante (1976), 162. 'I sing of' or 'let me sing of' is a common type of *incipit* also in Semitic hymns and narrative poems, see West (1997), 170–3.

first word, for instance RV 1. 146. 1 *trimūrdhā́nam saptáraśmim gr̥ṇīṣe ánūnam Agním*, 'the three-headed, seven-rayed one I exalt, the flawless Agni'; Anacreon, *PMG* 348. 1–3 γουνοῦμαί σ' ἐλαφηβόλε | ξανθὴ παῖ Διὸς ἀγρίων | δέσποιν' Ἄρτεμι θηρῶν, 'I supplicate you, deer-shooter, fair-haired daughter of Zeus, Artemis mistress of beasts of the wild'; *PMG* 885. 1 Πλούτου μητέρ' Ὀλυμπίαν ἀείδω | Δήμητρα, 'Wealth's Olympian mother I sing, Demeter'; similarly in Umbrian ritual, Tab. Iguv. VIa. 22 *teio subocau suboco, Dei Graboui*, 'thee I invoke, Jupiter Grabovius', and in the Gaulish curse-tablet from Chamalières, line 1 *andedíon uediíumi diíiuion risunartiu Mapon Arueriíatin*, 'by virtue of the Lower Gods I invoke Mapon Arveriatis'.[3]

In certain cases it is specified that the god is the first to be invoked, when others are to be added afterwards: RV 1. 35. 1 *hváyāmi Agním prathamám suastáye*, | *hváyāmi Mitrā́váruṇāv ihā́vase*, 'I call on Agni first for well-being, I call Mitra and Varuna hither for help'; 112. 1 *ī́ḷe Dyā́vāpr̥thivī́ pūrvácittaye*, | *Agním gharmám surúcam yā́man iṣṭáye*, 'I invoke Heaven and Earth for prior mindfulness, (then) Agni, bright blaze, to be eager in coming'; Aesch. *Eum.* 1 f. πρῶτον μὲν εὐχῇ τῇδε πρεσβεύω θεῶν | τὴν πρωτόμαντιν Γαῖαν, ἐκ δὲ τῆς Θέμιν, 'firstly among the gods in this prayer I venerate the primal prophetess Earth, and after her Themis'; Soph. *OT* 159 πρῶτα σὲ κεκλόμενος, θύγατερ Διὸς ἄμβροτ' Ἀθάνα, | γαιάοχόν τ' ἀδελφεάν | Ἄρτεμιν . . . | καὶ Φοῖβον ἑκαβόλον αἰτῶ, 'firstly invoking thee, daughter of Zeus, immortal Athena, and thy sister who holds the land, Artemis . . . and Phoebus the far-shooter I pray'. Sometimes, however, other gods are not mentioned, and the idea is just 'you are first in our thoughts', as in RV 1. 102. 9 *tuvā́m devéṣu prathamám havāmahe*, 'thee first among the gods we invoke', 8. 31. 14; Y. 29. 10, 31. 8; Theognis 1–4, 'O Lord, son of Leto, child of Zeus, never will I forget thee as I begin, nor when I cease: always I will sing of thee first and last and in between'.

This motif of 'not forgetting' to sing of the god is found twice in the Homeric Hymns (3. 1, 7. 58 f.). But it too is Vedic: RV 7. 22. 5 *ná te gíro ápi mr̥ṣye turásya*, | *ná suṣṭutím asuríyasya vidvā́n:* | *sádā te nā́ma svayaśo vivakmi*, 'I do not forget (my) praise-songs for thee the powerful one, not the eulogy for (thee) the divine, I who know: ever I proclaim thy name, self-glorious one'.

Vedic and early Greek agree further in a syntactic peculiarity that sometimes appears when two deities are invoked together. One is addressed in the

[3] Lambert (2003), 154 f. In *risunartiu* we have apparently a preposition *ri(s)* with the instrumental of *su-nartion* 'good manhood'. This may be an ancient sacral word, cf. RV 10. 104. 5 *táva sūnŕ̥tābhiḥ* 'by thy [Indra's] generosity'.

vocative, the other appended in the nominative with the copula *ca* or τε (both from *k^we): RV 1. 2. 5, 4. 47. 3 *Vā́yav Índraś ca*; *Il.* 3. 276 f. Ζεῦ πάτερ Ἴδηθεν μεδέων, κύδιστε μέγιστε, | Ἠέλιός θ', ὃς πάντ' ἐφορᾶις καὶ πάντ' ἐπακούεις; Aesch. *Sept.* 140, *Supp.* 26; Ar. *Nub.* 264 f. ὦ δέσποτ' ἄναξ, ἀμέτρητ' Ἀήρ . . . | λαμπρός τ' Αἰθήρ, σεμναί τε θεαὶ Νεφέλαι . . . | ἄρθητε, φάνητε. It is as if the one god is treated as being in the second person, and the other as in the third: 'O Vayu, hear, and (let) Indra (hear)'; a dual or plural verb normally follows.[4]

Occasionally the poet begins with a question: which god shall we honour? Or: how shall we praise him?

kásya nūnáṃ, katamásyāmṛ́tānām
mánāmahe cā́ru devásya nā́ma? . . .
Agnér vayám prathamásyāmṛ́tānām
mánāmahe cā́ru devásya nā́ma.

Whose now, of which of the immortals
do we bring to mind the dear god-name?
. . . Of Agni first of the immortals we
bring to mind the dear god-name. (RV 1. 24. 1 f.; cf. 4. 43. 1 f.)

ἀναξιφόρμιγγες ὕμνοι,
τίνα θεόν, τίν' ἥρωα, τίνα δ' ἄνδρα κελαδήσομεν;
ἤτοι Πίσα μὲν Διός, κτλ.

My lyre-mastering songs,
which god, which hero, and which man shall we resound?
Pisa belongs to Zeus, etc. (Pind. *Ol.* 2. 2, cf. fr. 29; Ar. *Thesm.* 104)

kathā́ dāśema Agnáye? kā́ asmai | devájuṣṭā ucyate bhāmíne gī́ḥ?

How should we sacrifice to Agni? What praise-song is uttered to the divine taste of him, the shining one? (1. 77. 1; cf. 43. 1, 120. 1; 4. 24. 1, 41. 1)

πῶς τάρ σ' ὑμνήσω, πάντως εὔυμνον ἐόντα;

How shall I hymn you, fit subject as you are in every respect? (*Hymn. Ap.* 19 = 207)

Praise of the god's status and powers

In most of the above examples, whether Vedic, Avestan, or Greek, the god's name is at once accompanied by honorific epithets in apposition. Further

[4] Cf. Pind. *Ol.* 10. 3 ὦ Μοῖσ', ἀλλὰ σὺ καὶ θυγάτηρ | Ἀλάθεια Διός, ὀρθᾶι χερί | ἐρύκετον ψευδέων ἐνιπὰν ἀλιτόξενον; *PMG* 884. 4 Παλλὰς Τριτογένει' ἄνασσ' Ἀθηνᾶ, | ὄρθου τήνδε πόλιν . . ., σύ τε καὶ πατήρ; Berthold Delbrück, *Syntaktische Forschungen* (Halle 1871–88), iv. 28; Renée Zwolanek, *Vā́yav índraśca. Studien zu Anrufungsformen im Vedischen, Avestischen und Griechischen* (Munich 1970).

development may take the form of one or more relative clauses, giving a characteristic structure:[5]

> śáṃsā mahā́m Índ^{a}raṃ, yásmi víśvā
> ā́ kṛṣṭáyaḥ somapā́ḥ kā́mam ávyan,
> yáṃ sukrátuṃ dhiṣáṇe vibhvataṣṭáṃ
> ghanáṃ vṛtrā́ṇāṃ janáyanta devā́ḥ;
> yám . . . ;
> inátamaḥ sátvabhir yó ha śūṣaíḥ . . .

> Praise great Indra, at whom all
> Soma-drinking tribes direct their desire,
> whom, intelligent, master-crafted, the two worlds,
> the gods bore, hammer of foes;
> whom . . . ;
> who, most mighty with his brave champions . . .
> (RV 3. 49. 1 f.; cf. 2. 4. 1; 4. 9. 1, 33. 1, 54. 1; 5. 6. 1, 16. 1, 18. 1; 6. 5. 1)

> Miθrəm vouru.gaoyaoitīm yazamaide . . .
> yim yazənte daiŋ́hupatayō
> arəzahe ava.jasəntō
> avi haēnayå xrvišyeitīš.

> Mithra of the broad pasture-lands we worship . . . [*ten more epithets*] . . .,
> whom the leaders of regions worship
> as they go off to battle
> against the bloodthirsty hordes.
> (Yt. 10. 7 f., cf. 10 f., 12 f., 17 f., 22, 25 f., etc.)

> *αἰδοίην χρυσοστέφανον καλὴν Ἀφροδίτην*
> *ἄισομαι, ἣ πάσης Κύπρου κρήδεμνα λέλογχεν.*

> Of the reverend, gold-crowned, lovely Aphrodite
> I will sing, who has been assigned the citadels of all Cyprus.
> (Hymn. Hom. 6. 1 f., cf. 10. 1 f., Hes. *Th.* 1 f., etc.)

The word order in the Avestan hymn, god's name—epithet—first-person verb—further epithets—relative clause, can be paralleled exactly in Greek, as in Hymn. Hom. 11. 1 f., 28. 1–4, 30. 1 f.; cf. Ar. *Thesm.* 1136–42.

The anaphoric series of relatives in the Vedic passage is paralleled in the formulaic eulogies of Ahuramazda in the Achaemenid inscriptions: *baga vazraka Auramazdā, hya imām būmim adā, hya avam asmānam adā, hya martiyam adā*, etc., 'a great god is Ahuramazda, who created this earth, who created that heaven, who created man,' etc. (DNa 1–3 et al.). It is found also in Hittite prayers: *ḫūmandakan udne kuis asnuskizzi, walliskanzi kuin,*

[5] Cf. Norden (1913), 168–76 (for Greek and Latin); Durante (1976), 46 f.

sallayaskan siūnas kuis sallis, utar kuēdani dassu, 'who controllest all lands, whom they constantly praise, who art greater than the great gods, whose word is strong'.[6] It is not so typical of early Greek hymns, but appears from the fifth century on, as at Soph. *Ant.* 781–4 Ἔρως ἀνίκατε μάχαν, | Ἔρως, ὃς ἐν κτήμασι πίπτεις, | ὃς ἐν μαλακαῖς παρειαῖς | νεάνιδος ἐννυχεύεις; Plaut. *Poen.* 1187 f.[7]

The virtues for which the deity is praised are of course very varied. But it is a fundamental property of gods that they have power, and it is a recurrent theme in hymns to the highest gods that their power is the greatest. 'Parmi les dieux, toi seule, déesse Soleil d'Arinna, (es) importante et grande . . . J'ajoute qu'il n'est pas de divinité plus importante et plus grande que toi' (*CTH* 376 i 31′–34′, trs. Lebrun (1980), 167 f.). 'No god, no mortal is greater than thou, Indra' (RV 6. 30. 4). 'For indeed none even in the past was ever born mightier than thou' (8. 24. 15). 'Thou alone art the king of all creation' (6. 36. 4). 'Thine is the power in heaven' (Archil. 177. 1). 'Seated under no one's rule does he exercise a lesser authority than others; he does not pay homage to the power of anyone sitting above him' (Aesch. *Supp.* 595–7). The Muses themselves, hymning Zeus on Olympus, sing of 'how far the noblest of the gods he is, and the greatest in power' (Hes. *Th.* 49).

His power resides in the thunderbolt, which is feared not only by us terrestrials but by the gods. Oceanus is the great father of all the rivers and springs, 'but even he fears great Zeus' bolt and his terrible thunder when he flashes from heaven' (*Il.* 21. 198 f.). This may have been a motif in Indo-European hymns to the thunder-god: compare RV 8. 97. 14, 'before thee all creatures, O god of the *vajra-*, (and) heaven and earth tremble in fear', with the only half-intelligible lines from the old Latin *Carmen Saliare*,

quome tonas Leucesie, prae tet tremonti
†quot ibet etinei de iscum tonarem†.

When you thunder, Leucesios, they tremble before thee,
all who . . .

Another ground for praising a deity is that only through his agency and good will certain desirable things happen. This is a rather unspecific feature, worth illustrating only where particular stylizations are involved. One such is the double negative formulation, 'not without thee (does so and so come about)'. RV 2. 12. 9 *yásmān ná ṛté vijáyante jánāso*, 'without whom the

[6] *CTH* 832. 2–4, cf. 6–9 = Lebrun (1980), 380. This is a Hittite version of an Akkadian hymn to Ištar; the Akkadian version of these lines, however, does not have relative clauses but simple predicates, see the edition by E. Reiner and H. G. Güterbock, *JCS* 21 (1967), 257 f. Parallel relative clauses also in *CTH* 383 i 5–10 = Lebrun, 310.

[7] More in Norden (1913), 171–6.

peoples are not victorious'; 2. 16. 2 *yásmād Índrād bṛhatáḥ kíṃ caném ṛté*, 'great Indra, without whom nothing'; 7. 11. 1 *ná rté tuvád amṛ́tā mādayante*, 'not without thee (Agni) do the immortals carouse'; 10. 112. 9 *ná ṛté tvát kriyate kíṃ canā́ré*, 'not without thee (Indra) is anything accomplished far off'; Hymn. Hom. 29. 4 *οὐ γὰρ ἄτερ σοῦ* | *εἰλαπίναι θνητοῖσι*, 'for not without thee (Hestia) are there feasts for mortals'; Pind. *Nem.* 7. 2 f. *ἄνευ σέθεν* | *οὐ φάος, οὐ μέλαιναν δρακέντες εὐφρόναν* | . . . *ἐλάχομεν ἀγλαόγυιον Ἥβαν*, 'without thee (Eleithyia) we see not the day, not the dark night, to obtain bright-limbed Youth'.[8]

The following strike a more personal note: RV 8. 24. 12 *nahí aṅgá nṛto tuvád* | *anyáṃ vindā́mi rā́dhase*, 'for indeed, O dancer, I find none other than thee for bounty'; *MBh.* 1. 223. 9 *na nas trātā vidyate'gne tvad anyaḥ*, 'no other protector is found for us than thou, Agni'; Y. 29. 1 *nōiṯ mōi vāstā xšmaṯ anyō*, 'I (the cow) have no herdsman other than you'; 34. 7 *naēcīm tə̄m anyə̄m yūšmaṯ vaēdā aṣ̌ā; aθā nå θrāzdūm!*, 'I do not know any such one other than you in truth; so protect us!'; 50. 1 *kə̄ mōi . . . θrātā vistō anyō Aṣ̌āṯ θβaṯcā?* 'who has been found as my . . . protector other than Truth and thee?'; Aesch. *Ag.* 163–6 *οὐκ ἔχω προσεικάσαι πάντ' ἐπισταθμώμενος* | *πλὴν Διός, εἰ τὸ μάταν ἀπὸ φροντίδος ἄχθος* | *χρὴ βαλεῖν ἐτητύμως*, 'I have nothing to compare, weighing everything up, but Zeus, if the useless burden is to be shed from my mind in very truth'. However, this cannot be called a typical motif in Greek, and if a source is to be sought, recent Graeco-Iranian contact seems a more probable solution than Indo-European inheritance.

Emphasis on the god's powers finds expression in anaphoric repetition of the second-person pronoun.

udne zik duttuskisi, tarḫuwilatar zikpat peskisi, zikpat ḫandanza anda genzū daskisi, zikpat mugawar, zikpat essatti, zikpat genzuwalas Istanus, nu genzu zikpat daskisi; ḫandanzakan antuḫsas tukpat assus, nan zikpat sariskisi.

Toi, tu ne cesses de diriger le pays, toi seul accordes la victoire, toi seul dans ton équité prends toujours pitié, toi seul, oui, toi seul donnes satisfaction à la supplication, toi seul (es) le Soleil miséricordieux, toi seul manifestes toujours de la pitié. A toi seul l'homme juste est cher et toi seul l'exaltes (*CTH* 372 i 3–10, trs. Lebrun (1980), 101).

tuvád vípro jāyate vājī́ Agne, | tuvád vīrāso abhimātiṣā́haḥ;
Vaíśvānara, tuvám asmā́su dhehi | vásūni rājan spṛhayā́yiyāṇi.
tuvā́ṃ víśve amṛta jā́yamānaṃ | śíśuṃ ná devā́ abhí sáṃ navante:
táva krátubhir amṛtatvám āyan, | Vaíśvānara, yát pitaró ádīdeḥ.
Vaíśvānara, táva tā́ni vratā́ni | mahā́ni Agne nákir ā́ dadharṣa.

[8] Cf also RV 1. 18. 7; 3. 30. 1; 9. 69. 6; Thgn. 171, Aesch. *Supp.* 823, *Ag.* 1487; more in Norden (1913), 157–9, 175, 349 f., 391 f. There are parallels too in Akkadian hymns: West (1997), 268 f.

From thee the victorious singer is born, Agni,
from thee heroes who defeat the foe;[9]
Vaiśvānara, do thou bring us
desirable treasures, O king.
Thy birth, immortal one, all
the gods cheer together as at a baby:
by thy power they attained immortality,
Vaiśvānara, when thou didst shine from thy parents.
Vaiśvānara, these great ordinances of thine,
Agni, none has (ever) challenged. (RV 6. 7. 3–5)

ὦ Ζεῦ, πάτερ Ζεῦ, σὸν μὲν οὐρανοῦ κράτος,
σὺ δ' ἔργ' ἐπ' ἀνθρώπων ὁρᾶις
λεωργὰ καὶ θεμιστά, σοὶ δὲ θηρίων
ὕβρις τε καὶ δίκη μέλει.

Zeus, father Zeus, thine is the power in heaven,
and thou dost oversee
men's deeds, wicked and lawful; thy concern,
all creatures' rights and wrongs. (Archil. fr. 177)[10]

A common predication of the deity is that whoever among mortals he favours enjoys success: 'for him whom ye two favour, Mitra and Varuna, the rain pours the sweetness of heaven' (RV 5. 63. 1, cf. 2. 25. 1–5; 5. 86. 1).

Aṣ̌i dāθre vohūm xᵛarənō
aēṣ̌ąm narąm yōi hacahi:
hubaoiδiš baoδaite nmānəm,
yeŋ́he nmāne Aṣ̌iš vaŋuhi
sūra pāδa nidaθaite.

Fortune, giver of good majesty
to those men that thou followest:
sweet-smelling smells his house
in whose house good Fortune,
the powerful, sets down her foot. (Yt. 17. 6)

[9] This recalls Hes. *Th.* 94–6, 'for from the Muses and far-shooting Apollo men are singers and citharists on earth, and from Zeus kings'.

[10] Cf. *CTH* 375 i B 5′–A 26′, 376 i 29′–56′ = Lebrun (1980), 122 f., 158 f.; RV 2. 1. 1–15; 3. 10. 1 f.; 4. 11. 3–5, 30. 1–3; 5. 8; 6. 26. 2–7; 9. 86. 28–30; 10. 153. 2–5; Yt. 10. 29f. *tūm . . . tūm . . . tūm . . .*, etc.; Thgn. 373–6, Soph. *Ant.* 787–94, Ariphron *PMG* 813, Aristotle *PMG* 842, etc. Latin examples may be due to Greek influence; material in Norden (1913), 149–60, 165, 172. We find the figure also in Lithuanian and Latvian: hymn to Pergrubius rendered in Latin by J. Maletius (1551) in Mannhardt (1936), 294 (cf. 361), *tu abigis hyemem, tu reducis amoenitatem ueris; per te agri et horti uirent, per te nemora et sylue frondent*; Jonval no. 890, 'Viens, Dieu, aide-moi | le matin à moudre le grain. | Tu as la force, tu as la vigueur, | tu as le bon conseil' (*tev spēciņis, tev varīte, tev gudrais padomiņš*); cf. no. 60.

'Fortunate is he whom the Muses love' (Hes. *Th.* 96 f., cf. *Hymn. Dem.* 486 f.). 'When men arm themselves for battle and slaughter, there the goddess (Hecate) comes and stands by whichever side she chooses to grant victory with her favour and hand them glory' (Hes. *Th.* 431–3).

Likewise, whoever honours the god, he rewards: 'him that prepares a sacrifice thou followest for well-being' (RV 5. 28. 2, cf. 2. 26. 3 f.; 3. 10. 3; 4. 12. 2; 5. 37. 4; 7. 90. 2); 'whichever of the two countries is the first to worship him . . ., to that one turns grass-land magnate Mithra' (Yt. 10. 9, trs. Gershevitch); 'to those too who till the surly grey (i.e. fish the sea), and who pray to Hecate and the strong-thundering Shaker of Earth, easily the proud goddess grants a large catch' (Hes. *Th.* 440–2).

Narrative elements

In the content too of the Greek and Vedic hymn there manifests itself a particular feature which does not seem to find analogies in other ancient cultures. In the literatures of the Near East hymnology and mythical narrative are two separate genres: the divinity is exalted in his mode of being and in his present activities and not, usually, in reference to events of the mythical past. Conversely the appeal to events of the past is one of the institutional features of the Vedic hymn, as of the Greek: the praise of the god is, so to speak, motivated historically through the more or less explicit allusion to his deeds, his origins, his relations with other gods or with men.[11]

Durante's statement about Near Eastern hymns is a little too absolute; one finds narrative elements, for example, in Psalms 89: 10, 99: 6–8, 105 f., 114, 135 f. But in principle he makes a sound point.

In certain hymns mythical matter is introduced with 'I celebrate', 'I will tell of', with the god's deeds rather than himself focalized as the object. RV 1. 32. 1 *Índrasya nú vīríyāṇi prá vocaṃ, | yā́ni cakā́ra prathamā́ni vajrī́: | áhann áhim, ánu apás tatarda*, etc., 'Indra's manly deeds I will now tell forth, the ones that the thunderbolt-god did first. He smashed the Serpent, pierced a path for the waters', etc., cf. 1. 154. 1; 2. 15. 1 (below); 10. 39. 5; Y. 45. 1 f. *at̰ fravaxšyā, nū gūšōdūm, nū sraotā . . . at̰ fravaxšyā aŋhə̄uš mainyū paourvyē, | yayå spanyå ūitī mravat̰ yə̄m aṇgrəm*, 'I will tell forth—now listen ye, now hear ye . . . I will tell forth the two Wills at the world's beginning, of whom the Liberal one speaks thus to the Hostile one'; *Hymn. Aphr.* 1 *Μοῦσά μοι ἔννεπε ἔργα πολυχρύσου Ἀφροδίτης*, 'Muse, tell me of the doings of Aphrodite rich in gold'.

Besides episodes in which a deity overcame an opponent or assisted a mortal in need, the myth of his or her birth is a typical object of narrative

[11] Durante (1976), 47 f. (translated).

reference: RV 10. 72. 1 *devā́nāṃ nú vayáṃ jā́nā | prá vocāma vipanyáyā,* 'the gods' births we will now tell forth in admiration'. Birth stories form the subject of the Delian portion of the *Hymn to Apollo*, the *Hymn to Hermes*, and the shorter hymn to Aphrodite.

A motif common to the Vedic and Greek hymns is the joy of the other gods at the new deity's birth: RV 2. 40. 2 'when these two gods (Soma and Pūṣan) were born they rejoiced'; 3. 1. 4 'the gods admired Agni at his birth'; *Hymn. Ap.* 134 f. 'all the goddesses looked on in wonder'; *Hymn. Pan.* 45 f. 'all the immortals were delighted, and especially Bacchic Dionysus'. When Zeus gave birth to Athena out of his head, 'all the immortals were struck with awe as they watched; before Zeus the aegis-bearer she sprang quickly down from his immortal head, with a brandish of her sharp javelin, and great Olympus trembled fearfully at the might of the Grey-eyed one' (Hymn. Hom. 28. 6–10). Similarly at Indra's birth 'heaven (and) earth trembled before him' (RV 4. 22. 4). The two words for 'trembled' (ἐλελίζετο, *rejata*) are perhaps cognate.[12] In the preceding verse of the Vedic hymn it is said that when Indra takes the eager *vajra-* in his arms, *diyā́m ámena rejayat prá bhū́ma*, 'heaven (and) earth he makes to tremble by his impetuousness'. Likewise Zeus nodded, in the famous lines of the *Iliad* (1. 528–30), μέγαν δ' ἐλέλιξεν Ὄλυμπον.

In the longer Homeric hymns the greater part of the poem is taken up by a long continuous narrative. This reflects the fact that they were the work of poets whose main business was narrative epic. These hymns were recited at festivals in honour of a deity, but not as part of the central religious ritual, in association with a sacrifice, when his or her praises might have been sung more intently by a chorus. In lyric hymns the narrative element is typically more allusive. The poet does not tell the story but summarizes it in a few lines with graphic images, or just refers to a part of it, the presumption being that it is known to the hearers; or if it is not, that merely demonstrates the superior learning of the poet. The story is not there for its intrinsic value as entertainment or instruction, but as a reminder of some aspect of the god's nature.

This allusive technique is also characteristic of the Vedic hymns, and probably a feature of Graeco-Aryan if not of Indo-European hymnic poetry.[13] Even where the Rishi dwells at length on a single story, as in RV 1. 32 on Indra's defeat of Vṛtra (quoted above, pp. 256 f.), it is a succession of vignettes rather than a progressive narrative.

[12] **leig*: Durante (1976), 41. Pindar changes the verb: *Ol.* 7. 38 Οὐρανὸς δ' ἔφριξέ νιν καὶ Γαῖα μάτηρ.

[13] Cf. Durante (1976), 164.

Of course several mythical events could be mentioned within the compass of one poem. If the poet chose to organize them into a series, the outcome might be what has been called an 'Aufreihlied', listing the god's accomplishments for his greater glory.[14] In the Rigveda such lists occur especially in hymns to the Aśvins (1. 112, 116–19; 10. 39) or to Indra (1. 51; 2. 15; 4. 30; 10. 48 f.). Let 2. 15. 1–9 serve as an example:

1 Now this great one's great,
this true one's true deeds will I tell forth.
At the Trikadrukas he drank of the pressed (Soma);
by it exalted, Indra smashed the Serpent.

2 In space he supported the high heaven;
he filled the two worlds (and) the air;
he made firm the earth and extended it:
this Indra did exalted by the Soma.

3 Like a dwelling he measured out the directions;
with his *vajra* he opened the river channels,
let them flow at will in their long-tracked paths:
this Indra did exalted by the Soma.

4 Surrounding the abductor of Dabhīti,
he burnt up all his weapon with kindled fire
(and) sent (D.) off with cattle, horses, chariots:
this Indra did exalted by the Soma.

5 He stopped that great Dhuni in his tracks,
he brought the non-swimmers safely across;
they emerged and went on to prosper:
this Indra did exalted by the Soma.

6 He made the Indus flow northwards by his power;
with his *vajra* he wrecked Dawn's wagon,
hewing through the speedless (wheels?) with the speedy:
this Indra did exalted by the Soma.

7 He knew where the girls were hidden,
the rejected one came to light and stood forth;
the lame one stood firm, the blind one saw:
this Indra did exalted by the Soma.

8 He cleft Vala, and the Angirases praised him;
he broke the fastnesses of the mountain;
he swept away the ramparts they had built:
this Indra did exalted by the Soma.

[14] F. R. Schröder, 'Eine indogermanische Liedform: das Aufreihlied', *GRM* 35 (1954), 179–85 = Schmitt (1968), 177–86; de Vries (1956), i. 439 f.; Schmitt (1967), 52–5, 138–41.

9 Thou didst put to sleep Cumuri and Dhuni,
smash the Dasyu, assist Dabhīti;
even the (old man) with a stick found gold:
this Indra did exalted by the Soma.

The best Avestan example of this style appears in the nineteenth *Yašt*, in the long mythical narrative about the history of the Kavi sovereignty. Part of it came to the heroic Kərəsāspa, 'who overcame the horned, horse-devouring, man-devouring, poisonous yellow monster . . . ; who killed Gandarəβa of the yellow heel, that swooped with gaping maw to destroy the material world of Truth; who killed the nine sons of Paθana, and the sons of Nivika, and the sons of Dāštayāni; who killed . . . (etc.)' (Yt. 19. 40–3).

In Greek the technique of serial allusion is adapted to more than one purpose. We have it in Zeus' recital of his own amours in *Il.* 14. 317–27, and in the passage of the *Hymn to Apollo* where the poet asks how he is to hymn the god, πάντως εὔυμνον ἐόντα:

Shall I sing of you as a wooer and lover,
of how you went to court the Azantid maid
in rivalry with godlike Ischys, Elatos' cavalier son,
or with Phorbas born of Triopas, or with Ereutheus,
or with Leucippus and Leucippus' wife,
you on foot and he on chariot—and he did not fall behind Triops?
Or of how first, in search of a place for your oracle for humankind,
you went over the earth, far-shooting Apollo? (208–15)

The chorus of Euripides' *Heracles*, lamenting the (apparently) imminent doom of Heracles' family, with himself absent and no prospect of his return, sings of his Labours in order, giving just a few lines to each:

Firstly he emptied Zeus' grove of the Lion,
and putting its tawny head over his back wrapped himself
in the dread beast's ruddy gape.
And one time the mountain-dwelling brood of wild Centaurs
he laid low with his deadly arrows, slaying them with his winged missiles:
fair-eddying Peneios is witness, and the wide untilled plains . . .
And by killing the gold-headed,
dapple-backed hind that preyed on the countryfolk
he brings lustre to the hunter goddess of Oenoe,

and so on through the series (*HF* 359–435). As with Kərəsāspa, it is not a god but a mortal hero whose deeds are celebrated here. But the recital is introduced rather formally as a praise-hymn, the chorus announcing that it proposes to sing Heracles' praises to crown his toils: ἐγὼ δὲ τὸν γᾶς ἐνέρων τ' ἐς ὄρφναν μολόντα παῖδ' εἴτε Διός νιν εἴπω | εἴτ' Ἀμφιτρύωνος ἶνιν | ὑμνῆσαι στεφάνωμα μόχθων δι' εὐλογίας θέλω (352–6). Another such recital, in the second person, appears in the cult hymn that Virgil describes as sung by the Salii in memory of Hercules' killing of Cacus (*Aen.* 8. 287–303).

It was argued in Chapter 6 that Heracles absorbed some of the mythology attached to the Indo-European storm-god, and that the story of Hercules and Cacus is a version of the same myth as that of Indra and Vṛtra. It is striking that this technique of serial allusion to mythical deeds is a feature of hymns to both Indra and Heracles. The coincidence is yet more telling when we find that their Nordic counterpart Thor is praised in the same style by tenth-century skalds:

> You broke the legs of Leikn,
> lamed Thrivaldi,
> overthrew Starkadr,
> stood over Gialpr's corpse.
>
> It hit on Keila's pate,
> Kiallandi you broke entire;
> before that you slew Lutr and Leidi,
> you made Buseyra bleed,
> you hobbled Hengiankiapta;
> Hyrrokkinn died earlier;
> yet sooner was the swarthy
> Svivor robbed of life.[15]

Perhaps all this reflects an ancient Indo-European tradition of hymns to the Storm-god.

'Hear us'

Hymns and prayers typically call upon the god or gods addressed to 'hear'.[16] We find this already in Hittite prayers, as for example in Mursili's Plague Prayers, *nusmas kuit memiskimi, numu istamasten*, 'what I am saying, hear me!'; *numu* ᵈU ᵘʳᵘ*Ḫatti* EN-*IA istamas, numu ḫuisnut*, 'Storm-god of Hatti, my lord, hear me, and save me'.[17]

In Indo-Iranian, Greek, and Messapic the traditional verb used is the local reflex of **ḱlu*, often in association with the god's name in the vocative and/or

[15] Vetrliði and Thorbiorn dísarskáld, quoted by Snorri in *Skáldsk.* 4 vv. 57–8.

[16] Schmitt (1967), 195–9; Campanile (1977), 63–5. So in some Semitic prayers: West (1997), 270 f.

[17] *CTH* 378(1) rev. 28′; (2) A rev. 21 = Lebrun (1980), 197, 208; cf. 376 A obv. 5′, 377 i 15 f., 384 ii 14 (Lebrun, 157, 181, 332).

with 'me' or 'my prayer': RV 1. 184. 2 *śrutám me . . . narā*, 'hear me, heroes'; 5. 78. 5; 6. 4. 7 *máhi naḥ śróṣi Agne*, 'hear our great (word), Agni'; 7. 62. 5; 8. 66. 12 *śáviṣṭha, śrudhí me hávam*, 'mightiest one, hear my invocation'; Y. 33. 11 *sraotā mōi*, 'hearken (ye) to me'; *Il.* 1. 37 κλῦθί μοι ἀργυρότοξε; 5. 115 κλῦθί μοι αἰγιόχοιο Διὸς τέκος Ἀτρυτώνη; Sappho 86. 5 κλ]ῦθί μ' ἄρας, 'hear my prayer'; Solon 13. 2 Μοῦσαι Πιερίδες, κλῦτέ μοι εὐχομένωι, 'Pierian Muses, hear me as I pray'; in Messapic inscriptions, as an introductory formula, *kl(a)ohi Zis.*[18] In Latin *audio* has taken over as the regular word for 'hear', and in sacral formulae recorded by Livy (1. 24. 7, 32. 6, 10) we find *audi Iuppiter.* Other verbs appear by lexical substitution in post-Homeric Greek poets: Pind. *Nem.* 7. 2 Ἐλείθυια . . . ἄκουσον, cf. Bacch. 17. 53; Aesch. *Eum.* 844 = 877 ἄιε μᾶτερ Νύξ.

Alternation between the second and third person is typical of the hymnic style, and the call for a god to hear may also appear in the third person: *CTH* 381 i 35 *numu siūnes isḫes kē uttār . . . istamasandu*, 'let the divine lords hear these my words'; RV 1. 122. 6 *śrutám me Mitrāvaruṇā hávemā́ . . . śrótu naḥ . . . Síndhur adbhíḥ*, 'hear these my invocations, Mitra and Varuna . . . ; let Indus hear us with her waters'; 5. 46. 6; 7. 44. 5 *śr̥ṇótu no daíviyaṃ śárdho, Agníḥ, śr̥ṇvántu víśve mahiṣā́ ámūrāḥ*, 'let the divine company hear us, (and) Agni, let all the enlightened buffaloes hear'; Y. 45. 6 *sraotū Mazdå Ahurō*, 'let Ahura Mazdā hear'; Aesch. *Supp.* 175 (quoted just below).

In a number of Vedic hymns the imperative 'hear' is reinforced by *sú* 'well', as in 1. 47. 2 *téṣāṃ sú śr̥nutaṃ hávam*, 'hear ye well their invocation'; 1. 26. 5 (= 45. 5; 2. 6. 1), 82. 1, 93. 1, 139. 7; 3. 33. 9; 4. 22. 10; 8. 82. 6. This idiom may strike us as a little strange, but it is exactly paralleled in Aeschylus' *Supplices*: ἀλλὰ θεοὶ γενέται, κλύετ' εὖ, τὸ δίκαιον ἰδόντες (77); ὕψοθεν δ' εὖ κλύοι (Ζεὺς) καλούμενος (175).

'Hear' implies 'hear and respond'. If a prayer is granted, it is clear that the deity did hear it. In Homer ὣς ἔφατ' εὐχόμενος, 'so he spoke in prayer', is routinely followed by τοῦ δ' ἔκλυε (Φοῖβος Ἀπόλλων, or whichever god), meaning not just that the god *heard* the prayer but that he or she *hearkened* to it and did what was wanted. We find just the same in the Russian *bylina* quoted on p. 278, where a princess prays to a river to let her ford it so that she can reach her husband, 'and the river gave ear to Marya, it let her ford it and go to her husband'.

[18] V. Pisani, *Le lingue dell'Italia antica oltre il Latino* (Turin 1953), 228–31; Haas (1962), inscriptions B. 1. 11, 48?; B. 2. 01. 1, 03. 1, 04. 1. Zis (perhaps borrowed from Oscan) is the Indo-European *Dyeus; *klaohi* or *klohi* is held to correspond to the rare Vedic *śróṣi* (Pisani), or to derive from **kleu-i̯e* (Haas, 175). The Greek athematic forms κλῦθι (singular) and κλῦτε (plural) correspond more closely to Vedic *śrudhí* and *śrótā*, though the expected forms would be *κλύθι and *κλεῦτε. See Schmitt (1967), 196 f.

'Look on us'

Less common than 'hear', but still documented on a wide front, is the appeal to the god to direct his gaze at those who seek his blessing or aid. So in a Hittite prayer to the Sun-goddess of the earth, *CTH* 371. 12′ f. *sakuwa lāk, nu āssu uttar istamas*, 'incline your eyes, and hear the good word'. From the Rigveda one may quote 3. 23. 2 *Ágne ví paśya bṛhatā́bhi rāyā́*, 'Agni, look here with great wealth'; from the Avesta Yt. 17. 15 *apa mąm apa.daiδya, frā.mąm aiβi.urvaēsayaŋuha marždikəm Aṣ̌iš bərəzaiti*, 'look here on me, show me favour, O high Fortune'; from Greek, Hes. *Op.* 9 κλῦθι ἰδὼν ἀΐων τε, 'hearken, seeing and hearing'; Aesch. *Sept.* 106–10 ὦ χρυσοπήληξ δαῖμον, ἔπιδε πόλιν . . . θεοὶ πολιάοχοι . . . ἴδετε παρθένων ἱκέσιον λόχον, 'O gold-helmed god, look, look upon your city . . . City-gods of the land, see the maidens' crouching supplication'; id. *Supp.* 79, 104, 531, 811, etc. In an Eddic poem the Valkyrie Sigrdrífa, awakened from her magic sleep by Sigurd, greets the light:

Heill Dagr, heilir Dags synir,
  heil Nótt oc nipt!
óreiðom augom lítið ocr þinig,
  oc gefit sitiondom sigr!

'Hail Day, hail Day's sons,
  hail Night and her kin!
With unwrathful eyes look on us from there,
  and give us who sit here victory!' (*Sigrdrífumál* 3)

A fifteenth-century chronicler describes a Volhynian bull-sacrifice performed to confirm a treaty. Those present smeared their hands and faces with the animal's blood and shouted '*Rogachina roznenachy gospanany*, quod interpretatur: Deus ad nos et animas [animal?] cornutum respice, iuramentum per nos promissum hodie persolutum.'[19]

'Come'

Very often the deity is implored not just to hear or see but to come, whether to take part in a religious ceremony or to provide first-hand assistance in some other need.[20] In a Luwian sacrificial ritual to rid the land of an epidemic a goat was consecrated to the god Sanda, and the master of the house, holding

[19] *Chronicon Dubnicense* ap. Mannhardt (1936), 119; Clemen (1936), 107. For Semitic parallels see West (1997), 270.

[20] Campanile (1977), 61–3; cf. West (1997), 271.

the axe, prayed 'Come, Sanda, and let the Innarawantes come with you . . . Come and eat, and we will take the oath.'[21]

A couple of examples from the many to be found in the Vedic hymns will suffice.

> Vā́yav, ā́ yāhi darśata,
> imé sómā áraṃkṛtāḥ:
> téṣām pāhi, śrudhí hávam.
>
> Vāyu, come, beautiful one;
> these Somas are prepared;
> drink of them, hear our invocation. (RV 1. 2. 1)
>
> pūrṇáṃ rátham vahethe mádhva ā́citaṃ:
> téna dāśvā́ṃsam úpa yātho Aśvinā!
>
> You ride the car full-laden with sweetness:
> on it come to the sacrificer, Aśvins! (1. 182. 2)

Cf. 1. 85. 6, 135. 2 f., 183. 5, 184. 5; 3. 58. 2; 4. 4. 1, 44. 4; 5. 83. 6; 7. 71. 2–4; 10. 15. 4 f. Sometimes the third-person imperative (or subjunctive or injunctive) is used, as in 1. 35. 10 *híraṇyahasto ásuraḥ . . . yātu arvā́ṅ*, 'let the golden-handed divinity . . . come hither'; 1. 1. 2, 5; 5. 11. 2.

There are several instances in the *Gāthās*, and others in the Younger Avesta: Y. 28. 3 *ā mōi rafəδrāi zavə̄ṇg jasatā*, 'come to my calls for support'; 29. 11 *Ahurā, nū nå avarə̄, ə̄hmā.rātōiš yūšmāvatąm*, 'Lord, now (come) down to us on account of our liberality, your followers' '; 49. 1 *Vaŋvhī Ādā, gaidī mōi, ā mōi rapā*, 'O Good Apportionment, come to me, support me'; 68. 9 'Hear our prayer, may it please you, fulfil it, come to our aid'; Yt. 10. 32 = 57 'Hear our prayer . . . come to our libations'; with third-person imperative, Y. 54. 1 'Let Airyaman the desired come (*ā . . . jaṇtū*) to the aid of Zarathushtra's men and women'.

From Greek we may quote, for example, Odysseus' prayer to Athena in the last lap of the foot-race, *Il.* 23. 770 κλῦθι θεά, ἀγαθή μοι ἐπίρροθος ἐλθὲ ποδοῖιν, 'hear, goddess, come as a good helper for my legs'; Alc. 34. 1–4 δεῦτέ μοι νᾶσον Πέλοπος λίποντε[ς, | παῖδες ἴφθ]ιμοι Δ[ίος] ἠδὲ Λήδας, | [– ∪ ω]ι θύ[μ]ωι προ[φά]νητε, Κάστορ καὶ Πολύδε[υ]κες, 'hither to me from Pelops' isle, doughty sons of Zeus and Leda, with [willing] heart appear, Castor and Polydeuces'; Anacr. *PMG* 357 ὦναξ . . . γουνοῦμαί σε, σὺ δ' εὐμενὴς ἔλθ' ἡμιν, κεχαρισμένης δ' εὐχωλῆς ἐπακούειν, 'Lord . . . I supplicate thee, come with good will and hear our acceptable prayer'.[22] Here, as in the Homeric example,

[21] *CTH* 757; Gurney (1977), 29 f. Cf. also *CTH* 422, 483 ii (trs. A. Goetze in *ANET* 355, 352).

[22] Cf. also Hes. *Op.* 2; Sappho 1. 5/25 (quoted below), 2. 1, 53, 128; Soph. *Aj.* 697, *El.* 115, *OT* 163–6, *Phil.* 829; id., *PMG* 737. 7; Anon. *PMG* 871, 934. 19, 935. 2, etc.; Norden (1913), 148; West (1978), 138.

'hear' and 'come' are closely associated, just as, for instance, in RV 5. 74. 6 *nū́ śrutám ma, ā́ gatam*, 'now hear me, come', and in a couple of the Avestan passages cited above.

In the Latvian songs too gods are asked to come.

Viens, Dieu, aide toi-même
à mener à terme le lourd travail.
Tu as, Dieu, la force, la puissance,
Tu as un esprit sage.

Pērkons allait par la mer,
la pluie tombait sur la mer.
Le laboureur priait Pērkons:
'Viens, Pērkons, en cette terre,
viens, Pērkons, en cette terre,
dans l'orge se sont flétris les germes.'[23]

The appeal to the god may be lent weight by the reminder that he has responded to similar ones in the past.[24] RV 8. 8. 6 *yác cid dhí vām purárṣayo | juhūré ávase narā, | ā́ yātam Aśvinā́ gatam | úpemā́ṃ suṣṭutím máma*, 'as in the past the Rishis have called upon you for help, O heroes, come, Aśvins, come to this eulogizing of mine', cf. 6. 35. 5; *Il.* 1. 453–5 'you heard my prayer before . . . so now too fulfil this wish for me', cf. 14. 234, 16. 236; Sappho 1. 5–25 *ἀλλὰ τυίδ' ἔλθ', αἴ ποτα κἀτέρωτα | τὰς ἔμας αὔδας ἀίοισα πήλοι | ἔκλυες . . . ἔλθε μοι καὶ νῦν*, 'but come here, if ever at another time too you heard my voice far off and hearkened . . . Come to me now too'; Soph. *OT* 165 f., Eur. *Alc.* 222–5. An old Russian harvest prayer, recorded by an Arab writer of the early tenth century, goes 'O Lord, who hast provided for us before, fulfil thy bounty for us even now'.[25]

'Come with——'

Sometimes the god directly addressed is asked to come or to act together with one or more others. The Luwian text quoted above already provides an example. In the Rigveda the accompanying deities are put in the instrumental case in comitative sense, in most cases reinforced with a word such as *sám* 'together', *sarátham* 'on the same chariot', *yujā́* 'yoked'.[26] Simple examples are 1. 1. 5 *Agnír . . . devó devébhir ā́ gamat*, 'let Agni come, god with the gods'; 1. 19. 1 *Marúdbhir Agna ā́ gahi*, 'come, Agni, with the Maruts'; 1. 6. 7 *Índreṇa*

[23] *LD* 6933, 33711 = Jonval nos. 60, 447; cf. nos. 24, 577, 667, 890 (quoted above, n. 10), 1112.
[24] Cf. Norden (1913), 151 f.; Durante (1976), 163.
[25] Ibn Rusta in C. H. Meyer (1931), 93. 32; Váňa (1992), 226.
[26] Zwolanek (as n. 4), 16–34.

sám hí dṛ́kṣase, 'so mayest thou (Sūrya) appear together with Indra'. Similarly in the *Gāthās*: Y. 28. 6 *Vohū gaidī Manaŋhā, dāidī, Aṣ̌ā, då darəgāyū*, 'come with Good Thought, give, O Truth, thy enduring gift'; 33. 7 *ā mā idūm, vahištā, ā xᵛaiθyācā, Mazdā, darəšatcā | Aṣ̌ā Vohū Manaŋhā*, 'come to me, Best ones, come, Wise One, in thine own person and confidently, with Truth and Good Thought'; cf. 50. 4, 7. In Greek the instrumental was merged in the dative, and in this usage it is typically reinforced by the preposition *σύν*: Hymn. Hom. 29. 7–11 *καὶ σύ μοι Ἀργειφόντα . . . | ἵλαος ὢν ἐπάρηγε σὺν αἰδοίηι τε φίληι τε | Ἱστίηι*, 'and you, Argus-slayer . . . be favourable and assist together with Hestia whom you love and revere'; Pind. *Pae.* 6. 1 f. *πρὸς Ὀλυμπίου Διός σε, χρυσέα κλυτόμαντι Πυθοῖ, | λίσσομαι Χαρίτεσσίν τε καὶ σὺν Ἀφροδίται*, 'by Olympian Zeus, O golden Pytho famed for prophecy, I pray you together with the Charites and Aphrodite'; *PMG* 871 *ἐλθ' ἵρ' ὦ Διόνυσε | Ϝαλείων ἐς ναὸν | ἁγνὸν σὺν Χαρίτεσσι*, 'come to the ceremony, Dionysus, to the Eleans' holy temple, with the Graces'.[27]

Some of the prayed-for visitations, if implemented, would have caused devastation on a regional or cosmic scale. At RV 7. 53. 2 Heaven and Earth are urged to come, with the whole divine race in train: *ā́ no Dyāvāpṛthivī daíviyena | jánena yātam!* And at 10. 64. 9 three great rivers: *Sárasvatī Saráyuḥ Síndhur ūrmíbhir . . . ā́ yantu*, 'let the Sarasvatī, the Sarayu, (and) the Indus come with their waves'. The instrumental *ūrmíbhiḥ* shows that it is not just disembodied river goddesses that are being invited but their waters too. One might take this as a flight of Indian extravagance, were it not that it has an exact parallel in an old Roman prayer recorded by Servius, *adesto Tiberine cum tuis undis*.[28] In the Avesta too we find a prayer for a river to come to the sacrificer (Yt. 5. 132).

Finding range and direction

It makes no difference whether the deity is near by or far away; gods hear as well, and come as readily, from any distance. 'We would voice a mantra to Agni, who hears us even from afar' (RV 1. 74. 1); 'the god Savitṛ comes from afar, banishing all difficulties' (1. 35. 3); 'if ever at another time too you heard my voice far off and hearkened' (Sappho 1. 5–7); Aesch. *Eum.* 297 'a god hears even from afar', cf. 397; the Dioskouroi 'easily rescue men from chilly death,

[27] Likewise in statements of gods' powers and activities, as Hes. *Th.* 253, 347, 444, 936, Alc. 364. 2, Pind. *Ol.* 6. 81.

[28] Serv. *Aen.* 8. 72; cf. Enn. *Ann.* 26 *teque pater Tiberine tuo cum flumine sancto*, imitated by Virgil l.c.; Eduard Norden, *Aus altrömischen Priesterbüchern* (Lund–Leipzig 1939), 178.

leaping in brightness from afar onto the forestays of firm-thwarted ships' (Alc. 34. 7–10).

The priest or singer does not know where the god is at the moment. Yet he feels that his call should carry some indication of its destination, and in the attempt to cover the alternatives he sometimes uses a formula such as 'whether you are far or near', 'come from near and far' (RV 1. 27. 3, 47. 7; 3. 37. 11; 4. 20. 1; 5. 73. 1; 8. 8. 14, 13. 15, 82. 1, 97. 4; Y. 45. 1). Often a series of possibilities is listed, creating a pattern that is documented in Hittite, Vedic, Avestan, and Greek.

> Wherever ye may be, O Cedar-gods, whether in heaven or on earth, whether on mountains or in rivers, whether in the Mitanni country or in the country of Kinza, the country of Tunip, the country of Ugarit, the country of Zinzira, the country of Dunanapa, the country of Idarukatta . . . *(and so on for ten more lines)* . . . the country of Lalha, in the Kashkean country or in whatever other countries—come ye now back to the Hatti land!

> Storm-god of Nerik, come from heaven, from earth; Storm-god of Nerik, come from the east, from the west . . . come to your festival.[29]

> If you are with Dīrghaprasadman, or if up there in the light of the sky,
> or if on the sea in the built house, come from there, O Aśvins . . .
> if today, Aśvins, in the west, if in the east you are, O givers of wealth,
> if with Druhyu, Anu, Turvaśa, (or) Yadu, I call on you: come to me!
> If you are flying through the air, O prosperous ones, or if along these two worlds,
> or if you mount your car at your inclination, come from there, O Aśvins!

(RV 8. 10. 1, 5 f.; cf. 1. 108. 7–12; 5. 60. 6; 8. 9. 12, 65. 1 f., 97. 5.) In 4. 21. 3 *ā́ yātu Índro divá ā́ pṛthivyā́*, 'let Indra come from heaven, from earth', we have a remarkably close parallel, in syntax as well as content, with the second Hittite passage quoted above, 'come from heaven, from earth' (*nebisaz daganzipaz ehuwa*).

> Even if you are, O truthful Rašnav, in the region Arəzahī, we invoke (you) . . .
> Even if you are, O truthful Rašnav, in the region Savahī, we invoke (you) . . .
> Even if you are, O truthful Rašnav, in the region Fradafšū, we invoke (you) . . .

(And so on for another twenty-six verses; Yt. 12. 9–37.)

> But whether in regions of the Libyan land
> beside the flowing Triton, her birth-river,

[29] *CTH* 483, trs. A. Goetze in *ANET* 352; *CTH* 386 (1) 7–19, ed. Lebrun (1980), 365. For other Hittite examples see *CTH* 377 i 8–10, ed. Lebrun (1980), 181; 406 i 40, ed. H. Hoffner, *Aula Orientalis* 5 (1987), 273; 716 §4–6, trs. B. J. Collins in W. W. Hallo–K. L. Younger (edd.), *The Context of Scripture*, i: *Canonical Compositions from the Biblical World* (Leiden–New York–Köln 1997), 164.

she sits with draped or walks with upright leg
to aid her friends, or like a bold commander
she reconnoitres the Phlegraean plain,
may she come: a god hears even from afar.
(Aesch. *Eum.* 292–7; cf. *Il.* 16. 514 f.; Ananias fr. 1;
Ar. *Nub.* 270–3; Anon. *PMG* 950a.)

Prayers

When the deity has been effectively invoked and lauded, it remains to ask him or her for boons. This completes a logical structure that is arguably Indo-European. The invocatory hymn to Telibinu read daily on behalf of the Hittite king exemplifies it well. Here it is in outline:

(*Summons to the god*) Now whether, esteemed Telibinu, thou art up in heaven among the gods, or in the sea, or gone to roam the mountains, or gone to the country of the enemy to battle, now let the sweet and soothing cedar essence summon thee: come back to thy temple! . . . Whatever I say to thee, hold thine ear inclined to me, O god, and hearken to it.

(*Praises, occupying about half of the whole*) Thou, Telibinu, art an estimable god; thy name is estimable among names; thy divinity is estimable among the gods . . .

(*Prayers, paraphrased*) Grant the king and queen and princes life, health, strength, long years, progeny, fertility of crops and livestock, peace and prosperity; transfer famine and plague to our enemies' lands.[30]

The proportions are very variable, depending on occasion and circumstances. If the prayer part is of a routine nature, it is often confined to the closing section of the composition; e.g. RV 1. 5. 10 'may mortals do us no bodily harm, hymn-loving Indra; as you have the power, ward off the death-blow'; 1. 6. 10, 16. 9, 116. 25, 159. 5; 3. 32. 17 = 34. 11; 4. 15. 9 f.; *Hymn. Dem.* 490–4, Hymn. Hom. 6. 19 f., 10. 5, 11. 5, 15. 9, 20. 8, 22. 7, 26. 12 f., 30. 18, 31. 17, Bacchyl. 17. 130–2, Timoth. *Pers.* 237–40.

The prayer texts that have come down to us are for the most part of a public nature. Blessings are requested not for a single individual but for a smaller or larger group: the circle of sacrificers, or the whole community or country. Individuals' prayers for themselves would not normally have been recorded and preserved unless they were of a literary or exemplary character, intended for public appreciation. Circumstances of transmission also favour re-usable prayers, that is, those asking for such general benefits as are always

[30] *CTH* 377; Lebrun (1980), 180–91.

desired rather than specific ones needed in some special situation. In some texts it is simply 'give us blessings': RV 4. 33. 11 *vásūni . . . dadhāta*, cf. 1. 15. 8; Theognis 5 ἐσθλὰ δίδου; Bacchyl. 17. 131 (quoted below).

The ancient formula 'herds and men', which was noticed in Chapter 2 under the heading 'Polar expressions', probably featured in prayers as collectivities for which protection was sought. Calvert Watkins has compared the Umbrian *ueiro pequo . . . salua seritu* (Tab. Iguv. VIa. 32, 42, al.) and the Latin variant *pastores pecuaque salua seruassis* with passages in Indo-Iranian hymns where men and cattle appear as objects of divine protection.[31]

In Greek literary prayers it is common for the speaker to remind the deity of the sacrifices and offerings he has made in the past: 'Hear me, Silverbow . . . if ever I have adorned your lovely shrine, or if ever I have burned fatty thighbones of oxen and goats for you, fulfil this prayer for me' (*Il.* 1. 37–41, cf. 8. 238–41, etc.). The Hittite kings in their prayers for deliverance from affliction emphasize their past pieties, their maintenance of temples and statues, the regularity of their offerings, and so forth. The motif is found in Akkadian and Hebrew too, and the Hittite and Greek uses of it might be accounted for as reflecting the influence of Semitic culture.[32] However, I have noted a few examples in the Indian epic: *MBh.* 8. 67. 20; *Rm.* 5. 51. 24; 6. 78. 31.

Sometimes a suppliant urges his appeal by telling the god 'this is something that lies in your power'. RV 1. 29. 2 *śácīvas, táva daṃsánā, | ā́ tū́ na Indra śaṃsaya | góṣu*, 'mighty one, thine is the power, give us, Indra, a claim to cattle'; 1. 5. 10 *ī́śāno yavayā vadhám*, 'being able, ward off from us the death-stroke', cf. 5. 71. 2; *Il.* 16. 514 κλῦθι ἄναξ, ὅς που Λυκίης ἐν πίονι δήμωι | εἶς ἢ ἐνὶ Τροίηι· δύνασαι δὲ σὺ πάντοσ' ἀκούειν, 'hear, lord, that art perhaps in Lycia's rich community, or in Troy: thou canst hear in every direction', cf. *Od.* 5. 25.[33] A Latvian example appears in a stanza quoted earlier, 'Viens, Dieu, aide toi-même | à mener à terme le lourd travail. | Tu as, Dieu, la force, la puissance, | Tu as un esprit sage.'

In certain cases the god's name or one of his titles—at least, as understood by the worshipper—itself implies his power to act in the manner desired, and this is pointed out by making an etymological play on it. RV 10. 36. 14 *Savitā́ naḥ suvatu sarvátātim*, 'Savitṛ [= Stimulator], stimulate well-being for us'; 10. 112. 10 *ráṇaṃ kṛdhi raṇakṛt*, 'create joy (of battle), O joy-creator'; Archil. 26 ὦναξ Ἄπολλον . . . καί σφας ὄλλυ' ὥσπερ ὀλλύεις, 'O lord Apollo [understood

[31] Y. 50. 1, Yt. 13. 10; AV 3. 28. 5 f.; 8. 7. 11; Watkins (1994), 652–5; (1995), 42, 210–13.

[32] West (1997), 273 f.

[33] For further Greek and Latin material cf. Norden (1913), 154, 221, and his note on Virg. *Aen.* 6. 117; West (1966), 283; a couple of Akkadian parallels in id. (1997), 273.

as "destroyer"] . . . destroy them (*ollye*) as you do destroy'; Aesch. *Sept.* 146 καὶ σύ, Λύκει' ἄναξ, Λύκειος γένου στρατῷι δαΐωι, 'and thou, lord Lykeios [understood as "wolflike"], be *lykeios* towards the enemy horde'.[34]

The worshipper or praise-singer hopes that the deity is pleased with his offering, and sometimes expresses this hope aloud, especially at the end of his hymn. RV 1. 12. 12 *imáṃ stómaṃ juṣasva naḥ*, 'be gratified with this our laudation'; 1. 73. 10 *etā́ te Agna ucáthāni vedho | júṣṭāni santu mánase hṛdé ca*, 'let these praises, lord Agni, be gratifying to thy mind and heart'; cf. 1. 10. 12, 16. 7; 4. 50. 10; Anacreon, *PMG* 357. 7 f. ἔλθ' ἡμιν, κεχαρισμένης δ' εὐχωλῆς ἐπακούειν, 'come to us and hear our favour-finding prayer'; Bacchyl. 17. 130 Δάλιε, χοροῖσι Κηΐων φρένα ἰανθεὶς ὄπαζε θεόπομπον ἐσθλῶν τύχαν, 'Delian god, be thy heart warmed by this Ceian dance and grant god-sent fortune'; Ar. *Nub.* 269–74 ἔλθετε δῆτ', ὦ πολυτίμητοι Νεφέλαι . . . ὑπακούσατε δεξάμεναι θυσίαν καὶ τοῖς ἱεροῖσι χαρεῖσαι, 'come, esteemed Clouds . . . respond, accepting our sacrifice and joying in the ceremony'; id., *Thesm.* 111, 313, 980; *Hymn. Curet.* 5 f. (refrain).

The end of the hymn is where the poet is most likely to make personal allusions to his patron or to himself.[35] The Vedic Rishis quite often identify themselves or their family in the last stanza of a hymn, as in RV 5. 1. 12, 7. 10, 22. 4, 33. 10, 40. 9, 64. 7, 81. 5; 7. 7. 7, 8. 7, 9. 6, 12. 3, etc.; 10. 63. 17, 64. 16 f., etc.[36] The Delian hymn to Apollo ended with the famous passage where the poet speaks of himself as a blind man from Chios (*Hymn. Ap.* 166–78). Bacchylides in the closing lines quoted above refers to the Cean chorus he has trained, and thus indirectly to his own provenance. He ends one of his Epinicians (3. 96–8) with a reference to himself as the 'honey-tongued Cean nightingale'. Here we are no longer in the hymnic genre, but it seems to have become a general convention that in lyric poems performed on public occasions, where the poet's personal concerns were not the main subject matter, he might refer to himself at the end or express there some personal viewpoint.[37] When Timotheus ends his citharodic nome *The Persians* with a substantial personal epilogue in which he names himself (202–36), we cannot separate this epideictic manifesto from the old Graeco-Aryan hymn tradition.

[34] Durante (1976), 153 f.
[35] Durante (1976), 182–4.
[36] Further references in Durante (1976), 183 f.; 'libro VI' in his n. 16 should read 'libro VII'.
[37] See Walther Kranz, *Stasimon* (Berlin 1933), 120–3.

MAGIC, CHARMS

Prayers are predicated on the belief that the gods are like human potentates who have the means to grant boons and may do so if asked nicely, or may decline to. Man proposes, God disposes. It is acknowledged that the outcome depends on the deity's will: RV 8. 28. 4 *yáthā vásanti devā́s, táthéd asat*, 'as the gods wish, so will it be', cf. 8. 20. 17, 61. 4; in almost identical phrasing, Y. 29. 4 *aθā nə̄ aŋhaṯ, yaθā hvō vasaṯ*, 'so it will be for us as he (Mazda) wishes'; *Od.* 14. 444 f. 'the god will grant one thing and ignore another, whatever his heart wishes'.[38]

The basic difference between a prayer and a spell, between religion and magic, is that the latter does not depend on persuasion. The incantation or ritual, if correctly uttered or performed, automatically produces the desired result. If supernatural powers are involved in bringing it about, they are not persuaded but compelled. If the magic is unsuccessful, some mistake must have been made in the words used or the actions executed. In hymns and prayers it is the content that counts, not the wording; as we have seen, new hymns were constantly being composed (until the point when the Veda became a sacrosanct text, to be memorized *verbatim*), and new prayers were made to suit circumstances. Spells and incantations, on the other hand, were esoteric knowledge, supposed to be fixed and unchanging.

Magic is no doubt a very ancient human craft, and *a priori* one might expect that the Indo-Europeans had practitioners of it. The expectation is confirmed by material to be considered in the remainder of this chapter. The practitioners would seem to have used spells and other magical techniques both for beneficent purposes such as healing or banishing evil things and for causing harm to enemies.

A survey of Indo-European magical arts might be very rewarding, but it lies beyond the scope of the present work. It would require a book to itself and more extensive research than anyone has yet conducted into the subject. All that is offered here is a review of some noteworthy points and comparisons concerning the verbal aspects.

Incantations: style and delivery

Our word 'incantation' suggests something sung or chanted, and in several Indo-European traditions similar vocabulary is used for spells as for songs. In

[38] On this motif cf. West (1997), 267.

Greek an incantation is ἐπαοιδή, ἐπῳδή, 'singing over' something or someone, and the corresponding verb is ἐπαείδω. Italic and Celtic share the root **kan-*: Latin *cano, canto, cantus, carmen* < **can-men*, all of magical incantations as well as of singing in general; Umbrian *ař̌kani kanetu* 'cantum canito' (Tab. Iguv. IV. 28); Irish *canaid* 'sings', applied often to uttering incantations. In Old Norse the ordinary word for 'song', *lióð*, can also mean a spell. Odin in *Hávamál* 146–63 catalogues eighteen magical *lióð* that he knows.[39]

Incantations are often metrical and/or marked by stylistic features such as repetition, symmetrical phrasing, assonance, and refrains.[40] Here is a Vedic example taken at random:

> asaú me smaratād íti, priyó me smaratād íti:
> dévāḥ, prá hiṇuta smarám: asaú mā́m ánu śocatu.
> yáthā máma smárād asaú, nā́múṣyāháṃ kadā́ caná,
> dévāḥ, prá hiṇuta smarám: asaú mā́m ánu śocatu.
> ún mādayata Maruta, úd Antarikṣa mādaya,
> Ágna, ún mādaya tuám: asaú mā́m ánu śocatu.
>
> Let him yearn for me, yes, my dear yearn for me, yes:
> gods, send yearning: let him burn for me.
> That he yearn for me, not I for him ever at all,
> gods, send yearning: let him burn for me.
> Send him wild, Maruts, Air, send him wild,
> Agni, send him wild: let him burn for me. (AV 6. 130. 2–4)

This is completely metrical. As an example of a non-metrical but structured incantation, full of anaphoric repetition, here is an Avestan mantra against demons:

> pāta.nō t̰biṣ̌yaṇtat̰ pairi Mazdåsca Ārmaitišca spəṇta[sca].
> nase daēvī druxš,
> nase daēvo.ciθre,
> nase daēvo.frakarš̌te,
> nase daēvo.fradāite;
> apa druxš nase,
> apa druxš dvāra,
> apa druxš vīnase.

[39] A commoner word for spell is *galdr*, from the verb *galan*, which is used of birds' singing. Cognate words are attested in Old High German and Old English for bewitching by means of spells. It has been inferred that among the Germans a special twittering or screeching voice was used for uttering incantations: de Vries (1956), i. 304 f.

[40] Cf. de Vries (1956), i. 302 f., 305–7; Gonda (1959), 220 f.; Schmitt (1967), 206–10; Watkins (1995), 197–240.

Protect us from the enemy, O Mazdā and holy Rightmindedness.
Begone, demon Lie,
begone, demon-sprung one,
begone, demon-created one,
begone, demon-established one;
away, Lie, begone,
away, Lie, depart,
away off, Lie, begone. (Srōš vāc 3; cf. Yt. 3. 7–9, 17; Vd. 20. 7)

Note the ordered increase in the length of phrases, from five to seven syllables in the first anaphoric sequence, and from five to six in the second.

Latin spells are marked by accentual rhythm, alliteration, and rhyme:

Ego tui memini: medere meis pedibus.
Terra pestem teneto, salus hic maneto
in meis pedibus.

Nouom uetus uinum bibo:
nouo ueteri morbo medeor.

Nec huic morbo caput crescat,
aut si creuerit tabescat.[41]

The old prayer to Mars recorded by Cato (*De agric.* 141), though not metrical, is formally structured, characterized by tricola (e.g. *mihi domo familiaeque nostrae*) and paired phrases, often alliterative: *uiduertatem uastitudinemque, fruges frumenta uineta uirgultaque, pastores pecuaque.* The same is true of the Umbrian sacral formulae in the Tabulae Iguvinae, as at VIb. 60 = VIIa. 49, *tursitu tremitu, hondu holtu, ninctu nepitu, sonitu sauitu, preplotatu preuiślatu.*[42]

Skírnir's curses on the giant maiden Gerðr in *Skírnismál* 25–36 give an idea of the style of Norse *galdrar.* Stanza 34 will serve as a sample:

Heyri iǫtnar, heyri hrímþursar,
synir Suttunga, siálfir ásliðar,
hvé ec fyrbýð, hvé ec fyrirbanna
manna glaum mani, manna nyt mani.

Hear, giants, hear, frost-ogres,
sons of Suttung, even Æsir folk,
how I forbid, how I forban
man-joy to the maid, man-use to the maid.

[41] Varro, *RR* 1. 2. 27, *LL* 6. 21; Marcell. *De medicam.* 8. 191.

[42] For extended stylistic analyses of these texts cf. Watkins (1995), 197–225. He translates the Umbrian phrases quoted above as 'terrify (and) make tremble, destroy (and) smash(?), fall upon (and) nullify(?), overcome (and) wound(?), trample (and) fetter' (223).

We noted in Chapter 2 the use of polar expressions, and in particular those of the type 'both X and non-X', 'both seen and unseen', to cover every possibility and leave no loophole. The idiom has a natural place in prayers and incantations; examples were quoted from the Atharvaveda, the Iguvine tablets, and Cato's prayer. Another stylistic feature arising from the same motive is the expression of a concept by a syzygy of two or three near-synonyms, as if to ensure that a solid block of semantic territory is occupied with no room for equivocation. So in the Avesta, Y. 26. 1 = 59. 18 = Yt. 13. 21 *ašāunąm . . . fravašayō staomi zbayemi ufyemi* 'the . . . Fravashis of the truthful I praise, I invoke, I sing'; 41. 1 *stūtō garō vahmə̄ṇg Ahurāi Mazdāi Aṣ̌āicā vahištāi dadəmahicā cīṣ̌mahicā ācā [ā]vaēdayamahī*, 'praises, hymns, prayers to Ahura Mazdā and best Truth we present and assign and dedicate', cf. 35. 5; in Cato's prayer, *precor quaesoque . . . uolens propitius . . . prohibessis defendas auerruncesque . . . duonam salutem ualetudinemque . . . lustrandi lustrique faciendi*. This is characteristic of Latin legal as well as hieratic style. A Nordic example is *hvé ec fyrbýð, hvé ec fyrirbanna* in the stanza quoted above.

Nine as a sacral number

I have mentioned the element of repetition, which is a means of insisting on what is being said or done and validating it as magically efficacious. Sometimes the repetition is formalized numerically, as when words have to be uttered or an action repeated three times.

Ovid, describing the ritual of the Lemuria, speaks of formulae that had to be spoken nine times (*Fasti* 5. 439, 443). The number nine, or by augmentation thrice nine, occurs often enough in Indo-European religious contexts to suggest that it was a traditional sacral quantity. Hesiod gives τρισεινάς 'thriceninth' as the correct name for the 27th day of the month. When Oedipus purifies himself at Colonus he is instructed to lay down thrice nine olive branches as an offering to the earth. Athenian seers prophesied that the Peloponnesian War would last thrice nine years, and told Nicias to wait thrice nine days following the lunar eclipse. Pythagoras is said to have spent the same period in the Idaean Cave as an initiate.[43] Several Delphic festivals were held every ninth year (eighth by our reckoning, but ἐνναετηρίς was

[43] Hes. *Op.* 814; Soph. *OC* 483; Thuc. 5. 26. 4; 7. 50. 4; Porph. *Vit. Pyth.* 17. More Greek material in W. H. Roscher, *Enneadische Studien* (Abhandlungen der philologisch-historischen Klasse der Königlichen Sächsischen Gesellschaft der Wissenschaften 26: 1, 1909). See further Hermann Diels, *Sibyllinische Blätter* (Berlin 1890), 40–3.

the official term). This sacral cycle recurs in Adam of Bremen's account of the great sacrifice at Uppsala: it took place every nine years, and nine heads of every male animal were offered.[44]

When portents appeared at Rome the pontifices declared a *novendiale*, a nine-day ritual period. In 207 BCE this was not enough, and they had thrice nine virgins go through the city singing an incantation (Livy 27. 37. 7). Varro says that the first of the spells that I have quoted from him above (*ego tui memini*) was to be recited *ter nouiens*.[45] In a poetic account of a private magical ritual an old woman binds together thrice nine threads of three colours (*Ciris* 371). In the Atiedian Brothers' ritual for Hontus Iovius the minister must at one point execute a *tripudium* nine times (*nuvis*, Tab. Iguv. IIa. 25).

There was an Old Prussian festival called *Sabarios* or alternatively *ant tryu dewinu*, 'Feast of the Thrice Nine', at which the master of the house took nine handfuls of every kind of crop that had been harvested, divided each handful into three, and threw them all in one heap. The Jesuit *Relatio* for 1600 contains an account of a Lithuanian sacrifice to the gods of the granary, in which a black sucking-pig was slaughtered, cooked, and eaten, and parts of the meal were carried into the granary together with thrice nine morsels of bread. A Lithuanian folk-tale tells how a young man who was plagued by an incubus was advised to cut down a young oak to make a wedge to block the chink by which the incubus got into his room, and to drive the wedge into place with a hammer made out of thrice nine pieces of iron. One of the Latvian songs goes 'Pour Ūsiņš je tuai un coq | aux neuf houppes de plumes, | pour que grandissent mes vaches, mes taureaux, | neuf fois plus nombreux.' Another: 'Menez votre troupeau, bergers, où vous le menez! | Menez-le dans le défrichage de Dieu: | vous ferez entrer trois génisses, | vous en ferez sortir trois fois neuf.'[46]

Nine often appears as a mystic number in Germanic myth, and in one Eddic passage an apparition of thrice nine Valkyries is described.[47] In Old Irish literature 'thrice nine' appears very frequently as a formulaic number, especially for groups of men or parties of retainers. Jocelin of Furness writes

[44] *Gesta Hammaburgensis ecclesiae pontificum* 4. 27 = Clemen (1928), 72. 4; Mannhardt (1936), 218. Dietmar of Merseburg (1. 9, quoted by Grimm (1883–8), 48) has heard report of a sacrifice in Zealand that took place every nine years and involved the immolation of ninety-nine men and the same number of horses, dogs, and cocks.

[45] *RR* 1. 2. 27. Cf. Marcell. *De medicam.* 8. 172, 10. 69, 15. 101, 23. 47, 28. 16.

[46] Mannhardt (1936), 568; 433 = Clemen (1936), 110; Schleicher (1857), 94; *LD* 30060, 28854 = Jonval nos. 700, 702.

[47] Gering–Sijmons (1927–31), i. 148; *Helgakviða Hiǫrvarðzsonar* 28. 1.

of a king who had thrice nine chariots in his train, superstitiously confident that this number would always secure him victory.[48] Heroes in battle often kill thrice nine men at one go, matching Patroclus' feat in the *Iliad* (16. 784 f.): 'three times he rushed at them . . . and thrice nine men he killed'.

Herbs

Many magical operations call for more than spells. The use of special herbs is often involved in addition. Latin poets speak of serpents being made to burst by incantations (Lucilius 575 M., Virg. *Ecl.* 8. 71, etc.), but in the *Rāmāyaṇa* (3. 28. 28) a club shattered by arrows is likened to a snake destroyed *mantrauṣadhibalaiḥ*, by the power of spells and herbs. Some of the poems in the Atharvaveda refer to or address the therapeutic herb with which a disease is to be treated. The combination of incantation and medication will be further documented below.

A mystique attaches to the culling of these potent plants. Pliny cites many special instructions on the matter: particular herbs must be picked before sunrise, at new moon, with two fingers of the left hand, without using iron, and so forth. He gives the Gaulish Druids as his authority for some of this, and European folklore provides more wisdom of the same kind.[49] By a device attested both in India and Italy, the spell itself includes a warranty of the plant's fitness for the intended purpose by stating how it was first discovered, collected, and ingested:

> suparṇás tvā́nv avindata, sūkarás tvākhanan nasā́ . . .
> Índro ha cakre tvā bāhaú . . .
> pāṭā́m Índ^a^ro ví aśnāt . . .
>
> An eagle found thee; a boar dug thee with his snout . . .
> Indra put thee on his arm . . .
> Indra ate up the *pāṭā* . . .
> (AV 2. 27. 2–4, cf. 4. 4. 1; 5. 14. 1; 6. 109. 3, 137. 1)
>
> Pastores te inuenerunt,
> sine manibus collegerunt,
> sine foco coxerunt,
> sine dentibus comederunt.

[48] *Vita S. Patricii* 5. 35f. (549B), *duxerat enim* [*rex Leogarius*] *ter nonies currus secum, quia fascinatio nugacitatis seducens cor eius persuaserat ei tali numero ubique provenire sibi omnem triumphum.*

[49] Plin. *HN* 20. 29; 21. 42, 143, 176; 22. 50; 24. 12, 103 f., 133, 170; 25. 21, 107, 145; 27. 140, etc.; Grimm (1883–8), 1195–9, 1202–9, 1673, 1676 f.

Herdsmen found you,
culled you without hands,
cooked you without fire,
ate you without teeth.[50]

The parallelism is astonishing; in both cases the herb is addressed with the statement of its history, as if to tell it that it has been exactly identified and cannot evade its duty.

Maledictions

In spells intended to harm or weaken another person two particular images of aggression appear repeatedly: binding and stabbing.

Binding spells are attested in India, Greece, and the Germanic north. In AV 4. 16, after some verses hymning the all-seeing and all-knowing god Varuna, the guarantor of justice, he is urged to apply all of his hundred fetters to the man who speaks untruth. This sounds like a general appeal for moral regulation of the world, but the last verse (9) goes

With all those fetters I bind you,
O so-and-so, of so-and-so's family, son of so-and-so [*fem.*];
and all of them in succession I assign to you.

Only the first and third verses are metrical; the second is a template to be filled in with the details of the particular person targeted. Other poems, such as AV 6. 63, 121; 7. 83, are for release from the bonds of Varuna or another deity.

Aeschylus' Erinyes sing a song with a refrain, designed to 'bind' their victim (ὕμνος δέσμιος σέθεν, *Eum.* 306, cf. 331 f. = 344 f.). This idea of binding is abundantly attested for Greek magic.[51] The one pronouncing the spell typically uses a performative first-person verb, as in the Vedic example, 'I bind (so-and-so)'.

Odin in the catalogue of his spells says 'I know a third one for when I have a great need of a fetter (*hapt*) against my enemies'; his fourth one enables him to release himself from fetters that others put on him (*Hávamál* 148 f.). The first of the two famous German incantations from the tenth-

[50] Quoted by Marcell. *De medicam.* 21. 3, cf. 28. 16; Pelagon. *Ars veterinaria* 121. 'Ate you without teeth' means 'swallowed without chewing', cf. Plin. *HN* 23. 110. I have assumed that the lines should refer to the remedy, though in Marcellus and Pelagonius they are strangely made to refer to the disease; so too in the Serbian, Russian, and Caucasian parallels adduced by Aarne (1918–20), iii. 44f.

[51] Cf. Plato, *Rep.* 364c, *Laws* 933a; Liddell–Scott–Jones, *Greek–English Lexicon* s.v. καταδέω (A) III; Gow on Theocr. 2. 3; Fritz Graf, *Magic in the Ancient World* (Cambridge, Mass. 1997), 118–25.

century Merseburg manuscript is such a releasing spell, apparently for a warrior in difficulties on the battlefield. It relates that certain women were sitting about: some were fastening fetters (*hapt heptidun*), some holding back the army, while some were pulling at the bonds to loosen them. Then: 'spring out of the bonds, escape the fighters!'[52]

The idea of stabbing by malediction is no doubt rooted in the practice of sympathetic magic and the stabbing of images of the victim.[53] It is possible that the Indo-European root *(*s*)*tig* 'pierce' had an ancient association with this, though the evidence is from comparatively late sources. In one Greek magical papyrus (*P. Mag.* 16. 15 and 64) στίξαι is used in a prayer for the victim's heart to be pierced. In the Neo-Phrygian tomb inscriptions there occurs a recurrent formula laying a curse on anyone who harms the tombs: με δεως κε ζεμελως κε Τιε τιττετικμενος ειτου, 'among gods and men by Tis(?) let him be *tittetikmenos*', which may mean 'stabbed to bits'.[54] In Gaulish the root came to mean generally 'bewitch', if it is correctly recognized in the text of the lead tablet from Larzac, *lunget-uton-id ponc ni-tiχsintor sies* 'let her release whomever they (the named sorceresses) have bewitched', and in the agent noun *an-digs* 'unbewitcher'.[55]

To ensure that the effect of the curse on the victim is comprehensive the parts of his or her body are sometimes enumerated.[56] 'With *vajra*- hundred-jointed, sharp, razor-pronged, strike at his shoulders, at his head, chop up his hair, strip off his skin, cut up his flesh, wrench off his sinews, wring his bones, strike down his marrow, undo all his limbs and joints' (AV 12. 5. 66–71). The great Paris magical papyrus describes a piece of love-magic in which a wax or clay image of the desired woman is made and various magic words inscribed on each part of it; then one must take thirteen bronze needles and stick them into different parts, saying 'I pierce your brain, N. N.—I pierce your ears.—I pierce your eyes.—I pierce your mouth.—I pierce your intestines.—I pierce your genitals.—I pierce your soles—so that you think of no one except me, N. N.' (*P. Mag.* 4. 296–328). A Latin *defixio* runs: 'Infernal Gods, I commend to you N. N.'s limbs, complexion, figure, head, hair, shadow, brain, brow, eyelids, mouth, nose, chin, cheeks, lips, word, face, neck, liver, shoulders, heart, lungs, intestines, belly, arms, fingers, hands, navel, bladder, thighs, knees, legs, heels, soles, toes'.[57]

[52] de Vries (1956), i. 321 f. This relates to the notion of the 'war fetter', to which we shall return in Chapter 12.

[53] On this topic cf. A. Audollent, *Defixionum Tabellae* (Paris 1904), lxxix f.; E. G. Kagarow, *Griechische Fluchtafeln* (*Eos* Suppl. 4, Lwów 1929), 12–16; F. Graf (as n. 51), 138–46.

[54] M. L. West, *Kadmos* 42 (2003), 78, 80.

[55] Meid (1994), 45 f.; Lambert (2003), 169, 172.

[56] Campanile (1977), 95 f.

[57] A. Audollent (as n. 53), 249 f.

Healing

A passage in the *Vidēvdāt* (7. 44; cf. Yt. 3. 6) distinguishes three types of healer: the knife-healer (*karətō.baēṣ̌azō*), the herb-healer (*urvarō.baēṣ̌azō*), and the spell-healer (*mąθrō.baēṣ̌azō*). Pindar ascribes all three techniques (but in reverse order) to Asclepius, who, he says, relieved all his patients' sufferings, 'treating some with gentle incantations, others with medicines swallowed or applied externally, while others he set on their feet by means of surgery'.[58] Darmesteter, who first noted the parallel, inferred that this triad was canonical in Indo-European medicine.

However, they should not be regarded as mutually exclusive methods. Incantations were sometimes, perhaps usually, employed in combination with hands-on therapy. We have already noted that certain Atharvavedic and Roman incantations refer to herbs whose efficacy they are designed to ensure. When the young Odysseus was gored by the Parnassian boar, the sons of Autolycus, his uncles, treated the wound and bandaged it expertly, while using incantation to stop the bleeding (*Od.* 19. 455–8). The Indian epic hero Yudhiṣṭhira, sorely wounded by arrows, is healed *mantrauṣadhābhyām*, by mantras and medicinal herbs (*MBh.* 8. 1063*. 15). The Irish mythical healer Míach (a counterpart of Asclepius, as we saw in Chapter 3) is associated with both: he re-attaches Núadu's severed hand with a spell, and after he is killed and buried 365 healing herbs grow from his grave.[59] In the *Táin* the wounded Cú Chulainn is visited by a person from a fairy mound who sings him into a three-day healing sleep. 'Then the warrior from the *síd* put plants and healing herbs and a curing charm (*slánsén*) in the wounds and cuts, in the gashes and many injuries of Cú Chulainn so that he recovered during his sleep without his perceiving it at all' (*Táin* (I) 2107–44, cf. (L) 3123, 3167–9).

AV 6. 25 is a charm against sores or skin eruptions of the neck and shoulders, 'the five and the fifty that gather on the nape areas . . . the seven and the seventy that gather on the neck areas . . . the nine and the ninety that gather on the shoulder areas . . .'. It is not clear whether the numbers are meant to be of different kinds of pustule or whatever. In any case there is a remarkable coincidence with references in German incantations to seventy-seven diseases, or in one case to 'ninety-nine and seventy-seven'.[60]

[58] *Pyth.* 3. 50–3. Cf. J. Darmesteter, *Ormazd et Ahriman* (Paris 1877), 293 n. 2; Campanile (1977), 88–91; Sergent (1995), 243 f.; Watkins (1995), 537–9.

[59] *Cath Maige Tuired* lines 133–46 Gray. It seems far-fetched to see an allusion to surgery in the manner of his death, his skull being cloven to the brain by his angry father Dían Cécht (J. Puhvel in Cardona et al. [1970], 378 f.; Watkins (1995), 539).

[60] A. Kuhn, *ZVS* 13 (1864), 128–35 (cf. 157), who illustrates the use of these and other multiples of eleven in other connections in the Veda. The Avesta speaks of 99,999 maladies (Vd. 22. 2, 6).

As in maledictions, so also in healing spells the parts of the body may be listed.

From your eyes, from your nose, from your ears, from your chin
I pull out the consumption in the head, from your brain, from your tongue.
From your neck, from your cervical vertebrae, from your discs, from your spine,
I pull out the consumption in the arms, from your shoulders, from your forearms.
From your intestines, etc. (RV 10. 163. 1–3 = AV 20. 96. 17–22, cf. AV 2. 33)

Irish prayers show the same principle in Christianized form, as in this one attributed to Mugrón:

Christ's cross over this face,
and thus over my ear;
Christ's cross over this eye;
Christ's cross over this nose.
Christ's cross over this mouth, [*and so on*].[61]

In another Vedic hymn the healing herbs are said to drive out the consumption from the sufferer in whom they 'creep on, limb by limb, joint by joint' (RV 10. 97. 12). What this means is that the disease is driven back from one organ to another until it is completely expelled. So in an Avestan purification ritual for one who has touched a dead body it is explained that successive lustrations with water, starting at the top of the head, drive the polluting demon down the body step by step until at last she is flushed out of the toes of the left foot (Vd. 8. 40–72, cf. 9. 15–26). Likewise in a Germanic charm, known in Old High German and Old Saxon versions from manuscripts of the ninth and tenth centuries; it is addressed to a worm supposed to be responsible for a malady:

Go out, worm, with your nine wormlings!
Out from the marrow to the bone,
from the bone to the flesh,
out from the flesh to the skin,
out from the skin to this shaft![62]

The belief in intrusive worms as the cause of diseases is common to many peoples. Three poems of the Atharvaveda (2. 31 f.; 5. 23) are directed against them. They all contain such pronouncements as 'I crush the worm', 'I slay you, worms'. Similarly in an Old Irish worm charm: 'I slay the creature, I slaughter the creature, I kill the creature'.[63]

[61] Gerard Murphy, *Early Irish Lyrics* (Oxford 1956), 32 (his translation).
[62] Both texts in Watkins (1995), 522 f. The Old High German version has 'the veins' instead of 'the bone'. On this theme of the ill being driven out part by part cf. also Lincoln (1986), 110–12.
[63] Watkins (1995), 521 f. Cf. Winternitz (1959), 115 f.

Legendenzauber

Some healing incantations begin in narrative mode, stating the mythical basis for the operation and so establishing its validity. This combination of myth and spell has been termed 'Legendenzauber'.[64] Here is an example from a Vedic charm against leprosy:

> The eagle was born first: | you were its bile.
> Then the Asura-woman, beaten in fight, | took form as the forest.
> The Asura-woman first made | this leprosy-remedy,
> this leprosy-destroyer. (AV 1. 24. 1 f.).

And another from one against arrow poison:

> The Brahman was born first, | ten-headed, ten-mouthed:
> he it was first drank the Soma, | he it was made the poison sapless. (4. 6. 1)

Cf. also 1. 35. 1; 2. 27; 4. 4. 1, 37. 1; 6. 30. 1, 68, 95, 113, 128. 1, 137. 1, etc.

Grimm cites a number of examples from German sources, mostly Christianized. They include a spell used by old women in Brandenburg to cure eye ailments and recorded by an eighteenth-century writer; in his Latin version it runs:

> Ibant aliquando tres puellae in via virente:
> prima noverat remedium aliquod contra suffusionem oculorum,
> altera noverat remedium aliquod contra albuginem,
> et tertia profecto contra inflammationem;
> eaeque sanabant una ratione omnia.
> —In nomine Patris, Filii, et Spiritus Sancti, Amen.

This was repeated in a raucous murmur again and again, with various gesticulations in front of the afflicted eyes.

The two Merseburg spells both belong under this heading. I have already cited the first, in which certain 'women', apparently battle-goddesses, were fastening or loosening fetters. The second refers more explicitly to pagan gods:

> Phol and Wodan were riding to the woods,
> when Balder's foal sprained his foot.
> Bechanted it Sinhtgunt, (and) the Sun her sister;
> bechanted it Friya, (and) Volla her sister;
> bechanted it Wodan as best he could.
> Like bone-sprain, like blood-sprain, like joint-sprain:
> bone to bone, blood to blood, joint to joint:
> so be they glued.

[64] Cf. Grimm (1883–8), 1247 f., 1698 f.; P. Thieme, *ZDMG* 113 (1963), 69–79 = *Kleine Schriften* (Wiesbaden 1971), i. 202–12; L. Alsdorf, *Journal of the Oriental Institute of Baroda* 13 (1974), 206 f.

The gods' incantations are to be understood as the source of the formula 'bone to bone', etc.

Many later versions of this spell have been recorded from Scandinavia and Britain (in English and Gaelic), and one each from Latvia and Russia.[65] The narrative opening is often preserved. One Swedish version still has Oden, and one from Benbecula has Bride, that is, St Brigit, who goes back to a pre-Christian goddess, but otherwise the pagan deities are replaced by Jesus. What is most persistent is the cluster of parallel phrases of the 'bone to bone' type, though with variation in the actual organs named: marrow to marrow, sinew to sinew, etc. It is attested also in Old Irish: the spell with which Míach re-attached Núadu's severed hand is given as *ault fri halt di ocus féith fri féth* 'joint to joint of it and sinew to sinew' (*Cath Maige Tuired* line 135 Gray).

Adalbert Kuhn identified a much older parallel in a passage in the Atharvaveda:[66]

yát te riṣṭáṃ, yát te dyuttám | ásti, péṣṭraṃ ta ātmáni,
Dhātā́ tád bhadráyā púnaḥ | sáṃ dadhat páruṣā páruḥ.
sáṃ majjā́ majjñā́ bhavatu, | sám u te páruṣā páruḥ,
sáṃ te māṃsásya vísrastam, | sáṃ snā́va, sám u párva te;
majjā́ majjñā́ sáṃ dhīyatām, | cármaṇā cárma rohatu;
ásṛk te asnā́ rohatu, | māṃsáṃ māṃséna rohatu.
lóma lómnā sáṃ kalpayā, | tvacā́ sáṃ kalpayā tvácam;
asthnā́ te ásthi rohatu: | chinnáṃ sáṃ dhehi oṣadhe.
sót tiṣṭha, préhi, prá drava | ráthaḥ sucakráḥ supavíḥ sunā́bhiḥ.
—práti tiṣṭhordhváḥ.

What of you is torn, what of you is broken (or) crushed,
let Dhātṛ put it auspiciously back together, joint with joint.
Together be marrow with marrow, together your joint with joint,
together your flesh's sundered part, together sinew, together your limb;
marrow with marrow together be set, with skin skin let grow;
blood with your blood let grow, flesh with flesh let grow.
Hair with hair together fit, with hide together fit hide;
bone with your bone let grow: set the severed together, O herb.
So stand up, go on, run on (as) a chariot well-wheeled, well-tyred, well-naved.
—Stand firm upright.

[65] A. Kuhn (as n. 60), 51–7, 151–4; Grimm (1883–8), 1231–3, 1694 f., 1868; Oskar Ebermann, *Blut- und Wundsegen* (Berlin 1903), 1–24 (the fullest collection of Germanic material); Carmichael (1928–59), ii. 18 f., 20 f.; iv. 214 f. Another variant appears in Peter Carey's novel *The True History of the Kelly Gang*, 82; in answer to an enquiry Mr Carey informed me that he found it in an old book of Irish popular lore.

[66] AV 4. 12. 2–6. I have adopted some variants from the Paippalāda recension (AV Paipp. 4. 15. 1–3), following Watkins (1995), 524, and made a couple of minor sandhi adjustments for the sake of the metre.

This was one of Kuhn's most famous discoveries.[67] The similarities in form and purpose between the Indic and Germanic incantations indicated, in his opinion, that they were relics of an Indo-European tradition.

We can accept this in principle, not in the sense that the Vedic hymn and the Germanic and Celtic spells are variants of a single text, but that the stylistic figure represented by 'bone to bone, blood to blood' was traditional in Indo-European healing incantations. We met this type of multiple polyptoton in Chapter 2, where it was illustrated with examples such as 'horse upon horse, army upon army, shield upon shield', and we saw that it had its place in a broader canvas of Indo-European poetic-rhetorical style; it is not something suited only to the healing of bodily organs.

As it happens, there is a Hittite–Luwian ritual text where the same figure is used in a different sort of therapeutic magic.[68] A ram was sacrificed and dismembered and the pieces arranged round the body of the human patient to draw out the sickness from each part into the corresponding part of the animal: 'head against head is arranged, throat against throat is arranged, ear against ear is arranged, shoulder against shoulder is arranged', and so on through a series of twelve down to the sole of the foot. The similarity with the Atharvavedic and European spells is only superficial, because they are not parts of the patient's own body that are being brought together. Yet after the sole of the foot the list continues, 'bone against bone is arranged, sinew against sinew is arranged, blood against blood is arranged'. These are no longer specific parts to go in a specific place. Possibly they have been added as a formulaic sequence from an incantation of the other type.

One further observation on the Vedic chant. After the healing formulae and the appeal to the herb, the patient is addressed as a man cured, in full running order like a chariot after servicing. The final, climactic phrase *práti tiṣṭhordhváḥ*, 'stand firm upright' is not metrical; it is what is said in plain prose after the incantation is complete: 'now get up, you're cured'.[69] But the words recall Pindar's verses about Asclepius setting people on their feet with

[67] A. Kuhn (as n. 60), 58–63 = Schmitt (1968), 20–5; cf. de Vries (1956), ii. 169–73; B. Schlerath in Schmitt (1968), 328–30; Schmitt (1967), 286–9; Durante (1976), 12 f.; Campanile (1977), 91–3; id. (1990b), 70 f.; K. G. Zysk in *Perspectives on Indo-European Language, Culture and Religion. Studies in Honor of Edgar C. Polomé*, ii (*JIESM* 9; McLean, VA 1992), 321–36; Watkins (1995), 523 f., 532.

[68] *CTH* 760 (1) 1 and 2; Manfred Hutter, *Behexung, Entsühnung und Heilung* (Freiburg i. d. Schweiz–Göttingen 1988), 32 f.; G. Beckman, *Orientalia* 59 (1990), 35 f., 45; cf. Watkins (1995), 249 f.

[69] The Paippalāda recension (4. 15. 7) has a somewhat different, fully metrical version: *rathaḥ sucakraḥ supavir yathaiti* | *sukhaḥ sunābhiḥ, prati tiṣṭha evam*, 'as goes a chariot well-wheeled, well-tyred, well-hubbed, well-naved, so stand firm'.

his incantations, medicines, and surgery: ἔστασεν ὀρθούς (*Pyth.* 3. 53), the same lexical elements as in *tiṣṭha urdhváḥ*. That the same words are used in Vedic and Greek for '(cause to) stand upright' is a trivial fact. What is much more interesting is that in both traditions the phrase is used as the expression of successful healing.

9

Cosmos and Canon

If chapters had subtitles, this one's would be something like 'Indo-European perceptions of the world, and their codification'. In the first part I deal with cosmology and cosmogony; in the second part with the forms of expression in which beliefs and opinions on these matters were typically encapsulated—not articulated poetic compositions but catechisms, proverbs, riddles, and the like.

COSMOLOGY

Heaven and earth

We saw in Chapters 3 and 4 that there was a fundamental opposition between celestials (gods) and terrestrials (humans), and that Heaven and Earth were paired as deities. Similarly heaven and earth are regularly coupled as a polar expression of the world about us. In Vedic they combine in the *dvandva* compound *dyā́vākṣā́mā* (RV 1. 35. 9, 52. 14, 61. 8, al.) or *dyā́vābhū́mī* (10. 65. 4, 81. 3). In Hittite *nēbis dēgan(na)* 'heaven (and) earth' is often used for 'the universe'; for example the god Wasezzili is told *nēbis dēgann-a* [*ḫarsi*], 'you hold heaven and earth'.[1] The Armenian fragment about the birth of Vahagn begins 'Heaven was in labour, earth was in labour', before adding 'the purple sea too was in labour', the sea being where the flame appeared that produced the divine hero.

Often the complementary terms are amplified to 'the heaven above' and/or 'the earth below'. So in Hittite texts: *nuza sēr nēbis sāit, katanma dēgan sāit*, 'the sky above was angry, the earth below was angry'.[2] Zarathushtra wonders,

[1] *CTH* 733, *KUB* 8. 41 ii 6 (E. Laroche, *JCS* 1 (1947), 187).

[2] *CTH* 327, *KUB* 7. 41 i 56 f., cf. iii 27 f. (H. Otten, *ZA* 54 (1961), 120, 130). Likewise in Akkadian, *Enūma eliš* 1. 1 f. 'When on high the heavens were unnamed, | (and) below, the earth unmentioned by name'.

kasnā dərətā zą̄mcā adə̄ nabåscā | avapastōiš? 'Who holds the earth below and the heavens from falling?' (Y. 44. 4). In Greek epic we find the formula γαῖα καὶ οὐρανὸς εὐρὺς ὕπερθεν, 'earth and broad heaven above'. In the Germanic poetic tradition the word for heaven was prefixed with *up-* 'above' to make it alliterate conveniently with 'earth';[3] this forms one of the most widely attested formulae of Germanic verse, as in the Eddic poems, *Vǫluspá* 3. 5 f. *iǫrð fannz æva né upphiminn*, cf. *Vafþrúðnismál* 20. 4 f., *Þrymskviða* 2. 6 f., *Oddrúnargrátr* 17. 5 f.; on the Swedish rune-stone from Skarpåker, *iarþ s<k>al rifna uk ubhimin*; 'earth shall be riven and heaven above'; in the Wessobrunn prayer, *ero ni was noh ûfhimil*; in the Old Saxon *Hêliand* (2886) *erda endi uphimil*; in Old English, *eorðan ic bidde and upheofon* (*ASPR* vi. 117. 29, cf. *Andreas* 799, *Crist III* 968, *Psalms* 101. 22). Conchobar in the *Táin* ((I) 3448) swears by 'the sea before them, the sky above them, the earth beneath them'.

An idiom characteristic of Indo-Iranian, but also found in Old English, is the addition of deictic pronouns: 'this earth, that heaven'. So in the Rigveda, *imé dyā́vāpṛthivī́*, 'this heaven and earth' (4. 56. 3); *iyáṃ dyaúḥ, pṛthivī́ mahī́*, 'this sky, the great earth' (8. 40. 4); in the Avesta, *aiŋ̊håsca zəmō avaiŋ̊heca ašnō*, 'of this earth and that sky' (Y. 1. 16); *imą̄mca zą̄m . . . aomca asmanəm* (Yt. 13. 153). The Achaemenid inscriptions proclaim the greatness of Auramazdā, *hya imām būmim adā, hya avam asmānam adā*, 'who created this earth, who created that sky' (DNa 1, DSe 1, etc.). In Old English poetry we find *þisne middangeard* 'this middle enclosure', i.e. the earth (*Beowulf* 75, 1771); *on þysse eorðan* (*Maxims B* 2); *on þisse foldan* (*Solomon and Saturn B* 298).

For the whole universe the Vedic poets use the phrase 'all this' or 'this whole': *víśvam idám* (RV 1. 98. 1; 10. 58. 10); *víśvā tā́* (2. 24. 11); *sárvam . . . idám* (10. 129. 3); *idáṃ sárvam* (AV 10. 8. 6). Sometimes it is expanded to 'all this that moves', *víśvam idáṃ jágat* (RV 8. 40. 4, AV 6. 44. 1 = 77. 1), 'this whole, what has been and what is to be', *idáṃ sárvaṃ yád bhūtáṃ yác ca bháviyam* (RV 10. 90. 2), or 'all this, whatever is on the earth', *idám víśvam . . . yát kíṃ ca pṛthivyā́ ádhi* (5. 83. 9); similarly in the Avesta, 'all this that is between earth and heaven', *vīspəm imat̰ . . . yat̰ aṇtarə zą̄m asmanəmca* (Yt. 10. 95). Corresponding expressions are used by early Greek philosophers and poets and by Plato: τάδε πάντα 'all this' (Xenophanes B 27, Heraclitus B 64, Empedocles B 35. 5, cf. Aesch. *Cho.* 985, fr. 70. 2); τάδε (Parmenides B 19. 1); τοῦτο τὸ πᾶν (Emped. B 17. 32); τὰ νῦν ἐσορῶμεν ἅπαντα (id. B 38.

[3] Meid (1991), 20. Any vowel alliterates with any other, including Norse *io* or *ia* (*jo*, *ja*) < *e. On the Germanic formula see L. Lönnroth in Ursula Dronke (ed.), *Speculum Norroenum* (Odense 1981), 310–27.

2); τὸν κόσμον τόνδε 'this set-up' (Heraclitus B 30); τὸ ὅλον τοῦτο (Pl. *Gorg.* 508a); τὸ πᾶν τόδε (id. *Tim.* 29d, al.).[4]

Stony skies

Alcman and other Greek poets refer to an obscure figure Akmon as the father of Ouranos, the personified Heaven.[5] Normally ἄκμων means an anvil; it can also signify the head of a battering-ram, or in Cypriot speech a pestle, so in each case a block of stone or metal designed to withstand a battering. The cognate word in other languages means 'stone': Vedic *áśman-*, Avestan *asman-*, Lithuanian *akmuõ*. But in Avestan *asman-* and its synonym *asan-* (Vedic *áśan-*) also have the meaning 'heaven', as do *asman-* in Old Persian and related forms in Middle Iranian dialects.[6] In the view of some scholars Germanic **hemena-* (from which come Gothic *himins*, Old English *heofon*, etc.) derives from the same proto-form.[7] The inference has been drawn 'that Indo-European **h₂eḱmōn* meant both "stone" and "heaven", and . . . that this was no mere homophony but that the notion of stone sky was part of the Indo-European world view'.[8]

Certainly there is nothing improbable in an ancient people's having believed in a solid firmament. There was a Babylonian concept of three heavens made of different semi-precious stones, and there are hints of a metallic sky in the Hebrew Genesis and the Younger Avesta.[9] In Homeric formula the sky is of bronze (χάλκεος, πολύχαλκος) or iron (σιδήρεος). These may be Bronze and Iron Age modifications of the more primitive conception of a stone sky.

One source of the idea may have been the observation or delusion that certain stones had fallen from the sky. We noted in Chapter 6 the widespread belief that they come down with the thunder and lightning. The word *áśman-* is used among others of Indra's weapon, and in Lithuania the

[4] See further West (1971), 196, 243.

[5] Alcm. *PMGF* 61, cf. Hes. fr. [389], etc.; Pfeiffer on Call. fr. 498; V. J. Matthews on Antim. fr. 51.

[6] H. W. Bailey, *Zoroastrian Problems in the Ninth-Century Books* (Oxford 1943), 125.

[7] From **ḱemen-o-*, built on *(*h₂*)*ḱmen-*. Cf. R. Wachter, *HS* 110 (1997), 17 f.; M. C. Beckwith, *HSCP* 98 (1998), 97; rejected by R. S. P. Beekes, *EIEC* 547b.

[8] M. C. Beckwith (as n. 7), 95. Cf. H. Reichelt, *IF* 32 (1913), 23–57; Durante (1976), 59 f.; Beckwith, 91–102.

[9] Alasdair Livingstone, *Mystical and Mythological Explanatory Works of Assyrian and Babylonian Scholars* (Oxford 1986), 86; West (1997), 139 f.; Wayne Horowitz, *Mesopotamian Cosmic Geography* (Winona Lake 1998), 263; A. R. George, *The Babylonian Epic of Gilgamesh* (Oxford 2003), 865; Yt. 13. 2; H. W. Bailey (as n. 6), 127.

thunderstone can be called *Perkūno akmuõ*, 'Perkunas' stone'. This makes a possible link between the senses of 'stone' and 'sky'.[10]

If ἄκμων was an old word for the sky, like *asman-* in Iranian, it might have been personified as Akmon, and the rival names Akmon and Ouranos then harmonized by making one the father of the other, much as Hyperion was made the father of Helios. Both names, of course, were partial replacements for the original *Dyeus.

In other parts of the Indo-European territories a different word took on the meaning 'sky'. This was **nébhes-* 'cloud' (Vedic *nábhas-*, Greek νέφος), which became the word for 'sky' in Hittite (*nēbis-*), Slavonic (**nebo*), Latvian (*debess*), and Celtic (Old Irish *nem*, Welsh *nef*, Breton *neñv*; Ben Nevis, Britain's highest peak, is 'the Mountain of Heaven'). The same semantic shift has taken place between Norse *ský* 'cloud' and English *sky*. It reflects a different way of thinking, or a different focus, from the conception of the stone heaven.

Body imagery

There is a Vedic word *nā́ka-* signifying the surface of the sky, that which appears fiery by day (RV 5. 17. 2, 54. 12) or decorated with stars by night (1. 19. 6, 68. 10; 6. 49. 12). It is sometimes combined with the genitive *diváḥ* (1. 34. 8; 9. 73. 4, 85. 10). It was evidently conceived as convex, like an animal's back: it has a 'back' (*pṛṣṭhám*, 1. 125. 5; *sā́nu*, 8. 103. 2), and at 3. 2. 12 it is equated with *divás pṛṣṭhám*, 'heaven's back'. This latter phrase occurs in eight other places in the Rigveda. At 1. 115. 3 the Sun's horses are described as mounting it. We find the same image in Euripidean lyric. Zeus changed the course of the sun in the time of Atreus, τὰ δ' ἕσπερα νῶτ' ἐλαύνει θερμᾶι φλογὶ θεοπύρωι, '(since then) he chases the westward back (of the sky) with the hot flame of his divine fire' (*El.* 731). And in a fragment of the *Andromeda* (114) Night is addressed as one journeying far in her chariot, ἀστεροειδέα νῶτα διφρεύουσ' αἰθέρος ἱερᾶς, 'riding across the starry back of the holy air'. Plato (*Phaedr.* 247b) speaks of souls rising up to heaven and landing on its back, ἐπὶ τῶι τοῦ οὐρανοῦ νώτωι.

The metaphor is more commonly used in Greek of the sea; ἐπ' εὐρέα νῶτα θαλάσσης is a Homeric formula, and the image remains alive in tragedy (Aesch. *Ag.* 286, Eur. *Hel.* 129, 774). This is paralleled in Old English

[10] Cf. J. P. Maher, *JIES* 1 (1973), 441–62. A Jesuit record from 1583 (Mannhardt (1936), 435) attests the cult in Lithuania of a 'saxum grandius' under the name of Akmo, but we do not know whether it was supposed to have any connection with the sky.

verse: *ofer wæteres hrycg* (*Beowulf* 471, cf. *Solomon* 19); *ȳða hrycgum*, 'on the waves' backs' (Exeter Riddle 4. 33).

Pindar and others speak of the 'back' of the earth, meaning its broad, rolling surface.[11] So too AV 4. 14. 3 *pṛṣṭhā́t pṛthivyā́ḥ*. We may refer also to the Vedic use of *sā́nu*, a word employed for the part of a horse or a demon that is whipped or belaboured (RV 6. 75. 13; 1. 32. 7, 80. 5 f.; 6. 39. 2) or for the highest part of a mountain or rock. The *diváḥ sā́nu* (1. 54. 4, 58. 2 al.) seems not to be significantly different from the *divás pṛṣṭhám*. But there are also references to *bhū́myāḥ* or *pṛthivyā́ḥ sā́nu*, the *sā́nu* of the earth, that is, its surface (1. 62. 5; 2. 31. 2; 6. 48. 5; 7. 7. 2, 36. 1; 9. 63. 27, 79. 4; 10. 75. 2; *urviyā́ḥ . . . sā́nau* 1. 146. 2).

There is other imagery in which the earth is treated as having bodily parts. In a hymn to Agni (Fire) it is said that when he spreads through the forest, fanned by the wind, he 'mows Earth's hair' (*rómā*, RV 1. 65. 8). The mountains are *vṛkṣákeśa-*, 'tree-tressed' (5. 41. 11), a compound paralleled by Greek δενδρόκομος, δενδροέθειρα, applied to mountains and vales (Eur. *Hel.* 1107, Ar. *Nub.* 280, Tim. *Pers.* 106). κόμη and κομάω are often used of trees and plants, and sometimes of the land on which they grow.[12] In Norse poetry the vegetation can be called *hadd Iarðar*, 'Earth's hair' (*Biarkamál* fr. 7. 1, *Edd. min.* 32). 'The wood it is called among men, but wolds' mane among gods' (*vallar fax*, *Alvíssmál* 28). The word for 'wold', *vǫllr*, related to German *Wald*, seems in fact to be cognate with a series of words for 'hair' in other languages: Old Irish *folt* (also of foliage), Welsh *gwallt*, Church Slavonic *vladĭ*, Old Russian *volod'*, the underlying meaning being perhaps 'shaggy covering'.[13]

In other Norse kennings stones are 'Earth's bones', *foldar bein* (Thiodolf, *Ynglingatal* 19. 10) or *Hlóðuniar bein* (Vǫlu-Steinn ap. *Skáldsk.* 57 v. 315. 4; cf. *Gylf.* prol. 1). The same oracular expression appeared in one of the earliest Greek tragedians: Γῆς ὀστοῖσιν ἐγχριμφθεὶς πόδα, of someone who tripped on some stones (Choerilus, *TrGF* 2 F 2). In a version of the Flood myth followed by Ovid (*Met.* 1. 348–415) Deucalion and Pyrrha, anxious to repopulate the world after the cataclysm, were instructed to throw their great mother's bones over their shoulders. Pyrrha was horrified, but Deucalion guessed correctly that their 'great mother' was Earth, and her bones stones.[14]

There are several references in the Rigveda to Earth's *nā́bhi-*, 'navel' (1. 59. 2, 143. 4; 2. 3. 7; 3. 5. 9, 29. 4; 9. 72. 7, 82. 3, 86. 8; 10. 1. 6). It is not a remote,

[11] See B. K. Braswell, *A Commentary on the Fourth Pythian Ode of Pindar* (Berlin–New York 1988), 102.

[12] *Hymn. Dem.* 454 with N. J. Richardson's note.

[13] PIE **wol-to-*; *IEW* 1139 f. On the hair–vegetation analogy cf. Lincoln (1986), 16 f., 88.

[14] On the bone–stone analogy cf. Lincoln (1986), 16.

mythical location; it is the fire-pit at the place of sacrifice where Agni blazes and forms a link with heaven. In Greece too the Navel of Earth, Γῆς ὀμφαλός, was a feature of a religious site—Delphi. This seems more than a coincidence. But it is not necessarily the result of inheritance from Graeco-Aryan times. The term 'navel of the earth' occurs also in Hebrew, and in Asiatic shamanism, which may be where it was originally at home.[15]

As for Earth's bones, hair, and back, if they are Indo-European images, it must be granted that they do not form elements of a coherent system, as the hair grows on the back and the bones are scattered about on it.

World pillar, world tree

There are a number of Vedic references to a prop or support (*skambhá-*, *skámbhanam*) of the sky. Some of them are clearly figurative. The world is pictured as being created anew each day by the dawn sacrifice, when Agni or Soma or Indra and Soma bring up the dawn and sun, prop up the sky, and spread out the earth (RV 6. 72. 2, cf. 9. 74. 2, 86. 46; 10. 111. 5); the Sun is the prop of heaven that supports the firmament (4. 13. 5). Varuna is said to hold heaven and earth apart with a pillar (8. 41. 10, cf. 6. 70. 1). When we read that Vishnu propped up the sky after taking his three famous cosmic steps (1. 154. 1), or that Indra after killing the dragon propped heaven and earth further apart (5. 29. 4, cf. 6. 44. 24, 47. 5; 'like a pair of wheels with the axle', 10. 89. 4), it is doubtful whether we are to think of a physical prop that still exists as a structural part of the universe. But it is a plausible assumption that behind this abstract imagery lies a more primitive concept of a world pillar that held up the sky like the timber prop of a house or yurt.[16]

In Greek myth the sky is supported on Atlas' head and shoulders (Hes. *Th.* 517–20, 746–8), but there is a concurrent notion of a pillar or pillars (ibid. 779, Ibycus, *PMGF* 336), in some passages awkwardly combined with Atlas (*Od.* 1. 52–4, [Aesch.] *Prom.* 348–50).

In connection with the hypothetical god *Aryomen in Chapter 3 I mentioned the Saxon cult pillar known as Irminsûl, noting that the element *irmin-* in compounds seems to have a cosmic or universal connotation. *Irmansûl*, plural *-sûlî*, also occurs in Old High German glosses, rendered as *colossus, altissima columna, pyramides.* The Saxons' pillar was of wood, and impressively tall. The ninth-century monk Rudolf of Fulda says of it:

[15] Cf. Durante (1976), 112; West (1997), 149 f. The Homeric 'navel of the sea' (*Od.* 1. 50, of Calypso's isle) has a parallel at *MBh.* 3. 21. 16, where, however, the phrase refers not to an island but to a coastal bay.

[16] See further Macdonell (1898), 11, 14, 120.

Truncum quoque ligni non parvae magnitudinis in altum erectum sub divo colebant, patria eum lingua Irminsul appellantes, quod Latine dicitur universalis columna, quasi sustinens omnia.[17]

Presumably this visible, tangible pillar was not really believed to be holding up the sky, but was a representation of the mythical pillar at the world's centre.

Taken together, this Vedic, Greek, and Germanic evidence might be considered to point to Indo-European status for the concept. But the inference is by no means certain. The Greek myth might be derived from the Near East, and the Indic and Germanic ideas of a pillar from the shamanistic cosmologies of the Finno-Ugric and other peoples of central and northern Asia.[18] Here the pillar of the sky is symbolized by the pole supporting the human dwelling, or by a separate sacred standing pole. It is a form of the *axis mundi* associated with the shaman's passage between higher and lower worlds.

The idea of the world tree is also at home in this context.[19] Within the Indo-European orbit this appears notably in the cosmic tree of Norse mythology, known as the Ash (of) Yggdrasil. The gods meet at it daily to confer. Its branches extend across the whole world and over the sky. Dew falls from it onto the earth. Its three roots grow among mankind, among the Frost Giants, and over Hel. Various creatures live in it and feed on it, including the dragon Nidhogg, who eats away at the Niflheim root.[20]

Is this the development of an Indo-European conception, or an import from north Asiatic cosmology? Certain details point towards the latter alternative.[21] If the world tree was an Indo-European idea, it has left few traces elsewhere. In Indo-Iranian texts there are references to a mythical tree that drips the immortal fluid Soma/Haoma, but it is not pictured as a mighty cosmic tree uniting upper and lower worlds; in the Veda it is located in the third heaven, in the Avesta it stands in the fabulous but terrestrial lake Vourukaša from which all rivers flow. According to a later Pahlavi source an evil lizard lurks beneath it, trying to get at the Haoma.[22] There is perhaps an

[17] *Translatio S. Alexandri* 3, ed. B. Krusch, *NGG* Phil.-hist. Kl. 1933, 426. 12. For other sources see Grimm (1883–8), 115–19; Clemen (1928), 48. 17, 54. 20, 61. 14, 67. 19–23, cf. 68. 31. Cf. also de Vries (1956), ii. 386–91; Davidson (1964), 196; (1988), 21–3.

[18] For the Near Eastern evidence see West (1997), 148 f.; for the central Asian, Uno Holmberg, *Der Baum des Lebens* (Helsinki 1923), 12–33; cf. de Vries (1956), ii. 388; Mircea Eliade, *Shamanism. Archaic Techniques of Ecstasy* (Princeton 1964), 259–66.

[19] Cf. U. Holmberg (as n. 18), 51–70; M. Eliade (as n. 18), 117–22, 269–71.

[20] *Vǫluspá* 19, 27, 47; *Grímnismál* 29–35, 44; *Gylf.* 15 f.; de Vries (1956), ii. 380–5; Davidson (1964), 190–6; Lorenz (1984), 237–41, 243.

[21] Cf. U. Holmberg (as n. 18), 67; L. Sternberg, *ARW* 28 (1930), 149.

[22] RV 10. 135. 1, AV 5. 4. 3, *Chāndogya Upaniṣad* 8. 5. 3; Yt. 1. 30, *Sīh rōcak* 1. 7, 2. 7, Vd. 20. 4; *Bundahišn* 18, 27. 4.

analogue to this in the Hesperides' tree which grows golden apples, has a guardian serpent at its base, and is located close to Atlas who supports the sky (Hes. *Th.* 215 f., 334 f., 518). When Greek poets speak of the 'roots' of the earth or sea, the metaphor might go back to a forgotten notion of a world tree.[23] The strange cosmology of Pherecydes of Syros involved a winged oak upon which was hung the embroidered robe of Earth; but wherever Pherecydes got this idea from, it can hardly have been from any ancestral Greek tradition.[24]

The cosmic serpent

The serpent or dragon that resides at the base of the Iranian tree Gaokərəna, the tree in the Hesperides' garden, and the Nordic Yggdrasil has a negative personality. The Greek monster denies access to the life-giving apples; the Iranian one seeks the elixir for himself; Nidhogg erodes the tree's structure and will eventually cause it to collapse.

There are other references to a cosmic serpent who is not associated with a tree but lurks in the depths of the waters. 'The Serpent of the Deep', *Áhir budhnyàḥ*, is mentioned a dozen times in the Rigveda and actually invoked as a deity. *Budhnyà-* is the adjective from *budhná-* 'base'; the noun is related to Greek *πυθ-μήν*, which is occasionally found in a cosmic sense, referring to the bottom of the sea, earth, etc.[25] The creature is associated with waters (RV 6. 49. 19), indeed born in them (*abjā́-*, 7. 34. 16). He sits in darkness in the depths of rivers (*budhné nadī́nām*, ibid.).[26]

No myth is related about him in the Veda, and as a recipient of prayers he is clearly distinct from Vṛtra, the water serpent overcome by Indra (Chapter 6), though they might originally have been the same. We saw that Vṛtra had something in common with Typhoeus/Typhaon and Python, the monsters struck down by Zeus and Apollo respectively. V. N. Toporov has argued that both of these names contain the same root (**b^hud^h-* or **d^hub^h-*) as the Vedic *budh-ná-*.[27]

In later Indic myth the earth lies sunk in the ocean between one creation and the next, surrounded by the vast coils of the serpent Śeṣa, who is a form

23 Cf. West (1966), 351; H. S. Schibli, *Pherekydes of Syros* (Oxford 1990), 70.

24 Cf. West (1971), 27, 55–60; H. S. Schibli (as n. 23), 69–77.

25 Hes. *Th.* 932 with West (1966), 414.

26 The other passages are 1. 186. 5; 2. 31. 6; 5. 41. 16; 6. 50. 14; 7. 35. 13, 38. 5; 10. 64. 4, 66. 11, 92. 12, 93. 5. Cf. Macdonell (1898), 72 f.; Hillebrandt (1927–9), ii. 305 f.; Watkins (1995), 460–2.

27 Followed by Watkins (1995), 461 f. The variations in the quantity of the [u] (short in *budhná-*, *πυθμήν*, *Τυφωεύς*, *Τυφάων*, but long in *Πύθων*, *Τυφῶν*) are problematic.

of Vishnu. At other times this Śeṣa supports the earth (*MBh.* 1. 32. 20–4; 3. 187. 10, 194. 9 f.; cf. 5. 101. 2 f.). The motif of a huge serpent in the waters who encircles the earth recurs in other traditions. In Greek there is the uncanonical myth of Ophion or Ophioneus, which so far as we can see first appeared in the above-mentioned, eccentric cosmology of Pherecydes. Ophion and his consort previously ruled in heaven, but Chronos (Kronos) fought him and drove him into the waters of Ogenos (Oceanus), where he remains.[28] In Nordic myth there is Iǫrmungand, the Miðgarð Serpent, who was smitten on the head by Thor, as was Vṛtra by Indra, and who lies in the sea surrounding all lands (p. 259). The biblical Leviathan came to be understood as a monster coiled round the earth, presumably by conflation with a non-biblical myth of separate origin.[29]

A less explicit but much earlier piece of Germanic evidence is provided by a decorated bronze razor from near Roskilde, Denmark, dated to about 900 BCE. In the left half of the field is the sun's ship, facing right, and in the right half, also facing right, an enormous serpent, its body in a series of coils, within which are solar designs.[30] Is this meant to convey that the sun passes through the monster's body at night? This would be like the account in the Egyptian funerary text *Amduat*, according to which Reʿ rides through the underworld each night in his boat but also, in the Twelfth Hour, undergoes rejuvenation by passing through the length of a serpent, emerging from its mouth at sunrise.[31] Whether or not this interpretation of the scene on the razor is close to the mark, the serpent clearly has cosmic status, and its juxtaposition with the ship suggests that it is in the sea.

If the Indo-Europeans had a myth of a great serpent of the watery deeps, we must confess that we do not know what it signified. In the first place we cannot be sure whether it was located in a river or rivers, as is the Vedic *Áhir budhnyàḥ*, or in a lake or the sea. In a river its purpose might have been to

[28] Pherecydes DK 7 A 11, B 4 = F 73, 78–80 Schibli; Call. fr. 177. 7 f.; Ap. Rhod. 1. 503–6; West (1971), 20–3, cf. 40–50; H. S. Schibli (as n. 23), 78–103.

[29] Ps.-Bede, *De mundi constitutione, Patrol. Lat.* cx. 884 *alii dicunt Leviathan animal terram complecti, tenetque caudam in ore suo*; so in the Irish saga *Togail bruidne Dá Derga* 56, 'the Leviathan that surrounds the globe and strikes with its tail to overturn the world' (trs. Koch–Carey (2000), 176). But Rabbinical lore also comes into the question, cf. Dillon (1948), 29 n. 30.

[30] F. Kaul in Meller (2004), 61 (centre left), 63.

[31] Erik Hornung, *Ägyptische Unterweltsbücher* (2nd edn., Zurich–Munich 1984), 185–8. The serpent's name is given as 'Der *Ka* dessen, der die Götter leben läßt', but according to Hornung it is certainly the same as the serpent 'Weltumringler' that made an appearance in previous sections of the work (ibid. 149 and 178). In the illustrations of the Eleventh Hour (174 f. Abb. 13) this 'World-encircler' is shown held up by a row of twelve gods ahead of the solar boat, its body in many coils. Apart from the presence of these gods, the arrangement of boat and coiling serpent, both facing to the right, is extraordinarily similar to that on the Danish razor made some two thousand years later. How to account for this I do not know.

account for the winding course of the stream. In a lake or sea it might have been to account for the turbulence of the water by the lashing of its tail. The idea that it encircled the whole earth would seem to presuppose the belief that the earth was surrounded by water: we can document this view for India (first in RV 9. 41. 6), Greece, and early medieval England and Scandinavia (*Beowulf* 93, *Gylf.* 8), but we have no sufficient ground for attributing it to the Indo-Europeans.

The land of the blest

We saw in Chapter 3 that the special food or drink which exempts the gods from old age and death is usually obtained from a particular source in a remote region. In general there is a tendency to imagine that peripheral parts of the earth may contain elements of paradise and be inhabited by a people free from the hardships and taints that affect us.

In the *Mahābhārata* there are several references to such places. Beyond the Himalaya live the Northern Kurus, a mythical saintly race.[32] Also in the north is *Śvetadvīpam*, the White Island; those go there who are devoted to Vishnu and die in battle at his hands. Its inhabitants shine white like the moon, and require no food.[33] Greek parallels spring to mind at once: the virtuous Hyperboreans who live beyond the North Wind, and the White Island in the Black Sea to which in the epic *Aethiopis* Achilles was translated after his death in battle at the hands of Apollo and Alexander.

In Ketumala and Jamvukhanda, on the west side of Mt Meru, men shine like gold and live for ten thousand years without pain or sickness (*MBh.* 6. 7. 29–31). Meru is the mountain about which the sun circles in post-Vedic myth. The people in question, therefore, are somewhere toward the sunset. Their long and idyllic life recalls those of Hesiod's Golden and Hero Races (*Op.* 109–19, 157–73; cf. Pind. *Ol.* 2. 70–4, fr. 129). The Heroes are located in the Isles of the Blest, beside Oceanus, generally thought of as being in the west. These isles cannot be distinguished from the Elysian plain to which Menelaus is to go instead of dying, where life is easy and there is neither snow nor rainstorm but only gentle westerly breezes (*Od.* 4. 561–8).

The counterpart in Irish legend is the Land of the Living (*tír na mbeo*) or Land of the Young (*tír na n-óg*), located in the western sea. It is a country 'where there is neither sickness nor age nor death; where happiness lasts

[32] *MBh.* 1. 102. 10, 113. 7; 6. 8. 2; cf. 5. 109; 12. 185. 8 f. Cf. Hermann Oldenberg, *Das Mahabharata* (Göttingen 1922), 84; Pisani (1969), 63 f., 144–6.

[33] *MBh.* 12. 322. 7–326, 331; *Rm.* 7 App. I 3. 267 ff.; cf. Pisani (1969), 146–55; W. Ruben, *Sitz.-Ber. Ak. Wiss. DDR* 1973 (24), 24.

forever and there is no satiety; where food and drink do not diminish when consumed; where to wish for something is to possess it; where a hundred years are as one day.'[34]

Celestial river

Homeric rivers sometimes have the puzzling epithet δι(ε)ιπετής. Adjectives in -πετής (*es*-stem) normally mean 'falling' in some defined way, but this does not go well with the apparent locative διί, which should mean 'in the sky'.[35] Alternatively it may be interpreted as 'flying', like -πέτης (*a*-stem) in ὑψιπέτης, ὠκυπέτης. It must have been so understood quite early, because we also find διιπετής applied to birds (*Hymn. Aphr.* 4). 'Flying in the sky' is a clear and coherent concept. But what sense does it make in reference to rivers?

It is evidently an old, stereotyped formula that may reflect an obsolete piece of cosmology. Heinrich Lüders collected Vedic evidence for the idea of celestial rivers, in particular a celestial Indus. One passage that he cited in this connection was RV 2. 28. 4, where it is said of the rivers *váyo ná paptū raghuyā́ párijman*, 'swift as birds they fly their circuit'.[36] Whether this particular verse refers to rivers in heaven is disputable. But certainly the river Sarasvatī is summoned to the sacrifice 'from high heaven, from the mountain' (5. 43. 11 *divó bṛhatáḥ, párvatāt*); she fills not only the terrestrial regions but the broad atmospheric spaces (6. 61. 11). In post-Vedic mythology the Ganges is conceived as having its source in heaven (*MBh.* 3. 107. 21–108. 18; 5. 109. 6; 13. 27. 71, 89). It flows in the sky among the gods (*MBh.* 1. 158. 18; *Rm.* 1. 36. 7; it fell from the sky, ibid. 41. 22–42. 16). In the Avesta the holy river Arədvī is said to have come down to earth from the stars at Ahura Mazdā's command (Yt. 5. 85, 88).

Two Mycenaean gold rings, usually dated to Late Helladic II, are embellished with cult scenes. In the sky is the sun (in one case also the moon), and this celestial field is demarcated by a wavy band which looks more like a river than anything else.[37] It has been suggested that it represents the Milky Way,

[34] Dillon (1948), 101, cf. 104 f.; Vendryès (1948), 308.

[35] The long second vowel in the compound is the regular outcome of metrical lengthening. The critic Zenodorus spelled the word διειπετ-, which is also written in the papyrus of Euripides' *Hypsipyle* fr. 752h. 31 (cf. fr. 815); but this would imply an old dative, as in δι(ε)ίφιλος, which would be inexplicable. On the problems of the word cf. Schmitt (1967), 44–6, 221–36; E. Risch, *Gnomon* 41 (1969), 325 f.; J. T. Hooker, *IF* 84 (1979), 117–19.

[36] H. Lüders, *Varuṇa* (Göttingen 1951–9), 138–44, 146–51. Lüders was exercised by the interpretation of δι(ε)ιπετής (677–9), but it was his posthumous editor L. Alsdorf who, in the annotation on p. 143, adduced RV 2. 28. 4 as the key to it.

[37] M. P. Nilsson, *The Minoan-Mycenaean Religion* (2nd edn., Lund 1950), 179 fig. 83; 347 fig. 158.

but if so it is surely the Milky Way conceived as a celestial river. The Milky Way was a conspicuous feature of pre-industrial skies, and its irregular course across the firmament, with some side-channels and dividing as if to flow round islands, might well suggest a river. In Vedic cosmology it was the bright ocean of heaven, the reservoir of celestial waters, the source of the rivers that flow down from the Himalaya.[38] If such a concept goes back to Graeco-Aryan times, the obscure Homeric formula finds a possible elucidation.

Moon and stars

The common Indo-European word for the moon is reconstructed as *$meh_1n(e)s$- (Vedic *mā́s-*, *mā́sa-*, Avestan *māh-*, Greek μείς, all meaning 'moon, month', Latin *mēns-is*, Old Irish *mí* 'month', etc.).[39] It is related to the verbal root *meh_1 'measure', and it is a masculine, implying an active role as 'the measurer (of time)'. The sense 'month' tended to become dominant, while other formations, often feminine, came into use in different areas for 'moon': Greek μήνη and σελήνη (**selas-nā*, 'mistress of radiance'), Old High German *mānīn*; Latin *lūna*, Old Irish *luan*, Church Slavonic *luna* (all from **louks-nā*, 'mistress of light'), etc. These suggest a personified figure Moon, though she, unlike Sun and Dawn, seems to have had no significant role in Indo-European mythology.

The ancestral word for 'star' was *h_2ster-, giving Hittite *ḫaster-*, Vedic *stár-*, Greek ἀστήρ, Armenian *astł*, etc. It was a masculine, perhaps originally meaning 'burner', with a collective form * $h_2st(e)r\bar{a}$, as represented by Greek ἄστρα, proto-Celtic **sterā* (Middle Cornish *steyr*, Welsh *ser*, etc.).[40]

It can be assumed that the study of astronomy was not much developed among the Indo-Europeans, and probably only a few individual stars and star-groups had established names. One that we can trace back to Graeco-Aryan is 'the Bears' or 'the Bear' for Ursa Major. In Sanskrit this prominent northern constellation is usually called the Seven Rishis; probably so already in RV 10. 82. 2. But according to the *Śatapatha Brāhmaṇa* (2. 1. 2. 4) it was formerly known as *ṛ́kṣāḥ*, 'the Bears' (masculine plural), and the stellar *ṛ́kṣāḥ* of RV 1. 24. 10 and *Taittirīya Āraṇyaka* 1. 11. 2 are presumably to be so understood. In Greek it is a single she-bear, ἡ Ἄρκτος. The variants can be

[38] M. Witzel, *Bulletin d'Études Indiennes* 2 (1984), 213–79; P. Olivelle, *Upaniṣads* (Oxford 1996), xlvi.

[39] On the forms see Scherer (1953), 61–73; id. in Mayrhofer et al. (1974), 190; R. S. P. Beekes, *JIES* 10 (1982), 53–7; id. in *EIEC* 385.

[40] Scherer (1953), 18–29; C. Watkins, *Die Sprache* 20 (1974), 10–14; A. Pârvulescu, *ZVS* 91 (1977), 41–50; *EIEC* 543.

reconciled on the assumption that 'the Bears' were a she-bear and her two or three young, and that the Greeks referred only to the mother.[41]

But the Latin designation *Septentriones* may also reflect a very old conception of these stars. *Triones* were oxen, originally, it would seem, threshing oxen, who plodded round in a circle trampling the corn or turning a mill-wheel—an apt likeness of the constellation that circles round the Pole. The same picture is attested in India, in the *Bhāgavata Purāṇa* (4. 8), where Dhruva ('Fixed'), who is to be transformed into the Pole Star, is told that he will stand immobile 'like the mill-post round which the oxen go to thresh the corn'. He then betakes himself to Vishnu's seat, the polar axis, round which the stars go like oxen.[42]

In Homer the Bear has the alternative name of the Wagon (*Ἄμαξα*, *Il.* 18. 487 = *Od.* 5. 273). Like many Greek names of constellations, this may have been taken over from Babylonian nomenclature.[43] To be sure, it is paralleled by Latin *Plaustrum* and by many designations in European languages, especially Germanic (Wagen, Wain, etc.).[44] But these may be modelled on the Latin, and the Latin on the Greek. In any case the shape of the constellation suggests a wagon more readily than a bear or a group of animals. It may have been so designated already in Indo-European times; but we cannot infer this from the agreements.

The name of Sirius, the brightest of the fixed stars, may provide another Graeco-Aryan link. In the Avesta it is venerated as the star Tištrya, especially in Yt. 8, which is devoted to it. The Vedic Tiṣíya (RV 5. 54. 13; 10. 64. 8) is very probably the same. Bernhard Forssman derived these forms by dissimilation from **tri-str-iyo-*, 'belonging to the Tristar'; the 'Tristar', he suggested, was the Belt of Orion, a prominent line of three stars that points down towards Sirius. Eric Hamp more persuasively understands it of the large equilateral triangle formed by the bright stars Procyon, Betelgeuse, and Sirius itself, which, as the

[41] Scherer (1953), 131 f.; id. in Mayrhofer et al. (1974), 187 f. Plurals were probably typical for Indo-European constellation-names. Scherer sees the Bears as going back to a hunting society, and he raises the possibility that the Greek Arktouros, the Bear-watcher, is an original part of the same complex. A. Pârvulescu, *JIES* 16 (1988), 95–100, maintains that *ṛ́kṣāḥ* simply meant 'stars' and never the Bear.

[42] Scherer (1953), 134–6, who notes that a similar conception of the Pole is found among central Asiatic peoples. O. Szemerényi, *Scripta Minora*, i (Innsbruck 1987), 53 f. (from a conference paper given in 1961), thinks that *Septentriones* originally had nothing to do with oxen but was from **septemsteriōn-*, 'seven-star group'; similarly E. Hamp in L. Heilmann (ed.), *Proceedings of the Eleventh International Congress of Linguists* (Bologna 1974), 1051, who explains Old Irish *sechtarét* 'Arctus' in the same way. But see C. Watkins, *Die Sprache* 20 (1974), 11; A. Scherer in Mayrhofer et al. (1974), 187 n. 9.

[43] West (1997), 29 f. The Akkadian name is *ereqqu*, 'Wagon'.

[44] Material in Grimm (1883–8), 724–6, 1508; A. Scherer (1953), 139–41; A. Pârvulescu, *JIES* 16 (1988), 102 f.

most brilliant of the three, would be *Tristriyos, the Triangle Star. Meanwhile H. Fischer had argued that the Greek *Σείριος* could also be derived from the reduced form **tisrio-*, by way of **tīrio-* > **sīrio-*, remodelled under the influence of *Σειρήν*.[45]

The Pleiades are such a conspicuous little cluster that they must always have been singled out for attention. There is a probable Bronze Age representation of them on the Nebra disc (p. 208). But we cannot reconstruct an Indo-European name for them.[46]

The descriptive names given to stars or constellations sometimes prompted identifications with mythical figures and stories about how they came to be translated to the sky. But they were essentially fanciful and non-definitive, not bound up with any serious belief in the cosmic significance of stars and their groupings. A lexical association shared by Indo-Iranian, Greek, and Latin suggests that the stars were seen as ornamental as much as anything. It involves the root **peiḱ* seen in Vedic *piś* 'adorn', *péśas-* 'adornment, embroidery', Avestan *paēs* 'adorn, colour', Greek *ποικίλος* 'decorated, multicoloured', *ποικίλλω* 'make variegated, embroider', Latin *pingo* 'colour, paint'. In the Rigveda we find *pipéśa nā́kaṃ stṛ́bhiḥ*, '(Agni) has adorned the firmament with stars' (1. 68. 10); *aruṣásya duhitárā vírūpe: stṛ́bhir anyā́, pipiśé sū́ro anyā́*, 'the red one's daughters [night and day] are distinct in appearance: one is adorned with stars, the other from the sun' (6. 49. 3). In the Avesta the compound epithet *stəhrpaēsah-* 'star-ornamented' is applied to Mithra's chariot (Yt. 10. 143) and to the heaven (*asman-*) that Ahura Mazdā wears like a garment (Yt. 13. 3). Euripides speaks of the *ἀστέρων ποικίλματα* (*Hel.* 1096), and Critias of the starry body of heaven as 'the fair ornamentation by Time, that expert craftsman' (*TrGF* 43 F 19. 33 f. *τό τ' ἀστερωπὸν οὐρανοῦ δέμας, | Χρόνου καλὸν ποίκιλμα, τέκτονος σοφοῦ*). The collocation *ποικίλον ἀστερόεντα* already occurs in Homer (*Il.* 16. 133 f.), though only in a description of Achilles' breastplate. Seneca (*Med.* 310) speaks of the stars *quibus pingitur aether*.[47]

[45] B. Forssman, *ZVS* 82 (1968), 49–60; H. Fischer, *MSS* 26 (1969), 19–26; E. Hamp (as n. 42), 1048. Note that Hamp dispenses with the initial laryngeal of the 'star' root, explaining it as a prefix meaning 'one'. This is one of several stretched points in his argument, which nevertheless remains engaging.

[46] The semantic connections suggested by Scherer (1953), 141–4, between Vedic *kṛ́ttikāḥ*, Greek *Π(ε)λειάδες*, and Latin *Vergiliae* are too tenuous to command conviction. However, there is something to be said for the argument (ibid. 146–9) that the Greek and Latin names for the Hyades (*Ὑάδες*, *Suculae*, sc. sow and piglets) go back to a common source, whether Indo-European or Mediterranean. Cf. W. Gundel, *RE* viii. 2615–17; O. Szemerényi, *ZVS* 71 (1954), 216 f.; Scherer in Mayrhofer et al. (1974), 186.

[47] The material is collected by P. Jackson, *IF* 106 (2001), 122–5.

COSMOGONY

This idea of the stars being added to the firmament as decoration implies a divine craftsman responsible for the creation of the cosmos in its present form. In the two Avestan passages cited above, heaven and Mithra's chariot, besides being *stəhrpaēsah-*, are *mainyu.tašta-*, 'fashioned by Spirit', where *taš* is the root considered in Chapter 1 under the heading 'poetry as carpentry'. Zarathushtra had earlier used it of Ahura Mazdā's creation of the cow and other things (Y. 29. 1 f., 6 f., 44. 6 f., 47. 3, 51. 7). It appears also in those verses of Critias where the star-decorated sky is called the work of Time, that expert τέκτων.

A more basic Indo-European verb for divine creation is *$*d^heh_1$*, which means to set in place, lay down, or establish. We find it in Hittite of the gods who *nēbis dēgan dāir*, 'established heaven (and) earth';[48] in the *Gāthās*, Y. 44. 3 *kasnā x^vəṇg strəmcā dāṯ advānəm?* 'Who made the path of the sun and stars?' 5 *kə huvāpå raocåscā dāṯ təmåscā? | kə huvāpå x^vafnəmcā dāṯ zaēmācā?* 'What skilful artificer made the regions of light and dark? What skilful artificer made sleep and waking?' 7 *vīspanąm dātārəm* 'maker of all things'; and similarly in the Old Persian inscriptions, of Ahuramazda *hya imām būmim adā, hya avam asmānam adā*, 'who created this earth, who created that sky' (DNa 1, DSe 1, etc.). The Vedic creator god Dhātṛ has his name from the same verb. In early Greek it appears as τίθημι, for example in Hes. *Op.* 173d Ζεὺς δ' αὖτ' ἄ]λλο γένος θῆκ[εν μερόπων ἀνθρώπων, 'and Zeus created another race of men'; Alcman *PMGF* 20 ὥρας δ' ἔθηκε τρεῖς, '(Zeus?) made three seasons'. In Alcman's idiosyncratic cosmogony (*PMGF* 5 fr. 2 ii–iii) Thetis, whose name can be analysed as $*d^heh_1$- with an agent suffix but who is otherwise a sea-nymph, appears to have played a demiurgic role, as if a female counterpart of Dhātṛ.

The idea of a created world is untypical of early Greek thinking. Hesiod and other theogonists spoke rather of the world coming into being through a series of 'births' of cosmic deities.

> First Chaos was born (γένετο), and then broad-breasted Earth . . .
> From Chaos Erebos and dark Night were born,
> and from Night in turn Aither and Day were born,
> whom she bore in union of love with Erebos. (Hes. *Th.* 116–25).

Such genetic language is common in the Rigveda, for example at 6. 48. 22 *sakṛ́d dha dyaúr ajāyata, sakṛ́d bhū́mir ajāyata*, 'just once was the sky born,

[48] See J. Catsanicos, *BSL* 81 (1986), 134–7.

once was the earth born'; 2. 19. 3 *ájanayat sū́riyam*, 'he [Indra] brought the sun to birth'; 2. 20. 7; 3. 31. 15; 10. 90. 9 f., 13, 129. 3, 6, 190. 1 f., etc.

However, this was apparently felt to be compatible with craftsmanship: 4. 56. 3 *sá ít suápā bhúvaneṣu āsa, | yá imé dyā́vāpṛthivī́ jajā́na*, 'he was a skilful artificer among beings, who generated this heaven and earth', where *suápas-* corresponds to Zarathushtra's *huvāpå* (above; the second element of the compound is the same as Latin *opus*). And while the Iranian prophet uses *dā* (*$d^h eh_1$) in the passages quoted, there are other places where he uses genealogical language, as in Y. 44. 3 *kasnā ząθā ptā aṣ̌ahyā paourvyē?* 'Who was the father-begetter of Truth in the beginning?' (cf. 45. 4, 47. 3). There is a similar alternation between the ideas of generating and making in some of the Greek cosmogonies. Alcman's Thetis seems to have been a creator, but she was one of a series of deities who were born. Pherecydes' Chronos (Time) 'made' fire, wind, and water, but he made them out of his seed (DK 7 A 8 = F 60 Schibli). The oldest Orphic theogony had a genealogical framework, but within this it had Zeus operating as a designer and craftsman; it used the verb μήσατο, 'contrived', suggesting deliberate intelligence.[49]

Before heaven and earth

Echoes of an Indo-European cosmogonic narrative have been found in RV 10. 129. 1 f.,

> Neither non-being was nor being was at that time;
> there was not the air, nor the heaven beyond it . . .
> Neither death was nor the immortal then,
> nor was there the mark of night and day,

in comparison with two Germanic texts, the Wessobrunn Prayer,

> This I have learned among men, the greatest of wonders,
> that earth was not, nor heaven above,
> nor tree < > nor mountain there was,
> not a single <star>, nor the sun shone,
> nor the moon gave light, nor the bright sea,

and the verses in the *Vǫluspá* (3) about the beginning of the world:

[49] Orph. fr. 16. 1 f., 155. 1 Bernabé. Cf. Parmenides DK 28 B 13 μητίσατο; Y. 54. 1 'I pray for Truth's reward, the desirable one that Mazdā conceived (*masatā*)'. The notion of creation is sometimes expressed by other verbs, some of them going in the direction of particular crafts. So in Hittite, *Song of Ullikummi* III A iii 40 *nebisanmukan kuabi daganzipanna sēr weder* 'when they built heaven and earth above me', *wede-* being the usual verb for building an edifice, erecting a stele, etc. Snorri writes that the All-father (Odin) *smiðaði himin ok iǫrð ok loptin*, 'fashioned heaven and earth and the air' (*Gylf.* 3, cf. 8, 13).

There was not sand nor sea   nor the cool waves;
earth was nowhere   nor heaven above;
Ginnunga Gap there was,   but grass nowhere.

Besides the general parallelism in the series of negative statements, we may note the specific correspondence between the Germanic formula 'nor heaven above' (*noh ūfhimil, né upphiminn*) and the Vedic *nó víomā paró yát,* literally 'nor the heaven which (is) beyond'.[50] A fourth text may be added from Greek:

Χάος ἦν καὶ Νὺξ Ἔρεβός τε μέλαν πρῶτον καὶ Τάρταρος εὐρύς,
γῆ δ' οὐδ' ἀὴρ οὐδ' οὐρανὸς ἦν.

There was Chasm and Night and dark Erebos at first, and broad Tartarus,
but earth nor air nor heaven there was.   (Ar. *Av.* 693 f.).

Aristophanes must have known the motif from a serious cosmogony current in his time. The analogy between the Hesiodic *Χάος* 'Chasm' and the Nordic *Ginnunga Gap* 'Gaping(?) Opening' has often been noted; Aristophanes' *Χάος ἦν* matches *Gap var Ginnunga* in the *Vǫluspá.*

The solitary Twin

That Eddic passage alludes to Ymir as the primal being, and to the sons of Bur (Odin, Vili, and Vé) raising up the earth and fashioning Miðgarð, the habitable world. Ymir was a frost giant. From the sweat of his two armpits came a man and a woman, and one of his legs made love to the other and fathered a six-headed son, ancestor of giants. Odin and his brothers killed Ymir and made the earth out of his flesh, the mountains from his bones, the trees from his hair, the sky from his skull, and the sea and lakes from his blood.[51]

Ymir's name is thought to mean 'Twin'. But whose twin could he have been, seeing that he was a unique creature? The answer may be 'his own', in the sense that he was bisexual, a combination of male and female. The story that one of his legs begot a son with the other looks like a half-understood or bowdlerized paraphrase of procreation by self-fertilization.

This interpretation is supported by a Germanic and an Iranian parallel. The Germanic one is the poetic tradition reported by Tacitus (*Germ.* 2. 2)

[50] The three texts were compared by Güntert (1923), 333; H. H. Schaeder, *Die Weltliteratur* 18 (1943), 84 f. = Schmitt (1968), 79 f.; Schmitt (1967), 204–6.

[51] *Vafþrúðnismál* 21, 33, *Grímnismál* 40 f., *Gylf.* 5–8. I take the couple born from the armpits to be the first humans, though Snorri leaves them unexplained and later provides a separate account of the creation of the first man and woman from two logs (*Gylf.* 9).

concerning a divine figure Tuisto who grew out of the earth to become the father of Mannus, the ancestor of all the Germans. Tuisto's name is understood to mean 'twin' or 'hermaphrodite'.[52] The assumption that he was bisexual and able to fertilize himself explains how he was able to beget Mannus on his own.

Another figure called Twin plays a role in Indo-Iranian myth as the first mortal man or the first king. This is the Vedic Yama, the Avestan Yima, a name considered to be cognate with Ymir.[53] He is the son of the solar deity Vivasvat or Vīvahvant. Some accounts give him a sister, also called Twin (Yamī, RV 10. 10; Yimeh in Pahlavi sources), with whom he has incest, or at least she pleads with him to do so. She is evidently a secondary figure, and it is shrewdly surmised that originally the myth featured not a pair but a single androgynous creature capable of procreation by himself.[54]

Yima, after a blessed reign on earth, lost his majesty and was sawn in two by a certain Spityura (Yt. 19. 46),[55] though there is no record of what became of the halves. In India it is not Yama but another primal man, Purusha, who suffers an analogous fate; *púruṣa-* is another word meaning 'man'. According to the famous hymn RV 10. 90 he was sacrificed by the gods and the cosmos was made out of him, the heaven from his head, the air from his navel, the earth from his legs, and so forth.

Some scholars regard the legend of Romulus and Remus as another relic of the Indo-European cosmogonic myth. Remus, it is claimed, was originally *Yemós 'Twin', the same as Yama, Yima, and Ymir, and the initial was changed for alliterative purposes. He was after all a twin. His killing had been essential to the foundation of the world, and the myth was transferred to the foundation of Rome. It is also pointed out that according to one tradition Romulus himself was killed by the senators and his body cut into pieces and disposed of secretly.[56] The senators here would, I suppose, correspond to the gods in the original myth who sacrificed the giant or proto-human.[57]

52 Güntert (1923), 324–6, cf. 334 f.

53 Cf. Güntert (1923), 336–8; de Vries (1956), ii. 363 f.; Ernout–Meillet (1959), s.v. *geminus*; Meid (1991), 20 f. On Yama cf. Macdonell (1898), 171–4; Oldenberg (1917), 280 f.; Oberlies (1998), 386–90.

54 Güntert (1923), 320–2.

55 Yt. 19. 46. Scholars say that Spityura was a brother of Yima, but I do not know the source for this.

56 Dion. Hal. *Ant.* 2. 56. 3 f.; Livy 1. 16. 4; Plut. *Rom.* 27. 6; W. Burkert, *Historia* 11 (1962), 356–76; J. Puhvel, *History of Religions* 15 (1975), 146–57; B. Lincoln, ibid. 137–9; id. (1986), 42–5; Oberlies (1998), 389 f.

57 In the reconstruction of Puhvel and others the Twin is slaughtered by his brother, as Remus is by Romulus and Yima by Spityura (if he was a brother). As I see it, he originally had no brother.

For Zarathushtra Yima was a sinner, the first to distribute portions of the cow for consumption (Y. 32. 8); in other words, the practice of cow-sacrifice was mythically projected back to the first mortal king. In a later Iranian account the killing of a primal ox and of a primal man (now called Gayōmart, 'Mortal Life') go together, being both brought about by Ahriman. From the ox's organs and seed came all plants and animals, and from Gayōmart's came minerals and Mahryaγ and Mahryānaγ, the father and mother of humankind. This pair grew from the earth in the form of a rhubarb plant, joined together and identical—another version of the primal hermaphrodite.[58] The bull sacrifice had a similar cosmogonic association in Roman Mithraism, as the monuments indicate.[59]

Some comparativists believe that it was already an integral part of the Indo-European myth. They point out that there is a pre-cosmic cow in the Norse story. She was called Auðhumla, she was formed from melting ice like Ymir, and she fed him with her milk (*Gylf.* 6). But nothing is said of her being sacrificed. It is possible that that was her original role, as Ymir's sustenance does not seem a sufficiently pressing mythological need to justify the invention of a cow. But as it stands, the cosmogonic bovine sacrifice is attested only in Iranian tradition, and there not in its earliest documents.

In the myth of 'Twin' there seems to be a merging of two distinct concepts. On the one hand there is the primal hermaphrodite who generates the first humans, and on the other the primal giant who is divided into two or more parts to make the parts of the world. If we ask why the same figure should play both roles, as both the Nordic Ymir and the Iranian Yima seem to do, the answer may perhaps be that originally the bisexual being, rather than giving birth to men and women, was divided in two, a male half and a female half, like the primeval double creatures pictured by Aristophanes in Plato's *Symposium* (189d–193d). The prototype of this separation of the sexes could be seen in the separation of Father Sky and Mother Earth; we are all descended from that divine pair as well as from the first human couple.

It is not possible to reconstruct in detail the process by which the extant versions developed from a better integrated archetype. But the shared features in the Indic, Iranian, and Germanic accounts point to an Indo-European

[58] *Greater Bundahišn* 4, 6, 14; text and translation of these sections, with parallel passages from Zātspram, in (R. Reitzenstein and) H. H. Schaeder, *Studien zum antiken Synkretismus aus Iran und Griechenland* (Studien der Bibliothek Warburg 7, Leipzig–Berlin 1926), 214–33. This ninth-century Pahlavi work drew its cosmogonic material from the lost *Dāmdāt Nask* of the Avesta. The Cow and Gaya-marətan- are associated in Y. 68. 22, Yt. 13. 86, *Visprat* 21. 2 as venerable figures.

[59] R. C. Zaehner, *The Dawn and Twilight of Zoroastrianism* (London 1961), 128.

myth in which the origin of man was bound up with the creation of the world from the body of a giant or proto-human killed and carved by the gods.

CANON AND CATECHISM

The myth of the world's construction from the body of the primal Twin must have been transmitted as a coherent narrative, not necessarily always in poetic form, but probably so for the most part. There is less basis for assuming that Indo-European poets expounded cosmological or other philosophical doctrines in verse, or indeed that there was any integrated system to be expounded. Caesar (*Bell. Gall.* 6. 14. 3–6) says that those studying to be Druids in Gaul had to learn a large quantity of oral poetry, and that they were taught about the transmigration of souls and much about cosmology and theology; but even if this is true, it is not matched by evidence for a corresponding genre in other Indo-European traditions. What seem more characteristic media for the transmission of popular, poetic, or priestly wisdom (insofar as it was not embedded incidentally in hymnic and narrative compositions) are simple, small-scale forms such as lists, catechisms, proverbs, and riddles.

As for lists, we noted in Chapter 1 the practice of codifying traditional material in the form of verse catalogues, the learning of which perhaps formed part of the poet's training. A more distinctive type of canon, used especially for precepts and philosophical aphorisms, but to some extent also for the codification of legend, takes the form 'there are three (or some other number) so-and-sos', this pronouncement being followed by the explanation of what they are. Examples occur from India to Ireland.

There are three measures, bull of the Bharatas, that they say apply to men: low, middling, and good ... There are three kinds of people, king: good, bad, and middling; one should properly charge to them three kinds of tasks. Three hold no property, king: the wife, the slave, and the son, whatever they obtain belongs to him who owns them. They say, and a *paṇḍit* should know, that a king who is powerful should avoid these four: he should not consult with dimwitted men, woolgatherers, sloths, and flattering bards.[60]

Of five I partake, of five I do not partake: of good thought I partake, of bad thought I do not partake; of good speech I partake, of bad speech I do not partake, [*etc.*] (Y. 10. 16).

[60] *MBh.* 5. 33. 50–9, continuing with more fours, then fives, and so on up to ten; further examples in 5. 35. 37–48, 64; 37. 25, 29 f., 33, etc.

The one dog's likeness is with eight: it behaves like a priest, it behaves like a warrior, it behaves like a cattle-farmer, [*and so on, each likeness then explained in turn*] (Vd. 13. 44–8).

From these four things came the types of women: one from a bitch, one from a bee, one from a hairy sow, and one from a long-maned mare: [*the characteristics of each in turn then explained*] (Phocylides fr. 14 West).

For there are ten things which overwhelm the falsehood of every sovereign ... sovereignty and worth, fame and victory, children and kindred, peace and life, destiny and tribes. ... There are four sovereigns: the true sovereign and the sovereign by his wits, the sovereign who takes possession with warbands and the bull sovereign [*these are then each in turn further defined*] (*Audacht Morainn* 56–62, trs. J. T. Koch in Koch–Carey [2000], 192 f.).

Three Fair Princes of the Island of Britain: Owain son of Urien, Rhun son of Maelgwn, Rhufawn the Radiant son of Dewrarth Wledig (*Trioedd ynys Prydein* 1, trs. Bromwich).

This last item comes from a Middle Welsh work consisting, in Rachel Bromwich's edition, of 96 triadic canons.[61] Its title means 'Triads of the Island of Britain'. The older material in it relates to the body of British saga tradition. The triads probably evolved as part of the teaching given in the bardic schools, serving as mnemonics encapsulating the essential facts.[62] There are many other Welsh triads; the form was extensively used in legal codes, and in a treatise on the poetic craft.[63]

Numbered canons may also appear in question and answer form:

'Yājñavalkya,' he said, 'tell me—how many graspers are there and how many over-graspers?' Yājñavalkya replied: 'There are eight graspers and eight overgraspers.' 'What are the eight graspers?' 'The out-breath is a grasper ... Speech is a grasper ...', etc. (*Bṛhadāraṇyaka Upaniṣad* 3. 2. 1–9, trs. P. Olivelle; cf. 3. 1. 7–10).

In general, wisdom is often presented as uttered by a sage or divinity in response to questioning. Zarathushtra composes a poem of twenty stanzas each containing a question to Ahura Mazdā, and all but the last begin with the same formula *taṯ θβā pərəsā, ərəš mōi vaocā, Ahurā*, 'this I ask thee, tell me straight, Lord' (Y. 44; cf. 31. 14–16). He is certainly following a traditional pattern, reflected also in the anaphoric series of *pṛcchā́mi tvā* ... 'I ask thee' (= Gāthic *θβā pərəsā*) in RV 1. 164. 34. In the Vedic poem the answers follow in the next stanza. There may have been another traditional pattern in which

[61] Rachel Bromwich, *Trioedd ynys Prydein* (2nd edn., Cardiff 1978).

[62] Bromwich (as n. 61), lxv–cvii.

[63] Bromwich, lxiii. It is likely that they were originally transmitted orally (ead., cviii). Cf. also Watkins (1995), 46 f.

the questions and answers alternated. Elsewhere Zarathushtra does frame questions that receive answers from on high (29. 2–8), and he claims to tell forth things that Mazdā has told him (45. 3, 5). In the Edda we find several examples of question and answer stanzas in symmetrical alternation, and here too the questions are prefaced by a repeated formula:

> Segðu mér þat, Alvíss: ǫll of rǫc fira
> voromc, dvergr, at vitir.
>
> Tell me this, Alvíss: about all beings' destinies
> I fancy, dwarf, you know. (*Alvíssmál* 9, 11, etc.).
>
> Segðu mér þat, Fiǫlsviþr, es ec þic fregna mon
> oc ec vilia vita.
>
> Tell me this, Fiǫlsviþr, that I shall ask you,
> and I should like to know. (*Fiǫlsvinnsmál* 7, 9, etc.)
>
> þegiattu, vǫlva, þic vil ec fregna—
> unz alkunna vil ec enn vita.
>
> Be not silent, seeress, I want to ask you—
> till I have full knowledge I want to know more. (*Baldrs draumar* 8, 10, 12)

The structure of the first and third of these, with a parenthetic supplement filling out the couplet, has been compared with Zarathushtra's 'this I ask thee, tell me straight, Lord'.[64]

A recurrent type of question concerns superlatives: what is the best thing, what is the greatest so-and-so? The Avestan hymn to Vərəθraγna begins with the tale that Zarathushtra asked Ahura Mazdā 'Who is the best-armed of the holy Yazatas?' The god answered, 'The Ahura-created Vərəθraγna, O Spitama Zarathushtra', and this exchange is repeated as a refrain (Yt. 14. 1, 6, 8, etc.). Similar questionings appear in the *Vidēvdāt*. In the third chapter Zarathushtra asks 'what place on earth is the most agreeable?' And then 'what place is the next most agreeable?' and so on to the fifth most agreeable; then 'what place is the most diagreeable?', and so forth. At the end of the Homeric catalogue of the Achaean ships the poet asks the Muse 'who was the best of them, of the men and the horses?' And the answers follow: 'the best horses were . . . And of the men the best was . . .' (*Il.* 2. 761–8). Among the so-called Akousmata which embodied the oral teaching of the Pythagoreans one category consisted in questions of the 'what is the most' type, with the answers: 'What is the most righteous act?—Sacrifice.' 'What is the cleverest thing?—Number; and secondly whoever gave things their names.'[65]

[64] Cf. Schmitt (1967), 36 f., 276 f.
[65] Iambl. *Vit. Pyth.* 82, with further instances. Cf. Ohlert (1912), 107–16.

This motif is also at home in poetic contests. In the *Certamen Homeri et Hesiodi* Homer is challenged to answer the questions 'what is best for mortals?' and 'what is finest for mortals?' (7), and again 'what is finest for mortals and what is worst?' and 'how would cities best be run?' 'What is the best thing to pray to the gods for?' 'What best thing grows in smallest space?' (11). In the Hesiodic *Melampodia* Melampous was probably asked 'what is the pleasantest thing?' and answered 'it is pleasant to . . . And it is also pleasant to . . . But pleasantest of all is . . .' (cf. frs. 273–4). The lake demon's testing of Yudhiṣṭhira contains several such questions (*MBh.* 3. 279. 36, 52, 54). In *Gylfaginning* (2 f.) king Gylfi's interrogation of the three presidents of Valhalla is introduced as a contest of learning, and his first question is 'who is the best or eldest of the gods?'

Elsewhere we find such wisdom offered apodeictically, without the preceding question:

> The finest thing is what's most right; the best is health;
> the nicest is to get the thing one craves.
> (Thgn. 255 f., cf. 425–8; *PMG* 890)

> Fire is best among the sons of men,
> and the sight of the sun;
> his health, if a man is able to have it;
> living without disgrace. (*Hávamál* 68)

> Wind is the swiftest thing in the air,
> thunder at times is the loudest . . .
> Fate is strongest, winter is coldest,
> spring frostiest—it is longest cold,
> summer sunniest, etc. (Old English *Maxims B* 3–11)

> Night is the darkest of weathers, necessity is the hardest of fates,
> sorrow is the heaviest burden, sleep is the likest to death.
> (*Solomon and Saturn B* 134 f.)

Proverbs

The Indo-Europeans, like other peoples, no doubt had much popular wisdom encapsulated in proverbs. It is doubtful, however, whether we can reconstruct any of it. It is not difficult to find examples of corresponding proverbs in different branches of the Indo-European tradition. But, to say nothing of the possibilities of independent creation, proverbs travel easily across borders, and one may often find just as good parallels in Arabic or Turkish.

Some proverbs current in modern Western languages can be traced back to Classical literature. There is a striking match between what Sophocles' Ajax quotes as a proverb, ἐχθρῶν ἄδωρα δῶρα, and the Danish proverb 'fjende-gave ingen gave', 'an enemy's gift is no gift'.[66] But the Sophoclean line found its way into the Paroemiographers, and learned transmission to the North is an all too obvious possibility. It is the same with Lithuanian proverbs such as 'one hand washes the other', or 'one swallow does not make it spring', both corresponding to familiar Classical adages.[67] In Old Irish as in Greek one finds the motif of the third wave (or some higher ordinal) that is bigger than the others and overwhelms one.[68]

Parallels between Greece and India might seem in principle more promising, but again it is difficult to find solid ground to build on. 'Put out the fire before it spreads' was a Greek proverb, applicable for example to a political situation such as a growing tyranny.[69] There is a similar one in the Indian epics: 'this blazing and grisly fire that is mounting, extinguish it now before there is war!' (*MBh.* 2. 56. 7; cf. *Rm.* 5. 45. 29). Are we to assume common inheritance? A few pages later the same sententious adviser cites a saying about the goat that scratched at the ground and dug up the lost knife with which its own throat was to be cut (*MBh.* 2. 59. 8). We have other Indian sources for this, the earliest of which is perhaps of the second century BCE. There is a corresponding Greek proverb αἲξ (or οἶς) τὴν μάχαιραν, 'the goat (or sheep) (found) the knife', and versions are attested later in Arabic and Ethiopic.[70] In this case the proverb does not allude to the typical behaviour of goats but to a fable, a tale of what a certain goat once did in a particular situation. Animal fables were popular in Greece from the archaic period on and at a later date in India; but it is fairly certain that they originated in the Near East and do not represent Indo-European heritage.

RIDDLES

We tend to think of riddles as a species of social diversion, something to amuse children and sharpen their wits. No doubt the more hackneyed ones always tended to finish up in that way. But in the ancient literatures riddles

[66] Soph. *Aj.* 665; G. Kallstenius in *Studier til Axel Kock* (Arkiv for Nordisk Filologi, Tillagsband til bd. 40, Lund 1929), 23 no. 36.

[67] Schleicher (1857), 162, 178.

[68] See P. Groeneboom's note on [Aesch.] *Prom.* 1015; Dooley–Roe (1999), 235.

[69] Alc. 74. 6 with schol.; Pind. *Nem.* 1. 24; Call. fr. 195. 23–6; Arnd Kerkhecker, *Callimachus' Book of Iambi* (Oxford 1999), 136.

[70] For the full material and discussion see Winfried Bühler, *Zenobii Athoi proverbia*, iv (Göttingen 1982), 233–44.

often appear as serious tests upon which weighty consequences hang, even matters of life and death. It may be that a hero has to answer a riddle posed by a supernatural creature, such as the Sphinx in the Oedipus saga, or Baba Yaga or a water nymph in Slavonic legends. He may, to win the hand of a princess, be required to solve a riddle posed by her or her father, or himself to pose one that she cannot answer. Riddles play an important role in stories of contests between poets or seers of the kind described at the end of Chapter 1. Besides the examples mentioned there we may cite the young priest Aṣṭāvakra's challenge to the wise Bandin in the *Mahābhārata*, and the contest between Marbán and Dael Duiled the *ollam* of Leinster.[71]

Sometimes these intellectual duels involve difficult questions that are not exactly riddles but call for special knowledge or mantic insight. I have mentioned the type 'what is the best thing for mortals?', where an answer is required that is not banal but at least thought-provoking. Yudhiṣṭhira's testing by a supernatural being who guards a lake (*MBh.* 3. 297) involves his answering a long series of questions, some of which are true riddles but most of which are theological and ethical, a veritable catechism. Odin's contest with Vafthrudnir is an examination of the giant's deep knowledge of cosmological and cosmogonic myth; he is finally defeated when asked what Odin whispered into Baldr's ear before he mounted the pyre, a secret known only to Odin himself.

In the Hesiodic *Melampodia* the seer Mopsus defeated Calchas by successfully answering the question how many figs there were on a tree in front of them; or, according to Pherecydes of Athens (fr. 142 Fowler), how many piglets a pregnant sow was carrying. (He not only gave the correct number, ten, but specified that one of them was female.) The same problem is posed in riddle form by Gestumblindi in his contest with King Heidrek: 'What is that wonder that I saw out there before Delling's doors? Ten tongues it has, twenty eyes, forty feet; that creature moves hard.' Heidrek replies correctly that it is a sow with nine piglets inside her, and the sow is killed to verify the number.[72] A similar feat is attributed to a Russian seer.

The more typical riddle is one that requires for its solution not private knowledge or second sight but intelligence, lateral thinking, and expertise in metaphor. We saw in Chapter 2 that the Indo-European poet was master of a special language and style that often obscured the plain identity of things under periphrases and symbols, a language that was in fact sometimes 'riddling', presenting to hearers unfamiliar with the code a challenge to

[71] *MBh.* 3. 133 f.; *Tromdám Guaire* lines 868–900 Joynt, paraphrased in Thurneysen (1921), 263 f. and Dillon (1946), 94 f.

[72] *Edd. min.* 110 st. 12; *Hervarar saga* 10 p. 49 Tolkien.

comprehension. It is not surprising that we find stories of poets measuring themselves against one another in contests both of riddling language and of mythological learning.

There is in fact a close affinity between the conventional metaphorical language of poetry and that used in riddles. When a Vedic poet begins a hymn to Agni with the announcement

> Longing they roused up the longing one
> like the husband of the house, the women who share a home;
> the sisters relished the dark one (and) the ruddy one, (RV 1. 71. 1)

the style is that of a riddle. But his fellow Rishis, and everyone who was accustomed to these hymns and knew the conventional metaphors and references, will have understood that the 'sisters' were the fingers operating the fire-drill and exciting the flame, while the feminine dark and ruddy ones were night and dawn.

Another hymn to Agni (10. 79) begins with several stanzas in this riddling manner.

> I saw his, the great one's greatness, the immortal's in mortal settlements.
> In various places his jaws open and close; insatiably munching they devour much.
> Hidden his head, apart his eyes; insatiable he eats the forests with his tongue . . .
> This truth I declare to you, Heaven and Earth: the born child devours his mothers.

His mothers (dual) are the two wooden components of the fire-drill (cf. 5. 11. 3; AV Paipp. 11. 1. 3). According to Plutarch there was a riddle in the Hesiodic *Wedding of Ceyx* (fr. 267) about the child devouring its parents, that is, the fire consuming the wood from which it was kindled. It looks as if this may have been at least a Graeco-Aryan if not an Indo-European riddle.[73]

Walter Porzig pointed out that the Vedic encoding imagery is to some extent systematic. Things that come in pairs or sets, like the fingers in RV 1. 71. 1 above, may be 'brothers' or 'sisters' (according to gender); anything travelling through the air may be a 'bird'; things that give nourishment may be 'cows'; the top of anything may be its 'head' and the bottom its 'foot'.[74] Such encryption was no doubt further developed in India than in Eurostan, though some forms of Greek poetry and the Norse skaldic tradition show

[73] K. Ohlert, *Philologus* 56 (1897), 612 f., who also quotes a Faroese and a north German riddle about the fire's crooked father(s) and hollow mother; id. (1912), 93.

[74] W. Porzig in *Germanica, Eduard Sievers zum 75. Geburtstag* (Halle/Saale 1925), 646–60, partly anticipated by Müller (1897), 87.

parallel tendencies. The brother/sister symbolism, at least, operates in the same way in Greek and Lithuanian riddles.[75]

The riddle's challenge is generally to identify a person, object, process, or event from a set of oblique statements about it couched in figurative language. The syntax is in itself unproblematic: the statements about the object follow each other in paratactic series, though they may seem to fit oddly together or to be contradictory. A teasing element of precision is often given by the inclusion of numbers, as in the above riddle about the sow.

Our modern riddles are regularly in question form, 'what is it that . . .?' This is an ancient type (*MBh.* 3. 133. 25, 297. 40 ff.; Theodectes, *TrGF* 72 F 18), but the more traditional form was apodeictic, consisting simply of obscure or paradoxical statements; the 'what is it?' was understood, or appended at the end.

One conventional device common to the Vedic, Greek, Persian, Germanic, and Slavonic traditions is to introduce the mysterious thing or situation as something that the propounder of the riddle has witnessed:

ápaśyam gopā́m ánipadyamānam
ā́ ca párā ca pathíbhiś cárantam;
sá sadhrī́cīḥ, sá víṣūcīr vásāna
ā́ varīvarti bhúvaneṣu antáḥ.

I saw a herdsman unrestingly
going to and fro on his paths;
clothed in the one-directional (and) the multi-directional,
he keeps turning about amid the creatures.
(RV 1. 164. 31, cf. 1, 43; 10. 27. 19, 79. 1 (above))

ἄνδρ' εἶδον πυρὶ χαλκὸν ἐπ' ἀνέρι κολλήσαντα
οὕτω συγκόλλως ὥστε σύναιμα ποιεῖν.

I saw a man welding bronze onto a man
so firmly as to make them of one blood.
(Cleobulina 1, cf. 2; *Anth. Pal.* 14. 19)

Likewise in some riddles quoted in Firdawsi's *Shāh-nāma*; in the Exeter Book, 13 *ic seah turf tredan, X wæron ealra, | VI gebroþor ond hyra sweostor mid*, 'I saw them treading the sward, they were ten in all, six brothers and their sisters with them', cf. 29, 34, 36, 38 *ic wiht geseah*, 'I saw a man . . .', etc.; *Heiðreksgátur* 30 *hest sá ek standa, hýði meri*, 'I saw a horse standing, the mare was whipping him'; cf. 8–16, 24, 32–4; in a Russian riddle, я видел

[75] Theodectes, *TrGF* 72 F 4, 'there are two sisters . . .' (= Night and Day); Schleicher (1857), 193 f., 211, 'two sisters come separately over a hill' (= the eyes); 'four brothers wear one hat' (= a Dutch barn); 'four sisters pee in a pit' (= a cow's teats).

какую чудовину, 'I saw a certain prodigy'.[76] I do not find any examples in Schleicher's collection of Lithuanian riddles, but there is the analogous pattern 'I went on my way and I found . . .', 'I went through the forest, I found . . .'.[77]

In another riddle attributed to the legendary Cleobulina the speaker's unusual apperception is not visual but auditory:

> *κνήμηι νεκρὸς ὄνος με κερασφόρωι οὖας ἔκρουσεν.*
>
> A dead ass struck my ear with its horned shank.

The reference is to the notes of a Phrygian hornpipe, made from an ass's tibia with a cow-horn attached. The phrase 'struck my ear' obscures the fact that sound is in question, but we have here a variant of the paradox that a dead creature gives voice through a musical instrument. There are several Greek texts that play on this idea, but it appears also in a Latvian riddle about a goat's horn: 'when I was still alive, I was not able to give forth a voice; when life was at an end, my voice began to sound'.[78] If there were Indo-European riddles on these lines, the horn is one of the likeliest instruments to have been their subject, beside the bone flute and the skin drum.

In the Latvian riddle the first-person pronouns and verbs refer to the thing to be guessed: it describes itself. This is by no means a rare type. We find it in Greek (Thgn. 257–60, *Anth. Pal.* 14. 2, 5, 35, 42, etc.), it is standard in the late Latin collections of Symphosius and Aldhelm, and common in the Old English and Lithuanian ones. It is not clear, however, whether it is of Indo-European antiquity. Its European distribution is compatible with a Classical origin.

Alternatively the subject of the riddle is described in the third person. In Greek and Old English, at least, it may be introduced by 'there is a certain creature that . . .' or the like. Such is the famous riddle of the Sphinx in the hexameter version that may have stood in the epic *Oedipodea*:[79]

[76] D. Sadovnikov, *Zagadki Russkago naroda* (St Petersburg 1901), 101 no. 987b. A similar 'I saw' occurs in Greek and Norse gnomic poetry, where it introduces a moral tale; cf. Thgn. 915/920, Soph. *Aj.* 1142/1150, Eur. *El.* 369, fr. 295; *Hávamál* 70. 4, 78. 2, 118. 2. This has Hebrew parallels: West (1997), 521.

[77] Schleicher (1857), 194, 196. Comparable is *Heiðreksgátur* 2, 'I went forth, I made an excursion, I saw . . .'. Another phrase is 'I know one who . . .': Eubulus fr. 106. 16 K.–A. *οἶδ' ἐγώ, ὅς* . . . ; Exeter Riddle 43. 1, 49. 1, 58. 1, *ic wāt* . . . ; Faroese riddle quoted by Ohlert (1912), 101, *eg veit ein fugl* . . .

[78] Thgn. 1229 f., 'a marine carcass that in death makes utterance with living mouth' (a conch); cf. *Hymn. Herm.* 38, Soph. *Ichn.* 299 f.; Philitas fr. 18 Sbardella; A. J. G. Bielenstein, *1000 lettische Rätsel* (Mitau 1881), no. 868.

[79] *Oedipodea* fr. 2* West, from Asclepiades of Tragilos, *FGrHist* 12 F 7a. Other examples of this type of opening: Antiph. fr. 194, Eubulus fr. 106, Theodectes *TrGF* 72 F 4; *Anth. Pal.* 14. 34; Exeter Riddles 50, 84.

> There is on earth a two-footed and four-footed creature with a single voice,
> and three-footed, changing its form alone of all creatures that move
> on earth and through the air and on the sea.
> When it walks supported on the most legs,
> then the strength of its limbs is feeblest.

The solution is man, who as a baby crawls on all fours and in old age uses a stick as a third leg. This riddle has a wide currency across Europe and beyond; it has reached Finno-Ugric peoples and Fiji.[80] It must be read against the background of the traditional Indo-European antithesis between two-footed and four-footed creatures (p. 100); one that belongs to both classes is deeply paradoxical from the start. But 'three-footed', of the man walking with a stick, also goes back to Indo-European riddling. We catch it in RV 10. 117. 8,

> ékapād bhū́yo dvipádo ví cakrame,
> dvipā́t tripā́dam abhí eti paścā́t.
>
> The one-footed (= the Sun) far outsteps the two-footed ones (humans),
> the two-footed catches up the three-footed from behind.

Hesiod in one of his most high-flown passages refers to a 'three-footed man', not intending it as a riddle, since he adds 'whose back is bent, and his head looks down at the ground', but as an inherited poetic locution (*Op.* 533; cf. Aesch. *Ag.* 81). An early Welsh poem speaks of an old man's staff as his third foot.[81]

Another type of riddle takes the form of a little narrative, like the 'I saw' ones but without the 'I saw'. There are examples among the Exeter Book riddles (22, 33, 46 f., 54, 86) and the *Heiðreksgátur* (17, 27; *Edd. min.* 112, 116 f.). Here is a Greek one:

> *αἶνός τίς ἐστιν ὡς ἀνήρ τε κοὐκ ἀνήρ*
> *ὄρνιθα κοὐκ ὄρνιθ' ἰδών τε κοὐκ ἰδών*
> *ἐπὶ ξύλου τε κοὐ ξύλου καθημένην*
> *λίθωι τε κοὐ λίθωι βάλοι τε κοὐ βάλοι.*
>
> There is a tale that a man who was no man,
> seeing and not seeing a bird that was no bird
> as it sat on a stock that was no stock,
> hit it and hit it not with a stone that was no stone.[82]

[80] See Aarne (1918–20), ii. 3–23.

[81] Red Book of Hergest col. 1029 = Kenneth Jackson, *Early Welsh Gnomic Poems* (Cardiff 1935), iii st. 30. 3 *trydyd troet y hen y ffon*; Clancy (2003), 113. For another family of riddles in which 'two-footed', 'three-footed', and 'four-footed' have a different reference see Aarne (1918–20), ii. 24–59.

[82] 'Panarces' ap. Clearch. fr. 95 Wehrli, cf. Pl. *Rep.* 479bc with schol.

The solution: a myopic eunuch, dimly descrying a bat that was clinging to a fennel-stalk, threw a pumice-stone at it but failed to make a direct hit. There is no reason to suppose that this delightfully silly conundrum is much older than the fourth century BCE, when it is first attested. Yet it has some recognizably Indo-European features. With its narrative mode and series of parallel members, in each of which something is mentioned only for its essence to be apparently negated, it shows a more than casual formal similarity to a widely diffused European riddle, first attested in a tenth-century manuscript at Reichenau, about snow melting in the sun:

> Volavit volucer sine plumis,
> sedit in arbore sine foliis;
> venit homo sine manibus,
> conscendit illam sine pedibus,
> assavit illum sine igne,
> comedit illum sine ore.

> There flew a bird without feathers,
> settled on a tree without leaves;
> there came a man without hands,
> climbed the tree without feet,
> roasted the bird without fire,
> devoured it without a mouth.[83]

This in turn recalls the Latin herbal spell quoted in the last chapter, 'Herdsmen found you, culled you without hands, cooked you without fire, ate you without teeth.' The subject matter of the three texts is so dissimilar that there can be no question of one being modelled on another. Rather they are all cast in the same inherited riddle form.

Further: the Greek riddle is based on an accumulation of apparent impossibilities, things that both are X and are not-X. In each case the solution turns out to be something on the margin between the opposed alternatives X and not-X. We have here something deeply rooted in Indo-European structures of thought and expression. In Chapter 2 we saw how pervasive was the use of binary oppositions to express totalities, many of them taking the form 'both X and non-X', which appeared to leave nothing unaccounted for. We saw too that occasionally a pair of opposites (though not of the 'X and non-X' type) was supplemented by a middle term, to stop a possible loophole. There are stories from several Indo-European traditions in which a set of apparently impossible conditions is laid down, framed in terms of exclusive polarities, and they then turn out to be fulfillable by means of intermediates. Indra binds

[83] Aarne (1918–20), iii. 1–48. Many of the variants have four lines, like the eunuch riddle, and Aarne argues that this was the original form.

himself in a treaty with Vṛtra under which the latter may not be killed 'with matter dry or wet, rock or wood, thunderbolt or weapon, by day or by night'. Vṛtra then supposes himself safe, but Indra finds the opportunity to kill him with foam (neither dry nor wet) at twilight (neither day not night) (*MBh.* 5. 10. 30–8). Lleu Llaw Gyffes in the *Mabinogion* cannot be killed either inside or outside a house, either on horseback or on foot. In a Lithuanian tale a traveller offers to marry a girl if she will come to him 'neither naked nor clothed, neither on horse nor on foot nor in a carriage, neither on the road nor the footpath nor beside the road, at once in summer and winter'. The girl succeeds in meeting these conditions, and Lleu's faithless wife in compassing his death, in each case by identifying actions and entities that (like the eunuch, the bat, and so on) are 'neither one thing nor the other'.[84]

Year riddles

Pumice-throwing eunuchs and Phrygian hornpipes are hazards to be encountered only in certain evolved cultures, and we may feel confident that they did not feature in Indo-European riddles. On the other hand many riddles in the older traditions refer to universals of human experience such as the elements and the seasons. This brings us back to the cosmological questions with which the present chapter began. Riddles on these topics involve metaphors that imply particular conceptions of how the world works. The posing and answering of such riddles is not far removed from the catechistic instruction that in some traditions contributed to the training of learned priests and poets. 'The greatest sage is he who knows the meaning of that which has six naves, twelve axles, twenty-four joints, and three hundred and sixty spokes' (*MBh.* 3. 133. 21).

It does not in fact require a great sage to see that this is the year, represented as a wheel or a wheeled vehicle. The year is a frequent subject of riddles across the Indo-European area and beyond, as appears from the detailed survey by Antti Aarne.[85] They are always based on the numbers of months, days, or other subdivisions.

Aarne distinguishes four models. The year is represented as (1) a spoked wheel; (2) a father with twelve children and 360 or 720 grandchildren; (3) a

[84] For further details see my paper in *JIES* 32 (2004), 1–9, where I use these stories and the riddle to explain why Baldr was killed by a blind god with a mistletoe missile, and Odysseus with the barb of a sting-ray. The offer of marriage to one who comes neither naked nor clothed (the answer is to come draped in a net) has Indic and German parallels; see Ohlert (1912), 56. A Gaelic oral version of the story of Diarmaid and Gráinne contains a set of provisos very like those of the Lithuanian tale: J. G. Campbell, *The Fians* (London 1891), 52 f.

[85] Aarne (1918–20), i. 74–178.

tree with twelve branches, each supporting numbers of birds' nests with eggs in them; or (4) a grand edifice with twelve rooms, etc. The last two models cannot be traced back further than the first millennium CE and seem to be less ancient than the first two, though the tree version enjoys a wide diffusion.[86]

The wheel model is well established in Vedic India. 'Twelve spokes, one wheel, three naves—who understands this? In it are fixed three hundred and sixty like dowels that do not wobble' (RV 1. 164. 48, cf. AV 10. 8. 4 f., *MBh.* 1. 3. 64 f., 150, 169, 173). The underlying concept is that the year revolves like a wheel, returning to the same point. The same ancient idea is presupposed in the Greek epic formula *περιπλομένων* or *περιτελλομένων ἐνιαυτῶν*, 'as the years revolved'. Euripides speaks of the 'wheel' or 'circle' (*κύκλος*) of the year (*Hel.* 112, *Phoen.* 477, al.).

In RV 1. 164. 11 f. the wheel image is combined with that of father and sons: on the twelve-spoked wheel stand the 720 sons in pairs, and they call it their father. In a Greek riddle ascribed to the sage Cleobulus of Lindos the year is a father with twelve sons, each of whom has thirty pale-skinned and thirty dark daughters, making a total of 720 grandchildren.[87] This genetic imagery is clearly archaic; we have seen that brothers and sisters were a traditional element of the metaphorical thesaurus. In another Greek riddle Day and Night are represented as two sisters, each of whom is also the mother and daughter of the other.[88] This again is very much in line with Vedic imagery: we saw in Chapter 5 that Dawn and Night are often called sisters in the Rigveda, and that Dawn is 'born' daily. I quoted the Latvian riddle: 'Two sisters who are at odds; one appears, the other runs away; one is white, the other black'.

In the 'Vedic' hymn in *MBh.* 1. 3. 60–70, at stanza 64, we again find the year-wheel, here with 720 spokes. But in the preceding stanza a quite different image is used, that of the Dawns as cows: 'Those three hundred and sixty milking cows give birth to one calf, and yield milk for it'. (The calf is the first dawn of the next year.) This is not presented as a riddle, but it might well have been. The lines in the *Odyssey* about the cattle of the Sun (12. 129–31),

> *ἑπτὰ βοῶν ἀγέλαι, τόσα δ' οἰῶν πώεα καλά,*
> *πεντήκοντα δ' ἕκαστα, γόνος δ' οὐ γίνεται αὐτῶν,*
> *οὐδέ ποτε φθινύθουσι, θεαὶ δ' ἐπὶ ποιμένες εἰσίν,*

[86] Aarne, 140–5, argues for its origin in the Persian–Arabic sphere.

[87] Diog. Laert. 1. 91 = *Anth. Pal.* 14. 101. For later versions of this riddle (French, Slavonic, modern Greek) see Aarne (1918–20), i. 102, 160–6.

[88] Theodectes, *TrGF* 72 F 4 = *Anth. Pal.* 14. 40; cf. ibid. 41. For a similar riddle found in Latin (*mater me genuit, eadem mox gignitur ex me*), German, and Latvian the solution is given as 'ice and water', but 'day and night' was presumably the original answer; cf. Ohlert (1912), 54 f.

(There are) seven herds of cows, and as many fair flocks of sheep,
and fifty in each; they give birth to no young,
and never perish, and there are goddesses to herd them,

have every appearance of being an old riddle, the 350 cows and 350 sheep standing (as Aristotle saw) for the days and nights of the lunar year. They may not have had that meaning for the poet of the *Odyssey*, but it is surely what they signified originally.[89]

THE WORLD WIDE WEB

We saw in Chapter 5 that the radiance of the morning sky and the starry splendour of the night sky were sometimes pictured, both in India and in Greece, as the raiments of Dawn and Night. In certain Vedic passages the creation of these fabrics is conceived as a continuing process. They are woven by the two goddesses themselves; the sun may also play a part. This is four-dimensional cosmology, with the time axis as an integral component.

The weaver [*fem.*, *sc.* Dawn] has rolled up again the spread-out (fabric);
in mid activity the craftsman has laid down the work. (RV 2. 38. 4)

With your best (steeds) you (Sūrya) come, tearing apart the weft,
pulling down the black garment, O god. (4. 13. 4)

A certain pair of maidens of different hue
attend the six-pegged loom and weave:
one draws out the threads, the other inserts them;
they do not break them off, they do not reach an end.
I, as they dance round, so to speak,
cannot distinguish which of them is ahead.
A male weaves it, ties it off;
a male has spread it out on the firmament. (AV 10. 7. 42 f.)

[89] Arist. fr. 175. For the Dawns as cows in Indo-European metaphor (and Slavonic riddle) cf. pp. 223 f. The seer Polyidus was famous for solving the riddle of a cow that changed colour three times a day, every four hours, from white to red to black (Hyg. *Fab.* 136. 2, cf. Aesch. fr. 116, Soph. fr. 395, Apollod. 3. 3. 1). His solution was 'a ripening blackberry'. But this does not fit the daily cycle given by Hyginus. In the Veda black, red, and white are the colours of the cows that represent night, dawn, and day. This must have been the original reference of Polyidus' riddle. Cf. Ohlert (1912), 91 f. He compares the Russian tale of Vasilissa, who on her way to Baba Yaga saw a white horse and rider, later a red one, and later a black one. She asked Baba Yaga about them, and the witch explained that they were 'my shining day, my red sun, and my black night' (Mannhardt (1875), 94 f.).

The six pegs of the loom (like the six wheel-naves of *MBh.* 3. 133. 21 cited above) represent the six seasons. The male is perhaps Sūrya.[90]

The notion of cosmic weaving is also found in Greek, applied not to the succession of day and night but rather to the seasonal clothing of the earth with vegetation and crops. It is first documented in that same cosmogony of Pherecydes of Syros in which we found a world tree and an oceanic dragon. The tree supported a wonderful robe which Zas had made, decorated with the earth and surrounding ocean, and which he had bestowed upon his bride Chthonie, the primal earth goddess. An Orphic poem entitled *The Robe* (*Πέπλος*), attributed to the Pythagorean Brontinus, apparently described the ploughing and sowing of the earth as a weaving process that produced her dress.[91]

In north European songs (German, Swedish, Baltic) the Sun's dress or the sunbeams are pictured as being spun or woven with gold threads. In this Latvian example both Sun and Moon are involved at the loom:

> Saule tendit la trame sur le métier
> debout au milieu de l'air;
> Mēnesis en courant dans le ciel
> emmêle la trame de Saule.[92]

Weaving was an ancient craft, familiar to the Indo-Europeans.[93] We saw in Chapter 1 that it was one of two forms of manufacturing activity that were applied metaphorically to poetic composition. The other was joinery, and in Graeco-Aryan more specifically chariot-building. It is noteworthy that in the Indic tradition, at least, the diurnal and annual cycles are conceived in imagery from the same two spheres, as weaving stretched out on the loom and as a spoked wheel or wheeled vehicle. In the *Mahābhārata* we find both in successive stanzas:

> Three hundred and sixty spokes are affixed to the nave in this abiding wheel,
> forever moving in a cycle of twenty-four fortnights, which the six boys keep turning.
>
> Two young women are weaving this colourful loom, forever turning back and forth their threads,
> turning them from black ones to white ones, which are for always the past creatures and the present. (1. 3. 150 f.)

With the patterned alternation of black and white we perhaps come close to the original inspiration of the cosmic weaving image. Early looms were often

[90] Cf. also RV 1. 115. 4; 10. 130. 1 f.; *Taittirīya Brāhmaṇa* 2. 5. 5. 3; *MBh.* 1. 3. 61; West (1971), 54 f.

[91] M. L. West, *The Orphic Poems* (Oxford 1983), 10 f., cf. 244 f.

[92] Mannhardt (1875), 216–19; *LD* 33941 = Jonval no. 302.

[93] See *EIEC* 572 f. (s.v. Textile preparation).

operated by two women, one on each side to pass the shuttle back to the other.[94] The goddesses Night and Day fit neatly into this role. If we now recall the ancient theory attested in the Vedas, and perhaps by the Trundholm sun-disc, that the sun travels to and fro across the sky, bright by day and dark by night (pp. 209 f.), it becomes obvious that this corresponds to the shuttle that the two sisters pass between them, drawing the alternate white and black threads. With this insight the whole weaving image becomes sharp and coherent. Of this beautiful prehistoric vision only fragmented echoes remain in the Rigveda and the other traditions at our disposal.

[94] Cf. E. J. W. Barber, *Prehistoric Textiles* (Princeton 1990), 84, 105 f., 113, 251; ead., *The Mummies of Ürümchi* (London 1999), 77–9.

10

Mortality and Fame

The gods are of heaven, and immortal; mankind is of the earth, and subject to death. Each of us is conscious that he is but one of a countless number who have lived, are living, or are yet to be born, and that his individual life is a brief detail in the long tale of generations, soon to be cut short and in all probability sunk in oblivion.

The Indo-European believed in a kind of afterlife, to be sure. He would go to join his forefathers, and with them receive homage from his descendants. But a limited number of great men—kings, warriors, seers—and even some women associated with them—lived on in the memory of the people, in poem and story. Their bodies and souls had passed away, but their name had survived death; they had achieved unfading fame. This was a prize that outstanding individuals could strive for and anticipate even in life. So Horace exults (*Carm.* 3. 30. 6–8):

> non omnis moriar, multaque pars mei
> uitabit Libitinam: usque ego postera
> crescam laude recens.

THE ORIGIN OF HUMANKIND

How did our terrestrial race come into being in the first place? The Indo-Europeans perhaps had no fixed and definite doctrine on the question. But as we saw in Chapter 4, there was a general idea that we are the children of Earth, the universal mother, whose fertility comes from Father Sky.

How is this parturition to be imagined? We see trees and plants growing up out of the soil, and there are myths according to which men, or a particular ancestor of men, grew up from the earth in tree form or came somehow from trees or plants. Hesiod's Bronze Race came ἐκ μελιᾶν, that is, from ash-trees or born of ash-tree nymphs. Of Pelasgus, the first man in Arcadian legend, we are told that 'dark Earth put him forth (ἀνέδωκεν) in the wooded mountains, so that there might be a mortal race'. There are other references in Greek sources to human origins from ash or other trees.[1] I mentioned in the last chapter the Iranian cosmogony in which mankind's first parents Mahryaγ and Mahryānaγ grew in the form of a rhubarb plant from the earth fertilized by the seed of Gayōmart. In the old German poetic genealogy reported by Tacitus (*Germ.* 2. 2) Tuisto, the father of Mannus from whom all the Germans descended, was *terra editus*, 'put forth from the earth'. In Eddic myth the first man and woman were Askr and Embla; the woman's name is obscure (possibly 'Elm'), but the man's certainly means 'Ash-tree'.[2] His Old English equivalent Æsc appears as the eponymous ancestor of the Æscingas.

Mannus is a form of the common Germanic word for 'man'.[3] He must have been conceived originally as the progenitor of all mankind, not just of the German peoples. The same root exists in Sanskrit: *mánu-* means a man, or mankind, and Manu(s) is a mythical divine ancestor. Here too he must have begun as the forefather of mankind as a whole, but he has become the representative of Aryan culture in opposition to that of the Dasus, India's dark-skinned aborigines.[4] He was considered to have been the first sacrificer and the establisher of the fire-cult (RV 5. 21. 1; 7. 2. 3; cf. 8. 63. 1). The parallelism between the German and the Indic figure points clearly to a common prototype, a primal 'Man' from whom all men were descended. There are perhaps traces of him in Iran and Anatolia too.[5]

In the Tacitean account Mannus is the son of Tuisto 'Twin', whom we have argued to be an androgynous being corresponding to the Nordic Ymir and the Indo-Iranian Yama/Yima. Ymir too gives birth to the first human pair. By analogy we might expect Manu to be the son of Yama. He is not, but the two are related, each being the son of Vivasvat. (The Iranian Yima is likewise son of Vīvahvant.)

The fact is that the Indo-Iranian Twin figure had lost his original cosmogonic significance. Withered remnants of it persist in the stories of his incest

[1] Hes. *Op.* 145; Asius fr. 8 W.; cf. F. Specht, *ZVS* 68 (1944), 191–3; West (1966), 221; (1978), 187.

[2] In the extant version (*Vǫluspá* 17 f.; *Gylf.* 9) the pair are not represented growing as trees but are found as logs by gods who endow them with life. Cf. de Vries (1956), ii. 371 f.; Dronke (1997), 123.

[3] For morphological analysis see N. Wagner, *HS* 107 (1994), 143–6; M. E. Huld in *EIEC* 366b. The word is perhaps related to **men-*/*mneh*$_2$ 'think'; cf. Nagy (1990), 70.

[4] Cf. RV 1. 130. 8; Oldenberg (1917), 151 n. 1.

[5] Iran: A. Christensen in *Festschrift für Friedrich Carl Andreas* (Leipzig 1916), 63–9. The Lydian proto-king Manes (Hdt. 1. 94. 3, 4. 45. 3; son of Zeus and Ge, Dion. Hal. *Ant.* 1. 27. 1) is a plausible counterpart, except that the manuscripts of Dionysius give *Μάσνην*, *Μάσνεω*, which Wilamowitz, *Kl. Schr.* iv. 63, contends is the true form.

with his sister and of his being sawn in two (Chapter 9). But he was remembered chiefly in association with the transition to mortality. Yima is portrayed as a world ruler in whose reign paradisiac conditions prevailed. There was no summer and winter, no old age, sickness, or death, but an unfailing abundance of food and water (Y. 9. 4 f., Yt. 15. 15–17, 19. 30–3, Vd. 2. 5). But he sinned, and his majesty departed stage by stage (Yt. 19. 34–8). Or the world became overcrowded with the swelling human and animal population: Ahura Mazdā prepared a killing winter, instructing Yima to build a stronghold and withdraw to it with the seeds of all the best men and women and animals and plants. He did so, and there the elect dwell, apart from this world (Vd. 2. 8–43). As for the Vedic Yama, he is celebrated as the one who marked himself off from the gods by renouncing immortality and opting for death as the price of having progeny (RV 10. 13. 4). He found the path for the many, the path that our fathers have trodden (10. 14. 1 f.). He is the king of the dead, to whose abode all go on the road that he established.[6]

The separation of the two races, the celestial and the terrestrial, is not absolute. It cannot be, so long as there are particular families that insist on their descent from a divinity. Indian Rishis traced themselves back to gods (RV 1. 139. 9; 7. 33. 11). Many of the heroes of Greek legend were sons or descendants of gods. The Scythian king Idanthyrsos claimed descent from 'Zeus' (Hdt. 4. 127. 4). Romulus and Remus were sons of Mars. Sundry Germanic kings and heroes boasted divine parentage or ancestry, especially from Odin/Woden.[7] The giantess Hyndla proposes to Freyja that they sit and talk 'of the lineage of princes, of those men who came from gods' (*Hyndluliόð* 8). Saxo tells of a Norwegian king Frogerus, 'ut quidam ferunt Othino patre natus', and of a Swede Haldanus Biargrammus who was held to be a son of Thor (4. 8. 1 p. 101; 7. 2. 3 p. 184). The British Royal Family's pedigree leads back ultimately to Woden, though they make little of it these days. There is no reason why such claims should not go back to Indo-European times.

Human and animal lifespans

The ideal length of a human life in Indo-European thinking is a hundred rather than the Psalmist's threescore years and ten or fourscore. 'A hundred autumns are before us, O gods, in which you have fixed the ageing of our bodies' (RV 1. 89. 9). 'That eye set by the gods, may we see it going forth in

[6] The Gauls claimed descent from 'Dis pater' (Caes. *Bell. Gall.* 6. 18. 1); in other words they identified their first ancestor with the lord of the dead. Is this a version of the same myth?

[7] Cf. Grimm (1883–8), 367 f., 1387, 1390; K. Sisam, *PBA* 39 (1953), 287–348; M. L. West, *The Hesiodic Catalogue of Women* (Oxford 1985), 20.

brightness for a hundred autumns; may we live for a hundred autumns' (ibid. 7. 66. 16, cf. 2. 18. 10; 3. 36. 10; 7. 101. 6; 10. 18. 4, 85. 39, 161. 2 f.; AV 3. 11. 2–4). Varro thought that *seclum* (*saeculum*) 'century' was related to *senex*, *quod longissimum spatium senescendorum hominum id putarunt* (*De lingua Latina* 6. 11). He was wrong about the etymology, but *saeculum* does originally seem to have meant 'lifetime', like its Welsh cognate *hoedl*. In an eighth-century Irish hymn the hundred-year unit is compounded: *ropo chétach cétblíadnach, cech cét diib ar úair*, 'may I live a hundred times a hundred years, each hundred of them in turn'. At Lithuanian christenings there is a toast 'may you live for the next hundred years'.[8]

Certain texts attest the belief that some other creatures live vastly longer. We noticed in Chapter 7 the 'Hesiodic' fragment according to which the crow lives nine human generations, the stag four times as long as a crow, the raven three times as long as a stag, the date-palm nine times as long as a raven, and the Nymphs ten times as long as the date-palm. The verses were often quoted in late antiquity and more than once rendered into Latin.[9] Classical influence probably lies behind similar canons recorded since medieval times from German, English, Irish, Scots Gaelic, and Portuguese written sources and popular wisdom, for example the Irish teaching that man lives nine times nine years, the deer three times as long as a man, the blackbird three times as long as a deer, the eagle three times as long as a blackbird, the salmon three times as long as an eagle, the yew three times as long as a salmon, and the world three times as long as a yew (= 59,049 years).[10]

However, neither Classical learning nor any other form of horizontal transmission can account for the extraordinary parallel between another Welsh text, the story of Culhwch and Olwen from the *Mabinogion*, and an episode in the *Mahābhārata*.

In the Indian epic it is related that the royal seer Indradyumna fell from heaven because no one any longer remembered his ancient fame. He asked the aged Mārkaṇḍeya if he recognized him. Mārkaṇḍeya did not, but advised him that there was a certain owl in the Himalaya who was older than himself and might know him. They went there. The owl said that he did not recognize Indradyumna, but that there was a crane living by a certain lake who was yet older. The owl accompanied them there. The crane too failed to identify the stranger, but said there was a tortoise in the lake who was his senior and

[8] Fer fio macc Fabri, ed. Kuno Meyer, *University of Illinois Studies in Language and Literature* 2 (1916), 569–71 = id., *Miscellanea Hibernica* (Urbana 1917), 19–21; Greimas (1992), 172. Cf. Pl. *Rep.* 615a; Schulze (1966), 147 f.; Campanile (1990b), 75 f., 94; Watkins (1995), 350 f.

[9] See R. Merkelbach–M. L. West, *Fragmenta Hesiodea* (Oxford 1967), 159.

[10] E. Hull, *Folk-Lore* 43 (1932), 378–83; J. Weisweiler, *ZCP* 24 (1954), 172 f.

might know more. The tortoise was called forth and after much pondering recognized the seer, who had formerly built his fire altars on its back.

In the Welsh tale King Arthur sends men to seek Mabon, son of Modron, who had been taken away from his mother ages before, when he was three nights old. They go and interrogate the Ouzel of Cilgwri, a bird so old that it has completely worn away a smith's anvil with its daily pecking. It knows nothing of Mabon, but tells them of an older creature who might know, the Stag of Rhedynfre, and it accompanies them there. The stag again knows nothing, but takes them to find a still older creature, the Owl of Cwm Cawlwyd. The owl in turn leads them to the oldest and most widely travelled creature in the world, the Eagle of Gwernabwy. Even he has heard nothing of Mabon. But he knows of an equally old creature, the Salmon of Llyn Llyw, and escorts them to it. The salmon is finally able to tell them where Mabon is imprisoned, and carries them there on its shoulders.[11]

The objects of the two quests are dissimilar, and the series of long-lived creatures do not agree in detail apart from the presence of an owl in both. Yet the narrative pattern is so alike and so distinctive that the resemblance is hard to account for except on the hypothesis of common inheritance. Like the Hesiodic verses, the stories presuppose a belief that creatures such as deer and certain birds may live many times longer than we humans. We may refer also to the Irish legend of Fintan mac Bóchra, a survivor of the Flood who knew the whole history of the western world and who spent hundreds of years in the shapes of a salmon, an eagle, and a hawk, and to his coeval, the Hawk or Crow of Achill.[12]

THE FATES

Individual human lives, as anyone can see, differ widely in length and fortune. For the most part the distribution of longevity and prosperity appears to be arbitrary; in other words, governed by divine agency. The Indo-Europeans seem to have believed that it was predetermined, not by a universal, all-encompassing Destiny that laid things down at the beginning of time, but by supernatural females attending the birth of each child and establishing the contours of its life then and there as it lay in its cradle. I do not know of any Indo-Iranian evidence for this idea, but it is found all over Europe, as well as

[11] *MBh.* 3. 191; *Culhwch and Olwen* 847–919. Cf. H. M. and N. K. Chadwick, *The Growth of Literature*, ii (Cambridge 1936), 572 f.

[12] R. I. Best et al. (edd.), *Anecdota from Irish Manuscripts*, i (Halle 1907), 24–39, trs. E. Hull (as n. 10), 392–402.

in Bronze Age Anatolia. In many traditions the goddesses determine fates by spinning.

Their names are different in different countries, but this is understandable. When deities are especially dangerous, it is common to avoid the name that is most truly theirs and to replace it with some substitute; we often find alternative names current at the same time. The important thing is the unity of the conception over such a large part of the Indo-European area, which makes it likely that it goes back to the deepest level of Indo-European.

Among the numerous deities of the Hittites and their Anatolian kinsmen are the Gulses, or in the Palaic language Gulzannikes, whose name comes from the verbal root *guls-* 'write'. They were 'goddesses of individual destiny, presiding at birth and acting as nurses, also in mythology creatresses of man'.[13] They appear repeatedly in mythical narratives in company with the Mother Goddesses called Ḫannaḫannes, and once also with Papaya and Isdustaya, goddesses who spin the threads of fate. In a ritual text for the erection of a new royal palace it is laid down that when the king enters into it, he commands an eagle to fly towards the sea and to report on who it sees sitting in field and forest. The eagle reports: 'I have looked. It is Isdustaya and Papaya, the ancient, infernal divinities, who are sitting huddled there.' 'So, what are they doing all the time?' 'She holds a spindle, they hold mirrors filled (with images); and they are spinning the king's years. And a shortening of his years, (even) a tally of them, is not to be seen!'[14]

While there are no spinster Fate-goddesses in the Vedas, there are certain passages in which the continuity of human life is conceived as a drawn-out thread or lengthening strip of fabric. One poet asks 'which god was it that put seed in man, saying *tántur ā́ tāyatām*, "let the thread (or warp) be extended"?' (AV 10. 2. 17). A sacrificer making an offering for offspring prays for his family to pass successfully along an unbroken thread (6. 122. 1 *áchinnaṃ tántum ánu sáṃ tarema*, cf. 2). The famous Vasiṣṭha family of Rishis weave the warp that Yama, the first man, set up on the loom (RV 7. 33. 9, 12).[15]

In the *Odyssey* (7. 197 f.) Alcinous says that once Odysseus has been brought home to Ithaca, he will experience whatever Aisa and the Spinners (*Κλῶθες* or *Κατάκλωθες*) spun for him with their flax at his birth. In the *Iliad* (20. 127 f., 24. 209 f., cf. 525) the same expression is used with Aisa or Moira as the subject: both words mean 'share, portion', and the goddess is

[13] Gurney (1977), 18. Cf. H. Otten–J. Siegelová, *Archiv für Orientforschung* 23 (1970), 32–8; Johann Tischler, *Hethitisches etymologisches Glossar*, i (Innsbruck 1977–83), 627–30; Jaan Puhvel, *Hittite Etymological Dictionary*, iv (Berlin–New York 1997), 239–44.

[14] *KUB* xxix. 1 i 50–ii 10; H. T. Bossert, *Die Welt des Orients* 2 (1957), 351 f.

[15] M. Lindenau, *Zeitschrift für Indologie und Iranistik* 1 (1922), 47.

at the same time the personification of what is allotted to one in life and the agent that allots it. Hesiod (*Th.* 904–6) registers a trio of Moirai, 'who give mortal men both good and ill'. Their names express their different aspects: Klotho 'Spinner', Lachesis 'Apportioner', and Atropos 'Inflexible'.[16] The three Moirai play a prominent role in modern Greek folk-tales, or did in the nineteenth century. They come on the third night after a child's birth and pronounce its destiny.[17]

At Rome the corresponding divinities are called the Parcae. The name may suggest 'the Sparing Ones', but that does not give an obvious sense, and Varro may have been nearer the mark when he explained it as related to *pario* 'give birth'; it may be contracted from **Paricae.* Their name then marks them as goddesses who attend at a birth. Their individual names are given as Nona, Decuma, and Morta, which may seem to express the blunt doctrine that the child is born in the ninth month or the tenth, or dead.[18]

Morta, however, may have had a wider reference. Livius Andronicus (fr. 23 Blänsdorf) used her name in translating a verse of the *Odyssey*. The Homeric line 'when the dread μοῖρα of death strikes a man down' became in Livius' version 'when the day arrives that Morta has proclaimed', *quando dies adueniet quem profata Morta est.* Morta appears here as the power that pre-determines the date of an individual's death by declaring it. It was natural for Latin-speakers to hear 'death' in the name Morta. But in origin it was very likely derived not from **mer* 'die' but, like Greek μοῖρα, from **smer* 'apportion'.[19]

The Parcae, like the Moirai, spin threads of fate. Everyone who has read Catullus' poem 64 remembers the refrain from their song at the wedding of Peleus and Thetis: *currite ducentes subtegmina, currite fusi*, 'run on, spindles, drawing out the threads for the weft'. It is possible that Catullus and other Latin writers such as Ovid (*Tr.* 5. 3. 25) and Petronius (*Sat.* 29. 6) took over the spinning image from Greek literature, and that it does not reflect native tradition. But the Latin evidence is not crucial to the argument, as we find the motif in various parts of barbarian Europe, not just in literature but in folk

[16] The second of these appears as a title of the Moirai in a late Spartan inscription, *IG* v(1). 602. 8 *Μοιρῶν Λαχέσεων*, and an apparent cognate *Logetibas* (dative plural) is taken to be a Messapic name for the Fates: Krahe (1955–64), i. 23, 84; ii. 90 no. 139; Haas (1962), inscr. B.1.47.

[17] Bernhard Schmidt, *Das Volksleben der Neugriechen und das hellenische Alterthum*, i (Leipzig 1871), 210–15; id., *Griechische Märchen, Sagen und Volkslieder* (Leipzig 1877), 67, 68, 98, 221; J. C. Lawson, *Modern Greek Folklore and Ancient Greek Religion* (Cambridge 1910), 121–30.

[18] Varro, *Res divinae* fr. 12a Agahd ap. Gell. 3. 16. 9; Caesellius Vindex ap. Gell. 3. 16. 11.

[19] The same root seems to appear with prepositional prefixes in the names of the Gaulish goddesses of abundance Canti-smerta and Ro-smerta (Lambert (2003), 150). The Cantismertas in the plural were perhaps equivalent to the Parcae (M. Lejeune).

belief, in circumstances where its presence is unlikely to be due to Classical influence.

In Nordic mythology the relevant figures are the Norns (*Nornir*), a name of unclear etymology. Like the Moirai, they give both good and ill.[20] They attend the birth of children and shape their lives. When Helgi the slayer of Hunding was born in Brálund,

> Night fell on the homestead, the Norns came,
> they who shaped his life for the lord;
> they ruled the prince should be most famous,
> and that he'd be held the best of warriors.
>
> They twisted strongly the strands of fate
> as castles crashed in Brálund;
> they separated the golden threads
> and fastened them in the moon's mid hall [the sky].
>
> East and west they concealed the ends—
> there the prince had the land in between;
> Neri's kinswoman cast to the north
> one fastening, bade it hold for aye.[21]

The power of fate is especially manifest on the battlefield, where some fall prey to death and others survive. In Homeric language the Moira of Death is said to come and stand by the warrior as he falls. The poet of the pseudo-Hesiodic *Shield of Heracles* (248–57) more graphically describes the *Κῆρες*, personifications of fated death, as horrible female figures present on the field and struggling to seize men as they fought, and then he or an interpolator has thrown in the names that belong to the Moirai, Klotho, Lachesis, and Atropos. In Norse mythology it is properly the Valkyries who have the task of choosing which warriors are to die and go to Valhalla. But the distinction between Norns and Valkyries becomes blurred, so that the Valkyries too can be portrayed as spinning men's destinies.[22]

The Norns also appear as three goddesses of fate who sit by the well of Urð at the foot of the cosmic tree Yggdrasil (*Vǫluspá* 20, *Gylf.* 15 f.). Urð corresponds to a word for fate found also in other Germanic languages. Old Saxon *wurth* is a gloss on *fatum*, and in the *Hêliand* is used for a person's

[20] Cf the runic inscription from Borgund (Sogn, Norway) quoted by de Vries (1956), i. 271, 'die Nornen bestimmen das Gute und das Böse, mir haben sie großes Leid bestimmt'.

[21] *Helgakviða Hundingsbana A* 2–4. On the Norns see Grimm (1883–8), 405–17; de Vries (1956), i. 270–3. On Germanic words for fate see D. H. Green (1998), 382–9. Another is represented by Old English *meotod*, Old Saxon *metud*, Norse *miǫtuðr*, from the root **med* 'measure, allot'; cf. Chantraine (1968–80), 675b; Meid (1991), 14.

[22] *Vǫlundarkviða* 1. On the Valkyries cf. de Vries (1956), i. 273 f.; Davidson (1988), 92–100.

fated death. In Old English Wyrd is a power that weaves destinies: *Rhyme Poem* 70 *me þæt Wyrd gewāf*, 'Wyrd wove that for me'; *Guthlac* 1350 f. *þrāg . . . wefen wyrdstafum*, 'the time woven on Wyrd's loom'. Later the Wyrds appear as a group, as in Chaucer, 'the Werdys that we clepyn Destiné' (*Legend of Good Women, Hypermnestra* 19), and most famously as the Weird Sisters in *Macbeth*.[23]

The word has a significant etymology. It is related to German *werden*, 'become', 'come about'. But in Latin the same verb means 'to turn', *uertere*; and in Vedic the middle form *vártate* has both senses, 'turns' or 'comes about', 'turns out' in such and such a way; the participle *vr̥ttá-* means 'turned, elapsed, happened'. This close semantic connection between turning and eventuating is surely relevant to the image of the goddesses' spindle that spins round as it twists the loose wool into a firm thread. In various languages the word for spindle or spindle-whorl is derived from the same verbal root: Sanskrit *vartanā* or *vartulā*, Old Church Slavonic *vrěteno*, Middle High German *wirtel*, Welsh *gwerthyd*. In the visionary cosmology of Plato's *Republic* (616c–17d) the planetary spheres, or rather hemispheres, are nested spindle-whorls on the great spindle of Ananke, and the three Moirai guide their revolutions. Perhaps the circling waters of Urð's well were also conceived as an analogue of destiny: Plutarch in his *Life of Caesar* (19. 8) records that German holy women prophesied by observing river eddies and taking indications from circling currents.

The Norns bear the individual names Urð, Verðandi, and Skuld (*Vǫluspá* 20, *Gylf.* 15), as it were 'Happened, Happening, and Due', representing the past, present, and future. Plato in the passage cited makes Lachesis sing of past things, Klotho of present, and Atropos of future, and the idea was perpetuated in later writers.[24] So it is likely enough that the Eddic names are due to Classical influence. On the other hand it should be borne in mind that 'past and future' or 'past, present, and future' were established Indo-European, or at any rate Graeco-Aryan, expressions of totality, especially in connection with divine or vatic knowledge (pp. 103 f.). It is a traditional formula that Plato is applying to the Moirai. This may have been a new combination; but the extent of the Fates' sway might have been stated in these terms at a very ancient epoch.

The spinster goddesses seem also to have been known in Germany. A spinning goddess is represented on a bracteate from south-west Germany, and a relief from Trier shows a trio of Mother goddesses, two of them holding distaffs or spindles. German ecclesiastical writers from around the tenth

[23] Cf. Brian Branston, *The Lost Gods of England* (London 1957), 64–71.

[24] Pl. *Rep.* 617c, [Arist.] *De mundo* 401^{b}18 (> Apul. *Mund.* 38), Isid. *Etym.* 8. 11. 92.

century denounce the people's foolish superstitious belief in the three sisters anciently called the Parcae, who determine a man's life at the moment of his birth, and for whom at certain times of year some women lay places at table in anticipation of a visit.[25]

The hymn of Fer fio macc Fabri cited earlier (n. 8) begins:

> Admuiniur secht n-ingena trethan
> dolbte snáithi macc n-áesmar.
>
> I call on the seven daughters of the sea
> who fashion the threads of the sons of long life.

Here is early Irish testimony to a group of goddesses, seven in this case, who 'fashion the threads' of life, evidently by spinning them.

In the Baltic area the goddesses of fate who spin or weave are well attested. According to a Lithuanian tale reported in 1839, 'The *dieves valditojes* ["ruling deities"] were seven goddesses; the first one spun the lives of men out of a distaff given her by the highest god, the second set up the warp, the third wove in the woof, the fourth told tales to tempt the workers to leave off, for a cessation of labour spoilt the web, the fifth exhorted them to industry, and added length to the life, the sixth cut the threads, the seventh washed the garment and gave it to the most high god, and it became the man's winding-sheet.' In another account the 'Spinstress' (*verpėja*) attaches the thread of each newborn child to a star. (We recall how the golden threads of Helgi's life were attached to the mid-point of heaven.) When the person is dying, his thread snaps and the star turns pale and falls as a meteor.[26]

The corresponding Latvian divinities are called Láimas, from the word for fortune.[27] They appear in hundreds of the mythological folk songs, most often in the singular but occasionally as a trio. The Láima comes to the newborn child's cradle and determines its life. Here is one stanza in which spinning imagery appears:

> Laima, Laima for the boy
> who is born to the world!
> For him Laima twisted the flaxen thread,
> steeping it in silver. (*LD* 1176 = Jonval no. 774)

The motif is widespread also in Slavonic folklore. The Russian Rožanicy or Roždenicy, the Czech Sudičky, the Polish Rodzanice, the Slovene Rojenice, the

[25] D. J. Shepherd in I. Carman–A. Harding (edd.), *Ancient Warfare* (Trowbridge 1999), 219–47 and 228 fig. 3; J. Colin, *Les antiquités de la Rhenanie* (Paris 1927), 183; M. Green (1986), 81; Clemen (1928), 65, 66.

[26] Grimm (1883–8), 416 n. 2 (from *Das Ausland*, 1839, no. 278); 722.

[27] Cf. Jonval (1929), 18–21 and nos. 742–1147; Gimbutas (1963), 197 f.; Biezais–Balys (1973), 417–20; Greimas (1992), 112–57.

Croat Rodjenice, the Serbian Sudjenice, the Bulgarian Narečnice or Urisnice, are supernatural females who appear at midnight within three days of a birth, mostly in threes, sometimes in a larger group, sometimes in the form of beautiful maidens, sometimes as grandmotherly old women, and pronounce destinies. They spin the child's fate as a golden thread, the eventual breaking or cutting of which will signify his death.[28]

In Albanian lore there are three old women, the Fatit (also called Mir or Ora), who appear on the third day after a birth and fix the child's fate. Phrases are used such as 'to tie off the destiny', 'predetermine the length of the thread of life', 'cut off the life'.[29]

Images of destiny

It is not hard to understand why spinning is such a pervasive image for the fixing of human destinies. It was a very ancient craft, and eminently suited to symbolize the conversion of loose, incoherent possibilities into something definite, something that, like a human life, grows continuously longer but sooner or later is cut off. The process is driven by the rotation of the spindle-whorl, and we have seen that there was an intimate connection in Indo-European speech between turning and eventuating.

The weaving image is a natural extension of the spinning. Thread is spun so that it can be woven into a fabric. It seems that in northern Europe the threads representing individual lives were sometimes imagined as being woven into a larger web. When the Norns at Helgi's birth fasten the threads east, west, and north, it is as if they are establishing his far-reaching importance in the world. Similarly in *Reginsmál* 14 Sigurd's fate-threads (*ørlǫgsímo*) are said to extend over all lands. In the terrible *Darraðarlióð* (*Edd. min.* 58–60, from *Njáls saga* 157) the Valkyries are represented as weaving the battle:

> Wide is the warp for the weapon-play,
> a cloud of wrath raining blood.
> Grey on the spears we here suspend
> the warriors' web, that with red weft
> we thralls of Odin all over thread.
> This web's warps are the guts of wights,
> weighted heavy with heads of men.
> Bloodstained darts it has for stays,
> the shafts are iron, the shuttles arrows:
> with weapons keen must the weft be tamped.

[28] N. Reiter in *Wb. d. Myth.* i(2), 177 f.; Váňa (1992), 125 f.

[29] Lambertz (1973), 477, 491 f., 494–6.

In *Beowulf* 696 f. the Lord is said to have granted the Weder-Geats *wīgspēda gewiofu*, 'webs of war-successes', that is, a victorious destiny. As we saw, Wyrd could also be said to 'weave' an individual's fortunes. The Norse words *auþna* 'fate, fortune, luck', *auþenn* 'fated, destined', Old English *ēaden, ēad*, are related to a verbal root meaning 'weave' (Lithuanian *áudmi*).[30]

For the fixing of destinies there are two alternative images that have already been touched on: oral pronouncement and writing. Morta in Livius Andronicus determines the day of death by declaring it in advance: *profata est.* Another Latin name for the Fates, *Fata*, expresses the same idea of destiny being fixed by pronouncement; *fatum* is what has been spoken and so fixed. The model is the pronouncement of the king whose word is law. Similarly in Greek an old poetic word for 'fated' is *θέσφατον*, literally 'god-spoken'. Like *fatum*, the word could also be used of oracles. There is a Lithuanian expression *taip Laima lėmė*, 'thus Laima has pronounced'.[31]

In cultures that have acquired the art, writing becomes a natural symbol of fixing things for the future. The Hittite and Palaic Fate goddesses, as I mentioned, take their name from the act of writing, and were presumably imagined to establish destinies by writing them down. Tertullian (*De anima* 39) records that on the seventh day after a child's birth the *Fata Scribunda* would be invoked, figures personifying destinies to be determined in writing. The Nordic goddesses at Urð's well are described as carving (runes) on wooden tablets (*Vǫluspá* 20). In *Beowulf* (2574 f.) we find the phrase *swā him Wyrd ne gescrāf | hrēð æt hilde*, 'Fate did not inscribe for him glory in battle'; the verb used, *gescrīfan*, is a loan from Latin *scribere*. One of the Latvian songs runs:

Bright, bright burns the fire
in the dark corner.
It is there that Laima is writing the life
for the little child. (*LD* 1196 = Jonval no. 769).

In nineteenth-century Greece and Albania the Moirai were often said to determine things by writing them. The image cannot go back to Indo-European, as the Indo-Europeans almost certainly had no knowledge of writing. The metaphor developed naturally and independently in the several poetic and mythic traditions.[32]

[30] Cf. Hermann Güntert, *Kalypso* (Halle 1919), 252 f.; *EIEC* 572. On the Fates as spinners or weavers cf. further Durante (1960), 238 n. 28; H. T. Bossert, *Die Welt des Orients* 2 (1957), 349–59; B. C. Dietrich, *Phoenix* 16 (1962), 86–101; Gamkrelidze–Ivanov (1995), 498; G. Giannakis, *IF* 103 (1998), 1–27; 104 (1999), 95–109.

[31] Greimas (1992), 114 f.

[32] For the Fates as writers cf. R. H. Klausen, *Zeitschrift für Altertumswissenschaft* 7 (1840), 226; Bernhard Schmidt (as n. 17, 1871), 215; Davidson (1988), 164.

DEATH

One's fated death, by definition, cannot be postponed or (one would suppose) advanced. But an idiom attested in Greek, Latin, Old Persian, Pali, Baluchi, Ossetic, Lithuanian, and several Slavonic languages, and so presumably current at least in the east and central Indo-European territories, suggests a distinction between the death that belongs to one as one's birthright, so to speak, and a premature death caused by violence, drowning, or some other manifest external agency. Someone who avoided the latter type and died naturally was said to 'die by his own death'.[33] The implied antithesis is an alien death. Are both types alike ordained by the Fates? If so, what is the status of the 'own death' that the murder victim is cheated of? I do not imagine the question was ever considered; but it points up a discrepancy between rival concepts.

Death as sleep; death as a journey

From one point of view death is a kind of sleep. 'Sleep', 'the eternal sleep', 'the sleep of death', etc., is widely used as a poetic metaphor or euphemism for death. In the Rigveda the causative stem (*ní*) *svāpaya-* 'put to sleep' is four times used of putting to death (1. 121. 11; 4. 30. 21; 7. 19. 4; 9. 97. 54); cf. *MBh.* 8. 31. 46 *svapsyanti*, 'they will sleep'. A slain warrior in the *Iliad* κοιμήσατο χάλκεον ὕπνον, 'fell into the bronze sleep' (11. 241); another simply εὕδει, 'sleeps' (14. 482). For Lucretius the dead man is *leto sopitus* (3. 904, cf. 920 f., 466, Catull. 5. 6, etc.). So *sofa* 'sleep' is used in Norse (*Sigrdrífumál* 34. 6), and in Old English *swefan* (*Waldere* A 31, *Beowulf* 2060, 2256, 2457, 2746); similarly we find *of slǣpe þǣm fæstan* 'out of that fast sleep' (*Andreas* 795); *deaðes swefn* 'the sleep of death' (*Genesis B* 720). In the Latvian songs death is often pictured as a sleep.[34] In the Armenian oral epic David rides to the tent of his enemy Melik and finds him sleeping. He tells the guards to wake him, but they say he is in the middle of a seven-day sleep and cannot be disturbed for four more days. David says 'I am not concerned with his sleep—call him quickly . . . I will put him to a lasting sleep' (*Sassountsy David* 273). Unsurprisingly, the image is not distinctively Indo-European. It

[33] Schulze (1966), 131–46 and 159 f.; R. C. T. Parker, *ZPE* 139 (2002), 66–8; M. L. West, *ZPE* 143 (2003), 70.

[34] *LD* 27414, 27520, 27528, 27531, 27638, 27707 = Jonval nos. 1214, 1207, 1213, 1164, 1160, 1201.

appears already in the Old Babylonian *Gilgamesh*, and in the prophet Jeremiah.[35]

But in imagining death people are not content with the idea of an endless sleep. The dead are generally represented as going somewhere. The 'somewhere' is commonly located below the earth. This is the logical corollary of the fact that in the fourth millennium, which is when the latest phase of undivided Indo-European has to be dated, and in all the lands that come into serious question as the original habitat, disposal of the dead was usually by inhumation. The deceased terrestrial returned to his Mother Earth. His tomb was a kind of house—the house of clay, as it is termed in a Vedic hymn (*mṛnmáya- gṛhá-*, 7. 89. 1). Indeed it was often constructed in the form of a house or chamber that was then covered over by a tumulus.

In mythological thinking the countless individual tombs merged into one place that all the dead go to, under a mountain or under the earth. Vedic, Greek, and Latin poets speak of the Lower Darkness. 'Whoever threatens us,' Indra is besought, *ádharaṃ gamayā támaḥ*, 'make him go to the lower darkness' (RV 10. 152. 4); *ádharam* is etymologically identical with Latin *inferum*. Another Vedic word for 'darkness' used in this connection, *rájas-*, corresponds exactly to the Greek ἔρεβος, the destination of Homeric departing spirits (*Il.* 16. 327, *Od.* 20. 356, etc.). The tragedians speak of the σκότος below the earth, the Latin poets of the *infernae tenebrae* (Virg. *Aen.* 7. 325, Hor. *C.* 4. 7. 25). The Germanic name for the place is Hel. Norse and Old English poets use the expressions 'he went to Hel', 'you sent my sister to Hel', 'Hel took him'. The word is related to a verb meaning 'conceal' and to Old Irish *cuile* 'cellar', 'underground chamber'.[36]

In some traditions the destination of the dead is known as the house of a certain figure. In Greek it is the house of Hades; I shall come back to the question of what the name Hades means. In Irish it is *tech nDuinn*, the house of Donn, who was perhaps the Dusky One, from **dhus-no-*, related to Latin *fuscus*. In India it is the house or domain or seat of Yama, that man who first accepted death. In the *Mahābhārata* warriors are often described as being sent to his abode (6. 50. 69, 73, 60. 28, 31, 71. 30, 75. 11, etc.).

The journey there is spoken of as going the way of no return. This expression in the Indian epics is paralleled in Greek and Latin poetry, and also in an Ossetic narrative. Similarly in a Hittite ritual text, in which the anger of the

[35] *Gilgamesh* OBV Meissner i 12′–15′ p. 276 George; Jer. 51. 39 = 57; cf. West (1997), 573.

[36] *Atlamál* 97. 7 *gekk til heliar*; ibid. 56. 9 *sendoð systr Helio*; *Beowulf* 1698 *þær hine Hel onfēng*. Cf. Grimm (1883–8), 313, 800–7, 1375, 1537–40; de Vries (1956), i. 91; Lorenz (1984), 100.

god Telibinu is sent by spells to the underworld, it is observed that 'what goes in does not come out again'.[37]

Crossing the water

The boundary between the worlds of the living and the dead was marked by a stream or a body of water, as frontiers between peoples often are in the upper world.

Certain Indic texts imply that the dead have to cross a river. One funeral ritual contains the verse, 'On the fearful path to Yama's gates there is the fearful river Vaitaranī: desiring to cross it, I offer the black cow Vaitaranī'. In a funeral hymn in the Atharvaveda we read, 'by fords (*tīrtháiḥ*) they cross the great down-courses (*pravátaḥ*), the way the sacrificers, the well-doers, go'. According to an Upanishad the lake Āra and the river Vijarā have to be crossed on the way to the world of Brahman.[38]

In the Homeric account of the land of the dead several formidable rivers are mentioned; they include the Acheron, which appears in other authors as a stream to be crossed by the dead.[39] From the late Archaic period we hear of the ferryman Charon. In Aristophanes' *Frogs* he is evidently a figure already well known to popular mythology. Here it is a great bottomless lake that has to be crossed.

The Latin word *tarentum* 'tomb', an archaism that survived in historical times only in connection with two Roman cult sites, meant by derivation 'crossing-place'.[40] It is cognate with Vedic *tīrthám*, the word used in the passage quoted above for the fords by which the meritorious dead cross (*taranti*) the rivers on the way to the other world. It is natural to suppose that *tarentum* had similar associations.

In Bohemia, Slovakia, and other south and east Slavic lands there are myths of a ferryman of the dead, and over the whole Slavic area from the ninth or tenth century onwards corpses were provided with coins in mouth or hand to pay their fare. A Jesuit source of the early seventeenth century records likewise

[37] *MBh.* 3. 131. 8 *panthānam apunarbhavam*; 7. 59. 18 *apunardarśanam mārgam*; 13. 70. 19 *viṣayam durnivartyam*, 'a domain hard to return from'; cf. RV 10. 95. 14 *ánāvṛt*; West (1997), 154 f.; Sikojev (1985), 127 f. The idea is not distinctively Indo-European, however; a common Sumerian and Akkadian name of the underworld was 'the Land of No Return', and the motif also occurs in the Old Testament (West, loc. cit.).

[38] A. Kuhn, *ZVS* 2 (1853), 316; AV 18. 4. 7; *Kauṣītakī Upaniṣad* 1. 3 f. Cf. Willem Caland, *Die altindischen Todten- und Bestattungsgebräuche* (Amsterdam 1896), 64, 121; Oldenberg (1917), 546 n. 1; Hillebrandt (1927–9), ii. 339 f.; Thieme (1952), 53; B. Lincoln, *JIES* 8 (1980), 52 f.

[39] *Od.* 10. 513 f.; Sapph. 95. 11–13, Alc. 38a. 2–3, 8; Aesch. *Sept.* 856.

[40] Watkins (1995), 347–53, who takes it to refer to overcoming death.

that at Baltic funerals the deceased was given two coins in his left hand to pay the ferryman for crossing the river.[41] In Russian laments the soul is represented as fording a stream.[42]

Seafaring peoples naturally made it the sea that had to be crossed. Odysseus has to sail across Oceanus to reach Hades. Procopius relates a Frankish or Celtic myth about how the souls of the dead are ferried over the sea to Britain. It is a regular duty that falls upon the boatmen according to a rota. They are summoned to the task in the middle of the night. They find strange boats waiting, fully equipped and weighed down with invisible passengers. They row out, and reach Britain with miraculous speed, in an hour, the voyage normally taking a day and a night. The ghosts disembark, and the boats return much lighter.[43] The body of Beowulf's father, Scyld, was laid in a ship that carried him away over the sea (*Beowulf* 32–52). The same was done with Baldr's corpse, only the ship carried the blazing pyre (*Gylf.* 49, from Úlf Uggason's *Húsdrápa*). Sinfiotli's body was ferried away across a fjord by a mysterious boatman (*Edda* p. 162 Neckel–Kuhn, *Frá dauða Sinfiǫtla*). The belief in a post-mortem voyage clearly underlies the practice of ship burial attested by archaeology in Scandinavia, England, and other countries where Northmen settled.[44]

As late as the nineteenth century, at Morar in the west Highlands, a Gaelic woman crofter's song, sung at the New Moon, referred to the fatal journey as 'going over the black water of the abyss'.[45]

Other traditions tell of a bridge. In Zoroastrian doctrine the soul after death has to cross the Arbiter's Bridge, which is broad for the virtuous but very narrow for the sinful. Similarly an old north English song sung at wakes referred to 'the bridge of dread, no brader than a thread'. Saxo (1. 8. 14 p. 30) tells how king Hading was taken by a witch to see the underworld, and how they crossed a bridge over a torrent of blue-black water, in which weapons of various kinds were being carried along. After Baldr was killed, Odin sent his son Hermóðr to Hel to offer a ransom for Baldr's release; Hermóðr rode for nine nights and then arrived at the bridge over the river called Giǫll. This

[41] Váňa (1992), 133; Mannhardt (1936), 444 (= Clemen (1936), 114), cf. 446, 452. On the ferryman motif cf. B. Lincoln (as n. 38), 41–59; A. R. George, *The Babylonian Epic of Gilgamesh* (Oxford 2003), 130 f. (Gilgamesh as ferryman of the dead); West (1997), 155 f.

[42] B. Lincoln (as n. 38), 51. He quotes one from Elsa Mahler, *Die russische Totenklage* (Leipzig 1935), 286, in which the Archangel Michael transports the souls of the righteous over a river of fire.

[43] *Bell. Goth.* 4. 20. 48–57. A Breton belief reported by Grimm (1883–8), 833, still has Britain as the destination of souls, but they travel there in an invisible flying wagon.

[44] Cf. Grimm (1883–8), 830–2, 1549 f.; de Vries (1956), i. 153 f.; Gelling–Davidson (1969), 156 f.; Davidson (1988), 169.

[45] Carmichael (1928–59), iii. 288, *thar abhainn duibh an aibheis.*

was guarded by a maiden to whom he had to declare his name and family (*Gylf.* 49).

In the Latvian songs it is a muddy marsh that has to be crossed, with no bridge or ferry. In one song (*LD* 34264 = Jonval no. 1169) the soul of a dead girl addresses the Mother of the Velanieši, the spirits of the dead, and asks how she is to get across. The answer comes, 'lift up your skirts, girl, and cross barefoot'. In another we read:

> Be ready, be ready, Mother of the Spirits,
> here comes the one you are expecting,
> her skirts black with the muddy water. (*LD* 27530 = Jonval no. 1182)

Gates, border control

'Then Hermóðr rode on till he came to Hel's gates.' Hel's walls, we are advised in another passage of *Gylfaginning* (34), are extremely high, and her gates strong. The Indian funeral text quoted above mentioned the gates of Yama. There are several references in Homer and Hesiod to the gates of Hades. Hades' house is 'wide-gated', εὐρυπυλές, and he himself is the gate-fastener, πυλάρτης. Baltic mythology too knows of gates or doors forming the entrance to the other world.[46]

It is natural that a dwelling should have a gate to go in by, and equally natural that this gate should be guarded, to ensure that the right people go in, and in the case of the underworld to ensure that they do not get out again. In Aristophanes' *Frogs* (464) Dionysus knocks on Hades' door and it is answered by the doorkeeper, who demands to know his name. In other Greek sources this doorkeeper was identified as Aiakos. In the traditional tales of the Ossetes the kingdom of the dead is entered by iron gates guarded by a doorkeeper called Aminon. The hero Soslan goes there because he needs to obtain leaves from a certain tree that only grows in the land of the dead. Aminon refuses to open the door for him because he has not died, but he breaks in by force.[47] In a Latvian song a girl asks her mother to bake her a loaf when she buries her so that she can give it to the Mother (or the children) of the Spirits for the opening of the door.[48]

[46] Mannhardt (1936), 59 (nine gates, thirteenth century), 62 f.

[47] Sikojev (1985), 45, 53, 116. For Near Eastern parallels see West (1997), 157 f.

[48] *LD* 27434 = Jonval no. 1156, cf. 27435, 27527, 27531 = J. 1157, 1163 f.; Mannhardt (1936), 62.

Beware of the Dog

As in the upper world houses are commonly guarded by a dog who repels those who have no business inside but allows in those who do, so in connection with the abode of the dead we hear in various Indo-European traditions of a dog (or dogs) who belongs to the proprietor and guards the entrance.[49] Classicists are familiar with Cerberus, who according to Hesiod (*Th.* 769–73) fawns and wags his tail at those who enter but devours any who attempt to leave. Different sources give him three, fifty, or a hundred heads. In the Vedas the way to the other world is guarded by Yama's two dogs, who seize the dead.[50] Each of them has four eyes, and they are described as spotted, *śabála-*: this, it has been suggested, was a deformation of a similar form **śarbára-*, corresponding etymologically to *Κέρβερος*. Kerberos, then, would originally have meant the Spotted One. It is consistent with this theory that *κέρβερος* is also the name of a type of bird and a kind of frog or toad.

In the Avesta (Vd. 13. 9, 19. 30) there is reference to two dogs that guard the bridge over which the dead must go to reach paradise. They assist the virtuous to pass, but not the sinner.

In Nordic mythology too a dog stands on the road to Hel. Odin meets it as he rides there to investigate the meaning of Baldr's sinister dreams. It has bloody marks on its chest, and it barks fiercely at him as he passes (*Baldrs draumar* 2. 7–3. 4). It is often assumed to be identical with the howling hound Garm who is bound at the entrance to Gnipa's Cave but will break free in the cosmic cataclysm of Ragnarøk.[51]

The Jesuit source on Baltic superstition cited earlier records that besides the money for the ferryman the corpse was provided with a loaf of bread for 'Cerberus', suggesting that in those parts too there lingered the notion of a canine guardian of the underworld. This seems to be a variant of the belief expressed in the Latvian song cited above. In Albanian folklore the world of the dead contains a three-headed dog who never sleeps.[52]

[49] Cf. B. Schlerath, *Paideuma* 6 (1954), 25–40.

[50] RV 10. 14. 10–12, AV 8. 1. 9, cf. 18. 2. 11 f.; Macdonell (1898), 173; Oldenberg (1917), 538; Sukumari Bhattacharji, *The Indian Theogony* (Cambridge 1970), 70 f.; Oberlies (1998), 469 n. 80. Cf. H. Hommel in *Aufsätze E. Kuhn gewidmet* (Munich 1916), 422; B. Lincoln, *JIES* 7 (1979), 273–85.

[51] *Vǫluspá* 44 = 49 = 58; *Gylf.* 51. Cf. E. Mogk in Roscher, ii. 1129 f.

[52] Mannhardt (1936), 444 = Clemen (1936), 114; Lambertz (1973), 469.

Pastures and herds

The Indo-Europeans were pastoralists, and it was pleasant to imagine that their broad pasture-lands would be replicated in the other world.[53] A Hittite mortuary ritual for a king includes the offering of a turf with the prayer:

Now, O Sun-god, confirm him in possession of this pasture! Let no one take it away from him (or) contest it legally! May oxen, sheep, horses, and mules graze for him on this pasture![54]

'Go to the meadow' was a Hittite expression for 'die'. In the Rigveda the land to which Yama has shown us the way is called a cattle-pasture, *gávyūti-* (10. 14. 2), and his Iranian counterpart Yima is *hvąθβa-*, 'having good herds' (Y. 9. 4 f., Yt. 5. 25, al.). Odysseus in *Odyssey* 11 sees the dead Achilles and Heracles going about in a meadow. Hades himself is κλυτόπωλος, 'having famous colts'. The Latvian dead are imagined as having their herds:

Qui poussait un cri si joliment
au sommet de la montagne des tombeaux?
—C'est la sœur qui poussait un cri,
gardant les vaches des Esprits. (*LD* 27714 = Jonval no. 1161)

Going to join the fathers

Dying was seen under another aspect as going to join those who have gone before. Hector in the *Iliad* (15. 251 f.), after being knocked out by Ajax with a rock, tells Apollo that 'I thought I was about to see the dead and the house of Hades this very day'. 'Going to (join) the majority' was a homely expression for dying in both Greek and Latin (Leonidas *AP* 7. 731. 6, Crinag. *AP* 11. 42; Plaut. *Trin.* 291, Petr. *Sat.* 42. 5). In Old Irish death was *techt do écaib* 'going to the dead'. A number of the Latvian folk songs (Jonval nos. 1153–64) speak of a deceased person as being taken to the Veļi, the spirits of the dead.

More specifically, dying meant going to join the fathers, the dead of one's own family. Antigone, condemned to death, says she is going to dwell with her parents (Soph. *Ant.* 867). The other world, in both Indian and Celtic conception, is the land of the fathers.[55] In Vedic funerary hymns the dead man is exhorted to go and join the fathers and Yama: *sáṃ gachasva pitṛ́bhih, sáṃ*

[53] Thieme (1952), 47–50.

[54] L. Christmann-Franck, *Revue hittite et asianique* 29 (1971), 72; V. Haas in J. M. Sasson (ed.), *Civilizations of the Ancient Near East* (New York 1995), iii. 2025 (his translation).

[55] Oldenberg (1917), 544, 547; Wolfgang Meid, *Die keltischen Sprachen und Literatur* (Innsbruck 1997), 66 f.

Yaména! (RV 10. 14. 8, cf. 154. 4). King Yama is called *saṃgámana- jánānām*, 'gatherer of peoples' (10. 14. 1). There is a formula *pitŕ̥bhiḥ saṃvidāná-* 'in union with the fathers' (RV 8. 48. 13; 10. 14. 4, 169. 4), literally 'finding oneself together with' them; it does not appear to be used of the dead, but one sees no reason why it should not have been, and Paul Thieme found here a very plausible etymology of Ἀΐδης, as the one who presides over meeting up. Vedic *sám* 'together' is from **sem*; as the first element of compounds in Greek this appeared with zero grade, **sm̥*, which developed by regular sound changes into [*ha*], as in ἀθρόος, ἁπλόος, etc. The Greek equivalent of *sam-u̯id-* would therefore be ἁ-Ϝιδ-.[56]

All Souls Day

The desire for reunion with the dead finds a different expression in the widespread annual festivals or calendar events at which the souls of the departed, and especially the departed ancestors, are supposed to return to the upper world for one day or a few days at the beginning of winter, or at the middle or end of winter. They are given food, and when their time is up they are told to depart.

In India festivals of the dead were held at New Moon or on special occasions such as anniversaries. At the 'Fathers' cake ritual' (*piṇḍapitryajñam*) pits were dug and food prepared for the souls. The sacrificer prayed, 'Come, you Fathers, you friends of Soma, on your deep old paths. Give us here good property, wealth and unharmed servants.' At the end of the ritual he would say 'Go, you Fathers, you friends of Soma, on your deep old paths'.[57] In Iran the Fravashis, the souls of the faithful, were supposed to revisit the earth for ten days at the end of winter, receive offerings, and dispense prosperity (Yt. 13. 49–52).

At Athens the festival in question was the one called Chytroi, which occupied the third day of the Anthesteria at the end of winter. At its conclusion the ghosts were expelled with the famous formula θύραζε Κῆρες, οὐκέτ' Ἀνθεστήρια, 'Out with you, spirits of death, the Anthesteria is over'.[58]

[56] Thieme (1952), 43–52, followed by Schmitt (1967), 50 f.; Durante (1976), 100; Puhvel (1987), 109, 231. *Contra*: E. Risch, *Gnomon* 41 (1969), 327; R. S. P. Beekes in *Mír Curad*, 17–19. Thieme took *pitŕ̥bhiḥ saṃvidāná* in AV 6. 63. 3 (= 84. 4) to refer to the dead man. But he is not the addressee: *uttamáṃ nā́kam ádhi rohayemám* does not mean 'besteige diesen höchsten Himmel' but 'make this man ascend to the highest firmament' (Whitney).

[57] Gobhila, *Gr̥hyasūtra* 4. 2. 3; Oldenberg (1917), 549–55.

[58] Ludwig Deubner, *Attische Feste* (Berlin 1932), 111–14; H. W. Parke, *Festivals of the Athenians* (London 1977), 116 f. For a modern Greek ritual of the same kind from Zakynthos cf. B. Schmidt, *ARW* 25 (1927), 74.

Arrian (ap. Eust. 1615. 3) described a feast of the dead among the Bithynians, who were perhaps of Thracian origin. The souls of those who had died abroad were called three times by name and invited to come up from below to share in the sacrificial meal.

At Rome there were two relevant festivals, the Parentalia[59] in February and the Lemuria in May. Offerings were put out for the souls of the ancestors, and they were supposed to come and feed while no one watched. Ovid gives the expulsion formula for the Lemuria as *Manes exite paterni*.[60]

No such custom, so far as I know, survived in Ireland in historical times. But it was believed that on the night before Samain (1 November) the fairy mounds opened and their inhabitants could be seen by mortal eyes.[61] This implies that the dead returned to the upper world once a year at that time.

In Germany the ghosts of the departed visited homesteads at Yuletide. A room was prepared for them and a table laid with offerings. A popular legend related that a man rode to a hill or mound at that season and invited the spirit who lived in it to a drinking feast.[62]

The Slavonic peoples had many festivals of the dead, the main ones being around the winter solstice and in spring. In Russia those honoured were the *rodítali*, 'the parents', but in Belarus they were *dzjady*, 'the grandfathers'. They were invited to the feast in these words:

> Ye sacred grandfathers, we call you,
> ye sacred grandfathers, come to us!
> Here is all that God has given . . .
> Ye sacred grandfathers, we implore you,
> come fly to us!

Afterwards they were given their marching orders:

> Ye sacred grandfathers! Ye have flown hither,
> ye have eaten and drunk,
> now fly away home again!
> Tell us, do you wish anything more?

[59] *Parentes*, in legal language, comprised parents, grandparents, and great-grandparents (Festus 247. 11 L.). In India it was these three generations that received offerings at the ceremony for the dead (Manu 9. 186). The same three were also covered by the Athenian law about providing for one's living *γονεῖς* (Isaeus 8. 32). Cf. Tritopatores as the name of the ancestral spirits worshipped in Attic cult; Schrader (1909), 23.

[60] Ov. *Fast.* 2. 533–616; 5. 419–92 (the expulsion formula: 443); W. Warde Fowler, *The Roman Festivals* (London 1899), 106–10, 306–10.

[61] Thurneysen (1921), 63.

[62] de Vries (1956), i. 449.

But better is it, that ye fly heavenwards.
Shoo! Shoo![63]

In Latvia and Lithuania the occasion could be at the time of a burial, or after a set period, or in autumn, especially All Souls Day. Meals were left out overnight for the souls, who were invited with prayers to come and partake. They might also be reproached for neglecting the protection of the family's crops and flocks. Afterwards they were turned away or requested to leave the house:

Vltimo scopant hypocaustum et expellunt animas ex hypocausto, alter arripit securim et parietes secat per quatuor angulos, easdem expellens, ne haereant in quodam loco.

Wann er nu gemeynet, daß sie wol gegessen, hat er den Pergel, wie man es hie zu Lande heisset, damit er das Fewr gehalten, auff der Thürschwellen mit einem Beil zerhawen und den Seelen geboten, daß sie jhres Weges gehen solten, sie hätten nu gegessen und getruncken, solten sich derwegen wieder an jhren Ort finden.[64]

We still have a relic of such old rituals in the modern celebration of Hallowe'en, to which various traditional pagan practices adhere, and the associated Christian feasts of All Saints and All Souls (1 and 2 November).

TRANSCENDING MORTALITY THROUGH FAME

Wyrce sē þe mōte
dōmes ǣr dēaþe: þæt bið drihtguman
unlifgendum æfter sēlest.

Let him strive, who can,
for glory ere death—that's for the liegeman
no longer living the best thing hereafter. (*Beowulf* 1387–9)

Deyr fé, deyja frændr, deyr sjálfr it sama:
ek veit einn, at aldri deyr: dómr um dauþan hvern.

[63] Schrader (1909), 26, after P. V. Šejn's account in a St Petersburg Academy publication of 1890; cf. J. Maletius, *Epistola de sacrificiis et idolatria veterum Borussorum Livonum aliarumque vicinarum gentium* (1551) in Mannhardt (1936), 298, with the annotation p. 306; Unbegaun (1948), 440; Váňa (1992), 226.

[64] Jesuit *Relatio* for 1606, Mannhardt (1936), 444 = Clemen (1936), 114; Paul Einhorn, *Historia Lettica* (1649), Mannhardt 487. Cf. *Statuta provincialia concilii Rigensis* (1428), § 19 in Mannhardt 156 = Clemen 101; J. Lasicius, *De diis Samagitarum* 48, 50 in Usener (1896), 104, 90 = Mannhardt 357, 359; other documents in Mannhardt 435 f. (= Clemen 109), 458, 467, 477 f., 501, 502, 504, 505, 507; Biezais–Balys (1973), 410, 441 f.; Greimas (1992), 38 f.

Cattle die, kinsmen die, oneself dies likewise.
I know one [*masc.*] that never dies: each dead man's repute. (*Hávamál* 77)

Trenghit golut, ni threingk molut.
Riches die, fame does not die.[65]

What is it that does not decay under the earth?—The name.[66]

These statements express what looks to have been an enduring attitude among Indo-European peoples from the earliest times. Fighting men were stimulated to deeds of valour, rulers to acts of justice and liberality, not by the prospect of rewards in the afterlife but by the anticipation of good repute in the present and the future. Praise by poets was the most potent mechanism for the diffusion and perpetuation of this repute. As kings and heroes of the past lived on in their songs, in the same way the best and greatest men of the present could hope to live on in the future. Their souls would go to join the majority and enjoy an unending communal existence in the great house below the earth. But they took little joy in this prospect. What fired them much more was the desire for an immortal name, for their individual achievements to be remembered on earth.

The key word was **ḱléwes-*, reflected in Vedic *śrávas-* 'glory', Avestan *sravah-* 'word, message', Greek κλέος 'fame, report', Church Slavonic *slovo* 'word', Old Irish *clú* 'fame', Tocharian A *klyu*, B *kälywe* 'fame'.[67] It was one of various derivatives from the root **ḱlu* 'hear, hear of'. To be heard of is to be famed: *eillt Wyned klywer e arderched*, 'the man of Gwynedd, his excellence is heard' (*Y Gododdin* 918). Hence the participle **ḱlutó-* may mean on the one hand 'heard, audible, sonorous',[68] on the other hand 'renowned', as in Vedic *śrutá-*, Avestan *srū̆ta-*, Greek κλυτός, Latin *in-clutus*, Armenian *lu* 'known'; with matching prefix in Avestan *frasrū̆ta-*, Greek πρόκλυτος (*Il.* 20. 204).

The **ḱléwes-* was not just something that extended between the poet and his audience. It was a property of the person famed. It could be conferred on him by a god, or he could put it on himself. In both cases, at least in Graeco-Aryan, the verb *$d^{h}eh_{1}$ 'place' was idiomatic: RV 1. 9. 8 *asmé dhehi śrávo bṛhát*, 'lay on us high fame'; 1. 40. 4 *sá dhatte ákṣiti śrávaḥ*, 'he lays upon himself unfailing glory'; Timocreon *PMG* 728 Μοῦσα, τοῦδε τοῦ μέλους κλέος ἀν' Ἕλλανας τίθει, 'Muse, set the fame of this song across Greece';

[65] Middle Welsh proverb in the Red Book of Hergest (Jesus College MS 111, late fourteenth century); H. Pedersen, *Vergleichende Grammatik der keltischen Sprachen* (Göttingen 1909–13), ii. 338.

[66] Lithuanian riddle in Schleicher (1857), 205.

[67] *IEW* 605–7; Euler (1979), 217–19.

[68] So (with long vowel) Old High German *hlūt*, English *loud*. Greek κλυτός sometimes has this sense, especially in Doric lyric; see M. L. West, *Glotta* 77 (2001), 128–30.

Hdt. 7. 220. 4 *βουλόμενον κλέος καταθέσθαι μοῦνον Σπαρτιητέων*, '(Leonidas) wishing to establish glory for himself alone of the Spartans', cf. 9. 78. 2.[69]

In Greek epic the typical subject matter of bards' songs is summed up as *κλέα ἀνδρῶν*, 'fames of men', that is, their famous exploits.[70] This use of the plural is paralleled in Vedic, where the plural *śrávāṃsi* is three times used of the 'glorious deeds' of Indra (RV 3. 30. 5, 37. 7; as the subject of eulogy, 8. 99. 2). The achievements of human heroes are not the concern of the Rigveda, but Indra is often praised in terms suitable to a human hero; he is called a *nṛ́* or *vīrá-*, 'a (real) man', he is *nṛmánas-* 'man-spirited', *nṛ́tama-* 'most manly', his exploits are *vīríyāṇi.* Oral epic about human heroes must have existed, and it would have been appropriate to refer to their famous deeds as *śrávāṃsi narā́m* (or *nṛṇā́m*), even if we cannot document the phrase.[71] A similar Old Irish expression may be quoted from the so-called Book of the Dun Cow (*Lebor na hUidre*, 10272): *comba luiet mo gníma eter clothaib neirt n-erred*, 'so that my deeds may count among the famous exploits of chariot-warriors', literally 'the fames of prowess of chariot-warriors'.[72]

Names

One's fame is inseparable from one's name. Someone achieving fame 'makes a name for himself'. The Vedic phrase *śrútiyaṃ nā́ma* 'famous name' (RV 5. 30. 5) is matched by Greek *ὄνομα κλυτόν* (*Od.* 9. 364, 19. 183). One is 'famed by name': RV 8. 46. 14 *Índraṃ nā́ma śrútiyam*, in Homer *ὄνομα κλυτός* (or *ὀνομάκλυτος*). Tocharian has the compound 'name-fame' (A *ñom-klyu*, B *ñem-kälywe*).[73]

The naming of a child was a solemn event, performed on the tenth day of its life.[74] A series of languages agree in using their reflexes of the phrase **$h_3$néh$_3$mn̥ d^{h}eh$_1$* (with dative) for the act of bestowing the name: Hittite

[69] More in Schmitt (1967), 71; Gamkrelidze–Ivanov (1995), 732. Also with the preverb *pári*, *περί*: RV 5. 18. 4 *śrávāṃsi dadhire pári*, Simon. epigr. 9. 1 Page *ἄσβεστον κλέος οἵδε φίλῃ περὶ πατρίδι θέντες*.

[70] *Il.* 9. 189, 524, *Od.* 8. 73; Hes. *Th.* 100 *κλεῖα προτέρων ἀνθρώπων*.

[71] F. Specht, *ZVS* 64 (1937), 1 = Schmitt (1968), 49, cited RV 5. 18. 5 *máhi śravo* (singular) . . . *maghónām* . . . *nṛṇā́m* and also the collocation *narā́ṃ śámsa-*, *nárāśáṃsa-*, 'praise of men', but these are semantically dissimilar. Cf. Schmitt (1967), 29 f., 93–101; Durante (1976), 50 f.

[72] Meid (1978), 20 n. 20. *Clothaib* is the dative plural of *cloth* < **ḱlutóm*. The word is often used in the plural in the sense of 'tidings'.

[73] Durante (1962), 32 ~ (1976), 95; Schmitt (1967), 55 f., 90–3; Watkins (1995), 65; W. Meid in *Mír Curad* 477–81. On the equivalence of **ḱlewes-* and name cf. Campanile (1990b), 89–91.

[74] Feist (1913), 301 f.; K. A. Eckhardt, *Irdische Unsterblichkeit* (Weimar 1937), i. 92–4; R. Schmitt in Ernst Eichler et al. (edd.), *Namenforschung*, i (Berlin–New York 1995), 616.

lāman dāi-, Vedic *nā́ma dhā-*, Avestan *nąmąn dā-*, Greek *ὄνομα τίθεσθαι*, Latin *indere nomen*, Tocharian A *ñom tā-*, B *ñem tā-*, Serbo-Croat *ime djesti*.[75] Another noteworthy concordance has been observed between the Vedic phrase *priyáṃ nā́ma* 'dear/favourite name' (RV 7. 56. 10; 9. 75. 1; 10. 84. 5, 123. 7) and the etymologically identical Old English *frēo nama* 'surname, cognomen'. This would appear to have been an Indo-European expression denoting an additional name chosen to distinguish an individual from namesakes.[76]

Indo-Iranian, Greek, Thracian, Illyrian, Balto-Slavic, Germanic, and Celtic names are very often two-part compounds, formed in similar ways to the compound adjectives typical of poetic language. Such names had an intrinsic element of grandeur, and were evidently characteristic of families and tribes that aspired to great things. The lexical components from which they are constructed often reflect the preoccupations of a warrior society.[77] A son's name sometimes contained one element taken over from his father's.[78]

The general conservatism of naming traditions may be judged by the extent to which names in different countries resemble each other in meaning or actually contain cognate elements. For example, the Avestan name Nərəmanah- corresponds to the Greek Ἀνδρομένης, and both to the Vedic epithet *nṛmáṇas-*, 'having the mind of a hero'.[79] Greek *Διογένης* 'of Zeus' race' is paralleled by Gaulish *Divogena* (*CIL* xiii. 571), *Divvogna* (ibid. 10024. 291); the second element also appears in Thracian *-zenes*, Venetic *-genes*.[80] Gaulish names in *-rix* 'king' can be compared with Indian ones in *-rājā*; in both cases (at any rate until the Roman conquest of Gaul) they were borne by actual rulers.[81] In Homeric names such as Echekles, Echepolos, Hektor, the first element, from **seĝʰ*, originally meaning 'conquer', is cognate with Sig(o)- in Germanic Sigemund, Sigurd, etc. Areïlykos, 'battle-wolf',

[75] R. Schmitt (as n. 74); Gamkrelidze–Ivanov (1995), 732.

[76] Schmitt (1967), 184 f. J. Puhvel in *Anatolia Antica. Studi in memoria di Fiorella Imparati* (Florence 2002), 671–5, points out that Latin *nomen proprium* may be another cognate, and he compares also Hittite *sanezzi lāman* 'sweet name'.

[77] Cf. Wackernagel (1943), 16; Durante (1962), 40–2; (1976), 102 f. Schramm (1957), 11, after Eduard Schröder, *Deutsche Namenkunde* (2nd edn., Göttingen 1944), 8, notes the tendency for Germanic names to be related to 'dichterische Ausdrücke für den Fürsten und Krieger'. Cf. id. 49, 60 f. (Greek, Germanic, Celtic, and Slavic names with '-battle' as the second element); 84 (weapon or armour as second element).

[78] R. Schmitt (as n. 74), 622, with examples from Avestan, Sarmatian, Thracian, Greek, and Germanic.

[79] See Schmitt (1967), 105–8.

[80] Cf. D. Ellis Evans, *Gaulish Personal Names* (Oxford 1967), 191–3; Lambert (2003), 129 f.; Lejeune (1974), 96. Compare also Old Irish Sogen (*o*-stem), corresponding to Sanskrit *sujana-* 'good, kind' (by origin 'noble, well-born'): J. Uhlich, *TPhS* 100 (2002), 422.

[81] Campanile (1977), 79.

corresponds in sense, and the second element etymologically, with runic Norse HaþuwulafR.[82]

Many names feature the horse.[83] Here we can find a number of correspondences, partly etymological, partly semantic, between Greek and Indic or Iranian names: compare Avestan Hvaspa- 'well-horsed' (and Indic Sauvaśva-) with *Εὔιππος*; Yuxtāspa- 'having yoked horses' with *Ζεύξιππος*; Vedic Śyāváaśva- 'having dark-brown horses' with *Μελάνιππος, Κυάνιππος, Ξάνθιππος*; Median Aspacanah- 'horse-lover' with *Φίλιππος*; Old Persian Asaçuta- 'horse-famed' with *Ἱπποκλῆς, Ἵπποκλος*. We need not suppose that there was a continuous tradition of each of these names, only that similar combinations kept suggesting themselves, given the common background and mindset.

There is a striking abundance of names containing the element **ḱlewes-* 'fame' or **ḱluto-* 'famous', sometimes identical with poetic epithets or corresponding to poetic phrases.[84] In the Rigveda we find, among others:

Suśrávas- 'of good fame' (1. 53. 9 f., also as an epithet); compare Avestan Haosravah- (Yt. 5. 49, al.), which later became Xusrav (Chosroes); Greek *Εὐκλῆς*; Illyrian Vescleves-.

Pr̥thuśrávas- 'of wide fame' (1. 116. 21); compare post-Vedic Uruśravas-; Greek *Εὐρυκλῆς*; perhaps Gaulish Verucloetius.[85]

Śrutáratha- 'of the famed chariot' (1. 122. 7); compare Mycenaean *A-mo-ke-re-*[*we*], interpreted as Harmoklewēs.

Deváśravas- 'having fame from the gods' (3. 23. 2–3); compare Greek *Θεοκλῆς, Θεοκλύμενος*.

Satyáśravas- 'of true fame' (5. 79. 1–3); compare Greek *Ἐτεοκλῆς*.

In post-Vedic India we find Dūreśravas- and Dūreśruta- 'far-famed', corresponding to Avestan Dūraēsrūta- (Yt. 13. 119), Greek *Τηλεκλῆς, Τήλεκλος*, and to epithets in the Atharvaveda (*dūráśravas-*), Avesta (*dūrāt̰ frasrūta-*), and Homer (*τηλέκλυτος*). The Avesta also knows a woman Srūtat̰.fəδrī (for *Srūta.fəδrī) 'of famed father', like Homeric *Κλεοπάτρη* (cf. *Πατροκλέης/Πάτροκλος*).

Altogether there are some 250 recorded Greek names connected with *κλέος*.[86] Some already appear in the Mycenaean tablets,[87] and an Etewoklewēs

[82] Cf. Schramm (1957), 79.

[83] Cf. Krahe (1955–64), i. 55, 63, 70 f.; Schramm (1957), 78, 100, 115; D. Ellis Evans (as n. 80), 197–200; Gamkrelidze–Ivanov (1995), 468, 471 f.; V. Blažek, *SIGL* 2 (1999), 21–3.

[84] Cf. Wackernagel (1943), 16; Durante (1962), 41 f. ~ (1976), 103; Campanile (1977), 82; id. (1990b), 104–6.

[85] Caesar, *Bell. Gall.* 1. 7. 3; D. Ellis Evans (as n. 80), 123 f.; Schmitt (1967), 75.

[86] Felix Solmsen, *Indogermanische Eigennamen* (Heidelberg 1922), 115.

[87] E. Risch, *ZVS* 100 (1987), 6 f.

appears (rendered as Tawagalawas) in the Hittite records. Roman names from this root are not numerous, but Cluvius, Clovatius, Cluatius, Cluentius, Cluilius may be cited.[88]

From other languages of ancient Europe we have Venetic Klutavikos and Klutiiaris; Illyrian Vescleves, Clevas, Clevatus; Gaulish names beginning with Clouto-, Cloto-, Cluto-.[89] There is a similar series of early German names: Chlodobert, Chlodochar (> Lothar, Luther), Chlodmar, Chlodowald, Chlodovicus (> Ludwig), Chlodulf (> Ludolf), Clotichilda.[90] A fifth-century runic inscription on one of the gold horns from Gallehus (Schleswig) gives us a Hlewaȝastiʀ 'having fame from guests', analogous to Greek *Κλεόξενος*. Later we have Norse names such as Hlédís and Hlébarðr, and a Welsh Clotrí (**ḱluto-rēg-*, 'famed king').

Fame won in combat

The winning of fame is associated especially with deeds of battle. The Vedic storm-demons, the Maruts, go forth 'like warriors, like ones hurrying ready for battle, like *śravasyávaḥ*, fame-seekers' (RV 1. 85. 8; cf. 132. 5). The Zoroastrian prays for victory and conquest of all wrong-thinkers and Daēva-worshippers 'so that I can obtain advantage and *vohu sravah*, good fame' (*Āfrīnakān* 1. 11).

Many passages of the *Iliad* might be cited. Two will suffice. When Hector's wife Andomache tries to persuade him not to go and fight outside the city wall, he persists in his resolve: he is schooled ever to be upstanding and fight in the front line, 'earning my father's great κλέος and my own' (6. 446). Achilles similarly rejects his mother's attempt to hold him back, saying that he will die when the time comes, 'but now let me earn good κλέος, and give the Trojan women cause to lament' (18. 121). Tyrtaeus (12. 31–4) preaches to the Spartans: 'His good κλέος is never lost (ἀπόλλυται), nor his name, but even below the earth he becomes deathless (ἀθάνατος), the man whom the furious War-god kills as he acts the hero and stands firm and fights for his land and his children'.

In the *Lay of Igor* (112) Svyatoslav remarks to his nephews, 'You have soon begun to harass the land of the Polovstians with your swords and to seek fame (*slavy*) for yourselves!' It is the same in the early Celtic literatures. At the great battle of Catraeth Heini the son of Neithon 'slew a great host to achieve fame'.

[88] F. Solmsen (as n. 86), 149.

[89] Lejeune (1974), 49, 249, 276; Krahe (1955–64), i. 61, 66, 68; Mayer (1957–9), i. 193, 359, ii. 66, 125; D. Ellis Evans (as n. 80), 180 f.

[90] F. Solmsen (as n. 86), 160, 162, 171; Schramm (1957), 18, 117.

A band of three hundred warriors wearing gold torques went to their deaths, but 'before they were slain, they slew; and till the end of the world they will be esteemed'.[91] In the *Táin* the old wounded warrior Cethern says, 'if I had my own weapons, the deeds I should do would be *airisiu co bráth*, a subject of story till Doomsday' (*Táin* (I) 3306).

So too in the Germanic world. In *Beowulf* (953–5) Hrothgar, who has decided to adopt Beowulf as a son, tells him 'you yourself have achieved it by your deeds that your reputation will live for evermore'. Snorri illustrates the *fornyrðislag* metre with the stanza:

> There are lays on the chieftain who reddens the lips
> of wolf and she-wolf and dyes weapons.
> This will live for aye, else man passes away—
> the heroes' praise— or the world cracks up. (*Háttatal*, v. 96)

We may quote too some verses from Saxo's Latin version of the lost *Biarkamál*:[92]

> gloria defunctos sequitur, putrique fauillae
> fama superstes erit, nec in ullum decidet aeuum,
> quod perfecta suo patrauit tempore uirtus.

> Glory follows the dead, our fame shall survive
> our crumbling remains, and what perfect courage accomplishes
> now, shall never fade in succeeding ages.

Fame valued above life

The hero's desire for fame is such that he willingly and knowingly buys it at the cost of his life. It is a typical motif in Indo-European epic and saga that the alternatives are explicitly put before the hero and he opts decisively for glory rather than length of days.

Achilles knows from his divine mother that he has the choice. If he stays on fighting at Troy, his life will be cut short but his fame will be imperishable; if he leaves and goes home, his fame is forfeit, but he will live into old age (*Il.* 9. 410–16). The lines appear in what is clearly an untraditional context: the poet makes Achilles use them to justify his temporary intention of abandoning the war and sailing home. But they must originally have been composed for a passage in which he embraced the glory option, in accord with his normal temper and with what happens in the event. He would have approved of the

91 *Y Gododdin* 1190, 1128 f.

92 Lines 177–9, from Saxo 2. 7. 16 p. 57, trs. P. Fisher; *Edd. Min.* 26.

Indic hero Karna, who declares outright, 'I choose fame on earth even at the cost of my life. The famous man attains to heaven, the inglorious man perishes' (*MBh.* 3. 284. 31), and on another occasion 'regarding fame as supreme in the world, I shall slay them or again, slain by the foe in battle, sleep' (7. 2. 15).

The Narts of the Caucasus were of the same persuasion. Having conquered all their enemies on earth, they resolved to challenge God himself. God sent a swallow with a message: 'If I defeat you, which do you prefer? Shall I wipe your race out completely, or do you want some descendants to remain, albeit inferior ones?' The Narts looked at each other and said, 'If he is going to destroy our race, let him do it completely!' There were some who objected, 'Better to have feeble descendants than none at all.' But Uryzmæg replied, 'No! Better to remain without descendants than to leave inferior ones. What do you want eternal life for? We don't need it. Let him give us eternal fame instead!' And all the Narts agreed with him.[93]

Irish and British heroes are of a like stamp. Cathbad declares that Cú Chulainn will be *airdirc* and *ainmgnaid*, conspicuous and known by name, but short-lived. He replies, 'if I can only be *airdirc*, I am content to live but a single day'.[94] Later in the *Táin* (3296 ff.) the severely wounded Cethern is given the choice: to lie as an invalid for a year and survive, or to have strength for just three days and three nights to attack his enemies. 'The latter is what Cethern chose.' The Novantian braveheart Cynddylig from Ayrshire

> had no desire for a happy little place in the world.
> This he sought: the acclamation of bards across the world's circuit,
> and gold, and great horses, and mead's intoxication. (*Y Gododdin* 820–2)

Fame conferred and sustained by poetry

In oral societies the warrior's long-term fame depended on the diffusion of stories and especially poems; the best stories were generally made into poems. Homeric singers spread the κλέος of heroic doings, ἔργ' ἀνδρῶν τε θεῶν τε, τά τε κλείουσιν ἀοιδοί (*Od.* 1. 338). Kleio is the name of one of Hesiod's Muses (*Th.* 77). Perhaps the Asopid Kleone (*Κλεϝ-ώνα), the eponymous nymph of the town Kleonai, was originally a goddess of poetry.

For the subject to survive, the song must survive. Thus the fame of the person celebrated becomes interlinked with the poet's own fame. As Ibycus advises Polycrates, 'you will have κλέος ἄφθιτον, unfailing fame, ὡς κατ'

[93] Sikojev (1985), 317 f.; a Circassian version in Colarusso (2002), 11.

[94] *Táin* (I) 638–41. The Irish epithets are compounds from elements whose Greek equivalents would be *περιδέρκετος and *ὀνομάγνωτος.

ἀοιδὰν καὶ ἐμὸν κλέος, so far as singing and my own fame can assure it' (*PMGF* S151. 47 f.). Pindar, bidding for reward from Hiero, says that if he is enriched, he is confident of achieving high κλέος for the future. 'We know of Nestor and Sarpedon ἐξ ἐπέων κελαδεννῶν, from resounding verses, that skilled craftsmen have built:

> ἁ δ' ἀρετὰ κλειναῖς ἀοιδαῖς χρονία τελέθει.
>
> It is through famous songs that excellence endures. (*Pyth.* 3. 110–15)

An early British bard avowed that 'as long as there are singers, Hyfaidd will be praised' (*Y Gododdin* 56). A thirteenth-century Irish poet makes the point at some length that if poetry disappeared, the people's knowledge of its past would be lost, the great fiery warriors forgotten. 'Conall and Conchobar live, because their praises live, and Fergus is with us still, his name being known abroad. . . . If poems did not give life to their deeds, however great, a pall would settle far and wide on Niall and Cormac and Conn.'[95]

The embedding of names in poetry

In life, in situations where a man's own name was not sufficient to identify him unequivocally, his father's was commonly appended, 'X (son) of Y'. In poetic narrative patronymics and patronymic expressions were extensively used, not only when a character was first introduced or when there might be ambiguity, but to make a fuller, more verse-filling phrase, or as a useful substitute for the primary name, a simple kenning. A verse from the *Mahābhārata* (7. 136. 1) will serve to exemplify both usages:

> tata Yudhiṣṭhiraś caiva Bhīmasenaś ca Pāṇḍavaḥ
> Droṇaputraṃ, mahārāja, samantāt paryavārayan.
>
> Then Yudhiṣṭhira and Bhīmasena the son of Pāndu,
> O great king, surrounded Drona's son on all sides.

Further examples of the solitary use were given in Chapter 2 ('Kennings'). Another artifice, also illustrated in that chapter, was to invert the normal order and place the patronymic before the name.

[95] Giolla Brighde mac Con Midhe, *A thechtaire thig ón Róimh*, stanzas 20–32, trs. Thomas Kinsella, *The New Oxford Book of Irish Verse* (Oxford 1986), 100–2. See further Durante (1960), 244–6 ~ (1976), 180–2. Anglo-Saxon nobles often eased their sons' path to poetic immortality by making sure that they had alliterating names: R. W. Chambers, *Beowulf. An Introduction* (3rd edn., Cambridge 1959), 316 f.; K. Sisam, *PBA* 39 (1953), 288, 300 f., 322 n.; de Vries (1956), i. 182.

The serviceability of the patronymic phrase as formulaic ballast to round off the verse appears in a structural pattern common to Greek, Old High German, Old English, Old Norse, and Russian, whereby the primary name is accompanied by a verb of speaking and then followed up by 'the son (or daughter) of X'.

> τὸν δ' αὖτ' Αὐτομέδων προσέφη, Διώρεος υἱός.
> (*Il.* 17. 474; cf. *Od.* 1. 383, 4. 660, 8. 132, etc.)
>
> Haðubrant gimahalta, Hiltibrantes sunu. (*Hildebrandslied* 14 = 36).
>
> Hiltibrant gimahalta, Heribrantes sunu. (ibid. 45)
>
> Unferð maþelode, Ecglāfes bearn. (*Beowulf* 499)
>
> Bēowulf maþelode, bearn Ecgþēowes. (ibid. 529 = 631 = 957)
>
> þá kvað þat Brynhildr, Buðla dóttir. (*Brot af Sigurðarkviðo* 8. 1)
>
> þá kvað þat Gullrǫnd, Giúca dóttir. (*Guðrúnarkviða.* 12. 1, al.)
>
> Young Shchelkan spoke, young Shchelkan Dyudentevich.
> (Chadwick (1932), 161. 57 f.).
>
> Tsar Azvyak replied, Azvyak Tavrulovich. (ibid. 162. 73 f.)

Many other verses have a similar structure, but with another title instead of the patronymic, as in *Waldere* B 11 *Waldere maþelode, wiga ellenrōf*, 'Waldere spoke, warrior strong in courage'; *Beowulf* 371 = 456 *Hrōðgār maþelode, helm Scyldinga*, 'Hrothgar spoke, protector of the Scyldings'; *Guðrúnarhvǫt* 4. 1 = 8. 1 *þá kvað þat Hamðir inn hugomstóri*, 'then Hamdir said this, the strong-minded', cf. *Hamðismál* 6. 1, al.; *Guðrúnarkviða A* 4. 1, 6. 1, al.

Besides the patronymic there is another type of surname that not only identifies an individual more certainly but at the same time recalls a major exploit: the designation 'slayer of X'. We saw in Chapter 2 that such titles could be used as kennings for a god or hero. Naturally they could also be used in conjunction with the primary name, even in prose texts, showing that this was no mere poetic ornament but part of the man's traditional identity. In the Avesta we have 'Θraētaona the slayer of Aži Dahāka' (Vd. 1. 17). Two of the Eddic poems are entitled *Lay of Helgi Hundingsbani*, that is, of Helgi slayer of Hunding. The phrase occurs once in the poetic text, but it had wider currency. The accompanying prose states that 'he slew king Hunding and was thereafter called Helgi Hundingsbani'.[96] Snorri refers no less matter-of-factly to Sigurðr Fáfnisbani, Sigurd the slayer of Fafnir (*Skáldsk.* 64).

[96] *Edda* p. 151 N.–K. Similarly Saxo 2. 5. 3 p. 47, (Helgo) *Hundingum Saxoniae regis Syrici filium . . . duello prostravit; ob quod Hundingi interemptor vocatus victoriae decus cognomine usurpavit.*

The idea 'slay' is often expressed in the old Germanic languages by the periphrasis 'become the slayer for' (with dative): Old English *tō bonan weorðan,* Old High German *ti banin werdan,* Old Saxon *te banon werðan,* Norse *at bana verða.*[97] There is a close parallel in Greek tragic idiom: *φονεὺς γενέσθαι τινός* (Aesch. *Ag.* 1648; Soph. *Trach.* 1207, *OT* 721). *φονεύς* and *bani* represent the same root with different stem suffixes. The effect of the periphrastic expression is to shift emphasis from the act of killing to the status assumed by the slayer. In the immediate situation it was a matter of his legal, social, and religious status. But from the perspective of ensuing poetic tradition it was a badge of fame—or infamy.

A thesaurus of glory

The preoccupation of Indo-European poets with fame has been recognized ever since Kuhn in 1853 put the Homeric phrase *κλέος ἄφθιτον* beside the Vedic *ákṣiti śrávaḥ* and *śrávo . . . ákṣitam,* 'unfading glory', and realized that they must go back to a common prototype in the parent language, and moreover in its poetry. Subsequently several other formulaic collocations involving **ḱléwes-* have been identified. We shall conclude the chapter with a succinct review of this material.[98]

By derivation, as we saw, the word meant 'being heard about', 'reputation'. A reputation may be good or bad. In Greek *εὐκλεής* 'of good repute' exists beside *δυσκλεής* 'of ill repute' and *ἀκλεής* 'of no repute'. *δυσκλεής* has cognates in the Avestan nouns *dus̆.sravahyā-* and *dǝus̆.srauuah-* 'ill fame' (implying the adjective **dus̆.sravah-*) and in the Old Irish *dochla* 'inglorious, infamous', *dochlatu* 'disrepute'. But the positive terms are more prevalent: Vedic *suśrávas-* = *εὐκλεής,* with the noun *sauśravasám* (and also *vásuśravas-*); Avestan *husravah-, haosravaŋham;* Old Irish *sochla, sochlach, sochlatha* 'renowned', *sochla* and *sochlatu* 'fame'. The corresponding personal names Suśrávas-, Haosravah-, *Εὐκλῆς,* Vescleves- have been mentioned above. The simple phrase 'good fame' has a similarly wide distribution, partly with lexical renewal: in Homer *κλέος ἐσθλόν* (replacing **ἐῢ κλέος*), in Avestan *vohu sravō* (Y. 30. 10, al.), in the Old Irish Laws *fó chlú* (< **wésu ḱléwos*).[99]

The various reflexes of **ḱléwes-* are often used without being specified as good or bad, and by default such fame is understood to be good. Its ideal properties are volume and extent over space and time. Volume is expressed by the phrase 'great fame', spatial extent by 'wide fame', and temporal extent by 'unfailing' or 'undying fame'.

[97] See Watkins (1995), 419–24.
[98] Cf. especially Schmitt (1967), 61–102.
[99] Cf. Schmitt (1967), 81–6; Meid (1978), 8.

'Great fame' is a natural collocation of words, and there is nothing necessarily poetic about it. However, it is established in Vedic and Greek poetry in lexically matching forms—*máhi śrávaḥ*, μέγα κλέος—and may fairly be considered an inherited formula.[100] In the *Mahābhārata* we find, with lexical replacement, phrases such as *mahatiṃ kīrtim* (3. 83. 106) or *yaśaḥ sphītam* ('abundant fame', 3. 120. 19). Old Irish has the *bahuvrīhi* compound *clu-mor*, 'of great fame, renowned'. One cannot put any weight on Latin *magna gloria* or Norse *mikil frægð* (*Gísla saga Súrssonar* 34).

In illustrating the process of lexical renewal in Chapter 2 I referred to the Vedic and Greek expressions for 'wide glory'. Homeric κλέος εὐρύ would be best matched by **urú śrávaḥ*, and this presumably once existed, since we find the expanded phrase *urugāyám . . . śrávaḥ* 'wide-going glory' (RV 6. 65. 6) and later a personal name Uruśravas-. But otherwise *urú* has been replaced in this collocation by *pṛthú*, the cognate of Greek πλατύ: *pṛthú śrávaḥ* (1. 9. 7; 7. 5. 8), and as a name Pṛthuśrávas- (1. 116. 21; 8. 46. 21, 24), analogous to Greek Εὐρυκλῆς. It survives in another Vedic compound of similar meaning, *uruśáṃsa*- 'of wide repute'; this has an Old Persian parallel in the title borne by the royal Benefactors, recorded by Herodotus as *orosangai*.[101]

Caesar (*Bell. Gall.* 1. 7. 3) mentions an envoy from the Celtic Helvetii whose name, Verucloetius, probably contains the same elements as **urú śravaḥ*/κλέος εὐρύ. British *clod* (**ḱlutom*) appears in analogous phrases in heroic poetry: *pellynnic y glot* 'far-reaching his fame' (*Y Gododdin* 1123; *Canu Llywarch* 1. 36 = Rowland (1990), 408/471); *mab Ywerit clod lydan* 'son of Ywerydd of wide fame' (Rowland (1990), 462 st. 2b). In *Beowulf* (18) we find, with a different noun but the same sense, *blǣd wīde sprang*, 'his glory leapt wide'.

Less obviously, fame may be characterized as 'high', perhaps on the principle that things high up can be seen from afar. In the Rigveda it is often *bṛhát* 'high, lofty' (1. 9. 7 f., 44. 2; 3. 37. 10, etc.), and sometimes *várṣiṣṭham* (4. 31. 15; 8. 46. 24) or *upamám*, 'the highest'. In Greek we find once κλέος ὑψηλόν (Pind. *Pyth.* 3. 111) and twice the superlative, ὑπέρτατον κλέος (Bacchyl. 17. 79; Soph. *Phil.* 1347). Perhaps more remarkable is the idea of its reaching up to the sky, which is both Vedic and Homeric: RV 1. 126. 2 *diví śrávo ajáram ā́ tatāna*, 'he has spread out his unageing fame in heaven'; 4. 31. 15 *asmā́kam uttamáṃ kṛdhi | śrávo devéṣu, Sūriya, | várṣiṣṭhaṃ dyā́m ivopári*, 'make our fame the uppermost among the gods, O Surya, the highest like the sky above'; *MBh.* 5. 88. 64 *yaśaś cāsya divaṃ spṛśet*, 'his fame will reach heaven'; *Il.* 8. 192 τῆς νῦν κλέος οὐρανὸν ἵκει, '(Nestor's shield,) the fame

[100] Schulze (1966), 258; Schmitt (1967), 77–80 with text references.

[101] Hdt. 8. 85. 3; Schulze (1966), 258 n. 2; Schmitt (1967), 72–5.

of which now reaches heaven', cf. *Od.* 8. 74, 9. 20, 19. 108; Ar. *Nub.* 461 κλέος οὐρανόμηκες, 'heaven-high fame'.[102]

The durability of fame is expressed by calling it 'unfading', 'undying', or 'unageing'. We will take first the famous parallelism of *ákṣiti śrávaḥ* (RV 1. 40. 4; 8. 103. 5; 9. 66. 7) or *śrávo . . . ákṣitam* (1. 9. 7) and κλέος ἄφθιτον.[103] The Greek phrase occurs once in Homer, in the passage about Achilles' choice of destinies cited above: it is what he will have if he stays at Troy. It is also what Ibycus promises Polycrates through the medium of his own lyrics, subject to their durability. The phrase appears further in a Hesiodic fragment, in Sappho, and in one literary and three epigraphic epitaphs.[104] It has been attractively argued that a Mycenaean woman's name written *A-qi-ti-ta* (MY Oe 103, KN Ap 639. 12) is to be read as $Ak^{w}t^{h}$itā, and that this must be a short name derived from a long compound one such as *$Ak^{w}t^{h}$itokleweyya.[105]

The verbal root *kṣi*/φθι (**$d^{h}g^{wh}i$*) meant 'perish, fade, fail'. Of the two alternative Vedic forms found with *śrávaḥ*, *ákṣiti-* and *ákṣita-*, the first combines the negative prefix with the feminine *i*-stem noun *kṣíti-*, corresponding to Greek φθίσις, while the second combines it with participial *kṣitó-*. The first is perhaps the more archaic type,[106] but both are clearly old, and it is the second that exactly matches Greek ἄφθιτος. In its application to fame it may have been a metaphor from an unfailing spring, as in both languages the word is used with that reference: RV 1. 64. 6, 8. 7. 16 *útsam . . . ákṣitam* 'the unfailing spring'; 10. 101. 6 *avatám . . . ákṣitam*; Hes. *Th.* 805 Στυγὸς ἄφθιτον ὕδωρ 'Styx's unfailing water'. The variant formula ἄσβεστον κλέος (*Od.* 4. 584, 7. 333) can be understood in the same way, as σβέννυσθαι is sometimes used of liquid flows drying up, and Simonides' phrase ἀέναον κλέος 'ever-flowing fame' (*PMG* 531. 9) is a similar image.

In the *Mahābhārata* we find instead of *akṣita-* the younger form *akṣaya-*, and instead of *śravas-*, *kīrti-* or *yaśas-*. But the one continues to be predicated of the other: *akṣayā tava kīrtiś ca loko sthāsyati* 'your fame will stand

102 Schmitt (1967), 73 n. 442. Cf. Simon. eleg. 11. 27 [φάτις δ' ἔχε]ν οὐρανομ[ήκ]ης.

103 A. Kuhn, *ZVS* 2 (1853), 467 (noted *en passant*); Wackernagel (1943), 16; Schmitt (1967), 61–9; Gregory Nagy, *Comparative Studies in Greek and Indic Meter* (Cambridge, Mass. 1974); Durante (1976), 8 f.; E. D. Floyd, *Glotta* 58 (1980), 133–57 (with careful analysis of the Vedic contexts, 135–8); M. Finkelberg, *CQ* 36 (1986), 1–5; E. Risch, *ZVS* 100 (1987), 3–11; A. T. Edwards, *CQ* 38 (1988), 25–30; Nagy (1990), 122–7; Campanile (1990b), 87–9; Watkins (1995), 173–8; K. Volk, *Classical Philology* 97 (2002), 61–8.

104 *Il.* 9. 413; Ibycus, *PMGF* S151. 47; 'Hes.' fr. 70. 5; Sapph. 44. 4; *CEG* 344. 2 (Phocis, *c.*600–550); *CEG* 2(ii). 1 (Athens, after 480); *GVI* 904. 2 (Rhodes, Hellenistic). Several later examples are collected by K. Volk (as n. 103), 63 f. Cf. also Thgn. 245 f., where the words are divided between two clauses, but the reference is again, as in Ibycus, to posthumous fame conferred by poetry.

105 E. Risch, *ZVS* 100 (1987), 9–11; questioned by Campanile (1990b), 105.

106 Schulze (1966), 258 n. 3.

imperishable in the world' (3. 42. 22); *kīrtir astu tavākṣayyā* 'let your fame be imperishable' (3. 77. 26); *yaśo 'kṣayam* (8. 738*. 3); with a different adjective, *kīrtim . . . śāśvatīm* 'continual fame' (3. 284. 35, 285. 2).

To be famed after death is a kind of immortality. In the preceding pages I have quoted a number of passages in which a man's fame is itself said to live, or not to die (Tyrtaeus, *Beowulf*, *Hávamál*, *Háttatal*, Welsh proverb). In the Rigveda we find the phrases *śrávo ámṛtyu* 'deathless fame' (6. 48. 12) and *śrávaḥ . . . amṛ́tam* 'undying fame' (7. 81. 6 = 8. 13. 12), besides *amṛ́tam nā́ma* 'an undying name' (5. 57. 5, cf. 6. 18. 7). There is no Homeric equivalent closer than κλέος ἄφθιτον, but Tyrtaeus in the passage cited (12. 31 f.) says that the hero's κλέος ἐσθλόν and his name never perish (ἀπόλλυται), and he himself, albeit below the earth, γίνεται ἀθάνατος, 'becomes deathless'. In Simonides and Bacchylides the phrase ἀθάνατον κλέος appears.[107]

As in the case of the gods, the idea of not dying is associated with that of not ageing. Both are combined in RV 3. 53. 15, where the Daughter of the Sun is said to have spread out among the gods her *śrávaḥ* that is *amṛ́tam ajuryám*, 'undying and ageless'. Compare also 1. 126. 2 *śrávo ajáram*, and 1. 117. 4 *ná vāṃ jūryanti pūrviyā́ kṛtā́ni* 'your [the Aśvins'] ancient deeds do not grow old'. Greek poets speak of κῦδος ἀγήραον and κλέος ἀγήρατον (Pind. *Pyth.* 2. 52; Eur. *IA* 567).[108] In a Norse poem we read

ok munu Írar angr of bíða,
þat er aldri mun ýtum fyrnask.

And the Irish will suffer a woe
that shall never grow old among men,

—that is, one that will never be forgotten.[109]

As the height of fame may be represented as reaching the ultimate limit, the sky, so its duration is occasionally predicted to extend until the end of the world. Theognis, after telling his friend Cyrnus that 'even after death you will not lose your κλέος, but have an ἄφθιτον name and ever be of interest to mankind', goes on to promise that he will be a subject of song for future generations as long as earth and sun exist (245 f., 251 f.). In the Indian epic there is talk of fame that will last as long as earth (*MBh.* 12. 54. 28); the story of Rāma will last as long as the mountains and rivers (*Rm.* 1. 2. 35). I have already quoted three passages from the northern literatures that show similar

[107] Simon. eleg. 11. 15 and 28, Bacch. 13. 65. Cf. Schmitt (1967), 69 f.

[108] Cf. Durante (1962), 35 n. 43; Schmitt (1967), 69 f.

[109] *Darraðarlióð* 8. 1–4 (*Edd. min.* 60). Here, as in RV 1. 117. 4 just quoted, the quality of not ageing is transferred from the poetic fame to the event itself. There is a very similar transfer from κλέος ἄφθιτον in Pindar, *Pyth.* 1. 94 οὐ φθίνει Κροίσου φιλόφρων ἀρετά, 'Croesus' friendly goodness does not fade'.

conceits. The Three Hundred in the gold torques will be esteemed *hyd orffen byd*, 'till the end of the world' (*Y Gododdin* 1129). Cethern, if he only had his own weapons, would do such deeds as would be 'a subject of story till Doomsday' (*Táin* (I) 3306). The praise of heroes *mun æ lifa, nema öld farisk . . . eða bili heimar*, 'will live for ever, unless mankind passes away or the worlds crack up' (*Háttatal* v. 96).

The evidence is perhaps too thinly scattered to warrant the conclusion that this was an Indo-European trope, especially as parallels can be found in the Near East.[110] But we have seen enough to establish beyond any reasonable doubt that the idea of posthumous fame was a pervasive theme of Indo-European poetry. Its predicates—good (or bad), great, wide, high, unfailing—may almost be said to form a formulaic system, not in the Parryist sense of being metrically complementary, but in the sense of being semantically complementary. The hero whose feats achieved acclaim and renown in his lifetime could hope that after the death of his body his name would remain: not perhaps explicitly 'to the end of the world', but indefinitely.

[110] See West (1997), 514 f.

11

King and Hero

In the long run these hopes were not realized. A hero's exploits might be celebrated in song for several generations or centuries, but in the end they were displaced from the repertory by newer themes, or the people to whom they had been of concern lost its identity or its taste for stories of old battles. Not a single name of an Indo-European hero has come down to us, only Greek heroes, Germanic heroes, Celtic heroes, and so on, and those only because the medium of writing came in time to preserve them before the oral traditions died.

The heroes of these surviving literatures, however, often have sufficiently similar characteristics to encourage generalization and reference to a traditional model. We should beware of setting up a stereotype, but we may fancy that we can get a notion of the sorts of hero likely to have played a leading role in Indo-European saga.

'Hero' is of course not a technical term but one of convenience. By it we mean generally a man of supreme physical strength and endurance allied to moral qualities such as fearlessness, determination, and a propensity for plunging into dangerous and daunting enterprises. He displays his abilities above all in fighting enemies of one sort or another.

In many traditions narratives about heroes also involve kings. A king may himself be a hero, but in most cases the roles are distinct. The outstanding hero—one may think of Achilles, Hector, Jason, Heracles, Arjuna, Beowulf, Cú Chulainn, Lancelot—is usually not identical with the king. The king is remembered for kingly virtues such as justice, prosperity, liberality, or his lack of them; the hero for achievement, for overcoming adversity (whether on the king's behalf or inflicted by him). He may be the king's champion; he may save the kingdom from disaster; he may in the end marry the king's daughter and become a king himself.[1]

[1] Jeffrey Gantz, *Early Irish Myths and Sagas* (London 1981), 9, remarks: 'Curiously, the kings of the Irish stories are not battle leaders: either they betray vestiges of divinity (Cú Ruí, for example) or they have a young champion as heir and rival.' On the relationship of king and hero cf. Miller (2000), 178–86.

This dichotomy probably reflects a reality of ancient societies. In the Roman war with the Sabines the kings of the two peoples were Romulus and Tatius, but the armies were led by Hostius Hostilius and Mettius Curtius. Strabo (4. 4. 3) writes that most of the Gallic polities in the pre-Roman age used to elect a chief (ἡγεμών) annually, and likewise one war commander would be chosen by the people. The two functions were separate. Tacitus reports of the Germans:

> Reges ex nobilitate, duces ex uirtute sumunt ... et duces exemplo potius quam imperio, si prompti, si conspicui, si ante aciem agant, admiratione praesunt.
>
> They choose their kings for nobility, their war-leaders for *uirtus* ... and the war-leaders are more admired for their conduct than their authority, for being bold and prominent and going out in front of the line (*Germ.* 7).

KINGS

'Kings' have yet to be defined. Historical Indo-European societies had rulers of different kinds at different times, but in their earliest phases the normal pattern everywhere was that one man was acknowledged as the ruler of a larger or smaller domain. Various titles are attested, most of them confined to a single language or language group, even where they have intelligible Indo-European etymologies. A couple are supra-regional. The Mycenaean and Greek *wanak(t)-* (also in Phrygian, but perhaps as an early loan from Greek) has a possible cognate in Tocharian A *nātäk* 'lord'. The reconstructed prototype is **w(n̥)natk-*, an odd-looking word that may be of non-Indo-European origin.[2]

The original MIE terms for 'king' and 'queen' are reconstructed from Indo-Iranian and Celtic evidence.[3] Vedic *rā́jñī* and Old Irish *rígain* 'queen' both go back to **(H)rḗĝn̥ih₂*; this should be the counterpart of a masculine **(H)rḗĝ-ō*/ **(H)rēĝn-*, which duly appears as Vedic *rā́jan-* 'king', and perhaps in Greek ἀρηγών 'defender'. These nouns were derived from the verbal root **(H)reĝ*, seen in Vedic *rā́ṣṭi*/*rā́jati* 'rules, directs', Latin *rego* 'I draw straight, regulate, rule', Gaulish *regu* 'I straighten', Old Irish *rigid* 'stretches; directs; rules'.[4] There also existed verbal rection compounds with *-*(H)rēĝ-* as the second element, meaning '-ruling, -ruler'. From these, Italo-Celtic (and perhaps to a limited extent Indo-Iranian) abstracted a free-standing **(H)rḗĝ-* which

[2] Cf. Gamkrelidze–Ivanov (1995), 654 f.; *EIEC* 329.

[3] Following the analysis of K. McCone, *Ériu* 49 (1998), 1–12.

[4] More in Kretschmer (1896), 126; *IEW* 854–7; *EIEC* 187a.

displaced the original *n*-stem as the word for 'king': Old Irish *rí* (genitive *ríg*), Gaulish *-rix* (in personal names, Dumnorix, Vercingetorix, etc.), Latin *rēx*, Vedic *rā́j*.[5]

It is striking that these old terms for the king and his consort are practically confined to the extremities of the Indo-European world, to Celtic and Italic in the west and Indo-Iranian in the east.[6] They must be archaic survivals from what was once a more general usage. There is in fact vestigial evidence from the central territories, for besides Greek ἀρηγών (if this is indeed cognate) a form of the old word probably appears in the Thracian royal name R(h)ēsos,[7] and a derivative in the Thracian place-names to be mentioned below.

The Latin adjective *rēgius* 'royal' has a parallel formation in Sanskrit *rājya-*. Its neuter **(H)rēg(i)yom* made a secondary noun: RV 7. 6. 2 *rājiyám* 'dominion', proto-Celtic **rīgion* > Old Irish *ríge* 'kingship, kingdom', Middle Welsh *riyđ*; from the Celtic came also Norse *ríki* 'kingdom, dominion, power', Old English *rīce*, Old High German *rîhhi* (modern *Reich*), etc. The neuter or the feminine appears too in place-names, no doubt marking where the king of a region had his seat. Ptolemy records two Ῥηγίαι in Ireland; there was an *Icorigium* between Trier and Cologne; there was the well-known R(h)egium in Calabria (correctly understood as βασίλειον by Strabo 6. 1. 6), besides others in Cisalpine Gaul and eastern Thrace; and, with a sound-change matching that in the name of Rhesos, a suburb of Byzantium called Ῥήσιον.[8]

The relationship between the word for 'king' and the verb meaning 'make straight, direct' is a strong clue to the original nature of the kingship. There is a clear semantic connection between making things straight, drawing straight boundaries, guiding something in a straight line, and governing justly and efficiently. The opposition of straight and crooked is one of the most basic of ethical images, reflected in many languages. From the same root as the verb we have, for example, Sanskrit *ṛjú-* 'straight, just'; Avestan *ərəzu-*, *ərəš*; Old Irish *díriug* 'straight', *recht* 'law'; Latin *rēctus* 'right, correct'. Using different roots but the same metaphor, Greek speaks of ἰθεῖα or εὐθεῖα δίκη, 'straight justice', and can express 'govern' by ἰθύνω, 'make straight'. The ancient **(H)rḗĝō*, therefore, like a Greek ἰθυντήρ, was a rector, a director, a corrector,

5 For a long time these were taken to represent the original form. Cf. for example Kretschmer (1896), 126 f.; Benveniste (1973), 307–12.

6 Gothic *reiks* [rīks] 'king' is an import from Celtic, as it presupposes the distinctively Celtic change from **rēg-* to **rīg-*; cf. D. H. Green (1998), 150 f. Old Prussian *rikis* came in turn from Germanic.

7 Cf. Detschew (1957), 393 s.v. Ρησκου-.

8 Ptol. 2. 2. 10, cf. O'Rahilly (1946), 14; *Suda* ρ 146, *Anth. Pal.* 9. 691 lemma; Detschew (1957), 393.

one who ensured that things ran true in his domain. There was a sacral aspect to his office, but religious ritual was determined and administered by a separate priesthood (see below).

In anthropological terms he would seem to have been a 'chief', 'that is the principal executive officer with some centralizing functions in what is still essentially a tribal society, based on kinship relations and often incorporating various smaller kinship-based social units. Thus a chiefdom is an autonomous political unit, usually comprising a number of clans living in settled villages or pastoral communities under the leadership of a paramount chief.'[9]

The evidence of several early Indo-European societies—Hittite, Vedic, Roman, Celtic, Germanic—suggests that the kingship may originally have been not hereditary but elective.[10] After all, the previous king's son might have been too young, or otherwise unsuitable, to act as an effective chief in an era before there was a developed apparatus of court officialdom or civil service. In any case the king depended in practice on the support and good will of a community of arms-bearing men. Generally it seems that the candidacy became limited, by custom or statute, to a particular family or group of families, and there must have been agreement on who elected the king and by what procedure. There would often be an heir presumptive during the king's lifetime. Iranian and Irish evidence indicates that he bore the title 'Second after the king'.[11]

The Queen

In many stories the kingdom comes with a woman: a man becomes king by marrying an existing queen or the widow or daughter of a king. Margalit Finkelberg has shown that this is a recurrent pattern in Greek heroic mythology, and there are numerous instances in early Irish history.[12] Saxo

[9] R. M. Rowlett, *JIES* 12 (1984), 193, with a reference to R. Carneiro in G. D. Jones–R. R. Kautz (edd.), *The Transition to Statehood in the New World* (Cambridge 1981), 37–79. Rowlett's article (193–233) is a survey of archaeological evidence for early Indo-European chieftains.

[10] Cf. K. Ohkuma, *JIES* 14 (1986), 231–43; Sergent (1995), 272 f.; for the Hittites, Trevor Bryce, *The Kingdom of the Hittites* (Oxford 1998), 91 f., 114; for Gaul, Strabo 4. 4. 3 cited above; for Germania, D. H. Green (1998), 121; for Ireland, Campanile (1981), 42 f. According to the *Togail bruidne Dá Derga* 11 (lines 122 ff. Knott) the men of Ireland would hold a bull-feast, 'that is, a bull used to be killed by them and one man would eat his fill of it and drink its broth and a spell of truth was chanted over him in his bed. Whoever he would see in his sleep would be king and the sleeper would perish if he uttered a falsehood' (Koch–Carey (2000), 168 f.). Cf. *Serglige Con Culainn* 22; McCone (1990), 168.

[11] Campanile (1981), 43–7.

[12] M. Finkelberg, *CQ* 41 (1991), 303–16; ead. (2005), 65–71, 91 f.; Bart Jaski, *Early Irish Kingship and Succession* (Dublin 2000), 69–71.

(4. 1. 16 p. 90) relates that Herminthrud, the queen of Scotland, offered herself to the young Danish king Amleth (Hamlet), saying that she herself would be rated a king but for her sex, and that whoever she saw fit to take as husband would be the king of her realm.

This mechanism does not necessarily contradict the elective principle. Where there was a woman of a status such that union with her was seen as desirable to legitimate the new king, the electors' choice of king was at the same time a choice of who should marry her. In the *Mabinogion* a king of France dies leaving an only daughter with the dominion in her hands. Llefelys, brother of Lludd the king of Britain, goes to seek her hand, sending messengers to the French nobles to explain his purpose, 'and by common counsel of the nobles of France and its princes the maiden was given to Llefelys, and the crown of the kingdom along with her'.[13]

Why were such marriages held to confer legitimacy on a new king? Several factors may be involved besides the ancient principle of matrilinear inheritance. It might seem right and natural, and in the interests of continuity, that the man who was going to take over the royal house should also take over the most royal female attached to it. Otherwise she might become an asset to a rival. A living king could hope to secure his borders or extend his influence by marrying his daughter to a friendly noble and setting him up as ruler of a neighbouring territory.

But there are signs that the queen was more essential to the kingship than is a modern sovereign's consort, who receives a noble title and much respect but is not an intrinsic part of the office. The correspondence between Vedic *rā́jñī* and Old Irish *rígain* points to the existence of an Indo-European title 'ruler-female', and it is not self-evident that the king's wife would merit such a special designation unless she had a particular role to play. The Hittite queen, the *tawananna*, not only exercised important functions in matters of cult and state, but held her position for life, even after her husband's death, and only on her own death passed it on to the current king's wife. Her next of kin in some circumstances formed essential links in the royal succession.[14]

In certain cases there is something divine about the queen. Peisetairos, the hero of Aristophanes' *Birds*, ends up as king of the new gods after Zeus is forced to cede his sceptre to the birds and give Peisetairos Basileia 'the Queen' as his bride. Basileia, it is explained, is a beautiful maiden and the custodian of Zeus' power, wisdom, and justice.[15] In several Irish legends the king's bride

[13] *Cyfranc Lludd a Llefelys* lines 15–29 (ed. B. F. Roberts, Dublin 1975).

[14] See M. Finkelberg, *Cosmos* 13 (1997), 127–41; ead. (2005), 71–9, 177–82.

[15] Ar. *Av.* 1534–43, cf. 1634, 1713, 1730, 1753. *Βασίλεια* has a short final alpha and therefore means 'Queen', not 'Kingship'.

is a goddess representing Sovereignty, or the land over which he is to be sovereign. For example, the five sons of Eochaid Mugmedón go out into the wild to hunt, make a meal, and find themselves in need of water. They go each in turn to a well, which is guarded by a repulsive hag. She demands a kiss as the price for water. Only the fifth brother, Niall, is willing to give her a proper kiss, and he even lies down with her, whereupon she changes into a girl of superlative beauty. She reveals that she is the Sovereignty of Tara, and Niall and his descendants will have it for ever.[16] Such symbolic unions seem to have had ritual status. The *Annals of Loch Cé* record that in 1310 Fedhlim the son of Aedh 'married the province of Connacht'. The idea that the king of Ireland was wedded to Ireland, and local kings to their own territories, persisted for centuries.[17]

The mythical heroine Medb, who cohabited with nine kings of Ireland and would not allow any king in Tara who did not have her to wife, was in origin an ancient goddess whom the king had to marry.[18] Her name is derived from *mid* (**med^{h}u*) 'mead', **Med^{h}w-ā*. She has a striking counterpart in the princess Mādhavī of the *Mahābhārata* (5. 113–17), whose name is likewise a derivative of *medhu*. Her impoverished father gave her in marriage to four successive kings, receiving a handsome bride-price of two hundred horses each time; she provided each husband with royal progeny before becoming a virgin again for the next one.[19] The Mead-queen of these stories seems to represent a ritual drink of mead with which the new king imbibed sovereignty. It is a drink (though only of water) that the Sovereignty-woman grants to Niall and denies to his brothers in the legend cited above. In other Irish texts too female symbols of sovereignty bestow a drink upon a man who is to be king, or kings are said to drink the sovereignty.[20] The proffering of a drink by a bride to her groom, and his acceptance of it, was a Celtic marriage custom signifying the couple's mutual consent to the union.[21]

[16] *Echtra mac n-Echach Muigmedóin* 9–17; W. Stokes, *RC* 24 (1903), 196–201; Koch–Carey (2000), 205–7; cf. McCone (1990), 109.

[17] See T. F. O'Rahilly, *Ériu* 14 (1946), 17–21.

[18] T. Ó Máille, *ZCP* 17 (1928), 129–46; cf. P. Mac Cana, *Études Celtiques* 7 (1955/6), 76–114, 356–413; 8 (1958/9), 59–65; Campanile (1981), 28–34; (1990a), 266 f.; (1990b), 42–5.

[19] Cf. Dumézil (1968–73), ii. 316–53; Puhvel (1987), 258–66; McCone (1990), 119 f. Mādhavī's story recalls the Greek myth of Mestra, whose father Erysichthon, afflicted by Demeter with an insatiable appetite and consequently bankrupt, married her to a succession of suitors, receiving cattle, sheep, and goats as bride-price. After each marriage she would change her shape, slip away, and return to her father ('Hes.' fr. 43). Mestra's name (*Μήστρη*) does not seem relatable to the 'mead' root, and her marriages do not appear to promote kingship.

[20] Cf. T. F. O'Rahilly, *Ériu* 14 (1946), 14–17; McCone (1990), 109; B. Jaski (as n. 12), 67 f. We may recall that Zeus swallowed his first wife Metis, 'Resource' (Hes. *Th.* 890. 899, fr. 343. 8–10).

[21] T. F. O'Rahilly (as n. 20), 15.

Let us return from these divine and symbolic queens to the human one. So far as we can make out, she played no part in the king's ordinary discharge of his duties, but she had an important role in certain religious ceremonies. Classical Athens provides a notorious example. The Athenian king (*basileus*) had long ceased to have any political significance, but he survived as a religious functionary. In the Choes festival of early spring his wife, attended by fourteen holy matrons, underwent a ritual marriage to Dionysus, god of growth and fertility, for the good of the community. As we shall see, the Indo-European king was held responsible for the fertility of land and livestock. In this Athenian rite his wife's mating with a god is somehow an essential contribution to his success. How it was enacted has long been a subject for speculation. It has been supposed either that the *basileus* himself stood in for the god or that the lady gratified herself with a statue or herm. It is also possible that the ritual involved, or had once involved, an animal representing the deity, a goat or a bull.[22]

A parallel detail may be discerned in the Indian royal ritual known as the Aśvamedha, utterly different though it is in other respects from the Greek ceremony. Jaan Puhvel has described it as a 'production with a cast of thousands, incorporating many adjutory rites and representing in a sense the sum of Ancient Indic sacrificial pageantry'.[23] Its preparation took a year. The central act was the sacrifice of a prize white or grey stallion which had had no contact with mares during that time and which had drawn the king's chariot. After it was killed and before it was dismembered, the principal queen lay down and passed the night with it under covers, and verses were chanted encouraging it to impregnate her. So here too the king's consort was required to enact a kind of supernatural coupling or *hieros gamos*.

King and horse

Scholars have noted an analogy between the Aśvamedha and a disgusting ritual recorded from twelfth-century Donegal. When a new king was consecrated, the people assembled and he, declaring himself to be a horse, copulated with a white mare in front of them. The animal was at once sacrificed and dismembered and the meat was boiled. A large barrel was filled

[22] We recall the myth of Minos' queen Pasiphae enclosing herself in a model cow in order to be impregnated by a bull. Obviously the Athenian rite featured nothing of this sort in historical times.

[23] In Jaan Puhvel (ed.), *Myth and Law among the Indo-Europeans* (Berkeley–Los Angeles 1970), 160–2; id. (1987), 269–72; cf. *MBh.* 14. 70–2. 74, 83 f., 86–91; *Rm.* 1. 11–13; A. B. Keith, *The Veda of the Black Yajus School entitled Taittirīya Saṅhitā*, i (Cambridge Mass. 1914), cxxxii–cxxxvii; Watkins (1995), 265–76.

with the broth. The naked king climbed into it and sat there, dipping his mouth in to sup, while the gobbets of boiled meat were distributed among the spectators.[24] There is no mention of a role for the queen, but the combination of royal horse sacrifice and royal copulation with the victim makes a striking parallel with the ancient Indian rite.

There is much evidence for horse sacrifice among Indo-European (as well as Finno-Ugric and Turkic) peoples.[25] It has no necessary connection with kingship, but it is related that the assumption of the Swedish kingship by the pagan Svein was ratified by the sacrifice, dismemberment, and consumption of a horse.[26] Puhvel has drawn attention to the Arvernian royal name Epomeduos, which combines 'horse' (**ekwo-*) with the 'mead' that occupied us above.[27] The Roman sacrifice of the October Equus, which took place in honour of Mars on the Ides of October, shows vestigial associations with royalty. The Campus Martius, the scene of the action, was the old *ager Tarquiniorum* (Livy 2. 5. 2), the horse's severed tail was taken quickly to the Regia so that the warm blood could drip on the sacred hearth there, and its head was fixed on the wall of the Regia (if the men of the Via Sacra succeeded in defending it from the men of the Subura). Dumézil noted another point of detail that makes a link between the October Equus and the Aśvamedha. The Roman event began with a chariot-race, and it was the right-hand horse of the winning pair that was chosen for sacrifice. Similarly for the Indian rite it was prescribed that the victim must 'excel on the right part of the yoke'.[28]

The motif of sexual congress between a man and a mare is documented sporadically elsewhere, though not in a way that clarifies its relevance to kingship. A rock drawing of the Bronze Age at Bohuslän in Sweden shows an ithyphallic winged man with a bird mask and a sword approaching a mare from the rear. The Gaulish horse goddess Epona is said to have been born after one Fulvius Stella, who did not care for women, copulated with a mare.[29]

[24] Giraldus Cambrensis, *Topographia Hiberniae* 3. 25; Koch–Carey (2000), 273; cf. F. R. Schröder, *ZCP* 16 (1927), 310–12; de Vries (1961), 243 f.; Puhvel (as n. 23, 1970), 163 f.; (1987), 273 f.; Campanile (1981), 35; McCone (1990), 117 f.; Watkins (1995), 265 f. In the Aśvamedha too the king has contact with the sacrificial horse-flesh: he sniffs the odour of the smoking fat, thus freeing himself from sin (*Rm.* 1. 13. 30). At the end of the ceremony he takes a purifying bath (*MBh.* 14. 90. 16, 91. 29).

[25] Cf. Grimm 47–9; Unbegaun (1948), 418; de Vries (1956), i. 364–6; M. Green (1986), 171 f.; Davidson (1988), 55 f.; *EIEC* 278 f.

[26] *Hervarar saga* 16. For Altaic horse sacrifices connected with kingship cf. E. R. Anderson, *JIES* 27 (1999), 379–93.

[27] J. Puhvel (as n. 23, 1970), 164, 167.

[28] Festus p. 190. 11 L.; ŚB 13. 4. 2. 1; W. Warde Fowler, *The Roman Festivals* (London 1899), 242, 247; G. Dumézil, *Revue des études latines* 36 (1959), 130 f.

[29] Gelling–Davidson (1969), 68 f.; Agesilaus *FGrHist* 828 F 1 ap. Plut. *Parall. min.* 312e.

We may also recall the Indian myth about the birth of the Aśvins (end of Chapter 4).

Before we leave the subject of the inauguration of kings, let us note in passing a point of Irish custom that may throw light on a Greek myth. Pindar (*Pyth.* 4. 72–96) relates that when Jason presented himself at Pelias' court in Iolkos, the usurper blenched on observing that the visitor wore only one shoe. He had been warned by an oracle to beware τὸν μονοκρήπιδα, the one-shoe man, who would depose him. Jason was the rightful claimant to the throne. Now in Irish bardic poetry the phrase 'the man of the one shoe' (*fear an énais*) or 'of the one golden shoe' (*fear an énais óir*) apparently refers to a claimant to the chieftaincy or to an inaugurated chief. The explanation lies in a practice mentioned in the *Annals of the Four Masters* under the years 1488 and 1589, whereby a claimant to the chieftancy of the O'Connors deposited a shoe as a token and had it replaced on his foot on his inauguration.[30]

King and priest

The construct of an Indo-European king from the eastern and western lexical evidence is given added solidity, in many scholars' view, by the presence beside him, in India and at Rome, of high-status priests with what are possibly cognate titles, Vedic *brahmán-*, *Latin flāmen*, which might both be derived from *$b^{h}la\hat{g}^{h}$(s)-men-*. The etymological equivalence has long been debated; it is not unproblematic, and sometimes rejected. Yet it is hard to dismiss the similarity of the words as fortuitous—they share the masculine suffix **-men-*, which is an archaic rarity—and the identification continues to be canvassed, albeit with reservations.[31] The case for it is strengthened by the fact that the Brahman and the Flamen Dialis were subject to a whole series of similar taboos.[32]

If this is accepted, we obtain a matching structure: *rā́jan-* + *brahmán-* ~ *rex* + *flamen*. The king, as we have seen, played a central role in some sacred ceremonies. The Hittite and Indian ritual texts abound with complicated prescriptions for his religious duties. But it was the chief priest, we may

[30] M. A. O'Brien, *Celtica* 2 (1954), 351–3; Watkins (1994), 668 f.; Dooley–Roe (1999), 232. Wearing one shoe plays a role in many rituals and superstitions, cf. W. Deonna, *Revue de l'histoire des religions* 56 (1935), 50–72; but the Irish custom seems the most relevant to Jason.

[31] Kretschmer (1896), 127–9; Georges Dumézil, *Flamen–Brahman* (Paris 1935); Benveniste (1973), 231 (*contra*); A. L. Sihler, *New Comparative Grammar of Greek and Latin* (New York–Oxford 1995), 198; M. E. Huld in Dexter–Polomé (1997), 179 f.; *EIEC* 451 f. Messapic(?) βλαμινι in a Greek inscription from Apulia (a priest, according to Haas (1962), 67) is also to be mentioned, though its meaning is not at all clear from the context.

[32] Listed in Puhvel (1987), 156 f.; *EIEC* 453.

assume, who laid down these prescriptions and counted as the supreme authority in matters of ritual.

Various other Indo-Iranian words denoting priests of one sort or another have apparent European cognates or analogues:

Vedic *hótar-* = Avestan *zaotar-*, 'pourer' of libations (*ĝʰéw-tor-*); cf. the Thracian proper name Seuthes; possibly the Messapic name *Hazzavoa*, *-voas*.[33]
Avestan *frabərətar-*, 'bringer' of offerings (**pro-bʰer-tor-*); Umbrian *arsfertur* (*ars* = 'to'); Messapic *tabaras*, fem. *tabara*.[34]
Vedic *pathikṛ́t-* 'path-maker' (for communication with the gods), a title applied to priests; Latin *pontifex*.[35]

Compare also Vedic *kaví-* and its cognates (Chapter 1, p. 28). These concordances suggest for Mature Indo-European an organized priesthood with different functions assigned to different ministers.

The wearing of white garments was an ancient and widespread mark of the sacerdotal office, attested at least for Italic, Celtic, and Germanic priests.[36]

The king's qualities

The king, as we saw, was by etymology a 'rector', one who made things go straight. Sometimes he was described in metaphorical terms as a charioteer or as the helmsman of a ship, that is, as one who guides a moving conveyance on the right course. The charioteer image is commonplace in the Rigveda, and occurs also in the Old Irish gnomic text *Audacht Morainn* (22), where the king is advised to be like the driver of an old chariot who uses his expertise to ensure that the vehicle runs true. The idea of the ruler as a helmsman (κυβερνητήρ) is familiar in Greek; our word 'govern' comes from Latin *gubernare*, 'steer' (a ship), 'control', which was a borrowing from the Greek κυβερνᾶν. The same image is expressed in different language when Eteocles in Aeschylus (*Sept.* 2 f., cf. 62) speaks of a monarch as 'plying the tiller at the city's stern', ἐν πρύμνῃ πόλεως οἴακα νωμῶν. It appears also in the *Rāmāyaṇa*: 'this royal majesty, founded on righteousness, belonged to him, the great and righteous king. And now it is adrift like a ship on the water without a helmsman' (2. 75. 6, cf. 82. 19). Ships and chariots, it will be

[33] So Ciro Santoro, *Nuovi Studi Messapici: Primo Supplemento* (Galatina 1984), 172 f.; id., *Archivio storico Pugliese* 41 (1988), 96–8. But the etymology of this name is very insecure.

[34] G. Redard in *Studia Indoeuropejskie. Mélanges Jan Safarewicz* (Cracow 1974), 191–5; C. Santoro, *Nuovi Studi Messapici*, ii (Galatina 1983), 182–6; id., *Archivio storico Pugliese* 41 (1988), 90 f.; Sergent (1995), 377 f.

[35] Cf. Campanile (1990b), 121–4.

[36] Grimm (1883–8), 1315 f.

recalled from Chapter 1, were ancient alternative images also in the sphere of poetry and song.

In several traditions the king is seen as a protector of the people. He is like a father to them: *Od.* 2. 47, 234, 5. 12 πατὴρ ὣς ἤπιος ἦεν; *Rm.* 2. 51. 12, 'like a father Rāma watched over the city, pondering what was advantageous for the people'. Under the best king men live fearlessly like sons in their father's house (*MBh.* 12. 57. 33). More picturesquely, the king is conceived as the herdsman of his subjects. We saw in Chapter 3 that this metaphor could be applied to gods, and that it was as much at home in Semitic as in Indo-European. The human ruler likewise can be called *jánasya gopā́-*, 'cowherd of the people' (RV 3. 43. 5, where it is parallel to *rā́jan-*); ποιμένα λαῶν, 'shepherd of peoples' (*Il.* 1. 263, 2. 85, and often); *folces hyrde* (*Beowulf* 610, 1832, 1849, 2644, 2981, *Finnesburh* 46); in Old Saxon *landes hirdi, uuerodes hirdi* (*Hêliand* 2743, 5549).[37]

Hesiod gives the following picture of the ideal king (*Th.* 84–92):

> Out of his mouth the words flow honeyed; and the peoples
> all look to him as he decides what is right
> with his straight judgments. His word is sure,
> and expertly he makes a quick end of even a great dispute.
> That is why there are prudent kings: when the peoples
> are wronged in their dealings, they make amends for them
> with ease, persuading them with gentle words.
> When he goes among a gathering, they seek his favour as if he were a god
> with conciliatory reverence, and he stands out among the crowd.

The qualities here described, a fine appearance, eloquence, wise and persuasive dispensation of justice, are all among those looked for in the ancient Irish king. According to *Audacht Morainn* (55) the king should be merciful, righteous, proper, conscientious, firm, generous, hospitable, of noble mien, steadfast, beneficent, able, honest, well-spoken, steady, true-judging. Other texts focus on physical beauty, wisdom, and martial prowess.[38]

The 'straight judgments' of the Hesiodic king reflect the original concept of the **Hrēĝō*, the rector. He decides what is right, διακρίνει θέμιστας; elsewhere we find the formula θεμιστοπόλοι βασιλῆες, 'kings that deal in (judgments of) right'. The Avestan phrase *ahura xratugūtō* (Yt. 8. 36) means very much the same, *xratu-* being the ruler's wisdom manifested in his judgments. In Ireland too the king was seen as the fount of justice. He had

[37] Cf. Schmitt (1967), 283 f.; H. Humbach, *MSS* 21 (1967), 23 f., 26; Durante (1976), 111; Campanile (1977), 25; for Semitic material West (1997), 227. For a collection of expressions in Old Norse poetry referring to the king as a defender or protector cf. *CPB* ii. 479.

[38] See McCone (1990), 121–4.

specialist lawyers to advise him, but the judgment was his unless he chose to delegate it.[39]

Where there is judicial authority, of course, there is always (except in the best regulated societies) the possibility of influencing it by means of gifts or bribes. The king or official who accepted them was perhaps said in Indo-European parlance to 'eat' them. The Hittite wisdom text known as the *Song of Release* contains two parables, really variants of a single parable, about a dog or another animal who stole a loaf from an oven, dipped it in oil, and ate it. It is explained that this stands for a governor who exacts excessive tribute and embezzles it, is denounced by the citizens, and has to 'pour out before his lord those items of tribute which he was continually swallowing'. Hesiod refers to *βασιλῆες δωροφάγοι*, 'gift-eating kings'. By a similar idiom a king might be castigated as *δημοβόρος*, 'eating the people' (*Il.* 1. 231); this is paralleled in a humorous simile in the Rigveda, where Agni (Fire) is said to eat the forests as a king does his dependants (1. 65. 7, *íbhyān ná rā́jā vánāni atti*), and also in later Sanskrit.[40]

The king's justice and the land's fertility

Justice and right were conceived as being not merely a function of human society but an alignment of the cosmic order. This fine abstract formulation is of course not ancient; it is our own attempt to give theoretical form to an ancient persuasion that finds expression in more concrete propositions. It is expressed particularly in the doctrine that the justice of the ruler conditions the fertility of the earth and livestock in his territory. We find this doctrine in the Indian and Iranian epics, and in Greek, Irish, and Norse literature, and it is also attested for ancient Burgundy.[41]

Where King Yudhiṣṭhira dwells, it is declared,

> there will be no people who are discontented, jealous, offensive in speech, or envious. Everyone will be avowed to his own Law.... There, no doubt, God Parjanya will rain in the proper season and the earth will bear rich crops and be free from plagues. The rice will be fine, the fruit juicy, the garlands fragrant ... Cows will be teeming, none of them lean or poor milk-givers; the milk, curds and butter will be tasty and whole-

[39] M. Gerriets, *Celtica* 20 (1988), 29–52; McCone (1990), 126.

[40] *Song of Release* §§18 f., 21 f., trs. Hoffner (1998), 71; Hes. *Op.* 39 *δωροφάγοι*; West (1978), 151; V. M. Apte in R. C. Majumdar (ed.), *The Vedic Age* (*The History and Culture of the Indian People*, i, London 1951), 433.

[41] It is not exclusively Indo-European, being also part of the ideology of Mesopotamian and Hebrew kingship. See West (1978), 213; (1997), 136. For other parts of the world cf. Frazer (1911–36), i. 353–6.

some. Water will be salubrious and foodstuffs delicious in the country where King Yudhiṣṭhira lives (*MBh.* 4. 27. 13–20).

Similarly in Rāma's reign all was benign, there were seasonal rains and good crops; there was no fire, flood, or disease; men lived for a thousand years and had a thousand children; the trees bore abundant flowers and fruits, and the cows gave abundant milk.[42]

Conversely an unjust king causes nature to withhold its bounty. According to the Turanian leader Afrāsiyāb in the *Shāh-nāma*, 'because of the tyranny of the Iranian king all good disappears into hiding; the wild ass does not bring forth at its due season, the eye of the young falcon is blinded, wild creatures stem the flow of milk to their breasts, water in the springs turns to pitch or dries up in the wells everywhere, the musk lacks perfume in its pod'. In a later episode Shah Bahrām by repenting of his harsh policies produces an immediate and spectacular increase in the yield of a cow that had been empty of milk.[43]

The disguised Odysseus tells Penelope that her fame is heaven-high,

> like that of some flawless king, who, god-fearing,
> ruling a numerous and doughty people,
> upholds justice, and the dark earth brings forth
> wheat and barley, and the trees are heavy with fruit,
> the sheep and goats give birth without fail, and the sea provides fish
> from his good leadership, and the peoples flourish under him.
> (*Od.* 19. 109–14)

Hesiod paints a similar picture in his description of the rewards of the just city (*Op.* 225–37). He does not refer specifically to kings, but in the context of his poem it is 'kings' who control the administration of justice.

According to Ammianus Marcellinus (28. 5. 14) it is an ancestral custom of the Burgundians to depose their king if the nation fares ill in war or if the earth gives poor crops. The ninth-century skald Einarr Skálaglamm praises Earl Hákon for restoring shrines that his predecessors had destroyed: 'now the gods receive their sacrifices again . . . the earth bears its fruits as before'. Snorri Sturluson tells of two kings who were sacrificed on account of continual bad harvests, and he comments that the Swedes hold their kings responsible in this matter. Elsewhere he writes that under a good ruler there are plentiful harvests both from the sea and the land.[44]

[42] *MBh.* 12. 29. 46–54, cf. 70. 6–24, 92. 6, 139. 9 f.; *Rm.* 6. 116. 82 ff.; Jan Gonda, *Ancient Indian Kingship from the Religious Point of View* (Leiden 1966), 7 f.

[43] Levy (1967), 96, 312.

[44] Einarr, *Vellekla* 15; *Ynglinga saga* 15, 43, cf. *Orkneyinga saga* 9; de Vries (1956), i. 203, 393–6; id. (1961), 236–8; Turville-Petre (1964), 191–3.

The same notions were current in the Celtic lands. Livy (5. 34. 2) tells of a legendary Gaulish king Ambigatus in the time of Tarquin: he was a model of virtue, with the consequence that the country became outstandingly fertile in both crops and men. In Irish eyes the essence of justice was *fír*, 'truth', and more specifically *fír flatha* or *flathemon*, 'the sovereign's truth'.[45] Its blessings as enumerated in *Audacht Morainn* include the following:

It is through the sovereign's truth that the mouth may taste the abundant fruit of the great forest; it is through the sovereign's truth that milk-yields of numerous cattle may be traded; it is through the sovereign's truth that there may be plenty of every high, tall grain; it is through the sovereign's truth that an abundance of the water's fish swim up streams; it is through the sovereign's truth that fair offspring, born of young women, are well begotten (17–21, trs. Koch).

There are many passages in Irish literature where good weather and abundant crops and livestock are connected with the virtue of the ruler, or bad weather, pestilence, and famine with his inadequacies.[46]

The king's liberality

Besides being a fountain of justice, the king was a whirlpool of wealth. He accumulated it and he distributed it, to reward his heroes and his poets. We noted evidence for the guerdon of poets in Chapter 1. Now we can take a wider view.

The king's gifts were typically of horses, cattle, or gold, this commonly in the form of rings and diadems. In a praise poem on an inscription the Indian King Skandagupta is celebrated as 'giver of many millions of gold and cows, all righteously acquired'.[47] Afrāsiyāb in the *Shāh-nāma*, attacked at night in his palace by Rostam, calls out 'Has sleep fettered all my warriors? Let all those champions who wish for a ring and a diadem hem them in on every side!'[48]

Posidonius described the carefree liberality of the Celtic chieftain Louernios or Louerios, who scattered gold and silver from his chariot for his followers to pick up. Cú Chulainn and Fer Diad are 'the two heroes . . . the two bestowers of gifts and rewards and wages in the northwestern world'.

[45] Cf. Campanile (1981), 36, 48–52; id. (1990b), 45 f.; Wolfgang Meid, *Die keltischen Sprachen und Literatur* (Innsbruck 1997), 39.

[46] McCone (1990), 108, 129 f., 139. C. Watkins, *Ériu* 30 (1979), 181–9 = id. (1994), 626–34, strikingly compares the *Audacht Morainn* passage with Vedic and Avestan statements in the form 'it is by truth that . . .': *ṛténa* . . . , RV 1. 2. 8; 4. 3. 9–12, al.; *tā bā aša* . . . *yaṯ* . . . , Yt. 5. 77.

[47] *Corpus Inscriptionum Indicarum* iii. 13. 11.

[48] Levy (1967), 171.

Urien of Rheged is praised in one of the poems ascribed to Taliesin as 'most bountiful of Christians: much you bestow on the men of this land. As you gather in, so you give away.'[49]

In the Germanic poetic traditions the giving of gold, especially rings or pieces broken from rings, is a commonplace motif. 'Giver of rings', 'breaker of treasure', and the like are formulaic phrases for kings and lords: Old English *bēahgifa, bēaga brytta, sinces brytta*, Old Saxon *bôggebo*, Norse *bauga deilir, spillir bauga, hringbroti*. The poems often refer to their engagement in this activity.[50] In the *Hildebrandslied* (33–5) Hiltibrant, discovering that the warrior facing him in battle is his son Hadubrant, takes off his arm gold rings that the Hun king had given him and offers them to his son to honour him.

A more singular demonstration of royal generosity appears in parallel Indic and Irish myths. A brahmin asked King Śibi for one of his eyes, and the king gladly gave him both. Indra restored his sight because he had always spoken the truth and granted petitions. The Irish poet Athirne asked King Echaid for his eye (he only had one), and Echaid at once plucked it out and handed it over; God afterwards gave him back both his eyes.[51]

THE HERO

His exceptional nature

When we read the *Iliad* we are impressed by Achilles' strongly emotional character; we are persuaded that he must have above average strength, stamina, and fighting ability because of his success in battle and the fear he inspires; we would be daunted to meet him face to face; yet we are not conscious of an uncrossable gulf separating him from human beings as we know them. Alexander the Great thought it feasible to be a second Achilles.

The signs are, however, that the Homeric epic—and this is the key to its greatness—has made a point of humanizing the heroes and portraying them naturalistically, suppressing the more outlandish and prodigious features that some of them may have had in earlier tradition. Only occasionally do traces of this older picture show through. Ajax in particular is called πελώριος,

[49] Posidonius F 170 Theiler (Strabo 4. 2. 3, Ath. 152de); *Táin* (L) 3287–90; *Canu Taliesin* 3. 1–5; Clancy (2003), 40.

[50] *Beowulf* 80, 1487, 1719 f., 1749 f., 1756 f., 1929–31, 1970, 2383, 2635; *Widsith* 73 f.; *Helgakviða Hundingsbana A* 9. 5–8; *Atlakviða* 37. 7, *Rígsþula* 38. 4–8, *Hyndlulióð* 28. 3; cf. Schramm (1957), 101.

[51] *Jātaka* 499; *Talland Etair*, ed. W. Stokes, *RC* 8 (1887), 48; compared by Dillon (1975), 89.

'huge, monstrous' (*Il.* 3. 166, 229, al.), and this adjective is sometimes applied to other heroes too, including Hector and Achilles. In Herodotus' story of the discovery of the bones of Orestes in Tegea (1. 67 f.), the coffin is seven cubits long and the skeleton fills it. The Irish had a similar notion of the colossal stature of the old heroes. At the beginning of *Acallam na Senórach* Patrick's priests, 'seeing Caílte and his men approaching, were seized with fear and horror at the sight of these enormous men, the warriors of an earlier age'. Later in the work the cairn of Garb Daire is dug up and his body and weapons found. His weapons and head are brought up, 'and the largest man of that host could find room to sit down on the bottom of the head'.[52] When Sigurd strode through a ripe cornfield the end of his scabbard only reached the tops of the ears; a hair from his horse's tail was seven yards long.[53]

The ancient heroes' size is matched by their terrific strength. More noteworthy than the fact itself are the means by which it is conveyed in traditional narratives. Diomedes, Hector, and Aeneas heft with ease rocks that two men could not carry, 'such as mortals are now' (*Il.* 5. 302, 12. 445, 20. 286). Similarly Cú Chulainn 'lifted Conchobar out of the ditch then. Six of our strong men in Ulster could not have lifted him out more courageously' (*Táin* (I) 508). Achilles' cabin has a door-bolt that takes three men to open and close, though Achilles can do it by himself (*Il.* 24. 453–6). Again an Irish saga supplies a parallel, with a door that takes nine men to close.[54]

Another measure of heroic strength links Irish with Iranian and Armenian tradition. The young Cú Chulainn goes to Conchobar to ask for arms. He tries out all of Conchobar's fifteen spare sets of weapons and breaks them all. Finally he is given Conchobar's own set, and they withstand his demands. It is the same with chariots: Conchobar gave him a chariot. Cú Chulainn put his hand between the two shafts and the chariot broke. In the same way he smashed twelve chariots. So finally Conchobar's chariot was given to him and it withstood the test. In the *Shāh-nāma* Rostam selects a horse for himself by pressing down on their spines till he finds one that does not buckle. And similarly in the Armenian epic Mher 'slapped the back of every horse; and every one of the horses dropped its belly to the ground', until at lasts he finds one that stands up to him.[55]

In some legends there appear individuals endowed with a single extraordinary faculty. For example, both in Greek and in Welsh myth we find a man so light of foot that he can run across the tops of reeds or standing

[52] Dooley–Roe (1999), 5, 64, cf. 166–9.

[53] *Vǫlsunga saga* 23; *Nornagests saga* 8; cf. Grimm (1883–8), 387, 1394.

[54] *Orgain Dind Ríg* 26, ed. W. Stokes, *ZCP* 3 (1901), 8/13.

[55] *Táin* (I) 616–52; Levy (1967), 50 f.; *Sassountsy David* 117 f. Cf. C. Monette, *JIES* 32 (2004), 64. The Armenian example may be derivative from the Persian.

corn without bending them,[56] and another who can see over vast distances.[57] The Welsh examples come in a long list of Arthur's warriors, many of whom have other wondrous peculiarities. In what follows, a quest is launched for Culhwch's unseen love, the giant's daughter Olwen, and six men are selected to go on it, each having a special talent: one could guide people through lands he had never seen before, one could make them invisible, one knew all languages, and so on. This is a typical story type, what Karl Meuli called the *Helfermärchen*, in which a band of people embark on an adventure, having among them certain individuals with exceptional abilities, and each of these enables them to overcome a particular danger.[58] This, I take it, is the type of narrative to which such persons properly belong. It is an ancient type, but we are not in a position to claim Indo-European antiquity for it.

Birth and infancy

To account for the exceptional nature of the hero an exceptional parentage was often invoked, usually a divine father or mother. But their parenting skills, if any, were not called in aid. In many cases the child was separated from his parents at an early age.

A common story motif, based on a real-life practice, is that the child is exposed, or an attempt is made to dispose of him in some other way. In real life the baby almost always perished. In story he invariably survives, suckled by an animal and/or found and reared by a herdsman, and eventually reappears to make his mark. I do not dwell on these familiar themes, which are neither confined to Indo-European traditions nor especially characteristic of the warrior hero as here defined.[59]

The heroic baby shows early signs of what he is to become. He typically has fair hair and flashing eyes. These are the outstanding features of Meleager ('Hes.' fr. 25. 5–7), of Grimvald (Paul. Diac. *Hist. Langobard.* 4. 37 *oculis micantibus, lacteo crine*), of the prototypical Jarl (*Rígsþula* 34, 'blond was his hair, bright his cheeks, piercing were his eyes like a young snake's'). Helgi's

[56] Iphiclus, 'Hes.' fr. 62; Sgilti Lightfoot, *Culhwch and Olwen* 239–44.

[57] Lynceus, who could see across the whole Peloponnese and detect the Dioskouroi hiding in a hollow tree, *Cypria* fr. 16 W.; Drem vab Dremidyt, 'Look son of Looker', who could see from Cornwall a gnat in Scotland, *Culhwch and Olwen* 261–3.

[58] Karl Meuli, *Odyssee und Argonautika* (Berlin 1921), 2–24 = *Gesammelte Schriften* (Basel 1975), ii. 594–610.

[59] Cf. H. M. and N. K. Chadwick, *The Growth of Literature* (Cambridge 1932–40), ii. 524; de Vries (1956), i. 179; McCone (1990), 181 f.; Sergent (1995), 219; West (1997), 439 f. For infants fed by wolves in particular cf. Sikojev (1985), 302; Dillon (1946), 24; McCone (1990), 191 f., 215–18.

keen eyes marked him out as a warrior on the first day of his life; he was already standing up in a cuirass.[60] The fair or yellow hair is characteristic of heroes in Greek epic (ξανθὸς Μενέλαος etc.) and in Irish and Welsh saga: *Táin* (I) 2345, 3593, 3606, (L) 165 (*findbuide, forórda*), 3474 (*bude*); *Cath Maige Tuired* 47 Gray (*órbuide* 'gold-yellow'); *Pwyll Prince of Dyfed* 546 (*kyuelynet oed a'r eur* 'yellow as gold'), *Math son of Mathonwy* 302 Ford (*brasuelyn* 'thick yellow'), *Culhwch and Olwen* 470.

Like gods, and for the same reason (p. 149), the child hero grows up with miraculous speed. This is typically expressed by saying that he grew at a multiple of the normal rate. We find this motif in Irish, Welsh, Persian, Armenian, Ossetic, and Serbo-Croat narratives. 'A week after the woman's lying-in was completed, the boy had two weeks' growth; and he maintained that increase for seven years, until he had reached the growth of fourteen years' (*Cath Maige Tuired* 75–7). 'Before he was one year old he was walking firmly, and he was bigger than a boy three years old who was of great growth and size. And the second year the boy was nursed, and he was as big as a child six years old' (*Pwyll Prince of Dyfed* 548–51 (trs. G. and T. Jones), cf. *Math son of Mathonwy* 327–34). 'After but a single month had passed, it was as though [Sohrab] was a full year old . . . At three years old he began the exercises of the battlefield; by his fifth year he had acquired the courage of lion-like men, and when he reached his tenth year there was no man in the land who would stand in combat with him' (*Shāh-nāma*, Levy (1967), 67 f.). 'The twin boys grew in a day as much as other children grew in a year . . . At one year of age they were as big as other children who were five years old' (*Sassountsy David* 15 f., cf. 160, 239). The Nart Batradz, the son of Hæmyts, 'grew as much in a month as other children in three years' (Sikojev (1985), 159, cf. 290 f.; Colarusso (2002), 306 f.). 'When the child was a year old, he was like another of four, and when the child was two years old, he was like another of eight' (*SCHS* ii, no. 32. 464–7).

Boyhood feats

Before he is of an age to perform on the battlefield, the hero typically shows his qualities in feats with animals. The newborn Heracles strangled two snakes that Hera had sent to kill him (Pind. *Nem.* 1. 38–47). While Achilles was with Chiron, 'often his hands threw the short iron javelin, and fighting swift as the winds he dealt death to ravening lions, killed boars, and brought their gasping bodies to the Centaur—six years old to begin with, and ever

[60] *Helgakviða Hundingsbana A* 6, cf. (for the eyes) *B* 2, 4; Gering–Sijmons (1927–31), i. 360.

after that. Artemis and Athena marvelled at him, that he killed deer without hounds or nets, by outrunning them' (Pind. *Nem.* 3. 43–52, paraphrased). Bharata diverted himself similarly: 'when he was six years old he would fetter lions and tigers, boars, buffaloes, and elephants to the trees, run about playing, riding, taming them' (*MBh.* 1. 68. 4). David of Sassoon, having as an infant burst his swaddling clothes and then the chains put on him to replace them, outruns foxes, martens, and hares (*Sassountsy David* 160, 194, 196). In an Abaza narrative the Nart Bataraz (the Ossetic Batradz) goes out at the age of two, chases and captures a deer with his bare hands, and comes back with it under his arm (Colarusso (2002), 307). The Danish hero Skiold as a boy captured a large bear without weapons, and attained his full manhood by the age of fifteen (Saxo 1. 3. 1 p. 11). A substantial section of the *Táin* is devoted to Cú Chulainn's boyhood feats; at the age of seven he drove a herd of deer into a bog, and then ran from his chariot and caught one of them. The boy Finn outran and caught two stags, and the sons of Usnech likewise used to outrun the deer. Peredur, the hero of a Welsh Arthurian romance, sees as a boy two hinds with his mother's goats, and thinking they are stray goats he rounds them up by his fleetness of foot and brings them home.[61]

Graduation to fighting against men comes at an early age. Egill Skallagrímsson killed his first man at the age of seven (*Egils saga* 40). Cú Chulainn's seven-year-old foster-son kills nine warriors per hour. His son Connla comes in search of his father on the seventh anniversary of his conception, and he is already a formidable warrior. Móen slew kings even as a boy—'it was the custom of high kings'.[62] In other traditions twelve is deemed an appropriate age for a hero to take up arms. Sigurd the Hart at this age slew twelve men in battle. Olaf Tryggvason launched his warship. Another Norse poem tells of a Hun army of twelve-year-olds and upwards. A Serbo-Croat heroic song too describes a twelve-year-old warrior of formidable prowess.[63]

Bigger animal challenges

If the boy hero measures himself against ordinary animals, the adult must distinguish himself by taking on an exceptional one. Heracles' tasks include

[61] *Táin* (I) 767–78; Koch–Carey (2000), 197; *Longes Mac nUsnig*, quoted by Dillon (1948), 14; *Historia Peredur vab Efrawc* p. 7. 21–8 Goetinck. Such hunting feats may reflect initiation tests, cf. Sergent (1995), 283 f.

[62] *Cath Étair*, ed. W. Stokes, *RC* 8 (1887), 55; *Aided óenfir Aífe*, ed. A. G. van Hamel, *Compert Con Culainn and Other Stories* (Dublin 1933), 11–15; Campanile (1988), 25 no. 1. 1, cf. 39 f. (n.).

[63] *Heimskringla* 2. 5; Hallfred Vandræðaskáld, *Ólafsdrápa* 1; *Hunnenschlacht* 14. 5 (*Edd. min.* 6), cf. *Hervarar saga* 12; Gering–Sijmons (1927–31), ii. 76; *SCHS* ii, no. 17. 61 (at line 101 he kills twenty-two of the enemy).

the overcoming of several beasts of familiar species but unique notoriety: the Nemean Lion, the Cerynian Hind, the Erymanthian Boar, the Cretan Bull, the mares of Diomedes. Theseus captures the Marathonian Bull. The expedition against the Calydonian Boar, in which Meleager proved himself, was one of the major Greek heroic legends. Odysseus as a youth killed a great boar on Parnassus (*Od.* 19. 428–58). Boar hunts are also a theme in Welsh and Irish saga. Arthur fought the boar Twrch Trwyth for nine nights and nine days (*Culhwch and Olwen* 1072). Diarmuid is drawn into the hunt for the Wild Boar of Benn Gulbán and is killed by it. A Fenian poem describes another great boar hunt, with a catalogue of the men who took part in it.[64]

The hero has a still greater opportunity to win fame where there is a dragon or monster to be dealt with. Now, of course, dragons are a protected species and it is illegal to harm them, but in the mythical era it was a pest that had to be eradicated. Heracles destroys the many-headed Hydra of Lerna. Perseus kills a monster to save a princess, a motif also to be found in Armenian and Lithuanian tales.[65] The theme of the dragon that guards treasure and is killed in order to obtain it is particularly characteristic of Germanic tradition.[66]

The archetypal Indo-European dragon-slaying myth is presumably the one discussed in Chapter 6, where the victor is the thunder-god and his victim the monstrous serpent that blocks the waters. We saw reason to think that Heracles took over features from the thunder-god and that his battle with the Hydra was an echo of the cosmic conflict. In this case we can see the divine myth transposed to the heroic plane. I do not suggest that all dragon-slaying heroes are faded thunder-gods, only that—seeing that dragons or colossal serpents are not a feature of the real world—the concept of slaying one as a heroic feat may have originated with the cosmic myth.

The hero in dialogue

At this point we may note a couple of typical formulae that may appear when someone encounters a person unknown to him or her. Even—indeed, espe-

[64] *Tóruigheacht Dhiarmuda agus Ghráinne*, summarized in Dillon (1948), 43–8; *Duanaire Finn* 17 (ed. E. MacNeill (Irish Texts Society 7, London 1908), 39–41 (text), 141–4 (trs.)).

[65] *Sassountsy David* 94–6 (brothers kill a dragon that guards a spring and exacts maidens as tribute); Schleicher (1857), 57 f.

[66] *Beowulf* 886 f., 2211 ff., 3051–7; *Skáldsk.* 40 (Sigurd and Fáfnir); Saxo 2. 1. 1–3 pp. 36 f., 6. 4. 10 p. 150; Grimm (1883–8), 689–91, 977–80, 1493 f., 1599 f.; de Vries (1956), i. 493 f.; Schramm (1957), 111. But a treasure-guarding snake can already be found in an ancient fable, Phaedrus 4. 21.

cially—when it is an opponent in battle, he is asked his identity and lineage.[67] Achilles demands of Asteropaios, τίς πόθεν εἰς ἀνδρῶν, ὅ μοι ἔτλης ἀντίος ἐλθεῖν; 'Who, from where among men are you, that have ventured to come against me?' (*Il.* 21. 150). In the *Odyssey* a variant of this verse occurs repeatedly: 'Who, from where among men are you? Where do you have your community and parents?' Similar double questions appear in the Indian epics: *ko 'si, kasyāsi?* 'Who are you, of whom are you?' (*MBh.* 1. 122. 19 v.l., cf. 139. 19, 142. 3, 160. 34; 13 App. 3. 203 post.; 'Who are you, who do you belong to, where do you come from?' (*Rm.* 3. 44. 30; 5. 40. 6, 47. 53). So in the *Gāthās* (Y. 43. 7), *ciš ahī, kahyā ahī?* '(when someone asks me) "Who are you, of whom are you?" '; in the *Hildebrandslied* (9–11), *her fragen gistuont fohem uuortum, wer sin fater wari . . . 'eddo welihhes cnuosles du sis'*, 'he began to ask in few words, who his father was . . . "or of what race you are" '; in Saxo (1. 4. 3 p. 14), *quod tibi nomen, | qua fueris, dic, | gente creata. :: . . . Tu quoque, quis sis | aut satus unde, | promito nobis*; and in Serbo-Croat heroic songs, 'O Border warrior, whence come you? From what country of the world are you? From what part of the world, and by what name do they call you?' (*SCHS* ii, no. 17. 516–19, cf. no. 18. 190–2, 259–61).

A man meeting a beautiful woman or girl in Greek or Indian epic is liable to ask wonderingly whether she is a goddess or some other class of supernatural being. 'Hail, Lady,' says Anchises, 'whichever of the blessed ones you are that arrive at this dwelling, Artemis or Leto or golden Aphrodite . . . or perhaps you are one of the Graces come here . . . or one of the nymphs, who haunt the fair groves and the waters of rivers and the grassy meads' (*Hymn. Aphr.* 92–9, cf. *Od.* 6. 149–52). Likewise Śamtanu: 'Art thou a Goddess, or a maiden of the Dānavas or Gandharvas, or perchance an Apsarā? Or art thou a Yakṣī, or a Snake sprite, or a mortal woman, slim-waisted lady?'[68]

On two occasions in the *Odyssey*, when Odysseus makes a request or asks a question that betrays him as a newcomer in the place, he receives the reply νήπιός εἰς, ὦ ξεῖν', ἢ τηλόθεν εἰλήλουθας, 'you are a simpleton, sir, or else you have come from a long way away'. There is a curiously exact parallel in the *Mabinogion*. Peredur comes to a broad valley in which a great, colourful concourse of people is encamped. He asks a miller for the reason, and is told,

[67] Cf. Schmitt (1967), 135–8; E. D. Floyd, *Word* 43 (1992), 399–409; id., *JIES* 20 (1992), 305–15.

[68] *MBh.* 1. 92. 30; cf. 1. 142. 3; 3. 61. 69, 114, 249. 2–4; *Rm.* 3. 44. 15 f.; 5. 31. 2 ff.; V. Pisani, *ZDMG* 103 (1953), 131 f. = Schmitt (1968), 161 f. In the *Odyssey* passage, after likening Nausicaa to Artemis, Odysseus goes on to say 'Thrice blessed are your father and mother, thrice blessed your brothers'. So the Nart hero Uryzmæg, meeting a boy who darts about more nimbly than the eye can follow and who is a joy to behold, thinks to himself 'Happy the man whose son you are!' (Sikojev (1985), 41).

'It is one of two things: either thou art a man from afar or thou art a fool.'[69] We can hardly infer on this slender basis that wayfarers' enquiries in Eurostan were liable to provoke the same bluff response, but the coincidence is worthy of remark.

THE HERO AND WOMEN

Although quite able to appreciate female beauty when he encounters it, the Indo-European warrior hero is not generally much interested in sex or involved with women.[70] He is mostly represented as unmarried; his *raison d'être* is competition with other males, and while women's intrigues may sometimes condition the events in which he plays a part, it can only detract from the atomic ferocity of his heroic persona if he is represented with a wife sharing his daily life. Richard Strauss could cast himself as the central figure both of a *Sinfonia Domestica* and of *Ein Heldenleben*, but it is not a convincing conjunction.

Many readers will think of Hector and his anxious, loving wife. But the Homeric epic has evolved to an exceptional level of sophistication and tasteful artistry; the characters are fleshed out with all kinds of realistic human detail to a degree unparalleled in other ancient traditions, and a figure such as Hector the family man is the product of this process. As ultimate hero he is outclassed by Achilles.

Yet a woman can have a functional (as opposed to a merely decorative or palliative) role in a hero's life, namely when she provides the motive for him to demonstrate his prowess. There are essentially two situations in which this is the case: when he seeks to win her as a bride, or when he seeks to win her back after an enforced separation.

Winning a bride

The Indo-Europeans probably recognized several forms of marriage, for example by priestly ceremonial, by capture, by cohabitation, or by negoti-

[69] *Od.* 9. 273 = 13. 237; *Historia Peredur vab Efrawc* p. 53. 4 Goetinck, 'mae y neill peth; ae tydi yn wr o bell, ae titheu yn ynuyt'.

[70] Noted by Miller (2000), 109 f., who speaks of 'the old notion that abstention from sex provides the ingathering of powers necessary to the successful fighter, which is widely current in the belief systems or traditions of many warrior societies'.

ation.[71] But these are not all of equal interest for the purposes of heroic narrative. It prefers an element of contest, of difficulties to be overcome. The premise is a woman so desirable that her hand is sought by many men of distinction.

In one type of myth winning her constitutes a challenge, not just because of the competition but because unsuccessful suitors must forfeit their lives. As with the life-or-death poetic contests mentioned at the end of Chapter 1, it may be doubted whether this was ever a real-life practice. But it makes for good stories.

Men who wanted to marry Hippodameia had to compete in a chariot-race against her father Oinomaos, and if defeated they were killed. Atalanta's suitors had to race on foot against her and lost their lives if she beat them; according to one version she chased them with a spear. The Scottish queen Herminthrud, until won by Amleth, had despised all her suitors and made every one of them pay with his head (Saxo 4. 1. 12 p. 88). The Nart heroine Gunda would wrestle with hers and humiliate those she defeated by cutting off their ears or branding them with a hot iron.[72]

In classical Indian literature a king's daughter is generally represented as selecting her own husband by the procedure called *svayaṃvara*, 'self-choice'.[73] When she reaches marriageable age her father makes a proclamation, and swarms of suitors—kings and princes from various regions—gather and enjoy his hospitality for a period of days. The damsel is displayed before them. More often than not they are required to undergo a contest or test of skill, and she will choose the winner as her husband, his 'manly deed' (*vīryam*) being regarded as the bride-price.

In several examples the contest involves stringing a powerful bow and performing a difficult feat of archery (*MBh.* 1. 175–9; *Rm.* 1. 65 f.; 2. 110. 37–52). There is a striking analogy here with the contest which Penelope sets for her suitors in the *Odyssey* and which the disguised Odysseus wins, whereupon he kills his rivals and recovers his rightful wife. The affair is in effect a *svayaṃvara*. It has been implied at various points in the poem that if Odysseus is written off, Penelope is free to choose her own husband (2. 87–105, 4. 770 f., 18. 285–9, 19. 524–9, 20. 341 f.). The test she prescribes is

[71] Cf. Feist (1913), 305–10; de Vries (1956), i. 185–7; Campanile (1990b), 114–20; id. in Ramat (1998), 12 f.; Gamkrelidze–Ivanov (1995), 658–61, 664 f.; Sergent (1995), 224–31; *EIEC* 369 f.

[72] Colarusso (2002), 364 (Abkhaz).

[73] On this see H.-P. Schmidt, *Some Women's Rites and Rights in the Veda* (Poona 1987), 76–109; S. W. Jamison, *Classical Antiquity* 18 (1999), 244–9; ead. in K. Karttunen–P. Koskikallio (edd.), *Vidyārṇavavandanam. Essays in Honour of Asko Parpola* (Helsinki 2001), 303–15. There is an allusion to the practice in RV 10. 17. 1.

quite similar to those employed in the Indian epics.[74] For reasons given below, however, I hesitate to conclude that the archery event is an Indo-European theme.

On several occasions in Greek myth a multitude of suitors come together in response to a proclamation and are assessed by the girl's father, who retains the right of decision. Danaos found husbands for forty-eight daughters in a morning by lining the girls up at the end of a racetrack, making the suitors race to them, and letting each man as he finished take his pick of those remaining. Antaios too made his daughter's suitors race for her, as did Ikarios when Penelope was to be married.[75]

The most celebrated of such gatherings was that of the suitors of Helen. According to the Hesiodic *Catalogue* her brothers the Dioskouroi organized the event. The chieftains came from all over Greece and the islands, each offering as high a bride-price as he could afford, and the Dioskouroi decided that she was to be given to Menelaus. Other authors, however, attest a version in which her father Tyndareos allowed her to choose whom she wanted, making it a real *svayaṃvara*.[76]

One of these writers, the mythographer Hyginus, includes in his cursory reference a detail of great interest: Tyndareos, he says, *arbitrio Helenae posuit ut cui uellet nubere coronam imponeret*. Helen was to signify her choice by placing a garland on the lucky man. This corresponds exactly to the Indian procedure as described in the epics. Once Damayantī had identified Nala, the man she wanted, among a group of divine lookalikes, she 'chose him according to the Law. Bashfully she touched the hem of his garment and hung on his shoulders a most beautiful garland; and thus the fair woman chose him for her husband'.[77]

A similar event is described in the *Shāh-nāma*. Caesar in 'Rum' decides that it is time for his daughter Katāyun to marry, and he assembles a large company of mature, distinguished men. She looks them all over and finds none of them to her liking. A further proclamation is made and another gathering of nobles and princes is convened. This time Goshtāsp is present. On seeing

[74] Gabriel Germain, *Genèse de l'Odyssée* (Paris 1954), 15–54; West (1997), 431–3; S. W. Jamison (as n. 73, 1999), 243–58. Vase paintings indicate that there was a myth of an archery contest for Iole, the daughter of Eurytos; see Gantz (1993), 435 f.

[75] Pind. *Pyth.* 9. 106–25; Paus. 3. 12. 1 f. If we believe Herodotus (6. 126–30), Cleisthenes of Sicyon invited quality suitors for his daughter Agariste from all over Greece and spent a year investigating their merits.

[76] Eur. *Iph. Aul.* 68–70, Arist. *Rhet.* 1401^{b}36 (Polycrates fr. 17 Sauppe), Hyg. *Fab.* 78.

[77] *MBh.* 3. 54. 26 (with one modification to van Buitenen's translation in the light of S. Insler, *JAOS* 109 (1989), 577); cf. 1. 179. 22 (with 1850*, 1852* from Southern manuscripts); Kālidāsa, *Raghuvaṃsā* 6. 86 f.; J. Przyluski, *JAs.* 205 (1924), 111–21.

him she says 'The dream I dreamed has now put up its head out of the void', and she goes and adorns his head with her coronet.[78]

We can find further parallels in northern Europe. I referred in Chapter 5 to the German May Day or Easter custom of auctioning pretty girls, each of whom became the 'May-wife' of the young man who offered most for her. It is now pertinent to add that in some places she signified her approval of him by attaching a bunch of flowers to his hat.[79] In one of the Latvian songs too a young girl expresses her desire to bedeck the hat of a suitor, and here it is perhaps a real marriage that is contemplated:

> Saule [the Sun] se couche le soir,
> parant les cimes de la forêt.
> Donne-moi, Dieu, pendant que je suis jeune,
> de parer le chapeau d'un prétendant. (*LD* 10482 = Jonval no. 985)

An alternative way for the girl in a *svayaṃvara* to make her choice appears in two barbarian settings described by Greek authors. Chares of Mytilene, a historian of Alexander, told the following romantic story (*FGrHist* 125 F 5). The Scythian king Homartes wanted to marry off his daughter Odatis, the most beautiful woman in Asia, and he invited his friends, kinsmen, and princes from his realm. After they had drunk deep, Odatis was called in and told that it was her wedding and that she should take a good look at all the candidates, fill a golden goblet, and give it to whichever one she most fancied. She cried and prolonged the process of mixing the wine, because she could not see Zariadres, the king from beyond the Tanais whom she had beheld in her dreams and fallen in love with but never met. But he turned up at the last minute, dressed as a Scythian. She gave him the cup, and he carried her off on his chariot, which was waiting near by. Chares said that the story was famous in Asia and depicted in shrines, palaces, and private houses.

After transcribing this from Chares, Athenaeus is reminded of a similar episode related by Aristotle (fr. 549). A local (presumably Celtic) king at Massalia was celebrating his daughter's wedding, 'and the wedding was done in this manner: after the dinner the girl had to come in with a cup of mixed wine and give it to whoever she wished of the suitors present, and the man she gave it to became the bridegroom'.

The giving of a drink, rather than the bestowal of a garland or bunch of flowers, recalls the Celtic custom noted earlier, by which a bride would proffer a drink to her groom. We saw that Irish kings might receive one from the personified Sovereignty whom they symbolically married. But it is the floral

[78] Levy (1967), 186 f. [79] Mannhardt (1905), i. 450–2.

variant that has the wider distribution—India, Greece, Latvia, Germany—and the stronger claim to represent a common Indo-European tradition.

If there was such a tradition, what was its status? Was the *svayaṃvara* anything more than a literary motif? Kim McCone has written that it 'hardly looks like a real institution'. 'In firmly patrilinear societies like those of ancient Ireland, Greece or India, not to mention the ancestral Indo-Europeans themselves, it would be strange indeed if the all-important kingship were left literally in the gift of a mere woman.'[80] He suspects that it all goes back to an archetypal sovereignty myth in which the woman who chose her consort was Sovereignty herself.

The German evidence may suggest an alternative explanation: that the myths reflect, not a historical method of aristocratic match-making for life, but a popular seasonal custom in which a girl chose a beau for the summer. We found reason in Chapter 5 to think that certain features of the mythology surrounding the Daughter of the Sun, including her wedding, were a projection of earthly festivities. We saw too that the competing suitors of Helen, her wedding, and her abduction, fitted into that model. Helen is the one bride in Greek myth who is said to have chosen her husband by putting a garland on him.

The myths of suitors running races for the hand of the Danaids or Penelope likewise make excellent sense in terms of ritual sports. We recall that at some places in Germany young men raced on foot to the Maypole, the winner becoming May King and partner to the May Queen.

The sword in the bed

It is a widespread motif that a couple sleep together for one or several nights with a sword laid between them as a guarantor of chastity. The purpose is the avoidance of adultery or incest, or the deliberate postponement of sexual relations till a prescribed period has elapsed or a task has been achieved, or to satisfy others that no coition has occurred.[81]

The best-known example is the Norse legend of how Sigurd slept chastely with Brynhild, laying his sword between them.[82] According to the *Vǫlsunga saga* they slept in this way for three nights. The same period is specified in the

[80] McCone (1990), 111.

[81] Cf. Jacob Grimm, *Deutsche Rechtsaltertümer* (4th edn., Berlin 1875–8), i. 232–5; B. Heller, *Romania* 36 (1907), 36–49; 37 (1908), 162 f.; J. Bolte–G. Polívka, *Anmerkungen zu den Kinder- und Hausmärchen der Brüder Grimm* (Leipzig 1913–18), i. 554 f.

[82] *Brot af Sigurðarkviðu* 19; *Sigurðarkviða in skamma* 68. Cf. Detter–Heinzel (1903), ii. 445; Gering–Sijmons (1927–31), ii. 231 f.

Danish story of King Gorm the Old, who married the English princess Thyra, the daughter of Ethelred. She insisted on three days' sexual abstinence before the marriage was consummated. The gallant Gorm respected her wishes and divided the marital bed into two compartments by placing a naked sword down the middle.[83]

In one of the Ossetic Nart sagas Axsartag's beautiful bride Dserassa mistakes his twin brother Axsar for her husband. Axsar does not disabuse her, but he does not abuse her either. He goes to bed with her at bedtime, but to avoid intimate contact he draws his sword from its scabbard and lays it between them (Sikojev (1985), 19). In the Armenian oral epic it is the woman who takes this step, in order to set her husband a challenge. Mher and Kohar celebrate their wedding with a seven-day feast. 'Mher went to Kohar's bed at night; she laid a sword between Mher and herself.—The King of the West is collecting a tax from us, she said; if you can put an end to that, I will be your wife, you will be my husband' (*Sassountsy David* 360).

Is the sword in the bed a traditional Indo-European motif? Not as such, because the article in question, a sword with a long sharp blade, did not exist until the technique of bronze-working developed to the point where it was possible to make such a weapon, that is to say, not until the second millennium BCE. The Indo-Europeans of the fourth or third millennium had daggers but not swords. A dagger would be less suited to the purpose.

However, the idea of the barrier separating a man and woman in bed may have existed before the invention of the sword. We find it at the extremities of the Indo-European world, in the Western Isles and India, with different objects forming the barrier. Diarmaid and Gráinne in an oral Gaelic account sleep separated by a cold stone. In India three days of sexual abstinence were required of newly-weds, and for those nights a perfumed staff, wound with cloth or threads, was laid between them.[84] Here, no doubt, we see the origin of the mythical motif, in a custom of real life.

Winning her back; the Husband's Return

If a wife is taken from her husband, a further field for heroic action is opened up. Helen's abduction is the basis for the central mythical cycle of Greek tradition, that revolving about the Trojan War. An abducted wife is a major theme in each of the two great Indian epics. The robbed husband (or

[83] Saxo 9. 11. 3 p. 267; cf. Davidson (1979–80), ii. 164.

[84] J. G. Campbell, *The Fians* (London 1891), 56; Āpastamba, *Gṛhyasūtra* 3. 8. 9; Oldenberg (1917), 88 n. 2, 253; Sergent (1995), 230.

husbands, in the case of the polyandrous Draupadī in the *Mahābhārata*) must go in pursuit and recover her by force of arms.

Stephanie Jamison has shown how this scenario may be understood in terms of the Indian warrior code.[85] Marriage by capture was a legitimate procedure if carried out in the proper way. Even if the woman was already married, you could take her for yourself provided that you announced your identity and intentions and fought and defeated her husband. But if she was taken without such a deed of valour, the abductor had no title to her. He had to be made to fight, and only if he then vanquished the first husband could he establish his position as the woman's rightful lord. Poetic justice, however, required his defeat.

The abduction of Helen can be seen in the same terms. Jamison draws attention to the striking parallelism between the episode in the *Iliad* (3. 161–244) where Helen, standing on the wall of Troy, identifies certain Greek heroes to Priam, and a scene in the *Mahābhārata* (3. 254) where Draupadī identifies to her abductor Jayadratha each in turn of her five husbands, the Pāṇḍavas, who can be seen coming in pursuit. This, Jamison argues, supplies what is required to legitimate the Pāṇḍavas' marital challenge, the formal announcement of their names and lineage. The corresponding passage in the *Iliad* reflects the same situation, even though the heroes that Helen identifies, Agamemnon, Odysseus, Ajax, and Idomeneus, do not include her husband Menelaus. The ensuing duel between Paris and Menelaus (3. 313–82), although aborted by the poet (otherwise the story would have come to a premature end), represents an essential element of the same complex. These sections of the Greek and Indic epics, Jamison submits in conclusion, both 'belong to an inherited Indo-European narrative pattern that has its roots in a particular societal institution—the fine line between legal and illegal abduction in the typology of Indo-European marriage'.

The thesis is appealing, though for 'Indo-European' it would be safer to say Graeco-Aryan. And a further reservation is in order. We shall see in the next chapter that the *Iliad* and *Mahābhārata* episodes can be placed in a larger category of heroic narrative scenes where a series of warriors are pointed out in turn or identified by their descriptions. There is no necessary connection with the reclaiming of a woman.

In another type of story the hero has been away for a prolonged period on some journey or adventure. Eventually it is assumed that he is not going to come back, and the woman, from choice or duress, is about to be married to someone else. Typically the hero receives word of what is going on and returns just in time, in disguise, because it is no straightforward matter to

[85] *Classical Antiquity* 13 (1994), 5–16.

re-establish his position in the changed situation. Sometimes he is conveyed home with extraordinary swiftness by a supernatural agency. He overcomes his rivals by a feat of valour and wins his wife back.

This story pattern, most familiar as the basis of the *Odyssey*, is widely attested in Europe and elsewhere, and well known to folklorists as the Husband's Return.[86] It appears in various medieval Germanic tales, in Serbo-Croat oral epic, and in at least one Russian *bylina* from the Kiev cycle.[87] However, there is no compelling case for claiming it as Indo-European. It is a prime example of the wandering folk-tale, diffused without regard to linguistic boundaries. The influence of the *Odyssey* is probable in at least some of the medieval versions. And the *Odyssey* story, like several of Odysseus' subsidiary adventures in that epic, is very likely not a piece of ancestral Greek tradition but a relatively recent import from abroad, perhaps picked up by Milesian explorers in the Black Sea region. It shows remarkable similarities to a story widely current in the epic poetry and popular narrative of the Turkic peoples of central Asia, the tale of Alpamysh.[88] The subject matter of the Alpamysh story can be traced back for many hundreds of years. There is no likelihood that it somehow derives from the *Odyssey*. So far as we can tell, it is indigenous to the Eurasian steppes. At the period relevant to the genesis of the *Odyssey* this region would have been occupied by Iranian peoples; the Turkic hordes came much later. But that does not mean that the story was of Indo-European antiquity or origin.

When Alpamysh returns home after escaping from seven years' captivity, preparations are afoot for his wife to marry his wicked half-brother. He goes to the wedding feast disguised as a beggar. There is an archery contest, in which the first challenge is to draw Alpamysh's old bow. Only he is able to do it. We noted earlier that this motif appears both in the *Odyssey* and in the two Indian epics in the context of a contest for a bride. But if in the *Odyssey* it is an integral part of a narrative deriving from the steppes and having no particular claim to be Indo-European heritage, the Indian epic may have it

[86] Cf. Kaspar Schnorf, *Der mythische Hintergrund im Gudrunlied und in der Odyssee* (Diss. Zurich 1879); Willi Splettstösser, *Der heimkehrende Gatte und sein Weib in der Weltliteratur* (Berlin 1899); Ludwig Radermacher, *Die Erzählungen der Odyssee* (Vienna 1915), 47–58; J. Tolstoi, *Philologus* 89 (1934), 261–74; O. Holzapfel in Kurt Ranke et al. (edd.), *Enzyklopädie des Märchens*, vi (Berlin 1990), 702–7; William Hansen, *Ariadne's Thread* (Ithaca–London 2002), 201–11 with further bibliography.

[87] A. B. Lord, *The Singer of Tales* (Cambridge, Mass. 1960), 121, 242–59; Chadwick (1932), 81–90, 'The Return of Dobryna'.

[88] On this cf. V. Zhirmunsky, *PBA* 52 (1966), 267–86; H. B. Paksoy, *Alpamysh. Central Asian Identity under Russian Rule* (Hartford, Conn. 1989), 119–57; Karl Reichl, *Turkic Oral Epic Poetry: Traditions, Forms, Poetic Structure* (New York–London 1992); id., *Das usbekische Heldenepos Alpomish* (Wiesbaden 2001).

from a similar source. This is in accord with the importance of the bow, the composite bow that requires great strength for its stringing, for this is at home above all among the steppe nomads, whether Iranian or Turko-Mongol.[89]

THE HERO AND HIS SON

As the essence of the hero is his prowess that others cannot match, there is not much scope for a son. It is no credit or joy to a man to have a son inferior to himself; but on the other hand a son who can equal him will detract from his aura of uniqueness.

Where a son does have a role, it is generally as a substitute for the hero, a replacement, or an avenger. Odysseus' son Telemachus stands up for his absent father's interests, doing his best to keep Penelope's suitors in check, though not yet capable of overcoming them. Neoptolemus comes to Troy after Achilles' death and in a sense fills the gap he has left, winning distinction but not the same level of supremacy and fame as his father. Orestes avenges the murder of his father Agamemnon, and that is the sum of his heroic achievement. In general, father and son do not operate together. Telemachus assists Odysseus in the fight against the suitors, but this is not his *raison d'être*, and it is not a customary feature of the Husband's Return.

The Sohrab and Rustum motif

Usually, then, the activity of a hero's son is separated in space or time from that of the hero himself. Sometimes he is brought up in another place and does not meet his father until he is already of fighting age. In many legends they meet in circumstances that lead them to fight each other, with the tragic result that the father kills his son, or the son his father. In some cases neither is aware of the other's identity; in others, only one of the pair knows who the other is.[90]

[89] Cf. G. Germain (as n. 74), 48 f.

[90] On the theme of the father–son combat cf. B. Busse, 'Sagengeschichtliches zum Hildebrandsliede', *Beiträge zur Geschichte der deutschen Sprache und Literatur* 26 (1901), 1–92; M. A. Potter, *Sohrab and Rustem: The Epic Theme of a Combat between Father and Son* (London 1902); Georg Baesecke, *NGG* 1940, Phil.-hist. Kl. (NF 3), 139–53; id., *Das Hildebrandlied* (Halle 1945), 51–5; J. de Vries, *GRM* 34 (1953), 257–74 = K. Hauck (ed.), *Zur germanisch-deutschen Heldensage* (Bad Homburg 1961), 248–84; id. in *Ogam* 50 (1957), 122–38; C. M. Bowra, *Heroic Poetry* (London 1952), 399; Olga M. Davidson, *Poet and Hero in the Persian Book of Kings* (Ithaca 1994), 128–41; D. A. Miller, *JIES* 22 (1994), 307–27; id. in E. C. Polomé (ed.), *Indo-European Religion after Dumézil* (*JIESM* 16, Washington, DC 1996), 109–30; id. (2000), 345–54.

The theme is most familiar to many English readers from Matthew Arnold's famous narrative poem *Sohrab and Rustum*, which is based on an episode from the *Shāh-nāma*.[91] In Firdawsi's epic Rustum, or Rostam, leaves a princess pregnant with a heroic son, Sohrab. When the lad is old enough he goes in search of his father. After many adventures he comes into his presence, but Rostam, not knowing that it is his son, denies that he is Rostam. They fight, and only after Rostam has dealt his son a mortal blow do they discover each other's identities.

Oedipus meets and kills his father in a chance encounter, neither knowing who the other is. But these are not warrior heroes, and the manslaughter is not the nub of the Oedipus myth. A better Greek example is the story of Telegonus, related in the lost Cyclic epic *Telegony*. He was born to Circe after Odysseus' year-long sojourn with her. She told him about his father, and when he was of an age he sailed to Ithaca to look for Odysseus. Taking the stranger for a raider, Odysseus fought him and was killed by Telegonus' unusual spear, which was made from the barb of a sting-ray. This was taken to fulfil a prophecy that death would come to Odysseus from the sea.

The motif appears also in the *Mahābhārata* (14. 78–80). Arjuna meets his death from a poisoned arrow shot by his son Babhruvāhana, whom he had fathered in a distant place and who had been brought up there.

The *Hildebrandslied* tells how Hiltibrant and his son Hadubrant met on the battlefield. Hiltibrant demands to know his opponent's name and lineage. Hadubrant names himself and says that he has been told his father was Hiltibrant, who departed to the east long ago. Hiltibrant intimates that they are close kin and offers his son gold rings off his arm as a token of honour. But Hadubrant, believing his father to be dead, thinks it is a trick. Hiltibrant realizes that they are doomed to fight and one to kill the other. The combat begins. Here the fragment of the old poem ends, but from later sources we gather that it was the son who was killed.

In the Irish and Russian traditions too it is the father who kills the son. Cú Chulainn has left Aife pregnant with a boy, Connla, and after seven years he comes in search of his father, showing aggression to all comers. Cú Chulainn comes against him to defend Ulster, dismissing a warning that it is his own son. The boy refuses to name himself, they fight, and Connla is killed. In the *bylina* of Ilya Murometz and Sokolniček the mighty hero Ilya at first fights against his son in ignorance, but then, on discovering his identity, spares his life. Subsequently, at his mother's instigation, the son returns to kill his father, but is killed himself.[92]

[91] *Shāh-nāma* 5. 14–20; Levy (1967), 67–80.

[92] *Aided óenfir Aífe*, ed. van Hamel (as n. 62), trs. Thomas Kinsella, *The Táin* (Oxford 1969), 39–45; P. N. Rybnikov, *Pesni* (2nd edn. by A. Ye. Gruzinski, Moscow 1909), i. 425–31, ii. 637 f.

Modifications of the basic theme appear in Armenian and Ossetic tradition. In the Armenian epic David unknowingly fights his son, the younger Mher, but there is a peaceful resolution (*Sassountsy David* 330–3). The Nart Uryzmæg is one day transported to a marvellous realm under the sea, where he is welcomed by people he realizes are his relatives, the family of Donbettir. Among them is a delightful boy, whom he quite accidentally, and through no fault of his own, kills. It turns out that this is his own son; his wife had given birth to him in Uryzmæg's absence and sent him to her parents' house for fosterage.[93]

Once again the question is whether these stories represent an inherited Indo-European theme or just a wandering folk-tale. Their distribution—India, Iran, Ossetia, Armenia, Greece, Germany, Ireland, Russia—matches the Indo-European map much more neatly than do the versions of the Husband's Return. On the other hand it is just the kind of dramatic motif that might readily be taken over from one people to another and attached to different national heroes. This is, I think, the prudent diagnosis.[94]

The hero's child as object of pathos

When a hero kills his own son, unwittingly or in the recognition that there is no other option, his own supremacy is confirmed, but that is not the point: the point is that it is a tragic outcome, above all for him. There are other types of story that draw their emotional power from the pathos inherent in the death of children—not lusty lads engaged in combat but helpless innocents.

Again it is the father who suffers most. This is especially the case where he is the killer, as in the myth of Heracles slaughtering his children in a fit of insanity, or the various stories of the man forced to sacrifice his own child.[95]

But a hero's children may also be killed by an enemy. Here we must take note of a distinctive and gruesome story-line that may be called the Thyestes motif. Classicists will recall that Atreus, whose wife had been seduced by his brother Thyestes, killed the latter's children and served them up to him in a casserole. When he realized what he was eating, he was horrified and overturned the table. Herodotus (1. 119) relates a similar story about Astyages and

[93] Sikojev (1985), 40–3.

[94] Cf. G. Baesecke (as n. 90, 1945), who argues for derivation of the Russian, German, and Irish versions from the Iranian.

[95] We may think of Agamemnon's sacrifice of Iphigeneia, or the Indian myth of Śunaḥśepa (A. B. Keith, *The Veda of the Black Yajus School entitled Taittirīya Saṅhitā*, i (Cambridge, Mass. 1914), cxl; Walter Ruben, *Die Philosophen der Upanishaden* (Bern 1947), 74 f.). For other Greek (and some Semitic) examples cf. West (1997), 441 f., 484 f.

Harpagus; whether this is genuinely Iranian material we do not know. The motif reappears in several other Greek myths, such as that of Procne and Tereus as it was treated in Sophocles' *Tereus*.

There are parallels in Nordic and Ossetic tradition. Sigurd's widow Gudrun was married to the Hunnish king Atli (Attila). After he treacherously killed her brothers, she slew the children she had had by Atli, mixed their blood into his beer, and fed him their roasted hearts, pretending it was veal. When she told him the truth, the hall was filled with moaning (*Atlakviða* 33–8, *Atlamál* 82–5; *Skáldsk.* 42).

Eddic scholars have naturally suspected the influence of Classical myth. But this can hardly be supposed in the case of the Caucasian legend. The surly and mean-minded Syrdon, having a grudge against Hæmyts, the hero of the iron moustache, steals his wondrous cow, takes it to his secret second home, slaughters it, and puts the meat in a cauldron to stew. The furious Hæmyts finds his way to the dwelling. Failing to catch Syrdon there, he kills his wife and twelve sons and throws their bodies into the stewpot. Syrdon returns, wonders where his family has gone, and sticks a large fork into the stew, only to discover what has happened.[96]

Another Greek story about a hero's child, while arousing pity and terror, has a happier outcome. Bellerophon's sons Hippolochus and Isander were in dispute over the kingship of Lycia and had to prove themselves in a feat of archery. The son of each was to lie on his back with a ring set up on his chest, and the challenge was to shoot through the ring without harming the boy. Hippolochus' wife refused to let her son take part in the dangerous enterprise, but his sister Laodamea supplied hers, Sarpedon, and because of this he, and not Hippolochus' son Glaucus, became the king. Everyone will be reminded of the Swiss legend of William Tell, who had to shoot an apple off his son's head. There are several earlier occurrences of the motif in Norse sagas and other Germanic sources.[97]

HOW TO KILL A HERO

A hero's legend is not complete without an account of his death. But he is, by definition, a difficult man to kill; and a quiet death in retirement is not the stuff of story. His demise, therefore, calls for special measures.

[96] Sikojev (1985), 258–61; a variant, ibid. 275; cf. Colarusso (2002), 144, 145.

[97] Sch. (T) *Il.* 12. 101 (cf. Erbse ad loc.), Eust. 894. 36; Saxo 10. 7. 1–3 pp. 274 f.; Grimm (1883–8), 380–3, 1393.

In real life your best chance of disposing of a formidable fighting man would be to surprise him in circumstances when he was especially vulnerable and defenceless, for example in his bath. This must have been done for real on occasion, and there are corresponding cases in legend. Agamemnon is hacked to death in his bath by his wife and her lover. Con Roí's wife disables him in the bath by tying his hair to a post so that the Ulstermen can attack him; he fells a hundred of them with his fists and feet, but is then killed with his own sword. Saxo relates how the tyrannical king Olo was assassinated in his bath by Starkather.[98]

In fair fight the hero will hold his own against normal human opposition, even if he is heavily outnumbered. When he engages a more than human antagonist such as a dragon, he may meet an honourable death, provided that he also dispatches the monster. Beowulf succeeds in killing the fire-breathing dragon, but he is wounded in the fight and dies from the reptile's venom (*Beowulf* 2711–820). Thor at Ragnarøk will fight against the Miðgarð serpent and vanquish it, but after taking just nine steps away he will fall dead from the poison it has spat at him (*Vǫluspá* 56, *Gylf.* 51). Fergus mac Léite kills the monster of the loch but dies of the wounds he sustains.[99] In a story from the Circassian Nart corpus the hero Warzameg kills a snake but then passes out from its poisonous breath, though he is subsequently revived by an eagle (Colarusso (2002), 27). The Greek myth about the death of Heracles represents a development of the motif. He is killed by what his wife Deianeira intended as a love charm, mixed from the venom of the Hydra and the blood of the Centaur Nessos, both creatures that Heracles had slain in the past.

Invulnerability; the weak spot

Certain heroes are especially difficult to kill because they have what every warrior would like, an impenetrable skin, and are impervious to ordinary weapons. But mythical difficulties are made to be overcome, and all these hardies come to grief in one way or another. The Trojan Kyknos was invulnerable, according to some authors; he prevented the Achaeans from landing and fought on, unmarked by spear or sword, until at last Achilles managed to strangle him with his helmet-strap (Ov. *Met.* 12. 72–144).

[98] *Aided Con Roí* II 6 f., ed. R. I. Best, *Ériu* 2 (1905), 24/25; Saxo 8. 6. 3 p. 221. Con Roí's hair must have been long; for this as a heroic motif cf. *EIEC* 253.

[99] *Imthechta Tuaithe Luchra* ⁊ *aided Fergusa*, ed. S. H. O'Grady, *Silva Gadelica* (London 1892), i. 251 f./ii. 284 f.; Thurneysen (1921), 546. Further examples are cited by Axel Olrik, *Ragnarök* (Berlin–Leipzig 1922), 56 f.

A method that enjoyed greater international recognition was to bury the obstinate brave under a mass of earth or stones. The Lapith king Kaineus, granted invulnerability by Poseidon, fought against the Centaurs, who vanquished him by battering him into the ground and sealing him in with a large rock.[100] A reference to Ajax being pelted with mud (Sophron fr. 31) is probably to be understood in the same terms, as there are other traces of a tradition that he was invulnerable.[101] In Norse myth the brothers Sorli and Hamdir travel to the court of Jormunrekk (Ermanaric) to avenge the death of their sister Svanhild, whom the Gothic king has married and put to death. They wear impregnable armour and wreak some havoc, until Jormunrekk sees what to do and gives the order to overwhelm them with a shower of stones.[102] The Nart hero Sosruquo is dealt with similarly in an Abaza legend: 'when his enemies realized they could not kill him, they buried him under the ground and erected a great tumulus over him' (Colarusso (2002), 266).

In various traditions the otherwise unassailable hero has one weak spot where he is vulnerable, usually in his legs or feet, and this is his downfall. The giant Talos who charged round Crete three times a day to guard it from attack had a body of bronze but a weakness at the ankle, where a vein ran close to the surface covered only by a thin membrane. Achilles too, according to late authors and earlier vase-paintings, was vulnerable only in the ankle or foot. Ajax in one tradition could be pierced only under his arm.[103] In the Indian epic Durvāsas has made Krishna invulnerable except through the soles of his feet; he is shot with an arrow under the heel, and his apotheosis follows.[104] Esfandiyar in the *Shāh-nāma* has a body of brass, but Rostam, using a special arrow as directed by the Simorgh bird, shoots him fatally through the eye.[105] The Nart hero Soslan was born from an inseminated stone, from which he emerged as a red-hot baby. After being tempered in cold water, wolf's milk, or molten steel, he was vulnerable only in his knees or thighs, which had been left untouched by the liquid, and his overthrow came when they were severed by a flying wheel.[106] In German legend Siegfried had a soft spot on his back

[100] Acusilaus *FGrHist* 2 F 22 = fr. 22 Fowler, and earlier art; Gantz (1993), 280 f.

[101] See the next paragraph.

[102] *Hamðismál* 25–31, *Skáldsk.* 42. For the motif of invincible armour cf. p. 157, n. 126.

[103] Gantz (1993), 364 f. (Talos), 625–8 (Achilles); Aesch. fr. 83 (Ajax), cf. Pind. *Isth.* 6. 47, apparently after 'Hes.' fr. 250.

[104] *MBh.* 16. 5. 19 f.; compared with Achilles by Walter Ruben, *Krishna. Konkordanz und Kommentar der Motive seines Heldenlebens* (Istanbul 1943), 236 f., 244; Pisani (1969), 203.

[105] Levy (1967), 207–11.

[106] Georges Dumézil, *Loki* (2nd edn., Darmstadt 1959), 160–81; Sikojev (1985), 73, 136, cf. 171/221, 291; Colarusso (2002), 52 f., 185 f., 259–65, 333, 388. W. Burkert, *Würzburger Jahrbücher für die Altertumswissenschaft* 5 (1979), 253–61 = *Kleine Schriften*, ii (Göttingen 2003), 87–95, brings the Caucasian myth into connection with the Hurrian–Hittite myth of Ullikummi, the stone colossus who was toppled by sawing through his ankles (pp. 262 f.).

where he could be hit, and his enemy Hagen was apprised of the fact (*Nibelungenlied* 899, 905, 980–2). Conganchnes ('Hornskin') mac Dedad had a skin so hard that the weapons bounced off him. But his wife, who was in league with his enemies, wheedled out of him the fact that he could be killed by driving red-hot iron spits through the soles of his feet into his shins. He was put to sleep with spells and the treatment was applied.[107] In Gaelic oral versions of the story of Diarmaid and Gráinne the hero can only be killed through the sole of his foot. After the hunting of a huge boar his enemy Fionn induces him to measure the length of the creature by stepping it out over the bristles, with fatal consequence.[108]

CONCLUSION

In treating of the king we were able to start from linguistic evidence and the certainty that kingship was an Indo-European institution. On this basis it seemed legitimate to interpret as reflecting common inheritance parallel features in the kingships known to various mythical and historical traditions. With heroes the situation is different, as we are not dealing with a specific institution. There was no Indo-European word for 'hero', at any rate in the sense in which we have been using the term. The hero is a creation of narrative art. What we have been seeking to identify are the typical colours in which he tends to be painted in the narrative traditions of Indo-European peoples, in the diffident hope that here too there may be something of a common ancestral heritage. We have tried to tread carefully, conscious of the power of horizontal transmission especially in the realm of stories and story patterns.

So far we have considered the hero as an individual and in relation to other individuals. In the final chapter a wider canvas is unrolled: heroic activity on the battlefield.

[107] *Aided Cheltchair meic Uthechair* 8 f., ed. Kuno Meyer, *The Death-Tales of Ulster Heroes* (Todd Lecture Series 1906), 26 f. Fer Diad too is 'horn-skinned' in *Táin* (L) 2641, cf. 2749.

[108] J. G. Campbell (as n. 84), 54, 56, 58 f.

12

Arms and the Man

Armed conflict has been a prominent feature of human history for many thousands of years. Indo-European peoples have done their share. Their extraordinary record of expansion may suggest that they have done rather more than their share at some periods. In the last fifty years or so there has been a scholarly reaction against the old idea of militant hordes swarming out of Eurostan with battle-axes held high and occupying one territory after another. It has been fashionable to deride this model and to put all the emphasis on peaceful processes of population and language diffusion. But when we consider the processes by which Arabic or the Turkic languages spread across vast areas in historical times, or by which Latin, starting from a small region of Italy, came to be the dominant language of half a continent; or how Celtic tribes in the last centuries BCE, and Germanic tribes from the fifth century CE, grew multitudinous and poured across the length and breadth of Europe; then it appears by no means implausible that similar bouts of aggressive migration in earlier eras played a large part in effecting the Indo-European diaspora.

After all, we saw in Chapter 10 that fame won in battle was a major preoccupation of Indo-European poetic and narrative tradition. There are constant references to battles and descriptions of fighting. They are especially extensive in the Homeric poems and the Indian epics. We have nothing comparable from ancient Iran, where only sacred literature was preserved, but even in the Avesta there are reminiscences of martial episodes such as the battles of the Kavi Vīštāspa and others (Yt. 5. 109–18; 9. 29–32; 19. 87). From the Old English corpus we may refer to pieces such as the *Finnsburh Fragment*, the *Battle of Brunanburh*, and the *Battle of Maldon*, besides passages in other poems such as *Genesis* 1982–2095. We shall find further illustrations of the narrative conventions in the other Germanic literatures, for example in the *Hildebrandslied* fragment and the Eddic *Hunnenschlacht*, as well as in the Irish sagas, *Y Gododdin*, the *Shāh-nāma*, *Sassountsy David*, the Serbo-Croat oral epics, and elsewhere.

It is true that no recognizable memories of the original homeland or the earliest migrations survived in the later poetries of which we have record. Whatever wars early Indo-European groups may have fought among themselves or against aliens were in time displaced from recollection by later crises, and the names of the oldest heroes were forgotten. Yet there are sufficient similarities in the depictions of warfare and fighting in the different traditions to suggest a considerable measure of continuity. There were of course historical changes in the arts of war over time—for example the development of the long sword, the horse-drawn chariot, and weapons with iron components—and these were naturally reflected in heroic poetry. But the tradition was conservative by nature, and the gradual reception of more modern elements did not wipe out the memory of more archaic ones.[1]

The war-band

In the Dumézilian scheme of things the martial function is one of the three basic compartments of Indo-European ideology, and according to the earlier form of Dumézil's theory the warrior class formed a distinct constituent of the Indo-European population. The early Celtic and Germanic world presents us with a more focused picture. A feature of these tribal societies is the war-band, formed from footloose young men who have not yet married and settled down. They live on the margins of society and follow their leader wherever he takes them, generally on raiding and looting expeditions.[2]

As Caesar represents it (*Bell. Gall.* 6. 23. 6–8), the Germans considered this a useful institution for exercising the youth and keeping it occupied. A prominent man would announce in the assembly that he planned an expedition, and volunteers would stand up and pledge him their allegiance, to general approbation. Tacitus (*Germ.* 13–15) describes a more permanent type of *comitatus* in which the followers remained with their leader when there was no fighting to be done, spending their time in eating and sleeping. If their own *civitas* was tediously peaceful, they would go off to seek action and glory among tribes at war. Sometimes a leader such as Ariovistus set out to conquer new territories with a force gathered from a number of tribes.

[1] For discussions of Indo-European warfare cf. Pictet (1859–63), ii. 188–234; J. P. Mallory in *EIEC* 629 f.; N. Plagne, *Études Indo-Européennes* 12 (1993/4), 65–131; 13 (1995), 149–92; Sergent (1995), 282–306. On warfare as portrayed in the Indian epics see Brockington (1998), 175–87, 404–8.

[2] Cf. Davidson (1988), 80–2; Sergent (1995), 291 f.; D. A. Miller in *EIEC* 632.

Similar enterprises were undertaken later among the Franks and Goths. An ancient common Germanic word for the war-band was **druhti-*, Frankish Latin *dructis*, Old High German *truht*, etc.[3] The Irish equivalent is the *fían*, which Kim McCone has described as 'an independent organization of predominantly landless, unmarried, unsettled and young men given to hunting, warfare, and sexual licence in the wilds outside the *túath* [tribe, people], upon which it made claims . . . to sustenance and hospitality and for which it might perform elementary police or military services where relations were not strained by hostility'.[4]

A more widely attested word for 'war-band' or 'army' was **kori̯os*, represented in Germanic **harja-* (modern German *Heer*), Middle Irish *cuire*, Lithuanian *kãrias* 'army', and in such personal names as Macedonian *Κόρραγος*, Thessalian *Κορρίμαχος*, *Μενέκορρος*. The Gaulish tribes *Tricorii* and *Petrucorii* were presumably formed from alliances of respectively three and four roving war-bands. The addition of the suffix **-nos*, which we met in Chapter 3 in connection with certain gods' names, produced **kori̯onos* 'leader of the war-band', from which came Greek *κοίρανος*, Old Norse *Herjan* (as a name of Odin), and the British tribal name *Coriono-totae* (*CIL* vii. 481, Hexham).[5] There is no clear representative of this lexical group in Indo-Iranian, but it was evidently pan-European.

The war-band, especially in the Celtic and Germanic areas, sometimes had a wild and frenzied character. The Nordic *berserkir* were systematic practitioners of battle fury, of 'going berserk' (*berserksgangr*). The word *ber-serkr* is traditionally explained as meaning 'bear-shirted', but Kim McCone has argued on philological and other grounds for 'bare-shirted', with reference to the fervid warrior's practice of fighting without armour, either lightly clad or naked.[6] Tacitus writes that the Germans mostly fight *nudi aut sagulo leues* (*Germ.* 6. 1). Other ancient authors tell of Celtic warrior groups that in their pride and valour disdained trousers and plaids and fought naked

[3] On this word and its cognates, and the Germanic war-band generally, see D. H. Green (1998), 107–12, 136 f.; M. J. Enright, *JIES* 32 (2004), 216–21.

[4] *Cambridge Medieval Celtic Studies* 12 (1986), 13; cf. McCone (1990), 203–11; Dooley–Roe (1999), xi–xiv.

[5] Perhaps Old Phrygian *kuryaneyon* (W-01c) = *κοιρανέων*? Cf. Krahe (1955–64), i. 57, 63; Mayer (1957–9), ii. 66 f., 182; Benveniste (1973), 91–4; K. McCone in Meid (1987), 115; Gamkrelidze–Ivanov (1995), 644; *EIEC* 30 f.; D. H. Green (1998), 84–6.

[6] K. McCone in Meid (1987), 106. Cf. *Ynglinga saga* 6, '(Odin's men) used to go without breastplates, furious as dogs or wolves, biting their shields, strong as bears or bulls; they slew men, and neither fire nor sword could injure them—this was called *berserksgangr*'; Saxo 5. 3. 9 p. 115, 7. 2. 7 p. 185, 7. 2. 11 p. 186; de Vries (1956), i. 454, 493; ii. 94, 97 f.; Davidson (1964), 66–9; (1979–80), ii. 76 f., 110, 111; (1988), 79–81; Puhvel (1987), 196.

with only their weapons. Naked warriors still appear here and there in the *Táin* and other Irish sagas, and are depicted on Celtic coins.[7]

Clothes make the man, they say. The warriors' rejection of human garb, together with their predatory life in the wild, assimilates them to wild animals, and they seem often to have been styled as wolves and to have consciously adopted a wolfish identity, clothing themselves in wolfskins and uttering terrifying howls. The Norse berserks are sometimes called *úlfheðnar*, 'wolf-skinned'. This is paralleled in the Old Irish martial sobriquet *luchthonn*, as well as in the Sanskrit name Vṛkājina 'Wolfskin'. Personal names based on 'wolf' occur widely among the Indo-European peoples, and like other theriophoric names such as those involving 'bear' or 'boar' they are interpreted with reference to the feral qualities displayed by the warrior.[8] In British, Irish, and Norse poetry 'wolf' is a laudatory metaphor for the warrior hero, and it appears also in Homeric similes for advancing battle-lines.[9]

In Homeric epic, while there are no professional *berserkir*, a few of the greatest heroes are from time to time visited on the battlefield by a mad raging fury that makes them invincible. This fury is called λύσσα, which is a derivative of λύκος 'wolf'. It is as if they temporarily become wolves.[10] In other Indo-European cultures the term 'wolf' is applied to brigands and outlaws who live in the wild.[11] This form of assimilation to the wolf is not unconnected with the widespread belief in lycanthropy, the idea that certain persons (women as well as men) on occasion transform themselves into wolves. This is often conceived to involve putting on a wolf-skin or wolf-girdle.[12]

[7] Polyb. 2. 28. 8; Diod. 5. 29. 2, 30. 3 (Posidonius F 169 Th.); *Táin* (I) 3367–85, 3937; *Togail bruidne Dá Derga* 25; M. Green (1986), 108; Davidson (1988), 88 f.; McCone (1990), 205, 213. For an Assyrian parallel cf. West (1997), 213.

[8] On theriophoric names cf. Felix Solmsen, *Indogermanische Eigennamen* (Heidelberg 1922), 157 f.; Krahe (1955–64), i. 70 f.; Mayer (1957–9), ii. 120 f.; Schramm (1957), 77–83; D. Ellis Evans, *Gaulish Personal Names* (Oxford 1967), 291 f.; Campanile (1977), 80 f.; K. McCone in Meid (1987), 118, 121 f.; Gamkrelidze–Ivanov (1995), 414, 416, 418; Sergent (1995), 296 f.; D. H. Green (1998), 80–2. The name of the Trojan Hyrtakos (*Il.* 13. 759, al.) possibly reflects Hittite *ḫartakka-* 'wolf' (Watkins (1994), 709). On warriors and animals cf. N. Plagne, *Études Indo-Européennes* 13 (1995), 150–67.

[9] *Il.* 4. 471, 11. 72, 16. 156; *Y Gododdin* 740; *Sigurðarkviða in skamma* 12. 3, cf. *Helgakviða Hundingsbana B* 37; Irish references in Campanile (1977), 80.

[10] West (1997), 213 f.; P. Sauzeau in Domenico Accorinti–Pierre Chuvin (edd.), *Des Géants à Dionysos. Mélanges . . . offerts à Francis Vian* (Alessandria 2003), 95–108.

[11] In the Hittite Laws (1. 37), 'you have become a wolf'; Vedic *vṛ́ka-*; Old Norse *vargr*. Cf. Michael Jacoby, *Wargus, vargr, 'Verbrecher', 'Wolf'. Eine sprach- und rechtsgeschichtliche Untersuchung* (Uppsala 1974); Puhvel (1987), 196 f.; K. McCone in Meid (1987), 119; Davidson (1988), 79; E. Campanile, *JIES* 7 (1979), 237–47; id. (1990b), 27–32; id. in Ramat (1998), 4 f. Alcaeus (fr. 130b. 9 f.) apparently refers to a certain Onomakles as a 'lone wolf' guerrilla who lived as a 'wolf-spearman' (λυκαιχμίαις) or in the λυκαιχμίαι; cf. *ZPE* 80 (1990), 3.

[12] On lycanthropy cf. Grimm (1883–8), 1093–8, 1629–31; Feist (1913), 332 f., 478 n. 2; Robert Eisler, *Man into Wolf* (London 1951); de Vries (1956), i. 237 f.; R. A. Ridley, *JIES* 4 (1976), 321–31 (Baltic and Slavonic); Gamkrelidze–Ivanov (1995), 408, 414.

It may be, as McCone has argued most fully, that this all reflects an Indo-European institution of initiatory character, by which boys after several years of fosterage joined the local war-band and became Wolves.[13]

Cattle raids

A form of aggression often celebrated in the Indo-European literatures is the cattle raid.[14] The domestication of the horse allowed the early pastoralists of the Eurasian steppe to herd much larger numbers of animals than before, roaming over a vaster area. It also provided a convenient means of driving off other people's flocks and herds. This was the easiest and quickest way to acquire wealth, which was commonly measured in cattle. But it was liable to provoke fighting.

Such was the association in Vedic India between warfare and cattle-rustling that *gáviṣṭi-*, literally 'desire for cows', often signifies an expedition to win them (e.g. RV 5. 63. 5; 6. 59. 7; 8. 24. 5). Other derivatives from the 'cow' root show parallel semantics: *gavyánt-*, *gavyú-*, *gavéṣaṇa-*, 'desiring cows, eager for booty'. RV 10. 38 is a prayer to Indra for support in battle:

> In this glorious battle, Indra,
> this energetic tumult, urge us on to win,
> in the cattle raid where among the bold beringed ones [warriors]
> the arrows fly in all directions for men's defeat (1).

In *MBh.* 4. 29–61 the princes of the Kurus take advantage of the absence of Virāta, king of Matsya, to drive off sixty thousand head of cattle. Cattle-raiding was a feature of life that Zarathushtra condemned; the Zoroastrian creed contains the declaration 'I abjure thievery and cattle-raiding, despoiling and devastating the Mazdayasnian clans' (Y. 12. 2; cf. Yt. 10. 38).

The earlier of the two great wars of Greek mythology, the Theban War, was fought according to Hesiod (*Op.* 163) *μήλων ἕνεκ' Οἰδιπόδαο*, 'on account of Oedipus' flocks'. One of Heracles' canonical Labours was the capture of Geryon's cattle, and cattle-rustling is a recurrent motif in Greek heroic legend.[15]

[13] K. McCone in Meid (1987), 101–54; McCone (1990), 213–18; id. in R. P. Das–Gerhard Meiser (edd.), *Geregeltes Ungestüm. Bruderschaften und Jugendbünde bei den indogermanischen Völkern* (Bremen 2002), 43–67; criticized by J. Untermann, *Kratylos* 34 (1989), 50 f.; S. Zimmer, *JIES* 32 (2004), 209 f.

[14] Cf. Dillon (1975), 121; B. Lincoln, *JIES* 3 (1975), 337 n. 4; Sergent (1995), 285 f.; *EIEC* 138b.

[15] e.g. *Il.* 1. 154, 11. 670–84, 20. 91; *Od.* 11. 288–93, 20. 51, 21. 18 f.; 'Hes.' fr. 37. 1–7, 193. 16–18 (with *Scut.* 11 f.), 204. 46–51; E. Cingano in Richard Hunter (ed.), *The Hesiodic* Catalogue of Women: *Constructions and Reconstructions* (Cambridge 2005), 147.

The cattle raid (*táin*) is a staple theme of Irish saga—the *Táin bó Cúailnge* (*Cattle raid of Cooley*) is one of several works that carry it in their title—and of early British poetry. Eithinyn the son of Boddwadaf 'attacked in force for the herd(s) of the East' (*Y Gododdin* 434, cf. 447). Urien of Rheged 'with his horse under him, set to raid Manaw, seeking spoils and plentiful plunder; a hundred and sixty of one colour of both cows and calves, milch cows and oxen'.

> They drove their spoils back from Taf's meadows;
> Captives complained; cattle lowed, bellowed . . .
> Splendour of sword-play, great the plunder
> at Caer Lwytgoed, Morial seized it,
> fifteen hundred cattle at battle's end,
> fourscore horses, and trappings as well.[16]

Strongholds

The sacking of an enemy stronghold is a climactic and sometimes conclusive achievement in war, and one that confers signal glory on the hero or heroes who accomplish it. It was certainly a feature of warfare from Neolithic times, and it is well reflected in Indo-European poetic traditions.

The strongholds in question, as regards the early millennia, were not castles but hill forts or other open spaces protected by walls of earth, perhaps reinforced with timber and stone, and serving as places of refuge for a community and its livestock.[17] Several (late) Indo-European words applicable to such enclosures can be identified.[18] The two most important for our purpose are those represented by Greek πόλις and πύργος.

The common classical sense of πόλις is 'community', 'city-state', but its older meaning was 'citadel, acropolis', as still in fifth-century Athens (Thuc. 2. 15. 6, al.). Nestor instructs his men how past warriors sacked πόλιας καὶ τείχεα, 'forts and walls' (*Il.* 4. 308), and πτολίπορθος '*polis*-sacker' was a traditional epithet of heroes. When Achilles claims 'I sacked twelve πόλῑς of men with my ships, and eleven more on foot in the fertile Troad, and from all of them I took much treasure', and when he recalls how he and Patroclus

[16] *Canu Taliesin* 5. 12–16, trs. J. T. Koch in Koch–Carey (2000), 345; *Marwnad Cynddylan* 38 f., 54 f., trs. Clancy (2003), 99. Cf. also *Kychwedyl am doddyw o Galchuynydd*, Koch–Carey, 356–8; *Moliant Cadwallon* 33, Koch–Carey, 362.

[17] Cf. Feist (1913), 143–6; M. Gimbutas in Cardona et al. (1970), 164–8; G. Costa, *SSL* 27 (1987), 151–75; *EIEC* 210 f., 629 f.

[18] Cf. A. Della Volpe, *JIES* 16 (1988), 195–208; Gamkrelidze–Ivanov (1995), 647–9; Sergent (1995), 185 f.; *EIEC* 199, 210.

sacked πόλῑς μερόπων ἀνθρώπων (*Il.* 9. 328, 18. 342), we should understand the word as referring to fortified places.

It has cognates in Vedic *púr-* 'rampart, wall, palisade' and Lithuanian *pilìs* (Latvian *pils*), 'fort, castle'. An Illyrian form appears in the place-name Polai or Pola.[19] The Indic word is incorporated in the compounds *pūrbhíd-*, *puraṃdará-*, 'breacher/burster of ramparts', applied mostly to Indra, the war-god who as leader of the Aryan invaders destroyed the strongholds of the native Dāsas.[20] The Aśvins are said to have assisted the hero Trasadasyu in his *pūrbhídyam*, his rampart-breaching (RV 1. 112. 14).

The other word, πύργος 'fortification, city wall, tower', is an early loanword in Greek from an unidentified, presumably Balkan source. Its closest cognates are in Germanic: Gothic *baurgs* 'castle, town', Old High German *burg* 'fortress', Old English *burh*, Old Norse *borg*. A Mitannian form perhaps underlies Urartian *burgana* 'palace, fortress', continued as Armenian *burgn*. The lexeme is related to a widely attested Indo-European word for 'high'.[21]

The Germanic word is used in the *Hildebrandslied* (52) of the scene of battles, and in the Edda likewise. In the world's first war, that between the Æsir and the Vanir, 'Odin hurled (his spear) and shot it over the host . . . breached was the encircling wall of the Æsir's *borg*' (*Vǫluspá* 24). In another poem Sigurd destroys Brynhild's *borg* (*Oddrúnargrátr* 18. 3–4).

Both in the Rigveda and in early Celtic poetry we find the motif of the 'hundred strongholds' as a marker of warfare on a grand scale. The Rishi Gṛtsamada celebrates Indra, *yáḥ śatáṃ Śámbarasya púro bibhéda áśmaneva pūrvī́ḥ*, 'who broke Śambara's hundred ancient fortresses as with a stone' (RV 2. 14. 6). The Arthurian hero Uther Pendragon is made to say in his death-song

> It is I who broke a hundred fortified towns;
> it is I who killed a hundred mayors of strongholds.

Cadwallon's campaign beyond Chester is summed up as 'a hundred warbands and a hundred bold soldiers, a hundred battles which conquered a hundred strongholds'. The Irish catalogue poem *Núadu Necht* records that 'Foglas was violent, who equipped a hundred forts' (*fuirec cét cathrach*).[22]

[19] Call. fr. 11. 6, Lyc. 1022, Strab. 5. 1. 9, al.; Mayer (1957–9), ii. 93.

[20] Oldenberg (1917), 153; Hillebrandt (1927–9), ii. 153–69; G. Costa, *SSL* 27 (1987), 157–65.

[21] Cf. Mayer (1957–9), ii. 31; Alfred Heubeck, *Praegraeca* (Erlangen 1961), 63–5; Chantraine (1968–80), 958; *EIEC* 210, 269.

[22] *Marwnat Uthyr Pen* 14, trs. J. T. Koch in Koch–Carey (2000), 300; *Marwnad Cadwallon* 10 (Rowland (1990), 447), trs. Koch–Carey, 359; K. Meyer (1913), 40/43 v. 12, trs. J. Carey in Koch–Carey, 55. For reduction of forts in Irish narrative cf. the poem on the Destruction of Dind Ríg (Campanile (1988), 26 no. 2), and the *Táin bó Flidais* (summarized in Thurneysen (1921), 319).

There was another Irish hero called Conn Cétchathach, 'Conn of the hundred battles'.

The reduction of a stronghold sometimes, no doubt, necessitated a siege. As Adolphe Pictet noted long ago, this is expressed in a series of languages as 'sitting at' or 'around'. He cited Greek προσ- or περικαθέζομαι, Latin *obsideo*, Old Irish *imm-said*, Old English *ymbsittan*, Old High German *umbisizan*, Lithuanian *apsėdėti*, Church Slavonic *obŭsiesti*, all based on the same Indo-European root **sed* 'sit'.[23]

THE HERO AS WARRIOR

Predicates

In the last chapter we constructed a general profile of the hero, a sort of *curriculum vitae*. We shall now look more closely at his behaviour in battle. We can say 'his', because however many men may be involved in the fighting, the tendency is always to focus on individuals, and very often on one central hero who makes the decisive contribution. When it is necessary to speak eulogistically of a whole corps, poets in several traditions may indicate that they are all individually men of quality by calling them 'chosen warriors': RV 4. 42. 5, 'me (Indra) the well-horsed heroes at contest, me the chosen ones invoke in the battle';[24] *Y Gododdin* 1158–60, 'when the nobles came . . . , the chosen men (*deetholwyl*) of every region in contention with Lloegr's mixed hosts'; *Beowulf* 205 f., Beowulf had with him 'chosen champions (*cempan gecorene*) of the Geatish people, of the keenest he could find'. Attila's praises were sung at his funeral by *Hunnorum lectissimi equites* (Jordanes, *Getica* 256).

It is a basic feature of the hero that he is a killer. In speaking of poetic compounds in Chapter 2 we mentioned the parallel epithets meaning 'man-slaying' that are applied to warriors and/or warrior gods in Vedic (*nṛhán-*) and Homeric Greek (ἀνδροφόνος). The Old Irish hero Conall too is a 'slaughterer', *oirgnech* or *oirgnid*.

By inflicting slaughter on the enemy the hero keeps it off his own side. With him in their front line they do not need the protection of a fortress, for he is their defending wall. Ajax is called the ἕρκος Ἀχαιῶν, the Achaeans'

[23] Pictet (1859–63), ii. 193. The preverbs in the Baltic and Slavonic compounds correspond to the Latin *ob*-.

[24] I follow Grassmann in taking *vṛtā́ḥ* as the participle of *vṛ* 'choose'. Geldner takes it as from *vṛ* 'enclose', translating 'wenn sie in der Schlacht umringt sind'.

protective enclosure (*Il.* 3. 229, 6. 5, 7. 211; cf. 1. 283 f. of Achilles). In another place he is called their πύργος, their battlement or tower (*Od.* 11. 556). Similar metaphors are commonplace in British heroic poetry: '(Morien) the battle lord, a fortress to the frightened army' (*Y Gododdin* 393, cf. 326, 422, 533, 772 f., 1244); *Moryen mur trin*, 'Morien the bulwark of battle' (*Cyvoesi Myrddin* 121); 'a broad shield, a fortress (*dinas*) for strong men, the best warrior is Caranfael' (Rowland (1990), 442 st. 92bc).[25] Cú Chulainn is called *in t-indellchró bodba fer talman*, 'the marshalled fence (*cró*) of battle of men of the earth' (*Táin* (I) 2213). Hrothgar is *eodor Scyldinga*, 'the Scyldings' shelter, enclosure' (*Beowulf* 428, 663, cf. 1044), and the corresponding Norse word, *iaðarr*, is used in similar expressions: *Fáfnismál* 36 *hers iaðar, Helgakviða Hundingsbana B* 42 *folcs iaðar, Lokasenna* 35 *ása iaðarr*. In this Germanic formula the metaphor has apparently faded, and the word has come to be hardly more than a synonym for 'leader'. In the Armenian oral epic, on the other hand, the old image is still alive: 'Mher, like a fort, had been holding back enemy kings' (*Sassountsy David* 343).[26]

A related but less common metaphor is that of the pillar. Pindar calls Hector Τροίας ἄμαχον ἀστραβῆ κίονα, 'Troy's uncombattable, unwarped pillar' (*Pyth.* 2. 81); near the beginning of the same ode he has praised Theron as the support (ἔρεισμα) of Acragas. In the same way Urien is called 'the pillar of Prydain (Britain)', and Rheithfyw 'the pillar of battle'. Similar phrases are used of Irish heroes and kings.[27]

Alarming symptoms

The hero's warrior fury manifests itself physiologically in exceptional body heat. Rāma, when ready for battle, burns like a smokeless flame (*Rm.* 3. 23. 15, 25 f., 27. 17). An Irish saga relates that 'this troop descended upon the green and sat there as one man, and the heat of the great valorous warriors was such that the snow softened and melted for thirty feet on every side' (*Mesca Ulad* 506 Watson, trs. Gantz). When the young Cú Chulainn comes to the

[25] Cf. also the *Lament for Pyll*, Rowland (1990), 409 st. 33; *Urien's Head*, Rowland, 477 st. 12 = Koch–Carey (2000), 352.

[26] On this imagery cf. Schramm (1957), 86–8; H. Humbach, *MSS* 21 (1967), 21–3, 26; Schmitt (1967), 282 f.; E. Campanile, *SSL* 14 (1974), 207; id. (1977), 120. Durante (1976), 114, notes that Vedic gods such as Indra and Agni are sometimes called a *púr-*, 'rampart, wall' (RV 1. 189. 2; 8. 69. 8, 80. 7; 10. 87. 22); the contexts are not military, but no doubt the metaphor could have been so employed.

[27] *Urien's Head* 16; *Y Gododdin* 67; Irish references in Campanile (1977), 120 f. Cf. the Royal Irish Academy's *Dictionary of the Irish Language* (Dublin 1983), s.v. *deil* II; Watkins (1994), 746 f.

stronghold of Emain Macha and threatens to kill everyone inside, they counter him by sending out naked women, so that he hides his face; they then seize him and throw him into a tub of cold water, which at once turns to steam and bursts. A second tub boils over; the third becomes warm and stabilizes his temperature (*Táin* (I) 802–18). The Nart hero Sosruquo is scorching hot when he is born and has to be cooled down with seven baths in cold water, which leaves him as hard as tempered steel.[28]

In several traditions we find the motif that a visible fire or light springs from the hero's body. When Athena confers on Diomedes a temporary dominance in the battle, she causes a flame to burn from his helmet and shield, from his head and shoulders (*Il.* 5. 4–7). Later she puts a golden nimbus round Achilles' head, with a flame burning from it up to the sky (18. 205 f., 214, 225–7). Livy (1. 39. 1–4) relates that when Servius Tullius was still a boy, a fire was seen to burn from his head as he slept. Someone came running with water to put it out, but the boy's mother stopped him. As Bhīma raged with longing for battle, 'flames of fire burst forth from all the orifices of his body, as from the hollows of a tree that is on fire'; he 'began to sweat with his inner heat. From the ears and the other orifices of the raging man fire issued forth, smoking and sparking' (*MBh.* 2. 63. 15, 64. 13; cf. 3. 261. 50; 8. 67. 7). Upon Cú Chulainn is seen the *lúan láith*, the 'hero's light'. At *Táin* (I) 69 it is said to be on his brow, at 433 to rise above his head. 'The torches of the war-goddess, virulent rain-clouds and sparks of blazing fire, were seen in the air over his head with the seething of fierce rage that rose in him . . . The hero's light rose from his forehead, as long and as thick as a hero's fist, and it was as long as his nose' (2265–73).[29] The motif occurs in an only slightly different form in Serbo-Croat oral epic: 'wherever I smote him, living fire leaped from Đelos̓'.[30]

The second of the passages quoted about Bhīma's outburst of fire continues: 'His face became fierce to behold, with its folds of knitted brows, as the face of Yama himself when the end of the Aeon has come' (*MBh.* 2. 64. 13). This facial distortion is again paralleled by a habit of Cú Chulainn's, though in the Irish narration it is intensified to a fantastic degree and becomes just one detail of a prodigious spasm that deforms his whole frame.

For it was usual with him that when his hero's flame sprang forth his feet would turn to the back and his hams turn to the front and the round muscles of his calves would come on to his shins, while one eye sank into his head and the other protruded. A

[28] Colarusso (2002), 53 (Circassian), 186 (Abaza), 388 (Ubykh). In the Ossetic version in Sikojev (1985), 70–3, the tempering takes place later, the heat being produced artificially.

[29] Cf. *Aided Con Chulainn* (Book of Leinster version), ed. W. Stokes, *RC* 3 (1876–8), 182; *Dictionary of the Irish Language* s.v. *lúan*; Campanile (1990b), 20–4.

[30] Salih Ugljanin, *SCHS* ii, no. 16. 111 f.

man's head would go into his mouth. Every hair on him would be as sharp as a spike of hawthorn and there would be a drop of blood on every hair.[31]

A further terrifying feature of heroes is their ability to utter a war-cry of overpowering volume, with devastating effect on the enemy's morale.[32] Achilles, with the divine flame rising from his head, goes from the Achaeans' defensive wall to the ditch and gives three mighty shouts (which Athena reinforces with her own voice), causing such confusion in the Trojan ranks that twelve men die in the press of their own spears and chariots (*Il.* 18. 215–29). Hanūmān advises Bhīma, 'when you go into battle, raise your lion's cry, and I will reinforce it with mine, uttering fearful roars that will rob your enemies of their lives' (*MBh.* 3. 150. 14 f., cf. 6. 42. 8–12). Cú Chulainn, seeing the four provinces of Ireland ranged against him,

> shook his shield and brandished his spears and waved his sword, and he uttered a hero's shout deep in his throat. And the goblins and sprites and spectres of the glen and demons of the air gave answer for terror of the shout that he had uttered. And Némain, the war goddess, attacked the host, and the four provinces of Ireland made a clamour of arms round the points of their own spears and weapons so that a hundred warriors among them fell dead of fright and terror in the middle of the encampment on that night (*Táin* (I) 2081–7, cf. 2238).

In one of the Ossetic Nart tales Batradz goes to Borata's house and lets out a great shout; it shakes the rafters, and plaster falls on the heads of the feasters, many of whom faint just from the shout (Sikojev (1985), 175). We may also note the episode in the Armenian epic where David is shot by his daughter, and she dies of fright at his cry of pain (*Sassountsy David* 334 f.).

Sometimes the hero is depicted not just as strong and brave but as the master of a special repertory of expert manoeuvres in hand-to-hand fighting. There is only perhaps a hint of this in Homer, when Hector declares that he is a fit match for Ajax, being well acquainted with battle and slaughter: 'I know how to ply the sere ox(hide) to right, to left . . . I know how to charge into the fray of swift horses, I know how to dance for fierce Ares in the standing fight' (*Il.* 7. 238–41). In Indian and Irish narrative there is a more elaborate and formalized body of techniques.

> Armed with that scimitar he suddenly began to career in circles over the arena, displaying, O monarch, the fourteen different kinds of manoeuvres . . . all those

[31] *Táin* (I) 1651–7, cf. 2245 ff.; *Fled Bricrenn* 27. In *Egils saga* 55 a Viking gives notice of his anger by lowering one eyebrow to his chin and raising the other to the roots of his hair; but this is probably something borrowed from Celtic, not an independent survival in Germanic tradition.

[32] Cf. Miller (2000), 230–2.

motions such as wheeling about and whirling on high, and making side-thrusts and jumping forward and leaping on high and running above and rushing forward and rushing upwards (*MBh.* 8. 18. 29 f.; cf. 7. 164. 143–7, where twenty-one types of movement are mentioned).

Cú Chulainn was taught a whole series of special feats by the supreme woman trainer Scáthach. They are listed in several texts. At *Táin* (I) 1714–19, where he is found practising them, they appear as

The ball-feat, the blade-feat, the feat with horizontally-held shield, the javelin-feat, the rope-feat, the feat with the body, the cat-feat, the hero's salmon-leap, the cast of a wand, the leap across the . . . , the bending of a valiant hero, the feat of the *gae bolga*, the feat of quickness, the wheel-feat, the eight-men feat, the over-breath feat, the bruising with a sword, the hero's war-cry, the well-measured blow, the return-stroke, the mounting on a spear and straightening the body on its point, with the bond of a valiant warrior.

Eagerness to fight

The heroic warrior of course stands firm against the enemy.[33] But more than that: the real hero actually delights in fighting.[34] The Vedic *samád-* and the Homeric *χάρμη* both mean by derivation 'rejoicing' but in regular usage 'battle'. Another Vedic word, *ráṇa-*, has both senses. When Achilles stays away from the battle in his anger against Agamemnon, he misses it: *ποθέεσκε δ' ἀϋτήν τε πτόλεμόν τε* (*Il.* 1. 492). The Aiakidai 'rejoiced in fighting as at a feast' ('Hes.' fr. 206). Archilochus, spoiling for a scrap with someone, says 'I crave the fight with you, as if thirsting to drink' (fr. 125). The Anglo-Saxon poet of *Exodus* (182) uses the same metaphor when he describes the Egyptian warriors as *þurstige þræcwīges*, 'thirsty for the violence of battle'.

The hero shows his zeal and courage by leading the charge and fighting in the front line.

ἀρτύνθη δὲ μάχη, σταν δ' ἀντίοι· ἐν δ' Ἀγαμέμνων
πρῶτος ὄρουσ', ἔθελεν δὲ πολὺ προμάχεσθαι ἁπάντων.
Battle was ordered, they stood opposed. Then Agamemnon
rushed in first, wanting to fight far in front of them all. (*Il.* 11. 216 f.)

[33] The epithet *yudhi-tiṣṭhat-*, applied to Bhīma at *MBh.* 3. 12. 51, means literally 'standing (firm) in battle', as does the name of the hero Yudhiṣṭhira. The same idea is expressed by the Homeric epithets *μενεχάρμης, μενεπτόλεμος* (found later as a personal name) and by the name of Menelaos, 'withstanding the war-host', and indeed by that of his father Atreus, 'he who does not flee'.

[34] Durante (1976), 114.

Mimnermus writes of a Smyrnaean hero of recent memory, 'Pallas Athena never had cause to fault his acid fury, when in the front line he hurtled through the battle's bloody moil' (14. 5–7). The sentence quoted from Tacitus in the last chapter may be repeated here: 'the war-leaders are more admired for their conduct than their authority, for being bold and prominent and going out in front of the line' (*Germ.* 7). Later Germanic poetry sustains this ethic. Hiltibrant 'was ever at the front of the host, fighting was ever dear to him' (*Hildebrandslied* 27). 'Never in the forefront did (Hrothgar's) far-famed valour fail, when the slain were falling' (*Beowulf* 1041 f.). 'Ever was Helgi Slayer of Hunding foremost in the war-host, where men were fighting' (*Helgakviða Hundingsbana A* 53). It is the same with the early Gododdin warriors. 'Wearing an ornament of rank, in the front line's array . . . he was a hero in deeds'. Cunedag likewise 'used to carry his shield in the vanguard'.[35]

The vow of abnegation

In some stories a hero is driven on by the compulsion to avenge the death of someone near to him, or to achieve some other self-set goal. To underline his dedication he may vow to deny himself some normal comfort or privilege until his purpose is accomplished. Achilles declares that he will not eat or drink until Patroclus is avenged, and he resists attempts to persuade him to fortify himself before the battle (*Il.* 19. 209, 303–8). Later he refuses the opportunity to wash Hector's blood off his body until Patroclus has had his proper funeral (23. 39–47). Karṇa vows not to wash his feet until he has slain Arjuna (*MBh.* 8. 5. 76, 46. 38, 791*. 6). The Chatti did not cut their hair or beards until they had slain an enemy in battle (Tac. *Germ.* 31. 1). The Batavian prince C. Julius Civilis, in obedience to a vow made when he took up arms against the Romans, dyed his hair orange and let it grow long until he had won a victory (Tac. *Hist.* 4. 61). Odin's newborn son Váli does not wash his hands or comb his hair before avenging Baldr (*Vǫluspá* 32 f., *Baldrs draumar* 11). Harald Fairhair vows not to cut or comb his hair until he has conquered all of Norway (*Heimskringla* 3. 4). Angantyr vows not to occupy his father's high seat till he has avenged him (*Hervarar saga* 11).[36]

[35] *Y Gododdin* 46 f., cf. 21, 39, 220, 418, 1214, 1239; *Marwnad Cunedda* 41, Koch–Carey (2000), 293. Cf. Campanile (1977), 122; (1990b), 62, who also cites several Vedic passages where Indra is represented as standing or fighting in front of his followers, and an Irish one about King Olaf of Dublin.

[36] On the motif cf. Karl Müllenhoff, *Deutsche Altertumskunde* (Berlin 1870–1900), iv. 414; Frazer (1911–36), iii. 261 f.

WEAPONS

A man's tools and weapons are extensions of his limbs. The warrior's weapons match his own virtues. As traditional narrative deals in warriors of high quality, the weapons and armour are also excellent. Indra's bow is 'well-made' (*súkṛta-*, RV 8. 77. 11), as are Mithra's bowstrings and arrows (*hukərəta-*, Yt. 10. 128 f.). Homeric helmets are likewise 'well-made' (*Il.* 3. 336 al. κυνέην εὔτυκτον), and spears are 'well-shaven' (*Il.* 10. 373 ἐΰξου δουρός, *Od.* 14. 225 ἄκοντες ἐΰξεστοι). So they are in the Avesta (*huxšnuta-*, Yt. 10. 24, 39). Mithra himself wields a 'well-fashioned' weapon (*hutāšta-*, Yt. 10. 141).[37]

The hero's fame is linked with his weapon. Odysseus and others are 'spear-famed', δουρικλυτός or δουρικλειτός. In another type of compound epithet the fame is predicated of the weapon itself: Apollo is κλυτότοξος, 'of the famous bow', a formation paralleled in the Vedic personal name and title of Indra *Śrutáratha-*, 'of the famous chariot'. In Irish we have *mac Ruide co rind-blaid*, 'Mac Ruide of the famous spear'.[38]

Certain heroes are associated with a particular, non-standard weapon. In Homer most warriors fight with throwing-spears, and with the sword after they have discharged their spears, but particular individuals such as Teukros and Pandaros are archers, and we hear of one Areithoos the Maceman, so called 'because he did not fight with bow and spear, but used to smash the battle-lines with an iron mace' (*Il.* 7. 140 f.). He belongs to the generation before the Trojan War, and the mace or club is an archaic, elementary weapon; later it became associated with Heracles. The obsolete word *wagro-* 'smasher' remained enshrined in the name of Meleagros, another pre-Trojan hero. The implement appears in other Indo-European traditions, but always as something exceptional.[39] We have discussed the storm-god's 'smasher' in Chapter 6. In the *Mahābhārata* it is the special weapon of Bhīma; its nature

[37] Bacchylides (18. 49) has ξεστοὺς ἄκοντας, which may be put beside the Eddic phrase *skafna aska* (*Atlakviða* 4. 2), literally 'shaven ash-trees'. The parallel would be more exact if he had had *ξεστὰς μελίας (as three times in Quintus of Smyrna we have ἐϋξέστῃς μελίῃσιν); μελίη 'ash' is routinely used in Homer for 'ash-wood spear', as are *askr* in Old Norse, *asck* in Old High German, *æsc* in Old English (*Beowulf* 1772, *Wanderer* 99, *Maldon* 43, etc.), and *onn* in early Welsh (*Y Gododdin* 316). Old English also shares with Greek the metonymy 'wood' (δόρυ, *wudu*) both for 'spear' (*Beowulf* 398) and for 'ship' (ibid. 216, 298, 1919).

[38] Edward Gwynn, *The Metrical Dindshenchas*, iii (Dublin 1908), 302. 57; Campanile (1977), 122 f.

[39] Cf. B. Schlerath, *Orbis* 24 (1975), 502–14; Campanile (1990a), 262 f., (1990b), 162 f.; Sergent (1995), 288 f.

and origin are described in 2. 3. 5–18. The Nordic hero Orvar-Odd fought with an oaken club (*Edd. min.* 58). The legendary Danish prince Gram, ignorant of iron, was armed with a wooden club, to which he attached a golden stud on learning that his enemy, the Swede Sigtrug, could only be vanquished by gold (Saxo 1. 4. 11 f. pp. 17 f.). Haldan used an oak cudgel with iron studs (7. 2. 1 p. 183).

To swing or hurl a massive club of wood, stone, or metal is a token of great strength. Even more so, to uproot a tree for the purpose. This is something of a commonplace. In Greek myth and art the Centaurs fight with fir trunks torn up from the ground. In the Indian epics it is a recurrent motif that mighty trees are pulled up from their roots and used, stripped or not of their branches and leaves, as bludgeons or missiles.[40] Similarly in an Ossetic tale about the hero Batradz: he is fighting the giant Tichifirt, and when they come to a wood, they tear up hundred-year-old trees, roots and all, and hurl them at each other.[41] In the Armenian epic David pulls up a tree to make a club (*Sassountsy David* 218, cf. 235, 349). In the Irish saga *Fled Bricrenn* (81) a giant comes to attack a fort, 'his hands full of stripped oaks, each of which would form a burden for a wagon-team of six', and starts casting them. Saxo's Haldan more than once pulls up an oak and fashions it into a club (7. 2. 9 f. pp. 185 f.; 7. 9. 11 p. 203).

The hero is often represented as possessing a unique weapon or piece of armour of a kind or quality not now available. Ajax is renowned for his great shield, constructed of bronze backed with seven layers of ox-hide from sturdy bulls (*Il.* 7. 219–23). Cú Chulainn's cuirass was made to a similar formula, being 'of hard leather, tough and tanned, made from the choicest part of seven yearling ox-hides' (*Táin* (I) 2219–21). Swords are of a wonderful sharpness, for which there is a distinctive criterion: the edge would cut a hair that floated against it on a stream. This is common to Irish and Norse literature, and we find something very similar in a Nart tale from the Caucasus. Socht's sword 'shone at night like a candle . . . It would sever a hair (floating) on water'.[42] Sigurd's sword Gram 'was so keen that he held it down in the Rhine and let a tuft of wool drift on the current, and the tuft parted like the water'.[43] In the Abaza story Sosruquo is trying to gain access to a giant's

[40] *MBh.* 3. 12. 39–49, 154. 46–51, 270. 13, 272. 14; 4. 22. 18–24; *Rm.* 3. 29. 16–19; 4. 16. 21; 5. 42. 11.

[41] Sikojev (1985), 180; cf. Colarusso (2002), 305.

[42] *Echtra Cormaic i Tír Tairngiri* 59 (*Irische Texte*, iii. 199); cf. *Togail bruidne Dá Derga* 128 (1230 Knott). The same is predicated of Cú Chulainn's shield-rim, *Táin* (I) 2235; of the barbs on the five prongs of Fer Maisse's javelin, *Acallam na Senórach* p. 196 Dooley–Roe. Cú Roí's axe was so sharp that it would cut hairs blown against it, *Fled Bricrenn* 91.

[43] Prose after *Reginsmál* 14; cf. *Skáldsk.* 40; *Þiðreks saga* 103–6.

fortress. A sword is hanging on the gate to bar entry. Sosruquo throws a horse-hair at it, but even that is cut (Colarusso (2002), 206).

The individuality of Sigurd's sword is underlined by the fact that it has its own name. This is a frequent feature of swords, and to some extent of other weapons and armour, in Germanic and Celtic tradition, and it can be found also in Avdo Međedović's epic *The Wedding of Smailagić Meho* (*SCHS* iii. 90).[44]

The weapon is often introduced with some account of its history, its previous owners, and so forth.[45] In many cases it was made by a special craftsman. Ajax's shield was made by Tychios (*Il.* 7. 220), Achilles' armour by Hephaestus. Waldere's sword Mimming was made by Weland (*Waldere* A 2), as was Beowulf's corslet (*Beowulf* 455). Several notable swords wielded by Norse heroes were made by dwarfs: Angantyr's sword Tyrfing (*Waking of Angantyr* 7, 18 = *Edd. min.* 15, 18), Hogni's sword Dáinsleif (*Skáldsk.* 50), and a pair bequeathed by Budli to his grandsons (*Hildibrand's Death-song* 2 = *Edd. min.* 53). Arthur's coat of mail was made by Wygar, an elvish smith (*aluisc smið*: Laȝamon, *Brut* 21131).

Weapons share their owners' blood-lust and are eager to do their work.[46] Pandaros' arrow leaps from the bow, καθ' ὅμιλον ἐπιπτέσθαι μενεαίνων, 'furious to fly among the throng' (*Il.* 4. 126). In the Indian epic arrows *gantum uśanti*, 'desire to go' (*MBh.* 5. 47. 96), and they drink blood (6. 49. 21, 69. 9, 78. 21, 80. 4; 7. 109. 25, 112. 28, al.). Spears 'yearn to get their fill of flesh' (*Il.* 11. 574, cf. 15. 542 f., 21. 70, 168). Diomedes' spear 'rages' in his hands (μαίνεται, 8. 111); Achilles' is 'angry' (ζάκοτος, Pind. *Nem.* 6. 53). Beowulf's sword sings out a greedy war-song as he brings it down on Grendel's mother's head (1521 f.). Another Anglo-Saxon poet speaks of the ash spears as *wælgīfru*, 'greedy for carnage' (*Wanderer* 100). Freyr's sword would fight by itself (*Skírnismál* 8. 4 f.; *Gylf.* 37). Thor's hammer Miǫllnir is *morðgiarn*, 'eager to kill' (*Hymiskviða* 36).

[44] Swords: *Beowulf* 1457, 2680; Saxo 2. 6. 11 p. 51; 2. 7. 19 p. 58; 4. 4. 7 p. 99; 7. 9. 11 p. 203; 7. 11. 10 p. 212; *Cath Maige Tuired* 777 Gray; *Acallam na Senórach* pp. 67, 193 Dooley–Roe. Spears: *Gylf.* 51, *Skáldsk.* 35 (Odin's spear Gungnir); *Acallam na Senórach* pp. 55, 95, 98, 170, 193 D.–R. A number of Germanic spear-blades from about the third century have names such as 'Attacker' inscribed on them in runes (de Vries (1956), i. 293; D. H. Green (1998), 186). Shield: *Táin* (I) 4046; *Acallam na Senórach* p. 170 D.–R. Helm and corslet: *Skáldsk.* 44. Arthur's named sword, spear, shield, and knife: *Culhwch and Olwen* 159–61. Cf. Miller (2000), 207–11.

[45] So with Meriones' boar's-tusk helmet, *Il.* 10. 266–71; Arjuna's bow, *MBh.* 4. 38. 39–41; Karṇa's, 8. 22. 36 ff.; Duryodhana's armour, 7. 78. 19; Yudhiṣṭhira's sword, 12. 160. 33–87; Wiglaf's sword, *Beowulf* 2610–25.

[46] Cf. de Vries (1956), i. 292 f.; Durante (1976), 144 f.; M. W. Edwards in the Cambridge *Iliad* Commentary, v. 51; Stith Thompson, *Motif-Index* D 1601. 4–5. 2. 'Furious' weapons in Akkadian: West (1997), 371.

We noted in Chapter 6 that the thunder-god's missile returns of its own accord after being thrown. The same useful property is ascribed to certain other weapons too. The poet of the *Iliad*, to be sure, reserves such paradoxical phenomena for divine agency, and when Achilles' spear is restored to his hand, it is by Athena's intervention (*Il.* 22. 273–7). But extra-Homeric myth told of Cephalus' javelin which *consequitur quodcumque petit, fortunaque missum non regit, et reuolat nullo referente cruentum* (Ov. *Met.* 7. 683 f.). In a battle fought between the gods and the Dānavas, led by Skanda, 'throw after throw the spear smote the foes in their thousands and then, as witnessed the Gods and the Dānavas, it returned again to Skanda's hand'.[47] In Irish legend the spear of Assal returs to the thrower's hand when he says the magic word 'Athibar'.[48]

As the hero's inner energy manifests itself in fire erupting from his body, so also may his weapons ignite. 'Blazing flames seemed to issue from the points of weapons, dazzling the eyes' (*MBh.* 9. 10. 18). The Nart Kandz has a sword whose blade flares with blue flame in the heat of battle, and a bow whose string emits red flames.[49] Belisarius' troops, encamped before the battle of Tricamarum, saw their spearheads ablaze with fire, which turned out to be a portent of victory (Procop. *Bell. Vandal.* 2. 2. 6). The Valkyries' spears radiate light (*Helgakviða Hundingsbana A* 15). The sorcerer Oddo made the enemy think that the Danish warriors' swords were flashing with fire (Saxo 5. 2. 4 p. 109). When Dubthach Dóel Ulad struck the butt of his great spear across his palm, 'a sack-measure of fiery tinder-sparks bursts out over its blade and over its tip, when its spear-heat takes hold of it' (*Mesca Ulad* 44, trs. Koch; cf. *Togail bruidne Dá Derga* 128 f. = 1232–53 Knott). The sword Dyrnwyrn 'Whitehilt', if drawn by a well-born man, would flame from hilt to tip.[50] Arthur's sword bore the image of two serpents in gold, 'and when the sword was drawn from its sheath as it were two flames of fire might be seen from the mouths of the serpents, and so exceeding dreadful was it that it was not easy for any to look on'.[51]

The warrior's close relationship with his weapon is such that he literally swears by it.[52] Parthenopaios swears on his spear, which he trusts and reveres more than a god or his eyes, that he will sack Thebes (Aesch. *Sept.* 529–31);

[47] *MBh.* 3. 221. 67, cf. 286. 16, 294. 24; *Rm.* 4. 12. 4 (arrow to quiver); 6. 47. 113 (spear), 97. 19 (the Brahma weapon).

[48] *Imthechta Clainne Tuirill* 3. 11, ed. R. Thurneysen, *ZCP* 12 (1918), 245 (trs.: 249).

[49] Sikojev (1985), 304; cf. Colarusso (2002), 290.

[50] *Thirteen Treasures* 1 in Rachel Bromwich, *Trioedd ynys Prydein* (2nd edn., Cardiff 1978), 240 f.

[51] *Breudwyt Ronabwy*, ed. Melville Richards (Cardiff 1948), p. 10. 27 ff., trs. Gwyn and Thomas Jones, *The Mabinogion* (London 1949), 144.

[52] Cf. S. Rożniecki, *Archiv für slavische Philologie* 23 (1901), 492–7; Watkins (1995), 417 f.

we have a sense of something wild and pre-Homeric. Euripides has Antigone swear on her sword (*Phoen.* 1677). The *Laws of Manu* (8. 113) state that a *kṣatriya*, a man of the warrior class, should swear by his chariot and weapons, and there are instances of such oaths in the *Mahābhārata* (5. 73. 14; 8. 50. 9). Ammianus Marcellinus (17. 12. 21) describes the Quadi as swearing an oath by their drawn swords, 'which they worship as *numina*'. Volund makes the Swedish king Nidud swear an oath 'by ship's sides, shield's rim, horse's withers and sword's edge' (*Vǫlundarkviða* 33). The Bohemian war-leader Vlaztislav in a bellicose speech swears by Mars, Bellona, and his sword-hilt.[53] Cú Chulainn swears *tar mó sciath* 7 *tar mó cloidim*, 'by my shield and by my sword' (*Fled Bricrenn* 99).

The Quadi were not alone in their weapon cult. The mythical warrior Kaineus worshipped his spear as a god, as do Mezentius and Turnus in Virgil and Capaneus in Statius.[54] The Scythians, according to Herodotus, worshipped the war-god in the form of an old iron scimitar,[55] while at Rome Mars was worshipped as a spear.[56] The author of an Irish mythical narrative avers that weapons used to be worshipped in olden times.[57]

There are various stories in which the same weapon is used successively by two or more heroes in different generations. But there are others in which a hero's weapon is so far identified with him that there can be no question of anyone else using it after him, and it has to be removed from the scene. Arjuna at the end of his career is instructed to throw his bow into the sea (*MBh.* 17. 1. 37–40). The sword of the Nart Batradz is dragged to the Black Sea after his death and sunk there; it rises up sometimes and causes lightning.[58] Arthur has to throw his sword Excalibur back into the lake from which it came in the first place. There is much evidence from Bronze and Iron Age Europe for weapons being thrown into lakes, rivers, springs, and bogs, as if they were prime prestige offerings.[59]

[53] Cosmas of Prague, *Chronica Boemorum* 1. 10 (C. H. Meyer (1931), 19. 6).

[54] Acusilaus, *FGrHist* 2 F 22 line 72 (?), sch. Ap. Rhod. 1. 57–64a, sch. D *Il.* 1. 264; Virg. *Aen.* 10. 773, 12. 95–100; Stat. *Theb.* 3. 615, 9. 549.

[55] Hdt. 4. 62. 2; cf. Eudoxus fr. 303 Lasserre, Mela 2. 15, Amm. Marc. 31. 2. 23 (Alans); further references in Grimm (1883–8), 1351. At Wolin in Pomerania a rusty old lance, alleged to be that of Julius Caesar, was still venerated in the twelfth century: C. H. Meyer (1931), 35. 14, 40. 24; Váňa (1992), 168.

[56] Plut. *Rom.* 29. 1; Georges Dumézil, *L'héritage indo-européen à Rome* (Paris 1949), 57 f.; id., *Les dieux des Indo-Européens* (Paris 1952), 111–17.

[57] *Cath Maige Tuired* 782 Gray. On the cult of weapons cf. Christopher Blinkenberg, *The Thunderweapon in Religion and Folklore* (Cambridge 1911), 39 f.; de Vries (1956), i. 95 f.; Gelling–Davidson (1969), 31–9.

[58] Georges Dumézil, *Loki* (2nd edn., Darmstadt 1959), 129.

[59] M. Green (1986), 139–44, 148.

HORSES

The partnership of man and horse goes far back into Indo-European prehistory.[60] The two are often coupled, especially in battle contexts: *Il.* 21. 16 πλῆτο ῥόος κελάδων ἐπιμὶξ ἵππων τε καὶ ἀνδρῶν, 'the noisy stream was filled pell-mell with both horses and men', 16. 167 ἵππους τε καὶ ἀνέρας, 17. 400 ἀνδρῶν τε καὶ ἵππων, cf. 8. 214, 10. 338, 17. 740, 19. 157; 9. 708 λαόν τε καὶ ἵππους, 11. 525 ἵπποι τε καὶ αὐτοί, etc.; in Old Persian, AmH 6 *huaspā humartiyā*, (Persia is a land) 'of good horses, of good men', cf. DPd 8, DSf 11, DSp 3, DZc 4; Yt. 10. 101 *aspaēca paiti vīraēca* . . . *aspa.vīraja*, (Mithra who is first to strike his club) 'at both horses and men . . . smiter of horse (and) man'; 19. 40 = Y. 9. 11 *aspō.garəm narə.garəm*, the 'horse-swallowing, man-swallowing' monster; Armenian *ayrewji, ayrowji* 'cavalry', literally 'man and horse' (*ayr* = ἀνήρ); Cic. *De officiis* 3. 116 *uiris equisque ut dicitur decertandum est*; Livy 3. 70. 6 *conficerent equos uirosque*, cf. 4. 33. 8, Mela 2. 86, Tac. *Ann.* 13. 57, etc.; *Y Gododdin* 745 *lledrudd llewyr a meirch a gŵr*, 'blood-stained throngs, both horses and men', cf. 1027; *Marwnad Cunedda* 24 'a swarm like an encircling hedge of men and horses' (trs. Koch); *Táin* (I) 2315 *cú* ⁊ *ech* ⁊ *dune*, 'hound and horse and man' (suffered alike in the slaughter), cf. (L) 3586 *formna bó, fer* ⁊ *ech roda slaidius ar cech leth*, 'the finest cattle, men and horses I slaughtered on every side'; *Hervarar saga* 14 *oc hió þá bæði menn oc hesta* . . . *enn dalir vóro fullir af hestom oc dauðom mǫnnom oc blóði*, 'and he hewed down both men and horses . . . and the dales were full of horses and dead men and blood'.

A poetic vocabulary for referring to horses developed at an early date. It is evidenced especially by parallel epithets and other predicates applied to horses in the Greek and Indo-Iranian texts.[61]

In the first place horses are typically swift.[62] The Vedic formula *áśvā(so)* . . . *āśávaḥ* 'swift horses' (RV 10. 78. 5, 119. 3; elsewhere in the instrumental plural and the accusative singular) shows exact etymological correspondence with Avestan *āsusca aspō, aspåŋhō* . . . *āsavō* (Yt. 13. 52 nom. sg., 17. 12 nom. pl.) and with Homeric ὠκέες ἵπποι, ὠκέας ἵππους, ἵππων ὠκειάων. An alternative Vedic expression of similar meaning is *ṛjrā́* . . . *áśvā* (dual, RV 1. 117. 14, 174. 5; 10. 22. 5), to which correspond the proper names Ṛjrā́śva- 'Swifthorse', Avestan Ərəzrāspa-; the cognate adjective in Greek is ἀργός, and

[60] On the Indo-Europeans and the horse see *EIEC* 273–9 with bibliography. On the formula 'horses and men' (mostly in this order) cf. É. Benveniste, *Bulletin of the School of Oriental Studies* 8 (1936), 406; J. Wackernagel, *Kl. Schr.* 435 f.; Schmitt (1967), 216.

[61] Cf. Schmitt (1967), 238–44; Durante (1976), 93 f.

[62] Schmitt (1967), 238–40; Schlerath (1968), ii. 162.

its application to horses has left an echo in the name of Menelaus' horse Podargos 'Swiftfoot' (*Il.* 23. 295). Achilles' horses Xanthos and Balios were born of the Harpy Podarge (not Podagre 'Gout', as printed in a recent book).

In the *Mahābhārata* the process of lexical substitution produces such variants as *śīghrair aśvaiḥ* 'with fast horses' (3. 6. 6), *śīghrair hayaiḥ* (3. 224. 17), *javanair aśvaiḥ* (3. 17. 16), *javanair hayaiḥ* (3. 233. 4), *hayān mahājavān* (3. 70. 4), much as in the *Iliad* we already find ταχέ' ἵππω (5. 356), ταχέες . . . ἵπποι (22. 464). Cú Chulainn's chariot was drawn by 'two swift horses' (*for dá n-echaib díana*, with the old Indo-European word for 'horse', *Táin* (I) 2287). In Senyllt's hall there used to be 'swift horses' (*mythfeirch, Y Gododdin* 567, cf. 3 *meirch mwth*, 1051 *meirch rhagfuan*). In a poem in the Book of Taliesin it is *meirch canholic* (*Cad Goddeu* 28).

The father of Achilles' horses was the West Wind, and they 'flew with the winds', that is, ran as fast as the wind (*Il.* 16. 149, cf. 19. 415). We meet 'wind-swift' horses also in the Rigveda (*vā́taraṃhas-*, 1. 181. 2; 8. 34. 17; cf. 1. 118. 1) and in the Indian epics.[63] Rostam's horse in the *Shāh-nāma* is 'wind-footed', like those which Tros rode.[64] The same token of speed is cited in Irish literature. Manannan's horse was as swift as the wind, while Cú Chulainn's chariot-team outstripped the wind and birds in flight.[65]

The Homeric gods' horses are 'swift-flying', ὠκυπέται (*Il.* 8. 42, 13. 24), and Achilles' horses that 'flew with the winds' were of divine birth. But ordinary horses too are said to 'fly' in the formula

> μάστιξεν δ' ἐλάαν, τὼ δ' οὐκ ἄκοντε πετέσθην.
>
> He goaded them to drive, and they flew with a will. (*Il.* 10. 530, etc.)

Similarly in the *Mahābhārata*, with the same word for 'fly':

> And as soon as the two of them had mounted
> that chariot the whole world adored, Dāśārha
> whipped up his thoroughbreds, effortlessly swift,
> and immediately they flew forward (*utpetur*), dragging
> the wondrous vehicle behind them, ridden
> by the Yadu bull and the two Pāṇḍavas. (10. 13. 7 f., trs. W. J. Johnson)

Cf. 3. 69. 21, 'Bāhuka prodded those excellent steeds in the right way, and they assumed their highest speed and seemed to fly in the air', and 3. 18. 2, 20. 9, 158. 25. In Venetic there is an adjective *ekvopetar(i)s* (*ekup-*), which some

[63] *MBh.* 2. 48. 22; 3. 69. 22; 5. 183. 17; *hayair vātasamair jave*, 2. 45. 56; *hayair vātajavaiḥ*, 3. 72. 9; *vātavegāḥ*, 5. 55. 12; *vāyostulyavegāḥ*, ibid. 13; *Rm.* 2. 35. 14.

[64] *Hymn. Aphr.* 217 ἵπποισιν ἀελλοπόδεσσιν ὀχεῖτο, cf. Simon. *PMG* 515, etc.; Levy (1967), 199.

[65] *Aided chlainne Tuirenn* (ed. E. O'Curry, *Atlantis* 4 (1863), 163); *Táin* (I) 764, cf. 2285.

have derived from a postulated **ekvopeś* 'cavalier', literally 'horse-flyer'.[66] In the Armenian oral epic a horse is described as flying like a homing pigeon (*Sassountsy David* 267).

Other epithets applied to horses in the Rigveda are *vājambharā́-* 'prize-winning' (1. 60. 5, al.) and *vŕ̥ṣapāṇi-* or *vīḷupāṇí-* 'strong-hooved' (6. 75. 7; 1. 38. 11; 7. 73. 4). Corresponding compounds are found in the *Iliad*: ἀεθλοφόροι ... ἵπποι (22. 162, al.; -φορος = *-bhará-*); κρατερώνυχας ἵππους (5. 329, al.). We noted in Chapter 3 that gods' horses have golden manes in both the Rigveda and the Greek epic.

Peleus, Tydeus, Nestor, and a couple of other heroes of the generation before the Trojan War bear the title ἱππότα, apparently a fossilized vocative used as a nominative in the epic language. It obviously connects them with horses, but as a derivative of ἱππο- the form is problematic. Rüdiger Schmitt compares Latin *eques equit-*. Others explain it as a haplology for *ἱπποπότης, or in Mycenaean **ikk^{w}opotās*, 'master of horses'. Except for the stem (for which compare δεσπότης) this would correspond exactly to Vedic *áśvapati-*, which is a title of Indra in RV 8. 21. 3 and found later as a personal name (*Rm.* 2. 1. 6, al.). If the latter view is correct, the inference is that there was a Graeco-Aryan poetic compound **ekwopoti-* (or the like), applicable to gods and heroes.[67]

In early Welsh literature the heroic status of horses is so far acknowledged that there is in the Book of Taliesin a poem, the so-called *Song of Horses* (*Canu y meirch*), which is a catalogue of heroes and their steeds, and several sections of the *Triads of the Island of Britain* are devoted to horses that were notable under one rubric or another.[68]

The close relationship presupposed between heroes and their horses is such that they can speak to each other at critical junctures. This motif—like the historical mastery of the horse—is the common property of Indo-Europeans and the Turkic peoples of central Asia. The horses are represented as intelligent, indeed wise, as well as brave and loyal, and often gifted with mantic knowledge.[69]

Even the *Iliad* poet, who on the whole avoids anything fantastic, admits an exchange of words between Achilles and Xanthos; the noble creature utters a well-founded prophecy of his master's death (19. 399–424). In an Eddic lay Skirnir tells his horse that it is time to go on a journey, and what the two possible outcomes are (*Skírnismál* 10). In another, Gudrun asks Sigurd's horse for news of him. 'Grani drooped his head then, hid it in the grass, the horse

66 Lejeune (1974), 85 f., 116, 120–3.

67 Cf. Schmitt (1967), 23, 130 f.

68 *Triads* 38–46; R. Bromwich (as n. 50), xcviii–cvii, 97–121.

69 See C. M. Bowra, *Heroic Poetry* (London 1952), 157–70 (speech: 165–70). Some out-of-the-way examples are cited by Grimm (1883–8), 392.

knew that his master was not living' (*Guðrúnarkviða B* 5). In several of the Russian *byliny* a hero speaks to the horse he is riding and receives a reply.[70] In a Serbo-Croat poem there is at least a one-sided dialogue. Halil speaks to his horse; 'it was a beast and could not speak, but it understood all he said' (*SCHS* ii, no. 16. 285–90; cf. no. 30. 488 ff.). The Nart heroes of Ossetic legend converse with their horses, who are capable of giving them good advice and information (Sikojev (1985), 200, 227, 231, 303–7). There are similar episodes in *Sassountsy David* (158 f., 262, 267 f.).

Chariots

The horses that are on speaking terms with humans are normally ridden horses. The *Iliad* passage is exceptional in that Xanthos is a chariot horse. It is typical of the Indo-Iranian, Greek, and Irish traditions that horses are not ridden but serve in pairs to pull chariots in which warriors travel about with a charioteer and ride to battle.

Despite the concurrence of far western with eastern evidence, this cannot be an early Indo-European practice, because, as I have noted elsewhere, the chariot with spoked wheels, light enough to be drawn at speed by horses, was not invented until shortly before 2000 BCE. It first appears in the Sintashta culture of the southern Urals. Chariot warfare spread widely in the Middle East in the first half of the second millennium and progressively into central Europe. The usefulness of chariots in battle was that they served as mobile platforms for archers, who discharged showers of arrows at the enemy and made a rapid withdrawal. After some centuries effective counter-tactics were found, and this form of warfare went out of fashion.[71]

It was typical of Vedic India, and the Indian epics, despite many fantastic elements, still give a more faithful picture than the Homeric tradition. Chariots are a constant feature of Homeric battle scenes, but their earlier function is more or less forgotten and they serve essentially as transport and escape vehicles for heroes who fight with spears and sword. Classical accounts of Gaulish and British chariot tactics are very similar to the Homeric.[72] In the Irish texts too chariots are much mentioned, but there is no archery and it

[70] Chadwick (1932), 54. 28 ff., 84. 114 ff., 112. 322 ff.

[71] Cf. Robert Drews, *The End of the Bronze Age* (Princeton 1993), 104–34; *EIEC* 627 f., 633; P. Raulwing in Meid (1998), 523–46; id., *Horses, Chariots and Indo-Europeans* (*Archaeolingua*, series minor, Budapest 2000); M. A. Littauer and J. H. Crouwel, *Selected Writings on Chariots, Other Early Vehicles, Riding and Harness* (Leiden 2002).

[72] On chariots in the Indic texts see Drews (as n. 71), 125; Brockington (1998), 176–8, 405 f.; on the Britons, Caes. *Bell. Gall.* 4. 33; Gauls, Diod. 5. 29. 1–3 (Posidonius fr. 169 Th.); Prop. 4. 10. 39–44.

is not clear what use they are in battle except as transport. Archaeological evidence for chariots in Ireland is in fact very slight, and some scholars have supposed that the part they play in battle narrative represents traditional memory of continental Celtic practice in the earlier Iron Age. In Campanile's view, 'les auteurs des sagas ont rappelé à la vie un objet archaïque, antérieur à la migration qui celtisa l'Irlande'.[73] Yet these Irish writers have a clear notion of a chariot's component parts, its breaking points, and the kinds of accident liable to befall its riders.

There certainly seems to have been an element of chariot lore carried along in the Irish heroic tradition. A. Hiltebeitel has noted that the relationship between the hero and his charioteer is very similar in the Irish and Indian traditions (and this is largely applicable to the Homeric picture too). The charioteer serves not just as the hero's driver but as his herald, friend, and confidant, providing him with advice, praise, or criticism as appropriate. Campanile has observed a further parallel of a technical nature: a verse of the Atharvaveda (8. 8. 23) indicates that the charioteer stood on the right side of the chariot, the fighter on the left, and Irish terminology points to the same arrangement.[74]

Indo-Iranian and Greek comparisons throw up certain parallelisms of diction. There is no common word for chariot: Vedic has *rátha-* (the cognate of Latin *rota*, 'wheel', Old High German *rad*, etc.); Avestan has both *raθa-* and *vāṣ̌a-* (from **varta-*); the Homeric words are ὄχεα (neuter plural), ἅρμα, and δίφρος (the last being properly the superstructure). But both Vedic and Greek (if we include the language of the tragedians) form phrases such as 'well-horsed chariot' (RV 1. 117. 2; 4. 45. 7 *ráthaḥ suáśvaḥ*; Eur. *Andr.* 1019 εὐίππους ὄχους); 'fine-yoked chariot' (RV 1. 113. 14, 117. 15; 4. 14. 3 *suyújā ráthena*; Eur. *Andr.* 277 ἅρμα ... καλλιζυγές); 'chariot with yoke of four (horses)' (RV 2. 18. 1 *rátho ... cáturyugaḥ*; Eur. *Hel.* 1039 τετραζύγων ὄχων; cf. Vd. 7. 41 *vāṣ̌əm caθruyuxtəm*). Indra's chariot-horses (*rathíyāso áśvāḥ*) are to bring him on his 'well-wheeled' (*sucakré*: 'chariot' is understood, RV 6. 37. 3, cf. 10. 85. 20; *MBh.* 2. 54. 4); the cognate adjective is used of a wagon in *Od.* 6. 58 ἀπήνην ... εὔκυκλον, [Aesch.] *PV* 710 ἐπ' εὐκύκλοις ὄχοις (cf. *Il.* 8. 438, 12. 58 ἐΰτροχον ἅρμα).[75] Someone equipped with a good chariot is *surátha-* (RV 1. 22. 2, al.), εὐάρματος (Pind. *Pyth.* 2. 5, *Isth.* 2. 17).

[73] Campanile (1990a), 261. For a thorough discussion of the question see J. P. Mallory in *Mír Curad*, 451–64.

[74] A. Hiltebeitel in E. C. Polomé (ed.), *Homage to Georges Dumézil* (*JIESM* 3, 1982), 92–104; Campanile (1990b), 15–19. However, there may have been both left-hand and right-hand chariots; see Drews (as n. 71), 126.

[75] Durante (1976), 94.

A recurring epithet of Homeric chariots is ποικίλος 'bright-coloured', sometimes with the addition of χαλκῶι 'with bronze', but sometimes on its own (*Il.* 5. 239, 10. 501, 13. 537, 14. 431), where it may be taken to refer to painting. In the Linear B tablets from Knossos the colour of chariots (vermilion, purple, red) is often noted, and it may have been significant for identification in battle.[76] Dawn's chariot in RV 7. 75. 6 is *viśvapíś-*, 'all-decorated', as is Mithra's in Yt. 10. 124 *vīspōpaēsa-*, where *-píś-*, *-paēsa-* represent the same root **peiḱ* as does ποικ-ίλος. In Dawn's case the colours are of course those of the morning sky, but the metaphor of the painted chariot no doubt had a grounding in real life.[77]

BATTLE NARRATIVE: SETTING THE SCENE

The narrator of a major conflict needs to give an account of the forces involved. Even if he is actually going to concentrate on the deeds of a small number of individuals, their achievement is the more significant, the greater the scale of the action as a whole. And their fame is not just a function of the numbers of men they kill, but of who they kill and in the context of what legendary event.

Hence a typical element in traditional battle narratives is a catalogue of fighting groups and their leaders. As examples we may refer to the Homeric catalogues covering both the Achaean and the Trojan confederations (*Il.* 2. 484–877); the long section of the *Udyogaparvan* (*MBh.* 5. 161–9) devoted to listing and evaluating the warriors and paladins who are to take part in the great war; the catalogue of the monkey contingents in the *Rāmāyaṇa* (4. 38. 10–35); the musters of the Ulstermen and the men of Ireland in the *Táin* ((I) 3455–97, 3948–81); the review of armies in *Sassountsy David* 314 f.[78]

Of course, if the conflict is conceived as involving thousands of men, there is no question of listing them all, only the notables. The poet of the *Iliad* asks the Muses to recite the names of the Danaans' leaders and commanders, confessing that 'as for the multitude, I could not tell of them or name them, not even if I had ten tongues and ten mouths, an unbreakable voice and a heart of bronze' (2. 487–90). This explicit exclusion of the masses from catalogues is routine in the *Mahābhārata*, and paralleled also in the *Táin*.

[76] M. Lejeune, *Minos* 9 (1968), 29; Drews (as n. 71), 126.

[77] Another divine chariot in the Rigveda is that of Ṛtam (Truth, Right), with which Watkins has compared Simon. eleg. 11. 12 ἅρμα . . . Δίκ[ης (*Ériu* 30 (1979), 181 ff. = (1994), 626 ff.; (1995), 16). It should be noted, however, that there is an ancient variant reading τέρμα.

[78] Cf. McCone (1990), 51; West (1997), 208. On catalogues more generally cf. H. M. and N. K. Chadwick, *The Growth of Literature*, i (Cambridge 1932), 276–83.

The names of the Snakes are very many, ascetic—I shall not mention all of them. But hear from me the chief ones (*MBh.* 1. 31. 4, cf. 52. 2 f.).

At this war of the Kurus many hundreds of thousands of kings foregathered, eager to fight in the battle. Their names are innumerable—not in a myriad years could their number be counted. But the chiefs have been mentioned, by whom hangs this tale (1. 57. 105 f.).

There are many thousands, myriads, and millions of warriors in your army, but hear from me the principal ones (5. 162. 18).

Their number is not known nor is it possible to count how many of the common soldiery fell there, but their leaders alone have been reckoned. Here follow their names (*Táin* (I) 2318).

Sometimes the number of an army is conveyed not with a vague reference to thousands and myriads, but by means of a multiplication sum, as in *Il.* 8. 562 f., 'a thousand fires burned on the plain, and by each one sat fifty men in the firelight' (cf. 2. 123–8). In a Norse heroic poem Angantyr asks Gizurr the size of the Hun army, and Gizurr tells him, 'Great is their multitude. There are six regiments of men; in each regiment, five Thousands; in each Thousand, thirteen Hundreds; in each Hundred, men reckoned four' (*Hunnenschlacht* 32; cf. Saxo 5. 7. 4 p. 130). And in an Irish text: 'A question: what is the number of the slain?' Lug said to Lóch. 'I do not know the number of peasants and rabble. As to the number of Fomorian lords and nobles and champions and over-kings, I do know: $3 + 3 \times 20 + 50 \times 100$ men $+ 20 \times 100 + 3 \times 50 + 9 \times 5 + 4 \times 20 \times 1000 + 8 + 8 \times 20 + 7 + 4 \times 20 + 6 + 4 \times 20 + 5 + 8 \times 20 + 2 + 40$, including the grandson of Nét with 90 men. That is the number of the slain of the Fomorian over-kings and high nobles who fell in the battle' (*Cath Maige Tuired* 724–41, trs. Gray).

In the so-called Teichoskopia of the *Iliad* (3. 161–244) the poet avails himself of a means to attach physical descriptions to the major Greek heroes. Priam stands on the wall of Troy with Helen, describes one after another of the men he can see below, and asks her to identify them, which she does. The same narrative technique is used in Indic, Celtic, and Norse texts. The most similar situation appears in the *Rāmāyaṇa*, where the king stands on a vantage-point and the leaders of the attacking army are pointed out by description and identified to him (6. 17–19, cf. 47. 11 ff.; cf. *MBh.* 15. 32). Dialogue scenes in which a series of heroes are described by one speaker and identified by the other are typical of the longer Irish sagas.[79] A variant of the

[79] Cf. *Táin* (I) 3205–82, 3589–3861; *Fled Bricrenn* 44–52; *Mesca Ulad* 33–47; *Togail bruidne Dá Derga* 75–140; Thurneysen (1921), 61.

technique is seen in the Welsh *Dream of Rhonabwy* (pp. 4–11 Richards), where the narrator himself describes a series of persons who come to Rhonabwy's attention, and in each case Rhonabwy asks someone who this is. In *Laxdœla saga* 63 Helgi's swain returns from a scouting foray to report that he has seen a company of men not far away who look like outsiders. He describes each one in turn, and Helgi is able to identify them all.

Sometimes it is determined before the battle begins which hero will fight which. In the Homeric Theomachy the gods are paired off against each other in advance (*Il.* 20. 67–74), and the actual battle conforms to the programme stated. In Aeschylus' *Seven Against Thebes*, perhaps following the model of the older epic *Thebaid*, a scout reports who is leading the assault on each of Thebes' seven gates, and Eteocles decides in each case which of his own men is to face the attacker; he himself will fight the ringleader, his own brother Polynices. There is a remarkable parallel in the *Rāmāyaṇa*. In 6. 21 a report comes to Rāvaṇa on the attackers of his city, concluding (35) 'So I have described the whole army of monkeys stationed on Mount Suvela; it is for you to decide what is to be done!' (cf. Aesch. *Sept.* 650–2). Then in 6. 28 scouts report to Rāma on which leaders are defending which gates, and Rāma names the leaders who will fight them. He himself will fight Rāvaṇa, as one of seven fighting in human form. Other passages in Indian epic where heroes are assigned specific opponents are *MBh.* 5. 161. 4–10; 6. 77. 11 ff.; 8. 31. 5 ff. In a story in *Acallam na Senórach* (p. 55 Dooley–Roe) the warrior Caílte enquires who is the most dangerous of the foes about to be fought, and on learning that it is Lir, declares that he will stand against him. Then Derg asks who are the next most dangerous, and when Donn and Dub are identified, he says he will oppose them.

Another typical preliminary to battle is the arming scene. Heroes put on their armour and take up their weapons. Each piece is mentioned in turn, often with details of its form, material, decoration, or history. Homeric examples are *Il.* 3. 328–39 (Paris and Menelaus), 11. 17–46 (Agamemnon), 16. 130–44 (Patroclus), 19. 364–98 (Achilles). From Indian epic we may quote this specimen:

> At their various positions the kings and princes put on their glistening and colourful armour, well worth the honour they paid it. Virāṭa's favourite brother Śatānīka donned a golden cuirass with an underlay of diamond-hard iron. Madirāśva, Śatānīka's junior, put on a hard, solid-iron coat of mail which was beautifully plated. The king of the Matsya himself wore a well-nigh impenetrable armour with a hundred suns, a hundred circles, a hundred dots, and a hundred eyes . . . [etc.] (*MBh.* 4. 30. 9–12; cf. 9. 31. 54).

Of Hiltibrant and Hadubrant we just hear briefly that

son and father   arranged their armour,
readied their war-guises,   girded their swords on,
the heroes, over their mail   as they rode to the battle.   (*Hildebrandslied* 4–6)

The arming of Cú Chulainn and his charioteer Láeg is described at much greater length (*Táin* (I) 2189–2244). Láeg's black mantle has had a distinguished career: 'Simon Magus had made it for Darius King of the Romans, and Darius had given it to Conchobar, and Conchobar had given it to Cú Chulainn, who gave it to his charioteer'.

THE TIME FRAME

Fighting normally takes place during the daylight hours, beginning early in the morning and continuing until it grows dark.

There was a great battle, Saturday morning,
from the time the sun rose till it set.[80]

In the *Iliad* (8. 53–6, 11. 1–14) as in the *Mahābhārata* (5. 183. 27; 6. 52. 1, 56. 1, 65. 1, 71. 1), dawn brings the renewal of the battle. It is a cliché of early Welsh poetry that the warriors start at dawn: 'Catraeth's men set out at daybreak' (*Canu Taliesin* 2. 1, trs. Clancy (2003), 39, cf. *Y Gododdin* 84, etc.); 'when Cadwal attacked, he used to raise up the battle-cry with the green dawn' (*Y Gododdin* 207, cf. 406); 'he arose early in the morning, when the centurions hasten in the mustering of the army' (ibid. 880).[81]

Homeric warriors may then expect to fight 'all day' (*Il.* 11. 279, 17. 384, 18. 453, 19. 168), 'till sunset' (19. 162). 'The sun set, and the noble Achaeans ceased from harsh battle' (18. 241 f.). Nightfall brings the duel of Ajax and Hector to an abrupt end (7. 282 = 293). Similarly in the *Mahābhārata* (7. 31. 77, 50. 1 f.) the armies retire when the sun sets, and in Ireland too that is the time to stop fighting (*Táin* (L) 3112 f., 3146, 3235).

But it need not be an undifferentiated slog from morning to night. Sometimes the narrator wants to demarcate different phases of the battle. Then he divides the day into two parts, with a transition in the middle of the day or the early afternoon.

While it was morning and the divine day was waxing,
the missiles fastened on both armies, and the horde kept falling;
but when the Sun was straddling the mid-heaven,
then father Zeus held up his golden scale-pans . . .   (*Il.* 8. 66–9, cf. 16. 777–80)

[80] *Gweith Argoet Llwyfein* 2 (Book of Taliesin 60), trs. Clancy (2003), 42.
[81] Cf. also ibid. 861, 915, 976; Rowland (1990), 414 st. 7ab = 456 st. 31ab.

Similarly in the *Mahābhārata* midday may mark the end of one phase of the battle (6. 45. 1, 55. 3 'after the forenoon had passed away, and the sun in his westward course had completed a portion of his path'; 68. 12, 73. 53, 80. 1, 85. 14). In the Book of Leinster version of the *Táin*, when Cú Chulainn has his great fight with Fer Dia, they go at each other 'from the grey of early morning to the middle of the day', neither gaining an advantage. Cú Chulainn then proposes a break and a change of weapons, telling Fer Dia that he has the choice of weapons until nightfall. They continue, and hurl their spears at each other 'from the middle of the day until the evening sunset'. The next day they fight without interruption 'from the grey of early morning until the evening sunset', and the third day likewise. At each day's end one proposes to the other that they break off, and the other agrees, 'if it is time'. On the fourth day they battle from dawn to noon; 'and when midday came, the rage of the combatants grew fiercer and they drew closer to each other'. This leads in to the concluding phase in which Fer Dia is killed.[82] When the Niflungs defended themselves against Atli's men, 'most of the morning they fought, till the mid day passed, | all the dawn and the day's beginning' (*Atlamál* 53). The Serbo-Croat and Armenian oral poets use the same convention. In Salih Ugljanin's poem on the Captivity of Đulić Ibrahim we twice hear that two forces 'cut one another to pieces until midday', 'hacked at one another a whole day till noon', when a dark cloud covered the area and obscured everything, and the same thing happens in a poem by Đemail Zogić.[83] And in *Sassountsy David* (73), 'they battled till noon, | and from noon till evening'. David fights Baron Asdghig until midday (319).

As in the *Táin* the warriors agree, when the due time comes, to stop fighting, so Hector, when the herald Idaios stops his duel with Ajax because night is falling, says, 'let us then cease fighting for today, as it is night; we will fight again at a later time' (7. 288–93). Elsewhere he tells the Trojans and allies, 'now night has stopped the fighting . . . Early in the morning we will arm ourselves and renew the battle' (8. 502/530 f.; cf. 18. 267/277/303). We find a similar programmatic pronouncement from Bhīṣma in *MBh.* 6. 60. 64–7.

Sometimes predictions are made of what will happen in the following day's battle.[84] Confident warriors declare 'you will see me tomorrow (doing so and so)' (*MBh.* 7. 53. 32, 37, 40, 43–5, 48; cf. *Rm.* 3. 26. 2; 4. 12. 33; 6. 333*. 20). Similarly Sohrab in the *Shāh-nāma*: 'tomorrow, when (Rostam) enters

[82] *Táin* (L) 3098–3294. Cf. also *Mesca Ulad* 66 (1006 Watson); *Acallam na Senórach* p. 55 Dooley–Roe.

[83] *SCHS* ii, no. 4. 1633, 1645; no. 24. 1296; trs. A. B. Lord in *SCHS* i. 111, 261.

[84] For example *Il.* 8. 535; *MBh.* 5. 160. 14; *Beowulf* 2939; *Táin* (L) 4584.

the contest with me, you will see the halter placed about his neck'. And Kamus: 'on the summit of the mountain tomorrow you will see a mound of dead Iranian warriors'.[85] The 'you will see' idiom is found also in the *Iliad*, when Agamemnon reproaches Menestheus and Odysseus for apparently hanging back from the battle line, and Odysseus retorts angrily, 'you will see, if you care to, the father of Telemachus mixing with the front line of the Trojans', whereupon Agamemnon soothes him and apologizes (4. 336–63). There is a very similar encounter in *MBh.* 5. 73–5. Keśava goads Bhīma with insinuations of cowardice, and the hero replies indignantly, saying 'you shall, when the crowded battle goes on, on the day of bloodshed, see the elephant and chariot drivers annihilated! You and all the world shall see me furiously finishing off brave bulls of the barons, pulling away the best of the best!'

Night is in general the time for sleeping and a break in the action. But more than once in the *Iliad* we find the motif that 'everyone else was asleep, but X did not sleep: he pondered in his heart . . .' (2. 1, 10. 1, 24. 677). It is a mechanism for introducing a new initiative into the action. In Book 10 it leads to a night raid on the Trojan allies' camp by two heroes, Odysseus and Diomedes. There is a remarkable parallel in the tenth book of the *Mahābhārata*, the *Sauptikaparvan.* Night comes, others sleep,

> But Droṇa's son, O Bhārata, overpowered
> by shame and wrath, could not sleep . . .

The man in question, Aśvatthāman, conceives a night attack to massacre the sleeping enemy, wakes his companions, and debates the plan with them (*MBh.* 10. 1. 32 ff., trs. Johnson). Objections are raised, but he will not be put off, and he sets out with two other heroes. They enter the enemy camp, cause havoc and slaughter, and return safely. The theme of a night attack in which enemy chieftains are killed in their sleep recurs in a lying story in the *Rāmāyaṇa* (6. 22. 18–34). The initial situation of the single wakeful ponderer is paralleled in an Eddic fragment (*Brot af Sigurðarkviðu* 12):

> All of them slept   when they came to their beds:
> only Gunnar was awake,   longer than all . . .

However, he is reflecting on something that has happened, not on a plan for action.

[85] Levy (1967), 77, 133.

SPEECHES

Altercations

Heroic battle narrative in the Indo-European traditions is not just an account of tactical movements, blows delivered, wounds sustained, bloody deaths. It contains a considerable amount of dialogue. A significant encounter between two warriors normally begins with a spirited exchange of words.[86]

When a hero is faced by a single opponent and is not busy felling anonymous multitudes, he will want to know who it is, if they have not met before. As noted in the last chapter, the question 'who are you?' is common in this situation. It may be combined with an assurance that whoever he is, he is doomed, as when Diomedes accosts Glaucus (*Il.* 6. 123–7, cf. 21. 150 f.):

> Who are you, my good fellow, of mortal men?. . .
> Unfortunate are they whose sons come against my fury.

Similarly Ashkabus to Rostam in the *Shāh-nāma*: 'What is your name? Who is it that must weep over your headless body?' (Levy (1967), 135).

Each is confident of victory and ready to denigrate his antagonist. He may warn him not to fight against his superiors (*Il.* 21. 486, cf. Hes. *Op.* 210; *MBh.* 7. 142. 14; 8. 17. 94), or remind him of a previous occasion when he was put to flight (*Il.* 20. 187–94; *MBh.* 8. 26. 66–9). He may boast, before or after dealing the fatal blow, that his foe's body will be eaten by the birds and dogs.[87] If he is hit by an arrow, he may dismiss it as a feeble effort: 'I think nothing of it, as if a woman had hit me or a silly child; blunt is the missile of a worthless coward' (*Il.* 11. 389 f.); 'you scratch me with arrows soft as flowers' (*Rm.* 3. 26. 12).

Often one of the combatants sums the matter up with a statement to the effect that 'now either I am going to kill you, or you me'. Sokos, son of Hippasos, tells Odysseus 'Today either you will exult over the two sons of Hippasos after killing the men we are and stripping us of their armour, or you will be struck by my spear and lose your life' (*Il.* 11. 431–3). 'Defeat us and win renown, or we will defeat you' (*MBh.* 6. 70. 14, cf. 77. 9; 8. 22. 30, 26. 52,

[86] For example *Il.* 5. 630–54, 7. 225–43, 20. 176–258, 21. 148–60, 22. 248–72; *MBh.* 6. 104. 40 ff.; 7. 117. 2 ff.; 8. 17. 49 ff., 42. 22 ff.; 9. 55. 27 ff.; *Rm.* 3. 28. 1–29. 15; *Shāh-nāma*, Levy (1967), 56, 72, 134 f., al.; *Hildebrandslied* 7–62; *Atlamál* 42 f.; Saxo 1. 8. 3 p. 26; *Táin* (I) 3015–80; Sikojev (1985), 294 f.; West (1997), 214–16; Miller (2000), 232–8.

[87] *Il.* 11. 452–4, 13. 831 f., 16. 836, 22. 335, 354; *Beowulf* 2940 f.; Saxo 1. 4. 5 p. 15, 5. 3. 4 p. 113; Sikojev (1985), 295. Also in the Epic of Gilgamesh and the Old Testament: West (1997), 215 f.

34. 8, 50. 19; *Rm.* 3. 26. 4). 'We shall not part like this until I carry off your head or until I leave my head with you' (*Táin* (I) 1350). 'Now my son will kill me, or I him' (*Hildebrandslied* 53 f.). 'Let us see which of us will be victor today and win armour' (ibid. 60–2). 'Today you will either die or have long fame among men' (*Waldere* A 8–11). Says Marko Kraljević to Musa the Highwayman, 'Today either you will perish, or Marko will perish' (Salih Ugljanin in *SCHS* i. 362. 96 f.). Sibdag Dev invites Mher into his tent and tells him 'Eat and drink until daybreak; then we will see which one of us God will favour' (*Sassountsy David* 130). In other cases the hero declares among his own companions that he is resolved to do or die.[88]

Before Paris embarks on the duel with Menelaus by which, it has been agreed, the whole issue of the war will be settled, his father Priam observes to all and sundry that 'Zeus knows, and the other immortals, for which of the two death is the fated outcome' (*Il.* 3. 308). Similarly Byrhtnoth calls his men to the battle, saying 'God only knows who (at the end) may control this battlefield' (*Battle of Maldon* 94 f.). The parallel is not of great significance, but it provides an opportunity to remark the expression 'God (only) knows', which is shared at least by Greek, Old English, Welsh, and Lithuanian.[89]

Exhortations

The supporting troops often need verbal encouragement from their leaders. Certain rhetorical elements and formulations recur in more than one tradition.

Homeric leaders regularly call upon their men to 'bethink yourselves of your courage' (*Il.* 6. 112, 8. 174, al., μνήσασθε δὲ θούριδος ἀλκῆς), and the same expression is used in describing warriors who faced up to the enemy (11. 566 μνησάσκετο θούριδος ἀλκῆς, etc.). A corresponding idiom is used in Old English verse. Hengest exhorts the Jutes in the Finnsburh fragment (11) *hicgeaþ on ellen*, 'think on courage' (cf. *Exodus* 218, *Maldon* 4). Beowulf grappling with Grendel *gemunde mægenes strenge*, 'bethought himself of the strength of his power'.[90]

[88] Cf. *Beowulf* 1490 f. 'I will win myself fame with (this sword) Hrunting, or death will take me', cf. 636–8, 2535–7, *Battle of Maldon* 208, 291–3; Saxo 2. 7. 4 p. 53, 3. 5. 2 p. 74.

[89] Ζεὺς οἶδεν, *Od.* 15. 523, cf. 14. 119, *Il.* l.c., Pind. fr. 94b. 33; θεὸς οἶδε, Pl. *Phdr.* 266b, *Rep.* 517b; *God āna wāt, Maldon* l.c.; *Meotud* (Fate) *āna wāt, Maxims A* 29, *B* 58; 'no one knows, save God and the world's sages | and diligent prophets', Cynddelw i. 95 st. 6 (trs. Clancy (2003), 146); Grimm (1883–8), 16 f.; Alfred Senn, *Handbuch der litauischen Sprache* (Heidelberg 1966), i. 307.

[90] *Beowulf* 1270, cf. 1530, 2678, 2689, *Maldon* 225. A similar phrase is found in an Old Babylonian hymn: West (1997), 228.

As Hector presses the Achaeans back towards their ships, Agamemnon shouts to them and reproaches them, asking them what has happened to the boasts they made when they were feasting and drinking in safety in Lemnos, when they swore they were supreme and could each stand up to a hundred or two hundred Trojans (*Il.* 8. 228–34; cf. 20. 83–5). Ælfwine urges the English in similar terms: 'Let us call to mind those declarations we often uttered over mead, when from our seat we heroes in hall would put up pledges about tough fighting' (*Maldon* 212–14). In Saxo's Latin version of the lost *Biarkamál* the Danish warrior Hjalti rouses his sleeping comrades to resist the treacherous attack of Hjorvard, and in the course of a long rhetorical address he says:

omnia quae poti temulento prompsimus ore
fortibus edamus animis, et uota sequamur
per summum iurata Iouem superosque potentes.

All those things we uttered in our cups from tipsy lips
let us deliver with valiant hearts, and follow the vows
we swore by Jupiter on high and the powers above.[91]

Other Homeric hortatory motifs find their parallels in the Indian epic. When Sarpedon sees his forces being worsted by Patroclus, he calls to them *αἰδώς, ὦ Λύκιοι· πόσε φεύγετε;* 'Shame, Lycians, where are you fleeing to?' (*Il.* 16. 422). Similarly Bhīṣma: 'Ye Kṣatriyas, where do ye go? This is not the duty of the righteous . . . Ye foremost of heroes, do not violate your pledges' (*MBh.* 6. 55. 79). When Agamemnon sees any of the Achaeans holding back from the fighting, he demands *τίφθ' οὕτως ἕστητε τεθηπότες ἠΰτε νεβροί;* 'Why do you stand thus in a daze like fawns?' (*Il.* 4. 243). And so Yudhiṣṭhira: 'Why do you stand thus as if stupefied?' (*MBh.* 7. 164. 50).

Not in Homer, but in the dramatists, urgent calls to attack or kill often take the form of an accumulation of imperative verbs with similar meaning: Ar. *Nub.* 1508 *δίωκε βάλλε παῖε*, *Av.* 365 *ἕλκε τίλλε παῖε δεῖρε*, Eur. *Or.* 1302 *φονεύετε καίνετε θείνετ' ὄλλυτε*; cf. Ar. *Ach.* 281–3, *Eq.* 247–52, [Eur.] *Rhes.* 675. This again is paralleled in the *Mahābhārata*, 7. 136. 9 *hata, praharatābhīta, vidhyata, vyavakṛntata*, 'slay, strike fearlessly, pierce, cut to pieces'; cf. 9. 11. 46, 17. 26. The redundancy is a natural expression of emotional intensity.[92]

[91] Lines 50–2, from Saxo 2. 7. 7 p. 54; *Edd. min.* 22.

[92] It can be explained in the same way in the Old Irish charm against worms adduced by Watkins (1995), 497 and 522, *gono míl, orgo míl, marbu míl*, 'I slay the creature, I slaughter the creature, I kill the creature'. (But see the remarks in Chapter 8 about repetition in spells.) John Penney reminds me of Tab. Iguv. VIb. 61 *tursitu tremitu, hondu holtu, ninctu nepitu, sonitu sauitu*, which 'would appear, whatever the precise meaning, to be hostile acts'. Cf. p. 328.

Poets knew many tales of heroes, and contrasts and comparisons between one and another must often have come into their minds. Rather than break the integrity of their narrative by referring to a different story in their own person, they preferred to let one of their speaking characters do it by way of admonition to another. Diomedes relates the myth of Lycurgus to Glaucus as a lesson against fighting an immortal (*Il.* 6. 130–40). Phoenix relates the story of Meleager to Achilles as an example of the danger of nursing wrath; he introduces it with the words 'Even so we used to hear of the famed deeds (κλέα) of the former warrior men' (9. 524 f.). Achilles tells Thetis he is not afraid of death, since not even Heracles could escape it (18. 115–21). So Narada consoled Srinjaya on the death of his son and urged the philosophical acceptance of death with a recital of great former kings who died (*MBh.* 12. 29. 13–136). Agamemnon chides Diomedes for his apparent lack of zeal for battle by comparing him unfavourably to his father Tydeus, who always liked to be in the forefront, 'as those who saw him say: I myself never met him or saw him, but they say he was outstanding'. A tale about Tydeus follows (*Il.* 4. 370–400). Similarly Gudrun goads her sons to avenge their sister, whom Jormunrekk had killed, by contrasting them with her brothers:

> You have not turned out like Gunnar and his brother,
> nor yet so minded as Hogni was:
> her you would have sought to avenge,
> if you had had the temperament of my brothers
> or the hard spirit of the Hun kings.[93]

EVENTS ON THE FIELD

Traditional battle narrative focuses on named individuals. But the larger picture that forms the background to the chief heroes' efforts needs to be sketched from time to time.

The moment when the combatants make contact is notable for the clash of shields.

> When they arrived and met in one place,
> they rammed together their (shield-)hides, spears, and furies of men
> bronze-corsleted; the bossed targes
> closed on each other, and a great clangour arose.
> (*Il.* 4. 446–9 = 8. 60–3, cf. 12. 339, Tyrt. 19. 14 f.)

[93] *Guðrúnarhvǫt* 3. Detter–Heinzel (1903), ii. 568, cite some parallels from the Sagas. For another Indic example of paraenetic exempla cf. *Rm.* 3. 62. 7–12.

Skapt mun gnesta, skiǫldr mun bresta, sing the Valkyries as they weave their web of war, 'shaft shall clash and shield crash' (*Darraðarlióð* 3, *Edd. min.* 59). Útsteinn challenges the sons of Úlf to battle with these words: 'Up we must rise, out we must go, and forcefully strike shields' (*Edd. min.* 71 no. 2). When Hiltibrant and Hadubrant have concluded their dialogue, they discharge their spears 'in sharp showers' (*scarpen scurim*) and then engage hand to hand: *do stoptû tosamane, staimbort chludun*, 'then they stepped together, the painted shields resounded'.[94]

We met the 'shower' or 'rain' metaphor in Chapter 2 in connection with various kennings for descending missiles. It is not restricted to the type of phrase discussed there. Besides the verse just quoted from the *Hildebrandslied*, it can be found in several passages of Old English poetry,[95] as well as in the *Mahābhārata*:

> tau tu tatra maheṣvāsau mahāmātrau mahārathau
> mahatā śaravarṣeṇa parasparam avarṣatām.
>
> Those two great bowmen then, great heroes, great car-warriors,
> rained on each other with a great arrow-rain. (*MBh.* 6. 112. 17)

In the Indian epics the clouds of arrows are often represented as obscuring the sun. Nothing like this occurs in Homer, but Hesiod describes the Hundred-Handers as 'over-shading' the Titans with their bombardment of three hundred rocks, that is, darkening their sky. There are occasional later Classical parallels, as well as an earlier Babylonian one.[96]

Common to Greek, Indic, and Serbo-Croat epic is the motif that at a certain stage it becomes difficult for the combatants to see what they are doing, either from the dust of battle or because of an abnormal darkness that descends on the battlefield.[97] 'Son did not recognize father, nor brother brother' (*MBh.* 6. 44. 2 f., 44 f., cf. 55. 37 f., 89. 23); and likewise in Đemail's

[94] *Hildebrandslied* 65, translation uncertain; some adopt Wackernagel's conjecture *chlubun*, 'clove'. Cf. also *Cath Cairnn Conaill*, ed. W. Stokes, *ZCP* 3 (1901), 208, 'when edges shall be against edges | and shields against shields'.

[95] *Elene* 117 *flāna scūras*, 'showers of arrows', cf. *Guthlac B* 1142. Snorri observes that 'missiles are frequently referred to as hail or snowfall or storm' (*Skáldsk.* 49).

[96] *MBh.* 4. 31. 6, 33. 18, 48. 19, 53. 26, 35; 5. 181. 31; 6. 42. 17, 51. 22, etc.; *Rm.* 3. 27. 9; Hes. *Th.* 716, Hdt. 7. 226, [Aesch.] fr. 199, Lucr. 2. 628; V. Pisani, *ZDMG* 103 (1953), 135 f. = Schmitt (1968), 166–8; West (1997), 297. In Herodotus it is the Persian archers who are said to blot out the sun, and Pisani, who overlooked the Hesiod passage, thought that it was a specifically Indo-Iranian image that the Greeks picked up from Persian ideology.

[97] *Il.* 5. 506 f., 16. 567, 17. 366–77 ~ 644–50; *MBh.* 3. 168. 14; 6. 42. 26, 53. 5, 67. 24; 7. 138; Salih Ugljanin in *SCHS* i. 111 and 193, Đemail Zogić, ibid. 261 f. (translations of texts in *SCHS* ii, no. 4. 1634 ff., 1646; no. 18. 1164 f.; no. 24. 1296 f.). Babylonian and Assyrian parallels in West (1997), 212.

poem, *da brat brata poznat' ne mogaše*, 'brother could not recognize brother'.[98] In this text the hero prays to God for a wind to disperse the fog, and God obliges, just as in *Il.* 17. 645 Ajax prays to Zeus to deliver the Achaeans from the obscuring mist, and Zeus does so.

We have noted in Chapter 2 the use in several traditions of compound polyptota to portray intense corporate action on the battlefield, 'spear against spear, shield against shield', and the like. Especially striking is the similarity between the *Iliad* and the *Mahābhārata* in the employment of the type

> Foot-soldiers were destroying foot-soldiers as they fled,
> and chariot-fighters chariot-fighters. (*Il.* 11. 150)
>
> Chariots engaged chariots, foot soldiers other foot soldiers,
> riders attacked riders, elephants elephants.
> (*MBh.* 4. 31. 8; further references on p. 115, n. 125)

The individual hero may find himself greatly outnumbered by the enemies confronting him, and yet hold his own. His situation may be underlined by the figure of speech that consists of juxtaposing the opposed terms 'alone' and 'many' or 'all': *Il.* 4. 388 *μοῦνος ἐὼν πολέσιν μετὰ Καδμείοισιν* 'being alone among the many Cadmeans', 15. 611 *πλεόνεσσι μετ' ἀνδράσι μοῦνον ἐόντα*, cf. *Od.* 20. 30, 22. 13; *Beowulf* 145 *āna wið eallum*, 'alone against them all', in this case not of a meritorious hero but of the savage Grendel; *Verba Scáthaige* 13 = *Tochmarc Emire* 79 *ba hóen fri slóg*, 'one against an army'.

It is a commonplace that the hero overcomes large numbers of opponents at one go.[99] Ajax 'pierced twelve men at close quarters before the ships' (*Il.* 15. 746). 'Seven Hogni hewed down with his keen sword, and the eighth he thrust into the hot fire' (*Atlakviða* 19). 'Eighteen, before they fell, they overcame, Bera's two boys and her brother' (*Atlamál* 53). Haldan, attacked by a gang of twelve men, made himself a club and killed them all; on another occasion Olo struck down the same number with his sword Løgthi (Saxo 7. 9. 11 p. 203; 7. 11. 10 p. 212). Cú Chulainn operates on a grander scale: 'a hundred warriors died by his hand . . . a hundred and forty-four kings were slain by him beside that same stream' (*Táin* (I) 1012); 'on each of the three nights that they were there, he killed a hundred of them' (1235, cf. 2067). Even more extravagant examples can be found in other Irish sagas and in the British tradition. 'Before the day [of his fatal battle] he was a hero in deeds . . .

[98] *SCHS* ii, no. 24. 1299. In *Sassountsy David* 102 f. Baghdasar fails to recognize his brother in the mêlée.

[99] Cf. West (1997), 212.

five fifties would fall before his blades, twenty hundred laid waste at one time' (*Y Gododdin* 47–51). According to Nennius (*Hist. Brittonum* 50) Arthur killed nine hundred men at Mt Badon. In the Armenian epic Sanasar faces sixty warriors and kills forty of them; his brother then arrives and kills the rest (*Sassountsy David* 86 f., 91). Nor does one have to look far in the *Mahābhārata* for parallels. 'Kuntī's son Yudhiṣṭhira struck down a thousand, while Bhīma showed seven hundred fighters the way to the other world. Nakula too dispatched seven hundred with his arrows, and the majestic Sahadeva three hundred champions' (4. 32. 24 f.).

It was noted in Chapter 8 that 'thrice nine' is a typical number in several contexts, and for men killed at one time. 'Three times he rushed at them . . . and thrice nine men he killed' (*Il.* 16. 785). 'Cú Chulainn cast the spear at him, and the butt-end towards him, so that it went through his head and through three times nine other men'.[100]

The Vedic gods are praised for their assistance in the Aryans' victories over the Dasyus, the earlier population of north India. In several places they are said to have made light for the Aryan: *urú jyótiś cakrathur Ā́riyāya*, 'you (Aśvins) made broad light for the Aryan' (RV 1. 117. 21); *ápāvṛṇor jyótir Ā́riyāya*, | *ní savyatáḥ sādi Dásyur Indra*, 'you uncovered the light for the Aryan, the Dasyu was left lying on the left, O Indra' (2. 11. 18); *tuváṃ Dásyūṁr ókaso Agna āja*, | *urú jyótir janáyann Ā́riyāya*, 'you drove the Dasyus from their homeland, generating broad light for the Aryan' (7. 5. 6). In prayers for help in battle Indra is bidden, *śévṛdham ádhi dhā dyumnám asmé*, 'make precious light for us' (1. 54. 11); *Índra dyumnáṃ suvárvad dhehi asmé*, 'Indra, make light as of the sun for us' (6. 19. 9). Durante has compared the Homeric use of 'light' as a metaphor for the relief or salvation that a hero brings to his troops when they are in difficulties on the battlefield. Ajax broke the Trojan line, φόως δ' ἑτάροισιν ἔθηκεν, 'and made light for his comrades' (*Il.* 6. 6). Here and in 16. 95 the verb is τίθημι, the cognate of *dhā* in the last two Vedic passages. Elsewhere the saviour 'becomes' a light for his side: αἴ κέν τι φόως Δαναοῖσι γένηαι, 'in the hope that you become a light for the Danaans' (8. 282, 11. 797, cf. 16. 39). The use of γενέσθαι may be linked with the causative participle from the same root in RV 7. 5. 6 *janáyan*, while the dative Δαναοῖσι is functionally parallel to *Ā́riyāya* in all of the first three passages. This was evidently a traditional form of expression in Graeco-Aryan heroic poetry.[101]

[100] *Aided Con Chulainn*, ed. W. Stokes, *RC* 3 (1876–8), 180; trs. Koch. Cf. *Togail bruidne Dá Derga* 1195, 1223, 1369 Knott; *Tochmarc Emire* 27, 86; *Mesca Ulad* 40; *Fled Bricrenn* 84.

[101] Cf. also *Il.* 15. 741, 17. 615; Durante (1976), 117 f.

Divine participation

The notion that war is a godless affair is modern. Ancient peoples assumed that their gods and their enemies' gods took an active interest in their armed struggles: what were gods for, if not to determine the outcome in situations of crisis and uncertainty? And as we noted in connection with hymns (Chapter 8), a god's help is generally conceived to require his coming to the scene. In the context of war, gods are sometimes represented as leading armies, sometimes as appearing in the midst of the fray, or as fighting disguised as mortals. The Hittite kings regularly claimed that the gods accompanied them to the field. Mursili II records in his annals that when he went to war 'my lady the Sun-goddess of Arinna and my lord Nergal and Mezzulla and all the gods ran before me'.[102] In the *Iliad* Ares and Enyo lead the Trojan battle-lines, or in another passage Apollo, while Poseidon leads the Achaeans (5. 592, 15. 307; 14. 384). The two armies depicted on Achilles' shield are led by Ares and Athena (18. 516).

The Indo-European divine Twins, the youthful sons of *Dyeus, were especially noted for appearing in battle on their white horses and bringing assistance or deliverance. I have cited the relevant Indic, Graeco-Roman, and Germanic material in the section about them in Chapter 4. It may be added that in a poem in the Book of Taliesin, celebrating the wars and cattle-raiding of Owein of Rheged, the young god Mabon is represented as appearing in battle on a white steed and killing all of the enemy within reach.[103]

In those traditions that tell of chariot fighting we here and there encounter the motif that a deity serves as the hero's charioteer.[104] Athena pushes Sthenelos out of Diomedes' chariot and takes up the reins and goad herself for the attack on Ares; the vehicle's wooden axle creaks under her weight (*Il.* 5. 835–40). The brigand Kyknos rides with his father Ares as driver ([Hes.] *Scut.* 59–61; cf. 441 *βρισάρματος . . . Ἄρης*). In the *Mahābhārata* Krishna serves as charioteer to Arjuna. In the great battle of Bråvalla or Bråvik between Harald Wartooth and his nephew Ring, Harald's charioteer Bruno turns out to be Odin in disguise. (The real Bruno has drowned elsewhere.) However, this cruel and cunning god is in fact supporting Ring, and no sooner has Harald realized who it is beside him than Odin dashes him out of the chariot and kills him (Saxo 8. 4. 8–9 pp. 219 f.).

Divine intervention is sometimes allowed to provide the ancient heroes with resources of kinds that real-life warriors must often have wished for:

[102] For Assyrian and Hebrew parallels see West (1997), 209 f.
[103] Koch–Carey (2000), 356–8.
[104] H. H. Schaeder, *Die Weltliteratur* 18 (1943), 83 = Schmitt (1968), 76 f.

temporary invisibility, instant transportation to a less dangerous spot. As with such motifs as the invulnerable armour, the unfailing sword, the missile that returns to its owner's hand, fantasy-wish is realized in myth. Invisibility is half rationalized as concealment in a conjured cloud or mist. This is a standard service afforded by Homeric gods to their favourites (*Il.* 3. 381, 20. 444, 21. 6, 597; *Od.* 7. 14). Caílte in the *Acallam na Senórach* relates how he and his companions were made invisible by a magic mist that rose about them, enabling them to listen to the conversation of another group without being seen (Dooley–Roe (1999), 145 f.). When the Nart Soslan rides to battle against Totradz, the wise woman Shatana, his mother, equips him, advises him, and sends with him a cloud to make him invisible, 'a cloud that only obeys a woman'. This enables him to overcome his enemy (Sikojev (1985), 297 f.).

Another familiar Homeric motif permits an important warrior in danger to be snatched away to safety by a deity (*Il.* 3. 380, 5. 445, 20. 325, 443, 21. 597). Similarly in the Avestan hymn to the Fravashis, the immortal souls of the faithful who ride like mounted warriors in the sky, we hear that when the king is surrounded by enemies he calls upon the Fravashis and they come to his aid and fly him home through the air like a bird.[105]

Given that gods may fight in mortal guise, it is only logical that a hero who is carrying all before him may on occasion be suspected of being really a god. Aeneas surmises this of Diomedes, and Pandaros replies that he cannot say for sure (*Il.* 5. 177, 183). The motif is paralleled in the *Rāmāyaṇa*, as well as in the Egyptian poem on the Battle of Qadesh.[106]

As the hero's prowess approximates to a god's, he may feel himself equal to any divine opponent. Capaneus, one of the famous Seven who attacked Thebes, declared that he would sack the city with or without God's will, and that not even Zeus' thunderbolt would stop him. So at least Aeschylus tells it (*Sept.* 427–31), no doubt following the tradition preserved in the epic *Thebaid.* Diomedes 'would even fight against Zeus' in the judgment of Iris and Apollo (*Il.* 5. 362, 457), and he does indeed fight against Aphrodite and Ares with Athena's envouragement. Dhṛṣṭadyumna claims that the Pāṇḍavas are invincible, even 'were we to face the Slayer of Vṛtra (Indra) himself in battle' (*MBh.* 3. 13. 119, cf. 8. 26. 42, *Rm.* 2. 20. 27). Uttara, having become Arjuna's chariot-driver and satisfied himself of the hero's quality, says 'I have found a battle companion and I can fight even with immortals' (4. 40. 15).

[105] Yt. 13. 69 f. The motif also appears in a pictorial story on two silver bowls of Phoenician workmanship, one found at Praeneste, the other in Cyprus; see West (1997), 100, 211.

[106] *Rm.* 6. 82. 24; West (1997), 361. In the Egyptian poem Ramesses boasts that he is taken to be Seth and his charioteer to be Sakhmet.

Archers

Although archery does not play a large part in Homer, we are able to observe a number of common features between its treatment there and in Indian poetry (and occasionally elsewhere). Arrows are characterized as 'winged', *parṇina-* (RV 6. 46. 11, *MBh.* 8. 18. 18), πτερόεις (*Il.* 4. 117, al.). They 'fly', *patayanti* (RV 6. 46. 11, 75. 11, 16), *patənti* (Yt. 10. 129), ἔπτατο (*Il.* 5. 99, al.).[107] Bows are 'shining', *rucira-* (*MBh.* 3. 116. 24, 266. 12), φαίδιμα (*Hymn. Ap.* 4). There are great bows which, like Odysseus', only an exceptional hero can draw (*MBh.* 3. 13. 69; *Rm.* 1. 30. 7–12).

Readers of the *Iliad* will remember the curious archery contest in the funeral games for Patroclus, when a ship's mast is set up on the sands and a live bird is tied to its top as the target (23. 850–83). Droṇa's archery test in *MBh.* 1. 123. 45–66 is more considerate of animal rights but takes a similar form. The target is an artificial bird attached to a treetop where it is hardly visible. Arjuna succeeds in decapitating it.

As the warrior goes to battle, the quiver rattles on his back (RV 6. 75. 5; *Il.* 1. 46). As he draws his bow, it is bent into a circle, κυκλοτερές (*Il.* 4. 124), *maṇḍala-*, *maṇḍalīkṛta-* (*MBh.* 1. 123. 60; 6. 104. 35; 7. 96. 5, 135. 41; 8. 15. 27, etc.; *Rm.* 3. 24. 15, al.). As he takes aim, he prays to the god of archery (*Il.* 4. 119–21, 23. 872 f.; *Rm.* 6. 78. 29 ff.). As he shoots, the bow twangs (*Il.* 4. 125 λίγξε βιός; *MBh.* 4. 40. 25; 7. 145. 44–6; 14. 76. 26; the earth trembles at the twang of Rāma's bow, *Rm.* 4. 35. 9).

But it is easily disabled by a blow. Teucer has one bowstring broken when Hector hits it with a rock, and another when Zeus himself snaps it as he is preparing to shoot Hector (*Il.* 8. 328, 15. 463). In the *Mahābhārata* bows are constantly being severed by super-accurate counter-fire (e.g. 5. 180. 26 f.). A similar incident is described by Saxo (6. 4. 9 p. 149). As Biorno is setting an arrow to his bowstring, three shots from Ano arrive: one severs the cord, one buries itself in his knuckles, the third hits his arrow.

Chariots

Chariots too are vulnerable. The shafts are liable to get broken (*Il.* 6. 39 f., 16. 370 f., *MBh.* 5. 182. 14; 6. 44. 5, 67. 37; cf. *Táin* 680, 866). The charioteer may be killed (*Il.* 5. 580, 8. 119–23, 312 f., 11. 161 f., 13. 396–9, 15. 451, 16. 737, 17. 610–19; *MBh.* 5. 183. 3 ff.), which may result in the horses bolting

[107] Spears too 'fly', at least in Greek and Old English: *Il.* 5. 282, 20. 88; *Maldon* 109, 150; *Elene* 140.

(*Il.* 6. 38–41, 11. 159–62, 15. 452; *MBh.* 6. 84. 12; 7. 88. 49, 93. 28). A horse may itself be wounded or killed (*Il.* 8. 81, 16. 467, Pind. *Pyth.* 6. 32; *MBh.* 5. 181. 29).

In a favourable case the warrior stranded by the failure of his transport may be rescued by another chariot (*Il.* 8. 90–115; *MBh.* 8. 32. 66, 44. 45). If his vehicle escapes mishap, the wounded or swooning warrior can be driven away to a calmer spot to recover (*Il.* 14. 429–32; *MBh.* 3. 19. 3; 5. 181. 15; 6. 54. 16 f., 79. 51 f.; 7. 39. 12, etc.). But in the overall picture, chariot losses loom large.

> Many were the proud-necked horses
> rattling empty chariots along the causeways of battle,
> in want of their good drivers, who lay on the ground
> more attractive to the vultures than to their wives. (*Il.* 11. 159, cf. 179)
>
> Many the chariots that [. . .] in the dust,
> many the bright-eyed [lads] trampled . . . (Alc. 283. 15 f.)
>
> Many were the elephants there deprived of their standards,
> and many car-warriors also deprived of their steeds . . .
> . . . others deprived of their cars. (*MBh.* 6. 51. 23 f., cf. 113. 13 f.)

Single combat

Nothing is more characteristic of heroic narrative than accounts of armed encounters between individuals, whether as independent events or within the framework of a battle. A typical sequence is: aggressive speeches from each combatant (sometimes preceded by an arming scene); attack with throwing-spears or other missiles, which are stopped by the opponent's shield; close combat with swords.[108] If heroes of the highest calibre are involved, the gods may be gathered to watch (*Il.* 22. 166; *Rm.* 6. 94. 13).

On occasion a champion may step forward and challenge anyone from the enemy side to fight him. So Hector does in the *Iliad*, Duryodhana in the *Mahābhārata*, Ashkabus in the *Shāh-nāma*, and an unnamed Slav in Saxo.[109]

In some cases it is agreed that the outcome of a single combat will settle the war. So it is with the duel of Paris and Menelaus (*Il.* 3. 67–75); the agreement is solemnized with sacrifices and oaths, and if the gods (that is, the poet) had not intervened to prevent the combat from coming to a clear conclusion,

[108] Cf. e.g. *Il.* 3. 326–80, 7. 206–82, 22. 248–330; *Shāh-nāma*, Levy (1967), 72 f.; *Hildebrandslied* 1–68; *Battle of Maldon* 134–42.

[109] *Il.* 7. 38–91; *MBh.* 9. 31. 9 ff.; Levy (1967), 134; Saxo 3. 5. 6 p. 74. The Biblical story of Goliath (1 Sam. 17. 8–10) is of the same kind; cf. West (1997), 214 f.

the Trojan War would have been terminated prematurely. In Roman legend the Romans and Albans agreed to let a combat between their sets of triplets, the Horatii and the Curiatii, decide which people was to rule over the other (Livy 1. 24 f.). The Germans, according to Tacitus (*Germ.* 10. 3), would set up a duel between a champion of their own and a captive from the people with whom they were at war, not as a substitute but as a prognostication for the coming conflict. Gregory of Tours tells that the Vandal and Alamannic invaders of Spain used the duel method to resolve their rival claims to the land and avoid a battle between kindred peoples. Further cases are related by Paulus Diaconus and Saxo, and I have noted one in a Serbo-Croat oral poem.[110]

A formal duel is often represented as being conducted in a specially marked out square or circle. For Paris' duel with Menelaus 'they measured out the place' (*Il.* 3. 315 χῶρον . . . διεμέτρεον). For Sohrab's fight with Rostam 'a narrow arena had been prepared' (*Shāh-nāma*, Levy (1967), 73). For Helgi's with Alf a field was 'hazled', that is, staked out with hazel rods.[111] Saxo makes several references to the preparation of such areas for duels.[112]

Despite the inconclusive end to Ajax's duel with Hector, the Achaeans deem him to have won, and at dinner Agamemnon honours him by giving him the best cut of beef, the chine (*Il.* 7. 321). This corresponds to a custom of the Celts, recorded by Posidonius, of honouring the best fighter with the best cut of meat. 'Anciently the champion (ὁ κράτιστος) got the thigh; and if anyone else laid claim to it, they engaged in a duel to the death' (Posid. F 171 Theiler ap. Ath. 154b, cf. 169 = Diod. 5. 28. 4). An episode of this kind is related in the Irish saga *Bricriu's Feast.* The mischief-maker Bricriu lays on a banquet for the Ulstermen with the intention of setting them against one another. He describes the 'champion's portion' (*mír curad*) that will be available—a feast in itself—and he leads three heroes separately to think it will be theirs. At the feast they quarrel and fight over it. The matter is adjourned, and the rivalry continues through various adventures and trials until at last Cú Chulainn is pronounced the winner.

[110] Gregory, *Hist. Franconum* 2. 2 (Clemen (1928), 27); Paul. Diac. *Hist. Langobard.* 5. 41; Saxo 3. 5. 2–6. 3 pp. 74–7; Suleiman Makić, *The Song of Baghdad, SCHS* i. 272 f./ii, no. 26. 400 ff. Cf. de Vries (1956), i. 429–31. The Goliath story is another example.

[111] *Helgakviða Hiǫrvarðzsonar* 34 prose; cf. *Kormáks saga* 10; Gering–Sijmons (1927–31), ii. 63 f.; de Vries (1956), i. 289.

[112] Saxo 3. 5. 6 p. 76 *circulatur campus*; 4. 8. 2 p. 101 *e diverso bina quadratae formae spatia cubitalibus figurata lateribus humi denotat . . . quibus descriptis assignatam uterque sibi partem complectitur*; 5. 5. 6 p. 128 *si alter dimicantium relato pede praenotati orbis gyrum excederet, perinde ac victus causae detrimentum reciperet.*

Doom and downfall

On two occasions in the *Iliad* Zeus makes drops of blood fall from the sky as a portent of death. The first is to presage the general carnage of the impending battle (11. 53 f.), the second is to honour his son Sarpedon who is about to be killed (16. 459). In the same way Indra sends showers of blood at the fall of Duryodhana (*MBh.* 9. 57. 48). Similar portents occur elsewhere in the Indian epics.[113] The motif of a rain of blood appears also with symbolic or metaphorical value in the Valkyries' weaving song preserved in *Njáls saga*: 'Wide is the warp for the weapon-play, a cloud of wrath raining blood'; 'all around are awful sights, gory clouds gather above' (*Darraðarlióð* 1, 9; *Edd. min.* 58–60). In an Irish saga druidical divinatory magic before a battle produces a dark cloud which sheds a rain of blood over the Ulstermen's camp.[114]

When Patroclus' death is at hand, Apollo gives him a terrific whack on the back, στρεφεδίνηθεν δέ οἱ ὄσσε ... τὸν δ' ἄτη φρένας εἷλε, λύθεν δ' ὕπο φαίδιμα γυῖα, στῆ δὲ ταφών, 'his eyes spun in a whirl . . . detriment seized his wits, his bright limbs lost their strength, and he stood dazed' (*Il.* 16. 792, 805 f.). Pisani has compared the demise of Droṇa in the *Mahābhārata*, where, amid a concerto grosso of portents, the hero's left eye and arm twitch and he becomes *vimanas*-, 'out of his mind, discomposed'.[115] This disorientation and paralysis that afflicts the man and lays him wide open to the forces of destruction is perhaps related to the distortion of perception with which the gods send awry the man they are set to destroy. The doctrine is familiar in Greek from post-Homeric texts such as Theognidea 403–6,

> the man whom God
> is purposely leading astray into great error,
> and easily makes him think that what is bad is good,
> and that what is worth while is bad,

and Soph. *Ant.* 622–5. It is paralleled in the Indian epics:

> When the gods deal defeat to a person, they first take his mind away, so that he sees matters wrongly. When destruction is imminent and his mind is beclouded, the wrong course appears as the right one and cannot be dislodged from his heart. When his destruction is near, evil takes on the appearance of good, the good appears as evil. (*MBh.* 2. 72. 8–10, and similarly 5. 34. 78 f.; cf. *Rm.* 3. 47. 27)

[113] Rains of flesh and blood: *MBh.* 6. 1. 21; 7. 6. 25, 95. 47. Portents including showers of blood: *Rm.* 3. 22. 1–15; 6. 26. 21 ff., 31. 3 ff., 41. 30 ff.

[114] *The Siege of Druim Damgaire* 114 f., ed. M. L. Sjoestedt, *RC* 43 (1926), 108 f. Cf. also H. R. E. Davidson in H. R. E. Davidson–W. M. S. Russell (edd.), *The Folklore of Ghosts* (Ipswich 1981), 157 f.

[115] *MBh.* 7. 192. 17–21; V. Pisani, *ZDMG* 103 (1953), 130 f. = Schmitt (1968), 159 f.

And in the *Shāh-nāma*: 'when the time arrives for a blow to strike a man, his mind is distracted and his senses go astray' (Levy (1967), 215).

In another Homeric passage Poseidon causes Alkathoos to fall to Idomeneus, *θέλξας ὄσσε φαεινά, πέδησε δὲ φαίδιμα γυῖα*, 'putting a spell on his bright eyes and fettering his limbs', so that he cannot run away or take avoiding action but stands rooted to the spot like a pillar or tree (*Il.* 13. 435–8). The verb *πεδάω* 'fetter' is used elsewhere of the intervention of Doom (*Μοῖρα*, *ὀλοιὴ Μοῖρα*) bringing a warrior to a standstill to meet his death (*Il.* 4. 517, 22. 5; cf. 19. 94 (Ate), *Od.* 3. 269, 18. 155). Durante has compared the Vedic metaphor of the 'fetter of Yama' or 'fetter of death', *Yamásya páḍbīśam* (RV 10. 97. 16, AV 8. 7. 28), *mṛtyóḥ páḍbīśam* (AV 8. 1. 4; 12. 5. 15; 16. 8. 27), and also the less specific 'bonds of death', found both in the Atharvaveda and in Old English.[116] But there is a more exact parallel for the Homeric image in the Germanic idea of the 'war fetter' that comes upon a man in battle and pins him down. In the *Harðar saga* (36) it is related that the *herfiǫturr* came upon Hord three times in a battle, and he managed to shake it off, but the fourth time he could not, and was killed. It is mentioned also in other sagas, and Herfiǫtur (a femininized form) is the name of a Valkyrie (*Grímnismál* 36).[117] In Chapter 8, in the general context of binding magic, we referred to the first Merseburg Spell with its depiction of certain supernatural females who fastened or loosened fetters on an army. The spell is apparently meant to free the warrior from such impediments. A version of the concept also appears in a medieval Slavonic chronicle, where a Bohemian witch advises her stepson, who is going into battle, of a magical procedure that will enable him to 'loosen the invisible ligatures with which, from the gods' anger, your people's horses will be tied and will fail and fall as if wearied from a long journey'.[118]

Minor warriors are killed at a stroke. With major ones it is a longer process, not always completed at one go. They may first suffer one or more damaging incidents from which they recover. Hector is on two occasions knocked down by a rock from the hand of Ajax; Bhīma is knocked off balance and temporarily stunned by one from the hand of the ogre Kirmīra (*Il.* 7. 268–72, 14. 409–20; *MBh.* 3. 12. 51). A wounded hero may pass out from pain, like Sarpedon (*Il.* 5. 696), Hector (11. 356, 14. 438), Cú Chulainn (*Táin* (L) 3379).[119] He may vomit blood: *Il.* 14. 437 *κελαινεφὲς αἷμ' ἀπέμεσσεν*, 15. 11 *αἷμ'*

[116] AV 8. 2. 2 *mṛtyupāśá-*; *Christ III* 1042 *deaþes bend*; Durante (1976), 111. In Vd. 5. 8 the man who dies is bound by the demon 'Bone-loosener', *Astō.vīδōtuš dim baṇdayeiti*; cf. Christian Bartholomae, *Altiranisches Wörterbuch* (Berlin 1904), 214.

[117] Further references in Gering–Sijmons (1927–31), i. 205; de Vries (1956), i. 322.

[118] Cosmas of Prague, *Chronica Boemorum* 1. 11 (C. H. Meyer (1931), 19. 25).

[119] David faints from grief in *Sassountsy David* 320.

ἐμέων, and with the same verb *MBh.* 9. 10. 54 *rudhiraṃ vaman,* 10. 9. 3 *vamantaṃ rudhiraṃ vaktrād,* cf. *Rm.* 4. 16. 20, 47. 19, al.

When the warrior falls for the last time, he is seen by Greek and Indian bards as embracing the earth: ἕλε γαῖαν ἀγοστῶι, 'he took the earth in his clasp' (*Il.* 11. 425, al.); he lays his arms on earth as if embracing a woman (*Rm.* 3. 29. 7, cf. 4. 20. 6, 23. 3). And if we maintain the traditional interpretation of the Homeric formula ὀδὰξ ἕλον ἄσπετον οὖδας (*Il.* 19. 61, al.) as 'bit the dust', we may compare *MBh.* 5. 21. 17 *bhakṣayiṣyāma pāṃsukān,* '(we shall be killed and) eat the dust'; 11. 19. 9 *pāṃsūn grasati,* 'gulps the dust'.[120]

At two climactic points of the *Iliad* the death of a great hero is marked with a couplet about the departure of his soul to the other world: 'the soul, flying from his face(?), was gone to Hades' house, lamenting its fate, forsaking manliness and vigour' (16. 856 = 22. 362). The last phrase at least must on linguistic grounds be a very old formula. Watkins has compared the lines at Beowulf's death: 'his soul departed from his breast(?) to seek the judgment of those steadfast in faith', noting that this obviously Christian formulation is likely to be an adaptation of an older pagan conception.[121] When Fergus mac Róich was killed, 'his soul passed out of him forthwith'.[122] Bhīṣma's life-breaths, unable to find another exit, leave him through his head (*MBh.* 13. 154. 6).

It is a conventional motif that when a leader is killed his followers turn to flight. This happens not only in the Greek[123] and Indian[124] epics but also in the *Shāh-nāma* (Levy (1967), 138), Old English (*Judith* 290–2), Old Norse (*Hervarar saga* 13, 14), and Irish (*Acallam na Senórach,* Dooley–Roe (1999), 182). Their opponents usually pursue them, but on occasion they gather round to marvel at the sight of the dead hero. So with Hector in the *Iliad* (22. 369–75) and probably with Penthesileia in the *Aethiopis* (cf. Qu. Smyrn. 1. 661–70); and so too with Karṇa in the *Mahābhārata* (8. 68. 3 f.).

A hero's horse or horses are as distressed by his death as anyone else. Achilles' horses weep for Patroclus (*Il.* 17. 426 f., 437 f.), and one of them hangs his head in anticipation of Achilles' own death, of which it has fore-

[120] But ὀδάξ originally meant 'clawing' according to Friedrich Bechtel, *Lexilogus zu Homer* (Halle/Saale 1914), 241–3.

[121] *Beowulf* 2819 f.; Watkins (1995), 499 n. 3.

[122] *Aided Fergusa maic Róich* 4, ed. Kuno Meyer, *The Death-tales of the Ulster Heroes* (Dublin 1906), 34, 7 *luid a anum as focétóir.*

[123] *Il.* 5. 27–37, 11. 744, 16. 290, 21. 206; for examples in the Epic Cycle see *CQ* 53 (2003), 8 n. 33.

[124] *MBh.* 3. 157. 70, 271. 18; 6. 54. 17 f.; *Rm.* 6. 44. 30 f., 46. 48, 66. 37, 97. 22.

knowledge (19. 405). Droṇa's horses shed tears when he is about to die.[125] Sigurd's horse Grani hung its head over the slain hero, and perhaps wept.[126] 'Upon David's death, Kourkig Jelaly went wild, | broke his rein tied to the tree, ran amuck, | trampled to death every man, | animal, and horse on his path, | until he reached Khantout Khanoun's door' (*Sassountsy David* 335).

The earth is sometimes said to drink the blood of the fallen. The image appears in a Hittite military oath: 'Then he pours out wine and says, "[This] is not wine, it is your blood, and [as the ea]rth has swallowed this, so shall the earth also sw[allow you]r [blood] and [. . .]." '[127] In Homer the effect of the shed blood on the earth is remarked, without the drinking metaphor: 'his dark blood flowed forth and soaked the earth' (*Il.* 13. 655, 21. 119). But in Aeschylus the earth drinks it (*Sept.* 736, *Cho.* 66, *Eum.* 979). So too in the Indian epic. 'If the Gandharvas do not free the sons of Dhṛtarāṣṭra peacefully, then earth today shall drink the blood of their king!' (*MBh.* 3. 232. 20; cf. 7. 166. 27; 8. 49. 112; *Rm.* 3. 2. 22, 29. 6). In an Old English poem it is written that 'feuding has existed among mankind ever since earth swallowed the blood of Abel' (*Maxims A* 192, trs. Bradley).

In the lurid episode in which Achilles exchanges words with and is pursued by the river Scamander, the latter complains that his stream is being blocked by the masses of corpses slain by Achilles (*Il.* 21. 218–20); that is in fact what causes him to overflow. The motif appears also in the new Archilochus elegy (P. Oxy. 4708), in which it is said that the Caicus was crowded with the Achaean dead when Telephus routed them in Mysia. It is paralleled in the Norse poem on the battle of the Goths and the Huns as paraphrased in the *Hervarar saga* (14): 'and the Goths slew and felled so many that the streams were blocked and tumbled out of their channels'. It recurs in Saxo's version of the lost *Biarkamál* (161 f.), *et corpora sparsa revolvit | elisus venis vapidum spumantibus amnis*, while in another passage of Saxo the sea itself is covered with bodies so that 'the harbours were choked and stank, the boats, surrounded by corpses, were blocked in and could not move' (5. 7. 5 p. 130).

Another means of expressing the horror of battlefield carnage is to evoke the carrion birds and the dogs or wolves who will enjoy feasting on the corpses. They are not normally described in the act (the reference to the eels and fishes feeding on Asteropaios in *Il.* 21. 203 f. is exceptional); it is more often a prospect with which to undermine your enemy's morale when you make your boastful speech at him (see above), or it is mentioned as the

[125] *MBh.* 7. 192. 20, noted by V. Pisani, *ZDMG* 103 (1953), 130 = Schmitt (1968), 159 f.; cf. *Rm.* 6. 65. 18.

[126] *Brot af Sigurðarkviðu* 7, *Guðrúnarkviða B* 5; it wept if *úrughlýra* in the second passage refers to Grani and not Gudrun.

[127] N. Oettinger, *Die militärischen Eide der Hethiter* (Wiesbaden 1976), 21, 74 f.

natural sequel to death in battle and left without its actualization being reported, though with a hint of the gratification that it will give the birds and beasts. Achilles' wrath consigned many warrior souls to Hades and made their bodies 'plunder' (ἑλώρια) for the dogs and all the birds, or with the ancient variant reading 'a feast' for the birds (*Il.* 1. 4 f.). Agamemnon's victims lay 'more attractive to the vultures than to their wives' (11. 162). Bodies not recovered will be κυσὶν μέλπηθρα, 'sport for dogs' (17. 255, 18. 179); they will 'sate' dogs and birds (8. 379, 13. 831, 17. 241). Similarly Helgi is characterized as a man *er opt hefir ǫrno sadda*, 'who has often sated the eagles' (*Helgakviða Hundingsbana A* 35).[128] An Anglo-Saxon poet describes the Assyrians lying slain by the Hebrew army, *wulfum tō willan and ēac wælgīfrum | fuglum tō frōfre*, 'to wolves' liking and carnage-greedy birds' comfort' (*Judith* 296 f.).

Vindictive victory

The hero's savagery towards his enemy does not abate once he has killed him. The *Iliad* poet himself seems rather to disapprove of Achilles' behaviour in piercing Hector's heels with leather straps and dragging his body behind his chariot to the ships (*Il.* 22. 395–404). It may have been a traditional motif in heroic narrative about chariot-warriors. At any rate it has a close parallel in Irish saga:

> Then Fergus put a spancelling band through Etarcomol's heels and dragged him behind his own chariot to the camp. Whenever Etarcomol's body went over rocks, one half would part from the other . . . Medb looked at him. 'That was not kind treatment for a young hound, Fergus,' said Medb. 'It is no source of annoyance to me,' said Fergus, 'that the mongrel should have waged battle with the great hound [Cú Chulainn] for whom he was no match' (*Táin* (I) 1378–84).

A yet more barbaric story is told about Tydeus, a hero of the Theban War. He had been wounded by Melanippus. When Amphiaraus killed Melanippus and brought back his head as a trophy, Tydeus split it open and passionately gobbled the brain, to the disgust of Athena, who was approaching to bestow immortality on him but now thought better of it.[129] Cutting off an enemy's head is a primitive practice, attested sporadically in several Indo-European traditions.[130] So is drinking his blood. Herodotus (4. 64. 1) relates that a Scythian drinks of the blood of the first man that he slays in battle, as well as

[128] More Norse material in Gering–Sijmons (1927–31), ii. 91.

[129] Sch. D *Il.* 5. 126, probably from the epic *Thebaid* (= fr. 9 Bernabé and West).

[130] Cf. M. Green (1986), 31; Campanile (1990a), 269–71; Bernard Sergent, *Celtes et Grecs*, i. *Le livre des héros* (Paris 1999), 165 f.

taking all his victims' heads back to the king as proof of his kills. Greek heroes do not drink their enemies' blood, but it is a recurrent motif in the Indian epics.[131] Cobthach the Slender killed Labraid's father and grandfather in one night and gave Labraid a piece of the heart of each and a goblet of their blood, and he consumed them (Dillon (1946), 7). Gwyn the son of Nudd killed Nwython and took out his heart, which he then forced Nwython's son Cyledur to eat (*Culhwch and Olwen* 993–6). Regin killed Fáfnir, drank of his blood, and roasted his heart. Then Sigurd cut off Regin's head, ate Fáfnir's heart, and drank the blood of both of them (*Fáfnismál* 26–39).

Herodotus goes on to say that in the case of their worst enemies the Scythians make their skulls into goblets, covering the outside with rawhide and the inside with gold (4. 65). The Celtic Scordisci are said to have drunk their enemies' blood from their skulls.[132] There is archaeological evidence for making skulls into cups from central Europe,[133] besides historical instances. The Cisalpine Boii famously did it with the skull of the consul designate L. Postumius in 216 BCE, and the Lombard king Alboin did it to the Gepid Cunimund in 567.[134] Further east, Chinese annalists record that in the second century BCE the king of the nomadic Yueji, who were perhaps Iranian or Tocharian-speakers, was killed and his skull made into a drinking vessel by Modun, ruler of the Xiongnu, probably a Turkic people.[135]

The evidence does not allow us to treat this as a distinctively or originally Indo-European practice; nor was it widely taken up in poetic tradition. It does make an appearance in the heroic mythology of the north. It was prophesied to the Ulstermen that they would gain strength from using Conall Cernach's huge skull to drink from (M. Green (1986), 31). Volund, the legendary smith of Nordic tradition, maimed and enslaved by the Swedish king Nidud, takes his revenge by killing Nidud's two sons, making their skulls into cups, chased with silver, and sending these to the king as gifts. The motif is borrowed for Gudrun's revenge on Atli.[136]

[131] *MBh.* 2. 61. 45, 68. 21, 29; 8. App. I 31, cf. 29. 13; 9. 60. 12; 10. 16. 30; *Rm.* 3. 2. 13, 18. 15; 6. 48. 69.

[132] Festus, *Breviarium* 9. 1; Amm. Marc. 27. 4. 4; Oros. *Hist. adv. paganos* 5. 23. 18; more in Zwicker (1934–6), 259. 5. Florus 1. 39. 2 ascribes the practice to Thracians but at once goes on to talk about the Scordisci. For drinking blood from skulls cf. M. Höfer, *Archiv für Anthropologie* NF 12 (1913), 63.

[133] A skull cup in a cave burial at Býčí Skála, north of Brno (Celtic, Hallstatt culture, *c.* sixth century BCE): J. V. S. Megaw, *Art of the European Iron Age* (New York 1970), 58 no. 35.

[134] Cn. Gellius fr. 26 Peters, Livy 23. 24. 12, cf. Sil. Ital. 13. 482 f.; Paul. Diac. *Hist. Langobard.* 1. 27, cf. 2. 28.

[135] Simaa Qian, *Shiji* 123, and Ban Gu, *Qian Han Shu* 96A, cited in Koch–Carey (2000), 37.

[136] *Vǫlundarkviða* 24; *Atlamál* 82; Gering–Sijmons (1927–31), ii. 19. For further material on skull cups, including Czech, Russian, Greek, and Italian folk-tales and historical Slavonic instances from 811 and 972, see Krek (1887), 759–71.

SIMILES

Our initial survey of similes in Chapter 2 may now be augmented by a collection of some types employed in battle contexts.

When Agamemnon slaughters the fleeing Trojans, it is 'as when ravaging fire falls upon dense woodland, and the wind blazes it up and carries it in all directions, and the thickets fall root and branch from the force of the fire's onset' (*Il.* 11. 155–7; cf. 15. 605 f., 20. 490–4). The Indian epic uses the same simile. Sātyaki says 'let them watch me . . . when I by myself kill the best Kuru fighters, as the doomsday fire burns down a dead wood!' (*MBh.* 3. 120. 10; cf. 6. 112. 88; 7. 3. 16, 13. 1, 20. 24). Narantaka mows the enemy down like a fire burning a forest (*Rm.* 6. 57. 65). More compendiously, a Homeric hero may be described as φλογὶ εἴκελος, 'flamelike' (*Il.* 13. 53, 688, al.). Rāma, 'adorned in his firelike armour, had the appearance of a smokeless flame flaring up in the dark' (*Rm.* 3. 23. 15). In Old Irish praise poetry the hero is sometimes called a 'red flame', 'fierce flame', etc.[137]

Alternatively he may be 'a powerful wave of the sea on the shore', 'a sea storm'. Lugaid 'rushed to their aid . . . , the roar of the vast sea'.[138] The metaphor corresponds to an ample Homeric simile: Hector falls upon the Achaeans like a huge wave falling on a ship (*Il.* 15. 624–8).

Immediately before this (618–21) the Achaean resistance to Hector has been compared to a great sheer cliff on the coast that withstands the keening winds and swollen waves that beat against it. When Antinous throws a footstool at Odysseus, the hero stands 'firm as a rock' and does not lose his balance (*Od.* 17. 463). We find comparable similes in the Indian epics and the early British heroic poems. Rāma stands firm under assault like a mountain under thunderbolts (*Rm.* 3. 24. 12). As a rock obstructs a torrent, so Kumbha withstands the onset of his adversaries under a hail of missiles (*Rm.* 6. 63. 27; cf. also *MBh.* 6. 59. 8, 74. 24, 88. 23; 7. 74. 28). 'No more than a stone of vast girth is shaken was Gwid son of Neithan moved' (*Y Gododdin* 386 f.). Merin was 'an unshaken rock before the host' (ibid. 742 f.).

In other passages the firm-standing one is likened to a great tree. The two Lapiths Polypoites and Leonteus stood defending the gate of the Achaean fortification 'like tall oaks in the mountains that withstand wind and rain at all times, fixed with their long thick roots' (*Il.* 12. 132–5). 'Tree of battle' is a

[137] Campanile (1977), 121; (1990b), 61 f. Cf. West (1997), 250.

[138] Campanile (1977), 121 f.; (1990b), 62; K. Meyer (1913), 40/43 vv. 9 f., trs. J. Carey in Koch–Carey (2000), 55.

kenning for 'warrior' both in early Welsh and in Norse poetry.[139] 'A golden oak was the outstanding Móen', an early Irish eulogist assures us.[140] The motif occurs in the Russian *byliny* in the form that a hero, surprised that his mighty blow has no effect on his enemy, wonders if his strength is failing and tries smiting a tree, which falls.

As a tree can be felled, either by a woodcutter or by a stroke of lightning, so can a warrior. Simoeisios, struck down by Ajax, falls like a poplar cut down by a joiner (*Il.* 4. 482–7, cf. 13. 178, 389). Indra struck down Vṛtra 'as an axe (does) the woods' (RV 10. 89. 7, cf. 1. 32. 5). Rāma, on hearing of his father's death, falls down in a swoon like a tree in the forest cut down by the axe (*Rm.* 2. 95. 9). Then again, Indra felled Vṛtra like a tree struck by a thunderbolt (RV 2. 14. 2, cf. 6. 33. 3; *MBh.* 2. 42. 21; 3. 271. 17), while Hector, laid out by a stone from Ajax's hand, falls like an oak under Zeus' thunderbolt (*Il.* 14. 414).[141]

Diomedes charging among the Trojans after sustaining an arrow wound is compared to a lion who leaps into a sheepfold, roused only the more by a wound from a shepherd, and causes havoc; a little later he is like a lion leaping among cattle (*Il.* 5. 136–43, 161; cf. 10. 485, 15. 630). Similarly when Bhīma sets upon Duryodhana's army he will be 'a lion invading a cowpen' (*MBh.* 5. 47. 15).[142] Sarpedon succumbing to Patroclus is like a bull being killed by a lion (*Il.* 16. 487, cf. 17. 542), and so too the demon Maṇimat 'was felled by Bhīmasena, as a bull by a lion' (*MBh.* 3. 157. 69; cf. 7. 152. 17).

The Trojans flee like cattle that a lion has put to flight (*Il.* 11. 172 f.), and the Karūṣaka chieftains deserted Śiśupāla 'running away like puny game at the sight of a lion' (*MBh.* 5. 22. 27). Timorous armies are elsewhere compared to deer (*Il.* 13. 102, 22. 1; *MBh.* 7. 148. 10, 45).[143] Or they are driven back like clouds by wind (*Il.* 11. 305 f., 16. 297–300; *MBh.* 7. 19. 32, 29. 34, 64. 57, 115. 20, etc.; like gnats by wind, *Sassountsy David* 349).

[139] *Guid gunet, Y Gododdin* 785; *hildimeiðr, Fáfnismál* 36; *Óþens eike* 'Odin's oaks', Egil Skallagrímsson, *Hǫfuðlausn* 8; elsewhere *Báleygs viðir* 'Odin's woods'.

[140] Campanile (1977), 119 f.; (1990b), 61.

[141] Cf. Durante (1976), 121. The tree simile could also be used of others besides warriors struck down by a god. In the preface to the Hittite story of Appu (§1; Hoffner (1998), 83) a deity is said to 'chop down evil men like trees'. In a hymn to Agni he is asked to 'bring the wicked one down as with the blade, O unageing king, like a tree of the forest with the cutting edge' (RV 6. 8. 5).

[142] For Assyrian and Hebrew parallels see West (1997), 219, 246 f.

[143] This very natural comparison is again found in Assyrian and Hebrew texts: West (1997), 248.

THE HERO'S FUNERAL

If there is one thing on which all human societies agree, it is that a death is not complete without a funeral. In heroic narrative thousands are killed without any mention of obsequies, and indeed, as we have seen, the expectation for many of them is that they will have none but be left abandoned to the appetites of birds and beasts. But when the greatest heroes die we find in several traditions an account of the funeral ceremonies that followed. In the *Iliad* there are the grand funerals of Patroclus and Hector, and that of Achilles was described at length in the *Aethiopis* (cf. *Od.* 24. 65–92). In the Indian epics there are a number of relevant passages.[144] In *Beowulf*, besides the funeral of the hero himself (3110–19, 3136–82), there are passages about those of other famous warriors, Scyld (26–52) and Hnæf (1107–24). In the more ballad-like style of the Eddic poems we would not expect anything of the kind. But in the *Sigurðarkviða* (65–70) Brynhild anticipates Sigurd's funeral (which will also be her own, as she has stabbed herself) and gives directions for it that serve the same poetic purpose as a narrative description. Snorri's telling of the story of Baldr, following Úlfr Uggason's *Húsdrápa*, includes an account of his funeral (*Gylf.* 49). Saxo refers to the royal funeral of Asmund (1. 8. 4 p. 27) and gives a fuller description of that of Harald Wartooth (8. 5. 1 p. 220).

Baldr and Scyld have untypical obsequies: they are laid in ships and committed to the sea. We have touched on this in Chapter 10. For the rest, there is a considerable measure of similarity among the various accounts. There is prolonged lamentation, especially by women. The hero is cremated on a pyre, a chieftain having first given the order to gather wood (*Il.* 23. 110–26, 24. 778; *Rm.* 3. 64. 27, 4. 24. 14; *Beowulf* 3110–14). His armour is committed with him,[145] and there may be other rich offerings, including animal and human victims. Patroclus' pyre receives—besides many sheep and cattle—four horses, two dogs, and twelve Trojan captives (*Il.* 23. 166–76). Baldr's receives the magic, self-reproducing gold ring Draupnir and his horse with all its harness. A company of servants and maids is to be burned with Sigurd in addition to Brynhild.

The hero's burnt remains are gathered in an urn, which is interred in a tumulus: so it is with Patroclus (*Il.* 23. 243–56), Achilles (*Od.* 24. 72–84), Harald (Saxo 8. 5. 1). In Beowulf's case no urn is mentioned; the remains

[144] *MBh.* 1. 118–19. 4; 11. 23. 37–42, 26. 25–43; 13. 154; 16. 8. 19–31; *Rm.* 2. 70; 3. 64. 27–35, 68. 1–6; 4. 24. 13–42. Cf. Brockington (1998), 226–9, 435–7.

[145] *Il.* 6. 418, *Od.* 11. 74 ~ 12. 13; *MBh.* 11. 23. 39, cf. RV 10. 18. 9 with Geldner's note; Jordanes, *Getica* 258 (Attila's funeral); *Beowulf* 1110 f., 3139 f., cf. 36–42; *Sigurðarkviða* 66; Saxo 8. 5. 1 p. 220.

are skilfully walled up in the barrow together with rings, jewels, and gold (3160–8). Harald's horse and arms are buried with him. Achilles' tumulus is situated on a headland by the sea so that it will be visible to mariners from afar, and almost exactly the same is said of Beowulf's (2802–8).

The funeral process extends over many days. Achilles is lamented for seventeen days before the pyre is lit (*Od.* 24. 63–5). For Hector it is agreed that there will be nine days of lamentation; the cremation will take place on the tenth day and the tumulus be built on the eleventh (*Il.* 24. 664–6, cf. 784–804). Pāṇḍu's mourners spend twelve nights lying on the ground in a state of impurity (*MBh.* 1. 118. 30). Daśaratha is mourned for ten days (*Rm.* 2. 70. 23). Ten days are spent on the construction of Beowulf's tumulus (3159).

We have the impression that we are dealing with variants of a common tradition, the source of which was not poetic fantasy but actual practice. As for the long duration of the ceremonial, we may note that the Hittite royal funeral ritual occupied fourteen days. It began with lamentation and sacrifices; the body was cremated on the third day, the remains transported to the grave chamber on the sixth.[146] In Vedic ritual the bones are gathered some days after the cremation, placed in a jar or other receptacle, and buried. Sometimes a tumulus was raised at a later date.[147] A 'Russian' (probably Viking) noble, whose funeral by the lower Volga in 922 was attended and described in great detail by the Arab writer Ibn Faḍlān, was laid in a covered grave for ten days until the funeral garments were ready. He was then finely dressed and taken to be propped up on the decking of his beached ship with all his weapons beside him. A dog, two horses, and other creatures were sacrificed and the carcasses put on the ship. One of the man's maids was laid beside him and put to death. Finally the ship with its cargo of death was burned. A tumulus was built over the spot and a wooden pillar set up on it with the names of the deceased and the king.[148]

The Scythian royal funerals as described by Herodotus (4. 71 f.) do not involve cremation, but they are long drawn out. The body is fenced round with spears, there are offerings of gold vessels and sacrifices of a concubine, various servants, and horses, and a great tumulus is built over them all. Caesar writes that at Gaulish funerals they put on the pyre whatever the deceased had valued, including animals,[149] and that it had earlier been the custom to burn with them their favourite slaves and dependants (*Bell. Gall.* 6. 19. 4 f.). Distinguished Germans, according to Tacitus (*Germ.* 27. 1), were cremated

[146] For the detail see L. Christmann-Franck, *Revue hittite et asianique* 29 (1971), 61–84; V. Haas in J. M. Sasson (ed.), *Civilizations of the Ancient Near East* (New York 1995), iii. 2024–7.

[147] Oldenberg (1917), 579–81.

[148] C. H. Meyer (1931), 88–92.

[149] Horses are specified by Comm. Bern. in Luc. 1. 451.

with their weapons and horse and a tumulus was raised. Pagan Prussian nobles were still cremated or interred with horses, male and female slaves, weapons, hunting dogs, and other precious offerings in the thirteenth century, as were Lithuanian kings even later.[150]

None of this evidence takes us back before the Late Bronze Age, and we cannot simply project it back to the proto-Indo-European era. The Indo-Europeans, in all probability, did not practise cremation, which first appears among the Hittites and spreads into Greece and northern Europe from the thirteenth century BCE.[151] On the other hand, the tradition of tumulus burial goes back into the fourth millennium and is characteristic of many of the cultures that feature in models of Indo-European expansion.[152] Burial with weapons and horses is also widely and early documented by archaeology.[153] Cremation is a separable element which, when introduced, could be prefixed to the older practice of interment in a tumulus. The heroic burials described in Homer, the *Mahābhārata, Beowulf,* and so on may be considered as regional manifestations of a broad current of tradition and practice common to most of the aristocratic societies of Late Bronze and Iron Age Europe.

Laments

Laments for the dead hero lend themselves to poetic treatment, and besides general references to ritual wailing and breast-beating by a body of women[154] we often find composed laments put in the mouth of someone who was close to the deceased. In the *Iliad* it is said that he or she *ἐξῆρχε γόοιο*, 'led the lamenting' (18. 316, 24. 723, 747, 761, cf. 721); the others present are treated as a kind of chorus giving responses (19. 301, al., *ἐπὶ δὲ στενάχοντο γυναῖκες*). Within this rather formal setting the poet gives us laments for Patroclus by Achilles and Briseis (18. 324–42; 19. 287–300) and for Hector by

[150] Sources in Mannhardt (1936), 41, 88, 123, 142 = Clemen (1936), 95. 20, 97. 25, 99. 16, 106. 35; cf. 174 = Clemen 107. 14; 334 f. Cf. Gimbutas (1963), 184–7.

[151] Sergent (1995), 232, 234 f., 354. For discussion of Indo-European funeral customs cf. Otto Schrader, *Reallexikon der indogermanischen Altertumskunde* (Strasbourg 1901), i. 102–18, 123–36; id. (1909), 16–29; Feist (1913), 311–17; Gamkrelidze–Ivanov (1995), 725–30; L. J. Hansen, *JIES* 8 (1980), 31–40; Sergent (1995), 232–8; K. Jones-Bley in Dexter–Polomé (1997), 194–221; *EIEC* 151 (agnostic).

[152] Especially Marija Gimbutas' imposing Kurgan theory, on which cf. Mallory (1989), 182–5; *EIEC* 338–41.

[153] Cf. Feist (1913), 316 f.; Turville-Petre (1964), 272; Gelling–Davidson (1969), 168; *EIEC* 279.

[154] A commonplace of Indo-European tradition; cf. Sergent (1995), 233. For India cf. AV 8. 1. 19; 12. 5. 48; 14. 2. 59–61 (women with loose hair who dance, wail, and beat their breasts); *MBh.* 9. 28. 64 ff.; 11. 26. 40; 16. 8; *Rm.* 2. 70. 21 f.; 4. 19. 20, 24. 27–9.

his wife twice, his mother, and his sister-in-law Helen (22. 477–514; 24. 724–75). In the Indian epics we have, for example, laments for Abhimanyu and Bhīṣma by their mothers (7. 55; 13. 154), for Abhimanyu by his wife (11. 20. 10–26), for Daśaratha by his son (*Rm.* 2. 70. 6–9), and for Vālin by his wife and daughter (*Rm.* 4. 24. 32–9, 40). Cú Chulainn sings a series of poetic laments for Fer Dia, his former friend whom he has now fought and killed (*Táin* (L) 3440–595). Poetic and rhetorical laments for the dead by men or women remained a common element in Irish saga narratives.[155] Gudrun sings a lament for Sigurd over his body (*Guðrúnarkviða A* 17–22).

While Beowulf's corpse burns on the pyre, a Geatish woman sings a lament; it is not given in direct speech but its subject matter is briefly indicated in the compressed style of the poem (3150–5; cf. 1117 f.). She sang 'how she sorely dreaded her days of [*illegible*], much slaughter, the people's terror, abuse and captivity'. This is a typical theme of women's laments when a hero and protector has fallen. Andromache laments that she is left a widow and her infant son an orphan who will suffer humiliation and deprivation; she anticipates the fall of Troy and the enslavement of its women (*Il.* 22. 483–507, 24. 725–38). Similarly, as Vālin is expiring, his wife Tārā laments: 'Once I was filled with happiness, but now, in my wretchedness, I must helplessly lead the life of a wretched, grief-anguished widow. And the delicate young warrior Añgada [*their son*], used to pleasure, indulged by me—what kind of a life will he lead?' (*Rm.* 4. 20. 14 f.; cf. *MBh.* 11. 25. 4). And as Andromache's two laments are both followed by 'So she spoke; and the women wailed upon it', so Tārā's is followed by 'Hearing her lament, those monkey women, afflicted with sorrow, surrounded wretched Añgada on all sides and wailed' (4. 20. 21).

Hector used to keep Troy's gates and walls safe, 'but now by the beaked ships, away from your parents, the wriggling worms will eat you, after the dogs have had their fill' (*Il.* 22. 508–11). Similar pathetic contrasts are drawn in the Indian epic. 'The scorcher of the enemy who would go in the van of the specially consecrated fighters now lies in the dust . . . now vultures sit around him' (*MBh.* 11. 17. 10–12). 'And here, face up, lies Durmukha, who killed brigades of the enemy . . . his face has been half eaten by the animals' (11. 19. 7 f.; cf. 22. 2, 25. 20 f.; *Rm.* 4. 20, 23. 1–16, 25–30, 24. 33–8).

Suttee

We have noted that the king's or hero's funeral is liable to involve the deaths of male and female servants, horses, and other animals. A recurrent motif of

155 Thurneysen (1921), 84.

more poignant moment is the voluntary death of the man's wife. This reflects a custom practised in a number of ancient Indo-European (and not only Indo-European) societies. There is already evidence suggesting it in burials of the Globular Amphora culture in north-central and eastern Europe, around 3400–2800 BCE.[156]

In Vedic India it is an 'old-established rule', *dhárma- purā́ṇa-* (AV 18. 3. 1), though after symbolically lying down beside her dead husband on his pyre the widow is apparently allowed to get up again and marry another.[157] It remained a Hindu ideal, however, for the 'true' wife (Sanskrit *satī*, from which English *suttee*). Krishna's four wives ascend his pyre in the *Mahābhārata* (16. 8).

It was certainly not practised in archaic Greece, and there is no mention of it in Homer. But Euadne's determination to leap onto Capaneus' pyre makes a dramatic scene in Euripides' *Supplices* (980–1071), and it is possible that the incident comes from the epic tradition about the Theban wars.

Among the northern Thracians, according to Herodotus (5. 5), a man had several wives, and on his death the one he was judged to have loved best had the much coveted honour of being put to death and buried with him. Propertius (3. 13. 15–22) ascribes a similar rivalry among wives to unspecified peoples of the East. Ibn Faḍlān, cited above, describes how a volunteer was found from among the dead man's maids to die with him. Another tenth-century Arab writer, Ibn Rusta, reports that if a man in 'Slavia' (*Ṣaqlabiyya*) died he was cremated and his ashes put into an urn, which was set on (in?) a mound. If he had three wives, the one who believed herself his favourite hanged herself and her body was thrown into the fire and burned.[158]

There is earlier evidence for suttee among Slavonic peoples. The Byzantine emperor Mauricius, or the author of the *Strategika* attributed to him, attests it around 600. Bonifatius in a letter of 746–7 avers that the Wends (*quod est foedissimum et deterrimum genus hominum*) consider that woman praiseworthy who commits suicide on her husband's death and burns beside him on the pyre.[159] Baltic wives, some of them at least, showed the same devotion. It is recorded that when in 1205 a Lithuanian war-band was slaughtered,

[156] J. P. Mallory in *EIEC* 227b.

[157] Cf. RV 10. 18. 8, AV 18. 3. 1–3; Oldenberg (1917), 576, 586 f.

[158] C. H. Meyer (1931), 93. 6–27.

[159] Mauricius, *Strategika* 11. 4; Bonifatius, *Epist.* 73 Tangl (*MGH* Epistolae selectae, i. 150. 22). Cf. also the anonymous Persian geographer in C. H. Meyer (1931), 94. 34 f.; Mas'ūdī, ibid. 95. 23–30 (both tenth century); Thietmar of Merseburg, *Chron.* 8. 3 (*MGH* Scriptores rerum Germanicarum NS ix. 494. 30, on the Poles; early eleventh century); Váňa (1992), 135 f., 252 f.

fifty women in one town hanged themselves on account of their husbands' deaths.[160]

For Germanic peoples the oldest testimony is that of Procopius (*Bell. Goth.* 2. 14) about the Heruli, that a woman was expected to hang herself beside her husband's tomb without much delay. In Eddic myth Brynhild joins Sigurd on his pyre. Saxo tells of the self-immolations of Asmund's wife Gunnilda (1. 8. 4 p. 27) and of Hagbarth's lover Sygne with all her maids (7. 7. 14 f. p. 197).[161]

Movses Xorenacʻi relates in his Armenian history (2. 60) that when Artašes died his wives and concubines committed suicide by his grave, and many servants and slaves also followed him to the other world. The Armenian oral epic also recognizes the motif of the widow's suicide (*Sassountsy David* 336).

Funeral games

Much of the account of Patroclus' funeral in the *Iliad* is taken up with the chariot-race and other contests that the Achaeans held in his honour, Achilles providing the prizes. Similar games followed Achilles' own funeral in the *Aethiopis*, and there are several mentions in the epics of other such occasions (*Il.* 22. 162–4, 23. 630–42, 679 f.; *Od.* 24. 97–9). The games for Pelias were a famous event celebrated in poetry. But funeral games were not reserved for mythical heroes. Hesiod attended funeral games for a warrior king of Chalcis of his own time (*Op.* 654–6), and many more great men were to be so honoured in historical times both in Greece and at Rome.[162]

A similar custom is documented for various other peoples.[163] Not all of them are Indo-European, but several are, and there seems no reason why it should not have been an ancestral tradition.[164] The wealthier Thracians' funerals, Herodotus tells us (5. 8), followed a pattern that is now familiar to us. The body was laid out for three days, there was lamentation, and many animals were sacrificed. Then it was cremated or buried and a tumulus was raised, after which there were contests of every kind, with the largest prizes being for single combat. Many Irish narratives refer to funeral games (*óenach ngubae*) as the sequel to burying a hero and marking his grave with a stele

[160] Heinricus, *Chronicon Livoniae* 9. 5 (*MGH* Scriptores, xxiii. 250. 34) = Mannhardt (1936), 30 = Clemen (1936), 93. 30; cf. Gimbutas (1963), 184–7.

[161] For Germanic peoples cf. H. M. Chadwick, *The Cult of Othin* (London 1899), 41–6; Gering–Sijmons (1927–31), ii. 276; de Vries (1956), i. 98, 138, 155.

[162] J. G. Frazer, *Pausanias's Description of Greece*, ii (London 1913), 549, amplified in Frazer (1911–36), iv. 92–6; L. Malten, *RE* xii. 1859–61; L. H. Jeffery, *The Local Scripts of Archaic Greece* (Oxford 1961), 91.

[163] Frazer (as n. 162, 1913), 549 f.; (1911–36), iv. 96–103.

[164] Cf. Sergent (1995), 236.

inscribed in the Ogam script. An Ossetic story relates that the Boratas sent an announcement round to all the villages saying that in three years they would celebrate a festival in honour of their ancestors, and that whoever wanted to honour their dead should start training for the horse races (Sikojev (1985), 301).

The emphasis on horse races, and in Greece on chariot races, which occupy the first and major place in the games for Patroclus and enjoyed the highest prestige in the great national games of historical times, harmonizes with an easy conjecture about the origin of the institution among the early horse-riding pastoralists of the Eurasian steppe. When the news went out that a notable man had died, men would ride from far and near to attend the funeral. What more natural at such a gathering than that they should then challenge one another to race their steeds and compete in other equestrian feats? At a later period, when chariots came into use, the racing urge would have been extended to these.

After the games are over, Achilles takes to tying Hector's body behind his chariot again and driving three times round Patroclus' tomb (*Il.* 24. 14–17). Some ancient writers explained that Achilles was a Thessalian and that it was a Thessalian custom to drag the killer of someone dear to one round his victim's tomb (Arist. fr. 166; Call. fr. 588). But elsewhere we find references to a ritual of honouring a dead king or hero by circling his tomb or bier, with no dragging of an enemy's body. Before the games the lamenting Myrmidons had driven their chariots three times round Patroclus' body (*Il.* 23. 13), and something similar seems to have been done when Achilles was about to be cremated (*Od.* 24. 68–70). In Apollonius Rhodius (1. 1057–62) the Argonauts and Doliones lament Kyzikos for three days, and then they parade three times round him in full armour, perform the funeral, and hold funeral games; his tomb remains a landmark. Mopsos too is honoured with the threefold circuit in armour (id. 4. 1535). Similar rites are performed for Pallas in Virgil (*Aen.* 11. 188 f.) and Archemorus in Statius (*Theb.* 6. 215–26), and indeed for Augustus (Dio Cass. 56. 42. 2).[165] Diodorus (19. 34. 6) describes how an Indian army processed in armour three times round the pyre of their commander Keteus before it was lit.[166] Jordanes records that after Attila was laid out and before he was interred, a troop of élite horsemen drawn from the

[165] For Rome cf. also Suet. *Claud.* 1. 4 (annual *decursio* round the tomb of Drusus); Luc. 8. 734 f. (Pompey).

[166] Ancient Indian funerary ritual was in fact acquainted with the practice by which Brahmans or women mourners circled the site of the pyre or the remains of the deceased three times. Cf. Willem Caland, *Die altindischen Todten- und Bestattungsgebräuche* (Amsterdam 1896), 24, 171; Oldenberg (1917), 582. Buddha's pyre is said to have burst into flame spontaneously when five hundred of his disciples passed three times round it.

whole Hunnish nation rode round his bier and sang his praises.[167] Following the construction of Beowulf's tumulus twelve warriors of noble birth ride round it, apparently delivering eulogies (3169–74). In a Nart tale translated by Dumézil, when Syrdon's enemy Sosyryko dies, he performs a travesty of the proper procedures. He beats his head about with a stick and laments, 'How am I to go on living, when you are no more?' Then he rides Sosyryko's horse to his grave and canters round it, improvising variants on the theme 'How your death delights me, Sosyryko!'[168]

These customs of honorific circumequitation throw some light on the remarkable Scythian procedure described by Herodotus (4. 72). On the anniversary of the royal funeral, he says, they kill the best fifty of the king's surviving servants and the finest fifty horses, stuff them, and set them up, supported on wooden cradles, in a circle round the tumulus, one rider to each horse.

Eulogies sung at funerals must have been one source that contributed to the traditions of heroic poetry. As the warrior's mortal husk decayed in the digestive system of Mother Earth, or floated up in a swirl of black particles towards Father Sky, his name continued its perilous quest for undying renown on the lips of men.

[167] Jordanes, *Getica* 256, *de tota gente Hunnorum lectissimi equites . . . in modum circensium cursibus ambientes facta eius cantu funereo tali ordine referebant* (there follows in 257 a précis of their dirge).

[168] G. Dumézil (as n. 58), 168; cf. Sikojev (1985), 144 f. An Ossetic custom is recorded by which 'the dead man's widow and his saddle-horse are led thrice round the grave, and no man may marry the widow or mount the horse thus devoted' (E. B. Tylor, *Primitive Culture* (4th edn., London 1903), i. 463 f.). For all these customs cf. Sam Eitrem, *Opferritus und Voropfer* (Christiania 1915), 9–13; W. Pax, *Wörter und Sachen* 18 (1937), 44–7; J. Cuillandre, *La droite et la gauche dans les poèmes homériques* (Paris 1944), 277, 284 f.

Elegy on an Indo-European hero

Urukleves now I call to mind,
the son of valiant Seghekleves,
who with his great thirsty spear
slew men and horses by hundreds.

Many a day he arose with the sun
and led the war-host to the field of blood:
there they fought like raging fire,
army against army, man against man.

He stood firm amid the missiles
like the oak of Perkunos under hail.
He broke ancient strongholds
and brought away wealth of cattle.

Hsugnos he slew, the son of Hsvekvos,
Vlqvo, Vlqvognos, and mighty Xnrmenes.
The black crows were glad of his work,
but a black cloud he set for the kinsfolk.

Well-joined was the dear name
you set on your son, Seghekleves:
wide in truth his glory spreads
under that heaven, over this earth.

He has gone the way of no return
to you and the Fathers in the mansion below,
but his name does not fail or grow old:
it lives in the mouths of us earth-walkers.

It will sound until Dieus' fair daughter
embraces her dark sister in one house,
or until the poets' woven songs
are sung no more in the kings' halls.

Bibliography

AARNE, ANTTI, *Vergleichende Rätselforschungen*, 3 vols., *FF* (= *Folklore Fellows*) *Communications* vol. 4 nos. 26–8 (Helsinki–Hamina 1918–20).

BADER, FRANÇOISE, *La langue des dieux, ou l'hermétisme des poètes indo-européens* (Pisa 1989).

BECKMAN, GARY, *Hittite Diplomatic Texts*, 2nd edn. (Atlanta 1999).

BENVENISTE, ÉMILE, *Indo-European Language and Society* (London 1973) (translated from *Le vocabulaire des institutions indo-européennes*, Paris 1969).

BIEZAIS, H., and J. BALYS, 'Baltische Mythologie', in *Wb. d. Myth.* i. 2 (1973), 375–454.

BROCKINGTON, J. L., *The Sanskrit Epics.* Handbuch der Orientalistik, ii. 12 (Leiden–Boston–Köln 1998).

CAMPANILE, ENRICO, *Ricerche di cultura poetica indoeuropea* (Pisa 1977).

—— *Studi di cultura celtica e indoeuropea* (Pisa 1981).

—— 'Die älteste Hofdichtung von Leinster', *Sitzungsberichte der Österreichischen Akademie der Wissenschaften*, Philosophisch-historische Klasse, 503 (1988).

—— 'Épopée celtique et épopée homérique', *Ollodagos* 1 (1990), 257–78 [= 1990a].

—— *La ricostruzione della cultura indoeuropea* (Pisa 1990) [= 1990b].

—— and C. ORLANDI, S. SANI, 'Funzione e figura del poeta nella cultura celtica e indiana', *SSL* 14 (1974), 228–51.

CARDONA, G. C., and H. M. HOENIGSWALD, ALFRED SENN (edd.), *Indo-European and Indo-Europeans* (Philadelphia 1970).

CARMICHAEL, ALEXANDER, *Carmina Gadelica*, 6 vols. (Edinburgh 1928–59).

CHADWICK, NORA K., *Russian Heroic Poetry* (Cambridge 1932).

CHANTRAINE, PIERRE, *Dictionnaire étymologique de la langue grecque* (Paris 1968–80).

CLANCY, JOSEPH P., *Medieval Welsh Poems* (Dublin 2003).

CLEMEN, CAROLUS, *Fontes Historiae Religionis Germanicae* (Berlin 1928).

—— *Fontes Historiae Religionum Primitivarum, Praeindogermanicarum, Indogermanicarum minus notarum* (Bonn 1936).

COLARUSSO, JOHN, *Nart Sagas from the Caucasus* (Princeton 2002).

DAVIDSON, HILDA R. ELLIS, *Gods and Myths of Northern Europe* (Harmondsworth 1964).

—— *Myths and Symbols in Pagan Europe* (Manchester 1988).

—— (with Peter Fisher), *Saxo Grammaticus. The History of the Danes, Books I–IX* (Cambridge 1979–80).

DETSCHEW, DIMITRI, 'Die thrakischen Sprachreste', *Sitzungsberichte der Österreichischen Akademie der Wissenschaften*, Linguistische Abteilung, 15 (1957).

DETTER, FERDINAND, and RICHARD HEINZEL, *Sæmundar Edda*, 2 vols. (Leipzig 1903).

Dexter, Miriam Robbins, and Edgar C. Polomé (edd.), Varia *on the Indo-European Past: Papers in memory of Marija Gimbutas* (*JIESM* 19, Washington 1997).

Dieterich, Albrecht, *Mutter Erde*, 3rd edn. (Leipzig–Berlin 1925).

Dillon, Myles, *The Cycles of the Kings* (Oxford 1946).

—— *Early Irish Literature* (Chicago 1948).

—— *Celts and Aryans: Survivals of Indo-European Speech and Society* (Simla 1975).

Dooley, Ann, and Harry Roe, *Tales of the Elders of Ireland* (Oxford 1999).

Drews, Robert (ed.), *Greater Anatolia and the Indo-Hittite Language Family* (*JIESM* 38, Washington 2001).

Dronke, Ursula, *The Poetic Edda*, 2 vols. (Oxford 1969, 1997).

Dumézil, Georges, *Servius et la Fortune* (Paris 1943).

—— *Mythe et épopée*, 3 vols. (Paris 1968–73).

Durante, Marcello, 'Epea pteroenta. La parola come "cammino" in immagini greche e vediche', *Atti della Accademia Nazionale dei Lincei: Rendiconti, Classe di Scienze morali, storiche e filologiche* 13 (1958), 3–14 (German version in Schmitt (1968), 242–60).

—— 'La terminologia relativa alla creazione poetica', ibid. 15 (1960), 231–49 (German version in Schmitt (1968), 261–90).

—— 'Ricerche sulla preistoria della lingua poetica greca. L'epiteto', ibid. 17 (1962), 25–43 (German version with some addenda in Schmitt (1968), 291–323).

—— *Sulla preistoria della tradizione poetica greca*, 2 vols. (Rome 1971, 1976).

Duval, Paul-Marie, *Les dieux de la Gaule* (Paris 1957).

Ernout, Alfred, and Antoine Meillet, *Dictionnaire étymologique de la langue latine*, 4th edn. (Paris 1959).

Euler, Wolfram, *Indoiranisch-griechische Gemeinsamkeiten der Nominalbildung und deren indogermanische Grundlagen* (Innsbruck 1979).

Feist, Sigmund, *Kultur, Ausbreitung und Herkunft der Indogermanen* (Berlin 1913).

—— *Vergleichendes Wörterbuch der gotischen Sprache*, 3rd edn. (Leiden 1939).

Finkelberg, Margalit, *Greeks and Pre-Greeks: Aegean Prehistory and Greek Heroic Tradition* (Cambridge 2005).

Frazer, J. G., *The Golden Bough*, 3rd edn., 13 vols. (London 1911–36).

Gamkrelidze, T. V., and V. V. Ivanov, *Indo-European and the Indo-Europeans* (Berlin–New York 1995).

Gantz, Timothy, *Early Greek Myth: A Guide to Literary and Artistic Sources* (Baltimore 1993).

Gasparov, M. L., *A History of European Versification* (Oxford 1996).

Gelling, Peter, and H. Ellis Davidson, *The Chariot of the Sun* (London 1969).

Gering, Hugo, and B. Sijmons, *Kommentar zu den Liedern der Edda*, 2 vols. (Halle/Saale 1927–31).

Gershevitch, Ilya, *The Avestan Hymn to Mithra* (Cambridge 1959).

Gimbutas, Marija, *The Balts* (London 1963).

—— *The Slavs* (London 1971).

Glob, P. V., *The Mound People* (London 1974).

Gonda, Jan, *Stylistic Repetition in the Veda* (Amsterdam 1959).

GREEN, DENNIS H., *Language and History in the Early Germanic World* (Cambridge 1998).

GREEN, MIRANDA, *The Gods of the Celts* (Godalming 1986).

—— *The Sun-Gods of Ancient Europe* (London 1991).

GREIMAS, A. J., *Of Gods and Men: Studies in Lithuanian Mythology* (Bloomington 1992) (translated from *Apie Dievus ir žmones: Lietuvių Mitologijos Studijos*, Chicago 1979).

GRIMM, JACOB, *Teutonic Mythology*, 4 vols. (London 1883–8) (translated from *Deutsche Mythologie*, 4th edn., Berlin 1875–8).

GÜNTERT, HERMANN, *Der arische Weltkönig und Heiland* (Halle/Saale 1923).

GURNEY, O. R., *Some Aspects of Hittite Religion* (Oxford 1977).

GUSMANI, ROBERTO, 'Le iscrizioni poetiche lidie', *Studi Triestini di Antichità in onore di Luigia Achillea Stella* (Trieste 1975), 255–70.

—— MIRJO SALVINI, PIETRO VANNICELLI (edd.), *Frigi e Frigio* (Rome 1997).

HAAS, OTTO, *Messapische Studien* (Heidelberg 1962).

—— *Die phrygischen Sprachdenkmäler* (Sofia 1966).

HAUDRY, JEAN, *La religion cosmique des Indo-Européens* (Milan–Paris 1987).

HILLEBRANDT, ALFRED, *Vedische Mythologie*, 2nd edn., 2 vols. (Breslau 1927–9).

HOFFNER, H. A., *Hittite Myths*, 2nd edn. (Atlanta 1998).

HOFMANN, ERICH, *Ausdrucksverstärkung* (Göttingen 1930).

ISHKOL-KEROVPIAN, K., 'Armenische Mythologie', in *Wb. d. Myth.* i. 4 (1986), 61–160.

JAKOBSON, ROMAN, *Selected Writings*, 8 vols. (The Hague–Paris etc. 1962–88).

JONVAL, MICHEL, *Les chansons mythologiques lettonnes* (*Latviešu mītologiskās daiņas*) (Riga–Paris 1929).

KAMMENHUBER, ANNELIES, *Die Arier im vorderen Orient* (Heidelberg 1968).

KOCH, JOHN T., and JOHN CAREY, *The Celtic Heroic Age. Literary Sources for Ancient Celtic Europe & Early Ireland & Wales*, 3rd edn. (Andover, Mass.–Aberystwyth 2000).

KRAHE, HANS, *Die Sprache der Illyrier*, 2 vols. (Wiesbaden 1955–64).

KREK, GREGOR, *Einleitung in die Slavische Literaturgeschichte*, 2nd edn. (Graz 1887).

KRETSCHMER, PAUL, *Einleitung in die Geschichte der griechischen Sprache* (Göttingen 1896).

KUHN, ADALBERT, *Die Herabkunft des Feuers und des Göttertrankes* (Berlin 1859).

KURYŁOWICZ, JERZY, *Metrik und Sprachgeschichte* (Wrocław 1973).

LAMBERT, P.-Y., *La langue gauloise*, édition revue et augmentée (Paris 2003).

LAMBERTZ, M., 'Die Mythologie der Albaner', in *Wb. d. Myth.* i. 2 (1973), 457–509.

LEBRUN, RENÉ, *Hymnes et prières hittites* (Louvain-la-Neuve 1980).

LEJEUNE, MICHEL, *Manuel de la langue vénète* (Heidelberg 1974).

LEVY, REUBEN, *The Epic of the Kings: Shah-Nama, the national epic of Persia by Ferdowsi* (London 1967).

LINCOLN, BRUCE, *Myth, Cosmos, and Society: Indo-European Themes of Creation and Destruction* (Cambridge, Mass. 1986).

LORENZ, GOTTFRIED, *Snorri Sturluson, Gylfaginning: Texte, Übersetzung, Kommentar* (Darmstadt 1984).

MCCONE, KIM, *Pagan Past and Christian Present in Early Irish Literature* (Maynooth 1990).

MACDONELL, A. A., *Vedic Mythology* (Strasbourg 1898).

MALLORY, J. P., *In Search of the Indo-Europeans: Language, Archaeology and Myth* (London 1989).

MANNHARDT, WILHELM, 'Die lettischen Sonnenmythen', *Zeitschrift für Ethnologie* 7 (1875), 73–104, 209–44, 281–330.

—— *Wald- und Feldkulte*, 2nd edn., 2 vols. (Berlin 1905).

—— *Letto-preussische Götterlehre* (Riga 1936).

MAYER, ANTON, *Die Sprache der alten Illyrier*, 2 vols. (Vienna 1957–9).

MAYRHOFER, M., *Kurzgefasstes etymologisches Wörterbuch des Altindischen* (Heidelberg 1953–80).

—— *Etymologisches Wörterbuch des Altindoarischen* (Heidelberg 1986–2001).

—— and others (edd.), *Antiquitates Indogermanicae: Gedenkschrift für H. Güntert* (Innsbruck 1974).

MEID, WOLFGANG, 'Das Suffix -*no*- in Götternamen', *Beiträge zur Namenforschung* 8 (1957), 72–108, 113–26.

—— *Dichter und Dichtkunst in indogermanischer Zeit* (Innsbruck 1978).

—— (ed.), *Studien zum indogermanischen Wortschatz* (Innsbruck 1987).

—— *Formen dichterischer Sprache im Keltischen und Germanischen* (Innsbruck 1990).

—— *Aspekte der germanischen und keltischen Religion im Zeugnis der Sprache* (Innsbruck 1991).

—— *Gaulish Inscriptions*, 2nd edn. (Budapest 1994).

—— (ed.), *Sprache und Kultur der Indogermanen.* Akten der X. Tagung der Indogermanischen Gesellschaft (Innsbruck 1998).

MEILLET, ANTOINE, *Les origines indo-européennes des mètres grecs* (Paris 1923).

MELCHERT, H. C., *Anatolian Historical Phonology* (Amsterdam–Atlanta 1994).

MELLER, HARALD (ed.), *Der geschmiedete Himmel* (Stuttgart 2004).

MEYER, C. H., *Fontes Historiae Religionis Slavicae* (Berlin 1931).

MEYER, KUNO, 'Über die älteste irische Dichtung', *Abhandlungen der Königlichen Preussischen Akademie der Wissenschaften* 1913 (6), 1914 (10).

MILLER, DEAN A., *The Epic Hero* (Baltimore 2000).

MÜLLER, F. MAX, *Contributions to the Science of Mythology* (London 1897).

NAGY, GREGORY, 'Perkūnas and Perunŭ', in Mayrhofer and others (1974), 113–31.

—— *Greek Mythology and Poetics* (Ithaca 1990).

NORDEN, EDUARD, *Agnostos Theos: Untersuchungen zur Formengeschichte religiöser Rede* (Berlin 1913).

NÜNLIST, RENÉ, *Poetologische Bildersprache in der frühgriechischen Dichtung* (Stuttgart–Leipzig 1998).

OBERLIES, THOMAS, *Die Religion des Ṛgveda, Erster Teil* (Vienna 1998).

OHLERT, KONRAD, *Rätsel und Rätselspiele der alten Griechen*, 2nd edn. (Berlin 1912).

Oldenberg, Hermann, *Die Religion des Veda*, 2nd edn. (Stuttgart 1917).

Olmsted, G. S., *The Gods of the Celts and the Indo-Europeans* (Budapest 1994).

O'Rahilly, T. F., *Early Irish History and Mythology* (Dublin 1946).

Pettazzoni, Raffaele, *L'Onniscienza di Dio* (Turin 1955), trs. H. J. Rose as *The All-Knowing God* (London 1956).

Pictet, Adolphe, *Les origines indo-européennes ou les Aryas primitifs: essai de paléontologie linguistique*, 2 vols. (Paris 1859–63).

Pisani, Vittore, *Lingue e culture* (Brescia 1969).

Puhvel, Jaan, *Comparative Mythology* (Baltimore 1987).

Ramat, Anna G., and Paolo Ramat, *The Indo-European Languages* (London–New York 1998) (translated from *Le lingue indoeuropee*, Bologna 1993).

Rhesa, L. G., *Dainos oder Lithauische Volkslieder* (Königsberg 1825; 2nd edn. with F. Kurschat, Berlin 1843).

Rowland, Jenny, *Early Welsh Saga Poetry* (Cambridge 1990).

Scherer, Anton, *Gestirnnamen bei den indogermanischen Völkern* (Heidelberg 1953).

Schleicher, August, *Litauische Märchen, Sprichworte, Rätsel und Lieder* (Weimar 1857).

Schlerath, Bernfried, *Awesta-Wörterbuch: Vorarbeiten*, 2 vols. (Wiesbaden 1968).

Schmitt, Rüdiger, *Dichtung und Dichtersprache in indogermanischer Zeit* (Wiesbaden 1967).

—— (ed.), *Indogermanische Dichtersprache*. Wege der Forschung, 165 (Darmstadt 1968).

Schrader, Otto, 'Aryan Religion', in James Hastings (ed.), *Encyclopaedia of Religion and Ethics* (Edinburgh 1908–26), ii (1909), 11–57.

Schramm, Gottfried, *Namenschatz und Dichtersprache: Studien zu den zweigliedrigen Personennamen der Germanen* (Göttingen 1957).

—— *Nordpontische Ströme: Namenphilologische Zugänge zur Frühzeit des europäischen Ostens* (Göttingen 1973).

von Schroeder, Leopold, *Arische Religion*, 2 vols. (Leipzig 1914–16).

Schulze, Wilhelm, *Kleine Schriften*, 2nd edn. (Göttingen 1966).

Sergent, Bernard, *Les Indo-Européens: Histoire, langues, mythes* (Paris 1995).

Sikojev, André, *Die Narten. Söhne der Sonne: Mythen und Heldensagen der Skythen, Sarmaten und Osseten* (Cologne 1985).

Thieme, Paul, 'Studien zur indogermanischen Wortkunde und Religionsgeschichte', *Berichte der Sächsischen Akademie*, Phil.-hist. Klasse, 98/5 (Berlin 1952) (= Schmitt (1968), 102–53).

Thurneysen, Rudolf, *Die irische Helden- und Königsage bis zum siebzehnten Jahrhundert* (Halle/Saale 1921).

Tristram, H. L. C. (ed.), *Metrik und Medienwechsel* (Tübingen 1991).

Turville-Petre, E. O. G., *Myth and Religion of the North* (London 1964).

Unbegaun, B.-O., *La religion des anciens slaves*. Les religions de l'Europe ancienne, 3 (Paris 1948), 389–445.

USENER, HERMANN, *Götternamen: Versuch einer Lehre von der religiösen Begriffsbildung* (Bonn 1896).

VÁŇA, ZDENĚK, *Mythologie und Götterwelt der slawischen Völker* (Stuttgart 1992).

VENDRYÈS, JOSEPH, *La religion des Celtes.* Les religions de l'Europe ancienne, 3 (Paris 1948), 239–320.

de VRIES, JAN, *Altgermanische Religionsgeschichte*, 2nd edn., 2 vols. (Berlin 1956).

—— *Keltische Religion* (Stuttgart 1961).

WACKERNAGEL, JACOB, 'Indogermanische Dichtersprache', *Philologus* 95 (1943), 1–19 (= *Kleine Schriften*, i. 186–204 = Schmitt (1968), 83–101).

WARD, DONALD, *The Divine Twins: An Indo-European Myth in Germanic Tradition* (Berkeley–Los Angeles 1968).

WATKINS, CALVERT, 'Indo-European Metrics and Archaic Irish Verse', *Celtica* 6 (1963), 194–249 (= (1994), 349–404).

—— *Selected Writings*, 2 vols. (Innsbruck 1994).

—— *How to Kill a Dragon: Aspects of Indo-European Poetics* (New York–Oxford 1995).

WEST, M. L., *Hesiod. Theogony* (Oxford 1966).

—— *Early Greek Philosophy and the Orient* (Oxford 1971).

—— 'Indo-European Metre', *Glotta* 51 (1973), 161–87.

—— *Hesiod. Works and Days* (Oxford 1978).

—— *The East Face of Helicon: West Asiatic Elements in Greek Poetry and Myth* (Oxford 1997).

—— 'An Indo-European Stylistic Feature in Homer', in A. Bierl, A. Schmitt, A. Willi (edd.), *Antike Literatur in neuer Deutung: Festschrift für Joachim Latacz anlässlich seines 70. Geburtstags* (Munich–Leipzig 2004), 33–49.

WINTERNITZ, MORIZ, *A History of Indian Literature*, 2nd edn., i (Calcutta 1959).

WÜST, WALTHER, *Von indogermanischer Dichtersprache: Probleme—Theorien—Pragmatisches* (Munich 1969).

ZWICKER, JOHANNES, *Fontes Historiae Religionis Celticae* (Berlin 1934–6).

Index